ALSO BY KEVIN R. C. GUTZMAN

Thomas Jefferson—Revolutionary

James Madison and the Making of America

The Politically Incorrect Guide to the Constitution

Who Killed the Constitution?: The Federal
Government vs. American Liberty from World War I
to Barack Obama (coauthored with Thomas E. Woods Jr.)

Virginia's American Revolution: From Dominion
to Republic, 1776–1840

THE JEFFERSONIANS

THE
JEFFERSONIANS

THE VISIONARY PRESIDENCIES OF JEFFERSON, MADISON, AND MONROE

KEVIN R. C. GUTZMAN

ST. MARTIN'S PRESS
NEW YORK

First published in the United States by St. Martin's Press,
an imprint of St. Martin's Publishing Group

THE JEFFERSONIANS. Copyright © 2022 by Kevin R. C. Gutzman. All rights reserved.
Printed in the United States of America. For information,
address St. Martin's Publishing Group, 120 Broadway, New York, NY 10271.

www.stmartins.com

Library of Congress Cataloging-in-Publication Data

Names: Gutzman, Kevin R. C. (Kevin Raeder Constantine), 1963– author.
Title: The Jeffersonians : the visionary presidencies of Jefferson, Madison, and Monroe /
    Kevin R. C. Gutzman.
Other titles: Visionary presidencies of Jefferson, Madison, and Monroe
Description: First edition. | New York : St. Martin's Press, 2022. | Includes bibliographical
    references and index.
Identifiers: LCCN 2022035070 | ISBN 9781250135452 (hardcover) | ISBN 9781250135476
    (ebook)
Subjects: LCSH: Presidents—United States—History—19th century. | United States—
    Politics and government—1801–1809. | United States—Politics and government—
    1809–1817. | United States—Politics and government—1817–1825. | Jefferson, Thomas,
    1743–1826. | Madison, James, 1751–1836. | Monroe, James, 1758–1831. | Republicanism—
    United States—History—19th century.
Classification: LCC E302.1 .G88 2022 | DDC 973.5—dc23/eng/20220727
LC record available at https://lccn.loc.gov/2022035070

Our books may be purchased in bulk for promotional, educational, or business use.
Please contact your local bookseller or the Macmillan Corporate and
Premium Sales Department at 1-800-221-7945, extension 5442, or by email at
MacmillanSpecialMarkets@macmillan.com.

First Edition: 2022

10 9 8 7 6 5 4 3 2 1

For Cyril

CONTENTS

A NOTE FROM THE AUTHOR

The Jeffersonians lived before standardization of capitalization, punctuation, and spelling. I have left their English as I found it.

PART I
THE BEGINNING

1

A House committee headed by Chairman Thomas Pinckney, Federalist of South Carolina, informed Vice President Thomas Jefferson that the House had at last elected him president.[1] One might have thought the Virginian would exult in his triumph, but that would be to mistake Jefferson. "In deciding between the candidates . . . ," he said, "I am sensible that age has been respected rather than more active and useful qualifications."

Only after several weeks' acrimonious dispute had the House at last broken the Electoral College deadlock between Jefferson and his running mate, New York's Senator Aaron Burr, by opting for the man all knew to be the Republican presidential candidate. Rumors held that Burr would make a deal with the outgoing House's Federalist majority: make me president, and I will maintain some of your measures my fellow Republicans find obnoxious. (Some leading Federalists took for granted that Burr would deal.)[2] Those rumors were false. Burr had refused any suggestion of switching party allegiances, as prominent Federalists told it, though this marked the death of any presidential aspirations Burr may have had.[3] One Federalist congressman said Burr's insistence that he would not come into the presidency as a Federalist would make it necessary for a President Burr to remove all Federalist appointees from office, and "I have direct information that Mr. Jefferson will not pursue that plan."[4]

Another possible result of the deadlock was that House Federalists would block any decision past Inauguration Day, thus reserving the position for some Federalist—perhaps the Senate president pro tempore. Unbeknownst to the public, radical steps might have been taken to prevent any such thing from happening. Jefferson's chief ally, James Madison, counseled his chieftain that Jefferson and Burr ought, if that happened, jointly to call for an early meeting of the new Republican Congress—which otherwise would not meet until December. The new House could then anoint Jefferson chief executive.[5] Not only did Madison advise Jefferson how he should act, but two Republican governors, including Jefferson's onetime law student James Monroe in neighboring Virginia, mulled sending their militiamen to Washington to install "the people's choice," Jefferson.[6] Federalists had better not try to thwart the popular will. (Left unclear in this plotting was how it could be illegitimate for Federalist representatives to vote against Jefferson in the House, as the Constitution empowered them to do.)

Also without the public's knowing it, Jefferson had told Madison in 1796 that in case of an Electoral College tie, his rival candidate John Adams should be given the presidency. After all, Jefferson then reasoned, Adams had always been his senior in politics. Far from demure, then, Jefferson may have been candid in concluding that his more advanced age accounted for his victory over Burr in early 1801.

May have been. We cannot be certain. Jefferson has not been called the "American Sphinx" for nothing.[7]

Jefferson's explanation of his election to Madison the day after the decisive February 17th vote reflected Jefferson's honest appraisal of the situation.[8] Federalists in the House had at last concluded, the vice president wrote, that they could not elect Burr, that any attempt to dispose of the presidency in some other way than by an election in the House "would be resisted by arms," and that "a Convention to reorganize & amend the government" would follow, and so they had caucused regarding what to do next. They might all have continued to oppose Jefferson, and they might all have joined the Republicans in electing Jefferson, but instead they had done neither. The Federalist representatives' behavior had disgusted all the Federalists outside the House, with even Alexander Hamilton and prominent Massachusetts Federalist Stephen Higginson Sr. acting, in Jefferson's words, as "zealous partisans for us."[9]

President John Adams endeavored till the end of his tenure to thwart the Republicans' hopes for a congenial transition. As Jefferson told it, "Mr A. embarrasses us. He keeps the offices of State & War vacant, has named Bayard M[inister] P[lenipotentiary] to France, and has called an unorganized Senate on the 4th. of March [inauguration day]." For his part, close observer Madison—never an Adams admirer—held, "The conduct of Mr. A. is not such as was to have been wished or perhaps expected. Instead of smoothing the path for his successor, he plays into the hands of those who are endeavoring to strew it with as many difficulties as possible; and with this view does not manifest a very squeamish regard to the Const[itutio]n."[10]

Jefferson's election a mere fifteen days prior to his inauguration had left him so pressed that he sent a letter to his intended secretary of war, Henry Dearborn, offering him the job the same day that he wrote informing Madison of the result.[11] The following day, Jefferson wrote imploring Meriwether Lewis to serve as his private secretary.[12] The young army captain's "knolege of the Western country, of the army and of all it's interests & relations" had made him especially fit for this post—which, Jefferson hastened to add, several other men had requested. While it would not pay well, it would put Lewis in contact with men whose acquaintance would help him later in his career (not least of them, it went without saying, Jefferson himself). A few days later, the president-elect informed Chancellor Robert Livingston of New York, who with Jefferson had been one of the five members of the congressional committee that drafted the Declaration of Independence, that he chose him to be minister plenipotentiary to France. Livingston soon accepted, and he would fill the post to momentous effect.[13]

About the same time, Jefferson repeated his observation about the popular effect of Federalist congressmen's machinations during the House proceedings. He then noted that Adams's calling the Senate, "imperfect as it will be on the 4th. of March," into session could lead to rejection of Jefferson's leading appointments. "This to be sure," he concluded, "would dismast our ship, before leaving port."[14]

Jefferson assured Representative Pinckney's delegation,

I know the difficulties of the station to which I am called and feel and acknowledge my incompetence to them. But whatsoever of understanding, whatsoever of diligence, whatsoever of justice or of affectionate concern for the happiness of man, it has pleased Providence to place within the compass of my faculties shall be called forth for the discharge of the duties confided to me, and for procuring to my fellow-citizens all the benefits which our Constitution has placed under the guardianship of the General Government. Guided by the wisdom and patriotism of those to whom it belongs to express the legislative will of the nation, I will give to that will a faithful execution.

On February 28, 1801, Vice President Jefferson resigned his office to make way for the Senate to select a new president pro tempore. Jefferson bade that body farewell in his characteristic way, noting that he "no doubt" had erred in his role as the Senate's president and holding that "for honest errors however indulgence may be hoped."[15]

Thus spoke Jefferson on February 28th. Due to the prolonged standoff in the House, if he put off writing it until certain of his election, Jefferson had only twelve days to prepare his First Inaugural Address for delivery on March 4th. Every indication is that he had not waited to begin writing it.

Jefferson's First Inaugural Address is one of only a handful of such speeches that repay a reading. Despite its sparkling eloquence and striking economy of expression, however, the mere text tells only part of the story. "The Revolution of 1800," as Jefferson later dubbed his party's electoral conquest, began before the new president laid his manuscript on the lectern.[16]

Part of that Revolution was a sharp shift in manners. The occasion of George Washington's first inauguration had become one extended celebration of the Continental Army's only commander-in-chief. En route from Mt. Vernon on the Potomac to Manhattan on the Hudson, Washington progressed from one festivity to the next.[17] Local militia detachments escorted him, young ladies fêted him, and leading citizens of towns through which he passed held celebratory balls in his honor.

It was Washington who decided, without prompting from the Constitution, that there ought to be a presidential speech in conjunction with the prescribed oath. With help from Representative James Madison, President Washington prepared and delivered a classic Virginian inauguration address.[18] It began with an avowal that he had not wanted nor felt qualified for the job, proceeded through a lengthy observation about an unnamed god's essential aid in winning the Revolution and establishing the Constitution, rested for a while on the idea that the success of the federal republic would depend on the morality of officeholders and of the people in general, stopped briefly upon a call for constitutional amendments to buttress individual rights, added a disavowal of any desire for a salary, and concluded with a prayer to "the benign Parent of the Human Race" to superintend the new government's activity. The whole ceremony took place before a crowd of onlookers on Wall Street—again at Washington's instigation.

Washington's Second Inaugural Address was four sentences long. It said that he was called again to enter upon the presidential office, that he someday would express his "high sense of . . . [that] distinguished honor," that the Constitution required that he take the oath prior to entering into the presidential office, and that witnesses to his taking it would be able to reprimand him in case he violated it.[19]

Washington's successor, John Adams, was already in the federal capital as vice president, so he could not have made a great progress akin to Washington's 1789 journey. He would not have been celebrated similarly anyway. Still he did his best to emulate the general, buying a $1,500 carriage with his new $25,000 presidential salary for the short trek to the Capitol. The powder in his scant hair was offset by his pearl suit, and he wore a sword at his hip. Liveried servants—whose fancy clothes Adams had purchased—accompanied him. When the president-elect entered the chamber, Vice President Jefferson had already been seated. Yet, perhaps for the only time, not the incoming president but his predecessor was the star of the show.[20]

Adams's address took a markedly different tack from Washington's First Inaugural.[21] He began by recounting the genesis of the Revolution and the supposed sources of the Articles of Confederation, which he said had been known to be inadequate early in their life. He then gave a stock Federalist account of the symptoms of the Articles' failure and a happy summary of the creation of the United States Constitution.

Adams noted that he had been absent—in England, as it happens—when the Constitution was written, and he (falsely) said that he had always praised it, in public as in private. (Vice President Jefferson, listening to this address, might well have recalled that Adams's first evaluation of it to Jefferson had taken the form of a list of its positive and negative attributes.)[22] In response to what had come to be common Republican criticisms of him, Adams took pains to say repeatedly that he had never advocated life terms for any Executive Branch or Legislative Branch official. He then described his policy aims in a general way and asked that the All-Powerful continue "His blessing upon this nation."

Thomas Jefferson's First Inaugural Address would be notably different from his predecessors' addresses.[23] He had several aims in mind. They shaped both his performance throughout the Inauguration Day and his First Inaugural Address itself.

In marked contrast to his predecessors, President-Elect Jefferson walked from his boardinghouse on Capitol Hill to the Capitol. Though he was preceded by a contingent of local militiamen with swords drawn, a few D.C. marshals, and a couple of Adams Cabinet members, Jefferson's procession struck contemporaries as calculated not to display the "pomp and pageantry" of the Washington and Adams inaugurations.[24] (Jefferson was to make a habit of his informality, often riding about the town unaccompanied. Although he kept a carriage at the White House stable, it was only used when his daughters came to Washington to visit. Not only did Jefferson ride around town on various errands, but the locals noticed him "fastening his horse's bridle himself to the shop doors." President Jefferson enjoyed local diversions including a tightrope act, horse races, plays, and scientific lectures.)[25] A description of the same setting early the previous October has it marked by hovels and "[a]ll the materials for building, bricks, planks, stone, & c. [*sic*]"

The U.S. Capitol was then "a large square, ungraceful, white building."[26] As only one wing of the Capitol, the Senate wing, had been completed, Jefferson would speak there. When he entered the room, the audience would have noticed that though certainly able to afford impressive clothing, Jefferson showed up at the big event dressed notably downscale, with no ceremonial sword in sight.

An eyewitness and a Jefferson acquaintance, Mrs. Margaret B. Smith, described the event this way:

> I have this morning witnessed one of the most interesting scenes, a free people can ever witness. The changes of administration, which in every government and in every age have most generally been epochs of confusion, villainy and bloodshed, in this our happy country take place without any species of distraction, or disorder. . . . I cannot describe the agitation I felt, while I looked around on the various multitude and while I listened to an address, containing principles the most correct, sentiments the most liberal, and wishes the most benevolent, conveyed in the most appropriate and elegant language and in a manner mild as it was firm. . . . The Senate chamber was so crowded that I believe not another creature could enter. . . . The speech was delivered in so low a tone that few heard it. . . . [27]

The party change in control of the Federal Government—a novelty in world history—stood out. It had occasioned no "confusion, villainy [or] bloodshed, in this our happy country."

Smith undoubtedly had not been alone in thinking that this was just the way things would work in America, thank God. In this she erred: the election of 1800–01 was a near-run thing. Though the Republican tandem of Jefferson and Aaron Burr outstripped its Federalist opponents, President John Adams's challengers tied each other in the Electoral College. Who would succeed Adams, no one knew.

Nowadays, according to the terms of the Twelfth Amendment, members of the Electoral College cast one vote for president and another for vice president. The Twelfth Amendment corrected a problem highlighted by the election of 1800. Under the Constitution as it came out of the Philadelphia Convention that framed it, each elector cast two undifferentiated votes. The Framers did not foresee the advent of political parties, and so they did not envision a scenario in which running mates each received votes from all of their party's electors—and thus had the same number of electoral votes.

In 1796 when Jefferson won the vice presidency by coming in second to

John Adams, he edged out Aaron Burr.[28] A few Virginian Republican electors' decision not to vote for Burr so that their man Jefferson would beat him accounted for the margin. Burr remembered his fellow Republicans' 1796 betrayal in November 1800. If some Republicans thought Burr ought to announce to the world that Jefferson ought to be the House of Representatives' choice, why should Burr have been among them? Through the entire thirty-six-ballot contest, Burr issued no public statement. Rumors circulated concerning supposed negotiations for Federalist support of a Burr presidency, but from what we can tell, Burr rejected any consideration of turning coat.

Meanwhile former treasury secretary Alexander Hamilton encouraged Federalist representatives to opt for Jefferson. "If there was a man in the world I ought to hate," Hamilton confided, "it is Jefferson. With Burr I have always been personally well."[29] He said more:

> *Jefferson* or *Burr*?—the former without all doubt. The latter in my judgment has no principle public or private—could be bound by no agreement— will listen to no monitor but his ambition; & for this purpose will use the *worst* part of the community as a ladder to climb to perman[en]t power & an instrument to crush the better part. He is bankrupt beyond redemption except by the resources that grow out of war and disorder or by a sale to a foreign power or by great peculation. War with Great Brita[i]n would be the immediate instrument. He is sanguine enough to hope every thing—daring enough to attempt every thing—wicked enough to scruple nothing. From the elevation of such a man heaven preserve the Country![30]

The Republicans did not have to be told that, however. They ought to be allowed the outcome they preferred after some kind of bargain was struck. So, Hamilton counseled, "Let our situation be improved to obtain from Jefferson assurances on certain points—the maintenance of the present system especially on the cardinal articles of public Credit, a *Navy, Neutrality*." When the House finally did elect Jefferson, the public did not know why. In later years the Delaware congressman whose switch from Burr to abstention had proven decisive gave an account of the bargain he had driven remarkably similar to Hamilton's suggestion. That congressman's version of history receives substantial support from the reality that President Jefferson ultimately provided all three items on Hamilton's wish list. Jefferson always denied having made a bargain.

Thomas Jefferson's First Inaugural Address signaled that party contestation should not continue at its accustomed pitch. He said in it that social life should return to normal—a state in which Jefferson's principles were recognized as Americans' principles. This tall, thin, unassuming man envisioned a different course for America's political elite—and for Americans at large. "Let us then, fellow citizens," he implored, "unite with one heart and one mind, let us restore to social intercourse that harmony and affection without which liberty, and even life itself, are but dreary things."[31] This was not mere verbiage: Jefferson ached for close relationships with intellectual peers—with fellow citizens and foreign members of the "Republic of Letters" disposed to share such relations with him.[32]

He continued by saying, "And let us reflect that having banished from our land that religious intolerance under which mankind so long bled and suffered, we have yet gained little if we countenance a political intolerance, as despotic, as wicked, and capable of as bitter and bloody persecutions." The extreme political acrimony of the 1790s had not arisen unprovoked, he insisted. It owed to divisions over the French Revolution. Republicans had been extremely hopeful that America's ally Louis XVI and his numerous soldiers who had fought in the American Revolution might succeed in reforming the land where a king could rightly say *"L'état, c'est moi"* into a constitutional monarchy. Jefferson, then the United States' ambassador, had participated in the early French reform efforts, and his hopes had proven the most enduring of all. Yet in the end Federalists saw their forecasts fulfilled as French republicanism degenerated into tyranny.[33]

As Jefferson put it, "During the throes and convulsions of the ancient world, during the agonising spasms of infuriated man, seeking through blood and slaughter his long lost liberty, it was not wonderful that the agitation of the billows should reach even this distant and peaceful shore; that this should be more felt and feared by some and less by others; and should divide opinions as to measures of safety. . . ."

Then came the passage most noted at the time and most often remembered since. Yes, Americans had been divided in the 1790s, but "every difference of opinion is not a difference of principle. We have called by different names brethren of the same principle. We are all republicans; we are all federalists."

Members of Jefferson's U.S. Capitol audience must have smiled, even gasped, at this. The Federalist Party, newly thrown into opposition, was gleeful. From such a man as they thought Jefferson to be—at least as they said he was—they would never have heard such a thing. He was a "Galloman," a Jacobin, a beast whose election, according to Connecticut's leading churchman, might mean the government would burn New Englanders' family Bibles and somehow make their "wives and daughters the victims of legal prostitution."[34] In France les Tricoteuses had stationed themselves on the Place de la Révolution day after day to watch as enemies of the Revolution were beheaded with that grisly, efficient invention of Dr. Guillotine. Perhaps the same fate lay in store for Federalist leaders.

But no. "If there be any among us," Jefferson intoned, "who would wish to dissolve this Union [that is, who were not federalist], or to change its republican form [i.e., who were not republican], let them stand undisturbed as monuments of the safety with which error of opinion may be tolerated, where reason is left free to combat it." American Republicans were not French Revolutionaries. His followers should think of their vanquished partisan foes as simply having come to a different appraisal of the situation. Soon enough, run-of-the-mill Jeffersonians would lament their leader's refusal to purge all of their defeated enemies from federal office and appoint Republicans in their places. He struggled to ignore them.

One ground of Federalist fear concerned the Adams administration's military buildup. Republicans had opposed it. Would they undo it? Perhaps they would. (Jefferson's intention to name the parsimonious Albert Gallatin treasury secretary certainly pointed in that direction.) Jeffersonians denied that palaces, crowns, and warships were the measure of national greatness. Unlike some leading Federalists, they did not murmur among themselves that only kings, lords, and large armies could keep a country safe. "I know indeed that some honest men fear a republican government cannot be strong," Jefferson held, "that this government is not strong enough. But would the honest patriot, in the full tide of successful experiment, abandon a government which has so far kept us free and firm, on the theoretic and visionary fear, that this government, the world's best hope, may, by possibility, want energy to preserve itself?" In other words, would a true American abandon republicanism out of fear that it might fail? "I trust not. I believe this . . . the strongest government on earth. I believe it is the only one, where every man, at the call of the law, would fly to the standard of the law, and would meet invasions of the public order as his own personal concern." There need not be a substantial peacetime army. Americans would defend the country if need be. Given his wartime experience as governor of Virginia, Jefferson cannot have been as certain of this as he tried to seem. Still, a hiatus in the Napoleonic Wars seemed an apt occasion to test the theory.[35]

Jefferson next described the United States as he understood them. Americans ought to hold to their "federal and republican principles," their "attachment to union and representative government." Their isolation from the Old World, their "chosen country, with room enough for . . . descendants to the thousandth and thousandth generation," their devotion to the principle that esteem followed achievement rather than inheritance, their "benign religion . . . inculcating honesty, truth, temperance, gratitude and the love of man, acknowledging and adoring an overruling providence" concerned for man's happiness—all of these signaled the likelihood of the American republican experiment's success.

"Still one thing more," he insisted, was needed for Americans to be "a happy and a prosperous people": a wise and frugal government. It would protect men from each other, "leave them otherwise free to regulate their own pursuits of industry and improvement, and . . . not take from the mouth of labor the bread it [had] earned." He summarized his little foray into political science by saying, "This is the sum of good government; and this is necessary to close the circle of our felicities."

In his penultimate paragraph Jefferson summarized his personal political philosophy, which by this time was Republicans' philosophy. He held that his fellow citizens had a right to understand his principles of government, and thus of administration. The first of these was "Equal and exact justice to all men, of whatever state or persuasion, religious or political." Careful observers of the political scene knew Jefferson as author of the Virginia Statute for Religious Freedom. That law had disentangled the Old Dominion's government from its former established church. It had also banned government discrimination based on religion. These Jeffersonian policies rested on the assertion that "Almighty God" had made man free in this regard. Equal justice would be done to Federalists too.[36]

Next Jefferson laid down in immortal language his devotion to "peace, commerce, and honest friendship with all nations, entangling alliances with none." An attentive Federalist might have thought this a paean to Hamiltonian neutrality. It was more. Jefferson here undertook, and his successors would continue, an experiment in foreign relations based not on nations' military capacity, but on liberal economics. Trade would improve man's lot, and so nations should remain at peace. Trading partners would be friends. Unforeseen developments overseas in time scuttled this new departure—though not Americans' attraction to it.[37]

Jefferson next pledged his devotion to "the support of the state governments in all their rights, as the most competent administrations for our domestic concerns, and the surest bulwarks against anti-republican tendencies" and "the preservation of the General government in its whole constitutional vigor, as the sheet anchor of our peace at home, and safety abroad." For Jefferson, federalism was a two-sided coin. To abandon either principle would mean the failure of the American Experiment. Scholars in our own day have been prone to wish away Jefferson's devotion to federalism, aka "states' rights." A recent account of the First Inaugural considers the principles Jefferson listed in this extended passage at length, omitting only one: his stated commitment to "the support of the state governments in all their rights."[38] Leaving out one of these two twinned principles, states' rights, while remaining attentive to "the General government in its whole constitutional vigor" has over time yielded a significantly distorted, far less republican constitutional system—one utterly unlike what Jeffersonians hoped the United States' would become. Jefferson's vow in this speech that both principles would be respected foretold much of American history over the next quarter century.[39]

Jefferson continued through a list of important American principles: free elections, majority rule, reliance on militia in peacetime, subordination of soldiers to civilian officials, "economy in the public expence," "the honest payment of our debts," open rather than secretive government, "freedom of religion; freedom of the press; and freedom of person, under the protection of the Habeas Corpus:—and trial by juries impartially selected." "These principles," he concluded, ". . . should be the creed of our political faith. . . ." He and his audience could not know it, but these would be the principles not only of Jefferson's administration, but of James Madison's and James Monroe's administrations as well.

While it is not apparent now, Jefferson honed that list of principles to cool the partisan flame of the 1790s, which still divided the country as he spoke. On one hand the opposition Federalists could be expected to dislike his insistence that militia, rather than professional soldiers, could be counted on to defend the country most of the time. On the other hand Federalists could be—in fact, were—relieved by his vow to ensure that the United States Government met its debt obligations. The New England religious establishment, in particular, could be counted on to dislike hearing that its bête noir, now in the chief executive office, intended to mete out justice to people of all religious persuasions, but Federalists generally should be pleased by Jefferson's statements about the rights of the minority—rights Republicans believed they had often been denied while Federalists held power.[40]

President Jefferson closed his address with an appeal for Americans' indulgence. Having held the highest subordinate offices, he said, "I have learnt to expect that it will rarely fall to the lot of imperfect man to retire from this station with the reputation, and the favor, which bring him into it." Jefferson had intended in a bipartisan gesture to compliment both of his predecessors, but John Adams had slipped out of town rather than participate in the day's solemnities, so he revised his address to make reference only to George Washington.[41] He thus said, "Without pretensions to that high confidence you reposed in our first and greatest revolutionary character, whose pre-eminent services had entitled him to the first place in his country's love, and destined for him the fairest page in the volume of faithful history," he hoped his countrymen would bear with him when he occasionally erred "through defect of judgment." He would never do so intentionally. He hoped his supporters and opponents both would see that he had done "them all the good in [his] power."

Then came one last surprise. The man from whom little old ladies in New England had been warned they must hide their family Bibles asked "that infinite power, which rules the destinies of the universe" to aid government officials in their tasks. Soon enough the statesman whose House election had at last broken "an awful and portentous silence"[42] and elicited celebrations across the country[43] was author of an address read by the cognoscenti all over America and in numerous European lands. The First Inaugural Address's admirers on the Old Continent saw to its publication in English, French, German, and Italian, at least.[44]

2

⁘

The federal Union over which Thomas Jefferson became president on March 4, 1801, was a land of hope and promise. Its southern boundary was at Spanish Florida, which in those days extended all the way to the Mississippi River. Though John Jay's diplomatic triumph at Paris in 1783 had unexpectedly given Americans the Father of Rivers as their western border, the pivotal ocean outlet at New Orleans remained the property of the Spanish monarchy—a hesitant participant on the American side in the Revolution.

The Electoral College in which Jefferson had tied Burr and the House of Representatives that chose between them represented the original thirteen states, plus Tennessee, Kentucky, and Vermont. Communication between the coastal United States and the areas beyond the Appalachians was slow, because roads were virtually nonexistent. From Bacon's Rebellion (1676) through the Carolina Regulation of the 1760s–1770s, Shays's Rebellion (1786), and the ratification campaign (1787–88) to the Whiskey Rebellion (1794) and on, East-West relationships had always been fraught. Inlanders believed their coastal brethren disdained, ignored, or exploited them, depending on the circumstance.

Besides distinctions between the coastal regions and the trans-Appalachian area, different parts of America also differed in other ways. So, for example, the longest-settled American region, the Tidewater Chesapeake, had come, through a combination of factors, to be almost entirely rural. Its economy centered on production of tobacco for export using slave labor, and numerous Tidewater counties had substantial slave majorities—several of two-thirds or more.

Tobacco planters dominated Virginia politics and society. Some of the great families, the fabled "FFVs" (First Families of Virginia), had large networks of kin owning tens of thousands of acres in numerous counties in Tidewater, Southside Virginia (the region below the James River, which bisects the Tidewater from west to east), and the Piedmont. Jefferson and Madison, respectively of the Randolph and the Taylor clans, hailed from Piedmont, Virginia. "Keep your land and your land will keep you," John Randolph of Roanoke, a cousin of Jefferson's prominent in Virginia Dynasty politics, remembered having his mother counsel him.[1] Randolph followed that advice to a T. His slaves took care of him too, and he requited them by freeing more than four hundred of them at his death. (Neither Jefferson nor Madison, far less careful with their money, did anything like that.)

A notably wealthy Virginian owned dozens of slaves. Madison owned more than a hundred. Jefferson owned more than two hundred at the height of his holdings. Both Madison and Jefferson expressed considerable uneasiness about this. Hard though it is for us to believe now, they were born into a world in which essentially no one had ever said slavery was wrong. Yet they grew to think it was as other citizens of the transatlantic "republic of letters" did. Besides Jefferson's cousin Randolph, George Washington freed his many slaves in his will. Large planters such as they were few and far between. Jefferson wrote that slavery was an evil that had to be, would be, abolished. He took substantial steps against it, as we will see. Yet he died enmeshed in slaveholding, and nearly all of his slaves were auctioned to satisfy his creditors. Madison's story was similar.

When Jefferson became president, tobacco remained a lucrative crop. Some great planters such as George Washington had begun the process of giving up growing John Rolfe's weed and transitioning to wheat. Virginia became a slave exporter, peopling Deep South states with bondsmen for money. John Randolph, for one, decried this practice. Being sold away from everything and everyone they knew was a terrible fate for slaves. Yet the practice continued. Though the most populous British colony in North America, Virginia by 1776 had no significant town. At the time of Jefferson's inauguration a quarter century later, it still had none.

From 1619 Virginia representatives met in its General Assembly, and they became a separate House of Burgesses in 1642. It was the first representative assembly in the Western Hemisphere. Planters—owners of significant numbers of slaves—dominated it from the first. In 1619 large landowners in Virginia employed mostly indentured servants, the overwhelming majority of whom were white. That changed in the 1680s, when improvements in the English economy and the Royal Navy's success in the Atlantic made white labor less readily available and slaves cheaper than before. The property qualification for voting seems to have been low enough that about half of white men qualified—which meant Virginia had a more democratic system than virtually any other place in the world, the New England colonies and a couple of Swiss cantons excepted.

New England, the second part of English North America settled, never had significant slave-based agriculture. Puritans and Separatists had no particular moral qualms about slavery, but the environment of Massachusetts was not conducive to it. With its scant arable land, harsh weather, and lengthy shorelines, and because New England's first settlers arrived as family units, New England early on came to be a land of small farms, sailing ships, and towns. Neither a very rich class nor a subordinated laboring class was much in evidence. The social elite ran town meetings, in which all male members of the local congregation were eligible to participate. Anyone who ran athwart the religious authorities would be shown the road to Rhode Island, the Isle of Errors. Quakers who returned after being expelled from Massachusetts Bay Colony suffered the draconian punishment of hanging, which prompted King Charles II to merge Plymouth and Massachusetts Bay into one colony, New Haven and Connecticut into another, and to ban such behavior. He also took control of selecting Massachusetts's governor and required the New England colonies to allow construction of Anglican churches.

Between New England and Maryland lay the Middle Colonies, three of which had been founded by Quakers (and thus never had a religious establishment) and the other of which, New York, was peculiar from the beginning. A Dutch colony, New Amsterdam proved too attractive a property not to draw England's attention. When the English conquered it, naming it for James, Duke of York (later James II/VII), English settlement meant it never had any significant religious majority. Nominally Anglican in the area around the city, its heterogeneous population meant New York never really required church participation. All four of the Middle Colonies' cultures centered on trade, particularly through the great ports of New York and Philadelphia. One significant distinction between the Quaker colonies and New York lay in the affectation of simplicity among the well-to-do Quakers. New York's rich always gloried in their riches. By the time the Revolution came, the Hudson River Valley and counties on Long Island featured significant slaveholdings, but after the war, the slave owners' political power did not match their economic majesty.

At the Revolution's start colonists began to take up in earnest the question of slavery's future. Essentially unchallenged, if not unremarked, through world history, slavery came to seem a moral error among a few Anglophones late in the seventeenth century. Pennsylvania colonists organized the first abolition organization, the Pennsylvania Abolition Society, in Philadelphia in 1775.[2] They elected sometime governor Benjamin Franklin its president in 1785, then asked him to present its cause to the Philadelphia Convention that wrote the Constitution. Though a member, Franklin seemingly did not present the abolitionist cause. He did, however, join in petitioning the First Federal Congress for abolition in 1790. By that time numerous states had acted against slavery—Vermont and Massachusetts by banning it, and several others by adopting "gradual emancipation acts," laws whose effect would be to eliminate the institution from particular states gradually. (The classic gradual emancipation act, signed into law by New York governor John Jay in 1799, freed New York slaves born after July 4, 1799, when they reached age twenty-eight for males and age twenty-five for females.)[3]

Virginia was not among them. Although Jefferson had cosponsored a gradual emancipation bill in the Virginia House of Burgesses in 1769, its overwhelming rejection by that body led him to put the cause on the back burner. However, he underscored his support for such a law in *Notes on the State of Virginia* (1781), saying that Virginia slaves eventually would be free, but he claimed to his death in 1826 that public opinion in the Old Dominion had not yet ripened to acceptance of such a reform.[4]

In general, states farther south were more resistant to abolition than Virginia. South Carolina and Georgia delegates insisted in the Philadelphia Convention that the Constitution include substantial protections for slavery, which anyway seemed to be on its last economic legs. However, Connecticut Yankee Eli Whitney's invention of the cotton gin meant that by the time of Jefferson's inauguration, the Deep South would become the heart of American slavery, which became more lucrative all the time. From those days to 1865, Virginia exported slaves to other states farther south and west. Jefferson, Madison, and their fellow Virginian James Monroe would have to deal with this matter repeatedly as presidents.

Jefferson asked Madison on December 19, 1800, during the pendency of the House election, to come to Washington.[5] Madison replied that he thought it inappropriate to put in an appearance not only before he had been nominated, but even before the presidential election had been decided. He added that his father's poor and declining health necessitated his staying at Montpelier.[6] On February 27th, James Madison Sr. died.[7] Though the oldest of his parents' large brood, James Madison Jr. had never owned his own home until his father died. He was fifty years old.

3

✣ ☼ ✣

By 1801 Jefferson and Madison had long been political allies. The two of them first worked together in 1779, when Jefferson embarked upon his governorship and Madison sat upon the Virginia Council of State—a kind of Cabinet appointed by the General Assembly. Similarly brilliant and bookish, though of substantially different casts of mind, they found each other's personalities highly congenial. If their political principles differed, they overcame those differences almost completely.

The popular movement that elected Jefferson to office, the Republican Party, reflected the programmatic goals of its figurehead and its main organizer. Contrary to expectation Jefferson became widely known as draftsman of the Declaration of Independence during the 1790s party conflict.[1] Elevating him to that august status was the work of the Republicans' chief organizer, James Madison.[2]

While Secretary of State Jefferson avoided public disputation, he did encourage others to take up the task. Most notably he paid Philip Freneau a State Department stipend to translate French—a language Jefferson spoke fluently—so that Freneau could launch a newspaper critical of Secretary of the Treasury Alexander Hamilton. Jefferson also aided Freneau by giving him "access to the foreign newspapers of the State Department," in addition to being "attentive to seemingly small matters of post offices, post roads, and postal rates, as well as a willing solicitor of subscriptions to" his paper.[3] Sometime Virginia U.S. senator John Taylor of Caroline (a Madison cousin) contributed numerous punchy and learned pseudonymous pamphlets to the cause as well.[4]

In a pinch Madison himself did the hard work of answering the indefatigable Hamilton. Hamilton had to be considered "a colossus to the antirepublican party," Jefferson said on one notable occasion, ". . . he is an host within himself. . . . In truth, when he comes forward, there is nobody but yourself who can meet him."[5] On at least one occasion Madison came away from such a contest thoroughly whipped.[6]

Republicans stood for a set of clear philosophical and policy positions. In fact their holding the positions antedated their organization as a party.[7] As prior to the Revolution, so in the 1790s Jefferson and the like subscribed to eighteenth-century British Opposition nostrums: they generally opposed war, standing armies, banks, taxes, debt, and Executive Branch influence over the Legislative Branch. They favored individual rights and decentralization of authority. The utility of written constitutions lay in limiting government power. Jefferson's claim that the "Revolution of 1800" had returned America to its rightful principles rested on the idea that each of these principles had been part of the Spirit of '76.

President Jefferson had considerable foreign policy experience. He had served as American minister to France during the Confederation period, and then he had been secretary of state in George Washington's first administration. He had traveled in Italy and England besides. James Madison, on the other hand, never left the United States.[8] Born to the richest planter in Orange County, Virginia, adjacent to Jefferson's Albemarle, Madison benefited from being a firstborn son much as Jefferson had. His father, James Sr., provided private tutors for the heir apparent until time came for the scion to head off to college. Sickly, thus averse to living in the Tidewater region where Virginia's College of William & Mary was located, James Jr. went to the College of New Jersey (now Princeton University) for intellectual finishing.

At Princeton, Madison proved remarkably studious. Both the New Jersey tradition of religious freedom and President John Witherspoon's Calvinism left lasting impressions on him—the latter perhaps not so much for its religious doctrine as for a certain skepticism about human nature. (Witherspoon was a Presbyterian clergyman.)

Madison followed the worsening Imperial Crisis closely, and eventually found himself in Virginia's May Convention of 1776. There, in his first elective office, he participated in drafting the first American declaration of rights and constitution, the Virginia Declaration of Rights and Constitution of 1776. His chief contribution as the youngest participant in that process was in persuading George Mason and their colleagues to substitute "free exercise" for Mason's "fullest toleration" in the Declaration's religious freedom article.

Madison next served in the new Council of State, a kind of Executive cabinet appointed by the General Assembly. His tenure began during the tenure of the Old Dominion's first republican governor, Patrick Henry, and carried into that of its second, Jefferson. By all accounts, the Jefferson-Madison friendship began then.

His tenure in the Continental/Confederation Congress (1780–83) played a key role in shaping Madison's mature constitutional vision. Congress lacked the fiscal resources to fund the war. Its diplomatic delegations could not be maintained without frequent requests for loans from the countries in which they were stationed. State governments complied half-heartedly from time to time. Congress had to relocate occasionally to avoid capture by the British, and soldiers threatened mutiny over arrears in pay.

Term-limited out of Congress, Madison returned to Virginia. He had persuaded his colleagues to send Jefferson as Benjamin Franklin's replacement at Versailles, and in the older man's absence Madison pushed several of Jefferson's Revisal of the Laws bills through the General Assembly. Among those the Bill for Establishing Religious Freedom took pride of place. Immediately after its passage, Madison wrote Minister Jefferson, "I flatter myself [we] have in this Country extinguished for ever the ambitious hope of making laws for the human mind."[9]

Unhappy with the state of Virginia's relations with the other states, Delegate Madison played the leading role in moving the General Assembly to instigate first the Mt. Vernon Conference of 1785 and then the abortive Annapolis Convention of 1786. The former succeeded in arranging an agreement between Virginia and Maryland concerning various matters related to their Potomac River, but attendance at the Annapolis Convention proved insufficient for the business of proposing to Congress and the states reforms to the commercial laws of the Union. Therefore Madison, fellow Virginian Edmund Randolph, and New York delegate Alexander Hamilton threw together a communication to Congress recommending another convention be called for Philadelphia the following year.

Congress complied. Meanwhile Madison applied himself to what one historian called his "research project."[10] Using several crates of related books he had had Jefferson send him from France, he dove into the history and theory of federal governments and the experience of the American federation. The products were a set of notes on confederations and a summary of the Confederation's flaws, "Vices of the Political System of the United States."[11] As had become his custom, Madison would be the best-prepared delegate in Philadelphia.

During the several months before the Philadelphia Convention's May 1787 opening, Madison also set himself another task: persuading George Washington to attend as a Virginia delegate.[12] Madison's success on this score seemed to him essential to success in creating a new federal constitution. While Pennsylvania and South Carolina had sent their most prominent statesmen to the Convention, Washington's imprimatur gave it the legitimacy it might otherwise have lacked.

Veteran of years in legislative bodies, Madison knew the importance of tactics, not to say legerdemain.[13] At his instigation his Virginia delegation prepared for the event's opening by drafting a set of fifteen resolutions outlining the changes to the federal constitution it had in mind. This "Virginia Plan," as it has come to be known, would have replaced the federal Confederation Congress with a national government featuring national legislative, executive, and judicial branches.

Though often called "the Father of the Constitution," Madison in fact had a sharply limited impact on the document's final form. For example, though he had envisioned a bicameral legislature in which both houses were apportioned by population, the lower house was elected by the people, and the upper house was elected by the lower house, and though the legislature in his proposal would have had a general legislative authority and a veto over all state laws, only two of these concepts—that there should be a bicameral legislature and that its lower house should be elected by the people—made their way into the Constitution. Madison repeatedly insisted that the large states would never accept state equality in the upper house and tried repeatedly to have his "favorite provision"—the veto over state laws—included. The final time he raised that last issue, it went down by a vote of ten states to zero. One prominent historian, Forrest McDonald, calculated that Madison lost on forty of seventy-one recorded votes in the Philadelphia Convention. Madison, in turn, called the Constitution "the work of many heads and many hands," perhaps recalling that he had called the congressional veto his favorite proposal.[14]

Madison did play the leading role in the process of ratifying the Constitution, particularly in Virginia.[15] With his thoughtful, dispassionate exposition of the Constitution, often building on arguments he had made under a pseudonym in *The Federalist*, he stood down Virginia's avatar of republicanism—and America's greatest orator—Patrick Henry. Having promised first the Richmond Convention and then his constituents that he would seek amendments in the First Congress, he pushed those through the House despite his colleagues' annoyance that he was taking up their time with so unimportant a matter for purely Virginian political reasons.[16]

Since the months leading up to the Philadelphia Convention, Madison had been in close cooperation with George Washington. The two of them had played key roles in Philadelphia. Now Madison served Washington as chief advisor, particularly when it came to selecting the men to hold appointed positions in the Executive and Judicial Branches. One of those choices, Madison's third recommendation for treasury secretary, was New Yorker Alexander Hamilton.

Madison knew Hamilton from Congress, Annapolis, and Philadelphia, besides their collaboration on *The Federalist*. The two of them had supported Robert Morris's efforts in Congress to finance the Revolution and the Confederation Government.[17] Likely they expected to cooperate closely during Washington's presidency. Their expectations proved mistaken.

Numerous historians have written excellent accounts of the party conflict of the 1790s Jefferson would one day lament in his First Inaugural Address.[18] Without their realizing it was happening, Madison, Hamilton, Jefferson, and eventually Washington were drawn into partisanship.[19] At root it resulted from differing ideas of what the American Revolution had been about.

In creating the Department of the Treasury, Congress required the first treasury secretary to propose a financial system for the new government.[20] Hamilton brilliantly did so. A practical man, as army officers generally are, Hamilton looked for an example the Federal Government might follow to the most successful country of his day: the United Kingdom. Unconcerned with philosophical niceties, Hamilton proposed that Congress emulate the British down the line. Hamilton's most perceptive biographer nicely captures Hamilton's attitude by using a couplet from Alexander Pope's "Essay on Man" as epigraph of his first chapter on Hamilton's tenure as secretary:

> For Forms of Government let fools contest;
> Whate'er is best administered is best.

Note that the couplet serves not only as a summary of Hamilton's attitude, but as a rebuke of his opponents.

Hamilton's proposals contemplated federal assumption of state debts, a tariff, funding the debt, an excise on whiskey, and chartering a national bank. He forecast several benefits from adoption of these measures, virtually all of which—such as a reduction of the interest the U.S. Government had to pay on its bonds following assumption of state debts—were borne out by experience. The result of assumption was that the Federal Government paid only 4 percent, rather than the former 6 percent, on the debt over the following decade—a savings of approximately one-third.[21]

Virginians, Thomas Jefferson ultimately most significant among them, had come under the sway of the English idea that government debt, war, and taxes were tightly interconnected.[22] A government at liberty to borrow would wage war, and an indebted government would impose stiff taxes. One generation's debt would weigh on succeeding generations. The dead would rule from the grave.

Ruminating on this matter and perhaps thinking of his late wife on the anniversary of her death seven years before, Jefferson on September 6, 1789, had written a letter to his friend James Madison. Jefferson was even more disposed than usual to ponder abstract truths at that point, because he had been aiding the Marquis de Lafayette in drafting his proposed French declaration of rights. He told Madison:

> The course of reflection in which we are immersed here on the elementary principles of society has presented this question to my mind; . . . , which I suppose to be self evident, '*that the earth belongs in usufruct to the living*': that the dead have neither powers nor rights over it. The portion occupied by any individual ceases to be his when himself ceases to be, and reverts to the society. If the society has formed no rules for the appropriation of it's lands in severality, it will be taken by the first occupants. These will generally be the wife and children of the decedent. If they have formed rules of appropriation, those rules may give it to the wife and children, or to some one of them, or to the legatee of the deceased. So they may give it to his creditor. But the child, the legatee, or creditor takes it, not by any natural right, but by a law of the society of which they are members, and to which they are subject. Then no man can, by *natural right*, oblige the lands he occupied, or the persons who succeed him in that occupation, to the paiment of debts contracted by him. For if he could, he might, during his own life, eat up the usufruct of the lands for several generations to come, and then the lands would belong to the dead, and not to the living, which would be the reverse of our principle. What is true of every member of the society individually, is true of them all collectively, since the rights of the whole can be no more than the sum of the rights of the individuals.[23]

("Usufruct," note, is a common legal term referring to a right to use property without impairing its value. A usufruct in a ski slope does not entitle the owner to strip-mine the mountainside.)

Madison, as was his wont, answered Jefferson with practical objections to his theory.[24] Historians have tended to conclude that the story ended there. What Herbert Sloan has shown, however, is that concern with debt—with

posterity's right not to be burdened by us—marked Jefferson's statesmanship ever after. Besides, his general attitude regarding the issue was pervasive among the Virginia ruling elite.

In response to Hamilton's assumption-and-funding proposal, which would
have raised the federal debt by adding the states' debts to it and providing
a permanent stream of revenue to service that debt, the Virginia political
elite howled with outrage. Patrick Henry and Richmond Ratification Convention Federalist Henry Lee sponsored House of Delegates resolutions
decrying Congress's exercise of powers not among those expressly granted
it.[25] In his brilliant study of Jefferson and debt, Herbert E. Sloan demon-
strates that not the formal constitutional question, but the perpetuation of
government debt—which in Britain might have been considered part of the
unwritten constitution—struck Hamilton's Virginia critics as assumption's
chief drawback.[26]

Ultimately Hamilton persuaded Jefferson and Madison that assumption
offered the sole hope of keeping the federal Union. On that basis, plus Hamilton's promises to compensate Virginia for debt it had already retired and
to help move the federal capital from New York to the Potomac River, they
agreed to persuade other Virginians to help assumption pass. Jefferson later
called that the biggest political mistake of his life. Why? It perpetuated the
federal debt. Given the chance in 1801, he would try to make things right.

Madison, chastened by his defeat in the election for Virginia's first U.S.
senators the year before and fresh off promising his constituents that in
case elected to the House, he would seek amendments making enumeration the basis of Congress's power, spoke up against Hamilton's next major
measure: the Bank Bill. Though Thomas Jefferson's Cabinet memorandum
for President George Washington is seen as the key document laying out
the strict construction/states' rights reading of the Constitution, Madison
made essentially the same argument weeks earlier in House debate. Congress had only the enumerated powers, Madison insisted. As the list in
Article I, Section 8 included no power to charter a bank, Congress had no
such power. Hamilton's House allies were wrong to claim that the General
Welfare Clause or the Necessary and Proper Clause gave Congress power
to charter a bank. The General Welfare Clause merely gave Congress
power to tax to fund exercise of the enumerated powers, while the Bank
Bill did not fall under the Necessary and Proper Clause because chartering
a bank was not necessary to exercise of any of the named powers. Madison also had privately counseled Washington to veto the bill by the time
the Cabinet considered the question. Jefferson's famous memorandum,

while characterized by Jefferson's trademark felicity of expression, said essentially the same thing.

Though their constitutional objections to Hamilton's stewardship would have been enough, the men who eventually became Jeffersonian Republicans found Hamilton's policies worrisome on other scores as well. That there should be a national bank and that the debt should be "funded" (serviced out of a dedicated stream of income) reflected Hamilton's propensity for copying British models. Funding the assumed state debts at par (that is, at face value) despite the wartime depreciation of state bonds and currency redounded to the benefit of the wealthy. Madison had tried to persuade fellow congressmen to redeem state instruments at discounted rates, but he met with defeat. Hamilton's friends, so the story went, benefited disproportionately. Madison, Jefferson, and others saw design in this.

At some point in this period, Madison shared with Jefferson his notes of Hamilton's June 18, 1787 Philadelphia Convention speech calling for a lifetime term for the president. Jefferson also recorded having been witness to an exchange between Vice President John Adams and Secretary Hamilton in which no sooner had Adams said of Britain's government, "Purge that constitution of its corruption, and give to its popular branch equality of representation, and it would be the most perfect constitution ever devised by the wit of man," than Hamilton had replied, "Purge it of its corruption, and give to its popular branch equality of representation, and it would become an *impracticable* government: as it stands at present, with all its supposed defects, it is the most perfect government which ever existed." As if that were not enough, Hamilton soon confided to Jefferson that, "the present government is not that which will answer the ends of society . . . and . . . it will probably be found expedient to go into the British form."[27] At least so Jefferson said.

We should note here that when Jefferson, Madison, Hamilton, and their contemporaries used the word "corruption," they had in mind a particular perversion of the British constitution: the ability of King George III, through his various appointment and patronage powers, to steer the House of Commons into support of his policy preferences. Though not personally corrupt, Hamilton seemed to Jefferson and his fellows to intend to corrupt Congress in this British sense.

Besides the assumption, funding, and Bank Bill issues, matters of foreign policy also divided the first few federal Congresses. George Washington's inauguration as the first president in 1789 nearly coincided with the first stirrings of what came to be the French Revolution, and soon enough the American political elite divided over what America's response ought to be. Hamilton, doubtless with an eye on the tariff revenue central to his financial program, stoutly resisted any measure that might alienate Britain—trade with which accounted for 90 percent of American trade. Secretary of State Jefferson, just back from five years as minister to France, took the opposite position. Not only did America have a mutual defense treaty with France, he insisted, and not only did both legal and moral obligations bind us to side with France, but after King Louis XVI was deposed so ought our republican faith. France, after all, was the only other significant republic in the world, and some of its leaders had fought on the American side in the Revolution.

Despite the facts that Jefferson was foreign minister and that he argued strenuously for a Francophile foreign policy, Washington ultimately issued a proclamation of neutrality. Crafted to avoid offending France (as, for example, by using the word "neutrality"), the proclamation of April 22, 1793, seemed a moral offense against France, if not a legal one. After all, the U.S.A. had a treaty obligation. So much the worse when Hamilton took to the papers to refer to it as the "Neutrality Proclamation."[28] Jefferson no doubt noted that in referring to it that way, Hamilton had (intentionally?) frittered away America's power to make the warring powers bid for its friendship.[29] Had he known of Hamilton's private assurances to the British minister, he would have been outraged.

Soon Hamilton took to the papers under the pseudonym "Pacificus" to defend the Neutrality Proclamation. His argument laid out a case for extensive Executive Branch discretion in making foreign policy. Jefferson, alarmed at yet more Anglophilic maneuvering, urged Madison, "For god's sake, my dear Sir, take up your pen, select the most striking heresies, and cut him to pieces in the face of the public."[30] Madison gave it his best effort, but even his most ardent academic admirers think Hamilton got the better of him. From the Republicans' "country party" perspective, Hamilton's insistence that the president shared, in some regards even dominated, constitutional policy making in the new government seemed reflective of his avowed admiration of Britain.

By this point the Republican Party was a going concern. Both among the political elite and among the people at large, Republicans recognized themselves as an organized group. James Madison's distaste for "faction" in *Federalist* 10 had yielded to the idea that party organization might be necessary, even inevitable. (Jefferson had said, "If I could not go to heaven but with a party, I would not go there at all,"[31] but as we have seen, he never got around to thinking of Republicans as a party.) However much the likes of

Jefferson may have resisted association with hoi polloi, the common man could associate himself with Jefferson.[32] Perhaps surprisingly Jefferson had not been known as "Penman of the Declaration of American Independence" before. It was in the political conflict of the 1790s that his partisans began to refer to him that way—to transform "the Continental Congress's press release on independence [in]to the statement of purpose for the American nation" and to emphasize the famous theoretical passage about men's equality in the state of nature.[33] Jefferson retired from the Cabinet at the end of 1793, leaving Madison to head up the Republican resistance in Philadelphia. Madison served out his current term and one more, retiring from federal service early in 1797.

4

✢ ⚙ ✢

adison soon sought election to a new office: state legislator. In the House of Delegates (formerly the House of Burgesses), he took several steps important to the national Republican Party's success. He drafted the law that changed Virginia's method of allocating presidential electors from a district basis to statewide/winner-take-all, which likely would deny John Adams any Virginia electoral votes in 1800. He pushed successfully for his and Jefferson's friend and ally James Monroe to be elected governor. (In those days Virginia's General Assembly elected its governor.) Most notoriously he followed up his secret draftsmanship of the Virginia Resolutions of 1798 with the *Virginia Report* of 1800 (sometimes called "Madison's Report").[1]

Madison would be the Jefferson Cabinet's first officer because of his close personal and political relationship to the president. There has been no other such relationship in American history: Jefferson and Madison not only were the closest of political allies, but each was the other's best friend. Though today's experts, armed with the mountains of private correspondence and political documentation each of them saved for us to study, notice various differences between Jefferson and Madison, their minds were so closely in tune as to seem indistinguishable to anyone in their own day. Besides this advantage Madison took to the office of secretary of state a determination to implement an experiment in foreign policy he had favored for nearly two decades. The United States, he and Jefferson agreed, would substitute economic might for military.[2] Presented with the lemons of inherent American military weakness, Madison would counsel Jefferson to make lemonade. To the feeble Federalist attempt to establish a naval force and give the U.S. Government means to pay for it, Madison told Jefferson—had told the voters—they ought to reply by eliminating it completely. In a day when Great Britain had more than eight hundred warships at sea, America should reduce a force that could be counted on one man's fingers.[3] Voters had rewarded the party with the low-tax program. Poetically, Madison would have to bear the burden of the predictable results as Jefferson's presidential successor.

The greatest of American historians, Henry Adams, distinguished between two wings of the Jeffersonian Republican coalition: the Southern and the Northern. Southern Republicans such as Jefferson and Madison rightly were called "Republicans," this great-grandson of John Adams wrote. Their northern allies, less concerned with constitutionalism, ought to be thought of as "Democrats."[4]

Primacy of place in that latter group went to the third glittering eminence of the Jefferson administration, Treasury Secretary Albert Gallatin. While unlike the other two members of the triumvirate in significant ways, this longest-serving major Cabinet officer in American history complemented Jefferson and Madison perfectly.

Gallatin became the rare exception to the old historians' saw that "dukes don't emigrate" by migrating to the United States from Geneva, Switzerland, at age nineteen in 1780.[5] His family came from Italian nobility, and his mother was a du Rosey. Having helped found the Genevan Republic, Gallatin's forebears had contributed five chief magistrates to their state in the sixteenth and seventeenth centuries.[6] As a result of his high birth, Albert enjoyed the best education Switzerland had to offer.[7]

Hungry for adventure, young Albert decided to embark for America. After seeing the northernmost American cities, including during a stint as a French instructor at Harvard College, he at last settled in western Pennsylvania and entered into business. Unlike the New England states, New York, South Carolina, Georgia, or Virginia, Pennsylvania in Gallatin's day could be called "democratic." As he explained, "In Pennsylvania, not only have we neither Livingstons nor Rensselaers, but from the suburbs of Philadelphia to the banks of the Ohio I do not know a single family that has any extensive influence. An equal distribution of property has rendered every individual independent, and there is among us true and real equality."[8] In this Pennsylvania differed markedly from Jefferson and Madison's Old Dominion.

Cold and isolated, the region Gallatin had chosen as his home ended up in the center of 1794's Whiskey Rebellion. While a hearty few like Albert Gallatin endeavored to establish businesses in his adopted home county, most of his neighbors farmed for home consumption. They also converted wheat to whiskey for transport across the mountains. This, so the story goes, is why his neighbors ultimately took the lead in the Whiskey Rebellion— which some Federalists dubbed "Gallatin's Insurrection."[9]

Told by the First Congress to propose a fiscal system for the new Federal

Government, Treasury Secretary Alexander Hamilton recommended among other measures establishment of an excise on whiskey. Rather than a flat tax, the law provided for a reduction of the rate of tax as the amount distilled rose. In other words it favored large, coastal distillers' interests over those of common inlanders such as Gallatin's neighbors in western Pennsylvania. Gallatin, by this time a member of the Pennsylvania Legislature, spoke out against the measure. He supported a legislative resolution to instruct Pennsylvania's U.S. senators (in those pre–Seventeenth Amendment days still elected by state legislators) to oppose Hamilton's bill, but the resolution failed in the Pennsylvania Senate.[10] He even proposed a constitutional amendment depriving Congress of power to tax goods moved from one state to another—also without effect.[11]

Still, in 1791 Gallatin accepted election as clerk of a Brownsville meeting Hamilton would characterize in 1794 as having been called to "confirm, inflame and Systematize the Spirit of opposition." The Brownsville meeting called a regional meeting for Pittsburgh. Though not attended by Gallatin, who was in Philadelphia as a legislator, that meeting urged popular "suasion" to prevent Pennsylvanians from becoming excise collectors.[12]

In 1792 Gallatin attended another Pittsburgh anti-excise meeting. Its resolutions said that attendees would "persist in our remonstrances to Congress, and in every other legal measure that may obstruct the operation of the Law until we are able to obtain its total repeal."[13] Thereafter, excise men fell under public intimidation and worse. Eventually Secretary Hamilton asked Attorney General Edmund Randolph to indict several ringleaders of excise resistance, including Albert Gallatin. Randolph conceded that the Pittsburgh resolutions had used "artful language" perhaps hinting at criminal behavior, but he concluded there had been no crime in assembling, remonstrating, petitioning, or otherwise opposing the Whiskey Excise in the ways Gallatin had. Looking back on these matters, Gallatin described his support of the Pittsburgh resolutions as his "only political sin."[14]

Gallatin moderated his public rhetoric after the Pittsburgh meeting. Yet nascent anti-administration sentiment seemed to have been undercut by the stridency of western opposition. Gallatin conceded that these events together had hurt his side in the congressional elections of 1792, confiding to a friend, "[W]e are generally blamed by our friends for the violence of our resolutions at Pittsburgh & they have undoubtedly tended to render the Excise law more popular than it was before."[15] Between mid-1792 and May 1794, Gallatin was away from western Pennsylvania attending the legislative session, attempting to retain his U.S. Senate seat, and marrying

Hannah Nicholson—the daughter of a high-ranking naval officer and already a sister-in-law of two Republican congressmen. Gallatin described Hannah as "neither handsome nor rich, but sensible, well-informed, good-natured, and belonging to a respectable and very amiable family. . . ."[16] In short she was precisely the kind of woman one would have expected Gallatin to marry. In describing her he nearly described himself.

When he did return, opinion in his neighborhood had reached high heat. Gallatin tried to tamp it down. At an August 1794 meeting of delegates from four Pennsylvania and two Virginia counties, Gallatin—once again elected secretary—spoke against the armed resistance some delegates openly urged. On September 10th, Gallatin's county issued a justification of its residents' position and behavior. Seemingly Gallatin's handiwork, it counseled compliance with the law.[17]

When Hamilton led federal troops out into western Pennsylvania, they had Gallatin's name on a short list of prime targets for arrest. One of Gallatin's biographers says that "Hamilton was browbeating witnesses for testimony that could implicate Gallatin in treason."[18] Meanwhile voters not only reelected Gallatin to the Pennsylvania Legislature, they elected him to the U.S. House of Representatives.

During the whiskey troubles, Gallatin had been elected to the U.S. Senate from Pennsylvania despite telling legislators he likely had not met the Constitution's citizenship requirement. He instantly found himself the center of controversy. Associating this immigrant with the Gallic nose and French accent (Federalists loved to mock it)[19] with the Whiskey Rebellion, his partisan opponents brought up the constitutional issue. Thanks to Senators John Taylor of Caroline, R-VA, and Aaron Burr, R-NY, the Senate opened its proceedings for the first time so that the public might witness the debate. On a party-line vote the Senate unseated Gallatin. He did not leave the Senate, however, without first landing a heavy blow upon Alexander Hamilton's stewardship of the Treasury Department.[20]

After his neighbors returned him to Congress in the wake of the Whiskey Rebellion, Gallatin quickly acquired a reputation as the one Republican who could match Alexander Hamilton's financial acumen. By the time Gallatin took his House seat in 1795, Hamilton had left his post, but his system remained in place. As he had said in the Pennsylvania Legislature, Gallatin wanted significantly lower federal taxes and spending. His three immediate goals, according to a recent biographer, were "frugality, accountability, and legislative oversight."[21] Gallatin's idea of frugal government bore no resemblance to twenty-first-century "frugality": he stood for substantial spending reductions.

Alexander Hamilton had said that a national debt could be a national blessing.[22] Representative Gallatin, on the other hand, soon dubbed Hamilton's funding system a "public curse." Covering borrowing with government bonds meant putting off the reckoning, which inflated public desire for government spending. Using this mechanism, he insisted, the Washington administration had covered up $2.8 million of growth in debt over the previous four years.[23]

The government's spending struck Gallatin as wasteful, particularly as it related to military matters. America could not compete with Britain, France, or Spain in the naval line, and so it should not try. If Gallatin had his way, the United States would pay off its debts first and turn to building a navy later. Besides that, lump-sum appropriations had allowed the Executive Branch to transfer money from one purpose to another—thus effectively taking Congress's power of the purse for itself. Gallatin wanted specificity in appropriations, and he got it while Republicans controlled the House. After party control shifted in 1797, Gallatin persuaded the speaker of the House to create the Committee on Ways and Means, the House's first permanent standing committee. Through that mechanism the House has had power to control federal spending as carefully as it wanted ever since.[24]

5

✦ ✵ ✦

allatin published his *Sketch of the Finances of the United States* in 1796.[1] In measured terms it attacked Alexander Hamilton's fiscal policies and proposed alternatives. As the historian of early American public finance, Thomas K. McCraw, put it, "Here, perhaps more than in any other single document of the era, one can see in high relief the differences in the two American schools of thought about a wide variety of issues." McCraw sees the *Sketch* as a kind of prospectus of the Jeffersonian ascendancy, at least through the War of 1812.

Gallatin's chief contentions in his *Sketch* fall into two categories: the theoretical and the particular. The theoretical claims he makes, typically of Republicans, are that debt corrupts public morality and that it inflates the financial class and the military, as it supposedly had done in eighteenth-century Britain. The particulars are that Hamilton's fiscal system had facilitated unnecessarily bloated federal spending and, in McCraw's words, "a deliberate increase in the national debt."

Gallatin noted that since 1789 the government's debt had grown from $75 million to $85 million. He made no mention of the fact that while the debt was growing by just over 13 percent, the economy and federal revenues had grown far more quickly, leaving the government in a far better fiscal position than it had been in at the time of Washington's inauguration. Had Gallatin taken account of this reality, he might have counseled his fellow congressmen, American voters, and, ultimately, the Jeffersonian presidents differently than he did.

Gallatin urged that the Federalists' ongoing program of building up the U.S. Navy, centering on construction of six frigates, be abandoned. He questioned the utility of having any navy at all. After upbraiding the Federalists first for their measures of defense against Indians to the west, then for their huge deployment of manpower against the Whiskey Rebellion, Gallatin at last turned to Hamilton's financial measures. Funding the federal debt at par, he said, had meant paying four times its then–market value, and assumption of responsibility for the state governments' debts ought never to have happened at all.

Gallatin also advocated a structural change to the federal tax system. Hamilton's system relied largely on tariffs, which fell most heavily on the overwhelmingly agricultural southern states. Gallatin therefore would have put significant reliance on a property tax. Finally he would have eased the terms of purchase for the federal lands. Such sales not only would have provided a relatively painless source of funds, but they would have sped migration of population into America's abundant open land.

Representative Madison reported to former secretary Jefferson that "Gallatin [is] a real Treasure in this department of Legislation. He is sound in his principles, accurate in his calculations & indefatigable in his researches. Who could have supposed that Hamilton could have gone off in the triumph he assumed, with such a condition of the finances behind him?"[2]

Like Madison, Gallatin had by this time married into a family (the Nicholsons of New York) that was in time connected to numerous members of Congress. Add his primacy among Republicans in regard to financial policy and his Pennsylvania constituency, and Gallatin had established himself as the obvious choice for the Jefferson Cabinet's number-two post.

The great difficulty in forming Jefferson's Cabinet lay in the new Department of the Navy. In short, understanding Republicans' (particularly Gallatin's) general hostility to naval expenditures, likely candidates recognized that the office would decline significantly in importance as Republican budget cutters worked their way with it. Having been rebuffed on that basis by Robert Livingston, Jefferson next asked Samuel Smith of Maryland to take the job, and he too declined.[3] The new president's eventual appointee, Smith's brother Robert, was the fifth man offered the job—and two of the first four turned it down twice. Along the way Jefferson confided to a correspondent, "I believe I shall have to advertise for a Secretary of the Navy." Robert Smith would prove a virtual cipher in the Cabinet.[4]

Not that it mattered. Jefferson moved quickly to cut military spending. Though sworn into office only on March 4, 1801, he was by June 20th writing Virginia's Governor James Monroe that

> We are preparing and carrying into execution all the reforms in economy we
> can. our navy partly selling off, partly laying up is now on an establishment
> of about half a million a year. it might have been reduced to 400,000. & still

kept three frigates in the Mediterranean, had the regulations of Congress permitted it. the marines will be dismissed in a few days to about 400. which will economise about 40,000. D. about the same sum is saved by the discontinuance of useless diplomatic missions. [He referred to embassies in The Netherlands, Prussia, and Portugal.[5]] in the erection of shipyards &c. some hundred thousands will be stopped.

Monroe likely would have found this heartening, though unsurprising. Perhaps startling to Jefferson's friend, however, would have been the president's news that "the expenses of this government were chiefly in jobs not seen; agencies upon agencies in every part of the earth, and for the most useless or mischievous purposes, & all of these opening doors for fraud & embezzlement far beyond the ostensible profits of the agency. these are things," he concluded, "of which no man dreamt, and we are lopping them down silently to make as little noise as possible." Anticipating Monroe's wonderment, he added that, "they have been covered from the public under the head of contingencies, quartermaster's department &c."[6]

Washington, D.C., is today the capital of the world's most important state. It is a major population hub, its own population ranking twentieth among American cities and its suburban areas extending well into neighboring Virginia and Maryland. On March 4, 1801, on the other hand, when President Thomas Jefferson took the oath of office, Washington, D.C., was a forlorn place, the Executive Mansion and Capitol Hill separated by a significant expanse of swamp. The uncompleted mansion in which President John Adams had lived for a month remained unfinished, so that his wife Abigail had thought nothing of putting up a clothesline in the East Room, which today is the most public room in the White House. Jefferson was well into his second presidential term before workmen completed the stairway to his house's second floor.

Try though they might, American officials failed to entice anyone not directly connected to the Federal Government to relocate to the capital. Semi-annual public land auctions routinely yielded less money than expected. Attempts first to persuade Congress and then to entice the public into funding a university there failed—the public lottery that was intended to fund it landing the lottery operator in jail. The chimera of a canal connecting the Potomac River that ran through the District of Columbia to the Ohio River also came a cropper. A British diplomat noted during James Madison's first presidential term that the American capital had "not a single great mercantile house," and even two decades later, the federal capital still lacked "all sights, sounds, [and] smells of commerce."[7]

It was not only businessmen who stayed away from the aspiring imperial center. The new town lacked lobbyists, out-of-town newspapermen, and, in general, American citizens. "Far more in evidence," says the leading historian of the town's early years, "were Indians, come to present grievances or to pay respects to the white father [that is, the president]."[8] Washington also had, as of 1820, "what was probably America's first soup kitchen," which graced the hill designated for Congress's home.[9]

One reason no one else relocated to the new federal capital is that the new government was seldom there either. The Supreme Court sat for a few months each year, other than which the justices spent much of their time "riding circuit"—that is, hearing intermediate-level appeals in their assigned geographic circuits. Congress too met only for a few months each year. Just as Secretary Madison had opted for the College of New Jersey in Princeton to avoid the Tidewater vapors, so President Jefferson told Secretary Gallatin that he would never spend the three sickliest months in Tidewater. This meant he would not be in Washington in the summer, as the reason for Alexandria, Virginia's location was that it was on the Potomac River's fall line (the farthest point inland to which a seagoing vessel could sail), thus on tidewater. Jefferson meant by this to instruct the Geneva-born western Pennsylvanian to flee town in the summer, but the herculean Swiss work ethic that helped make the treasury secretary so valuable an ally kept him at his desk even while his two senior colleagues summered at their Piedmont plantations: Montpelier and Monticello.

Anyone familiar with twenty-first-century imperial Washington will have to work to bear in mind that Jeffersonian Washington bore no resemblance at all to today's city. A better analogy would be to the seven villages in west central Italy described by Livy as precursors to "the glory that was Rome." In the eighth century BC, those hills were home to a few hundred proto-Italians. The federal Union's top officials lived generally in two clusters of housing units: virtually all of the Executive Branch employees near the Executive Mansion, and most of the legislators around the Capitol.[10]

A young Massachusetts senator, John Quincy Adams, noted in his diary that the 2.5-mile walk from his boardinghouse in the region of the Executive Mansion to the Capitol each day took him forty-five minutes.[11] The young senator felt gratitude the time that Vice President Aaron Burr stopped him on his way to offer a carriage ride. (He accepted the offer.)[12]

Almost uniquely among Executive Branch employees of the Jeffersonian era, Gallatin opted to live on Capitol Hill.[13] There he played a significant role in ushering the president's (meaning, in many of its most significant aspects,

Gallatin's) program through Congress. Members of Congress frequently visited his home, and he could easily walk to the Capitol and surrounding congressional boardinghouses. Though critics such as Henry Adams exaggerated the unity of the Republican Party, their characterization has more than a kernel of truth to it.

Upon being elected Jefferson faced several tasks. He immediately submitted the names of all of his Cabinet choices except a navy secretary and Gallatin to the Senate for confirmation.[14] (Remembering that a Federalist Senate majority had expelled Gallatin, and in light of the Federalist press's attacks on Gallatin, the president would hold off submitting his name until newly elected Republican senators made their appearance later in the year. For now a recess appointment of Gallatin would have to do.)[15] Besides secretaries of state, treasury, war, and navy, he would need a postmaster general (in those pre–Civil Service Reform Act days, an important patronage position) and an attorney general (not an appointed office until Reconstruction). He chose Levi Lincoln of Massachusetts for attorney general and Gideon Granger of Connecticut for postmaster general with an eye to the political intelligence concerning their region—the Federalists' last redoubt—that they could provide him. The Senate consented right away.

These top Executive Branch posts represented only the apex of the federal pyramid. While the president sat atop a picayune branch of a Lilliputian government in 1801, the absence of a permanent party structure and the political nature of all the appointments meant that Jefferson faced a set of related problems in staffing the government. In general he managed it better than most presidents, though not as well as, say, Washington did.[16]

When George Washington first staffed the high offices, he looked for several kinds of qualifications. The Electoral College had chosen Massachusetts's John Adams for vice president, so the Bay State was covered. Jay family lore says that when the general arrived in New York to assume the presidency, he stayed at John Jay's mansion. With the New Yorker's extensive experience in foreign policy and significant role in the ratification campaign no doubt in mind, Washington offered Jay, as the latter's son told it, "any office he might prefer." Perhaps surprisingly Jay opted to become the first chief justice of the Supreme Court.[17] Jefferson seemed an obvious second choice for what he at least expected to be the top Cabinet position (that is, once there came to be a Cabinet, as Washington himself decided there would be). The president and his then-ally Madison went to two other men with the idea of their serving as secretary of the treasury. When each declined, they settled upon Alexander Hamilton—nominally a New Yorker, but in reality a native of the West Indies without any particular emotional or cultural attachment to the Empire State. Washington kept Henry Knox, his chief of artillery during the war and at the time the Confederation Congress's war secretary, on in that post, and he selected Edmund Randolph to be attorney general. Not only had Randolph played key roles in both the Philadelphia Convention and Virginia's ratification battle, been attorney general of Virginia for ten years, and held that state's governorship, but he had for several years been Washington's personal attorney. As there would be no Justice Department until after the Civil War, the attorney general was to be the chief Executive Branch legal advisor, and so it would have been hard to find a better choice than Randolph.

In those days the vice presidency was seen as a Legislative Branch office. What Jay, Jefferson, Hamilton, Knox, and Randolph had in common was that each had distinguished himself in high office and supported the creation of the new government. (Washington likely had not seen Madison's correspondence with Jefferson about ratification and a bill of rights, else he might have looked elsewhere than to the marginally pro-ratification Virginian for a secretary of state.) With Madison advising him behind the scenes, all three authors of *The Federalist* would have important posts, formal or informal, in the Federal Government's early days. Ultimately Washington staffed the federal courts with prominent ratification-campaign Federalists too, again with Madison's help.

As political parties came into being in the 1790s, Washington's appointments seemed increasingly partisan. The general, enamored of Bolingbroke's conception of the "Patriot King" (a king above/outside the party system), could be forgiven for seeing critics of his administration as unfit for service in it.[18] John Adams followed the same practice, as indeed he might have been expected to do: the Republicans put up Jefferson against him, after all. Most historians see his offer of a British posting to Madison as calculated at once to smooth over partisan differences and to get the Republicans' slickest party operator out of the country.

When it came to it, then, when at last given their chance, many of Jefferson's supporters expected payback. Those people felt a certain discontent with the evenhanded posture Jefferson had taken in his First Inaugural. As one leader among them, prominent 1790s Virginia Republican congressman William Branch Giles, told Jefferson in a letter dated only twelve days into the new president's tenure, "Many of your best and firmest friends already suggest apprehensions, that the principle of moderation adopted by the administration, although correct in itself, may by too much indulgence, degenerate into feebleness and inefficiency."[19] If that happened, Republican morale would be sapped and Federalist vim restored. Federalists, Giles confided, "are not dead.—They only sleep."

What to do? Giles got to the point: "A pretty general purgation of office," he confided, "has been one of the benefits expected by the friends of the new order of things." Likely thinking that on reading this far Jefferson would have begun to feel a pang of discomfort, Giles hastened to add that "although an indiscriminate privation of office, merely from a difference in political sentiment, might not be expected; yet it is expected, and confidently expected, that obnoxious men will be ousted."

When first reading it, Jefferson might have thought that by "obnoxious," Giles meant not merely "Federalist," but "actively partisan." He would have been mistaken. Giles held that "from the prevalence of the vicious principles of the late administration, and the universal loyalty of its adherants in office, it would be hardly possible to err in exclusions; at the same time I highly approve of that part of your speech which recognizes justice, as the right of the minority as well as the majority."

Giles looked for a pretty broad removal of government placeholders, and he was not alone. Over and over again through his presidency, Jefferson would butt heads with supporters aggrieved at his temperate removal policy. Yet Giles's was not the sole Republican view. So, for example, Jefferson's old friend since his college days, Dr. Walter Jones, wrote shortly after the inauguration to share his opinion on the subject.[20] Not only had Jones been a friend of Jefferson's, but he had served as a representative in one of the two Congresses when Jefferson was vice president, and he would return for a four-term stint two years into Jefferson's presidency, so although he would never be as prominent as Giles, we may infer that his thinking reflected that of a substantial share of Jefferson's supporters.[21]

Jones allowed that he had found Jefferson's Inaugural Address passage noting the resemblance between "religious & political Intolerance" insightful. He was happy that Jefferson would not be giving vent to "all the fervor of vindictive Retaliation" that possessed some of their fellows. Yet, like the Peripatetic, Jones did not think "Forbearance" ought to be indulged "in its extreme Latitude." After all, voters had investigated the meaning of votes for Jefferson and for Adams, and their decision had to have its effect. "A society of conscientious Baptists," he noted, "would act very absurdly in electing for their Pastor, a lutheran Priest, tho in other respects a pious & virtuous man."

As Jones saw it, the top officials in the Executive Branch must share the president's views, because "to them he must impart his Confidential counsels and Commit his official responsibility." When it came to those lower on the totem pole, on the other hand, "Talent, diligence & fidelity seem to bound the claims of the state," and personal opinions ought to play no role. A man deprived of or denied office on the basis of "his private Judgment" would likely "foster in *his Party* the implacable obstinacy of martyrdom, which grows out of Persecution." A good republican will occasionally notice principled disagreement, but in making appointments he ought "to exhibit occasional proofs, that he aims not at the Extermination but the Reformation of his adversaries, at a System of Comprehension not of exclusion. . . ." Over time this approach would lead to widespread agreement "in every mind not eminently perverted, and gradually sink the spirit of Party, in a Common attachment to true Principles of Liberty & Right." Judicious appointments could even win converts.

Jefferson's reply to Jones's thoughtful ruminations on the challenge Jefferson faced when it came to appointments, the considerations he should bear in mind, and the course he ought to follow did not reach the length of Jones's.[22] It did make clear that the president understood the task facing him. "I am sensible," he wrote, "how far I should fall short of effecting all the reformation which reason would suggest and experience approve, were I free to do whatever I thought best. but when we reflect how difficult it is to move or inflect the great machine of society, how impossible to advance the notions of a whole people suddenly to ideal right, we see the wisdom of Solen's remark that no more good must be attempted than the nation can bear. . . ." His priorities would be "to reform the waste of public money . . . and improve some little on old routines."

6

✢ ❀ ✢

The new president had already paid considerable attention to appointments by the time he took the oath of office, drawing up lists of Adams's appointees, making notes on patronage problems in particular states, requiring State Department Chief Clerk Jacob Wagner to provide him a list of that department's clerks including a description of each man's duties, and otherwise methodically preparing for the task he faced. He continued on this path throughout his tenure.[1] Appointment issues would be a kind of leitmotif of his presidency, swelling to dominant volume from time to time and otherwise always humming along in the background. (Reverberations of some of Jefferson's patronage decisions would affect the Madison administration significantly.) Characteristically Jefferson hoped to strike some kind of medium. On one hand he would not throw out all of the old functionaries and replace them with new ones. On the other he could hardly be expected to leave things as they were. Federalist presidents had excluded Republicans from office, and the newly ascendant Republicans (whom Jefferson regarded as being the American people) ought ultimately to have a due proportion of federal offices. ("Ultimately" could be distant.)

Jefferson thought he had 316 employees under his power of removal.[2] Subordinates of those 316 could be replaced by the president's appointees, which meant they were at Jefferson's beck and call in case he decided to push the matter. Most of the three thousand or so other civilian workers in the Federal Government came under the authority of Postmaster General Gideon Granger, also a presidential appointee.[3] The selection of a New Englander for that patronage-heavy post reflected the president's calculations concerning the special care that would need to be taken to coax that homeland of Federalism into line.

Immediately upon entering office, Jefferson sent a letter to the "midnight appointees" informing them that they would never enter into their intended offices.[4] Jefferson regarded John Adams's and the Federalist Senate's appointment of these people in what were known to be the waning days of their tenure not only as an affront to the people that had chosen Republicans to control the Executive Branch and Congress in 1800–01, but as a personal unkindness by his onetime friend John Adams to him. The letter explained that Adams had selected these people "when so restricted in time as not to admit sufficient enquiry & consideration," and that since Jefferson had a right to "agents of his administration . . . on whom he ha[d] personal reliance," they would "therefore be pleased to consider the appointment[s they] ha[d] received as if never made."

Jefferson confided to one political ally, "[T]here is nothing I am so anxious about as good nominations, conscious that the merit as well as reputation of an administration depends as much on that as on it's measures."[5] He had learned this lesson from participation in and close observation of his presidential predecessors' administrations.

Different states would present their own unique patronage problems, as not only did Federalist strength vary from state to state, but some states' Republicans were divided into numerous groups. Thus Jefferson found himself in July 1801 writing to Republican U.S. Senator Wilson Cary Nicholas of Virginia that he heard nothing about removals from south of the Old Dominion, "in Delaware & Jersey they are moderately importunate: in Pennsylvania there is a strong pressure on us, & some discontent. but in N. York a section of the republicans is furious on this subject." Nicholas knew of the three Republican groups in the Empire State—Livingstonians, Clintonians, and supporters of Vice President Aaron Burr—"without my venturing a specification of them," and Jefferson had "the confidential sentiments of the most respectable persons of each." One New York Republican group "has opened a battery on us as you will see by the inclosed paper. you will be at no loss for the source of this": followers of Vice President Burr.[6]

Perhaps Burr thought that, as vice president, he could count on the president's support when it came to squabbles among New York Republicans. If so, he mistook Jefferson. To Nicholas, a Virginian and sometime confidant, Jefferson made clear that Burr had no claim to his loyalty: "we shall yield a little to their pressure, but no more than appears absolutely necessary to keep them together."

Ultimately Jefferson decided that the Clintonians and the Livingstonians had outstripped the Burrites, and so he cut Burr supporters out of the patronage in their state. Eventually Jefferson gave his behind-the-scenes support to George Clinton for Republican vice presidential candidate in 1804.[7]

Burr, recognizing that staying in the District of Columbia had become a political dead end, tried to buttress his political strength by running for governor of New York.[8] Alexander Hamilton, who had advocated Jefferson's cause against Burr during the 1801 presidential runoff in the U.S. House of Representatives, slandered his onetime friend during the latter's ill-fated governor's race as well. Burr demanded an explanation—that is, some kind of retraction of Hamilton's insinuations about Burr's character. Although Hamilton had given way in a similar context once before, he decided this time not to do so. Burr demanded "satisfaction." The "interview" was scheduled for Weehawken, New Jersey.

Though he had told a friend beforehand that he intended to waste his shot, Hamilton took hair-trigger pistols to the dueling ground. This became clear when one of his pistols misfired before the combatants assumed their places. In the event the greatest living Federalist missed the vice president. Aaron Burr took careful aim, then delivered a mortal wound. Hamilton died the next day.

Despite soon being indicted in both New York and New Jersey, Aaron Burr remained vice president. His role in the Virginia Dynasty drama had two more acts to play.

We have no surviving commentary from Jefferson concerning Hamilton's fate. Life's fleeting nature weighed on his mind in mid-1804 for personal reasons.

Jefferson married Martha Wayles on January 1, 1772, and they had two daughters who survived to adulthood: Martha and Mary, aka Maria. Mrs. Jefferson died as a result of complications from Mary's birth, and family lore says she exacted a promise from her husband on her deathbed that he would never remarry. Aged thirty-nine at the time, and with nearly forty-four years ahead of him, he never did.

By all accounts Jefferson invested considerable emotional energy in these daughters and their children. He also seems to have gotten along well with his sons-in-law, both of whom won election to Congress during his presidency and lived in the Executive Mansion with him at one point, though Martha's husband, Thomas Mann Randolph, was increasingly beset with mental or emotional issues as he aged.

It came as a shock to President Jefferson when Mary died, aged twenty-five years, early in 1804. His friend from college days and fellow eminent Virginia politician John Page wrote Jefferson a truly heartfelt note of condolence after waiting a little while.[9] As he explained, he had not wanted to intrude on Jefferson's "precious time which paternal tenderness could not but devote to bewailing the inexpressible loss of an inestimable Daughter! But I should be void of sympathetic Feelings, were I any longer to refrain from mingling my Grief, & that of my Family, with yours!" (Page used five exclamation points in this quite poignant eleven-sentence letter, a record in Jefferson's entire surviving correspondence.)

Pious Episcopalian that he was, Page drew Jefferson's attention to his own conviction that Maria was now "happy! And that our unavailing grief for lost happiness is to be unhappy indeed. Let us no longer be selfish," he counseled, "and make ourselves unhappy, because we could not detain her in this Vale of Sorrow. . . . Mrs. Eppes," John assured Tom, "was too dear to every one who had even once seen her, not to leave on their minds a long recollection of her, & a lasting impression of Grief for her loss." Everyone who had witnessed her father's "paternal delight in her, must be greatly afflicted till they can know, or hope at least, that you have found that consolation which they wish you to receive."

If that were not a beautiful enough statement, Jefferson responded with perhaps the most affectingly poetic passage he ever wrote. "Your letter, my dear friend, of the 25th ult.," he began, "is a new proof of the goodness of your heart, and the part you take in my loss marks an affectionate concern for the greatness of it. it is great indeed. others may lose of their abundance.; but, I, of my want, have lost, even the half of all I had."[10] Whatever expectations of a contented retirement he nurtured "now hang on the slender thread of a single life." After ruminating a bit on the passing of so many of their common college friends, Jefferson—for whom staying in Virginia's coastal Tidewater region (including Washington and Williamsburg) in the heat of the summer was anathema—invited Page to bring his family to Monticello to escape the sick season.

Maria Eppes's death also brought another unexpected event: a sympathetic letter from Jefferson's former friend Abigail Adams.[11] The wife of former president John Adams, Mrs. Adams had known Maria as a child who made quite a powerful impression on her. Thomas Jefferson, American minister to France, had left young Mary at home in the care of his sister when first he went with his older daughter Martha to France. Finding the separation unbearable, Jefferson père finally sent for his younger daughter. She was to travel by ship to England, then from there to France, in company of a slave woman.

Mary turned up in England not in the company of the person Jefferson had intended, but of a girl only slightly older than she, Sally Hemings. Abigail Adams thought this shocking. Still, over several days' stay, Mary made a strong impression on the frosty Yankee. Thus, despite the political acrimony between the House of Adams and Père Jefferson over the previous decade, Mrs. Adams felt impelled to tell him how sorry she was at his loss.

"Had you been no other than the private inhabitant of Monticello," she began, "I should e'er this time have addrest you, with that sympathy, which a recent event has awakened in my Bosom, but reasons of various kinds withheld my pen, until the powerful feelings of my heart, have burst through the restraint, and called upon me to shed the tear of sorrow over the departed remains, of your beloved and deserving Daughter, an event which I most sincerely mourn." Bygones had not exactly become bygones so far as she was concerned, but she had to commiserate with him anyway. She did so by recalling a touching scene between herself and young Maria, then aged nine years. "It has been some time since that I conceived of any event in this Life, which could call forth, feelings of Mutual sympathy, but . . . I have tasted the bitter cup, and bow with reverence, and humility before the great Dispenser of it, without whose permission, and over ruling providence; not a sparrow falls to the ground." She signed "her, who once took pleasure in Subscribing Herself your Friend ABIGAIL ADAMS."

Jefferson's response to Abigail Adams made clear that Maria had died loving her, and that he welcomed the opportunity "of expressing my regret that circumstances should have arisen which have seemed to draw a line of separation between us."[12] He artfully insisted that he and John Adams had never been rivals, for if either had retired from the contest, his supporters rather than supporting the other would have found a new champion for their principles. He surely must have realized he would provoke her ire by adding, "I can say with truth that one act of mr Adams's life, and one only, ever gave me a moment's personal displeasure. I did consider his last appointments to office as personally unkind." He went on to explain that since "they were from among my most ardent political enemies, from whom no faithful cooperation could ever be expected," Adams's appointment of them left Jefferson to choose between their obstruction of his administration if he did not remove them and "the odium of putting others in their places." However, he concluded, his displeasure at this act of the Adams administration's closing days had soon come to seem to Jefferson "something for friendship to forgive," and had been "cordially" forgiven.

Jefferson concluded his message with assurance he had hoped for an opportunity to "feel relief from being unbosomed" to her. He held Mr. Adams in "the same state of esteem & respect" as he customarily had, as well as feeling "a sincere attachment" to her—which is why he had taken the liberty of "open[ing] myself to you without reserve." Mrs. Adams replied with equal openness. First she claimed that John Adams had found on entering into the presidency that every appointive office had been filled by his predecessor, and that he had thought nothing of appointing fit people to all the appointive offices. She then leveled a return blast at him: winning an election against her husband had not in itself provoked "any enmity towards you Sir," but siccing James Thomson Callender on John Adams had "my utter abhorrence and detestation," because his tactics "were the blackest calumny and foulest falsehoods."

As to their friendship, she found the pardon of Callender and attendant reimbursement of his fine had "placed you in a light very different from what I once viewed you in." Callender's "basest libel" and "vilest Slander, which malice could invent" had earned him his punishment, to her eye, and for the president to reimburse him the fine "was a public approbation of his conduct" even if Jefferson had not publicly praised the wordsmith's writing. This "stab" to "the fair fame and upright intentions of" John Adams was insupportable. "This Sir," she thundered, "I considered as a personal injury. This was the Sword that cut asunder the Gordian knot, which could not be untied by all the efforts of party Spirit, by rivalship by Jealousy or any other malignant fiend."

Yet she took some solace in observing, "The serpent you cherished and warmed, bit the hand that nourished him, and gave you sufficient Specimens of his talents, his gratitude his justice, and his truth." Abigail Adams did not know the half of it. The blowback to which she referred was Callender's disclosure of Jefferson's relationship with the slave who had accompanied Maria from Virginia to Paris via the Adamses' English residence in 1787, Sally Hemings. In time—nearly two centuries later—the stories Callender told would damage Thomas Jefferson's carefully cultivated historical reputation extremely.[13]

After being rebuffed in his quest for a patronage post by the Virginia Republican high command at the beginning of Jefferson's administration, Callender had resolved to have his revenge. He turned his particular set of skills—those described by Abigail Adams in her letter to President Jefferson—on the man with whom he had been so angry in his correspondence with Secretary James Madison.

According to the leading scholar of the subject, "Sally Hemings had either six or seven children."[14] Virginians in the know thought Jefferson had fathered them. Although at least one newspaper editor had considered publishing it before, Callender in 1802 made this story, details of which he had gained from Jefferson's neighbors, public.[15] Another reason for Callender's decision to publicize this matter was his disgust with the easy interaction between upper-class white men and black women in Richmond. His first blast included several examples of the hostile anti-black rhetoric he would use in later installments:

> It is well known that the man, whom it delighteth the people to honor, keeps and for many years has kept, as his concubine, one of his slaves. Her name is SALLY. The name of her eldest son is Tom. His features are said to bear a striking though sable resemblance to those of the president himself. The boy is ten or twelve years of age. His mother went to France in the same vessel with Mr. Jefferson and his two daughters. The delicacy of this arrangement must strike every portion of common sensibility. What a sublime pattern for an American ambassador to place before the eyes of two young ladies! . . .
>
> By this wench Sally, our president has had several children. There is not an individual in the neighbourhood of Charlottesville who does not believe the story, and not a few who know it. . . . [16]

Annette Gordon-Reed describes Callender's tack as his series of attacks progressed as "accusing Thomas Jefferson of something on the order of bestiality," what with his reference to the supposed offspring of this liaison as a "litter," his invocation of a "pigstye," etc.[17]

Callender in the end said that he would be happy to go to court (as defendant in a libel suit) to prove the truth of his allegations about Jefferson. For obvious political reasons Jefferson maintained a stony silence on the matter. He did, however, concede in a private letter that Callender had struck the target in relation to another issue, that Jefferson once had tried to seduce the wife of a friend.[18] As the president wrote in mid-1805, "[W]hen young and single I offered love to a handsome lady. I acknolege its incorrectness. it is the only one, founded in truth among all their allegations against me."[19] Abigail Adams was more right than she knew. The embarrassment Callender inflicted on Jefferson must have been excruciating.

She closed her letter by mentioning "one other act of your administration which I considered as personally unkind," but forbore to name it, and with a claim that John Adams had not seen this letter. She bore Jefferson no malice, she said, but hoped to forgive and be forgiven, "in the true spirit of christian Charity."

Jefferson responded that he had not encouraged Callender in his scurrility any more than by giving a beggar money he encouraged him in "his vices."

Too, while prominent Federalist propagandists had levelled far more volleys at Jefferson than Callender had at Adams, Jefferson had never thought Adams to blame for them; he expected similar consideration. In fact the president said he had always vindicated Adams's character even while disagreeing with his politics.[20]

To Mrs. Adams's charge that Jefferson had liberated a journalist imprisoned under the Sedition Act, the president noted that he had liberated everyone in prison for violating that law, which he considered as no more valid than would have been a statute by which "Congress had ordered us to fall down and worship a golden image. . . ." He referred to that act as "the pretended Sedition law" because he considered it no law at all.[21] He had no idea, he said, what unkind act of his she found objectionable. Having heard from Mrs. Adams that she was referring to Jefferson's having fired John Quincy Adams from some minor post in the federal judiciary in Boston,[22] Jefferson explained that Congress had transferred power to appoint particular low-ranking officials from the (all Federalist) judges to the president, and that if he had realized John Quincy was among the men in question, he would have kept him on. He had appointed a proportionate number of Federalists, and surely would have preferred John Quincy Adams to the fellow Federalists he had appointed to those positions.[23]

In response to her continued complaints about his position on the Sedition Act, he now explained himself at length. "You seem to think," he began, "it devolved on the judges to decide on the validity of the sedition law," and that that should be the end of it. He had pardoned those convicted on the ground that while "The judges, believing the law constitutional, had a right to pass a sentence of fine and imprisonment," he, "believing the law to be unconstitutional, was bound to remit the execution of it; because that power [had] been confided to him by the constitution." His reading he based on the understanding that "[t]hat instrument meant that it's co-ordinate branches should be checks on each other," while her notion that the judges decided the question once and for all "would make the judiciary a despotic branch."

Having told her how he understood the respective constitutional duties of the three branches in respect to the others' actions, he went on to say a word about the meaning of the first ten amendments to the Constitution:

Nor does the opinion of the unconstitutionality and consequent nullity of that law remove all restraint from the overwhelming torrent of slander which is confounding all vice and virtue, all truth and falsehood in the US. The power to do that is fully possessed by the several state legislatures. It was reserved to them, and was denied to the general government, by the constitution according to our construction of it. While we deny that Congress have a right to controul the freedom of the press, we have ever asserted the right of the states, and their exclusive right, to do so.

He thought the states' defamation laws generally made sense, though some likely had "gone too far" by not allowing truth as a defense in a libel suit.[24]

Though she cannot have known either that Jefferson was the author of the first draft of the Kentucky Resolutions of 1798 or what he had said in the 1790 Cabinet debate over Hamilton's bank bill, and thus probably would not have known—what she must have suspected—that Republicans' federalism/states'-rights doctrine ran back to Jefferson, surely she was not terribly surprised by his position. What she thought of his assertion that his party and hers differed chiefly over the question of whether "the ignorance of the people" or "the selfishness of rulers independant of them" threatened America more, it would be nice to know. He concluded with an insinuation that he had never intended to break off his friendships with her and John and with "prayers for [their] health and happiness."[25] In reply Abigail told Thomas that she knew there was "not a more difficult part devolves upon a chief Majestrate, nor one which Subjects him to more reproach, and censure, than the appointments to office. and all the patronage which this enviable power gives him, is but a poor compensation for the responsibility to which it Subjects him." She happily accepted his explanation of the Quincy Adams matter, then closed the exchange with an expression of wishes similar to his.[26] Not until 1812 would Monticello and Quincy correspond again.

7

⊹ ⊛ ⊹

The second anomalous patronage scenario played out in the second state in which Republicans were riven by faction: the other Middle States battleground, Pennsylvania. The key figure in the drama there was Jefferson's treasury secretary, Albert Gallatin.

Within a short time of Jefferson's inauguration, William Duane visited from Philadelphia to request certain patronage favors. Although overwhelmingly preponderant, Pennsylvania Republicans fell into two groups—one led by the journalist Duane, and the other, more aristocratic faction in the city aligned with Gallatin since his days as a state legislator. Duane, at the head of the popular group, rested his importunities on his tie to Benjamin Franklin and his services to the Republican Party during the Federalist era.[1]

Gallatin in the earliest days of the administration counseled Jefferson against politically motivated appointments. This advice extended to Duane, whom Gallatin described as overcome by "the persuasion that he alone had overthrown Federalism."[2] Duane, in Gallatin's telling, "thought himself neither sufficiently rewarded nor respected." Meantime the pro-Jefferson governor of Pennsylvania, Thomas McKean, found himself in a patronage dispute with Michael Leib, whom Gallatin understood to be a tool of Duane. As editor of Pennsylvania's leading newspaper, the Philadelphia *Aurora*, "he easily gained the victory for his friends."

As early as spring 1803, Duane's paper began blasting away at Madison and Gallatin. Soon enough he leveled his guns at Alexander Dallas, the U.S. attorney for Philadelphia, and McKean. As a result of being understood to be (as he in fact was) sympathetic with McKean and Dallas in this intra-party feud, Gallatin found himself on the outs with Duane and Leib—that is, with the majority faction. Not one to concern himself overmuch with such matters when he thought himself in the right, Gallatin would in the end suffer significant indignities and disappointment at the hand of Leib—by then a leader of the Senate "Invisibles."[3] Duane's allies in the U.S. Senate would prevent President James Madison from making Gallatin secretary of state, or even minister to Russia; Gallatin blamed them in addition for the death of the Bank of the United States in 1811.[4]

After years of watching aghast, and even organizing formal protests,[5] as federal judges and grand jurors descended into creatively partisan behavior and the lame-duck Federalist Congress and president created numerous new judicial posts to staff with their co-partisans, the president had arrived at a determination to appoint only Republicans to the non-judicial posts in the Judicial Branch. "The only shield for our Republican citizens against the federalism of the courts," he insisted, "is to have the Attornies & Marshals republicans." Recommendations for such posts should be of men "the most respectable & unexceptionable possible," of course, but "especially let them be republican."

In the crush of business in his first days as president, Jefferson took a pair of steps that were to have considerable lasting moment. As he recounted it in a letter to his appointee Justice William Johnson a couple of decades later, soon after his inauguration he went to the secretary of state's office at the State Department.[6] On the secretary's desk he found a stack of undelivered commissions for judges intended to be appointed pursuant to the lame-duck Federalist Congress's Judiciary Act of 1801—the so-called Midnight Judges. Jefferson immediately decided not to deliver the commissions. Among the disappointed aspirants to office when this gambit became clear to the public would be Chief Justice Marshall's brother James Markham Marshall, Adams's choice for one of the new federal circuit court judgeships,[7] and one William Marbury.

As Jefferson explained the matter, he experienced not a moment's pause in deciding not to deliver these commissions. An appointment, he held, took effect only upon the commission's delivery. Withholding the commissions would be the end of it. Besides, the president and his supporters thought the outgoing Federalist congressional majority had passed this law and created the new judgeships entirely to throw up an obstacle to implementation of the incoming Republicans' program. At least one prominent Federalist, Senator Gouverneur Morris, privately admitted that was true, saying the Judiciary Act of 1801 grew out of the fact that Federalists were "about to experience a heavy gale of adverse wind." Since this was so, he asked, "Can they be blamed for casting many anchors to hold their ship through the storm?"[8] As we shall see, Federalists' public pose on this question was all one of injured virtue, and one of the men for whom John

Adams had intended the commissions Jefferson held back, William Marbury, intended to make something of it.

Also in the first flush of his inauguration, Jefferson halted a prosecution under, and pardoned everyone who had been convicted under, the Federalists' Sedition Act of 1798.[9] Those still in prison were released.[10] Reimbursing them for their fines would be a more complicated matter.[11] Perhaps of most interest in this connection were Thomas Cooper, former congressman Matthew Lyon of Vermont (who had been reelected while in federal prison), and James Thomson Callender.

Jefferson pardoned Callender on March 16th.[12] His ground for doing so was the Sedition Act's unconstitutionality—the case for which underlay the Virginia and Kentucky Resolutions of 1798, the latter secretly drafted by Vice President Jefferson.[13] By the end of April, Callender had concluded he had a grievance against Jefferson: despite his badgering the president ("you will perceive the expediency of its being done as early as possible"), his fine had not been remitted.[14] He wrote to Secretary Madison how happy he was to have someone in the Cabinet he felt "an attachment for" (Madison), and to express in rather vitriolic terms his unhappiness with Jefferson. "I now begin," he said, "to know what Ingratitude is."

In a bit of heat Callender relayed to Madison the supposed observations of several prominent Virginia lawyers—Edmund Randolph, Governor James Monroe, and perhaps John Wickham[15]—who had expressed confidence that his fine would be reimbursed. "President as he is," the journalist warned, "He may trust me, if he pleases, that I am not the man, who is either to be oppressed or plundered with impunity. Mr. Jefferson has said that my Services were considerable; that I made up the best Newspaper in America . . . with other things of that kind. . . . I had no more idea of such mean usage than that mountains were to dance a minuet."

Come to think of it, Callender added, there was something the president might do for him:

> I have just heard that Mr. Davis of Richmond has got notice that he is to quit his Situation in the Post office; that this in one of the few situations which I would think myself qualified to fill; and that it would just about afford a genteel living for an œconomical family. It Cannot be pretended that I am too late in application. But, indeed, my dear Sir, I have gone such desperate lengths to serve the party, that I believe your friend designs to discountenance and sacrifice me, as a kind of Scape Goat to political *decorum*, as a kind of compromise to federal feelings. I will tell you frankly that I have always

Suspected that he would serve me so; and so rooted has been my jealousy
Upon this head, that if ever I am to be the better of the new administration,
I shall be much disposed to ascribe it entirely to you.

We can only imagine how James Madison received this letter. Perhaps he gasped. Maybe it made him angry. Good-natured sir that he was, likely he laughed. The sheer affrontery of an assaultive demand that a pardoned felon's fine be reimbursed him more quickly, followed immediately by the serious suggestion that the fellow be given a lucrative appointment, stands out among the dozens of requests for appointments in the surviving records of the Jeffersonian era.

It seems that Callender had a bit of an inkling that he had taken the wrong tack, for backtracking, he immediately wrote a paean to Jefferson. He referred to "the high idea of the President's wisdom . . . which I have always had," and a president than whom "surely a wiser man . . . does not exist." "His probity is exemplary. His political ideas, Are, to the minutest ramification, precisely mine. I respect and admire him," Madison must have been pleased to learn, "exceedingly." Yet, alas, Jefferson had "on various occasions treated [Callender] with such ostentatious coolness and indifference, that [Callender] Could hardly say that [he] was able to love or trust him."

Madison could rest confident that Callender would not breathe a word of his discontentment to anyone (well, other than Randolph, Monroe, Wickham, or, finally, Madison—besides, if the chance recurred, Jefferson again). At last having vented all of these feelings, Callender concluded by telling Madison that he could take his time responding to the idea about the Richmond post office. Madison wrote to Governor Monroe that "Callender I find is under a strange error on the subject of his fine, and in a strange humor in consequence of it." Madison said that Jefferson shared Madison's appraisal of the situation.[16] Monroe looked into the matter and answered, "The fine was paid by the Marshall, by subscription, and when it was heard that the money was with-held from Callendar as above, some of the same pe[r]sons who had contributed to raise that sum, were willing to contribute to raise a like sum a second time" to remit his fine. Callender had actually been paid, though he apparently had mistaken the payment for "a loan only."[17]

Madison knew that Monroe had been present at Callender's June 1800 trial. Callender must have been aware of the governor's attendance as well. By Monroe's account the presiding judge in the Richmond Federal Circuit Court, Supreme Court Justice Samuel Chase, had essentially fixed the Republican newspaperman's case. An attorney himself, the governor gave an account of cruel judicial behavior. First Chase asked Callender how much he had in assets, to which Callender replied that he had no notable debts and approximately $200 to cover expenses for himself and two children; upon conviction, Chase handed down a sentence of imprisonment until March 4th (the last day of John Adams's presidential term and the day the Sedition Act expired) and a fine of . . . $200.[18]

"It is impossible to give you an adequate idea," Monroe's account began, "of the violence, illegality & injustice of the Judge's conduct thro the whole of the tri[al]. He dictated & imposed new rules of evidence never heard of before, insulted the council for the prisoner & I may say [si]lenc'd them . . . , and hurried the trial to the a[bove] conclusion with a precipitation wh: seem[e]d to confound [every]one, even the boldest advocate of the adm[inistratio]n." Callender had not borne his ordeal well. Republicans, and Americans at large, would not forget Justice Chase's conduct of the Callender trial. President Thomas Jefferson would see to it.

Callender visited Governor Monroe in Richmond again. Monroe noted the poor man's seemingly irrational, personal animosity toward President Jefferson, whom he blamed for the delay in reimbursing him his fine. Callender "intimated his services in support of the republican cause, spoke of the ingratitude of the republicans who after getting into power had left him in the ditch." Monroe now held it a poor idea to raise the money by subscription, as Callender seemed unlikely to "acquit the Executive tho' five times the sum shod. be advanc'd him, and that in case he attacks the Ex: he might state these circumstances or advances, to the discredit of the govt. & its friends." Wisely, Monroe allowed that "the President & yrself cannot be too circumspect in case he comes to Georgetown in yr. conversations with him; for I think nothing more doubtful than his future political course."[19]

The delays in Callender's reimbursement continued. The federal marshal at Richmond found himself $2,000 in arrears in his official account, and thus could not give Callender the money.[20] Eventually Treasury Secretary Albert Gallatin also had a role in the drama.[21] The journalist became increasingly agitated, as became perfectly clear to the three extremely high officials involved. At some point along the way, Madison came to the obvious conclusion that Callender's "imagination & passions ha[d] been . . . fermented." Whatever efforts had been made in Callender's behalf, Madison estimated, he appeared likely "not to be satisfied in any respect, without an office." Madison at least had divined the source of the pestiferous wannabe-postman's urgency: he had been smitten with a Richmond woman "in a sphere above him" and had "flattered himself & probably been flattered by others into a persuasion that the emoluments & reputation of a post office, would obtain her in marriage." Despite imploring, hectoring, and threatening everyone at the pinnacle of the Republican Party and the Federal Government, however, "he is sent back in despair." Madison could only regret that "[i]t has been my lot to bear the burden of receiving & repelling his claims." Certainly Madison did not know the significance of his own confessed inability to say how Callender would respond to the blunt treatment he had dealt him.[22]

Monroe answered that he had "endeavored to tranquilize [Callender's] mind, and bring him to view the cause of his disquietude with more temper and candor." He had tried to show Callender that the president had always been well disposed toward him, both before and since the recent election. He had walked Callender through the problems with the marshal at Richmond. Callender under prodding had conceded that he "had no greater claim on [Jefferson] than on any other person" for his work on Republicans' behalf, but he had insisted some office would stand him in good stead. Absent that and weary of journalism, perhaps he could become an attorney. (He named one of Richmond's foremost attorneys, saying he "cod. soon make as much noise as" he.)[23] Would Monroe help him identify an attorney under whom he might study? Monroe told Madison that Callender probably could do it (!), "especially if his friends wod. contribute a fund to defray the expense of his board & cloathing for a year." (Surely the governor, the secretary, or both must have laughed at this.)[24]

The Republican high command never satisfied Callender in his desire for a significant appointment. Perhaps he at last realized that Jefferson, Madison, and Monroe thought such a post, to borrow Madison's phrase, "in a sphere above him." (They generally sought out "persons from the same reputable social class of gentlemen upon whom the Federalists had depended" for appointments.)[25] In the end Callender would show them.

8

✤ ☼ ✤

Besides this consideration, Jefferson's appointments policy when it came to non-Cabinet offices reflected one other: the president's opposition to nepotism. Not only had John Adams put teenager John Quincy in a foreign service post in Europe during the Revolution, but by the time the Adams administration ended, there were several of his relatives in appointed positions. Abigail Adams even upbraided Jefferson for not having kept one of them on. Jefferson resolved to be as pure as Caesar's wife in this regard. As he explained to one relative, "The resolution [against nepotism in appointments] you so properly approve had long been formed in my mind. the public will never be made to believe that an appointment of a relative is made on the ground of merit alone, uninfluenced by family views. . . . mr Adams degraded himself infinitely by his conduct on this subject, as Genl. Washington had done himself the greatest honor. with two such examples to proceed by, I should be doubly inexcusable to err." Yes, this probably would be unfair to the president's relatives, "but the public good which cannot be effected if it's confidence is lost, requires this sacrifice. perhaps too it is compensated by sharing in the public esteem." Perhaps in relief, the president-elect closed by saying how much he respected his kinsman for having taken this view of the matter.[1] In time Madison and Monroe followed Jefferson's example.

After only a few days in office, Jefferson wrote to his friend and former Continental Congress colleague Benjamin Rush, a Pennsylvania physician, about the appointments problem.[2] "Some removals must be made for misconduct," he said, pointing to a Philadelphia marshal notorious for choosing jurors predisposed to convict. He estimated that of "thousands of officers," those falling into this category numbered "probably not 20." He also intended to reappoint officials Adams had cashiered for insufficient solicitude to Adams's political needs. In the end he would have removed some, but not so many as his allies would have liked, and "after the first unfavorable impressions of doing too much in the opinion of some, & too little in that of others, shall be got over, I should hope a steady line of conciliation very practicable. . . ." He hoped that this reasonable course would win over the vast majority of Americans heretofore Federalist.

The most notable flare-up of consternation with Jefferson's appointments policy came from the home state of the most rabid anti-Jeffersonian organization in the country: Connecticut. Only in connection with that state had Jefferson concluded that "a general sweep seems to be called for on principles of justice & policy. their legislature now sitting are removing every republican even from the commissions of the peace & the lowest offices. there then we will retaliate. whilst the Feds are taking possession of all the state offices, exclusively they ought not to expect we will leave them the exclusive possession of those at our disposal. the republicans have some rights: and must be protected."[3] The Connecticut flare-up pleased Jefferson, then, because it provided him the opportunity he had long been looking for of explaining to Republicans how he intended to use his appointments power to give them their fair share of the appointed offices.[4] Irked by the replacement of one of their own with a Republican as Collector for the port of New Haven, eighty of that town's most prosperous merchants on June 18, 1801, fired off a remonstrance to the president.[5] The late Federalist incumbent, they said, had performed the duties of his office "with a promptness integrity and ability satisfactory to the mercantile Interest of the district." This "promptness and ability," they hastened to add, were "not to be found in his successor." (At least they did not impugn the new fellow's integrity.)

The New Haven merchants' message amounted to this: while the old fellow had done his job well and pleasingly, the Jefferson appointee's seventy-eight years of age weighed heavily on him—so heavily that his lifelong ignorance of accounting, the tax laws, and "the forms of doing mercantile business" had now joined to them "an alarming loss of eyesight" that left him barely able to sign his name. Sure, he remained mayor of New Haven, besides town clerk and a judge of the county court, but this should not be mistaken for his knowledgeable neighbors' endorsement of his abilities. He had not entered into any of those other offices recently, and Connecticut voters were "not in the habit of neglecting those who once enjoyed their confidence, by a long course of usefulness."

Perhaps, the merchants guessed, President Jefferson had appointed Samuel Bishop in the expectation that his son would perform the actual work of his office. If so, they wanted the president to know that Bishop Jr. was "odious to his fellow citizens" and utterly unfit for the post. (Somehow the New Haven petitioners omitted to mention that young Abraham Bishop had run afoul of New Haven't leading lights not by lacking competence and integrity, but by daring to oppose their position in the matter of the Yazoo lands. He called New England's Georgia land speculators "robbers," saying "they scorn the paltry plunder of pocket-books, and watches—they aim at houses and lands—strike at the foundation of many generations,—and would destroy families, root and branch."[6] (Ironically, this question would divide the Republican Party in Jefferson's second term, as we shall see.) Having said all of this, the New Havenites reminded Jefferson of his Inaugural Address avowal of an intention to "promote the general welfare without regarding distinction of parties." To them this meant Jefferson would not "continu[e] . . . a father utterly unqualified for the office, or . . . a son so universally contemned." If Jefferson really wanted "to restore harmony to social intercourse," as he said, he would heed the petitioners' request.

The president took this as an opportunity to explain his appointments policy to the public at large.[7] "Declarations by myself, in favor of *political tolerance*, exhortations to *harmony* and affection in social intercourse, and to respect for the *equal rights* of the minority, have, on certain occasions, been quoted & misconstrued into assurances that the tenure of offices was to be undisturbed." Could that really be what he had meant? He granted (charitably, let us note) that the merchants had not made this mistake before adding that "it leads to the explanations which [their remonstrance] calls for."

His answer to the mistaken criticism justified the course he intended to follow. During the Adams administration, Republicans had been "excluded from all office" (that is, denied appointments), so that by the time Jefferson became president, nearly all federal offices were held by Federalists. "When the public sentiment at length declared itself, & burst open the doors of honor & confidence to those whose opinions they more approved; was it to be imagined that this monopoly of office was still to be continued in the hands of the minority?"

Jefferson denied that it was "*political intolerance* to claim a proportionate share in the direction of the public affairs" and rejected the implication that Federalists could not "*harmonize* in society unless they ha[d] every thing in their own hands." He also made the seemingly obvious point that if Republicans' recent electoral victory meant there had to be reallocation of government offices, the obvious way to begin was by removing appointees hurriedly installed by the outgoing Federalists in hopes that they would be able to obstruct Republicans' program. "Mr. Goodrich," he asserted, "was one of these."

In light of the necessity that some Republicans should be installed in federal office, how could vacancies be made without removing Federalists? "Those by death are few. by resignation none. can any other mode then, but by removal, be proposed?" Though he did not like it, Jefferson considered such replacements his "duty," and he would endeavor to "injure the best men least . . . with the least private distress. . . ." He would try to ensure that the burden was "thrown, as much as possible, on delinquency, on oppression, on intolerance, on antirevolutionary adherence to our enemies."

Though it likely seemed rhetorical to his audience, our familiarity with Jefferson's private correspondence gives us ample reason to believe his insistence to the New Haven merchants that "[o]f the various Executive duties, no one excites more anxious concern than that of placing the interests of our fellow citizens in the hands of honest men, with understandings sufficient for their station." It was, he continued, the most difficult. No man knew enough characters in every corner of America to rely on his own judgment. A president must rely on others' counsel.

Contrary to their insinuation, in the matter of Samuel Bishop, "time was taken, information was sought, and such obtained as could leave no room for doubt of his fitness." Jefferson knew before appointing him that "his understanding was sound, his integrity pure, his character unstained. and the offices confided to him," which the merchants had described as insignificant, in fact were "public evidences of the estimation in which he [was] held by the state in general, & the city & township particularly. . . ." Not only was he a town clerk and justice of the peace, but Bishop remained mayor of New Haven (an office from which the Connecticut Legislature could at any time have removed him), a judge on an important court with both civil and criminal jurisdiction whose decisions generally were not subject to appellate review, and the only local probate judge—which meant that he had authority over "all the property real & personal of persons dying." These last two offices, in which his tenure was annual, had been given to him most recently the month before the merchants' remonstrance.

"Is it possible," Jefferson asked, "that the man to whom the legislature of Connecticut has so recently committed trusts of such difficulty & magnitude 'is unfit to be the Collector of the district of Newhaven,' tho' acknowledged, in the same writing, to have obtained all this confidence 'by a long course of usefulness'?" To the objection that his appointee's age unfitted him for the office in New Haven, Jefferson answered that "our [Benjamin] Franklin" had remained "the ornament of human nature" when significantly older. In the event he proved too old to perform his assigned duties, whether in person or via supervision of other people, the president could be counted on to remove him.

A few days after his public self-justification, Jefferson wrote to his chief New Haven Republican contact to thank him for the information he had used to refute the merchants' assertions.[8] Since the critics had leveled their blast at "that class of removals which every reasonable man of whatsoever party has approved; I mean those which were made by a preceding administration in their last moments, & with a view either to force their successors to work with thwarting cooperators, or to incur odium by removing them," Jefferson "was glad the remonstrants . . . took the measure they did." That the New Haven merchants had given him an opportunity to underscore his commitment to the principles they said he had violated made him all the happier. He thought the exchange left him better positioned to pursue his appointments policy, as now the public would understand his principles clearly. (Even at this point, however, Jefferson had not decided whether Republicans were entitled to a proportionate share of appointive offices in each state, or only to a proportionate share in the country as a whole.)[9]

In the same letter Jefferson offered an appraisal of the Republicans' fortunes in each of the New England states. Rhode Island, he said, "is entirely republican." Vermont would at that year's elections be "threefourths." Massachusetts Republicans would win a majority, with even "N.H. coming fast up." The sole laggard, in his estimation, was the Nutmeg State. As its government rested on "a subordination of the civil to the Ecclesiastical power," Jefferson supporters' situation there would be "desperate for long years to come." Connecticut's "steady habits," he reasoned, "exclude the advances of information & they seem exactly where they were when they separated from the Saints of Oliver Cromwell. and there your clergy will always keep them if they can." The president's political antennae proved quite sensitive over the following years, as Connecticut's electoral votes would not be cast for a Republican until James Monroe's reelection in 1820—the first presidential election after adoption of the Connecticut Constitution of 1818, which disestablished the Congregationalist Church.

9

That disestablishment came to Connecticut at so late a date cannot be blamed on Jefferson. He in fact took pains to hurry the process along. His chief intervention into the Land of Steady Habits's political system came on January 1, 1802.

That date earned immediate national renown as the occasion of a notable instance of gift-giving. On that day Elder John Leland of Cheshire, Massachusetts, presented to President Jefferson a cheese "more than four feet in diameter, thirteen feet in circumference, and seventeen inches in height," weighing "1,235 pounds," and, as some said, "emblazoned with Jefferson's favorite motto: 'Rebellion to tyrants is obedience to God.'"[1] Located in the remote, downtrodden part of the Bay State that had spawned Shays's Rebellion, Cheshire stood out as an island of Republican unanimity in a huge sea of Federalism at the polls in 1800. The local citizenry sent Leland and the cheese to Jefferson as an emblem of their joy at his election. Perhaps the local Congregationalist-Federalist establishment had beaten them down, but with Jeffersonian Republican electoral victory in 1800–01, the dawn seemed to have broken.

Leland and his culinary delight drew substantial attention on their southward progress. On the appointed day "two dray horses" pulled the cheese down the rude, unfinished capital's main street. Jefferson, clad in his favored republican black, "stood in the White House doorway, arms outstretched, eagerly awaiting the cheese's arrival." Newspapers of the day loved the story, and some authorities say that Federalist mockery of Leland's gift introduced adjectival use of the word "mammoth" into American English. When used derisively in connection with Leland's cheese, it carried connotations suggestive of the supposedly "exaggerated, impractical" nature of Republicans' political principles.[2]

Consider this typical bit of Federalist, Jefferson-related whimsy:

In this great cheese I see myself portray'd
My life and fortunes in this useless mass,
I curse the hands, by which the thing was made,
To them a cheese, to me a looking-glass.
Once I was pure—Alas, that happy hour,
E'en as the milk, from which this monster came,
Till turn'd by philosophic rennet sour
I barter'd virtue for an empty name. . . .

Like to this cheese, my outside, smooth and sound,
Presents an aspect kind and lasting too;
When nought but rottenness within is found,
And all my seeming rests on nothing true.[3]

The president greeted Leland and company with a rare public address.[4] He saw the cheese as "an ebullition of republicanism in a state where it had been under heavy oppression." Happily, he wrote to a son-in-law that day, oppression of religious minorities was "rapidly passing away," and he hoped soon to see "all the New England states come round to their antient principles"—except for "the real Monarchists & the Priests. . . ."[5]

Historian Daniel Dreisbach notes that awareness of several precedents could have inspired Jefferson's Massachusetts admirers. "In the late 1760s," he writes, colonists' admiration of English radical John Wilkes led different groups of them to send him gifts of "tobacco, 'curious hams,' and other agricultural produce," Nantucket admirers of the Marquis de Lafayette awarded him a 500-pound cheese, and residents of Norleach, England, had given King George III a 1,350-pound cheese in 1792—a story that had been recounted in the *Gazette of the United States* in October 1801.[6] Perhaps this history explains the weird impulse that struck Berkshires Jeffersonians that year.

Jefferson had adopted a policy against accepting gifts while president. This necessitated his paying Leland $200 (out of his $25,000 annual salary) for the cheese. Besides money out of his pocket, the Mammoth Cheese would also inflict another cost on Jefferson: its presence in the Executive Mansion. As late as New Year's Day 1805, visitors to the President's House received servings of this Republican culinary delicacy, and one contemporary account said the last of it was being eaten later that year. (Another held that it was unceremoniously deposited in the Potomac River before New Year's Day.) We can only hope, then, that an 1802 report of maggots' appearance in the cheese was untrue. (One does wonder how Jefferson, a gourmand to his marrow, could have stood the odor of such a specimen in his house. Then again, even the most refined gentleman's olfactory sense received far more . . . stimulation then than Americans would find bearable today.)[7]

However significant the story of the big cheese may have been at the time and may be now, it has been overshadowed utterly by another event of that day. This one, too, bears on the relationship between religious minorities and popular majorities.

In October 1801 Baptists in eastern New York and western Connecticut, the Danbury Baptist Association, wrote President Jefferson "to express our great satisfaction, in your appointment to the chief Magistracy in the United States."[8] After asserting their commitment to freedom of conscience in language similar to that used by Jefferson in the Virginia Statute for Religious Freedom,[9] they went on to lament their own state's omission to accommodate religious dissent. Connecticut's colonial charter, they explained, had been retained "as the Basis of our government," and that meant "religion [was] considered as the first object of Legislation. . . ." If dissenters from the Establishment had any religious rights at all, they were "favors granted, and not . . . inalienable rights." In order to enjoy religious freedom even as favors, they continued, they had first to submit to "such degrading acknowledgements as [were] inconsistent with the rights of freemen."

Though they would not have known how irksome Jefferson found the Connecticut Establishment to be, the Danbury Baptists explained to him that it was unsurprising men who wanted "*power & gain* . . . under the pretence *of government & religion* . . . should reproach their chief Magistrate [Jefferson], as an enemy of religion Law & good order because he [would] not, dare[d] not assume the prerogative of Jehovah and make Laws to govern the Kingdom of Christ"—that is, would not call days of thanksgiving, prayer, and/or fasting. As these men and their organization had recently commenced a petition drive aimed at eliminating religious establishment in the Nutmeg State, they might have found themselves sympathizing with Jefferson as the subject of their oppressors' criticism even had he not been a prominent proponent of religious liberty. Though he was not "the national Legislator," the Baptists told Jefferson, and thus could not personally relieve them of Connecticut laws' unjust burden, they hoped that the president's good example would so affect America and the world that "Hierarchy and tyranny [would] be destroyed from the Earth"—even from Connecticut. ("Hierarchy" here retained its original meaning of "government by ecclesiastical rulers.")

Knowing of the Massachusetts Baptists' approach, Jefferson drafted an answer to the Danbury Baptists' kind letter.[10] He then sent his draft to his postmaster general and his attorney general, two New Englanders on whom he relied for advice concerning matters related to New England, for commentary.[11] Jefferson explained that he took public addresses as opportunities for "sowing useful truths & principles among the people, which might germinate and become rooted among their political tenets."[12] (Jefferson knew the example of his actions while president could affect public opinion too. This helps to account for his having himself inoculated against smallpox in Washington in June 1801 and, since that experiment had failed, repeating it on himself and about two hundred other people at and near Monticello that August.)[13] Postmaster General Gideon Granger replied that it would "undoubtedly give great Offence to the established Clergy of New England" and "delight the Dissenters," but as "[i]t [was] but a declaration of Truths which [were] in fact felt by a great Majority of New England, & publicly acknowledged by near half the People of Connecticut, . . . his mind approve[d] of it." As the Baptists and Jefferson hoped, so Granger believed that the principles Jefferson espoused in his draft would "germinate among the People" and help to remedy their errors on the question of the proper relationship between government and religion. Therefore he would not change a thing about it.[14] When it was his turn, Attorney General Levi Lincoln counseled Jefferson to remove the passage of his draft explaining on constitutional grounds Jefferson's policy not to issue executive proclamations for days of prayer and fasting. Lincoln said the people of all five New England states were accustomed to observing such days, including Republicans.[15] Jefferson had heeded that advice by the time he issued his response to the Danbury Baptists later that day.[16]

Perhaps what will surprise Americans of the early twenty-first century about this story is that it drew little attention in Jefferson's day. No New England newspaper published it, and even the Danbury Baptist Association's minutes let it pass without notice.[17] In general liberty-minded Americans in the days of the Jeffersonian presidents tended to echo the Virginia Statute for Religious Freedom—the religious freedom—related document Jefferson mentioned on his gravestone—when the issue came up.

Jefferson began by noting that he and the Baptists shared a belief that "religion is a matter which lies solely between Man & his God."[18] Good lawyer that he was, he could not resist redundantly adding that "he owes account to none other for his faith or his worship," and next generalized to the idea that "the legitimate powers of government reach actions only, & not opinions." Then came his memorable assertion, familiar to us from the

Supreme Court's 1947 decision in the case of *Everson v. Board of Education*,[19] that, "I contemplate with sovereign reverence that act of the whole American people which declared that *their* legislature should 'make no law respecting an establishment of religion, or prohibiting the free exercise thereof,' thus building a wall of separation between Church & State."

Having loosed his metaphor upon the world, Jefferson concluded his letter with statements obviously intended to clarify its meaning. First, characteristically, he located the spread of religious freedom within his understanding of history generally by saying that it was inevitable ("I shall see with sincere satisfaction the progress of those sentiments which tend to restore to man all his natural rights . . .") and that it would cost society nothing (". . . convinced he has no natural right in opposition to his social duties"). Then, so he would not be misunderstood as saying that American government must be irreligious, he closed by "reciprocat[ing]" the Danbury Baptists' "kind prayers for the protection & blessing of the common father and creator of man" before at last "assur[ing]" them "of [his] high respect & esteem."

President Jefferson would in the coming years repeatedly take opportunities to remind the public of his views concerning the proper relationship between government and religion, church and state. Calling the Revolution to mind on one occasion, he claimed that "vassalage in religion and civil government" had been one predicament, the "recollection" of which would "unite the zeal of every heart, and the energy of every hand, to preserve that independence in both which, under the favor of heaven, a disinterested devotion to the public cause first achieved. . . ." In another instance he told a group of Virginia Baptists that when he thought back through the country's founding, "no portion of it gives greater satisfaction . . . than that which presents the efforts of the friends of religious freedom, and the success with which they were crowned. We have solved by fair experiment, the great and interesting question whether freedom of religion is compatible with order in government, and obedience to the laws. And we have experienced the quiet as well as the comfort which results from leaving everyone to profess freely and openly those principles of religion which are the inductions of his own reason, and the serious convictions of his own inquiries." Jefferson consistently closed such communications with prayers to "the same almighty Being" as his correspondents had invoked—no doubt with the didactic function of his official behavior in mind.[20]

How effective these efforts to instruct the public were in Jefferson's day may come as a bit of a surprise. So, for example, Thomas Jefferson as governor of Virginia had never issued a call for a day of prayer and/or fasting.

Despite his presidential predecessors' example, he would not do so as federal chief executive either. People noticed.

On April 20, 1802, a correspondent who signed himself "S" wrote from Baltimore to upbraid him.[21] Washington and Adams had issued such calls, the unknown citizen noted, and yet, "It is with extreem Reluctance that I must say, that nothing Similar to this has ever occurred Since Your administration, I am at a loss Sir to know what Your objections can be to Such a Step." After all, "Such a thing is Servicable to Society." If Jefferson did not issue such a call soon, people might infer that "the eroneous misrepresentations which are in Circulation in regard to your Religious principals, are too well founded. . . ."

One lesson of this story is that what are now taken to have been landmark events did not seem so important at the time. While Jefferson's most famous public pronouncement about government and religion, his letter to the Danbury Baptists, has been central to discussion of the First Amendment's Establishment Clause since the 1940s, it apparently went unremarked, at least by a concerned citizen such as "S," in Jefferson's day.[22]

10

✦ ❊ ✦

As he accepted the Cheshire Baptists' cheese and corresponded with their bedraggled brethren in and near Danbury, Jefferson also set off on a new departure for the Executive Branch. The Constitution says of the president in Article II, Section 3, Clause 1 that "[h]e shall from time to time give to the Congress Information of the State of the Union, and recommend to their Consideration such Measures as he shall judge necessary and expedient." During the first two presidents' administrations, this had been translated into an annual speech to a joint session of Congress, each house of which replied with a formal written statement of its own.

As secretary of state under George Washington and vice president during John Adams's administration, Jefferson had felt discomfort over Executive Branch ceremony. Carriages, honor guards, ceremonial swords, stylish suits, and the like struck him as . . . monarchical. When the time for his first annual message came then, Jefferson was ready. The Seventh Congress opened on December 7, 1801, and on December 8, the president sent his secretary, Meriwether Lewis, to deliver his message to the speaker of the House and the president of the Senate. The cover letter explained Jefferson's new departure by saying that the crude circumstances in which the Federal Government found itself in its rude new capital "render[ed] inconvenient the mode . . . practiced" to that point, besides which he did not want to impose on them the need to respond regarding matters they had not yet considered.[1]

Jefferson and his team had worked on the address for several days. Jefferson began to prepare by writing notes on the Bank of the United States and government revenue.[2] When he had served in Washington's Cabinet, the pattern had been for the secretaries to submit passages to the president for his approval. Jefferson adopted the opposite model of sending his secretaries draft text to critique, telling them that he would welcome both substantive and verbal criticism.[3] Turning to the address, he wrote out passages on

naturalization,[4] on appointments policy,[5] on the judiciary and naturalization,[6] on annual payments on the federal debt,[7] and on the caseload of the
federal circuit (that is, intermediate appellate) courts,[8] which appeared in
the final address either in part or not at all.

The fair copy draft of the message included marginal headings: "Peace";
"Indians"; "Tripoli"; "Algiers. Tunis"; "Census"; "Finances"; "Economies";
"Appropriations"; "Army"; "Navy"; "Navy Yards"; "Fortifications"; "Agriculture Manufactures Commerce Navigation"; "Sedition act"; "Judiciary";
"Juries"; and "Naturalisation." Reading through these headings, a Cabinet
member would have known more or less what to expect: that Jefferson welcomed peace, looked forward to further incorporation of the Indians into
trans-Appalachian American society, had news for Congress on the progress of the navy's work in the Mediterranean, intended to continue on the
path he had already started down of paring back the military, had pardoned
Sedition Act convicts, looked to repeal of the Judiciary Act of 1801 (with the
concomitant budget savings), and favored repeal of the Federalists' exact-
ing 1798 revisal of the immigration laws (which had extended the period of
residence required prior to citizenship from the previous two to a record
fourteen years).

The president received extensive feedback from his Cabinet, heeding
some suggestions and deciding not to follow the rest. So, for example, his
New Englander attorney general advised him that in light of the impression
common "in the northern States, that the Administration & the Southern
States, are hostile to our navigation & commerce," it might be wise to include a suggestion that Congress consider what legislation might be helpful
to those important interests.[9] Jefferson heeded this suggestion.

A new day had dawned, Jefferson began: "the wars & troubles, which
have for so many years afflicted our sister-nations, have at length come to
an end. . . ."[10] While Americans thank "the beneficent being who has been
pleased to breathe into them the spirit of conciliation & forgiveness," he
said, they also "are bound, with peculiar gratitude, to be thankful to him
that our own peace has been preserved through so perilous a season. . . ."
Peace having come, the former combatants would see that their mistreat-
ment of neutral countries should be considered "as founding just claims of
retribution. . . ."

Having considered relations with the Europeans, Jefferson next considered America's relations with the domestic Indians. He held that the Indians
were benefiting from the transition from their traditional ways to the settled, agricultural ones he hoped they eventually would adopt.[11] In fact the

president told Congress that "they are becoming more & more sensible of
the superiority of . . . dependence [on the practice of husbandry and of the
household arts] for clothing & subsistence, over the precarious resources
of hunting & fishing. . . ."

The paper's next two sections dealt with policy truly foreign. First Jefferson described relations with Tripoli, the sole exception "to this state of
general peace with which we have been blessed." That "least considerable
of the Barbary states" had made demands the United States had refused
to meet because they were "unfounded either in right or in compact" and
had declared war when America failed to heed its ultimatum. Jefferson
"sent a small squadron of frigates into the Mediterranean," he said, carrying a message of peaceful intentions along with orders to defend American
merchant shipping.

What the *Enterprise* found on arriving at Gibraltar was that "our commerce in the Mediterranean was blockaded." Under Lieutenant Andrew
Sterrett, the ship defeated a Tripolitan corsair commanded by Admiral Rais
Mahomet Rous, killing or wounding more than half of the enemy crew (inflicting, in Jefferson's words, "a heavy slaughter of her men") in a three-hour
battle. Contrary to accepted naval behavior, the Africans twice lowered
their flag as a symbol of surrender, then opened fire when the American
ship approached. Somewhat astoundingly, the Tripolitans lost sixty men,
the Americans none during the battle. Judging that he lacked authority to
take the enemy ship as a prize, Sterrett ordered her masts cut down and her
cannons thrown into the sea before permitting her to return to Tripoli. Seeing his ship humbled thus, Pasha of Tripoli Yusuf Karamanli ordered the
admiral beaten, bedecked with a necklace of sheep entrails, and forced to
ride through the town seated backwards on a donkey.[12] Jefferson explained
the release of the ship and crew by saying that Congress had not authorized
the Executive to undertake more extensive military operations, and so defense had been the limit of Sterrett's action. (Here he covered for the young
lieutenant, a Federalist, in a way that would soon draw Federalist ire—as
we shall see.)

In his next section the president noted that relations with the other Barbary states were not satisfactory either. He provided Congress information
on which to base its policy in this regard.

Jefferson held that the decennial census's results would enable Congress to reallocate representation and taxation among the states. America's population grew so quickly that it would double within twenty years
if trends continued. The prospect, he said, struck Americans not as an

augury of future military strength, but as it foreshadowed "the settlement of the extensive country, still remaining vacant within our limits," and in relation "to the multiplication of men, susceptible of happiness, educated in the love of order, habituated to self-government, & valuing it's blessings above all price."

Another happy topic logically followed. As the population grew, so did importations and the related tariff revenue, which anyway would have been somewhat greater during the post–Peace of Amiens lull in the wars of the French Revolution and Napoleon because of a temporary cessation of the antagonists' interference with American merchant shipping. Thus he held that "we may now safely dispense with all the internal taxes, comprehending excises, stamps, auctions, licenses, carriages and refined sugars: to which the postage on newspapers may be added to facilitate the progress of information. . . ." Even so, he said he expected to be able to pay off the federal debts faster than the Federalist administrations had planned. George Washington had said in his first State of the Union Address that "[t]o be prepared for war is one of the most effectual means of preserving peace."[13] Jefferson took the contrary position for two reasons: first, that "sound principles" did not support taxing Americans "for wars to happen we know not when," and second, that maintaining the old policy could lead to wars "which might not perhaps happen but from the temptations offered by that treasure."

Promising to lay an accounting of federal expenditures before Congress, the president noted that he had already "begun the reduction of what was deemed unnecessary. the expenses of diplomatic agency," he said, "have been considerably diminished. the Inspectors of internal revenue . . . have been discontinued. several agencies, created by Executive authority, on salaries fixed by that also, have been suppressed, and should suggest the expediency of regulating that power by law. . . ." Remarkably, in other words, Jefferson wanted Congress to rein in the presidency when it came to creating new Executive positions. In case Congress wanted to conduct a cost-benefit analysis of all federal positions, "they may be assured of every aid & light which Executive information can yield." He believed there was a "general tendency to multiply offices and dependencies, and to increase expense to the ultimate term of burthen which the citizen can bear," and so elected officials should "avail [them]selves of every occasion which presents itself for taking off the surcharge. . . ." Doubtless remembering what he had seen in France, he did not want it to be "seen here that, after leaving to labour the smallest portion of it's earnings on which it can subsist, government shall itself consume the whole residue of what it was instituted to guard." In case he ever lost his way, Treasury Secretary Gallatin would promptly push him back onto the straight and narrow.

From a twenty-first-century viewpoint, the following section of this address is perhaps most spectacular of all. Tax receipts "entrusted to our direction" ought to be guarded by multiple "barriers against their dissipation, by appropriating specific sums to every specific purpose susceptible of definition. . . ." In other words rather than giving the president a large sum for a general purpose, Congress ought to designate particular sums for specific purposes and forbid "all applications of money varying from the appropriation in object, or transcending it in amount. . . ."

Turning in the next section to the army, Jefferson announced that the war secretary's report showed that far fewer men than were currently in the service would suffice to man the existing garrisons, and that "for the surplus no particular use can be pointed out."[14] In light of the country's gigantic perimeter, keeping them on as a standing army for defensive purposes would be unavailing; only the militia could fill that function. Therefore the laws for regulating the militias (an expressly delegated power of Congress) should be attended to, and the president and legislature should not "now, or at any time, separate until we can say we have done every thing, for the militia, which we could do, were an enemy at our door." Heirs to country party ideology, Republicans distrusted standing armies, and so Jefferson intended to step up training for militia units.[15] As he had said in his First Inaugural Address, Jefferson disfavored standing professional armies, but as Republicans embarked upon their new venture of ruling the Union, their leader would not have them ignore the necessity of keeping the militia in good fighting form.

Americans could expect, he said in the next section, that they would disagree about naval expenditures. "[A] small force," he said, "will probably continue to be wanted, for actual service, in the Mediterranean," but "whatever annual sum beyond that you might think proper to appropriate . . . would perhaps be better employed in providing those articles which may be [stored] . . . and be in readiness when any exigence calls them into use." The following section, on navy yards, was of the same bent. Jefferson thought there had been provision for more than necessary, and so he had delayed the related expenditures pending the present Congress's consideration of the issue. He also thought fortification and garrisoning of the specified American ports so enormous a project that Congress ought to reconsider whether it was worth the cost. The main sectors of the American economy might come into Congress's cognizance as well, "within the limits of your constitutional powers," his next section said.

In the section of his draft headed "Sedition Act," he had noted that each of the departments was to exercise its own judgement, in some circumstances without any check from the others, and that the Constitution had erected, "as a further security for itself, against violation even by a concurrence of all the departments . . . [provision] for it's own reintegration by a change of the persons exercising the functions of those departments." He had weighed the claims of citizens appealing to the Constitution against the Sedition Act, and he now found that the act violated the Constitution. "[C]onsidering it then as a nullity," he said, "I have relieved from oppression under it those of my fellow-citizens who were within the reach of the functions confided to me."

Apparently hoping to smooth any ruffled Federalist feathers, Jefferson intended to concede that though he acted pursuant to his "zealous devotion to" the Constitution, erroneous interpretations might flow from "inadvertence, . . . panic, or [the] passions of a moment." Whatever accounted for the Sedition Act, he hoped his pardons would reassure the states that "the General government views [the Constitution] as the principle of it's own life." The legislatures of Virginia, Kentucky, Tennessee, and Georgia, besides one house of North Carolina's, had been heard. Perhaps the president knew that South Carolina's legislature and governor had supported Virginia in this cause as well.[16]

In the end this section did not appear in the version of the message that was presented to Congress. Although we have no surviving explanation of this editorial change, we may infer that Jefferson judged both that including it likely would spur partisan animosity and that his exercise of judgement in a manner he described as without any check from another branch did not require any new explanation. Indeed, everyone knew why the Sedition Act convicts had been pardoned, as disagreement over that law's constitutionality had been one of the chief political issues between Republicans and Federalists for more than three years.

Jefferson took up the topic of "the least dangerous branch," which had played a prime role in the crisis of 1798, in his next section. "The judiciary system of the United states, and especially that portion of it recently erected, will of course present itself to the contemplation of Congress." To assist in that task, he had provided figures on the numbers of cases decided by each federal court since its creation and the number it had pending at the time of enactment of the Judiciary Act of 1801.[17] In his "Juries" section, and perhaps with the Cabell Presentment of 1797 in mind, Jefferson referred to jurors' "impartial selection" as "essential to their value" before posing the question whether jurors should continue to be chosen by marshals responsible to the president, by federal judges, or by minor functionaries dependent on the judges in those states where that was the custom. His implication was that no, they should not.[18]

In his final substantive passage Jefferson turned to the problem posed by the Federalists' partisan immigration reform of 1798, saying, "I cannot omit recommending a revisal. . . ." In light of the typical life expectancy, a fourteen-year residency requirement was "a denial to a great proportion of those who ask it," as they died before attaining eligibility. Besides that, it counteracted the policy pursued by several of the states since their first settlement, "and still believed of consequence to their prosperity." He wondered whether Americans of his dye would "refuse to the unhappy fugitives from distress, that hospitality which the savages of the wilderness extended to our fathers arriving in this land." Pulling at his audience's heartstrings (and with an echo of Thomas Paine), he asked, "shall oppressed humanity find no asylum on this globe?"[19] While the Constitution's residency requirements for officeholders made sense, surely citizenship could be extended to anyone showing he intended permanent residency.

This first new-style annual message closed with a paean to Jeffersonianism:

I indulge the pleasing persuasion that the great body of our citizens will cordially concur in honest and disinterested efforts, which have for their object to preserve the general & state governments in their constitutional form & equilibrium; to maintain peace abroad, & order & obedience to the laws at home; to establish principles & practices of administration favorable to the security of liberty & property; & to reduce expenses to what is necessary for the useful purposes of government.

11

⊰ ⬡ ⊱

Congress had, by January 1, 1802, not taken any roll-call votes, as the laggardliness of four Republican senators in coming to the capital meant Jefferson had had to hold off on submitting his chief nominations.[1] When finally they did arrive at the Capitol, Jefferson tendered the Senate a list of his recess appointees. His introductory note asked that the regular appointments of them all to office be confirmed. Heading the list were Albert Gallatin for treasury secretary, Robert Smith for navy secretary, and Gideon Granger for postmaster general. All except some justices of the peace for the District of Columbia were confirmed in the regular course of business. A test vote on one of the nominations was 16–14, validating Jefferson's calculation that he should make Gallatin's initial appointment during a Senate recess and put off making a regular appointment until the new Republican Senate majority materialized in Washington.[2]

President Jefferson and Treasury Secretary Gallatin shared an understanding of the fiscal priority facing the government: in the words of Jefferson, "extinguishment of the public debt, before we engage in any war." Having achieved that goal, Jefferson believed, America could pay for any war out of existing revenues, never having to raise taxes to meet wartime necessities. It would also in that case be able to pursue a program of domestic improvement in peacetime without substantial exertion. On the other hand if the debt were not paid while the Republicans had the chance, it likely never would be. Future generations then would rue that they should "be committed to the English career of debt, corruption & rottenness, closing with revolution."[3] Gallatin replied that he would recall of his Cabinet tenure that "[t]he reduction of the public debt was certainly the principal object in bringing me into office. . . ."[4]

Gallatin set to work at this task as soon as he received his recess appointment. Already on March 14, 1801, he sent the president a detailed "Estimate of Receipts and Expenditures for 1801."[5] Gallatin envisioned slashing the naval budget ("laying up the frigates"), cashiering a number of marines, repealing the Judiciary Act of 1801 (saving money by eliminating the new judicial posts), paring back the diplomatic corps, and cutting the "Barbary expenses."[6] He drew Jefferson's attention to the section of his Estimate bearing on the army and navy. Significant savings had to be achieved in those line items "in order to render a repeal of all the internal duties practicable" and to pay off the Dutch loans of Revolution days on schedule. Responsible statesman that he was, Gallatin proposed to keep the taxes until Congress had made the spending cuts.

On March 16, 1802, Jefferson signed the Military Peace Establishment Act into law. This statute had several components. It axed the army's staff and most senior officers, who of course were all Federalists, besides reducing the number of regiments, which meant further reduction in the number of army officers, and thus allowed Jefferson to remove some of his most senior and vociferous critics from government service. It also created the United States Military Academy.[7] All of these elements contributed to what Jefferson described to Speaker Nathaniel Macon as the army's "chaste reformation."[8]

Jefferson had several goals for his new academy, some of which he achieved and some of which he did not. The president hoped soon to persuade Congress to relocate the new school for army officers from West Point, New York, to Washington, D.C. For various reasons, the most important of which centered on Republicans' allergy to expenditure, he failed at this.

On the other hand Jefferson did both Republicanize the officer corps and professionalize it. Though his predecessors had been Federalist, thus likely to have drawn military appointees from among the Federalist elite anyway, their party's dominance of the elite colleges reinforced that tendency. In short the pool of potential officers skewed heavily in the Federalist direction. From the beginning West Point provided what its leading historian described as "a source of future Republican officers." By the end of his administration, "Jefferson's appointees achieved a majority in every rank (from ensign to brigadier general) except major."[9]

Here then is one way to square the circle of Jeffersonian creation of a national military academy. Another part of the formula must be Jefferson's belief that, as he put it, "whatever enables us to go to war, secures our peace." This Washingtonian postulate, it seems, was not only Washingtonian.[10] "A military academy purged of its monarchical and aristocratic tendencies"[11] would help secure the peace.

Though long the subject of partisan sniping from proponents of the

Federalists' ship-building program, Gallatin told Jefferson that it would have to be for experts in such matters, not for the treasury secretary, to decide which military spending should be reduced. (I use the adjective "military" in its broad, twenty-first-century sense, "related to an armed force," not the more restricted sense of Jefferson's day, "related to an army.")

As in those days it only met for a few months each year, Congress would not take up the administration's recommendations until it reconvened in December 1801. That first Jeffersonian congressional session did yeoman's work. True, it took up what became the Twelfth Amendment—a corrective to the constitutional provision that had resulted in the lengthy process of choosing between Jefferson and Aaron Burr early in 1801—without passing a proposal for the states to consider ratifying. That matter would be resolved only in the following Congress, which first met in October 1803, and with ratification of the Twelfth Amendment by the necessary number of states as of June 1804—just in time for the 1804 election.[12] The session did, however, confirm Gallatin's appointment as treasury secretary and numerous other appointments, adopt most of Gallatin's fiscal proposals, and replace the Judiciary Act of 1801 with the Judiciary Act of 1802—that last on February 13, 1802.[13] Republicans thereby not only repealed the Federalist provision that with the next retirement of a justice, the Supreme Court would shrink from six to five members (a flagrantly political attempt to deny Jefferson an appointment—and thus keep the high court 100 percent Federalist), but also purported to deny the "Midnight Judges" their offices. This meant, among other things, that the justices would now once again serve not only on the Supreme Court, but as members of the intermediate federal circuit courts of appeal.

One might have expected the Supreme Court to respond to this counter-reform in some way. When the Virginia General Assembly had reorganized Virginia's state courts several years before, the judges had declared the law unconstitutional.[14] What would Chief Justice John Marshall and his colleagues do now?

They discussed the matter. The first sign of it in Marshall's surviving correspondence appears in his letter to Justice William Paterson of April 6, 1802, nearly two months after Congress passed the law.[15] Perhaps surprisingly, it was not the tenure issue—that Congress had eliminated the posts of several judges appointed to serve "during good behaviour"—that bothered Marshall. "I confess I have some strong constitutional scruples," he confided. "I cannot well perceive how the performance of circuit duty by the Judges of the supreme court can be supported." He wished the justices had had an opportunity to take stock of the new law prior to acting as intermediate-court judges pursuant to it but thought that their doing anything about this problem had been foreclosed now.

Within a couple of weeks, Marshall had changed his mind.[16] Writing to Paterson a second time, he disclosed that his research had led him to "an opinion which [he could not] conquer that the constitution requires distinct appointments & commissions for the Judges of the inferior courts from those of the supreme court." He hoped his fellow justices would offer their opinions so that Marshall could "communicate [them] to each judge." He would abide by their opinion.

What Marshall contemplated was that the lot of them would refuse to abide by the new law. "The consequences of refusing to carry the law into effect," he admitted, might "be very serious." Yet, he believed the other justices would do their duty, as would he. Still, "the conviction of duty ought to be very strong before the measure [was] resolved on." He asked Paterson to forward Justice William Cushing the similar letter he had written for him, besides writing one of his own.

Later that week the most bombastically partisan of all the justices, Samuel Chase, wrote the chief justice a lengthy missive on the same subject.[17] Marshall probably found it unsurprising that Chase argued strongly for taking a stand against the change in the system contemplated by the new judiciary law. If it were possible, Chase began, he would prefer that the justices meet to discuss the problem and then present their objections to Jefferson himself—as the Jay Court had presented a similar problem to President George Washington in 1792.[18]

Chase's first objection to the law was that although Congress perhaps had authority to abolish the new courts the outgoing Congress had just created (though he had "*great doubt*"), he had "*no doubt*" that Congress lacked power to deprive the new circuit judges of their places or pay except through the impeachment process. "The distinction of taking the Office from the Judge, and not the Judge from the Office," he concluded, "I consider as puerile, and nonsensical."

Chase said in passing that Congress cannot vest original jurisdiction in the Supreme Court over any class of cases other than those the Constitution does—an interesting foreshadowing of the court's decision in *Marbury v. Madison* the following year. He also classified the Constitution as "*limited* . . . because (in Art. I S. 9.) it expressly *prohibits* Congress from making certain *enumerated Laws*. . . ." Those limits, he continued, would be useless if not to be enforced "by the *Judicial* power." These ruminations would have their echoes in the case of *McCulloch v. Maryland* (1819). If any federal judge could be removed by Congress, either directly or by abolition of his position, he would be "dependent on" Congress, and therefore not able to exercise judicial review as he ought.

The Supreme Court justices, Chase thought, should not sit on the circuit courts of appeals pursuant to the new judiciary act for three reasons. First, since the new circuit courts were essentially the old circuit courts, the old judges still held their offices—leaving no circuit duty for the justices to perform. For a justice to serve in one of those purportedly removed judges' place would violate the Constitution. Second, if a justice served as a circuit judge under the new law, he would be deciding that the new law was constitutional; in case he thought the law unconstitutional, he would be violating the Constitution by removing the circuit judge from office. Third, he denied that a Supreme Court justice could constitutionally serve as a judge on an inferior court. His argument was that such justice did not hold a commission to serve as an inferior-court judge, and that a justice could not accept such a commission. By his reasoning a justice would in that case have been made into a circuit judge by Congress without the president's having played his designated Article II role in appointing such judges. Besides that, he would act as an inferior-court judge without having taken an applicable oath of office.

Chase concluded that he would not accept the new circuit duties he had been assigned unless his brethren disagreed with his reasoning. He hoped the justices might meet in Washington to arrive at a common resolution of this question. Probably the district judges would agree.

Justice Cushing reasoned entirely opposite to Chase.[19] He had considered Chase's arguments carefully. Yet eleven years' precedent of Supreme Court justices serving on circuit courts had answered the question whether they might do so, he thought. Further, for a justice to refuse to serve as a circuit judge would not restore either the office or the salary of one of the circuit judges displaced by the Judiciary Act of 1802, so the justices would have no responsibility at all in that regard. Presenting their concerns to Jefferson could not help, as the law had already been adopted, the legislature was not in session, and neither Jefferson nor, certainly, the Federalist justices could make Congress change its decisions.

Justice Bushrod Washington agreed with Cushing, to Marshall's disappointment.[20] "I have no doubt myself but that policy dictates this decision [acquiescence in the new state of things] to us all," Marshall then told Paterson. Still, "[j]udges . . . are of all men those who have the least right to obey her dictates." He would go along with the majority, and he would inform Paterson of Justice Alfred Moore's views.[21]

In the end the justices rode circuit in the fall of 1802 without raising the constitutional issue.[22] On January 1, 1803, the Supreme Court in *Stuart v. Laird*[23] answered an argument for reversal of an earlier circuit-court order on the ground that "the judges of the supreme court have no right to sit as circuit judges, not being appointed as such, or in other words, that they ought to have distinct commissions for that purpose," as Justices Cushing and Washington had written they ought to do. Justice Paterson's opinion for the Court said, "To this objection, which is of recent date, it is sufficient to observe, that practice and acquiescence under it for a period of several years, commencing with the organization of the judicial system, affords an irresistible answer, and has indeed fixed the construction. It is a contemporary interpretation of the most forcible nature."

The practice of the Federalist era in American politics had been raised to constitutional status. "Of course, the question is at rest," the justice concluded, "and ought not now to be disturbed." Whatever the new government had done in its earliest days, without giving much thought to constitutional questions, would be presumed constitutional. This argument would be heard again later in the Jeffersonian period, in perhaps the most unexpected of contexts. In some contexts, it was the political elite that invoked Federalist practice as binding precedents; in others, it was common people who saw things that way.

12

⊹ ⚙ ⊹

Chief Justice Marshall and his associates did not know it, but what seemed to them a low point for Federalism struck the resident of what is now 1600 Pennsylvania Avenue rather differently. While they planned a response to the Judiciary Act of 1802, President Jefferson dreaded the impending publication of Marshall's *The Life of George Washington*. The late general's papers had been entrusted to his nephew Justice Washington, and Jefferson feared the impact of a popular, slanted version of Washington's life based on the hero's personal correspondence. He asked Joel Barlow, the famous Connecticut Republican writer, to enter the lists against Marshall.[1]

"Mr. Madison & myself have cut out a piece of work for you," the president wrote from the Executive Mansion, "which is to write the history of the US. from the close of the war downwards." The Republican high command dreaded a biased account of the battle with Hamiltonianism—one that put them in a bad light. Thus their friend should answer.

The chief justice had abundant materials on which to base his work, Jefferson knew Barlow would be thinking, but "we are rich ourselves in materials, and can open all the public archives to you." Marshall had George Washington's papers, but Jefferson and Madison had the best account of the Philadelphia Convention, Madison's, besides Madison's and Jefferson's own extensive papers, including their correspondence and Jefferson's several memoranda of his experience in Washington's Cabinet. In addition, as Jefferson pointed out, the archives were at their disposal. Besides providing these sources, Jefferson and Madison would be available to Barlow "for verbal communication."

The catch was that he would have to relocate to Washington. Knowing that Barlow shared not only his principles, but his loathing of Federalism, Jefferson guessed that learning Marshall's book was "intended to come out just in time to influence the next presidential election" would seal the deal.

George Washington had, on reading Barlow's *Vision of Columbus,* an epic poem about America, branded its author "a genius of the first magnitude . . . and one of those Bards who hold the keys of the gate by which Patriots, Sages, and heroes are admitted to immortality,"[2] but Jefferson never knew how ironic his invitation to Barlow thus was. Washington's correspondence remained unavailable to him.

Jefferson at the beginning of his intellectual life thought historical study a pointless diversion, but by 1802 he changed his mind.[3] Now he believed it necessary to understand the Revolutionaries' experience as they had, because only thus could Americans defend their legacy. All the materials to which he offered Barlow access had been collected for this purpose.

Barlow disappointed him, however. He did not accept Jefferson's invitation in time for the 1804 election, so "the perversions of truth necessary to be rectified," as Jefferson described them to Barlow, were left to local newspapers to address. Nor indeed did any other Republican accept the task of answering Marshall's book in Jefferson's lifetime.

Also early in 1802 Jefferson signed into law an abridgement of the length of residency required preliminary to naturalization. As he had noted in his State of the Union message in December, Federalists had extended it to fourteen years by legislation of 1798, but now Republicans in Congress cut it back to five. Together with the repeal of that same year's Alien Act, the defeat of an 1801 attempt to reenact the expired Sedition Act, and Jefferson's pardons for those convicted under that law, this meant that the entire suite of repressive legislation that had provoked the Virginia and Kentucky Resolutions had expired or been repealed.[4]

President Jefferson faced another significant problem early in his presidency. This one had to do with the "peculiar institution" of the Southern states, specifically of Virginia. Just as the presidential election of 1800 had come to a head, Virginia seemingly had been the site of the largest slave conspiracy in American history. A slave on a plantation near Richmond, Gabriel Prosser, had organized many (he would claim well over a hundred) slave men to rise against their masters. Their plan was to march on the capital on an appointed evening, seize the state armory with the aid of the black man who was on watch there, abscond with the Commonwealth's store of weapons, and use them to take control of the city.[5]

Highly unfortunate in their timing—the appointed night, August 30, 1800, proved to be the occasion of the heaviest rainstorm in memory[6]— Gabriel and his coadjutors were captured. After the first few of what would be a lengthy series of trials, several of the insurgents were hanged. Rumors that white Frenchmen had been involved originated with the slave participants themselves. Distant Federalists chortled in private that now the Francophile Virginia Republicans were receiving a share of "liberty and equality."[7]

By September 15, 1800, Governor Monroe concluded that the bulk of the participants had been captured and the danger to the state had passed. After discharging the bulk of the militia called into service for the occasion,[8] Monroe wrote to his political patron, Vice President Jefferson. "We have had much trouble with the negroes here," he began. "The plan of an insurrection has been clearly proved, & appears to have been of considerable extent. 10. have been condemned & executed, and there are at least twenty perhaps 40. more to be tried, of whose guilt no doubt is entertained. It is unquestionably the most serious and formidable conspiracy we have ever known of the kind: tho' indeed to call it so is to give no idea of the thing itself." He had at first kept the news secret, but then had employed the full power of the state "to intimidate" potential participants.

Monroe wrote not merely to inform Jefferson, but to ask his advice. "Where to arrest the hand of the Executioner," he noted, was "a question of great importance." A confessed conspirator who had aimed to kill his master could never "become a useful servant." Besides, Virginia had "no power to transport him abroad." Clearly having found the whole affair distasteful, he concluded that he could not "say whether mercy or severity [wa]s the best policy in this case, though where there [wa]s cause for doubt it [wa]s best to incline to the former council." What to do?

Jefferson confided to Monroe that even at Monticello, "where every thing has been perfectly tranquil," though "a familiarity with slavery, and a possibility of danger from that quarter prepares the general mind for some severities, there is a strong sentiment that there has been hanging enough."[9] Clearly with an eye to Republicans' prospects in that year's federal elections, the vice president pointed out that "the other states & the world at large will for ever condemn us if we indulge a principle of revenge, or go one step beyond absolute necessity. . . ." After all, though free Virginians had their "rights," the slaves' goal—freedom—made them sympathetic in the eyes of many outside onlookers. The puzzle was made more difficult, as Jefferson saw it, by the essential impossibility of safely reincorporating Gabriel's followers into Virginia society.

Jefferson hoped the General Assembly would provide for the remaining conspirators' "exportation." He considered this "the proper measure on this & all similar occasions." Jefferson had for twenty years by this point been devoted to the concept of colonization—freeing all slaves and moving them outside Virginia and/or America in the ordinary course of life.[10] Slaves had the same right to liberty as anyone else, and so they must eventually be freed. He believed, however, that whites' distaste for blacks and slaves' loathing of whites (which he said whites earned anew every day) meant the two races could not live peacefully together. Thus he looked to a day when the blacks might be sent abroad. Gabriel's conspiracy made the general issue urgent.

At its next session the Virginia General Assembly first authorized sale of condemned slaves beyond the bounds of Virginia, then took up the matter of what to do with "persons obnoxious to the laws or dangerous to the peace of society," resolving to have the governor raise it with his friend the president.[11] Their idea was "obtaining by purchase lands without the limits of" Virginia to which the slave rebels might be sent. "The idea of such an acquisition," Monroe explained to now-President Jefferson, "was suggested by motives of humanity, it being intended by means thereof to provide an alternate mode of punishment for those described by the resolution, who under the existing law might be doomed to suffer death."

Monroe told Jefferson that he thought the resolution contemplated moving the convicts in question to the Federal Government's western lands, but he did not see that it ruled out deporting them from America altogether. He thought "or dangerous to the peace of society" could be read as including more people than "persons obnoxious to the laws," but said he would not state an opinion on that question.

Read it in the broader way, Monroe continued, and "vast and interesting objects present themselves to view." He then ruminated on the condition of Virginia—the relationship of society as a whole to slaves—more generally. "It is impossible not to revolve in it," he said, "the condition of those people, the embarrassment they have already occasioned us, and are still likely to subject us to."

By "embarrassment," he referred not to abashment, but to difficulty—notably during the American Revolution, when Lord Dunmore's Proclamation had thrown Virginia slave owners off their guard, driving them into supporting independence, and numerous Virginia slaves—some Jefferson's own property—had fled into the British Army. He also referred, of course, to Gabriel's Rebellion itself. Such problems would likely recur.

"We perceive," the governor continued, knowing Jefferson to be sympathetic, "an existing evil which commenced under our colonial System, with which we are not properly chargeable, or if at all not in the present degree. . . ."[12] Then-Burgess Jefferson had with "A Summary View of the Rights of British America" (1774) intended to instruct Virginia's congressmen to upbraid King George III for not approving Virginians' attempts to stanch slave imports, and he had more famously intended in his draft Declaration of Independence (1776) to rebuke George for inflicting slavery on the colonies. The germ of accuracy in those charges had been that contemporary Americans had not made the decision that slavery should come to North America. No doubt familiar with Jefferson's old claims, Monroe here conceded that Virginians of 1801 might bear some responsibility for slavery's existence in the Old Dominion—though certainly "not in the present degree."

"We acknowledge," he said, "the extreme difficulty of remedying it." Jefferson had written in his sole book, *Notes on the State of Virginia* (1781), that freeing Virginia's slaves without deporting them, which in the nineteenth century was called "colonizing" them, would "produce convulsions which [would] probably never end but in the extermination of the one or the other race."[13] No doubt Monroe shared his trepidation, as he referred to "obstacles which become more serious as we approach them." Still, if the General Assembly were to act "in the extent to which it is capable, with a view to adopt the system of policy which appear[ed] to it most wise and just, . . . it [was] necessary that the field of practicable expedients be opened to its election, on the widest possible Scale." On the basis of this passage, the editor of Monroe's papers describes this letter as "the first known instance of JM expressing his support for the idea of general emancipation in Virginia."[14]

So he wanted Jefferson's help. Could Virginia obtain some of the United States' western lands for the purpose? If so, "on what terms?" If "a friendly power" might make appropriate territory available, "and [be] willing to facilitate the measure by co-operating with [Virginia] in the accomplishment of it," he would like that information too. Perhaps the president could inquire of foreign countries with lands nearby regarding this project. Indeed he would do so. Monroe could not have known that Jefferson's first response to news of Gabriel's plot was to exclaim, "We truly are to be pitied!" Jefferson understood the deplorable situation in which white Virginians found themselves just as Monroe did.[15]

At the General Assembly's request Jefferson hoped to obtain permission from the British to send survivors of Gabriel's Rebellion to their new west African colony of Sierra Leone. In conveying this message to the American minister to Great Britain, Federalist holdover Rufus King, Jefferson made a notable point.[16] The people the General Assembly looked to transport, as Jefferson had it, were "not felons, or common malefactors, but persons guilty of what the safety of society, under actual [meaning current] circumstances, obliges us to treat as a crime. . . ." From the point of view of Sierra Leone, however, these people would be desirable immigrants: "they are such," the president held, "as will be a valuable acquisition to the settlement already existing there. . . ."

Of course, he ruminated, transporting so many people to Africa could be quite expensive. Why not then allow them to enter into indenture agreements, "as the Germans & others do who come to this country poor, giving their labour for a certain term to some one who will pay their passage." Ships' captains might be attracted into this business by the prospect of carrying items in commerce between that country and this one. King should pursue this issue with His Majesty's Government. In fact King should inquire not only for information about sending the recently rebellious slaves, but about sending others not involved in Gabriel's conspiracy to Sierra Leone. The general population of people emancipated in Virginia were not "a selection of bad subjects," but generally either a master's entire stock of slaves or "such individuals as have particularly deserved well. the latter is most frequent."

King may not have known it, but Jefferson had been urged to replace him as America's minister to the Court of St. James's. Jefferson closed his letter by assuring King that he hoped for smooth relations with the British and that Secretary Madison's expressions of contentment with King's performance reflected the president's own views. No doubt Jefferson saw both domestic and diplomatic benefits to keeping King in place. His continuance in what in those days of primitive means of communication could be a significant policy-making post served as a powerful symbol of Jefferson's intention to tamp down the former partisan divisions. Besides, the facts that his party's Anglophile tendency was known in Whitehall and that King had established a reputation of his own there could only help the administration's effort to keep American-British relations on a good footing.

Unfortunately both aspects of Jefferson's initiative toward King came to naught. First, the Sierra Leone colony's proprietors communicated that its internal situation was so unstable, its military resources were so puny, that it could not risk taking in the people Jefferson had in mind to send.[17] Second, frustrated by his inability to persuade Secretary Madison to allow him to negotiate a revision and extension of the Jay Treaty's commercial provisions, King resigned his post and headed back to America.[18] In the end the president decided the obvious thing to do with slave insurrectionaries was to send them to Haiti. Nature, he said, intended Haiti "to become the receptacle of the blacks transplanted into this hemisphere."[19]

13

❖ ☼ ❖

Jefferson's inauguration ushered in more than surface changes to American government, though it certainly brought those.[1] When it came to policy formulation, Jefferson's methods of politics would be highly personal. In later years he liked to recall that though he and the members of his Cabinet frequently discussed policy matters in detail, they had never come to significant disagreement. As Jefferson recalled his experience to a subject of Napoleon whom he quite admired a few years after the fact, "the [Jefferson] administration, which was of eight years, presented an example of harmony in a cabinet of six persons, to which perhaps history has furnished no parallel. there never arose, during the whole time, an instance of unpleasant thought or word between the members. we sometimes met under differences of opinion, but scarcely ever failed, by conversing & reasoning, so to modify each other's ideas, as to produce an unanimous result."[2] (Jefferson perhaps erred in this judgment, as Gallatin could attest.)

The new president also used social occasions at the president's house differently from Washington. Republicans had come to see the first president's twice-weekly *levées* as of a piece with what they saw as the monarchist tenor of Federalist policy. Stiff and formal, Washington's experiment in republican interaction with the federal chief executive had looked more regal than would have been appropriate to, among others, Jefferson, Madison, and Gallatin. A footman led the invited visitors into the presence of President and Mrs. Washington and arranged them in a semi-circle facing the formally dressed hosts in the front of the room. The president, stationary, then engaged each in turn in a brief snippet of conversation. Two or three times back and forth across the semi-circle, with Mrs. Washington having taken her turn with them as well, and the guests were led out of the room.

When the Federal Government moved to the District of Columbia during President Adams's closing weeks in office, Jefferson became part of the

Capitol Hill boardinghouse culture. The night of his First Inaugural Address, he returned to his boardinghouse and sat at the end of the common table farther from the fireplace, after the egalitarian (republican) fashion. When he took up residency in the Executive Mansion (now known as the White House), he continued to strike a plebeian pose, for example by dressing informally as a matter of . . . well, if not of policy, certainly of calculation.

At the upper reaches of his branch of the government, the situation would be novel in a way not often remarked. While Washington had chosen his Cabinet members largely on the basis of merit, with ratification-campaign Federalism another requirement, and while Adams's decision to keep Washington's Cabinet on yielded a situation in which Adams too had serious personnel problems atop his administration, Jefferson entered office with the intention to have only extremely able fellow Republicans among his top advisors. The less important Cabinet posts were one thing (the New Englanders chosen largely because they were New Englanders, the navy secretary selected virtually out of desperation), but Madison and Gallatin stood alongside their chief among the three ablest members of their party.[3] If Jefferson, man of the Enlightenment, saw things in bright, clear colors, and Madison, a genius of political science, added occasional shading, Gallatin would be the numbers cruncher the other two could not.

The president and his subordinates handled relations with Congress similarly. While on one hand Jefferson had drawn back from formal interaction by terminating the tradition of an annual in-person address relaying information on the state of the Union, on the other hand he substituted intimate interaction with rotating, selected members of Congress for Washington's stilted, formally unrepublican *levées*. Those summoned before the general and his wife had enjoyed tightly limited opportunity for exchanging a few words with him, but now Jefferson's guests stayed for lengthy dinners of French food and fine wine at the First Gourmand's table—and on his nickel, no less. If the District of Columbia was a (not very) dignified cow pasture, dinner with Jefferson could one day reasonably be compared by President John F. Kennedy to a party with a score of the Western Hemisphere's leading intellectual lights.[4] Not only was Jefferson remarkably brilliant, but his chef had French training, and the host had the full Article II Executive Branch powers.

A faulty speaker before a large assemblage, Jefferson shone at the dinner table. On one hand, conducting politics in this setting helped him avoid the ridiculousness of John Adams trying to ape George Washington. On the other, here he could display all of the ingratiating manners and copious knowledge

he had picked up as a Virginia squire's scion, a young man invited to frequent dinners at the colonial governor's palace with Small and Wythe, and
a diplomat in France during the waning days of *ancien régime salon* society.

A leading scholar of the presidency described Jefferson's dinners this way:

> As a method of cultivating the acquaintance of legislators without violat-
> ing the norms of distance and decorum expected between the two elective
> branches of government, these dinners were both functional and unique.
> Their uniqueness flowed from the skill with which Jefferson pursued his
> political purposes while outwardly avoiding the merest breath of politics.
> The dinners gave every appearance of being purely social occasions, and
> Jefferson's charm, hospitality, and his excellent taste in food and wine as
> well as in the selection of his guests managed to veil from all but the most
> detached of witnesses the full extent of political advantage that these eve-
> nings afforded their host![5]

The same author goes on to note that when Congress was in session, Jefferson typically alternated between Republicans-only and Federalists-only
dinners, with the effects that the former group became more unified and the
latter found themselves less stridently opposing the president. Federalists
and perverse Republicans alike bemoaned the dinners' effects, but still they
attended. The president's ingratiating ways struck everyone.[6]

His contemporaries and scholars since have delighted in tales of Jefferson's White House dinners, but not all participants were impressed. Massachusetts's junior senator, John Quincy Adams, sometimes found Jefferson's
company pleasing, sometimes found it perplexing, on some occasions de-
picted the president as ridiculous, and in at least one instance seems to have
taken a perverse pleasure in being unhelpful to his host. Fortunately Adams
recorded some of his interactions with Jefferson in his voluminous diary.[7]
The felt imperative to maintain only "a cold and formal intercourse of official station" resulting from what Adams understood to have been Jefferson's "perfidy in his personal relations with my father" colors his accounts.[8]

Adams expressed perplexity concerning Jefferson's remarking about the
French Revolution in late 1804 "how *contrary to all expectation* this great
bouleversement had turned out" [emphasis in the original]. Because the Republicans had earned their reputation in the 1790s as the party friendly to
the French Revolution, including by using observances of its important an-
niversaries as party holidays, Jefferson's comment struck Adams as somewhat astonishing. "It seemed," he had Jefferson saying, "as every thing in

that country for the last twelve or fifteen years had been a DREAM; and who could have imagined that such an *ébranlement* would have come to this? He thought it very much to be wished that they could now return to the Constitution of 1789, and call back *the Old Family*. For although by that Constitution the Government was much too weak, and although it was defective in having a Legislature in only one branch, yet even thus it was better than the present form, where it was impossible to perceive *any limits*." No doubt anticipating that his reader would find it hard to believe an account of Jefferson coming to this conclusion, Adams closed the story by insisting that "I have used as near as possible his very words; for this is one of the most unexpected phases in the waxing and waning opinions of this gentleman concerning the French Revolution."

Adams found Jefferson ridiculous in a conversation in which the president first said, in Adams's words, that he thought "both French and Spanish ought to be made primary objects of acquisition in all the educations of our young men." That should pose no problem, the president hurried to add, because (again in Adams's words) Spanish "was so easy that he had learned it, with the help of a Don Quixote lent him by Mr. Cabot, and a grammar, in the course of a passage to Europe, on which he was but nineteen days at sea." Adams, who knew several foreign languages, considered this claim quite foolish, concluding with, "But Mr. Jefferson tells large stories. . . . You never can be an hour in this man's company without something of the marvellous like these stories. His genius is of the old French school. It conceives better than it combines. He showed us, among other things, a Natural History of Parrots, in French, with colored plates very beautifully executed."

Adams also recorded a conversation in which Jefferson lamented the difficulty he had run into in trying to staff the territorial government of Louisiana. Francophone lawyers willing to go be judges in that newly American land had proven impossible to find, and Jefferson "would now give *the creation*" for an able, young one. After a few more details, the senator concluded his entry by saying, "I could easily have named a character fully corresponding to the one he appeared so much to want. But if his observations were meant as a *consultation* or an intent to ask whether I knew any such person I could recommend, he was not sufficiently explicit. Though if they were not, I know not why he made them to me."

Jefferson also innovated, shall we say, when it came to formal diplomatic dinners. In Europe, diplomats' precedence depended on, among other things, particular countries' status and a given diplomat's rank. The third president resolved to turn this system upside down. He caused a diplomatic furor.

As Secretary of State Madison related it, Jefferson's new system "had gone on for three years without a whisper or a suspicion that it was disrelished" when Anthony Merry arrived as the new minister from the United Kingdom.[9] The first time Merry and his wife were at the White House, when it came time for the party to remove to the dining table, the president as was his custom instead of taking Mrs. Merry by the hand selected a Cabinet member's wife to accompany him. When the Merrys put in their first appearance at Madison's house a few nights later, Madison followed Jefferson's example. "It soon appeared that umbrage had been taken."

The Spanish minister found the resulting social tension irksome and intervened with Madison. Might not the American government follow the European custom of preferring foreign ministers over Americans? Madison thought that "the pêle mêle readily occurred as the most convenient in itself, and the most consonant to the principles of the Country." On formal state occasions the ministers as a group would be afforded a particular space and left to sort out their arrangement for themselves.

When Madison told Merry of these decisions, Merry went into an elaborate complaint about the treatment he had received, "some of which," Madison scribbled, "had never been dreampt of." Most notable to Merry was that on first meeting Jefferson, he found that although he had dressed in formal diplomatic garb of "deep blue coat with black velvet trim and gold braid, white breeches, silk stockings, ornate buckled shoes, plumed hat, and a large sword," the president wore plain morning clothes: "not merely in an undress," Merry reported to his superior, "but *actually standing in slippers down at the heels*, and both pantaloons, coat, and under-clothes indicative of utter slovenliness and indifference to appearances and in a state of negligence actually studied." (He left out the awkwardness resulting from Jefferson's not having been in the appointed office at the appointed time.)[10] Madison replied that the only other foreign minister who had arrived in Washington during Jefferson's tenure, the Dane, had been received in the same way. Merry answered that his higher rank meant he should have been shown greater respect than the Danish minister.

Like Madison most historians breeze past the possibility that Jefferson's insult to Merry, thus to Britain, was indeed "studied." In light of the famous episode in which King George III had been notably rude on meeting then-Minister Jefferson for the sole time, it seems entirely possible that the president intentionally reciprocated the slight. Thomas Jefferson was not one to forget such an insult, particularly from that source.[11]

Merry had several other complaints related to seating, reception, and guest lists on several occasions subsequent to his first meeting with Jefferson (particularly regarding having been invited to an event at which the French chargé, with whose country Britain was once again at war, had been in attendance). Madison, clearly perturbed by what he was describing, concluded that part of his account by saying that he had told Merry, "In this country people were left to seat themselves at table with as little rule as around a fire."

Perhaps the gravamen of Merry's lengthy set of complaints centered on that having to do with the formalities (not) shown to his wife, who after the surprise of not having been taken by the hand by the president at the time for dinner found herself being ignored once again at Madison's house a few days later. He had been told before departing England to expect better.

Madison took pains to explain to Merry that the British diplomats back home who had told him what to expect must have briefed him on the old (Federalist) dispensation. Jefferson was of course at liberty to conduct such matters as he wanted, and Madison had to follow the president's lead, whatever he might have done in private life. More important, usage was all in such matters. In Russia, military rank took precedence over diplomatic and noble; in Rome, ecclesiastical rank came first; in Prussia's capital, domestic rank was favored over foreign; and in England, hereditary rank came first. Besides that, Jefferson and Madison had not treated Mrs. Merry any worse than "what had been experienced in the case of the American Minister on a farewell dinner given him & his lady by Ld. Hawksbury, at which Mrs. King was postponed to the lady of the ex Minister Dundas." Even George III's levies had a good portion of the pêle mêle about them.

Madison's account of the conversation included a very interesting passage in which, after telling Merry that although the American usages to which he objected had been created without very much thought, this trouble with Merry had led the administration to consider the difficulties in European courts concerning the different ranks of diplomats, the different prominence of the various kingdoms, and the endless trouble, sometimes extending even to war, that had arisen among the Old Continent's powers over these issues. European disagreements of this type "were many of them unsettled to this day," Madison wrote, and "[i]t was not to be expected that we should willingly enter into such a labyrinth."

Merry concluded by saying that although he thought he had been treated reasonably, "it was the standing duty of a public Minister to maintain his rights & his rank in every thing." Therefore "he must retire (in what degree is not yet ascertained); but that if his Govt. should direct him to wave his pretensions, he & Mrs. M. would with the greatest readiness & pleasure return fully into society." Madison said the British government must have known of the Jeffersonian ceremonial, as it had had Chargé Thornton on station here for years.

Madison felt particularly unhappy with the likely impression upon people in Britain that he and Jefferson had been partial to France in all of this, when in fact "a marked attention was meant to be shewn" to Merry. He hoped Merry could stay in place, because "I really think favorably of him as a medium of conciliatory & useful communication," despite the fact that this situation did not reflect well on him. Madison made "great allowances for" Mrs. Merry's influence. Whatever else might have been made of this matter, Madison "blush[ed] at having put so much trash on paper."

Four weeks later Madison updated Monroe on the Merry kerfuffle.[12] Madison had sounded out Merry regarding the likelihood Merry would dine with Jefferson alone, with little luck. The secretary took this as reflecting new British suspicion in the wake of the final adjustment of the Louisiana and other matters with France. Whatever Whitehall might hear from Merry, Madison hoped that Monroe could convince the British that America's government recognized its natural interest in establishing friendly relations with the United Kingdom.

Madison said the government intended to maintain its policy. Since the Spanish minister, the Marquis de Yrujo, had been joining Merry in all of his protests, they might be brought to the realization that prior to the Constitution, precedence had been given to foreign governments in the order in which they had recognized the United States—which obviously did not seem a policy Spain and Britain would wish the Americans had maintained. Where in his previous missive to Monroe he had closed by alluding to Mrs. Merry, this time his final statement was, "The manners of Mistress Merry disgust both sexes and all parties."

So said President Jefferson's number-two man. Others saw Mrs. Merry entirely differently. Vice President Burr, who though elected to extremely high office as a Republican did not share Jefferson's goal of establishing a particular kind of republican capital on the banks of the Potomac, found her quite impressive. Margaret Bayard Smith described Mrs. Merry's attire, which was entirely out of place in the Spartan little village on the Potomac, after saying that it "attracted great attention," as

> . . . brilliant and fantastic, with satin with a long train, dark blue crape of
> the same length over it and white crape drapery down to her knees and open

at one side, so thickly cover'd with silver spangles that it appear'd to be a brilliant silver tissue; a breadth of blue crape, about four yards long, and in other words a long shawl, put over her head, instead of over her shoulders and hanging down to the floor, her hair bound tight to her head with a band like her drapery, with a diamond crescent before and a diamond comb behind, diamond ear-rings and necklace, displayed on a bare bosom.

Her physique was "rather masculine," and she was "rather free and affable in her manners, but easy without being graceful." Rather than a complement to her husband the minister, Mrs. Merry seemed to Mrs. Smith "so entirely the talker and actor in all companies, that her good husband passes quite unnoticed; he is plain in his appearance and called rather inferior in understanding."[13]

President Jefferson blamed the Merry problem entirely on Mrs. Merry, whom he called a "virago." As the president saw it, soon after arriving she had "established a degree of dislike among all classes which one would have thought impossible in so short a time." The French minister agreed.[14] Whatever her place in Washington society, such as it was, Mrs. Merry certainly impeded the functioning of her husband's office—which after all was the only reason the two of them went to Washington.[15] The minister played his assigned role in Washington awkwardly until he was recalled from America by Britain's foreign minister for giving tacit approval to an intrigue of Aaron Burr—on which more hereafter.

If the "Etiquette" affair, as Madison and Monroe referred to it in correspondence, made any impression in Britain, Monroe did not notice it. He relayed to Madison from London a few months afterward the story of having bumped into a noble lord who inquired after Merry, saying (as Monroe reported) "that he wished him well and hoped he succeeded." From this Monroe deduced that "he knew nothing of the Etiquette story, tho' he is in the diplomacy of the country, & at present a lord in waiting: I inferr'd from that circumstance that the government gave no eclat to the incident. . . ." Unlike politicians in the little village on the Potomac, those on the Thames had important matters to attend to.[16]

Historians have differed on the question of how Jefferson succeeded so notably in eliciting passage of his program from the first Republican Congress. Writing at the end of the nineteenth century, John Quincy Adams's grandson Henry Adams gave much of the credit (though he did not see it exactly as credit) to Jefferson's cousin, Virginia's Representative John Randolph of Roanoke.[17]

This Jefferson cousin made an odd floor leader, and indeed an odd spectacle. With his pubescent face, his high-pitched voice, and his tall, thin frame, he appeared somehow unwell—as indeed he was. Still in his twenties when Jefferson became president, Randolph commonly strode across the floor of the original House chamber wearing spurs and followed by numerous hunting dogs. On one occasion Randolph took the Senate floor with "six or seven overcoats" hiding his body, then proceeded to remove them one at a time, piling them in a heap. (An unfriendly newspaper thereafter mocked him as in the habit of disrobing on the Senate floor.)[18]

Draw him into debate, however, or even unintentionally draw his attention, and any member, no matter what his origin or how great his eminence, stood to be verbally lacerated. Not only a Randolph (the clan of Thomas Jefferson, John Marshall, Continental Congress Speaker Peyton Randolph, Philadelphia Convention Framer Edmund Randolph, and innumerable other prominent and powerful Randolphs), but, unlike Jefferson, a descendant of Pocahontas, John Randolph of Roanoke recognized no superior—social, political, oratorical, or intellectual. With no wife or children to distract him from his politics and his studies, Randolph as orator ranged through ancient and modern history and literature for illustration of his arguments. If ever Congress hosted a quicker wit, his name has been lost to us. On one notable occasion then-Senator Randolph's refusal to recant an insult to Secretary of State Henry Clay—no legislator, according to the Virginian, could answer to a high Executive Branch official for what he said in parliamentary debate—led to a duel. Four shots were fired. Randolph's coat sustained the sole injury. Clay did not know it at the time, but the excellent shot from Virginia had explained to a common friend the day before the "interview" that he intended to miss. Clay's large brood and devoted wife would mourn his passing, Randolph confided, but no one would mourn him. Though Clay insisted after the first exchange of shots that the seconds reload, the secretary missed the senator once again, and Randolph intentionally missed him the second time too.[19]

In another remarkable instance Randolph stood across the House chamber as Dolley Madison's brother-in-law Representative John Jackson referred to Randolph as "my colleague." He instantly said, "I am not the gentleman's colleague." Jackson corrected himself: "Very well . . . John Randolph." Speaker Nathaniel Macon, from the chair, called Jackson to order for referring to a member by name. "Sir, I know of no more appropriate appellation unless it is the descendant of Powhatan [Pocahontas's father]," Jackson spluttered. Randolph let the matter drop.[20]

Some contemporaries not in political sync with Randolph found his behavior on the House floor quite off-putting. One such, Senator William Plumer of New Hampshire, described his impression of the Republican congressman during an 1803 debate: "John Randolph Jr of Virginia is evidently the leader of the Democrats in the House. The manner in which he exercised this authority today, was very disgusting, & excited my indignation. Profuse in censuring the *motives* of his opponents—artful in evading their arguments, & peremptory in demanding the vote—sitting on his seat insolently & frequently exclaiming *I hope this motion will not prevail*—or when it suited his views, *I hope this will be adopted*."[21]

The great historian Forrest McDonald, whose inveterate and avowed Hamiltonianism did not impair his authorial style, described Randolph thus: "a man of pure political principles, he was also a bit crazy, and was devoid, as well, of ability to compromise."[22] Such a man seemed unlikely to serve as floor leader, or what we would now call majority leader, in the long run. Randolph's preeminence among congressional Republicans barely endured through Jefferson's first term. More Jeffersonian than Jefferson, Randolph bolted from the Republicans to head America's first third party, which Randolph—no democrat, he—dubbed the "Tertium Quid." (If you did not speak Latin, and so did not understand the name, too bad for you.) History knows those of like mind with Randolph, whether they remained within the Jeffersonian fold or not, as the "Old Republicans."[23]

14

The year 1803 was to be marked by the most significant developments of Jefferson's presidency. The first concerned the federal judiciary.

John Marshall and his colleagues had in the end accepted that repeal of the Judiciary Act of 1801 could not be undone, a position made explicit in *Stuart v. Laird* (1803). The matter did not end there, however, because restoring Supreme Court justices' circuit-riding duties was not the sole effect of the new Republican majority's Judiciary Act of 1802. It also eliminated the new judicial positions created by the 1801 law.

Besides Article III circuit judgeships, the Judiciary Act of 1801 also set up new justice of the peace positions in the District of Columbia. Among the commissions President Jefferson had decided not to deliver was one for a new justice of the peace, William Marbury. Unlike the Supreme Court justices, Marbury decided to contest the matter. Although justice of the peace is not an important position, the litigation Marbury launched would result in one of the most famous court opinions in history.[1]

On behalf of Marbury and two others, former Washington and Adams attorney general Charles Lee prayed the Supreme Court for a writ of mandamus, a particular type of court order, to be issued to Secretary of State James Madison. A mandamus would have been used to order an Executive Branch official to perform a mandatory duty he had omitted to perform. Though the stakes for Marbury and his fellows, Robert T. Hooe and Dennis Ramsay—petty judicial posts in a tiny town—cannot have seemed very important, the petition to Chief Justice John Marshall and his colleagues raised the explosive issue whether the Federalist Supreme Court, fresh from knuckling under in regard to the abolition of the circuit court judgeships created by the Judiciary Act of 1801, would dare to issue a command to Secretary Madison—and, through him, to President Jefferson himself. The Supreme Court announced in December 1801 that it would hear oral arguments, but the Republicans' repeal of the Judiciary Act of 1801 was joined to abolition of the June 1802 term, so that *Marbury v. Madison* did not come before the court until February 1803. When at last the court heard argument, two of the six justices did not participate. No one appeared as counsel on behalf of the administration.

Likely a contemporary justice in Chief Justice Marshall's position would recuse himself from a case with the same facts. Marshall told his brother that he had, as secretary of state in the Adams administration's closing days, possessed the disputed commissions and decided not to deliver them, as he believed nomination and confirmation rendered them superfluous, and both the signed commissions' existence and the constitutional requirements for an appointment to be effective would be at issue in *Marbury*. Too, as Charles F. Hobson, the editor of Marshall's papers, asserts, "Marshall's not delivering [the commissions] provided President Jefferson the opportunity to withhold them." Besides that, "the very bringing of the action, which coincided with the meeting of the first session of the new Congress under a Republican majority, hastened the repeal of the judiciary act [of 1801] and prompted the accompanying act by which the Supreme Court lost a term. . . ." Yet Marshall led the court in this matter.

As had by this point become customary, the chief justice read the opinion of the court, from which none dissented. It began by saying the case presented three questions:

> "Has the applicant a right to the commission he demands?" "If he has a right, and that right has been violated, do the laws of his country afford him a remedy?" and "If they do afford him a remedy, is it a *Mandamus* issuing from this court?"

In considering the first question, Marshall in the opinion notes that the president [Adams] has done everything the Constitution contemplates his doing to make these appointments valid. "The last act to be done by the President," he reasons, "is the signature of the commission. . . . His judgment, on the advice and consent of the Senate, has been made, and the officer is appointed." Since "[s]ome point of time must be taken when the power of the executive over an officer, not removable at his will, must cease," and an act of Congress provides that after the president has signed commissions, the secretary of state "shall affix the . . . seal to all civil commissions, to officers of the United States, to be appointed by the President," Marshall concludes that Congress believed the president's constitutional role in appointments, like the Senate's, ended prior to the delivery of the commission. The appointment became valid then. "The subsequent duty of the Secretary of State is prescribed by law, and not to be guided by the will of the President." The secretary's role in the process "is a ministerial act which the law enjoins on a particular officer for a particular purpose."

Although the administration had sent no one to argue its case, Marshall says that the court considered all the arguments it could conjure in behalf of an alternative conclusion. Thus "it has been conjectured that the commission may have been assimilated to a deed, to the validity of which, delivery is essential." While that type of document does not take effect until delivered, he asserted, the commissions in question became effective when signed and sealed. A president could require aspirant appointees to proceed to some particular place instead of awaiting delivery of commissions, and that would be within his discretion. "A commission," then, "is transmitted to a person already appointed. . . ." Marbury, in short, came into his office when the president signed and the secretary sealed his commission. Given the office's term, he had "a right to hold for five years." To deny him his commission was "violative of a vested legal right."

The next question the court considered was whether there was a legal remedy. In this case, Marshall intoned, the court did not face a situation in which Secretary Madison exercised the president's constitutional political discretion on his behalf. Such cases would not be reviewable by the federal courts. "But when the legislature proceeds to impose, on that officer, other duties; when he is directed peremptorily to perform certain acts; when the rights of individuals are dependent on the performance of those acts; he is so far the officer of the law; is amenable to the laws for his conduct; and cannot at his discretion, sport away the vested rights of others." Because Marbury's commission had been signed and sealed after presidential nomination and Senate confirmation, he had a right to the commission, "a refusal to deliver which is a plain violation of that right, for which the laws of his country afford him a remedy."

At last the court reached the question whether the remedy for the injury of which Marbury complained was a writ of mandamus. Having decided that it was, Marshall at last considered the issue, "Whether it can issue from this court." The Judiciary Act of 1789, written by the two chief authors of the Constitution's judicial article—one later chief justice, the other also later a justice—while they were senators, purported to empower the Supreme Court "to issue writs of mandamus, in cases warranted by the principles and usages of law, to any courts appointed, or persons holding office, under the authority of the U. States." Madison fit that description. The only remaining question concerned the Act's constitutionality.

The Constitution in Article III, Section 2 assigns the Supreme Court original jurisdiction—that is, jurisdiction over cases begun in the Supreme Court rather than appealed to it—"in all cases affecting ambassadors, other public ministers & consuls, and those in which a state shall be a party. In all other cases," it concludes, "the supreme court shall have appellate jurisdiction." The court read this list as exclusive—that is, as foreclosing an option in Congress of assigning the Supreme Court original jurisdiction over cases not listed. If the list were not exclusive, the court reasoned, there would have been no reason to include it in Article III, Section 2, and a reading rendering a constitutional provision meaningless must be disfavored. Further grounds for reading the provision as exclusive lay in the general structure of the Judicial Branch established by Article III: that it had a supreme court with particular types of original jurisdiction and appellate jurisdiction over "such inferior courts as Congress [might] ordain and establish."

In order for the Supreme Court to issue a writ of mandamus, then, issuing such a writ must be an exercise of appellate jurisdiction or "necessary to enable them to exercise appellate jurisdiction." Since the statutory provision in this case purported to empower the Supreme Court to hear suits for writs of mandamus as an original matter, not on appeal, the statutory provision seemed to be unconstitutional. This raised the question whether the Supreme Court could issue such a writ anyway.

The court next outlined what remains the classic argument for the power of judicial review—the characteristically American power of judges to refuse to enforce statutes (to "strike them down") on the ground that they are unconstitutional. First, it observed that "[t]he question whether an act, repugnant to the constitution, can become the law of the land, is a question deeply interesting to the United States; but happily not of an intricacy proportioned to its interest." "The distinction between a government with limited and unlimited powers" is that in a limited government, constitutional "limits . . . confine the persons on whom they are imposed. . . ." "Certainly all those who have framed written constitutions, contemplate them as forming the fundamental and paramount law of the nation, and consequently the theory of every such government must be, that an act of the legislature, repugnant to the constitution, is void."

In a case where a statute runs afoul of a constitution, "the constitution, and not such ordinary act, must govern the case to which they both apply." The alternative course—enforcing the statute anyway—"reduces to nothing what we have deemed the greatest improvement on political institutions—a written constitution. . . ." This is particularly hard to accept since under the U.S. Constitution, federal courts' jurisdiction "is extended to all cases arising under the constitution"[2] What, the court asks, would the judges' oath to uphold the constitution signify if they were to enforce unconstitutional statutes anyway?

Chief Justice Marshall and his colleagues issued Mr. Marbury no writ.

Some have credited John Marshall with an outstanding exercise of judicial legerdemain in *Marbury v. Madison*. How ingenious to exercise the power of judicial review while carefully avoiding giving James Madison (and Thomas Jefferson) an opportunity to ignore a court order to issue Marbury his commission. As Hobson notes, however, we have no reason to think the court did not believe what its opinion said: that Section 13 of the Judiciary Act of 1789, despite its august parentage, was unconstitutional. Yes, the president probably would have liked to thumb his nose at Federalists on the high bench, with whom his quarrel was not yet concluded, and yes, disappointing Marbury denied Jefferson the opportunity to ignore a Supreme Court order, but that does not mean Marshall's court did not believe what it said.

Others have thought that the controversy over *Marbury* in 1803 must have centered on the Supreme Court's claim to the power of judicial review. They miss that lower federal courts, including Supreme Court justices on circuit duty, had repeatedly exercised that power before.[3] In fact we have no evidence that this aspect of what the court did in this case aroused any controversy at all.[4]

What outraged Republican partisans about *Marbury v. Madison* in 1803 was the gratuitous legal lecture that preceded the jurisdictional section of the court's opinion. Federal courts, unlike state courts, have limited jurisdiction. Before a federal court hears a case, it must be persuaded that it has jurisdiction. That question is decided first. Too, within the federal Judicial Branch, inferior courts have original jurisdiction, and the Supreme Court generally hears cases only on appeal. There are, as we have seen, a few special exceptions—a few classes of rare cases that can originate in the Supreme Court rather than making their way there on appeal.

Rather than start with the question whether the Supreme Court properly could hear a suit for a writ of mandamus as an original matter, as one might have expected it to do, the opinion Marshall read began with a lengthy lecture directed at Secretary Madison—and through him, President Jefferson. Marbury had a right to the commission, the all-Federalist court began; there is a remedy for someone in his position, to whom an official such as Madison will not give his commission despite his right to it; and . . . this court cannot give him what he is entitled to. In fact there is nothing it can do to make Madison (and Jefferson) give the commission to him.

Republicans generally heard this as of a piece with the justices' enthusiastic support for the Sedition Act of 1798 and the Federalist congressional majority's Judiciary Act of 1801. It was another salvo at the Republicans from the federal judiciary, which frustratingly could not be thoroughly reformed by the Jeffersonians. But the struggle between the Jeffersonians and Marshall's court was not over. The most important rounds remained to be fought.

15

The year 1803 also saw the most important success of the entire Virginia
Dynasty period: the Louisiana Purchase. This greatest of all land sales
seemed to Jefferson and Madison to validate their long-standing approach
to foreign policy, to which they now would be even more deeply committed.
Their partisan opponents, on the other hand, thought all along that the Republicans approached the questions of the Mississippi navigation and access
to the port of New Orleans all wrong. They bewailed Jefferson's triumph.

As Thomas Jefferson explained in his First Inaugural Address, the
Republicans' would be a frugal government reliant chiefly on goodwill and
commercial intercourse to maintain the peace with foreign countries. The
military establishment would be slight, military adventures few. In his Second Annual Address, Jefferson told the Congress that Republicans' policy
for extinguishing the federal debt was "substituting economy for taxation,"
and he intended to continue on that path.[1]

The most interesting part of the drafting process for that annual address
must be Secretary Gallatin's response to the draft Jefferson sent him.[2] Notably, Gallatin denied that the American naval forces deployed in distant
waters needed "a legislative sanction" "to act offensively in case of war declared by other Barbary powers." Rather, he thought, "the executive has a
right, & is in duty bound, to apply the public force which he may have the
means legally to employ, in the most effective manner to annoy the enemy."
He went on to add that the commander of the Mediterranean squadron had
orders "drawn in conformity to that doctrine . . . and that was the result of
a long cabinet discussion on that very ground." (Gallatin's memory served
him well on this point.)[3] Pointing to a passage in the previous year's address
that had provoked Alexander Hamilton's ire, the treasury secretary said it
"adopted a different construction of the constitution," though Gallatin did
"not recollect" "how that took place."

In that same December 1802 message Jefferson also made mention of the Spanish government's cession of Louisiana—the entire area bounded by Texas in the south, the Rocky Mountains in the west, the Mississippi River in the east, and Canada in the north—to France. Via the secret Treaty of San Ildefonso, signed between the French Republic and Spain on October 1, 1800, Louisiana became France's property once again.[4]

Substitution of the most world's most powerful nation for the decrepit Spanish Empire as America's western neighbor meant a complete revolution in the geostrategic situation. Republican leaders had expected that if not soon, certainly eventually the weight of the United States' population growth and resultant conversion of virgin North American land to farmland were going to lead to a transfer of legal title to Louisiana from Spain to the new republic. Though Spain since the days of the conquistadors dominated the map of the Western Hemisphere, the extreme disjunct between Madrid's fiscal and population resources and the size of its geographic possessions meant that it could pose little danger to America on one hand or to Republicans' anticipated territorial expansion on the other.

France could not in this sense have been more unlike Spain. Possessed of the world's best farmland, Europe's largest population, enormous armies reformed by Lazare Carnot, and a ruler, Napoleon Bonaparte, combining military brilliance in a class with Alexander the Great and Julius Caesar with seemingly superhuman energy for administration and unlimited ambition, France posed a great danger to Americans' republican dreams of the future. American statesmen immediately regarded French possession of Louisiana as a threat to America's geographic aspirations. If once Bonaparte placed a significant garrison in Louisiana, denial of the great Gulf of Mexico port to the United States might prove permanent.

On coming into office, President Jefferson immediately dispatched Robert R. Livingston to Paris as American minister plenipotentiary to the French Republic. This highly capable Hudson River land baron and state chancellor, like Jefferson a scion of his state's leading family, was the sole Jeffersonian among his relatives—and thus a welcome addition to the Republican Party. Secretary James Madison told Livingston in a letter dated September 28, 1801, to let France know that though America felt "anxiety . . . to maintain harmony and confidence with the French Republic," any return of Louisiana to France from Spain—which had acquired it at the end of the Seven Years War—would make this difficult to achieve due to the "collisions more or less inseparable from a neighbourhood under such circumstances. . . ." Madison hurried to add that it could "not be the interest of this Country to favor any voluntary or compulsive transfer of the possessions in question from Spain to Great Britain."[5]

Madison said that in light of the frequency with which France and Britain were at war and the American slaves' understanding that the French were "patrons of their cause," French control of Louisiana might well make American citizens think a closer tie to Britain in their interest. This could "possibly produce a crisis in which a very valuable part of [France's] dominions would be exposed to the joint operations of a naval and territorial power"—that is, of Britain and the United States. He left it to Livingston to decide whether and how to raise these points with French officials.

Madison's instructions to his agent in France went further. In case France were to become proprietor of Louisiana again, he was to endeavor to obtain French guarantees of American access to New Orleans or, what Jefferson and Madison considered more likely, title to the Floridas, particularly West Florida, if they were in French possession, or French aid in obtaining them from Spain if they were not. He stressed the significance of West Florida, "through which several of our rivers, particularly the important river Mobille, empty themselves into the Sea." If Spain was never to cede the Floridas to France, Livingston was to endeavor to secure French help in obtaining them from Madrid. Exactly how France might aid the Americans in wresting that territory from Spain went unsaid, but Livingston was to coordinate efforts along these lines with his colleague at the Spanish capital, the South Carolinian Edward Pinckney. The chief Jeffersonian goal was simple enough: acquisition of New Orleans and so much of the adjacent territory as would make that possession secure, all without involving the new republic in the whirl of Europe's endless cycles of war-making.

Jefferson himself wrote Livingston a lengthy missive on the Louisiana issue the following year.[6] It laid out his administration's policy on the matter, and the president's thinking about it, in detail. France, Jefferson said, would in obtaining Louisiana transition from "our natural friend" to "our natural and habitual enemy." The reason was obvious: "there is on the globe," he wrote, "one single spot, the possessor of which is our natural and habitual enemy. it is New Orleans, through which the produce of three eighths of our territory must pass to market, and from it's fertility it will ere long yield more than half of our whole produce and contain more than half our inhabitants. France," he mused, "placing herself in that door assumes to us the attitude of defiance." The retrocession from Spain made all the difference. "Spain might have retained it quietly for years. her pacific dispositions, her feeble state, would induce her to increase our facilities there, so that her possession of the place would hardly be felt by us. . . ." In fact, she might soon have sold it to us. "[N]ot so can it ever be in the hands of France," whose "impetuosity of . . . temper," when juxtaposed to "our character, which though quiet, & loving peace & the pursuit of wealth, is high minded, . . . enterprizing & energetic as any nation on earth," will make it "impossible that France and the US. can continue long friends when they meet in so irritable a position."

What then was to be done? Jefferson held it inevitable that "the day that France takes possession of N. Orleans fixes the sentence which is to restrain her forever within her low water mark. it seals the union of two nations [America and Britain] who in conjunction can maintain exclusive possession of the ocean. from that moment we must marry ourselves to the British fleet & nation." What form this would take seemed obvious to Jefferson: "we must turn all our attentions to a maritime force, for which our resources place us on very high ground. . . ." The moment hostilities between France and Britain resumed, as resume they eventually must, "the United British & American nations" would exclude France from North America. New Orleans would "be wrested from her."

Jefferson, for America, did not desire this outcome. Rather, he held that "it is one which this measure, if adopted by France, forces on us, as necessarily as any other cause, by the laws of nature, brings on it's necessary effect." Here Jefferson sounded every bit like the penman of the American Revolution, the young rhetorician who with fellow Patriot leaders always explained events as forced upon his people by British authority. Just as George III had made America independent, leaving to the Americans only public declaration of it, so Napoleon Bonaparte could drive the United States into a new union with Britain—than which nothing could have been more shocking from the pen of Thomas Jefferson.[7]

The mature Jefferson continued to look upon France as America's natural friend. His country remained "bound to France by the interests and the strong sympathies still existing in the minds of our citizens." He mentioned all of this, he told Livingston, not "as a menace, but as consequences not controulable by us. . . ." In case France considered continued possession of Louisiana essential to its interests, America would take "ceding to us the island of New Orleans and the Floridas" as calculated to ensure the continued happy proximity of the two nations, removing "the causes of jarring & irritation between us. . . ."

At last Jefferson closed this lengthy letter by guessing that all of these ideas would already have occurred to Livingston, then adding that he had writ-

ten him about them anyway in order to underscore "the importance we affix
to this transaction." America was abuzz over the New Orleans problem, he
said, and "perhaps nothing since the revolutionary war has produced more
uneasy sensations through the body of the nation." Still, Americans felt great
attachment to France and hoped it could be worked out. Finally, Pierre S.
du Pont de Nemours (hereafter, du Pont) should be seen as a sincere friend
to both countries and potentially helpful go-between.

Jefferson entrusted this letter for delivery to a French friend of his, du
Pont. Though eventually the forebear of the prominent American Du Pont
family, du Pont de Nemours at the time was a Frenchman well affected toward
the United States and Jefferson. Opening the letter to Livingston and reading it en route to France, he immediately intuited that passing its contents
along to Bonaparte would be a disaster. The first consul would receive it
as an insult and not respond well. Besides, American possession of New
Orleans and the Mississippi would likely lead to American conquest, either
private or official, of Mexico; that would not be conducive to the long-term
health of American republicanism. He counseled the president to offer to
purchase Louisiana instead; likely that would yield both New Orleans and
the Floridas.[8] Jefferson answered Du Pont that his intention had not been
"that the observations [he] made should be considered as menaces."[9] He who
foresees a storm and warns of it, the president insisted, is not the cause of
it, "nor can [his] admonition be a threat." France would indeed forever be
America's friend, as had been expected, if only she did not come into possession of New Orleans.

Turning to Du Pont's ideas, Jefferson said that no one in America contemplated the conquest of "an enlargement of our territory beyond the Mis-
sisipi," and that it would at present be considered "to be almost as great a
misfortune as a contraction of it on this side." As to purchasing the territory at issue, "we are too poor to pay any sum which France would feel. we
are in debt, and wish to pay our debts." The only expedient he could conjure for this purpose was that the U.S. Government might assume France's
responsibility under the Convention of 1800 for paying American ships'
owners millions of dollars in compensation for ships illegally seized in the
West Indies. Du Pont was to share all of these considerations with Minister Livingston, who was still to consider Madison's instructions binding.[10]

Honor certainly was involved, but so was interest. Although "perhaps a
dozen" American boats had stopped at New Orleans in 1792, that number
passed five hundred in 1802.[11] If residents of Kentucky and the rest of the

American west lost the right of deposit, their livelihoods would be lost; so too would those of shippers and merchants in the great American cities of New York, Baltimore, and Philadelphia, among others.

Jefferson decided, at the turn of the year 1803, to send James Monroe as Envoy Extraordinary to France.[12] His mission: to purchase New Orleans or some such site as a port of deposit for America on the Mississippi River at the Gulf Coast.[13] From our vantage point, that Jefferson and Madison sent Monroe on this errand seems rather ho-hum. Of course the United States bought Louisiana. In its time, however, as one skeptical historian put it, "[i]t was pie-in-the-sky diplomacy if ever such existed. Given Napoleon's ambitions, Monroe had about as much chance of buying New Orleans as he had of buying Paris. Even Jefferson felt, except in his most euphoric moments, that it was a futile gesture and that war with France would still be necessary. And yet the mission resulted in the most spectacular diplomatic coup in American history."[14]

16

✢ ✿ ✢

October's events in New Orleans continued to rile up Westerners, and Monroe was tailor-made for the assignment. First, he had been an authentic hero in the American Revolution, leaving the College of William & Mary in 1776 to join the Continental Army and winning eternal fame as hero of the Battle of Trenton, General Washington's first significant victory, by the end of the year. Seriously wounded at the battle's climax, Monroe carried a musket ball in his forearm for the rest of his life. His role was immortalized in Emanuel Leutze's famous painting *Washington Crossing the Delaware* (1851), in which he is shown, standing right behind Washington, holding an American flag.

Monroe also had led the Confederation Congress opposition to Secretary of Foreign Affairs John Jay's 1786 request for that body's authorization to sacrifice American access to the Mississippi River, then property of Spain, for access to Spanish colonial ports in the Caribbean. While Jay believed the United States would make only token use of the Mississippi for the foreseeable future, and thus could afford to do without it for a quarter century, he calculated that the Spanish Caribbean trade offered a substantial profit to (mainly Northern) shipping, mercantile, and farming interests right away. Congressman Monroe, on the other hand, read this as a New York City man's attempt to trade off inland interests, in fact natural rights, for Yankee/ Northern gain, and so opposed it. The Congress ultimately voted by a bare, sectional majority to change Jay's instructions as he had requested. Several significant politicians, including not only Monroe but Patrick Henry, became opponents of the constitutional reform movement culminating in ratification of the U.S. Constitution as a result of these events. His role made Monroe a special favorite of Westerners for the rest of his life.

Not only would the Americans most affected likely welcome Monroe's appointment, but so would France. Monroe had served in 1794–96 as American

minister to France. During that time, he repeatedly expressed his support
for the French Revolution. In the end President Washington recalled him
from Paris on the ground that Monroe's public Francophilia might damage
relations with the other leading European power, Great Britain. Since the
Republican ascendancy had reoriented American foreign policy in France's
direction, a man such as Monroe's time had come again.

President Jefferson explained the reasons for Monroe's appointment in
a message dated January 13, 1803.[1] Like Jefferson when appointed secretary
of state by Washington in 1790, Monroe learned of his nomination only after
the Senate had given its consent.[2] "[T]he agitation of the public mind," Jefferson told him, "on occasion of the late suspension of our right of deposit
at N. Orleans is extreme. in the Western country it is natural and grounded
in honest motives. in the seaports it proceeds from a desire for war which
increases the mercantile lottery. . . ." Besides selfish motives among groups
not generally supportive of his administration, Jefferson confided that he saw
political motives among his partisan opponents. War, if Jefferson could be
coaxed into it, would "derange our finances" or "attach the Western country to" the Federalists. This would ease their way back into power.

While public agitation produced "remonstrances, memorials &c. . . .
thro' the whole of the Western country & signing by the body of the people,"
diplomatic steps ongoing in Europe and Washington "do not satisfy their
minds." Thus Monroe must head off to Paris.

What this initiative could produce, Jefferson could not say. Monroe would
therefore take "discretionary powers." He knew the thinking of Jefferson and
Madison well and in detail, and to that he added "the unlimited confidence
of . . . the Western people; & generally of the republicans everywhere. . . ."
No one else would fit the bill. In fact congressional Federalists had been "silenced" by the appointment already, and "the country will become calm as
fast as the information extends over it." To flattery Jefferson added the warning that "were you to decline, the chagrin would be universal, and would
shake under your feet the high ground on which you stand with the public. indeed I know nothing which would produce such a shock. for on the
event of this mission depends the future destinies of this republic." Failing
to purchase New Orleans, Monroe might have "to cross the channel (that is,
make arrangements with Britain) as a prelude to inevitable war": "we shall
get entangled in European politics. . . ."

Jefferson closed by noting that France's problems in the West Indies made
this a particularly propitious moment for Monroe to go thither. Napoleon's

problems on St. Domingue, a hitherto highly lucrative slave colony whose slaves were in full revolt, meant he needed money, and quick.

The Republican high command put on quite a show in sending Monroe to France. Monroe told the chief French diplomat in Washington, Louis Pichon, that failure in Paris would lead Monroe to depart immediately for London. Pichon also received an invitation to a public dinner at which Senator Samuel Smith toasted Monroe with, "Peace if peace is honorable, war if war is necessary." Pichon, impressed, recounted these developments for Talleyrand.[3]

Meanwhile the British prime minister, Henry Addington, approached the American minister to the U.K., Rufus King.[4] He asked how the United States would receive British occupation of New Orleans in case of a renewal of the European war. King replied that while happy to see any French design on that territory thwarted, the American government would "see it in the possession of England" only "with much concern." Spain remained America's preferred neighbor, particularly as the administration expected Spanish possession of New Orleans to lead to American "in the ordinary course of things." Even if that occupation resulted in a transfer of Louisiana to the United States, King said, this apparent collusion between the United States and Great Britain would implicate America in an anti-French gambit, thus potentially damaging America's relations with France—an outcome America wanted to avoid. In King's account Addington concluded by saying that England had no intention of claiming the territory and would indeed prefer for it to end up in the possession of the United States. Despite this news from King, James Madison, for one, found the notion of Britain giving New Orleans to the United States unbelievable.

King concluded that Britain would have no part in pressuring either France or Spain on America's behalf. As he explained to Madison, "England abstains from mixing herself in it, precisely from those considerations which have led her to acquiesce in others of great importance to the Balance of Europe, as well as her own repose." Britain in fact saw advantage to herself in ongoing proximity between France and the United States, because it "would keep the latter in a perpetual state of jealousy with respect to the former, and of consequence unite [the United States] in closer bonds of amity with Great Britain."[5] Jefferson privately conceded, "The day that France takes possession of New Orleans . . . seals the union of two nations who in conjunction can maintain exclusive possession of the ocean. From that moment we must marry ourselves to the British fleet and nation."[6]

So long as the peace endured, then, America could hope for nothing in particular in regard to Louisiana. If the war did recommence, however, and if France denied America the right of deposit at New Orleans, Livingston and James Monroe (who was sent to Paris with the special mission of resolving the Louisiana issue) should press the British for "concurrence" in it. The American diplomats were to offer King George's government nothing in particular, but a vague promise of special commercial access to Louisiana. None of this seemed likely, as France had avowed its intention to leave America in possession of the same commercial rights at New Orleans as it had enjoyed during the Spanish intendancy there. Why Britain would agree to what the Americans were to offer remains unclear; they had nothing much to gain from it.[7]

Livingston advised Madison in May 1802 that French forces' departure for Louisiana had been delayed by a dispute between that country and Spain over Louisiana's boundaries. France held that Louisiana included the Floridas, he advised, while Spain excluded that portion of the Spanish Empire.[8] From February 1802 to the end of the year, Napoleon's plans for North America had to be kept on the back burner. More pressing matters intervened.

Bonaparte's vision for French Louisiana was characteristically grand. Its colonization was "among the most favourite projects of the first Consul." As Livingston found on arriving in Paris, Napoleon "Saw in it a new Egypt; he Saw in it a Colony that was to counterbalance the Eastern establishments of Britain; he Saw in it a provision for his Generals, and what was more important in the then State of things he Saw in it a pretence for the ostracism of Suspected enemies," who could be stationed in Louisiana to get them away from Paris.[9]

In the end Bonaparte's grand strategy collapsed. Hoping to resuscitate France's Western Hemisphere empire, he had dispatched the first of what would be over thirty thousand soldiers and sailors under the command of his brother-in-law, General Victor Emmanuel Leclerc, to St. Domingue. Leclerc and his men were to restore French government there and to re-enslave the rebels who had seized control of France's most lucrative colony.[10] What neither the general nor his master knew, however, was that tropical disease would ravage their expeditionary force, leaving only a few thousand fit for service, and in the end driving Leclerc to tell Bonaparte that both substantial reinforcements and a policy of outright butchery would be necessary to reestablishment of French authority on the island. Disease claimed his life too before the first consul's rejection of Leclerc's advice could become known to him.[11]

It was as a result of this that Napoleon's North American ambition was thwarted, the future of Anglophone culture on that continent made secure. Seeing that re-subjugation of the colony's Africans would require several tens of thousands of soldiers and a long, hard military campaign, and realizing in light of British naval superiority that renewal of European war could at any moment render St. Domingue impossible to defend anyway, Napoleon at a stroke decided to cut his losses. "Damn sugar, damn coffee, damn colonies!" he yelled.[12] "Irresolution and deliberation are no longer in season; I renounce Louisiana. It is not only New Orleans that I cede; it is the whole colony, without reserve."[13] France would take what it could get from the bothersome American diplomats who had been nagging his foreign minister, Catholic bishop-turned-republican-revolutionary-cum-Bonapartist-for-the-nonce (with more than one change in posture still ahead of him) Charles Maurice de Talleyrand-Périgord.

Livingston was Johnny-on-the-spot, then, when news arrived in Europe of the Spanish intendant's unilateral move on October 18, 1802, as the Kentucky Legislature communicated it to Jefferson, "forbid[ding] American Citizens to deposit their merchandizes and effects in the said Port, without having assigned to the United States an equivalent establishment on another part of the banks of the Mississippi." The Kentuckians closed their warlike communiqué by "pledg[ing] [them]selves to support, at the expense of [their] lives and fortunes, such measures as the honor, and interest of the United States [might] require."[14]

On March 2, 1803, Madison sent Monroe and Livingston what proved to be their ultimate instructions for negotiation with Talleyrand.[15] They might spend as much as ten million dollars (fifty million French "livres tournois," plus assumption of responsibility for some debts the French owed to Americans), he advised. They should obtain New Orleans and the Floridas (today's state of Florida, plus the coastal regions of Alabama and Mississippi, in addition to the portion of today's state of Louisiana east of the Mississippi River) "or as much thereof as the actual proprietor can be prevailed on to part with." As had become customary among Republicans, Madison classified American aims as "natural and . . . convenient" (which was alternative to "imperial"). Though the administration had undertaken a program of severe military retrenchment, France likely would see the wisdom of avoiding having America's "Colossal growth" thrown into the British scale—that is, America could have her cake (spending and tax reductions) and eat it too (expect France to accede to American demands because of the United States' military potential).

France would have noticed the great uproar in the United States over the Spanish intendant's decision to revoke America's right of deposit. It would want to avoid any conflict with America, and so hope to resolve the looming issue. The conjuncture of the St. Domingue difficulty and "the languishing state of the French finances" should ease the negotiators' path. Madison went on to explain how the French government's evident calculation that the Western states ultimately would become friendly to France's government at New Orleans instead of to the United States was mistaken. Then he laid out the proposal his agents should tender to Talleyrand, the main elements of which were that France would cede the Floridas and New Orleans, besides various related islands; the two powers would share the Mississippi navigation; and the inhabitants of the ceded territory would ultimately be incorporated into the American population "on an equal footing." While he could wish Spain would be party to the pact, Madison said, the potential for delay meant the United States would not insist on that. This last point would have serious consequences through the nineteenth century's second decade.

Though loath to grant it, Madison said Livingston and Monroe might guarantee the west bank of the river to France rather than "have the negotiation fail." Absent any sale, the Americans were at least to obtain a guarantee of the right of deposit. So too the negotiators should endeavor to regularize American access to "suitable deposits at the mouths of the other Rivers passing from the United States thro' the Floridas," besides "the free navigation of those rivers by Citizens of the United States." In a letter of April 18th, Madison clarified that war would only be necessary if France seemed determined to deny American navigation of the Mississippi or the right of deposit.

By the time these instructions reached Livingston and Monroe, the matter had already been resolved. François Barbé-Marbois, another of Bonaparte's ministers, offered Livingston "the whole of Louisiana" on the day of Monroe's arrival—thus before Monroe could play any role in the matter.[16] As Livingston rushed to tell Madison, he had taken the Spanish intendant's revocation of the American right of deposit at New Orleans as an opportunity to impress upon Bonaparte's mind the likelihood that America would use that as an occasion to seize New Orleans and the Floridas and that "Britain would never suffer Spain to grant the Floridas to France even were she so disposed, but would immediately seize upon them as soon as the transfer was made. . . ." Once deprived of the Floridas, France would lose any benefit from possession of Louisiana, which anyway would be "indefensible as it possesses not one port even for Frigates."[17]

Livingston went on to explain that he had developed for French consideration the effect on the European balance of power, particularly the balance of naval power, should Britain seize Louisiana and the Floridas. "These reasons," he scribbled excitedly, "have had I trust the desired effect. Mr. Talleyrand asked me this day . . . whether we wished to have the whole of Louisiana." Somewhat discombobulated, Livingston "told him no, that our wishes extended only to New Orleans & the Floridas. . . ." Pressing the point, the wily Frenchman, no doubt amused at Livingston's error, "said that if they gave New Orleans the rest would be of little value, & that he would wish to know 'what we would give for the whole.'" When Livingston spat out the figure "twenty Millions," Talleyrand answered "that this was too low an offer" and Livingston should mull it over and "tell him to morrow." Knowing of Monroe's arrival, Livingston asked for time to consult with him, then see Talleyrand again the second day. The conversation ended with Talleyrand saying that "he did not speak from authority, but that the idea had struck him."

Livingston sent Monroe an enthusiastic letter of welcome on hearing of his arrival in France.[18] Livingston told Madison that he had made clear to the French the possibility that Americans had already seized New Orleans, as Senator James Ross, F-PA, had proposed resolutions in the Senate authorizing Madison to raise fifty thousand militiamen to seize New Orleans for a deposit.[19] With Monroe's arrival Livingston told his French interlocutors that they should push "the train we are now in" (that is, the process that had nearly reached a conclusion before Monroe's arrival) "& which I flatter myself we shall be able on the arrival of Mr. Monroe to pursue to effect. I think from every appearance that war is very near at hand, & under these circumstances I have endeavored to impress the government that not a moment should be lost least Britain should anticipate us."

Livingston still did not attach much significance to Louisiana Territory outside New Orleans. Rather, he told Madison that in case the deal were closed, they should immediately try to trade Spain "the west bank of the Mississippi . . . for the Floridas reserving New Orleans."

Monroe, a bit irked, considered the behavior both of Livingston and of the Frenchman in advancing the negotiation after learning of Monroe's mission but prior to Monroe's arrival contrary to "strict diplomatic etiquette," and thus a weak reed on which to rest the negotiation. While Monroe's notes showed that he hoped to spare himself and the administration "the charge of having lost by the measure taken, a brilliant opportunity of securing all our objects here," one might also infer that Monroe, ever alert to the possibility of political advancement, wanted to ensure that he reaped some of the glory of impending events.[20] Livingston too chafed at being in tandem, taking time both to gripe to the secretary of state about the titles assigned to him and Monroe and to confide to Madison that "Mr. Monroe having been compelled when here to be well with the party then uppermost and who are detested by the present rulers it will be some time before they know how to estimate his worth. . . ."[21]

In the end, though he thought of them as representing "the Jacobin Government of America, so dangerous to the repose & safety of European Systems,"[22] Bonaparte did the deed with Livingston and Monroe.[23] Thrilled, they covered the treaty with a letter to Secretary of State Madison conceding that "[a]n acquisition of so great an extent was . . . not contemplated by [their] appointment," but insisting the offer had been too good to refuse.[24] By removing the threat of France or Britain as a neighbor, they hoped that they had not only obtained the territory, but separated America from the European state system. "We make in fine," they concluded, "a great stride to real and substantial independence. . . ." In doing so they also bade fair to cement the American Union.

In a private letter Monroe told Madison that Bonaparte had presented the American ministers an all-or-nothing choice. Anyway, he continued, the navigation fees and real estate value would have made it a good deal even at as much as three times the price. Perhaps now, he mused, the Federal Government could keep the Louisiana Territory unsettled until the American lands east of the river had been filled with population. He guessed, rightly as it turns out, that Federalists who had clamored for forcibly seizing the desired territory would "declaim ag[ain]st the govt. & its agents for getting too much. But the clamor will not avail them," he concluded. "It will disgrace them." Rufus King had stayed on in Britain, Monroe heard, awaiting the outcome of the Louisiana negotiation. An American in Paris had told Monroe that while "we could not give too much for this territory; that the object was vast and ought to be embraced; that it wod. not be, by our admn. from the want of spirit to such an enterprize." Livingston had been difficult, and seemed perturbed, but unless he took a hostile tack deserved all the plaudits flowing from his role in achieving this outcome.

As he pondered the Louisiana Purchase, Monroe arrived at the conclusion that not Livingston, he, or the two of them, but the Jefferson administration deserved the credit. As he said, France decided on the measure before he arrived, and if Livingston had been the spur must have decided on it much sooner. "I consider this transaction as resulting from the wise and firm tho' moderate measures of the Executive & congress during the last Session," he told three sympathetic senators. Maintaining friendly relations with France had yielded this result.[25]

Yet the weary received no rest: asked to clarify Louisiana's eastern boundary, Talleyrand replied only, "you have made a noble bargain for yourselves & I suppose you will make the most of it."[26] Likely Talleyrand calculated that the United States and Spain would disagree whether Louisiana included any or all of West Florida, which would be a bone of contention between the two—to France's benefit—for the foreseeable future. Monroe left immediately for Spain, where he was "to treat with his Catholic Majesty for such portions as he owns of Florida."[27] He thought the Louisiana Purchase reduced the Floridas' value to Spain, which should be reflected in their price.[28] The problem would not be resolved anytime soon.

17

⊹ ⊛ ⊹

While the French mission proceeded, President Jefferson had raised a point of discussion in his Cabinet.[1] He wanted to know whether the Federal Government had authority to purchase New Orleans and the Floridas from France.[2]

Attorney General Lincoln thought the problem could be avoided by the simple expedient of having France agree to extend the boundaries of the Mississippi Territory and Georgia. If the U.S. Government did not purchase the territory itself, he contended, no constitutional issue would arise. This would avoid "risking the doubtful attempt, so to amend the constitution, as to embrace the object; or hazarding the ratification of the treaty, from an opposition to such an amendment. . . ." It would also dodge the question of the status of the newly incorporated people in the United States, as they would be citizens of the affected states.

Apparently the issue that had perplexed Jefferson concerned the nature of the federal Union. As Lincoln put it, "the opinion" was "that the Genl. Govt. when formed, was predicated on the then existing *united* States, and such as could grow out of *them*, & out of *them* only, and that its authority, [was], constitutionally, limited to the people composing the several political states Societies in that union, & such as might be formed out of them. . . ." A "direct independent purchase" might then strike "the Eastern States" as threatening, from a constitutional point of view, while "the proposed indirect mode" need not. (Remember that one reason Jefferson appointed Lincoln attorney general was to have New England political counsel.) Politically this enlargement of particular states would avoid the possibility of rousing Northerners' ire as the probable addition of numerous new southern states would. Both the Federalists and the New England states, though open to a measure calculated to secure the Mississippi Navigation and the deposit at New Orleans, would likely oppose a measure sure to augment Southern strength in Congress.

Secretary of the Treasury Albert Gallatin cut through Lincoln's arguments with characteristic force.[3] He could not see any difference between acquiring territory for the United States and entering into a treaty extending the territory of the United States. He also did not see obtaining territory to be added to the Mississippi Territory as significantly different, from a constitutional point of view. If the president and Senate could not constitutionally annex territory, they could not do so in either guise, and in fact Lincoln's alternative seemed more dubious. "As to the danger resulting from the exercise of such power," he said, "it is as great on his plan as on the other. What could on his construction, prevent the Presidt. & Senate, by treaty annexing Cuba to Massachusetts or Bengal to Rhode Island . . . ?" Any constitutional problem must flow from an original understanding of the Constitution as "confined to the then existing territory of the Union, and *that* excludes a possibility of enlargement of one State as well as that of territory common to the United States."

"But does any constitutional objection really exist?"

Nothing in the constitutional language concerning treaty powers excludes acquisition of territory by treaties, he reasoned, "whilst, on the contrary, the existence of the United States as a nation presupposes the power enjoyed by every nation of extending their territory by treaties. . . ." The Constitution says how treaties will be made and how such territories may be either governed by Congress or admitted to the Union. Besides this, he continued, the Constitution gave all of the powers the Articles of Confederation had placed in nine states to Congress, and power to admit new territories to the Union had been given to nine states by the Articles. Gallatin easily disposed of Lincoln's reading of the Territories Clause. If it had only applied to property the United States owned at the time of ratification, the cessions from North Carolina and Georgia in the interim could not have been accepted. In his summation Gallatin did admit that the Tenth Amendment complicated the problem, adding that although he thought the War, Treaty, and Territories Clauses seemed to settle the matter, he was not entirely certain.

Jefferson, in turn, thought, or at least said, that "there is no constitutional difficulty as to the acquisition of territory: and whether, when acquired, it may be taken into the union by the constn as it now stands, will become a question of expediency."[4] Yet he thought it "safer not to permit the enlargement of the Union but by amendment of the constitution." Next up, then, would be the project of adopting another amendment.

When the question moved from the theoretical into the practical column, however, the president took a different position. Now he confided to his old Revolutionary colleague John Dickinson, "There is a difficulty in this acquisition which presents a handle to the malcontents among us, tho' they have not yet discovered it. our confederation is certainly confined to the limits established by the revolution. the general government has no powers but such as the constitution has given it; and it has not given it a power of holding foreign territory, & still less of incorporating it into the Union." It thus was necessary, not merely "safe," to amend the Constitution. In the meantime the money must be spent and the people's pardon begged, "as we have treated, for a thing beyond the constitution, and rely on the nation to sanction an act done for it's great good, without its previous authority. . . ."

On July 3rd Jefferson learned for certain that a Louisiana treaty had been agreed.[5] On July 5th Alexander Hamilton's house organ, the *New-York Evening Post*, published his op-ed column saying that there was not much to credit the administration with in buying Louisiana, but what credit there was ought to go to Livingston, with none at all for Monroe, as the deal had been agreed before Monroe had had any input.[6] Sometime in early July, Jefferson drafted an amendment empowering the government to enter into the French treaty for the Louisiana Purchase.[7] Around July 9th Madison gave Jefferson a draft amendment of three sentences: one making Louisiana "part of the U. States," one empowering Congress to annex "other adjacent territories which shall be justly acquired," and a third empowering Congress "to sever from the U.S. territory not heretofore within the U. States. . . ."[8] By July 9th Jefferson could tell Gallatin that he had "sketched an amendment to the constitution" Congress could propose to the states.[9] However, Jefferson also told Gallatin that "our minds" remained "to make up" before the administration's path had been chosen in this regard and others related to the prospective Purchase.

Jefferson's first draft said first that the "Province of Louisiana" was made part of the United States; second, that "the rights of occupancy in the soil, and of self government," would remain with the local Indians "as they now exist" (that is, subject to their abandonment, which would leave "the full rights of possession . . . property & sovereignty" to the Americans), and that the U.S. Government was entitled to exchange trans-Mississippi lands in its possession for cis-Mississippi lands in Indians'. In addition the U.S. Government would have full power to regulate intercourse "between the Indian inhabitants and all other persons." The portion of the Purchase Territory lying south of 31 degrees latitude could be made into a territory with its own government or added to another whenever Congress judged appropriate, but the rest could not be similarly disposed of "until a new amendment of the constitution shall give it that authority."

Jefferson's second draft comes down to us in a manuscript altered by James Madison's addition of a final section to it.[10] Closely patterned on the first draft except in its division into several sections (in a way reminiscent of the U.S. Constitution), it closed with Madison's new provision covering "[t]erritories Eastwd. of the Mississippi & Southward of the U.S. which may be acquired by the U.S."

One reason Jefferson set aside this highly detailed proposal must have been Secretary Robert Smith's observation that "I am greatly pleased with the ideas suggested in the proposed amendment[. . . ,] But I am rather inclined to think that they ought not all to be ingrafted upon the Constitution."[11] He went on to provide examples of scenarios in which an amendment like Jefferson's could turn out to straitjacket Congress in situations in which it needed discretion. His counterproposal said simply that the territory purchased from France was property of the United States as if it had been its territory at the time of the Constitution's ratification and that the northern part could not be erected into a state or states absent a new amendment.

Madison drafted an alternative, quite brief (three-sentence) amendment at the same time.[12] Jefferson had it in hand when on August 17th he received an urgent note from Minister Livingston.[13] Dated June 2nd, it relayed alarming news from Paris.

Although the French government had ratified the treaty, Livingston explained, First Consul Bonaparte now thought it a mistake. "I [am] persuaded," Livingston wrote, "that if he could conveniently get off he would, he insists that our whole debt does not exceed four millions and that we have got twenty. . . ." After recounting various technical objections the French leader had raised regarding the details of ratification and payment and describing various circumstances in which, per Bonaparte, the treaty would be void, Livingston's coded message said, "[H]e appears to wish the thing undone. . . ." "[W]e must," Livingston said, "as far as we can soothe the youthful Conqueror whose will knows no resistance. . . ." There must be no delay and no objection to any aspect of the treaty, but rather expeditious ratification of the agreement as soon as practicable. In fact Bonaparte regretted having sent a ratified copy of the treaty "before you had agreed to ratify it. . . ." Because the U.S. Senate had ratified the Convention of 1800, which ended the Quasi-War, only after removing one article, Bonaparte was claiming the right to change this treaty up to the moment when the U.S. Government had formally agreed to it.[14]

Jefferson's response to Livingston's letter was first to write immediately to a close congressional ally, Senator John Breckinridge, R-KY, asking him to keep their previous communication private, and to urge friendly senators from his part of the country to be on hand when the Senate next convened so that the Louisiana Purchase Treaty might be ratified immediately. He also wrote to Secretary Madison telling him that in light of Livingston's information, "I infer that the less we say about constitutional difficulties respecting Louisiana the better, and that what is necessary for surmounting them must be done sub silentio."[15] In his reply Madison guessed that France did not really want to back out of the agreement, but instead wanted to see whether America and the British had arrived at some kind of meeting of the minds regarding Louisiana.[16]

Gallatin considered a volte-face on Bonaparte's part out of the question: "I feel not . . . any apprehension that France intends seriously to raise objections to the execution of the treaty: unless intoxicated by the hope of laying England prostrate, or allured by some offer from Spain to give a better price for Louisiana than we have done, it is impossible that Bonaparte should not consider his bargain as so much gained for nothing; for, however valuable to us, it must be evident to him that, pending the war, he could not occupy Louisiana, & that the war would place it very soon in other hands." Gallatin also told Jefferson he agreed with Jefferson's conclusion that "we have a right to claim that part of West Florida which was part of Louisiana." Jefferson had persuaded him. As usual Gallatin had seen to the financial arrangements, complicated as they were.[17]

Besides these constitutional matters and the political problem that would face the coming Congress, the Louisiana Purchase presented practical questions. No one knew Louisiana's precise boundaries, for example. Nor did Americans know exactly how the place had been governed. Neither France nor Spain had ever conducted a census of its inhabitants. As one provision of Jefferson's draft amendments highlighted, the government would need "to explore & ascertain the geography of the province, it's productions and other interesting circumstances." (How thrilling this prospect must have been to the author of *Notes on the State of Virginia*!) Learning and instituting would have to coincide, as the people living in Louisiana would have to have government.

Meanwhile Jefferson developed his thinking about the treaty more fully in a letter to Senator Breckinridge.[18] As he had to Dickinson, Jefferson relayed to the Kentucky senator his understanding that America's plausible claims under the treaty extended west to the Rio Grande and, with more force, east to the Perdido River "between Mobile and Pensacola." "[T]hese claims," he said, "will be a subject of negociation with Spain, and if, as soon as she is at war, we push them strongly with one hand, holding out a price in the other, we shall certainly obtain the Floridas, and all in good time." The Great Powers' constant war-making meant that the United States would have its way sooner or later. In the meantime America would insist on the same natural right to travel down the rivers that ran into the Gulf of Mexico east of Louisiana as it had insisted upon in relation to the Mississippi.

Jefferson informed Breckinridge that New Englanders had begun to protest the gigantic territorial acquisition Talleyrand had handed him, saying that "propositions are made to exchange Louisiana or a part of it for the Floridas," but he thought such proposals silly: America would have the Floridas in the end anyway. Unilateral control of the Mississippi, he insisted, was "very important to our peace." Federalists lamented that the entire Mississippi Basin, including that river's tributaries as far north as Ohio, might in time form a separate "new confederacy" and instigate "a separation of it's Eastern waters from us." Jefferson saw this as no problem. First, it was extremely unlikely. Second, "if it should become the great interest of those nations [states] to separate from this, if their happiness should depend on it so strongly as to induce them to go through that convulsion, why should the Atlantic states dread it?" After all, "the future inhabitants of the Atlantic & Mispi states will be our sons. we think we see their happiness in their union, & we wish it," but "if they see their interest in separation, why should we take side with our Atlantic rather than our Mispi descendants it is the elder & the younger son differing. god bless them both. . . ."[19]

For the nonce the southernmost section of the Territory would "be immediately a territorial government & soon a state. but above that, the best use we can make of the country for some time will be to give establishments in it to the Indians on the East side of the Mispi in exchange for their present country. . . ." The government could sell off the Indians' former lands as this process developed, thus peopling the cis-Mississippi lands rather than allowing the more remote newly acquired territory to draw off American population. "[W]hen we shall be full on this side," he ruminated, "we may lay off a range of states on the Western bank from the head to the mouth, & so range after range, advancing compactly as we multiply."

Jefferson's thinking here reflected his understanding of the relationship between population density and cultural advancement. Observation led him to conclude that population density was associated with development. As he put it:

[L]et a philosophic observer commence a journey from the savages of
the Rocky mountains, Eastwardly towards our seacoast. these he would
observe in the earliest stage of association living under no law but that of
nature, subsisting and covering themselves with the flesh and skins of wild
beasts. he would next find those on our frontiers in the pastoral state, raising
domestic animals to supply the defects of hunting. then succeed our own
semibarbarous citizens, the pioneers of the advance of civilisation, and so
in his progress he would meet the gradual shades of improving man until
he would reach his, as yet, most improved state in our seaport towns this in
fact is equivalent to a survey, in time of the progress of man from the infancy
of nation to the present day.[20]

It would be best if possible, then, for government to endeavor to try to
shepherd new settlers into denser settlements, perforce closer to the east,
than to open the entire Louisiana Territory to sparse settlement throughout.

Jefferson's letter to Breckinridge arrived at last at his relaying his concern
for constitutional nicety to his close ally the senator. Both houses of Congress would have to approve the Louisiana Purchase Treaty, he said, and
having done so, they would need to "appeal to *the nation* for an additional
article to the constitution, approving & confirming an act which the nation
had not previously authorised." Neither the president nor the Congress had
had authority for what they had done, and so "the legislature" must ignore
"[m]etaphysical subtleties, and risking themselves like faithful servants, must
ratify & pay for it, and throw themselves on their country for doing for them
unauthorised what we know they would have done for themselves had they
been in a situation to do it." Jefferson drew an analogy, familiar to land bar-
ons such as he and the senator, of a guardian for a young heir who stood to
come into substantial lands upon attaining the age of majority who purchased
the lad neighboring property in the meantime. Though not strictly authorized to do so, the guardian might throw himself on the newly adult fellow's
mercy, asking him to accept responsibility for the purchase because it had
been made in his interest. The amendment Congress would propose for the
states' ratification in the wake of ratifying the treaty, Jefferson closed, would
"not weaken the constitution," but "more strongly mak[e] out its lines."

Breckinridge's reply was everything Jefferson could have hoped.[21] Of course
the treaty would be ratified. There could be no hesitation. Yes, some might
calculate that this accession would alter relations among the nation's sections
in an undesirable way, but gaining control of so enormous a territory—two
hundred million acres!—rather than risk its being controlled by another,

perhaps hostile, power, really was astoundingly good. And all this "without . . . the expence of a single dollar (for the port of Orleans will of itself reimburse the 15 Millions of dollars in the 15 years) is an achievement, of which the annals of no country can furnish a parallel.—As to the Floridas," he continued, "I really consider this acquisition as of no consequence for the present. We can obtain them long before we shall want them, & upon our own terms." The constitutional question that struck Jefferson did not merit Breckinridge's mention.

The Kentuckian-by-way-of-Virginia's view did not command universal support among Republican senators, however. Jefferson broached the matter with his close acquaintance Senator Wilson Cary Nicholas of Virginia in conversation. Nicholas mulled it over and sent a lengthy reply.[22] The nub of it was that Nicholas thought power to purchase territory clearly covered by the Constitution's grant of power to enter into treaties, as that power was a general power limited only by the Constitution's express prohibitions; in other words he read the matter oppositely to Jefferson, who saw the treaty power as having implicit limitations he never really spelled out.

Nicholas also offered Jefferson political advice. The president should not publicly stake out a position regarding the constitutional matter prior to the Senate vote on the treaty, he said. In case he did, Nicholas judged it "very probable" that the treaty would be defeated, and if it were not defeated, "great use wou'd be made with the people, of a wilful breach of the constitution."

Jefferson wrote Nicholas again a few days later.[23] Here he gave his home-state senator (and eventual kinsman) the fullest extant explanation of his thinking on the question of the Louisiana Purchase and the Constitution. After noting that Monroe had written from Paris warning that the matter must be hurried through the Senate, as Bonaparte was thinking better of it, and that Talleyrand had told Madison the same in "an unusual kind of letter," Jefferson addressed the obvious answer to the president's own constitutional qualms. Yes, Jefferson said, he felt "the force of the observations you make on the power given by the Constn to Congress to admit new states into the Union, without restraining the subject to the territory then constituting the US." However, he thought this point outweighed by the facts that the Treaty of Paris "fixed" "the limits of the US," which was the country for which "the constitution expressly declares itself to be made." He read these facts as indicating that the Treaty Clause and the Territories Clause did not give Congress power to acquire territory and admit it to the Union as a state or states. The most powerful part of his argument was that in which he said, "I do not believe it was meant that they might receive England, Ireland, Holland &c into it, which would be the case on your construction."

Then Jefferson came to his general approach to constitutional interpretation: "when an instrument admits two constructions the one safe, the other dangerous, the one precise the other indefinite, I prefer that which is safe & precise. I would rather risk an enlargement of power from the nation where it is found necessary, than to assume it by a construction which would make our powers boundless." In one of his most famous statements about constitutional interpretation, he closed with, "[O]ur peculiar security is in the possession of a written constitution. let us not make it a blank paper by construction." It was foreseeable that a government with enumerated powers would be found to need powers not delegated, he insisted. The proper remedy was amendment. The Republican leadership found itself in what nowadays would be called a "teachable moment," he thought: "I confess then I think it important in the present case to set an example against broad construction by appealing for new power to the people." If other Republican officials disagreed with him, he concluded, he would bow to their judgment.

18

Jefferson called Congress back into session on October 17, 1803, three weeks earlier than the statutory date.[1] The chief subjects he intended for Congress to consider were the French treaty, the situation of the Indians in Louisiana, governance of that new possession, and America's neutral posture in the renewed European war. Once again Madison and Gallatin in particular offered extensive substantive criticisms of the presidential message for the opening of the new Congress, criticisms which Jefferson in most cases heeded. Dearborn's and Lincoln's impress was clear upon the message's face as well. Perhaps of most interest is that Madison at one point in the drafting process referred to "suspensions of intercourse," aka economic embargo, which Gallatin and Lincoln called by different names. It is difficult to tell whether including this notion was Jefferson's idea, but after Gallatin and Lincoln objected strongly, Jefferson left it out of his final version. The embargo idea, alas, did not die in late 1803.[2]

As had become customary, Jefferson relied almost completely on Gallatin's input when it came to the financial section of the Annual Message. He also took Madison's advice to hold off on submitting the treaty to the House until the Senate had ratified it, as Madison thought the constitutional allocation to the Senate alone of power to consent to a treaty required this delay.[3]

In those days Congress met for only a few weeks each year, so being called back into session early posed a substantial inconvenience. After apologizing for this inconvenience, Jefferson turned directly to the Louisiana Purchase.[4] The suspension of the deposit during the last congressional session had sent Americans into great agitation. Friendly Spain quickly resolved the issue. France having come into possession of the entire Louisiana Territory, Jefferson dispatched diplomats with congressional authorization to spend $2 million "as part of the price." Bonaparte, seeing that "liberal arrangements . . .

might . . . permanently promote the peace, friendship & interests of both," agreed to sell the Louisiana Territory.

Though not all of the members would have known about Jefferson's conversations and correspondence with Senators Nicholas and Breckinridge and the members of the Executive Council, those who did may have arched an eyebrow on hearing the clerk read the president's nonchalant statement that "[w]ith the wisdom of Congress it will rest to take those ulterior measures which may be necessary for the immediate occupation, & temporary government of the country. . . ." To amend or not to amend, it seemed, was to be Congress's question. The president publicly offered no recommendation. He did, however, point out the pressing need for Congress to decide how Louisiana's residents would be governed, "for confirming to the Indian inhabitants their occupancy & self-government, establishing friendly & commercial relations with them," and for measures "for ascertaining the geography of the country acquired."

Besides pointing to the urgent need to resolve the Louisiana issue, Jefferson also brought Congress up to speed in relation to the progress of his Indian policy. The Kaskaskias of the Midwest, reduced to very few by war and disease, had yielded their land to the United States in exchange for "patronage & protection." As Jefferson hoped would become universal, these Indians had decided to exchange their traditional ways for life "in an agricultural way." As in the French case, Jefferson hoped the Senate would ratify the treaty and both houses would fund compliance. "With many of the other Indian tribes," he said, "improvements in agriculture & household manufacture, are advancing. . . ."

Even with the expense of the Louisiana Purchase, Jefferson contentedly noted, the government's entire debt should be extinguished within thirteen years. Jefferson had switched from the Federalist administrations' practice of favoring discharge of domestic over discharge of foreign loans to the opposite bias. He also had not found it necessary to expend the funds Congress had provided him for hostilities along the Mississippi in the wake of the Spanish intendant's action. He closed with a happy reflection on the United States' geostrategic situation and an oblique warning to all Americans not to become involved in the European wars in any way. "[W]e should be most unwise indeed," he held, "were we to cast away the singular blessings of the position in which nature has placed us, the opportunity she has endowed us with, of pursuing, at a distance from foreign contentions, the paths of industry, peace, & happiness, of cultivating general friendship, and of bringing collisions of interest to the umpirage of reason, rather than of force. . . ." If the Europeans would have it, America would be a neutral power trading with all; if not, she would appeal to "reason." Having won so fair a prize as the inner third of the North American continent without firing a shot, the administration concluded that military power was indeed, with the exception of a few ships to deal with Barbary states, superfluous. How foolish the Federalist presidents had been.

A new U.S. senator, William Plumer of New Hampshire—at the time a Federalist, but eventually to become a Republican—took a jaundiced view of the first day's proceedings.[5] The most partisan Republicans reprobated Speaker Nathaniel Macon for his unbiased performance in the speaker's chair, and thus divided the House on the question of who should be speaker this time around. The president deigned to inform the Senate that he would forward the Louisiana Purchase Treaty and conventions to the House "when these shall receive the constitutional sanction of the Senate," thus "tak[ing] it for granted that the Senate w[ould] sanction them." "No language," Plumer seethed, "could be more improper for a President than this—& no one in this Country ever before assumed it[.] He not only publicly pledges himself to ratify the treaties if the Senate should advise thereto, but takes it for granted that the Senate will sanction them[.]" The ground of Plumer's objection was that "As far as his influence can extend this is destroying the freedom of opinion in the Senate on that subject[.]" Jefferson would make clear soon enough that his laying a treaty before the Senate for its consent implied he would agree to it if the Senate ratified it—as the president's lieutenant James Monroe would learn to his regret. Plumer closed his journal entry for the day by noting that what would become the Twelfth Amendment had been introduced in the House by Representative John Dawson, R-VA.

If any other Republicans saw any constitutional difficulty in connection with the Louisiana Purchase, they kept mum.[6] One junior Federalist senator, Massachuetts's John Quincy Adams, pursued it. On October 21, 1803, "I called at the Secretary of State's Office. . . . I asked him whether the Executive had made any arrangements with any member of either house to bring forward the proposal for an Amendment to the Constitution to carry through the Louisiana Treaty."[7] According to Adams, after he offered to handle the matter in case no one else was going to do so, Secretary James Madison replied that although "he did not know that it was universally agreed that it required an Amendment of the Constitution," he would, had he been a member of Congress at the time, "have seen, no difficulty in acknowledging that the Constitution had not provided for such a case as this." As to the propriety of proceeding without first obtaining an amendment, Madison said (in markedly Jeffersonian language) "[t]hat it must be estimated by the magnitude of the object, and that those who had agreed to it must rely upon the candour [meaning indulgence] of their Country for Justification." Adams's diary says that he told Madison he "agreed, but urged the necessity of removing as speedily as possible all question on this subject." Madison, if Adams is to be trusted, concurred in that sentiment as well.

Adams found manifold difficulties not only with the Louisiana Purchase Treaty, but with various measures considered alongside it. He particularly objected to the enabling bill maintaining the Spanish form of government there for the short term, merely substituting Jefferson for Carlos IV as Louisiana's autocrat. As Dumas Malone put it, "Alone among the Federalist senators from New England he approved of the purchase, but he had qualms about what was happening to the rights of the inhabitants of Louisiana."[8] He wanted a constitutional amendment authorizing purchase of Louisiana and a referendum of the territory's residents prior to accession of the Purchase.[9]

As Attorney General Lincoln had warned Jefferson by mail from his Worcester, Massachusetts, home a month before, "Republicans [in New England] are, I believe, universally pleased with the purchase, indeed, many of them are more than pleased with it."[10] Thus far the good news. As for the majority Federalists, they were "vexed, disappointed, mortified, enraged." Postmaster General Granger had confided in Lincoln his impression that "one half the federalists approve of the cession. I am satisfied he is mistaken, & greatly overstates the number." Eminent men in his part of the Bay State said that the Mississippi navigation, America's great interest in Louisiana, "was ours before the late treaty." As to the kingdom Livingston and Monroe had bought, it would "prove very injurious to U.S. that they are too extensive already, containing more territory than we know what to do with, can dispose of, or Govern, that the [said?] country, is principally a sunken swamp of no value. . . ." Opening up so large an area would "draw from the existing states their useful inhabitants" before Louisiana should "finally become independent. . . ." In sum, "I am satisfied the ratification of the treaty . . . will meet with every obstacle in the power of the opposition."

Senator William Plumer, Adams's fellow Yankee Federalist from New Hampshire, laid out the Federalist arguments Lincoln had heard in the final Senate debate on the treaty on October 20th. After showing that the treaty submitted to the Senate for its ratification purported to give the United States what France did not at the moment possess, clear title to Louisiana, and that even this gift did not have specific boundaries, Plumer objected that "[w]e have already, without Louisiana, more uncultivated lands than we can sell. Our territory," he added—perhaps somewhat surprisingly—"was before this treaty too extensive, our settlements too sparse, for the security of our government." The Louisiana Territory could not be governed as a New England Yankee thought appropriate, he moaned, reasoning from New England practice, homely metaphors, and the famous teaching of Montesquieu's *The Spirit of the Laws*:

> Our republican government derives its authority & momentum from the frequent meetings of the mass of the people in town & county assemblies. An extension of the body politic will enfeeble the circulation of its powers & energies in the extreme parts. A piece of our coin, an eagle, may be extended to the size of a coach wheel, but its beauty & use will be destroyed. If the bed of the *North River* was ten times as wide as it is, that noble stream, would lose both its force & usefulness. The testimony of history and the very nature of things unite in declaring that a republican government established over a large extensive country cannot long exist.

He concluded with the dire forecast that "the ratification of this treaty & the possession of that immense territory will hasten the dissolution of our present government. We must form different empires, & the form of our governments will then result more from the circumstances of the times in which the change is effected, than the will of the people or the fitness & propriety of the measure."[11]

Plumer spoke for much New England opinion when he objected to the pending treaty on constitutional grounds. Sounding every bit the Jeffersonian, he held that "[t]he constitution is in its form as well as in its nature a *federative* government. It may," he held, "be fitly compared to a company in trade consisting of several partners. And with as much propriety might a *new* partner be admitted, & the *firm* of the company changed, without the consent of each of the old partners, as to admit a new State, formed from without the limits of the original territory, into the Union, without the previous consent of each State." Granting Jefferson's public statements about the extent of Louisiana's territory and the grandeur of the natural resources found there, Plumer objected on precisely that basis. He warned that New Englanders "know their importance, they know their rights, they feel the high rank that they are entitled to hold in the Union—and they have too

much pride tamely to shrink into a state of insignificance." Here, we now
know, was an accurate forecast.

After making these general points, Plumer turned to particular provisions
of the Constitution—for uniformity of import duties, making natural born
citizenship a condition of eligibility for the presidency, and confiding power
to admit new states to the Union exclusively to Congress—and showed how
the treaty, with its special guarantees for Louisiana, would violate them. As
Plumer told the story, Virginia's Senator John Taylor of Caroline, the prominent Republican pamphleteer of the 1790s and House of Delegates sponsor of
the Virginia Resolutions of 1798, stood during the debate and said, "That he
would, like an attorney who exceeded the authority delegated to him by his
client, vote to ratify the treaty, *& throw himself upon the people*, & request the
States so to amend the Constitution as to admit Louisiana into the Union."
A decade earlier Taylor would not have accepted this type of argument from
Alexander Hamilton in relation to the Federal Government's assumption
of responsibility for the state debts. Neither would President Jefferson, who
as we have seen was the father of the simile (what might today be called the
"talking point") on which Taylor here relied.

Plumer closed his argument by lamenting a new burden this treaty would
impose, the necessity to maintain an army in Louisiana. The weight of this
requirement would fall largely on New Englanders, "without their deriv-
ing any advantages from it." Besides that, "it will encrease the patronage, &
enrich the minions, of the Executive"—which again, not so long before, Taylor, Jefferson, and their fellows would have bewailed. He then pointed out
that the Senate had devoted less attention to this treaty "than they allowed
themselves on the most trivial Indian contract." "Twenty three democrats
[that is, Jeffersonians] voted in favor of the resolution, & the seven federal
senators against it."

Plumer's argument reflected Northern sentiment in general. As former
senator Gouverneur Morris, another aristocrat from New York, explained
it to Livingston,

I like well your treaty with France. It is in my opinion one of the best we
have made.[12] Our party, though with numerous exceptions, opposed it; for
one reason, that it cost money the greater part of which we to the northward
must pay, and it gains territory which will, in their apprehension, by giving
strength to the Southern representation, diminish the Eastern [meaning
New England] influence in our councils. They dislike it, also, because it
has strengthened an administration they abhor.[13]

France had vowed to Spain that it would never cede possession of Louisiana. When news of the impending transfer of title reached Madrid, Spain protested. Not for the last time in dealing with Bonaparte, or indeed in losing the various parts of their empire, Spanish statesmen must have been put in mind of Thucydides's "Melian Dialogue." "[T]he strong," the Athenians told the men of Melos, "do what they can, while the weak suffer what they must." Since Spain had come into its New World possessions in so disreputable a way, it had little ground for complaint; it had merely moved from one position in Thucydides's account to the other. Jefferson prepared to seize New Orleans by force if Spain held up its retrocession to France. It did not.[14]

Senator Adams proposed an amendment authorizing adding new territory to the Union in the following congressional session. Only three senators—two Federalists and a Republican—supported his motion. Breckinridge explained to him in a Senate speech that to attempt to adopt such an amendment was impractical, because the deadline for paying France what was owed likely would pass before the amendment's ratification. Adams later wrote that his experience as a constitutionalist in the Louisiana Affair showed that Jefferson and Madison had been motivated purely by politics in the 1790s. Here had come a matter of more constitutional moment, involving exercise of greater undelegated power, than any of the 1790s, and their response was to do nothing. Leaving aside the self-serving nature of Adams's evaluation (which came in 1828, as Jeffersonians were decrying his latitudinarian First Annual Message and other initiatives as president), one may infer that Breckinridge's position, as usual, reflected the thinking of Jefferson, Madison, and Gallatin on the general issue.[15]

19

✦ ☸ ✦

nbeknownst to Jefferson and his allies at the time, "*certain leaders* of the Federal party" lit upon a plan in the wake of the Louisiana Purchase "to effect a dissolution of the Union, and the establishment of a Northern confederacy" as their answer to what seemed likely to be a permanent Republican majority.[1] (This was nothing new from that quarter. As early as 1794 Federalist Senators Rufus King of New York and Oliver Ellsworth of Connecticut had broached the idea of a north-south split with Virginia's Senator John Taylor of Caroline.)[2] As John Quincy Adams explained, this campaign rested on the claim that the Louisiana Purchase was unconstitutional, and in fact "formed . . . a new confederacy, to which the States, united by the former compact, were not bound to adhere. . . ." Because this new situation "was oppressive to the interests and destructive to the influence of the Northern section of the confederacy," the northern states had a "right and duty . . . to secede from the new body politic, and to constitute one of their own." The parties to this effort went so far as to recruit a military commander.

Adams's version of events in 1828, during the final year of his presidency, was that learning of the New England secessionist plot "alienated [him] from the secret councils of those leaders of the Federal Party," into which he "was never initiated." New York's Rufus King, the Philadelphia Convention Framer and former senator who had just returned from his stint as American minister to the Court of St. James's, told Adams that Timothy Pickering, once George Washington's third secretary of state, had tried to recruit Alexander Hamilton to participate, but both King and Hamilton disapproved of the project. Pickering had more luck with New Hampshire's Senator William Plumer, then a Federalist. As Plumer recalled decades later, during the 1803–04 session of Congress "several of the Federalists, Senators and Representatives, from the New England States, informed me that they thought it necessary to establish a separate government in New England; and, if it should be found practicable, to extend it so far south as to include Pennsylvania. . . ."[3]

As the former senator remembered, his secessionist New England congressional colleagues had several complaints about the federal Union. First, the Three-Fifths Clause gave "the slave-holding States" more weight in the U.S. House of Representatives "than was just and equal"; second, federal taxation and expenditures operated to transfer money from "the Northern States" to "the Southern and Western States"; and third, the Louisiana Purchase meant that "the Northern States" were soon to have their "weight and influence" in Congress "annihilated." In response to these problems, they said, the target states would one at a time cease to participate in Congress, "and gradually withdraw . . . from the Union, establish custom-house officers to grant registers and clearances to vessels, and eventually establish a Federal government in the Northern and Eastern [that is, New England] States. . . ." They hoped that if the whole region cooperated in secession, "it would in due time be effected without resorting to arms."

As Plumer told it, plans were afoot to meet at Boston in autumn of 1804. "The leading Federalists in New England" (the so-called Essex Junto) then would start the process. "Alexander Hamilton of New York had consented to attend that meeting." When Plumer discussed this general idea with leading New Hampshire Federalists that year, however, he found most of them "decidedly opposed." Hamilton's death at the hand of Aaron Burr meant the plot could not go forward in the same way, but neither did it put the planning to an end. Plumer favored all of these actions at the time, though he later came to oppose the concept. However accurate Plumer's appraisal of the situation then and his recollection of it a quarter century later, New England separatism did not end in 1804.

Hamilton had ruined himself at the highest reaches of Federalist politics by torpedoing John Adams's reelection campaign in 1800. In 1803 his favorite, oldest son's death in a duel sent him into a prolonged depression. Meanwhile Jefferson's decision to favor the Clinton-Livingston coalition in New York over Burr's political friends left the vice president at sea. Burr seems to have cast about for new allies in the run-up to the February Republican congressional caucus to select the party's ticket for 1804. So, for example, a prominent Massachusetts Republican reported to Jefferson early in 1804 that Burr had broached the idea of a coalition between Burrites and Federalists in the 1804 presidential election: "our friends," he quoted Burr as saying, "must join the federal vote."[4]

A few days later Vice President Burr visited the president in the Executive Mansion.[5] According to the president's account (which of course was intended for posterity, meaning us), Burr explained that on moving to New York, he had found the state under the control of the Livingstons and Clintons, "two rich families," and that he had stayed out of their way until they solicited his aid in the 1800 elections. "He lent it without any view of promotion," Jefferson has him saying, and "his being named as a candidate for Vice-President was unexpected by him."

Burr has a reputation as a bit of an oily operator, and Jefferson's account of this conversation played a large part in making that a lasting reputation. According to Jefferson, Burr said, "He acceded to [being named as a candidate for Vice-President] to promote my [meaning Jefferson's] fame and advancement, and from a desire to be with me, whose company and conversation had always been fascinating to him." Since their election, however, the Clintons and Livingstons had disseminated "the calumnies which I had seen published," in which "Hamilton had joined, and had even written some of the pieces against him."

Burr noted that "his attachment to me had been sincere, and was still unchanged, although many little stories had been carried to him, and he supposed to me also, which he despised. . . ." Burr wanted assurance from Jefferson that the "attachments" remained mutual. He supposedly told Jefferson that because his remaining politically active would disrupt the New York Republican organization, he had decided to retire, but that he thought to "shrink from the public sentence" would not reflect well on him. Therefore he hoped Jefferson could confer some "mark of favor" upon him as he departed.

Jefferson told Burr that his general rule had been to stay out of contests for party nomination, let alone for electoral votes, and that the one exception he had made was working to ensure Burr received votes from all of Virginia's electors in 1800. His justification for that exception was that "I thought any failure there might be imputed to me."

Jefferson's account of this conversation reflects quite poorly on Burr, of whom he clearly came at some point to have a highly negative opinion. (More on that anon.) For example, he closes by noting that "Colonel Burr must have thought that I could swallow strong things in my own favor, when he founded his acquiescence in the nomination as Vice-President, to his desire of promoting my honor, the being with me, whose company and conversation had always been fascinating with him, &c. I had never seen Colonel

Burr till he came as a member of Senate. His conduct very soon inspired me with distrust. I habitually cautioned Mr. Madison against trusting him too much." He went on to add that during the Washington and Adams administrations, "whenever a great military appointment or a diplomatic one was to be made, he came post to Philadelphia to show himself, and in fact that he was always at market, if they had wanted him. . . . there never had been an intimacy between us, and but little association." His exertions on behalf of the Republican Party in New York in 1800 accounted for whatever favor Jefferson had shown him.

That George Clinton won the party's favor in 1804 comes as no surprise, then. Although his nephew DeWitt Clinton handled the day-to-day politics, George had by 1804 served as governor of the Empire State for a total of two decades. Perhaps Jefferson kept his preferences to himself, but his longstanding denigration of Burr to Madison must have had its effect. The party, after all, was Jefferson's party—certainly in Washington, where the decision was made.

Jefferson delivered his Fourth Annual Message to Congress as the month-long presidential voting season began.[6] Notable sections concerned the ongoing naval war with "the barbarians of Tripoli," potential hostilities with Tunis, early provisions for governance of the Louisiana Territory, and implementation of the Jeffersonian experiment in reliance on gunboats for defense of American ports. Jefferson looked to "adding to their number from year to year, as experience shall test their utility, until all our important harbors, by these and auxiliary means, shall be insured against insult and opposition to the laws." Reflection on the economy of this policy led him directly into a happy account of the retirement of another large tranche of the government's total debt in the past year.

Jefferson's ticket won an easy victory at the polls against Federalists Charles Cotesworth Pinckney, the head of one of the most prominent families in South Carolina, and Rufus King, a native of Massachusetts now high up in the New York political elite, both of them Philadelphia Convention Framers. The Republicans swept all of the states except for Delaware and the remaining Federalist redoubt, Connecticut, which thus became the only two states that voted against Thomas Jefferson for president all three times he was nominated. (Both Delaware and Connecticut remained among the handful of states that held no popular vote for electors in 1804.) Even Massachusetts ended up in the Republican column. The elections for Congress yielded equally lopsided results: a 27–7 Republican edge in the Senate and a 116–25 margin in the House.[7] The tax cutting, the end of the Alien and Sedition Acts, and particularly the Louisiana Purchase had made Thomas Jefferson politically invincible. For a moment.

By the end of 1804, Jefferson arrived at the determination that he would retire after his second presidential term. His first grave concern about the U.S. Constitution in 1787 had been that presidents had no term limit, and he hoped that by following George Washington's precedent he could help to establish a two-term limit as a kind of unwritten rule. When his long-time political ally John Taylor of Caroline wrote to him as the year closed to express hope that rumors of Jefferson's planned departure were erroneous then, Jefferson pointed to this issue as justification of his plan. He might also have said that he longed for home and that repairing to Monticello for several weeks at the peak of each summer did not satisfy that longing. Neither he nor Taylor would have considered this an appropriate justification, however.[8]

In his Second Inaugural Address, Jefferson once again staked out a new role for such speeches.[9] His First Inaugural Address had reminded Americans of his party's principles and told them what Republicans intended to do in power. This speech would recap the administration's successes and mark the trail for his second term. As he put it, "The former one was an exposition of the principles on which I thought it my duty to administer the government. The second, then, should naturally be a *compte rendu*, or a statement of facts showing that I have conformed to those principles. The former was *promise*: this is *performance*."[10]

So after noting that "[t]he suppression of unnecessary offices, enabled us to discontinue our internal taxes" and that "[t]he remaining revenue on the consumption of foreign articles, is paid cheerfully by those who can afford to add foreign luxuries to domestic comforts," he rhetorically asked "what farmer, what mechanic, what laborer, ever sees a tax-gatherer of the United States?" He looked forward to a day when the country's debt was paid, "the native right of soil within our limits" "extinguish[ed]," and "a corresponding amendment of the constitution" made so that the government could devote part of its revenue to "rivers, canals, roads, arts, manufactures, education, and other great objects within each state." So great would federal revenues become in a future day as a result of significantly greater "population and consumption" that war's expenses could be covered by the simple expedient of suspending expenditures on inessential purposes—"without encroaching on the rights of future generations, by burdening them with the debts of the past. War will then be but a suspension of useful works, and a return to a state of peace, a return to the progress of improvement."

Turning to his Louisiana triumph, Jefferson first noted the likelihood that the Purchase would pay for itself, then responded to warnings it would lead to the breakup of the Union by asking, "But who can limit the extent to which the federative principle may operate effectively?" Drawing on Madison's argument in *Federalist* #51, he posited, "The larger our association, the less will it be shaken by local passions" before concluding with two conmmon-sense rhetorical questions: "in any view, is it not better that the opposite bank of the Mississippi should be settled by our own brethren and children, than by strangers of another family?" and, "With which shall we be most likely to live in harmony and friendly intercourse?"

Jefferson had devoted considerable thought to the fate of American Indians in the United States, and he updated Congress "with the commiseration their history inspires." The president described them as "Endowed with the faculties and the rights of men, breathing an ardent love of liberty and independence, and occupying a country which left them no desire but to be undisturbed" until they encountered an irresistible "stream of overflowing population from other regions. . . ." As for him had by now become customary, the displacement of Indians from the United States became a natural phenomenon akin to a river flowing to the sea or a wind blowing across a plain. In the face of it, "humanity enjoins us to teach them agriculture and the domestic arts; to encourage them to that industry which alone can enable them to maintain their place in existence, and to prepare them in time for that state of society, which to bodily comforts adds the improvement of the mind and morals." With these goals in mind, the U.S. Government had provided farm implements, instructors in basic mechanical arts, and "the aegis of the law against aggressors from among ourselves."[11]

In the concluding two paragraphs of this, his final public address, Jefferson struck a contemplative pose. There remained some Americans who did not agree with the majority, he conceded, but in time even they would participate in "the union of sentiment now manifested so generally." Their "disposition to do so," he said, was "now gaining strength" and "facts are piercing through the veil drawn over them; . . . our doubting brethren," he insisted, "will at length see, that the mass of their fellow citizens . . . think as they think, and desire what they desire. . . ." Until they came around, "let us cherish them with patient affection" until "truth, reason, and their own interests, . . . at length prevail . . . and . . . complete that entire union of opinion, which gives to a nation the blessing of harmony, and the benefit of all its strength." In other words the End of History would be an Era of Good Feelings. Surely the day was not far off. He closed with an invocation of the God who had led Americans' ancestors "as Israel of old, from their native land," led them to North America, and helped them arrive at this juncture, to whom he asked listeners to pray to guide their government so that it could "secure to you the peace, friendship, and approbation of all nations."

20

Jefferson's hopes were destined to be blasted. After nearly unmitigated success in his first term, he would encounter a string of frustrations in his second. A good part of the difficulty he encountered came from overseas, as the Napoleonic Wars' destructive power left the Americans no choice but effectively to take a side, while substantial domestic political problems divided Jefferson's own coalition. At the center of the latter storm was a Republican congressman, and not only was he a Republican, but he was a Virginian— even Jefferson's cousin. Not without reason did contemporaries say that John Randolph of Roanoke was more Republican than Thomas Jefferson himself. Randolph certainly thought he was more Republican than James Madison, the organizer of the Republican Party and Jefferson's secretary of state. That judgment crystallized in his mind over the first great shock to the Jeffersonian Republican majority: the injection of the Yazoo issue into federal politics.[1]

The Yazoo Scandal centered on Georgia's attempt to sell its western lands, which at the beginning of the mess in 1795 extended north of Spanish Florida (which included the entire Gulf Coast east of the Mississippi River) all the way west to the Mississippi. By a law passed and signed into law on January 7, 1795, four land companies obtained thirty-five million acres of land—an area larger than twenty-six of today's states—for $500,000 in gold and silver coin. All but one member of the Georgia Legislature had been bribed.[2]

Then followed a raucous, apparently sometimes violent political campaign in Georgia to undo the outrageous sale of most Georgia public lands for a song. At the next legislative session the Georgia Legislature—purged of the corrupt members—passed a law undoing the land sale law and ordering all the Yazoo documents destroyed. "These and the original copy of the act," says the leading Yazoo Scandal historian, "were burned in the public square of Louisville, the site of the legislative session."[3]

Perhaps that would have been the story's end, but for the identities of the people who had bought the Yazoo lands—and of the people to whom they had sold them. Shareholders in the four land companies that were the first subsequent purchasers included Philadelphia Convention Framers of the U.S. Constitution Robert Morris (now a U.S. senator and reputedly the wealthiest man in America) and James Wilson (by this time a U.S. Supreme Court justice), another senator, two U.S. representatives, a state supreme court justice, a U.S. district court judge, and several other prominent men. They hailed from all over the country, though mainly from Georgia and Pennsylvania.

Rather than hold the land, the land companies quickly sold most of it "throughout the country and especially in the Boston area." Leaders of the New England Mississippi Land Company, chief northeastern purchaser, included future Jefferson administration postmaster general Gideon Granger, among several other prominent political folk. The day the Georgia Legislature passed the repeal act, the New England Mississippi Land Company bought eleven million acres for $1,138,000, which gave the original purchasers profit well in excess of 500 percent.[4]

Subsequent purchasers denied having had any knowledge of the fraud in the original land ordinance. Georgia authorities vehemently insisted that was impossible, as the scandal surrounding the original law had received widespread publicity and the repeal act had been immediately publicized throughout the country by the Georgia government.[5] The Georgia government also insisted that the question of who held title to particular lands in Georgia depended on decisions made in Georgia politics and, if it came to that, Georgia courts.

Because many of the subsequent purchasers of the titles to Yazoo lands resided in the northern states and many of them possessed substantial political influence or power, Congress intervened. On March 2, 1795, the Senate instructed the attorney general to report on the validity of Georgia's title to the Yazoo lands supposedly owned by purchasers under the repealed act. That same day the U.S. House of Representatives authorized President Washington to negotiate federal purchase of Georgia's western lands.[6]

On March 25, 1795, at the height of the contest between the Washington administration and its Republican critics, the leading Federalist, former treasury secretary Alexander Hamilton, offered his assessment of the legal aspect of the Yazoo Scandal. (Surely he did not produce this opinion unbidden.) Hamilton pointed to the portion of Article I, Section 10 of the Constitution that says, "No state shall . . . pass any . . . law impairing the obligation of contracts . . . ," the Contracts Clause. This provision of the Constitution was included to prevent states from adopting "stay laws" of the kind every state had adopted at one point or another during the Revolution—laws saying, for example, that for the next x months, no farm foreclosures would be allowed in the state of y. Creditors in this scenario composed a "minority" of the kind James Madison had been concerned to protect from local majorities in *Federalist* #10.[7]

Yet Hamilton's opinion regarding the Yazoo matter made a new departure: it is the first known argument that not only private contracts, but contracts to which states are parties come under the Contracts Clause.[8] In another remarkable move Hamilton assumed that the sales the Georgia Legislature had been bribed to make were valid contracts.[9] Hamilton had no trouble reaching the conclusion that the Contracts Clause barred an honest legislature's immediate revocation of a law made in such complete derogation of republicanism as the fraudulent Georgia Yazoo land sale law of 1795. He wrote that "it may be safely said to be a contravention of the first principles of natural justice and social policy, without any judicial decision of facts, by a positive act of the legislature, to revoke a grant of property regularly made for valuable consideration, under legislative authority, to the prejudice even of third persons . . . innocent of the alleged fraud or corruption. . . ."

Two years later President John Adams signed into law a bill authorizing the president to appoint three commissioners to negotiate a settlement of the issue with Georgia. In 1798 Georgia adopted a new state constitution contemplating sale of its western lands to the United States. "Yazoo men" favored such negotiation by the Federal Government, as they recognized the futility of trying to obtain payment for their claims from the reigning anti-Yazoo party in Georgia politics. Adams's commissioners reached no accommodation with Georgia, however.[10]

A House amendment of 1800 told the federal commissioners to "investigate" claims arising from the Georgia sale and to propose a compromise measure. A Senate committee headed by a pro-speculator senator, Georgia's James Gunn, would have amended that language to instruct the commissioners to "settle . . . any claims which are or shall be made by settlers, or any other persons whatsoever." This proposal split both houses of Congress on party lines, passing by 19–8 (15 Federalists and 2 Republicans among the 19, 7 Republicans and only 1 Federalist among the 8) in the Senate and meeting rejection by a vote of 46–34 (with 26 Federalists and 1 Republican among the "yea" voters whose party affiliations are known, while 29 Republicans and 10 Federalists (8 of the latter from the South) were among the "nay" voters whose party affiliation is known) in the House. Federalist Representative John Marshall of Richmond, Virginia, cast his vote in favor of the Gunn language. In light of his later role in this controversy, it is a shame that no record of his speech explaining his vote survives.

Thus Congress in 1800 merely directed the federal commissioners to investigate the Yazoo claims. There matters stood when Thomas Jefferson took the presidential oath of office on March 4, 1801.[11]

Jefferson, Madison, and Gallatin must have recognized that their political interests all lay on the side of the Yazoo land companies. Georgia, after all, had been firmly in the Republican camp, but the New England states went for John Adams in both 1796 and 1800. So Gideon Granger—not only a connected Connecticut politico but a substantial Yazoo land speculator who would be the speculators' chief Washington lobbyist—became postmaster general in 1801. Jefferson appointed his two chief lieutenants, Madison and Gallatin, along with Attorney General Levi Lincoln (another New Englander), as the Federal Government's commissioners to negotiate with Georgia regarding its western lands. The commissioners arrived at an agreement with Georgia in 1802 according to which the U.S. Government purchased Georgia's western lands for $1.25 million. The United States also agreed to buy out all Indians still holding land titles in Georgia and to use one-tenth of the land it had purchased from Georgia to compensate the Yazoo claimants.[12]

Secretary Gallatin's close friend Representative John Randolph of Roanoke, R-VA, would have none of it. Despite knowing that on the Federal Government's end the Yazoo compromise had been almost entirely Gallatin's doing, Randolph for three years put the blame squarely on Madison, with whom he would be a political enemy for the balance of his life.[13] His position cut straight to the heart of the matter. He insisted that even if Georgia had a right to sell lands still in Indians' possession (which he denied), "the contract being laid in corruption and fraud, was null and void, *ab initio*; that consequently the question of notice was not material to the question of title, in the hands of third persons [that is, subsequent purchasers], since the original grant being obtained by bribery and fraud, no right could rest under it; and that the grantees of 1795 could not sell a greater or better title than they themselves possessed."

Randolph laid out this position in a scalding January 29, 1805 speech in which he blasted not only the "Yazoo men" whom he had seen lobbying Congress on behalf of subsequent takers, notably the Yankees who had bought Georgia land titles from original holders under the corrupt law, but—by implication—the Jefferson administration itself.[14] For months prior to this speech, relations between Randolph and his cousin the president, once those of closest alliance, had been increasingly strained. Now Randolph leaned in the direction of breaking with the administration over what he saw as its iniquitous connection to "a few Yazoo men."

Randolph took particular aim at Gideon Granger in this address. Noting the postmaster general's role in the controversy over the Connecticut Reserve during the Adams administration, "by which the Nation were swindled out of three or four millions of acres of land, which, like other bad titles, had fallen into the hands of innocent purchasers," Randolph rebuked him as "seem[ing] to have an unfortunate knack at buying bad titles. His gigantic grasp," the congressman sneered, "embraces with one hand the shores of Lake Erie and stretches with the other to the bay of Mobile. Millions of acres are easily digested by such stomachs. Goaded by avarice, they buy only to sell, and sell only to buy. The retail trade of fraud and imposture yields too small and slow a profit to gratify their cupidity. They buy and sell corruption in the gross. . . ." Now the game was being played with "the patrimony of the people."

Granger served not only as an agent of the New England Mississippi Land Company, recall, but also as a member of a Republican president's Cabinet. In those pre–civil service days, when every postal position in the country was an appointive position and the Federal Government exercised remarkably few functions, Granger exercised a unique national power in Jefferson's behalf. "This same agent," Randolph fumed, "is at the head of an executive department of our Government, subordinate indeed in rank and dignity, and in the ability required for its superintendence, but inferior to none in the influence attached to it." After pointing out that a senator had retired from the Senate to accept a subordinate position in Granger's department, Randolph wailed, "Sir, when I see this tremendous patronage brought to bear upon us, I do confess that it strikes me with consternation and dismay. Is it come to this? Are Heads of Executive Departments of the Government to be brought into this House with all the influence and patronage attached to them, to extort from us now what was refused at the last session of Congress?"

At last Randolph reached his speech's climax: "Is the voice of patriotism lulled to rest? That we no longer hear the cry against an overbearing majority, determined to put down the Constitution, and deaf to every proposition of compromise? . . . [I]f the enmity of such men be formidable, their friendship is deadly distinction, their touch pollution. What is the spirit against which we now struggle? Which we have vainly endeavoured to stifle? A monster generated by fraud, nursed in corruption, that in grim silence awaits his prey. It is the spirit of *Federalism!*" (Imagine the hush, the shock, that must have swept the old House chamber.) "That spirit which considers the many, as made only for a few, which sees in government nothing but a job,[15] which is never so true to itself as when false to the nation." For Federalists to support the pending proposal, as they did "almost to a man," came as no surprise. Most of the measure's proponents had always been "the unblushing advocates of unblushing corruption." But the Republican members, "acting with your adversaries" on principles "the voice of the nation has put down, which I did hope were buried never to rise again, in this section of the Globe," "filled" Randolph "with apprehension and concern." If this bill passed, Randolph insisted no congressman should ever again speak ill of the Adams administration: "I should disdain," he thundered, "to prate upon the petty larcenies of our predecessors, after having given my sanction to this atrocious public robbery. Their petty delinquencies will vanish before it, as the stars of the firmament fade at the effulgent approach of a summer's Sun."

Randolph dominated discussion of the Yazoo bill from the day it was reported to the Committee of the Whole House, January 28, 1805. In the end he brought the House to refuse the Gallatin plan in March 1806. Only the Supreme Court's 1810 decision in *Fletcher v. Peck*, more or less along Alexander Hamilton's lines, prodded Congress to give the land companies a $4 million settlement.

21

_❁

In February 5, 1805, Congressman Randolph called the House's attention to what proved to be the final act in the Jeffersonians' war on the Federalist Judicial Branch: the impeachment of Justice Samuel Chase. Impeaching Chase would not be the first such blow Republicans struck, however. They had impeached in the House and convicted in the Senate a U.S. district judge, New Hampshire's John Pickering. Jefferson referred various Department of the Treasury documents about Pickering's conduct in a recent trial to the House on February 3, 1803. As a Pickering-sympathetic historian described it, "[I]n this particular trial Judge Pickering had been thoroughly intoxicated, and . . . in this condition he had threatened spectators, bullied witnesses, silenced the district attorney, rendered an arbitrary decision in favor of his Federalist friends, and refused to grant an appeal. Even if his verdict were just, his behavior had been scandalous."[1] Some sense of the problem presented by the Pickering impeachment can be gathered from the account left by a senator, William Plumer—also a Federalist from New Hampshire—of his own role in organizing the Senate trial.[2] As the senator told it, he objected to a motion that senators participating in Pickering's Senate trial swear to "do impartial justice, according to *Law*." If senators had to "take the Oath proposed," he explained, "it will then be incumbent on the House of Representatives to prove that John Pickering has committed an offence against *law*, & that perhaps they cannot prove—for I understand the Judge is deranged—*& I know of no law that makes derangement criminal*." No other senator voted to sustain his objection.

Representative Joseph Nicholson, R-MD, Randolph's closest House ally and another close Jefferson ally, served as the House impeachment manager (that is, chief prosecutor) in the Pickering trial. At the trial an attorney appeared with a letter from Judge Pickering's son insisting that the judge was insane, had been for three years, and could not attend the trial as a result.

(There is no record of anyone's having asked the son why the judge did not resign his office or some legal agent did not resign it on his behalf.) Counsel for Pickering's son said the judge "was then wholly incapable of appearing before the court [meaning the Senate], of making a defence, or of giving authority to any person to appear for him"—in other words, of enjoying the rights to due process of law and trial by jury.[3]

So what to do? The Judiciary Act of 1801 provided a mechanism for another federal judge to serve in place of a judge suffering disability, and in fact this provision had been used in regard to Pickering. Republicans had since triumphantly repealed that law in 1802 without making an exception for that salutary provision or substituting anything similar. Senator John Quincy Adams of Massachusetts summarized the situation the Senate faced for his colleagues' benefit thus: "You require a man to plead for another who is incapable of appointing a representative, & who in fact is no longer a man. Will you consider his non-Appearance as a default—as a confession of the truth of the articles of Impeachment?"[4] Senator William Cocke, R-TN, replied that as the Constitution said a judge was to receive compensation for his "services" and a madman could provide none, Judge Pickering ought to have no compensation. Cocke favored proceeding to a trial. On the following day, March 5th, Senator George Logan, R-PA, asserted that the law talk had misled the Senate. In an impeachment, it was not a court of law, but "a *court of enquiry only*," and if the Senate found Judge Pickering actually incapable of performing the functions of his office, it ought to remove him.[5]

Finally Senator Robert Wright, R-MD summarized the proceedings by saying that he had at first considered it a criminal trial, "the second day, mixt both criminal & civil," but at last thought it "altogether a civil process." That being so, "If judge Pickering was now here as mad as Bedlam it would make no difference—I would remove him—he holds his office during good behavior—Madness surely is not good behavior."[6] Apparently the Senate majority agreed with him, as it voted 19–7 the following day to convict Judge Pickering, thus removing him from office.[7] The Senate refused to print the trial record.[8] That was a Saturday. The following Monday, March 26, 1804, John Randolph's committee reported articles of impeachment against Justice Samuel Chase.[9]

Federalist propaganda of the day said Pickering's impeachment marked the beginning of a wholesale campaign of removal of Federalist judges, but the foremost historian of the era, though an ardent Federalist, concedes that "there is nothing to prove that this was then the intent of the majority."[10] Still, one can see why Randolph's success in persuading his House colleagues to

impeach a Supreme Court justice the day Pickering was convicted would
have led Federalists to think so even if they had had no other evidence.

Samuel Chase was the great exception to the general rule among President George Washington's appointees to high federal office: although a signer
of the Declaration of Independence, he had been an Antifederalist during
the campaign over ratification of the U.S. Constitution. He also stood out
among his Supreme Court brethren, as we saw in considering the justices'
response to repeal of the Judiciary Act of 1801, as inclined to be impolitic.
Had he won the day, his fellow justices would have joined him in flouting
the Judiciary Act of 1802 by refusing to ride circuit again.

Chase also came into conflict with one of his colleagues in the notable
case of *Calder v. Bull* (1798). The justice there said that not only the Constitution, but general political principles theoretically could form the basis of
his refusal to allow a statute to be enforced. In a day when the justices still issued seriatim opinions instead of generally joining in one general opinion of
the court, this pronouncement from Chase elicited a blistering rebuttal from
Justice James Iredell, once the foremost ratification campaign Federalist in
North Carolina. Natural law must not be the basis of judicial rulings, Iredell
said, because natural law was no law at all. No two men agreed about what
the particulars of natural law were. If general principles not reflected in the
Constitution were to be reflected in the law, Iredell concluded, they would
have to be put there by elected legislators as reflecting the will of voters.[11]

Republicans surely most have found this exchange notable. Their outrage was stoked by Chase's grand jury charges and his conduct of criminal
trials under the Sedition Act, the chief symbol in Republican martyrology
of Federalist tyranny. Chase was not alone among pre-Revolution of 1800
Supreme Court justices in delivering political harangues in the form of grand
jury charges.[12] His specimens of the genre, however, featured a particular
strain of bombast.

One grand jury charge by Chase in particular, delivered in Baltimore
on May 2, 1803, caught President Jefferson's eye. "The independence of the
national Judiciary is already shaken to its foundation, and the virtue of
the people alone can restore it," Chase fulminated to his captive audience.
Then he turned to the recent elimination of his state of Maryland's property requirement for voting, which he feared would "certainly and rapidly
destroy all protection to property; and all security to personal liberty," before ultimately "our republican constitution will sink into a mobocracy, the
worst of all possible governments." He concluded by blaming the promul-
gation of "modern doctrines by our late reformers, that all men in a state

of society are entitled to enjoy equal liberty and equal rights." Pressing his anti-Lockean doctrine home, the justice told the grand jurors that "there could be no rights of man in a state of nature previous to the institution of society; and that liberty, properly speaking, could not exist in a state of nature"—which, anyway, was "a creature of the imagination only, although great names" stood for "a contrary opinion."[13]

Which "great names" and what "late reformers"? It is not hard to guess.

Eleven days after Chase's charge, President Jefferson wrote to Representative Joseph H. Nicholson that "you must have heard of the extraordinary charge of Chace [sic] to the grand jury at Baltimore. ought this seditious & official attack on the principles of our constitution, and on the proceedings of a state, to go unpunished?[14] and to whom so pointedly as yourself"—a prominent attorney who happened to be a leading Republican member of the U.S. House of Representatives—"will the public look for the necessary measures?"

Jefferson closed his letter to Nicholson by saying that "it is better I should not interfere." Nicholson, wondering whether he should interfere, ran the question by his and Jefferson's trusted ally Speaker of the House Nathaniel Macon. As Nicholson stood a good chance of being tapped as Chase's Supreme Court replacement in case of a Senate conviction, Macon counseled him against taking the lead in this matter. Macon also hazarded the question whether "error of opinion" alone could form a valid basis for an impeachment.[15]

Thus the matter fell to John Randolph of Roanoke. When he brought a motion of impeachment before the House on the day of the Pickering conviction, Federalists demanded charges, and Republicans denied them. On what was seen as a party vote, Republicans, including both of Jefferson's sons-in-law, voted overwhelmingly to impeach Justice Samuel Chase. He remains the only Supreme Court justice ever impeached.

Perhaps John Randolph was a superb orator and a formidable party chieftain, but he was no attorney. He did have the nominal aid of four fellow House members, Nicholson among them, in drafting the articles of impeachment and presenting the case before the Senate. He seems barely, if at all, to have availed himself of it. Instead the House—and Washington generally—proceeded directly from several days' listening to Randolph lambaste various House members, high Executive Branch officials, and fellow citizens as "Yazoo men," which was temporarily laid aside for this purpose, to the Chase matter. As Washington was a mere village at the time and politics the leading (virtually only) industry, the Senate Republicans were not exactly thrilled with Randolph at the moment either.

In other words Randolph had prepared his ground poorly. He was not helped in this regard by the Republicans' Senate whip, William Branch Giles of Virginia. Giles was a wondrous phenomenon—an extremely successful politician during a lengthy career who was utterly impolitic. The day would come when Randolph and Giles were at loggerheads, but for now they cooperated in leading the attempt to bring down Chase. As Senator John Quincy Adams, F-MA, told it, he overheard a conversation during the pendency of the Chase trial in which Giles explained that "not only Mr. Chase, but all the other Judges of the Supreme Court, excepting the one last appointed [the sole Jefferson appointee to this point, South Carolinian William Johnson, on whom more hereafter] must be impeached and removed. He treated with the utmost contempt the idea of an *Independent* Judiciary—Said there was not a word about such an Independence in the Constitution, and [the justices'] pretensions to it were nothing more nor less than an attempt to establish an Aristocratic despotism in themselves."[16]

Startlingly, Giles went even further, saying (in Adams's words) that "a removal by impeachment was nothing more than a declaration by Congress to this effect—You hold dangerous opinions, and if you are suffered to carry them into effect you will work the destruction of the Nation—*We want your offices*; for the purpose of giving them to men who will fill them better." The senator to whom Adams heard Giles offer this assessment of the posture in which Congress found itself, Israel Smith, R-VT, insisted (again in Adams's words) that "*honest error of opinion*, could not as he conceived be a subject of impeachment." (Recall that this was Speaker Macon's assessment as well.) Adams, dour pessimist that he was, concluded his scene with a forecast of Giles and Randolph's success in removing not only Chase, but the other Federalist justices from office. Such was "the present state of things."

Senator William Plumer, F-NH, recorded a conversation with President Jefferson on Thursday, January 5, 1804, as the Chase matter was being discussed in the House.[17] After telling Jefferson that "I had no doubt the judge [Pickering, whom Plumer had known for decades] was *insane*, & ask[ing] him whether insanity was good cause for impeachment & removal from office, He replied, 'If the facts of his denying an appeal & of his intoxication, as stated in the impeachment are proven, that will be sufficient cause of removal without further inquiry.'" Plumer said Jefferson responded to his question about there being a House inquiry into impeaching Chase by saying, "*I have heard so.* . . . There are three cases to which I suppose the House would refer, Fries, Cooper & Callender—But the conduct of Judge Chase was, perhaps the most extrordinary in the trial of Callender—He there refused to admit Col Taylor, late one of your senators, as a witness for Callender, because he could not prove the whole of the case." Then Jefferson mused, "This business of removing Judges by impeachment is a *bungling way.*"

Two days later Plumer described the House of Representatives proceedings of January 5th and ruminated on how Federalists could have prevented them. Randolph had moved "[t]hat a Committee be appointed to enquire into the official conduct of Samuel Chase . . . & to report their opinion, whether the said Samuel Chase hath so acted in his judicial capacity, as to require the interposition of the constitutional power of this House." A Federalist motion for "time to investigate it—to examine precedents" was denied. Rather the House appointed a seven-man committee with Randolph as chairman.[18]

Sounding much like his colleague Adams, Plumer scribbled that Jefferson had long intended to destroy the Judicial Branch's independence. The Judiciary Act of 1802 Plumer took as a long stride toward that goal. "At the last session of Congress," Plumer recalled, "Mr. Jefferson told me that the Constitution ought to be so altered as that the President, on application of Congress should have authority to remove any Judge from office." Amending having been "found to be a tedious process—the good work of *reform* cannot be delayed—The president & his Cabinet agree that impeachment conviction & removal from office is necessary. . . ."

Representative John Wayles Eppes in the House echoed his father-in-law the president's statement about Chase's conduct of the Callender trial "to me [Plumer] in private conversation," "that it was [here he quotes Eppes] *indecent & tyrannical.*" Chase both excluded a witness's testimony on strange grounds and "[b]y a system of conduct *peculiar to himself* . . . deprived the prisoner of the aid of Council. . . ." Plumer concluded his journal entry for that day by lamenting that the Supreme Court had not declared the Judiciary Act of 1802 unconstitutional as it related to abolition of the circuit judgeships, saying that "then was the time for the Judges of the Supreme Court, to have taken their stand against the encroachments of Congress & of the Executive."

Presiding over the Chase impeachment in the Senate would be Vice President Aaron Burr. On July 12, 1804, he had shot and killed former treasury secretary Alexander Hamilton. Where formerly all who met him noted his fine manners, splendid person, and cultural polish, Plumer on December 5th said that since the Senate had convened for the fall session, he had "attentively watched the conduct of Aaron Burr. . . . He appears," Plumer thought, "to have lost those easy graceful manners that beguiled the hours away the last session—He is now uneasy, discontented, & hurried. So true it is, 'Great guilt never knew great joy at heart.'"[19] Though doubting Burr would ever "rise again" after his term ended on March 3rd, he thought the vice president "a very extraordinary man," one very adept at manipulating the public, "& considering how little restraint laws human or divine have on his mind, [it] is impossible to say what he will attempt—or what he may obtain."[20]

Plumer had struck the mark: the Chase trial would be only the penultimate act in the drama of Aaron Burr's political life.

Justice Chase prepared for his impeachment trial by recruiting some of the ablest lawyers in the country to defend him. By the time the proceedings concluded, they included Maryland's Luther Martin (who in time would do good service to the Federalist cause by showing up in his cups to make a pro forma argument for the contrary side in one landmark Marshall Court case, *Fletcher v. Peck*, and drastically mischaracterizing the Republican position in another, *McCulloch v. Maryland*); Charles Lee, the last Federalist U.S. attorney general; and three other prominent Federalist attorneys.[21]

For their part the House managers relied almost entirely on Randolph—who, again, was no lawyer at all. Thus the Virginia congressman boasted that the articles of impeachment (analogous in such cases to an indictment) had been "drawn by my own hand." It showed. Randolph's presentation of the House's case against Chase has been generally panned as well.

The House presented eight articles of impeachment:[22]

1. That in the Fries trial Chase had presented a written opinion of law tending to bias the jury against Fries before his counsel was heard, that he had refused to allow Fries's counsel to cite certain American and English precedents, and that he had prevented Fries's counsel from addressing the law, thus attempting to deny Fries his right to have the jury determine on the law, after which Fries was condemned to death.
2. That Chase had denied a Callender juror's request to be excused from the jury because he was biased against Callender.
3. That Chase had refused to let John Taylor of Caroline testify for the Callender defense on the ground that Taylor's testimony would not go to every element of the charge.
4. That Chase had in various ways interfered with defense coun-

sel's presentation of Callender's defense, as by frequently inter-
rupting them, using rude expressions toward them, refusing to
grant them a continuance to procure witnesses, requiring them
to submit to Chase in writing proposed questions for Taylor, etc.

5. "That he awarded a capias agt. the sd Callender and not a summons, as by the law of Virginia he ought to have done." (The
   distinction here was between a writ requiring that he be taken
   into custody and transported and a mere order for Callender
   to appear.)

6. "That he adjudged Callender to be tried at the same term in
   which he was indicted contrary to the laws of Virginia."

7. That he refused to discharge a grand jury in Delaware until he
   had made the U.S. attorney seize the files of a particular "seditious printer" in New Castle.

8. That, in the Baltimore grand jury charge of which Jefferson had
   complained to Nicholson in the first place, Chase "delivered an
   intemperate & inflammatory political harangue, to excite the
   fears & resentment of the jury & the people of Maryland agt.
   their State government & constitution," besides which he in the
   same address "endeavoured to excite the odium of said jury &
   of the people of Maryland agt the government of the United
   States, by delivering opinions, highly indecent, extrajudicial and
   tending to prostitute the high judicial character with which he
   was invested to the low purpose of an electioneering partisan."

When a few days later Justice Chase first appeared before the Senate,
Plumer recorded the discussion between him and the vice president about
Chase's need for time to prepare his defense, then concluded, "It is indeed a
humiliating scene to behold an *aged man, a Judge* of the Supreme Court of
the United States . . . bro't to trial as a criminal—Arraigned before a Court,
the president of whom is a fugitive from Justice—& stands indicted as a
MURDERER!"

22

❖ ⚙ ❖

Justice Chase and his counsel presented to the Senate on May 4, 1805, detailed answers to the articles of impeachment against him. The reporter noted that "[t]he Chamber of the Senate, which is very extensive, was soon filled with spectators, a large portion of whom consisted of ladies, who continued, with little intermission, to attend during the whole course of the trial."[1] Senator Plumer observed that "[t]he Reading took up two hours & a half—It is a very able answer indeed."[2] The learned defendant and his eminent lawyers put on quite a display of legal learning. It takes up fifty pages of small type in the *Annals of Congress*, the Jeffersonian era analogue of today's *Congressional Record*. The House managers' one-sentence reply said simply that the House remained convinced that Chase had "commit[ted] the numerous acts of persecution, oppression, and injustice, of which he stands accused," and repeated the House's insistence that the Senate try him on its articles of impeachment.[3]

In laying out the grounds of the various articles of impeachment and presenting two witnesses on Saturday, February 9, 1805, Randolph got hung up both on the facts and on the law. In regard to the facts, Fries's attorneys both testified that they had withdrawn as counsel in his case because they thought that President Adams would more likely pardon a convict who had been reduced to defending himself than one who had enjoyed assistance of counsel. In regard to the law, he unnecessarily made a comparison of murder to high treason, which requires only overt acts—not any particular state of mind. As Plumer noted, "This speech is the most feeble—the most incorrect that I ever heard him make." Besides that, he fell into insulting John Adams (whose son was a senator, thus a judge and juror, in this trial) and likely did not thrill Vice President Burr, who, again, stood indicted for murder.[4]

As the trial progressed, Randolph proved to have "a tedious circuitous method of asking questions—they are often imperative."[5] Although generally pleased with all of the defense witnesses and displeased with Randolph and Burr's performances, Senator Plumer did have harsh criticism for one leading Federalist participant: Chief Justice John Marshall. Plumer "was much better pleased with the manner in which his brother testified than with him. The Chief Justice really discovered [that is, displayed] too much caution— too much fear—too much cunning—He ought to have been more bold—frank & explicit than he was. There was in his manner an evident disposition to accommodate the Managers. That dignified frankness which his high office required did not appear. A cunning man ought never to discover [that is, display] the arts of the *trimmer* in his testimony."[6]

Plumer presumably did not know that Marshall was, like President Jefferson, a Randolph on his mother's side. He almost certainly did not know that besides being relatives, Marshall and Randolph were close friends. In the course of Randolph's questioning, Marshall testified to several facts that helped the House's case. For example, the chief justice said that he "never knew it requested [by a judge] that a question should be reduced to writing in the first instance [that is, before counsel have posed the question to the witness] in the whole course of my practice,"[7] which strongly supported the fourth article of impeachment. Later in his testimony, when Randolph asked whether Marshall had "ever . . . know[n] a witness deemed inadmissible . . . because he could not narrate all the circumstances of the crime charged in an indictment . . . and could only prove a part of a particular charge, and not the whole of it," Marshall replied, "I never did hear that objection made by the court except in this particular case."[8] This certainly supported the third article of impeachment, the one about exclusion of John Taylor of Caroline's testimony. Marshall also said that he thought he had heard Chase during the Callender trial use the terms "young men, or young gentlemen," toward defense counsel—though he could not be certain, because he had "heard it so frequently spoken of since the trial."[9] If Marshall "trimmed," then Plumer ought to have been pleased with it, as the hedging tended in Justice Chase's favor.

Senator John Quincy Adams wrote prior to the trial that the charges against Chase pointed to no "corruption, or turpitude." Perhaps with that in mind, Chase's counsel, Joseph Hopkinson, told the Senate that it must, in deciding the case, remember that "another dread tribunal," "posterity," would weigh the senators' votes. In general history has been kind to the men who acquitted the justice, but a powerful argument to the contrary was made by historian Raoul Berger.

Chase, as Berger quotes the justice's fellow circuit judge Richard Peters, "was forever getting into some intemperate and unnecessary squabble," so that Peters "never sat with him without pain."[10] Yes, other Federalist judges had during the Adams administration issued splenetically partisan grand jury charges, but that was no excuse.[11] So too the judgment of history has generally been against those, like Chase, who advocated passage of the Sedition Act, which certainly makes it difficult to excuse his railroading (if the anachronism may be allowed) of Sedition Act defendants such as James Callender and Thomas Cooper.[12] As Berger describes Chase's conduct in regard to Callender, he "selected the victim, announced his determination to punish him for his 'atrocious and profligate' libel, procured his presentment by the grand jury, refused to excuse jurors who confessed their bias against the accused, at every step identified himself with the prosecution, and took every means to disconcert, discredit, and disable counsel for the defense."[13] If the Republican scuttlebutt was true, Berger omitted that Chase carefully stacked the Callender jury with Federalists.[14] One might argue that Chase's conduct in the Fries matter was even worse.

Yet the Senate acquitted the judge, who sat on the United States' highest court until his death in 1811. "The Senate's votes," as one historian put it, "ranged from unanimous acquittal on one count to 19-to-15 for conviction on the Maryland address."[15] Dumas Malone pointed out that although Federalists of the day considered President Jefferson the éminence grise of the Chase impeachment, with Hamilton's *New-York Evening Post* among other Federalist newspapers saying so,[16] "there seems to be no evidence that the President himself sought to bring any influence to bear on his wavering partisans."[17] Perhaps the reason for this was to be found in the administration's new attitude toward Randolph, whom it may have been maneuvering to hang out to dry, as he repeatedly took positions hostile to it in the early days of the Eighth Congress's second session.[18] On the other hand the reason may have been that, as Plumer jotted down in the trial's aftermath, Jefferson seemed to have "a great and primary object . . . never to pursue a measure if it becomes unpopular." Plumer gave Jefferson's hands-off posture toward the Chase impeachment as an example.[19]

As John Quincy Adams described the affair's climax,

At half-past twelve o'clock [on March 1, 1805], the Court met. . . . Mr. Burr ordered the civil officers in the upper galleries to turn their faces toward the spectators, and to seize and commit to prison the first person who should make the smallest noise or disturbance. He then directed the Secretary to read the first article of impeachment, which being done, he called upon each

Senator by name, and put the question as agreed upon. The same course was pursued with all the succeeding articles. . . . After a short pause, the Vice-President said . . . "there not being a constitutional majority who answer 'Guilty' to any one charge, it becomes my duty to declare that Samuel Chase is acquitted upon all the articles of impeachment. . . ." The Court then immediately adjourned; and thus terminated this great and important trial.[20]

John Randolph returned to the House straightway and "pronounced . . . a violent phillippic against Judge Chase & against the Senate—& he concluded with offering a resolution proposing an Amendment to the Constitution of the United States" requiring the president to remove any federal judge at the request of both houses of Congress. "Mr Randoph & Nicholson were very warm & passionate in the debate. . . ."[21]

Adams in his diary described a conversation later that day with a Republican senator, William Cocke of Tennessee. Cocke

. . . spoke with much severity of Mr. John Randolph and his conduct upon this impeachment, and various other subjects; charged him with excessive vanity, ambition, insolence, and even dishonesty, which he exemplified by the misrecital of the Virginia law referred to in the fifth article of the impeachment, which he said must have been intentional. He told me that he had always been very sorry that this impeachment was brought forward, and though, when compelled to vote, his judgment had been as unfavorable to Mr. Chase as that of any member of the Court, he was heartily glad of the acquittal, which it appeared to him would have a tendency to mitigate the irritation of party spirit. He said that Mr. Randolph had boasted with great exultation that this was *his* impeachment—that every article was drawn by *his* hand, and that *he* was to have the whole merit of it; though, if the facts were so, it was not a very glorious feat for a young man to plume himself upon; for the undertaking to ruin the reputation and fortune of an old public servant, who had long possessed the confidence of his country, might be excusable, but was no subject to boast of.

Senator Adams also found Secretary Madison in a conversation soon after the event "much diverted [that is, amused] at the petulance of the managers on their disappointment."[22] In light of Randolph's course thereafter, Madison perhaps had occasion to regret his initial reaction to the Chase outcome. Anyway he and the other Cabinet members always maintained a studied silence in public when it came to the Chase impeachment. As Madison explained it, "they did not I believe intermeddle during the trial with a subject exclusively belonging to another Dept., and now that the Constl. decision has taken place, it would be evidently improper for themselves to pronounce for public use their opinion of the issue. . . ."[23]

Two days later, looking back on the congressional session just ended, Adams described the Chase impeachment as its "most remarkable transaction." He said it was "a party prosecution" and reveled in his appraisal that it had "issued in the unexpected and total disappointment of those by whom it was brought forward."[24] Even if it had been true that the entire Republican Party acted in this matter on the basis of the same motives as did Senator Giles (which, as we have seen, President Jefferson certainly did not), it would be impossible to accept Adams's conclusion that "a sense of justice" accounted for Chase's acquittal. The hanging judge of Messrs. Fries, Callender, and Cooper deserved to be removed from office.

In *Federalist* #79 and #81 Alexander Hamilton had explained that while judges would, under the U.S. Constitution, have no set terms of office, impeachment would be a remedy for gross judicial misbehavior. Ratifiers in several states took the same position. The Chase acquittal forever wrote that option out of American politics. As Jefferson described the post-Chase impeachment situation, "Impeachment is a farce which will not be tried again."[25] He later said that "experience has . . . shewn that the impeachment [our constitution] has provided is not even a scare-crow," so that the supposed checks and balances among the three branches of the Federal Government were reduced to a system in which "to one of them alone the right to prescribe rules for the government of the others" had been given.[26] In the twenty years remaining to the Virginia Dynasty, this problem would take on pressing urgency.

No one knew it at the time, but the Senate vote in the Chase impeachment was the high-water mark of the Jefferson presidency. "It was here," as Henry Adams said, "that the Jeffersonian republicans fought their last aggressive battle, and, wavering under the shock of defeat, broke into factions which slowly abandoned the field and forgot their discipline." What their defeat meant was that not the people through their constitution and representatives would have their way, but for three decades to come, "[t]he people were at the mercy of their creatures," as "Chief Justice John Marshall and his associates would disregard their will, and would impose upon them his own."[27]

The day after the Senate concluded the impeachment trial, Vice President Burr resigned his office. He first cleared the Senate chamber's galleries, then delivered a farewell address explaining his behavior as presiding officer. Although he had intended to stay on until this congressional session's conclusion the following day, an incipient illness seemed to require his resignation.[28] "For each individual senator he entertained & felt a spirit of friendship, & he trusted that the regret on parting was mutual." "Several," according to Senator Plumer, "shed tears very plentifully."[29] Senators may have thought that American public affairs had seen the last of Aaron Burr. If so, they were mistaken.

23

✢ ❁ ✢

Soon after the conclusion of the Eighth Congress, and thus of his first term as president, Jefferson received welcome news from the Mediterranean Sea. He had in the first days of his presidency dispatched a substantial flotilla thither with the purpose of protecting American shipping. The mission had at last been a complete success.

Since his time as minister to France (1784–89), the president had been concerned to bring an end to Barbary States' practice of essentially requiring ransom in exchange for allowing minor European powers' ships to ply the Mediterranean trade safely. In the absence of regular payments, they seized those small powers' ships and enslaved the sailors.[1] As Jefferson and John Adams reported from England to Confederation Secretary for Foreign Affairs John Jay:

> We took the liberty to make some inquiries concerning the Grounds of their pretentions to make war upon Nations who had done them no Injury, and observed that we considered all mankind as our friends who had done us no wrong, nor had given us any provocation. The Ambassador [of Tripoli to France] answered us that it was founded on the Laws of their Prophet, that it was written in their Koran, that all nations who should not have acknowledged their authority were sinners, that it was their right and duty to make war upon them wherever they could be found, and to make slaves of all they could take as Prisoners, and that every Musselman [that is, Muslim] who should be slain in battle was sure to go to Paradise. That it was a law that the first who boarded an Enemy's Vessell should have one slave, more than his share with the rest, which operated as an incentive to the most desperate Valour and Enterprise. . . .[2]

The system logically consequent to this belief had undergirded the North African states, by Jefferson's time only nominally provinces of the Ottoman Empire, for three hundred years.[3]

Ultimately, Minister Jefferson found himself at odds with his friend the minister to the Court of St. James's, John Adams. If Adams had his way, Congress would fork over reasonable annual payments to the four North African Muslim powers. As far as Jefferson was concerned, this humiliation had to stop. He therefore tried to organize a league of minor naval powers to enforce their freedom of the seas, casting his eye toward Stockholm, Lisbon, Copenhagen, Berlin, and some Italian city-states. In the end, with the notable exception of a treaty with Morocco, his effort came to naught.[4]

But now he was president, and as historian Norman K. Risjord put it, while Federalist administrations had been nationalist in the sense of working to augment the domestic power of the Federal Government, Republicans would be nationalist when it came to foreign policy.[5] This distinction was manifest in Republicans' policies of extending the country's boundaries and standing up to foreign aggression.

So, early in his first year as president, Jefferson wrote Madison, "I am an enemy to all these *douceurs*, tributes & humiliations. . . . I know that nothing will stop the eternal increase of demand from those pirates but the presence of an armed force, and it will be more economical & more honorable to use the same means at once for suppressing their insolences."[6] As early as November 1801, Jefferson had publicized the feats of Navy Lieutenant Andrew Sterrett. Two days after Secretary Gallatin arrived in Washington on May 13th to assume his new post at the Treasury Department, Jefferson held a Cabinet meeting in which all agreed to send three frigates to the Mediterranean "to superintend the safety of our commerce, and to exercise our seamen in nautical duties." The Federalists' new Peace Establishment Act authorized the president to take these steps.[7] The U.S. Navy and Marine Corps were about to write a glorious chapter of their history on "the shores of Tripoli." The Algerine and Tripolitan pirate states would receive their comeuppance at American hands.

In its early stages the Jeffersonian naval policy in the Mediterranean was a bit of a debacle. When, nearly two years after the 1801 Cabinet vote to dispatch substantial naval forces, the president polled his Cabinet on Gallatin's proposal to pay Tripoli tribute rather than persevere in the naval policy—the treasury secretary insisted it was a "mere matter of calculation whether the purchase of peace is not cheaper than the expense of a war"—all voted "aye." Nevertheless Jefferson determined that yes, he would be willing to bribe Tripoli's ruler, but absent a reasonable accommodation, war there would continue to be.[8]

By the middle of 1803, the American commodore Edward Preble had called what would in time be an irresolvable problem to Washington's attention. The British Royal Navy considered itself at liberty to interrogate American sailors, even those who were U.S. Navy personnel, about their citizenship and to impress them—that is, force them into the Royal Navy—on the spot. Not only did British officers facilitate desertion from American ships, but one described the British policy as being to "afford protection to every man who has an opportunity to claim it, and will say he is an Englishman."[9] Though he resented this treatment, Preble realized that the picayune American navy could not dispute the matter with the British, and so he transferred his base of operations from Gibraltar to Syracuse—which was not a British possession.

The next significant naval news to reach Washington concerned loss of the frigate U.S.S. *Philadelphia*, commanded by Captain William Bainbridge. On October 31, 1803, en route to participate in a blockade of Tripoli, it ran aground off that Barbary capital and, though seriously damaged by Bainbridge's crew in anticipation of its capture, ended up in the possession of the Tripolitan pasha. Bainbridge and his men would remain captive for nineteen months. Their capture set the scene for the most daring naval exploit of the age.[10]

Commodore Preble recognized the severely awkward position in which the *Philadelphia*'s misfortune left him. What was intended as an American show of force to open up commercial possibilities for the New World republic had gone from failure to fiasco. Though his letters to Bainbridge via the Danish consul at Tripoli expressed sympathy for the captain, Preble told Secretary of the Navy Smith, "Would to God that the Officers and crew of the *Philadelphia* had one and all determined to prefer death to slavery; it is possible such a determination might have saved them from either!"[11]

He wrote to Secretary Smith in December that the *Philadelphia* would be destroyed—a particularly difficult job for his force of a frigate, a brig, and three schooners, "comprising in all," as historian Ian W. Toll put it, "about 100 guns and seven hundred men." Although "it will undoubtedly cost us many lives, . . . it must be done." Bainbridge wrote that a force of several small boats with combustibles should be sent into Tripoli Harbor under cover of darkness, and that once the force reached its position the task "could be easily effected." Lieutenant Stephen Decatur, commander of one of Preble's three schooners, volunteered to lead the mission.[12]

Preble would have preferred to recoup his lost ship, but he adjudged that task impossible. Therefore he would send Decatur and his group upon a captured Tripoline ketch to sail into the harbor and destroy *Philadelphia*. The ketch he renamed *Intrepid*.[13]

Preble's orders for Decatur said, in part, "Board the Frigate *Philadelphia*, burn her, and make your retreat good." His men were to start fires in various rooms of the ship and, "After the Ship is well on fire, point two of the 18-pounders shotted down the Main Hatch and blow her bottom out. The destruction of the *Philadelphia* is an object of great importance. I rely with confidence on your Intrepidity & Enterprize to effect it."[14]

The eighty-man crew's performance in the Bay of Tripoli was superb. They sailed in the night directly into the city's harbor, the huge majority of the men crammed belowdecks. When at last they had sailed to within vocal range, their Maltese pilot shouted for permission to compensate for loss of the ketch's anchors by tying to the frigate. Yes, came the reply. When the *Intrepid* had approached so close that men aboard *Philadelphia* could see *Intrepid*'s decks, they noticed an anchor there and saw some of the Americans lying prone on the deck. An Arab voice shouted "Americanos!"

The Maltese pilot urged Decatur to order boarding, but the steely American barked, "No order to be obeyed but that of the commanding officer." Finally within range, Decatur yelled, "Board!" The combat lasted ten minutes. The attackers relied on swords, pikes, and knives alone, lest the noise of gunfire draw Tripoline reinforcements. About a score of the enemy dared to stand their ground. Only one survived the fight, and his prognosis was grim. American casualties were one man wounded.

Then the Americans went from room to room, dispersing the combustibles and setting them afire. The conflagration spread so quickly that they had to scramble down to the *Intrepid*, Decatur of course last among them. It took a while for *Intrepid* to work her way clear of *Philadelphia*, a time during which the locals had at last been roused to cannon fire. Characteristically, their cannonade missed the mark. "Once out of range of the enemy guns," concludes the best account, "they laughed, joked, sang, and paused to watch the spectacle of the still-blazing *Philadelphia*."

At last the flame found the *Philadelphia*'s rigging, the tar of which conducted the fire quickly up the mastheads. The masts fell into the bay at 11:00 PM. Seven hours later the inferno could still be seen forty miles out to sea.[15] When word of the Americans' feat reached British ears, Admiral Horatio, Lord Nelson, the greatest of admirals, pronounced what Decatur had done "the most bold and daring act of the age."[16] In six months Decatur would be a captain, having been given a two-rank promotion. He also had become a national celebrity.[17]

Back home in Washington, President Jefferson learned of the *Philadelphia*'s capture a month after Decatur's mission.[18] The U.S. Navy's gallant accomplishment of destroying an American frigate drove home an ironic lesson: that ships of the line like the *Philadelphia* were not cost-efficient. Why not rely on small gunboats deployed up and down the American coast instead of spending serious money on a small number of big seagoing ships? Jefferson and Gallatin eventually yielded to this siren's song, which "cost the navy millions in appropriations."[19] Commodore Preble would return to Washington to be fêted by the highest officials of the government,[20] but his service would for years be deprived of the funding it required.

In the meantime Jefferson requested and Congress provided authority for "equipping, officering, manning, and employing such of the armed vessels of the United States, as may be deemed requisite" for reprisal. He ordered four more frigates to sea.[21] The First Barbary War had not ended yet. That would require a second spectacular American military feat. This involved a bit of American meddling in Tripolitan politics.

The current pasha, America's enemy Yusuf Karamanli, had come to power a decade earlier by fomenting a coup against his brother Hamet while the latter was away from the city. America could take sides with Hamet Karamanli, who would march upon Tripoli from the landward side at the head of a force of Arabs and Mamelukes. Hamet vowed that in case of success, he would free all of his state's Christian slaves, allow the Americans to garrison one of the chief batteries guarding his capital's harbor, and free the United States of any obligations of tribute or ransom forevermore. Yusuf would suffer the fate customary in such cases: hanging.[22]

So a local force participated in bringing the First Barbary War to its successful conclusion. Once an Egyptian force commanded by American diplomat William Eaton made its way from Alexandria, Egypt, to Tripolitan Derna (on "the shores of Tripoli") en route to Benghazi, this threat, the presence of Hamet Karmanli's force on the Gulf of Sidra, and news that five American frigates would make their appearance at the beginning of the next campaign season drove Yusuf to negotiate. He conceded that he knew the Americans would take the city if it came to that. Reckoning that once installed, Hamet was unlikely to hold power in Tripoli, America paid no tribute and no peace bribe, but it did pay a $60,000 ransom for the number of Americans held captive by Tripoli in excess of the Tripolitans held by the United States. America had her Mediterranean trade once again, though the president's dreams of a neutral naval coalition to suppress Barbary piracy forever never reached fruition. The United States would have to confront the matter on its own again during the Madison administration.[23]

Dealing with the Barbary states was one thing. Relations with the major European powers proved to be quite another. President Jefferson and Secretary of State Madison expected, as their second term in tandem began, for foreign affairs to play a significant part in their next four years' stewardship. Having won glory via the Louisiana Purchase, they anticipated a new triumph in connection with West Florida.

That was the name of the Spanish province stretching from the Perdido River to the Mississippi River—essentially, the coastal portions of today's states of Alabama and Mississippi, plus the part of Louisiana east of the Mississippi. Jefferson and Madison calculated that their success in buying the enormous Louisiana Territory from France, most powerful nation in the world, augured well for their chances of prying relatively small West Florida from Spain. If France had Europe's ablest leader, best farmland, and largest population, after all, Spain had few natural resources, a sub-mediocre king, and few people. Because Spain bordered France and had for generations played second fiddle in a family entente with the senior branch of the Bourbon dynasty ruling in Paris, and because Napoleon's recent abandonment of St. Domingue (now Haiti) meant he would not recoup the revenue stream thus lost to France, it seemed entirely likely that Emperor Napoleon would facilitate American success in prying West Florida from Spain.

As we have seen, the American negotiators Monroe and Livingston asked the French foreign minister, Talleyrand, whether he agreed that the Louisiana Territory purchased by them from France included West Florida, and he gave an obscure non-answer. Napoleon was not one to respect a country shorn, as Jeffersonian America by design was, of whatever paltry military assets it had possessed. Besides that, the events of the first year of Jefferson's second term, 1805, hardened Napoleon's disposition to side with France's traditional ally Spain in whatever diplomatic difficulty it might encounter with the United States.

Although he had impressed all of Europe with his Italian victories of 1796, 1797, and 1800, it was in 1805 that Napoleon established himself as one of the great captains of history. His smashing Austerlitz Campaign, beginning with a superlatively brilliant encirclement of Austria's fifty-thousand-man army at Ulm and capped by his destruction of a combined Russian-Austrian army at Austerlitz, since immortalized in Count Leo Tolstoy's *War and Peace*, put him on the road to complete domination of Europe.

Further complicating the diplomatic picture from America's point of view was an event toward the end of the year off Cape Trafalgar in southwestern Spain. There a smaller British fleet under the command of Vice Admiral Horatio, Lord Nelson destroyed the combined fleets of France, Spain, and The Netherlands, capturing or destroying eighteen ships in history's most decisive naval battle.[24] This outcome made Britannia ruler of the waves for the nonce—if she could man her warships.

From the great powers' point of view, America did not much matter. France's master had his eye on completing his subjugation of Europe (which he did with a crushing defeat of Prussia's armies in 1806 and a win over a combined Russian-Austrian army, thus bringing about a Russian peace, in 1807) as a necessary prelude to reducing Britain, while the British determined to use their naval supremacy to defend their home islands and undermine Napoleon's Continental System. American attempts to bring one or the other of the main combatants to diverge from the path it was on proved futile. Predictably. The end of Jefferson's administration did not mark any great turning point in this course of affairs. Rather, Secretary Madison's succession to the presidency came at a point of ignominious American acquiescence.

America had profited handsomely from its neutrality through Jefferson's first term. It traded with both of the leading belligerents under cover of the slogan "Free ships make free goods," which stood for the idea that while a belligerent's ship could rightly be interdicted by its enemy, a neutral party's shipping was to be left alone. Not only could the Americans trade their wares and crops with the British home islands and Napoleonic Europe, but American ships traded freely with the belligerents' New World colonies as well. In the middle of 1805, that course of business came to a crashing halt.

The *Essex* decision of July 23, 1805, resuscitated strict enforcement of the so-called Rule of 1756.[25] Under that rule the British Admiralty declared impermissible in wartime any trade that would have been prohibited in peacetime. In other words, for example, if France had not allowed neutral (American) ships to trade between French Caribbean colonies and the French homeland prior to resumption of hostilities in 1803, Britain would not allow such trade in wartime.

Although this general policy had been on the books prior to the *Essex* decision, Britain had allowed Americans to skirt it via the fiction of the broken voyage. Thus, while an American ship could not take, say, sugar directly from Guadeloupe to Bordeaux in wartime without running afoul of British policy because it had not been allowed by France's mercantile laws to do so in peacetime, if the American ship stopped at, say, Philadelphia en route, unloaded the sugar at the American port, and then reloaded it for the Atlantic voyage, this was treated not as a voyage from the French island colony to the French port, but as transportation of American goods from Philadelphia to France. The British navy treated it as two voyages rather than one. What the *Essex* holding did was put an end to this fiction. From now on the Royal Navy would treat the broken voyage as the ruse it was, which meant that an American merchant ship bound from Guadeloupe to Bordeaux and its cargo were apt to be seized and sold by His Majesty's Government regardless of whether the ship had stopped in an American port on its way.

The *Essex* decision reflected more than a single British judge's calculation about American ships and the French trans-Atlantic trade, however. In a pamphlet entitled *War in Disguise; or the Frauds of the Neutral Flags*, Englishman James Stephen laid out an understanding of the Jefferson administration's trade policy notably similar to American Federalists'. Since they carried to and from the French Empire goods that the Royal Navy would otherwise interdict, the Americans and other neutrals were benefiting from aiding Napoleon in what amounted to a war over Britain's survival. The British had no reason to tolerate this behavior.

The *Essex* decision and the pamphlet virtually coincided with the epic victory off Cape Trafalgar and with stepped-up British impressment of sailors from American merchant ships. This British practice—stopping American ships at sea, questioning the crew members, and forcing those identified as British into the Royal Navy on the spot—stoked considerable animosity in the United States. As the president described the situation, "What an awful spectacle does the world exhibit at this instance. One nation bestriding the continent of Europe like a Colossus, and another roaming unbridled on the ocean."[26] Secretary Madison had told Minister Merry even before the *Essex* decision that retraction of the British impressment policy was an essential precondition of an improvement in British-American relations. Impressments, Madison confided to Monroe, were an "evil" to which Americans felt "growing sensibility." Although the secretary instructed Monroe to ensure that Whitehall did not take American complaints about impressment to be "marks of illiberal or hostile sentiments towards Great Britain," he wanted his representative to convey the depth of American concern.[27] The imperative to respond to this situation would dominate the attention of the Cabinet and Congress to a growing degree through the balance of Jefferson's presidency—and into that of his successor.

24

Meantime American diplomatic efforts in Europe reached a kind of climax. James Monroe proceeded from Paris to Madrid with the idea of wringing from the feeble Spanish government acquiescence in the American claim that the Louisiana Territory included West Florida. Foreign Minister Talleyrand allowed Monroe to be on his way on the three-week journey across the Pyrenees, then sent him a communication making clear that no, Napoleon's government did not agree with the American position: West Florida remained Spanish. It did not form part of the Louisiana Purchase.

France's reasons for taking this position are easy to divine. For one thing, so long as the Floridas remained in Spain's hands, France might again have use of them. For another, difficulty in the relationship between America and Madrid would likely be to France's advantage, as Talleyrand could serve as a kind of broker between them. This calculation assumed, reasonably, that Jefferson could not conceivably be brought to a rapprochement with the British. Finally, France almost certainly guessed that the Americans could be brought to provide yet more gold for the emperor's coffers if that were what it took to add the Floridas to their territory. The secretary of state captured the administration's position clearly when he confided to the French minister to Washington that "when the pear is ripe it will fall of its own accord."[1] Talleyrand at last flatly told the new American minister in Paris, John Armstrong, on December 21, 1804, that the Americans' claim to the Floridas had absolutely no basis.[2]

That John Armstrong Jr., formerly a senator from New York and by this point a relative of the Livingstons by marriage, should have become American minister to France is one of the truly jaw-dropping developments in American political history. This was the same John Armstrong who as a colonel in the Continental Army had played the leading role in the Newburgh Conspiracy, that nearly successful attempt by disgruntled officers to organize a march in force from their upstate New York encampment to the seat of Congress, where they were to extract back pay from that body by what can only charitably be called a mass act of false arrest. A harsher appraisal is that they intended treason.

Hearing of these plans and informed in advance of those officers' meeting to finalize their plans, General George Washington famously—and of course without being invited—strode into the meeting, marched straight to the lectern, fumbled around in his breast pocket, pulled out the spectacles virtually no one had known he wore, and as he put them on said, "I have not only grown gray but almost blind in the service of my country."[3] Only by the margin of the Great Man's intervention did the United States at that precarious moment dodge the fate of so many other republics in the form of what amounted to a military coup, or at least military coercion of the Confederation Congress.

John Quincy Adams judged Armstrong's appointment to be a disreputable act. As he described the Senate confirmation of Armstrong in a March 17, 1806 diary entry,

> There was nothing said this day in his favour. The Speakers against him were Mr. Smith of Maryland, Mr. Pickering, Mr. Wright and myself; who closed the debate. The votes were 15 to 15—And the Vice-President decided in favour of the appointment—Mr. Adair of Kentucky left his seat to avoid voting—He was averse to the appointment, but had not the courage to vote against it; and by his weakness, this shameful transaction was accomplished. Of the 15 members who voted for this nomination two thirds at least answered with faltering voices—I consider it as one of the most disgraceful acts of Mr. Jefferson's Administration. . . . [4]

Armstrong would hold this important post until 1810.[5]

Although possible political motivations for this appointment seem obvious, that a president so sensitive to the possibility of military usurpation in a republic should have made this choice is strikingly, even shockingly, out of character. Armstrong's generally sympathetic biographer explains it by observing that Armstrong not only belonged to the Livingston family, but wrote skillfully and knew world affairs. Too, like Jefferson and Madison, Armstrong possessed the means to support himself in what in that day was a costly position.[6]

In the end Armstrong's tenure as minister to France had two notable effects. First, he appears at the emperor's invitation in Jacques-Louis David's momentous masterwork *Le Sacre de Napoléon*.[7] More important, Armstrong's ministerial service, when joined to his stint as a senator and his Livingston connection, qualified him for a significant position in the Cabinet, which he would hold to great—and woeful—effect in the Madison administration.

With the failure of his Spanish mission, Monroe became available for a new post in Great Britain, where he joined William Pinkney in endeavoring to negotiate some modus vivendi with the mother country. The British government's new posture toward the United States promised to make that difficult. Madison, following lengthy discussions with Jefferson and his fellow Cabinet secretaries, repeatedly sent lengthy letters instructing the two of them to ensure an end to impressment—the British practice of on-the-spot conscription of sailors on American merchant vessels whom British naval officers identified as British. In case it could be helpful, Madison relayed to Monroe that "Incidents are daily occurring which otherwise may overcome the calculating policy of the Present Executive, & provoke the public temper into an irresistible impetus on the public Councils."[8]

Soon enough Madison informed Monroe that "In the American seas . . . the scene . . . I fear is growing worse and worse." Congress perhaps would legislate an exclusion of any ship believed to have participated in impressment from American ports, which it only delayed doing in hopes of a negotiated end to such behavior.[9]

Madison first hoped that an end to impressment might be achieved through informal agreement.[10] After relaying the insistence on an end to impressments, Madison at last sent Monroe formal instructions and a draft agreement.[11] The draft contemplated resolution of several outstanding issues between the two countries, notably that neither should force a citizen/subject of the other residing within its territory into its navy; that their warships should try to remain out of cannon range of each other; that "contraband of war" subject to seizure should include only certain enumerated items obviously useful by military forces; that a "blockaded port" would be only a port actually blockaded by the other party's navy; that neither party should give sanctuary to deserters from the other's armed forces; and a few more suchlike provisions.

Most notably, each party was to be prohibited from carrying away "any seamen or soldiers" from the other's territory, and no impressment of any sailor not then "in the Military service of an enemy" of the impressing party was to be allowed. Madison listed this as his first and optimum suggested provision of any agreement. An alternative, "Second and Ultimatum Article I," allowed one of the parties to take men off the other's ships "in cases where they may be liable to be so taken according to the law of nations; which liability however, shall not be construed to extend in any case to seamen, or seafaring persons being actually part of the crew of the vessel in which they may be. . . ."

Monroe approached the new British premier, Lord Hawkesbury, in his first meeting with him after he succeeded to the premiership about a potential treaty addressing matters arising as a result of the present war and those opened up by the expiration of Jay's Treaty. Hawkesbury suggested the Jay Treaty form the basis of new negotiations, and he appeared startled by Monroe's blunt rejection of the idea. Monroe told him that people in Britain knew the present American administration disliked some features of Jay's handiwork, and the lord said perhaps they should put the matter off, to which Monroe agreed.[12]

Hawkesbury agreed to Monroe's suggestion that some elements of the trade relationship could not be regularized while the war continued, pointing to the slave rising of St. Domingue as illustrative. Monroe suggested America and Britain enter into an interim agreement on the matter of trade, but he rejected the lord's idea of simply extending Jay's Treaty while hostilities continued.

Nothing came of it. A change of ministry in the U.K. if anything brought in a new government less congenial to the United States. Thus in the winter of 1805 Madison sent Monroe his conclusion that "[t]he procrastinations of the British Ministry in meeting you effectively, on the subjects proposed in your project for a Convention betray a repugnance to some of them, and a spirit of evasion, inauspicious to a satisfactory result." Merry had by now used "language on several late occasions [which] strongly opposed the expectation that Great Britain will ever relinquish her practice of taking her own subjects out of neutral vessels."[13] The Republican high command would remain similarly insistent. Perhaps war would be the outcome.

The president's general position in regard to the European broils can be found in a letter he sent to Minister Monroe on January 8, 1804.[14] The British diplomat Edward Thornton, echoing long-standing Federalist appraisals, had said that America favored France over Britain, but Jefferson denied it. "[W]e are anxious to see England maintain her standing," the president insisted, "only wishing she would use her power on the ocean with justice. if she had done this heretofore, other nations would not have stood by & looked on with unconcern on a conflict which endangers her existence."

Contrary to what Englishmen thought, Jefferson confided that "we are not indifferent to it's issue, nor should we be so on a conflict on which the existence of France should be in danger. we consider each as a necessary instrument to hold in check the disposition of the other to tyrannize over other nations." Contrary to the Hamiltonian bent of most accounts of Jefferson's foreign policy career, he endeavored during his presidency to adhere to a policy that served the interests not of France, but of the United States. Along these lines he later in that same year reached out to Emperor Alexander I of Russia with a request that he use his influence to help establish international agreement on the trading rights of neutrals when the great ongoing war at last reached its end.[15]

Jefferson's Fifth Annual Message, which he dated December 3, 1805, came to Congress in the interim between Napoleon's smashing victory at Austerlitz the day before and arrival of that news in Washington. The president described the international scene as one in which the major powers "are in commotion and arming against each other" and warned Congress that "the countenance of some of them toward our peaceable country threatens that even that may not be unaffected by what is passing on the general theater."[16]

After a passage describing the proliferation of privateers lurking off the American coast and occasionally committing acts of aggression against American ships, Jefferson described the failed attempts to negotiate compensation to the United States from Spain for the injuries done "during the former war." He made clear that the Mississippi and Orleans Territories had been sites of Spanish incursion and injury and called on Congress to grant him discretion to reorganize the militia so that only the youngest cohort would be exposed to being called up in case of full-blown hostilities. When it came to America's harbors, he thought numerous additional gunboats and several well-placed cannon could put the country in readiness. Finally in this vein he noted that the Executive had purchased materials for building ships of the line as Congress had directed and suggested a ban on "exportation of arms and ammunition."

The president next vaunted the U.S. military's feats against Tripoli. After mentioning his "high satisfaction," he asked that Congress expand the peacetime numbers of navy captains and lieutenants so that he could give the younger men "a just reward" for their outstanding performance. He told the legislators that relations with Tunis seemed apt to result in a mutually satisfactory agreement, so that most of America's naval force could be recalled from the Mediterranean. He would leave a smaller one until all was well.

Indian relations that year cast a promising light across the Ohio country and much of the South. In regard to the Ohio, in particular, Jefferson rejoiced that the United States now possessed virtually all of both banks from its source to its mouth. The Indians continued to progress in adoption of farmers' ways, thus in needing less of the huge expanses of land formerly used as hunting ground. "They are becoming sensible," Jefferson wrote, "that the earth yields subsistence with less labor and more certainty than the forest, and find it in their interest, from time to time, to dispose of parts of their surplus and waste lands for the means of improving those they occupy. . . ."

Alluding to the Voyage of Discovery, then under way, the president informed Congress that various Indian peoples from the Louisiana Territory "come charged with the assurances of their satisfaction with the new relations in which they are placed with us, of their disposition to cultivate our peace and friendship, and their desire to enter into commercial intercourse with us." He would provide Congress a full account as soon as he could. He closed his message with a glowing account of progress in retiring the national debt, a hint that some of the surplus should be spent on armaments and ships, and a vow that in this, his second term, he would work diligently "to secure the liberty, property, and personal safety of our fellow citizens, and to consolidate the republican forms and principles of our government."

Though Jefferson presented matters in his characteristically optimistic way, all was not well among Republicans. John Randolph, in particular, found new reasons for objecting to the administration's policies. Appointed chairman of the committee to which the House referred Jefferson's message, Randolph went to see Jefferson. In the congressman's account, Jefferson told Randolph that he wanted $2 million to buy Florida. (In his memorandum of the preceding Cabinet discussion of Spanish affairs, Jefferson presents this initiative as his own idea.)[17] Randolph recalled having exploded to Jefferson that he would not agree to any such appropriation, as it was totally at odds with the confrontational tone of the annual message, and he continued that, anyway, "after the total failure of every attempt at negotiation, such a step would disgrace us forever."[18]

Randolph soon made his determination to oppose this gambit clear to his congressional colleagues. As one of the most devout anti-Jeffersonians in the country, Senator Timothy Pickering of Massachusetts, explained to his fellow High Federalist Fisher Ames in a mid-March letter, "On Saturday, while the doors were closed, Mr. Randolph said that about the middle of December, he called on Mr. Madison, who told him that the French government had forbidden our negotiating directly with Spain: that we must negotiate through the medium of the French government which wanted money; and that we must give it.—Randolph added—'I had not much confidence in him (Madison) before, and from that time I have had none;' at that moment, with an indignant motion, throwing his hat across the hall!—You will connect this anecdote with the secret appropriation of 2 millions."[19]

President Jefferson did not scruple concerning the ultimate payee in this scenario. Whether Spain's despot or France's ultimately received the money did not seem to him to make any notable difference. The territorial acquisition he had had in mind since his administration's earliest days had come into sight, and he wanted to strike.[20]

Randolph had had enough. He would not be party to paying France for Spanish property against the wishes of Spain, not even if Jefferson held that the only alternative way to obtain the desired patch of Deep South land was war. Randolph saw Madison as the puppeteer, Jefferson as the puppet. Here was the creeping Federalism that had to a growing degree replaced the Republicanism of 1798 in the country's policy, Randolph thought, and he would have none of it.[21]

Another way of reading it, Henry Adams's way, is that here at last Randolph had the handle he could use to prevent James Madison's election to the presidency. Adams's reading is that Madison was right in estimating that America faced a choice between giving France $2 or $3 million for the Floridas, on the one hand, and war with France and Spain, on the other. So, Chairman Randolph delayed taking action, and when his friend Gallatin came to him after several days with a document titled "Provision for the purchase of Florida," Randolph turned his back on him, insisting that if the president wanted such a measure, he should not leave it to Congress to adopt the unmanly posture before the public of trying to buy what the president's message said should be obtained using other means. His committee adopted instructions to its chairman to ask the secretary of war what kind of appropriation he would need to reinforce America's defenses on the Florida border.[22]

Matters came to a head when Congressman Randolph met with his cousin the president at the White House. Pressed for a resolution—a House capitulation—Randolph thundered "that he too had a character to support and principles to maintain." At last the matter had been decided: this meant war between John Randolph of Roanoke and Thomas Jefferson.

What a sorry scene the congressional conclusion to this development made. In a closed House session, Randolph remained the preeminent figure, and although the debate over the $2 million appropriation ended with a vote in the administration's favor, several members openly regretted having to support the president's measure. Randolph's friend Nicholson, though voting for the measure, said he hoped the negotiation would fail. Randolph

carried a majority of Jefferson's and his home-state delegation on a preliminary vote (12–10), and a measure favored by Jefferson passed chiefly on the
strength of Northern support for the first time. The Senate soon endorsed
the measure, and Madison wrote Armstrong on March 13, 1806, authorizing
him to spend $5 million on the Floridas and much of Texas, with $2 million the limit on what could be paid up front.[23] That this attempt to purchase territory from Spain at this point came to naught made the rift in the
party all the worse.

25

❖

Lacking military assets to impose its will and ignored in its appeals to what it took to be common morality, both in regard to impressment and when it came to the carrying trade, the Jefferson administration could have been at a standstill. For James Madison, the mastermind of domestic political architecture, however, his friend the president's English Problem appeared as another puzzle for a statesman of the kind that had absorbed him during the critical period between the Treaty of Paris in 1783 and George Washington's inauguration in 1789. And so he did what he had done before: he produced a highly learned written argument.

Titled *An Examination of the British Doctrine, Which Subjects to Capture a Legal Trade, Not Open in Time of Peace*, this 1806 pamphlet laid out the Jefferson administration's answer to the *Essex* decision.[1] Madison attempted in it to prove that "As a nation not engaged in the war remains in the same relations of amity and of commercial pursuits, with each of the belligerent nations, as existed prior to the war, . . . the war could not affect the intercourse between the neutral and either of the belligerent nations; and that the neutral nation might treat and trade with either, or both the belligerent nations, with the same freedom as if no war had arisen between them." (That last, ironically, looks a lot like the *Essex* holding.)

The leading study of Madison's pamphlet calls it "the fullest and most authoritative statement of the Jefferson administration's position on neutral rights." It is "an exhaustive illustration of the illegality of the Rule of 1756," and it "had little impact on the course of events" in Madison's day, which perhaps accounts for the fact that it "generally has been ignored or dismissed by scholars." Those who ignored Madison's production erred, however, because the influence of Madison's book ran through a highly influential 1836 treatise, and "through it the subsequent development of international legal thought."[2]

Madison faced a daunting task. The balance-of-power scenario on which Emer de Vattel's *The Law of Nations* rested had collapsed before the genius of Emperor Napoleon and Lord Nelson; natural-rights arguments drew little attention (given law's evident impossibility in a world of contending states), and a scheme depending on the preponderant power's will left maritime matters up to Britain. Somehow Madison wanted to carve out a role for the weak United States and show that Britain should concede that piddling power's rights.[3]

"With the exception of Great Britain alone, all the powers of Europe, materially interested in the maritime law of nations, have given a recent and repeated sanction to the right of neutrals to trade freely with every part of the countries at war," he wrote. This immediately raised the problem of seeming Francophile—a risk Madison did not want to run. He avoided it by pointing to agreements freely entered into among various states; those, he said, made up "a law of themselves." It was only through their consent that states helped form this body of law. "The spirit of treaties," he wrote, "is, with few, if any exceptions, at all times more just, more rational, and more benevolent, than the spirit of the law derived from practice only."

Madison's complaint was with what he described as the *Essex* court's claim that, "It is right in Great Britain to capture and condemn a neutral trade with her enemies, disallowed by her enemies in time of peace, for the sole reason that her force is predominant at sea. And it is wrong in her enemies to capture and condemn a neutral trade with British colonies, because their maritime force is inferior to hers. The question no longer is, whether the trade be right or wrong in itself, but on which side the superiority of force lies?" Here, Madison said, stood a legal edifice based on nothing more than force, open to shifting considerably as a result of "the comparative state of naval armaments, which itself may change at every moment, may depend on the event of a battle, on the skill of an admiral, on the tack of the wind; one of those thousand casualties which verify the admonition, that the battle is not always given to the strong, any more than the race to the swift." Well might an American secretary of state have called this consideration to British cognizance.[4]

Yet whatever arguments Madison mustered—and at more than 250 pages, his pamphlet at least can be judged lengthy—His Majesty's Government might well have had the attitude captured in Stalin's famous quip, "How many divisions does the pope have?" Britain and France fought for life and death. Justice for America, if then being denied, could wait. (A British official could also wonder, of course, just how unjust it would be to deny Americans the profit, the benefit, of trading with Britain's enemies in wartime as those enemies had not allowed in peacetime. Even at this temporal and geographic remove, then, the British position seems reasonable.)

On January 29, 1806, the House passed Gregg's Resolution, which called for forgoing commercial intercourse with Great Britain. It was with this as backdrop that Monroe returned to England at the middle of the year. He was soon joined by William Pinkney, and the two were charged with negotiating a new treaty with the British. Although a mutually beneficial trade agreement would be the Americans' chief object, their superior Madison underscored the imperative to come to an agreement concerning impressment. For President Jefferson this provision would be a sine qua non of an overarching agreement.

The timing could hardly have been worse. Monroe arrived on the same day as the *Essex* decision was announced, July 23, 1805.[5] The end of the "broken voyage" ruse posed a serious problem for American commerce and diplomacy, as all involved recognized. Monroe first spoke with the new British prime minister, Lord Harrowby, on August 3rd.[6] The Brit, apparently feeling Monroe out, asked what the status of Jay's Treaty should be understood to be. Monroe, as a Republican, of course had no affection for that agreement, which had been the subject of intense partisan rancor in the United States during the Washington administration (as Harrowby no doubt knew).

Harrowby suggested that the two parties stipulate Jay's Treaty would remain in effect until two years after the end of the current war. As Monroe reported to Madison,

I told his Lordship that I had no power to agree to such a proposal; that the President animated by a sincere desire to cherish and perpetuate the friendly relations subsisting between the two countries, had been disposed to postpone the regulation of their general commercial system, 'till the period should arrive when each party enjoying the blessings of peace, might find itself at liberty to pay the subject the attention it merited: that he wished those regulations to be founded in the permanent interests, justly and liberally viewed, of both countries; that he sought for the present only to remove certain topics which produced irritation in the intercourse, such as the impressment of seamen, and in our commerce with other powers parties to the present war, according to a project which I had had the honor to present his predecessor some months since, with which I presumed his Lordship was acquainted.

Monroe said Harrowby wanted to avoid that topic, though he gave the impression of finding the American position acceptable. Harrowby did, however, suggest that the ministry could adopt Jay's Treaty as the rule of its interaction with America, which forced Monroe to respond, speaking in as elliptical a way as in the passage above, that both sides surely had reason to consider that treaty inadequate, that the U.S.A. understood its own interests better now than it had then, and that (as Monroe had told the recently departed British foreign minister) America would want to negotiate a totally new trade agreement with Great Britain. Monroe tried to draw Harrowby's attention to a draft treaty he had tendered, but the lord said it was a complicated matter, he had other urgent business, and so on.

"I told him," Monroe reported, "that the most urgent part of the Subject was that which respected our seamen." Noting that the problem was reciprocal, Monroe conceded, "His government claimed that deserters from their ships in America were not restored to them; ours that our seamen were impressed in their ports (those of G.B.) and on the high seas, in our vessels and sometimes in our bays and rivers; that such injuries ought to be put an end to and that we were willing to adopt a fair and efficacious remedy for the purpose."

Harrowby answered with what would remain the British position for years to come. It showed a shrewd understanding of American public opinion. "He said he was afraid, however well disposed our Government might be to give the aid of the civil authority to restore deserters to their vessels in the U. States, that little advantage could be derived from such a stipulation. The bias and spirit of the people would be against it, with us, as it was here, under favor of which deserters would always find means to elude the most active search of the most vigilant peace officers." If the Briton knew anything much at all about the history of the United States during the previous forty years, Monroe's protestation that an agreement along the lines of what he had suggested would indeed be reciprocally enforceable, because "our people were very obedient to the law in all cases," must have made him smile.

If Monroe's account of this discussion approximated what had really happened, then Harrowby had not understood the chief point on which the American minister had insisted. Harrowby wrote an account of it to Anthony Merry the next day, and although he gave a bit more detail than Monroe had about the exchange concerning the idea of continuing to treat Jay's Treaty as in effect, he did not mention impressment at all.[7] As Jefferson and Madison insisted this matter be resolved, the lord's apparent determination to forge ahead without addressing it would mean the two countries could not agree.

Monroe gave British prime minister Lord Hawkesbury, who did not reply in the small time left to him in his high office, a full plan for resolving the impressment issue on April 7, 1804, and then relayed the same material to his successor, Lord Harrowby, on May 27th or 28th.[8]

By the dawn of the following year, Madison could relay to Monroe that "The perseverance of the British Government in the principle which licenses the depredations on our commerce in Colonial productions, with the losses already sustained and still apprehended by our merchants, has produced a very general indignation throughout this Country, and makes it necessary that you should renew and extend your remonstrances on the subject." To help Monroe present his case more forcefully, he enclosed a copy of "*An Examination of the British Doctrine . . . ,*" which seems to have had no more effect coming from Monroe than it had coming from Madison himself. He told Monroe he would soon relay various memorials from American merchants, which somehow he imagined would "assist [Monroe's] endeavours to make on the British Government the impression which the occasion call[ed] for."[9] Whether Monroe too expected American pamphlets and petitions to sway H.M. Government, we do not know. Monroe did, however, believe that Jefferson's annual message for 1805 had impressed the British ruling class generally with the idea that insofar as friction had arisen between the two countries, the culpability lay on Britain's end.[10]

On February 6, 1806, Monroe wrote to Madison a bit perturbed.[11] He had heard that he was to be joined by a minister plenipotentiary, and he said that such appointments were universally read as negative judgments on diplomats already in place. He therefore explained to Madison why, in light of the European scene in 1805, he had judged it essential to stay in place. He closed with a request for "the necessary powers" and "explicit" instructions regarding the position he was to take regarding the principle that free ships made free goods and with a warning that although the new foreign minister had always been friendly toward the United States, his Cabinet consisted of jarring elements.

Soon thereafter Monroe had occasion to take a remarkable, though minor, step in connection with his friend John Randolph of Roanoke. Randolph's deaf-mute nephew John St. George Randolph, son of John's late brother, had traveled to England for special educational attention unavailable in the United States.[12] He arrived in the company of a trusted Randolph slave, Essex White. A month after first encountering him, Minister Monroe wrote White a passport identifying him as "a domestic of the Honorable John Randolph" and "a citizen of the United States." As late as 1859, this April 15, 1806 passport was published in a New Hampshire newspaper as evidence that a slave had been treated as a citizen by a high government official.[13]

Soon after that, coincidentally, President Jefferson wrote a rather cryptic letter to Monroe advising him not to take sides in any ongoing political developments in America. The president had to remain neutral due to his station, he said, but this was in conformity with his "friendships." What he meant was that since breaking with the administration, Randolph had begun to knock Madison and vaunt Monroe. "[S]ome of your new friends," Jefferson informed him, "are attacking your old ones out of friendship to you, but in a way to render you great injury." Guessing—though of course not knowing—that Monroe would find this intimation rather opaque, the president guardedly added that, "in a few weeks I shall be able to write less enigmatically. in the mean time," he concluded, "be cautious what & to whom you write, that you may not be allied to operations of which you are uninformed."[14]

As if that were not enough, he then followed up with this bombshell: "Mr. Nicholson's resolutions" (that is, Randolph's ally Representative Joseph Nicholson's resolutions calling for a ban on importation of select British goods—to go into effect in November)[15] "will be passed this week by a majority of 100. . . . when past I shall join Mr Pinkney of Maryland as your associate for settling our differences with Gr. Br."

Perhaps having read Monroe's perturbed February 6th letter to Madison, Jefferson—who would have preferred to leave Monroe in place by himself, but who felt pressured by Congress to dispatch a second[16]—told Monroe that "it is desirable for your own as well as the public interest that you should join in the settlement of this business, and I am perfectly satisfied that if this can be done so as to be here before the next meeting of Congress it will be greatly for your benefit." He closed with his "affectionate salutations & assurances of sincere & unalterable friendship."

John Taylor of Caroline and Randolph both soon wrote apprising Monroe of political schisms and backstage (if anything Randolph did could remain backstage) machinations.[17] Taylor confided, "A third party, between the federalists and republicans, recruited from both is appearing in force," and noted that in some states, divisions concerned disputants' attitudes toward Monroe. (For example, he noted that "The Clinton party of New York are said to be in your favor—the Livingston your foe.") Randolph was rather more unreserved: "There is no longer a doubt, but that the principles of our administration have been materially changed. . . . Suffice it to say, that every thing is made a business of bargain & traffick, the ultimate object of which is to raise Mr M—n to the presidency. To this the old republican party will never consent—nor can N.Y. be brought into the measure. Between them & the supporters of Mr M. there is an open rupture. Need I tell you that they (the old republicans) are united in your support?" Monroe's behavior would vindicate the belief "that the government can be conducted on open, upright principles, without intrigue or any species of disingenuous artifice." Randolph urged Monroe to return to America forthwith so that "a character which has proved invulnerable to every open attack, should triumph over insidious enmity."

Meanwhile, after what Monroe described individually as several promising meetings marked by an evident resolution on the British side to bring the ongoing legal dispute between the United States and United Kingdom to a close, Foreign Secretary Charles James Fox, long understood to be sympathetic to the United States, died. There followed several fruitless meetings in which, according to their British opposite numbers Lords Holland and Auckland, Monroe and Pinkney presented the American position on impressment quite vehemently—even going so far as to say that unless it were resolved, "all the other objects of Negotiation were of so secondary a nature that it would not be material to proceed with them,"[18] before the discussion of that subject at last broke down. Although the two lords agreed to a provision that impressment from ships at sea would be discontinued, the Admiralty and the king's advocate insisted on striking that provision, and so it was removed.[19] Holland and Auckland ultimately told the Americans that although they maintained "the same friendly and conciliatory disposition, which has marked every step of the negotiation," they could not surrender their country's historic claim to a right of impressment, particularly in the midst of so threatening a war. Despite this, they concluded, they wished to proceed with negotiations on the other matters under discussion.[20]

Monroe and Pinkney wrote Madison a lengthy description of the situation. It ended with their resolution to conclude a treaty on the other matters of discussion, namely trade with the colonies of the hostile parties, limitation on the types of scenarios in which a blockade could be said to exist, and the extent of American territorial waters. American trade with India could be put on a good footing too, they thought, as could trade with British colonies to the United States' north, though the West Indies trade would likely not be made so readily available as the Americans might hope.[21] The Monroe-Pinkney Treaty was agreed on December 31, 1806, and transmitted by the American negotiators to Secretary Madison on January 3, 1807. Though the treaty included no agreement that Britain would halt its practice of impressment, Monroe and Pinkney said, the British had pledged "it's practice would

nevertheless be essentially if not completely abandoned." In subsequent conversations the British negotiators had insisted "that in their judgement [the
Americans] were made as secure against the exercise of their pretension by
the policy, which their gov¹ had adopted in regard to that very delicate and
important question, as we could have been made by treaty." However, they
continued, congressional action "to check desertions from the British service" would be essential to British perseverance in this change of policy. The
treaty also included no provision concerning compensation for shipowners
injured by British actions contrary to the law of nations.[22]

Just as this lengthy negotiation came to an end, Emperor Napoleon issued his Berlin Decree, according to the terms of which the French ruler
purported to lay Great Britain and Ireland under blockade. As Nelson's
victory at Trafalgar had essentially swept the seas of French naval vessels,
this blockade could be only nominal. Its purpose was to exclude all trade
between Britain and Ireland, on one hand, and Europe, on the other. The
British government responded by declaring that trade between any French
or allied port and another French or allied port would be disallowed by the
Royal Navy, and that any ship found engaging in such trade would be considered lawful prize for the Royal Navy and British privateers.[23] In short the
Great Powers' policies would curtail American trade significantly.

26

✦ ✿ ✦

The first significant communication to Monroe describing President Jefferson's impression of the Monroe-Pinkney Treaty came from the top administration ally in the Senate, William Branch Giles of Virginia. He wrote on March 4th that although "it would give me great pleasure, to have it in my power to assure you that [the contents] were acceptable to the government and people of this country . . . this is not the fact.—The obvious tendency of the explanatory note, and the silence respecting seamen, have excited universal disappointment & astonishment." Although "High and unabated confidence in our commissioners" precluded arriving at a final appraisal "until their own inducements for consenting to such a measure sh[ould] be known," the initial response had been quite negative.[1]

When at last Monroe heard directly from Jefferson, he cannot have been pleased. Jefferson first summarized the most significant terms, then said, "[B]ut depend upon it, my dear Sir, that it will be considered as a hard treaty when it is known. the British Commis[rs] appear to have screwed every article as far as it would bear, to have taken every thing, & yielded nothing." Here Jefferson seems to have been fixated on his firm requirement that the impressment issue be resolved. He certainly did not grant credit to his negotiators for what one scholar called "terms . . . so favorable in other respects, even more than Jay's Treaty a dozen years earlier, that Monroe and Pinkney believed that the document would be acceptable to the president. The re-export trade was confirmed. . . . The British accepted a narrow definition of contraband and agreed to give appropriate notice of blockades. And as a further mark of accommodation they agreed to indemnify any merchant whose ship was detained in violation of the treaty. The price for these concessions," he concludes, "was minimal."[2] Nevertheless Jefferson had determined not to agree to any treaty that did not resolve the impressment issue, so he closed by saying that now at last Monroe could have his wish of coming home, and that when he did Jefferson had in mind for him to become governor at New Orleans, "the 2^d office in the US. in importance." He closed with the formulae that denoted close friendship in those days, but Monroe must surely have felt the sting of having his intense, long-running labors' fruits judged unworthy by his leader.[3]

Madison first saw the treaty when it was presented to him by the new British minister in D.C., thirty-year-old David Erskine, son of the lord chancellor.[4] Merry's recall would have been a positive enough sign of Fox's intention to improve relations with the Americans even if he had not chosen so august a father's son, and one with an American wife to boot, to succeed him. The course of negotiations culminating in the treaty, then, must have come as a bit of a shock. On February 1, 1807, Madison heard that Monroe and Pinkney had agreed to leave the impressment issue aside. He summoned Erskine and told him that a resolution of the impressment issue was absolutely imperative. Never could the United States agree that a few seamen's loss to the Royal Navy weighed in the balance with thousands of sailors' loss to American merchant shipping. Rather, he said, the cost to America "infinitely outweighed the inconveniences that might be incurred by the British" if the matter were resolved. Besides, in that event, the U.S. Government would strain to turn over British deserters. The president thought the American nation would prefer no treaty to such a treaty, and the Cabinet agreed with him unanimously.[5]

Jefferson gave the Senate only the outline of the treaty. The Federalist *United States Gazette* guessed that his reason for not submitting the treaty for Senate ratification was to avoid elevating Monroe above Madison in popular esteem.[6] Madison floated the idea in Cabinet deliberations of offering the British exclusion of Britons from American ships' crews in exchange for an end to impressment, but when Secretary Gallatin reported back "chiefly on the federal hospital tax deducted from seamen's wages," the Cabinet learned that of sixty-seven thousand sailors in the American merchant marine, nine thousand were British—including half of those in the foreign trade. In other words excluding them would be unfeasible. The Anglophone powers faced an irresoluble obstacle to improved relations—one that easily could lead to war.[7]

Of particular interest to Monroe must have been an insightful account of the political scene he received soon after from John Randolph's chief House ally, Joseph Nicholson.[8] The Marylander noted that Britain considered her existence dependent on the right of impressment, and so a resolution of the issue satisfactory to Jefferson probably could not be reached. Whatever the president decided would receive popular approval, however, and in fact "[t]he President's Popularity is unbounded" and "his Will is that of the Nation. His Approbation seems to be the Criterion by which the

Correctness of all public Events is tested." He could submit Jay's Treaty to the Senate and, although it would be opposed by all of the Federalists, it would be ratified easily, "although heretofore so odious to some of us." "Such," Nicholson confided, "is our present Infatuation."

There were, however, exceptions to the general rule, Nicholson believed. "There is a portion who yet retain the Feelings of 1798, and who denominate the old Republican party. These men are personally attached to the President, and condemn his measures when they think him wrong. They neither wish for, nor expect anything from his extensive Patronage. Their public service is intended for the public Good, and has no View to private Emolument or personal Ambition. But it is said, they have not his confidence, and I lament it."

While Monroe had been engaged in his unavailing Spanish, French, and British diplomacy, Jefferson had the pleasure of welcoming Meriwether Lewis, William Clark, and the Corps of Discovery back from its transcontinental journey. A lifelong ethnohistorian (trailblazing archaeologist and linguist, besides biologist) and sub rosa participant in the European countries' scramble for new territory, Jefferson from an early point in his life wanted more information about the Indians and the landscape of the great American West.[9]

As early as January 1803, then, he and his private secretary Lewis—a native of Jefferson's home county, Piedmont Virginia Albemarle—discussed preparations for the eventual trip.[10] Lewis, whom Jefferson had by now come to know well, seemed an obvious choice because, as the president put it, he was "brave, prudent, habituated to the woods, & familiar with Indian manners & character." Though "not regularly educated," Jefferson wrote, he "possesses a great mass of accurate observation on all the subjects of nature which present themselves here, & will therefore readily select those only in his new route which shall be new. He has qualified himself for those observations of longitude & latitude necessary to fix the points of the line he will go over."[11] On the eighteenth of that month, the president made a confidential request for funding "for the purpose of extending the external commerce of the US" to Congress. He invoked the Commerce Clause as constitutional justification.[12] To lead the soldiers along with Lewis, he chose Revolutionary War hero General George Rogers Clark's younger brother William. Between them Lewis and Clark possessed an excellent combination of the skills that would be needed for success on a journey through territory much of which had never been visited by European man before.

So much before the Purchase. Afterward President Jefferson envisioned its achievement of several different goals. Perhaps most important were to "establish federal sovereignty with the Indians and survey the land for federal control." Instead of insisting that it exhaust those tasks, however, Jefferson looked for this to be the first of several expeditions—ultimately there were five—that would map out a route to the Pacific and establish good relations with the local Indians.[13]

Before their departure Lewis and Clark were supplied a number of friendship medals—medallions with a profile image of President Jefferson on one side and clasped hands on the other. They were to explain to the leaders of each Indian band they encountered that not the king of Britain, France, or Spain, but now the president of the United States was their chief political, military, and if need be diplomatic reliance, and then they were to award its chief a friendship medal. Jefferson also intended for the Corps of Discovery to return with a lexicon from each Indian people it had encountered. He gave the commanders a list of English words to use.

We should not think that attempts at information-gathering and friendly, trade-based diplomacy marked Jefferson's exclusive approach to American Indian peoples. Far from it. Rather, in connection with tribes nearer by, he hoped to persuade the Indians to accept that they were going to be swamped under whites' superior numbers, and so they would "in time either incorporate with us as citizens of the United States, or remove beyond the Mississippi." They ought to accept that farming in the Americans' way yielded more comfort, and so their extensive remaining lands could be sold to the newcomers. In other words, like most Jeffersonian conundrums, that of how both whites and Indians could benefit from the situation they faced seemed to hold out the prospect of a resolution advantageous to all involved. Ohio statehood in 1803 seemed to vindicate this faith.[14]

In our day of easy cross-country travel and readily available geographic information, the task these thirty-one soldiers undertook is hard to comprehend. Two aspects of their charge can help us to understand. First, among the specimens the president instructed them to bring back was a mastodon, which the Indians said roamed wild in northwestern North America. Second, they were to find the Northwest Passage—the river route from Saint Louis to the Pacific Ocean. They of course failed to capture a mastodon, and when they reached Lemhi Pass on today's Montana-Idaho border and looked westward, they saw only many miles of additional mountains. As historian Stephen Ambrose put it, "It was Lewis's unhappy task to tell the president that his hope for an all-water route linking the Atlantic to the Pacific was gone." Instead Lewis sent word that between the Missouri and the

Columbia waters lay "a passage of 340 miles, 200 along a good road, the other 140 'the most formidable part of the tract . . . [over] tremendious mountains which for 60 mls. are covered with eternal snows.'"[15] Lewis, ever sparing in his verbiage, added only that he was bringing nine Indian lexicons, numerous types of furs, a "pretty extensive collection of plants," and a Mandan chief—leaving it to the president and his scientist friends to imagine all that he and Clark had discovered. They would learn soon enough.[16]

On December 2, 1806, Jefferson had his sixth State of the Union message delivered to Congress.[17] He lauded Lewis and Clark for their success, concluding that "Messrs. Lewis and Clarke [sic], and their brave companions, have by this arduous service deserved well of their country," before describing the progress of other expeditions in mapping the Mississippi River and Red River.

Probably the most noteworthy passage of that address, however, concerned the institution of slavery. Article IV of the Constitution excepted from Congress's Commerce Clause power the power to ban slave imports prior to 1808. Jefferson here called on Congress to exercise its power to do so beginning on January 1st of that year, saying, with a typical Jeffersonian flourish, that

> I congratulate you, fellow citizens, on the approach of the period at which you may interpose your authority constitutionally, to withdraw the citizens of the United States from all further participation in those violations of human rights which have been so long continued on the unoffending inhabitants of Africa, and which the morality, the reputation, and the best interests of our country, have long been eager to proscribe. Although no law you may pass can take prohibitory effect till the first day of the year one thousand eight hundred and eight, yet the intervening period is not too long to prevent, by timely notice, expeditions which cannot be completed before that day.

Congress passed just such a bill in that session, and Jefferson signed it into law—which meant that slave imports were illegal from the morning of January 1, 1808.

Envisioning the approaching moment when the federal debt would be extinguished, Jefferson suggested that "the great purposes of the public education, roads, rivers, canals, and such other objects of public improvement as it may be thought proper to add to the constitutional enumeration of federal powers" could be the subjects of constitutional amendment "because the objects now recommended are not among those enumerated in the constitution, and to which it permits the public moneys to be applied." Military expenditure could always be greater, he concluded, but to make it before it was necessary would mean "[o]ur resources would have been exhausted on dangers which have never happened, instead of being reserved for what is really to take place." Well organized militia units and short-term volunteers could always be ready to hand without eating out Americans' substance. So he said. Time would tell.

The other matter he mentioned was an incipient organization of "a great number of private individuals . . . to carry on military expeditions against the territories of Spain. . . ."[18] This enterprise has come down to us as Burr's Conspiracy. Even now, exactly what former vice president Aaron Burr had in mind remains impossible to determine, try though scholars have.[19] What we do know is that Burr by September 1806 had told a prominent man near Pittsburgh that "with two hundred men he could drive the president and Congress into the Potomac" and that "the separation of the Union must take place." His interlocutor reported the conversation to Jefferson.[20] As the president described the situation to Congress, "the criminal attempts of private persons to decide for their country the questions of peace or war" had made it necessary for him "to take measures for . . . suppressing this enterprise, for seizing the vessels, arms, and other means provided for it, and for arresting and bringing to justice its authors and abettors."[21]

As Burr's plans and machinations remain to some indeterminate degree unknown to us, so it seems we are in the dark regarding the extent of President Jefferson's knowledge of the subject. At some early point he decided Burr needed to be prosecuted for crimes of which, as the president saw it, he was guilty. Once he had the bit in his teeth, Jefferson just would not let go. For his part, Burr recruited a stable of prominent attorneys to aid him in his courtroom defense. Due to a jurisdictional quirk, Chief Justice John Marshall, Jefferson's powerful, tenacious adversary, presided over the trial. Here were the ingredients of what has long been called "the greatest criminal trial in American history and one of the notable trials in the annals of the law."[22]

Jefferson first took the Burr matter to his Cabinet in a meeting of October 22, 1806.[23] His *Anas* entry for the meeting says that Burr had come to Washington during the previous session of Congress seeking some kind of government post and, not finding one, confided in some people his plan to separate western states from the rest and make them "into an independent Confederacy." Suspicions had already been roused by Burr's travels in those states, Jefferson wrote. General William Eaton, various private citizens, and newspapers were among Jefferson's sources. The Cabinet and president agreed unanimously that the governors of Ohio, Indiana, Mississippi, and Orleans, besides the U.S. attorneys for Kentucky, Tennessee, and Louisiana, ought to be put on their guard that Burr must be "strictly watched." In case he "commit[ted] any overt act unequivocally," he should be "arrested and tried for treason, misdemeanor, or whatever other offence the act [might] amount to." So should any of his followers who might be found to have broken the law.

Complicating the Burr issue was the festering suspicion that Brigadier General James Wilkinson, the army's chief general and governor of Louisiana (that is, the Louisiana Purchase Territory north of today's state of Louisiana), was somehow involved. Burr had told Eaton that he was, and Jefferson recorded that "suspicions of infidelity in Wilkinson" had by this time "become very general." (Unbeknownst to the president, Wilkinson was given a cipher letter on October 8, 1806, in which Burr described Burr's force as ready to move downriver toward New Orleans. At the same time he got a letter from Burr's man Jonathan Dayton warning that the general's long-standing wrongdoings had been exposed at last, and that they would be disclosed to Congress at its next session.)[24] The Cabinet and president considered the matter again two days later, when they decided to send a secret agent through Kentucky after Burr to consult with the western governors and to arrest Burr if he found grounds for doing so. On arrival in Orleans Territory (today's Louisiana), he was to assume the governorship there. By the following day, however, Jefferson and the Cabinet decided not to write to the various high officials on the secret agent's route. They would instead leave to the agent the task of discussing the matter with them in person. Complete silence of state officials, members of Congress, and newspapers in the region regarding any action by Burr seemed to indicate that further focus on him was unnecessary.[25]

27

✦ ⚙ ✦

Jefferson and his Cabinet would have been far more upset if they had known the full details of Burr's filibustering career. The then–vice president had written to the British minister to the United States, Anthony Merry, in mid-1804. He wanted Great Britain to cooperate in a filibustering effort in the West. Most historians have followed Merry in thinking that Burr's point was to separate the western states and drive Spain out of those states.[1] Certainly that was Jefferson's ultimate position.

General Wilkinson responded to Jefferson's order to proceed to the Sabine in answer to Spanish encroachments by dithering until September. (Forrest McDonald thinks that the Randolph faction's attempt to have him removed from his position helps account for this behavior.)[2] Suspicious of Wilkinson and fielding demands from all types of residents of St. Louis for his removal, Jefferson apparently intended moving Wilkinson to the Sabine as a smooth way of easing the general out of his governorship. Wilkinson and congressional allies saw it that way too. Historian Merrill Peterson reads Wilkinson as having had trouble deciding whether to go ahead with the Burr conspiracy, on one hand, or turn against Burr and pose as the United States' hero, on the other.[3]

Instead of putting their forces into motion, General Wilkinson—whom we now know to have been on the Spanish payroll at the time—opted to betray Burr to Jefferson rather than launch a filibuster against neighboring Spanish territory. He almost instantly concluded an agreement with the Spanish putting off a final agreement on the border between the Louisiana Purchase and Florida, then dunned the Spanish $120,000 for his services.[4]

Things moved independently in the Upper South, where a Federalist U.S. attorney in Kentucky began a grand jury investigation of Burr on November 4, 1806, for violating the Neutrality Act of 1794. Burr, aided by a rising young attorney named Henry Clay, defended himself. The government failed to secure an indictment, in response to which "cheering erupted." On December 1 through 5, the U.S. attorney gave it another go, once again without securing an indictment. This time a public ball was held in Burr's honor.[5] The following day, Harman Blennerhassett and a number of Burr's other followers assembled on Blennerhassett's Island in the Ohio. The assemblage broke up when the threat of arrest became known.[6]

At New Orleans, Wilkinson assumed dictatorial powers in order to cloud the question of his own relationship to Burr's activities. He had the former vice president's three top collaborators—Samuel Swartwout, Peter V. Ogden, and Eric Bollman—peremptorily arrested and held incommunicado. When writs of habeas corpus were finally issued in their behalf, he put them on a ship to Washington. As one account has it, "He also jailed their attorney, the judge, the judge's closest friend, the editor of the *Orleans Gazette*," a former senator, "and some sixty other citizens. None were specifically charged, all were denied their legal and constitutional rights, and several were transported in chains away from the vicinage, where they had a constitutional right to a speedy and public trial, and were shipped in secret to Washington." President Jefferson, fabled defender of civil liberties, never uttered a peep of protest. Apparently swayed by the government's extreme measures that something grave must be up, the public scarcely did either.[7]

Wilkinson's decoded version of the cipher letter, doctored to implicate Burr and exonerate Wilkinson, came to Jefferson on January 18, 1807, with a cover letter in which Wilkinson advised Jefferson that Burr intended to provoke a revolt in Orleans Territory as a preliminary to his move on Mexico. That same day John Randolph of Roanoke got his House colleagues to inquire formally of the president what information he had about a conspiracy against the U.S.A. or a foreign nation and what he had done about it. Four days later the president sent Congress a special message. He told the nation, mostly on the basis of Wilkinson's letter, that Burr had committed treason.[8] The evidence made a kind of puzzle. "It is chiefly in the form of letters," he explained, "often containing such a mixture of rumors, conjectures, and suspicions, as render it difficult to sift out the real facts, and unadvisable to hazard more than general outlines, strengthened by concurrent information, or the particular credibility of the relater. In this state of the evidence, delivered sometimes too under the restriction of private confidence, neither safety nor justice will permit the exposing names, except that of the principle actor, whose guilt is placed beyond question." He had begun to hear in September of "designs . . . in the western country, unlawful and unfriendly to the peace of the Union; and that the prime mover in these was Aaron Burr, heretofore distinguished by the favor of his country."

As the president described them, Burr's designs centered on "the severance of the Union of these States by the Alleghany mountains" and "an attack on Mexico," which "might be carried on either jointly or separately." Finding that the first was impracticable, the locals not approving, Burr purportedly had decided to loot New Orleans and use the captured money and military supplies in an attack on Mexico. Various outcasts supported him, as did men deluded into believing the U.S. Government supported Burr too. It was with this information that Jefferson ordered arrest of all conspirators and seizure of all property intended to be used in the venture. The quick response of Ohio's Governor Edward Tiffin wrote finis to the entire enterprise.

Kentucky's government also acted quickly. Wilkinson found the population of New Orleans highly agitated over the exaggerated accounts of the support he would receive, given it by Burr. The president's message told Congress that rumors of foreign agency in Burr's Conspiracy had no basis. "These surmises," he wrote, "are, therefore, to be imputed to the vauntings of the author of this enterprise, to multiply his partisans by magnifying the belief of his prospects and support." Burr's three chief conspirators, he concluded, had all been arrested at Wilkinson's command. One was subsequently released pursuant to a writ of habeas corpus, and the other two were en route to the Atlantic coast for trial.

On February 13, 1807, the Supreme Court per Chief Justice Marshall freed Bollman and Swartwout on writs of habeas corpus.[9] Along the way it laid down a definition of "treason" according to Article III of the Constitution. When as a circuit judge in Richmond he presided at Burr's trial, Marshall would have to deal with this precedent.

The definitional question was what the expression "levying war" meant. The U.S. attorney reasoned that the Executive was the organ of the government charged with making war, and since President Jefferson had declared there was a state of war, there was. Marshall's decision said that "[t]o constitute that specific crime . . . , war must be actually levied against the United States. However flagitious may be the crime of conspiring to subvert by force the government of our country, such conspiracy is not treason . . . To conspire to levy war, and actually to levy war, are distinct offences. The first must be brought into operation by the assemblage of men for a purpose treasonable in itself, or the fact of levying war cannot have been committed." Bollman and Swartwout went free.

Once Aaron Burr arrived in Richmond, matters developed far differently.

First, the grand jury included several notable Republicans, including two U.S. senators and, as foreman, John Marshall's distant cousin John Randolph of Roanoke. Though a Republican more Catholic than the pope, Randolph admired his cousin the chief justice, who was a close friend. He despised James Wilkinson, on the other hand, whom he adjudged more deserving of indictment than anyone else.

Burr's trial would be a grand public spectacle. On Burr's side a "dream team" of eminent lawyers from several states, all under the command of their very adept lawyer-client, would enter the lists, while on the government's, a prominent Virginian attorney ran a prosecution everyone knew to be the brainchild of the president himself. Because the president had publicly deemed the defendant guilty, the throngs of spectators presumed him so.

The case of *United States v. Burr* (1807) is best known today for the argument over Burr's request to have the president of the United States issued a subpoena *duces tecum*—a court order to produce documents. How would this president, after all that had passed between his administration and the federal judiciary, respond? Might he take this as the opportunity Marshall's statesmanly opinion in *Marbury v. Madison* had denied him and flout the subpoena? He did not. Rather, although he noted that the press of government business prevented him from traveling to Richmond for the purpose, Jefferson sent the materials Marshall had commanded him to submit. He did so without ever conceding that duty required it, however.[10]

Besides that question, another matter that raised controversy concerned social life in Virginia's little capital "city." Small town as it was, and smaller still as its social elite was, it was difficult for attorneys on either side of a case to avoid each other in their off-hours. They did not even try. How unsurprising, then, that Chief Justice Marshall and Defendant Burr ended up at least briefly running into each other at a Richmond soirée. Republicans were (or feigned being) outraged. The authoritative account of the case concludes that here was an innocent coincidence.[11] We can be excused for being skeptical.

The Constitution's Treason Clause (Art. III, Section 3, Clause 1) says, "Treason against the United States, shall consist only in levying War against them, or in adhering to their Enemies, giving them Aid and comfort." It further says, "No Person shall be convicted of Treason unless on the Testimony of two Witnesses to the same overt Act, or on Confession in open Court." As Burr was not going to confess, trying him for treason would come to naught unless multiple witnesses testified to a specific act of his levying war against the United States.

But Burr had not been among the throng on Blennerhassett's Island.

Even if he had been, as the historian of the Burr trial R. Kent Newmyer explained, "nothing happened on Blennerhasset's Island, or anywhere else on the western frontier, that looked remotely like war levied against the United States." Since Marshall had "repudiated . . . the proposition that a conspiracy to commit treason was itself treason," that was the end of it.[12] To the president's extreme disgust, Burr was not found guilty, though the jury's holding of "not proved guilty under this indictment under any evidence submitted to us" implied that the court had manipulated the proceedings.[13] Jefferson blamed his cousin the chief justice, insisting that the outcome would "heap coals of fire on the head of the Judge"[14]—as Republican congressmen and newspapers were quick to do.

Through this period the president of course had to deal with mundane matters—appointments, debt service, and such. At one point, he responded to Secretary Gallatin's recommendation of an appointment by saying, "The appointment of a woman to office is an innovation for which the public is not prepared, nor am I."[15] Many, many moons would pass before one of Jefferson's successors took the step the immigrant European aristocrat master of the Treasury Department had suggested.

The main issue occupying the president's attention in his second term was the trans-Atlantic blowback from the Napoleonic Wars. The president's refusal to submit the Monroe-Pinkney Treaty for Senate ratification left matters in an awkward state, with America insisting on a return of the "broken voyage" doctrine and an end to impressment without being willing to help resolve the Royal Navy's desertion problem. Some historians have speculated that Jefferson expected Napoleon to solve his problem for him—to help the United States pry the Floridas from Spain's withered grasp and, through further military success and prolonged dominance of Europe, to make Britain in time more accommodating.[16] This miscalculation led him, and America, down the path that started with rejection of the Monroe-Pinkney Treaty and culminated in the War of 1812.

That is one way to see it. Certainly rejection of the Monroe-Pinkney Treaty did not have any obvious benefits. Yet Jefferson may have thought he had no real alternatives. The Berlin Decree had closed the Continent to any ship that had docked in a British port, and new British Orders in Council required American ships heading to Europe to pay British fees on their way. The treaty's provision denying America the right to impose sanctions would leave the country essentially defenseless against hostile British measures bearing unjustly on U.S. ships. Withal, Jefferson saw the treaty as holding out the prospect of an English-American entente against France, and he hoped the emperor would appreciate that Jefferson had rejected it. What might well result was "a war of commercial restrictions" between America and the United Kingdom, he wrote.[17]

Matters came to a head in what came to be known as the *Chesapeake-Leopard* Incident of 1807. The United States had for years been allowing other nations' ships free access to American ports for provisioning and for "succor to their sick & suffering." The chief beneficiary was the United Kingdom, not only because it had the largest fleet but because of the common language. Repeatedly, as Secretary Madison told it, the American government had filed official complaints with His Majesty's Government about Royal Navy officers' "continued course of insubordination to the laws, of violence to the persons of our citizens, and of trespass on their property."[18] Still they persisted.

On June 22, 1807, a Royal Navy warship took this habit of offense considerably further: to the point of open acts of war.[19] The frigate U.S.S. *Chesapeake* was one of America's frontline warships. Its crew of 381 included 329 officers and seamen and 52 U.S. Marines, besides various civilians (among them a ten-man Italian band). More than a score of the men were "on the sick list," and because the ship's captain did not contemplate any hostilities, its guns were "lashed up in case of heavy weather during the Atlantic crossing." Since the Tripolitan War's happy conclusion, America was at peace.

At several points, as *Chesapeake*'s officers later recalled, H.M.S. *Leopard*'s behavior off the Virginia coast at Norfolk seemed curious. Yet innocent explanations came to mind. When the British ship's captain asked to send an officer aboard, the American commander Commodore James Barron responded receptively. Receiving a demand to allow the British to muster the American crew—a preliminary to impressment, Barron replied that he had orders never to allow anyone but his ship's crew to muster its men. Had he known that the *Leopard* had in the previous twelve days impressed "seamen from several merchant vessels along the American coast," he probably would have been no more prepared for this turn of events than he was: impressment from a warship was a different matter entirely.

Only at this point did Barron take preliminary steps to prepare his ship for hostilities. Still, as the leading account explains:

Not a single gun was primed and ready to be fired. There were no powder horns on the gun deck, no matches in the match tubs, and not enough rammers, sponges, and handspikes to serve a full broadside. Sick men were still lying in hammocks slung between the spar deck guns. *Coils* of anchor cable, the armorer's forge, casks, ladders, furniture, lumber, baggage, and various other articles obstructed the lanes leading fore and aft on the gun deck. Orders were shouted and countermanded; men rushed back and forth; and precious minutes continued to slip away.

Very close by, *Leopard*'s commander at last shouted a warning across to Barron, who answered that he could not hear it. The British ship then fired a warning shot across *Chesapeake*'s bow, which Barron ignored. And all hell broke loose.

By the time Barron's colors were struck, his ship had taken three broadsides at close range. *Chesapeake* managed to fire only one round from one cannon in response. In fifteen minutes *Leopard* had killed three American crewmen and wounded eighteen, including Barron, one of whom would die shortly afterward. A boarding party then mustered the American ship's crew, of whom it decided to abscond with four. The *Chesapeake* limped back into port for repairs.

President Jefferson issued his angry *Chesapeake* Proclamation on July 2, 1807.[20] He began by noting that America had observed a scrupulous neutrality between the warring powers. He then noted the British naval officers' long-standing habit of abusing America's hospitality—and that "repeated representations to their government" had elicited "assurances . . . that proper orders should restrain them within the limit of the rights, & of the respect belonging to a friendly nation. . . ." Alas, he said, "those orders & assurances have been without effect; nor has a single instance of punishment for past wrongs taken place."

Building to its crescendo, Jefferson's woeful and enraged communication to his countrymen and the world said that "at length a deed, transcending all we have suffered, brings the public sensibility to a serious crisis, and forbearance to a necessary pause. A frigate of the US. trusting to a state of peace and leaving her harbor on a distant service, has been surprised and attacked by a British vessel of superior force, one of a squadron then lying in our waters to cover the transaction, & has been disabled from service with the loss of a number of men killed & wounded." All British vessels were to leave American waters immediately, and any American who gave them supplies would be punished to the fullest extent of the law.

By President Jefferson's account Americans had not been so outraged since Lexington in 1775. From north to south, they wanted war. So, for example, a public meeting on the subject at Abbeville, South Carolina, ended with adoption of a set of "Resolutions on the *Chesapeake-Leopard* Affair" by a native son recently returned from years of Yankee schooling—first at Yale College, then at Litchfield Law School.[21] His name was John C. Calhoun.

Calhoun's audience that day cannot have known that in mentioning "those in whom the Sovereignty of the country ultimately resides" in his resolutions' very first paragraph he took the ground on which he would often stand through more than four decades in all but the very highest public office. What they did hear was his invocation of "the torrent of our feelings," which drove them "to give vent to an indignation deep and universal." Far from "a pusillanimous people," Americans would now be found "a nation glorying in its Independence, united by a common and enthusiastic Patriotism; and resolute, by a joint exertion of strength, to maintain the united and indivisible interest of our common country."

Americans, Calhoun insisted, had no "wanton desire of war." Rather, "We have been the friends of peace. An habitual attachment to it is a deep-marked trait in our national character." Jefferson's "excellent Administration" had struggled to maintain it. Many nations had reciprocated. One exception, however, stood out: "Great Britain, by her repeated gross and flagrant outrages, the impressment of our citizens, capturing our vessels, and insulting conduct in our harbours, seems determined to demonstrate . . . that our Love of Peace . . . is only . . . stupid insensibility. . . ." There followed eleven resolves, among which were pledges to help enforce the president's proclamation, to take up arms if called upon, and to "renounce, as mere luxuries, all articles of foreign importation" if the Revolutionary-era economic boycotts should be reprised by the Federal Government at this time.

Although we have no record of Calhoun's oratorical performance that day, one man who had been present recalled that Calhoun "astonished everybody" and, as the best biography says, "laid the foundation for his enduring political popularity in the district." Soon enough he was a major national figure.[22]

As Congress was not in session, Jefferson had a decision to make: should he call a special session, which likely would lead to war, or should he wait for the legislature to reconvene on October 26?[23] Despite the public mood he chose the latter course.

By the time Congress reconvened, the furor had abated somewhat. Yet, in the time since the unpleasantness with the Royal Navy, the geostrategic picture had grown substantially darker. A British proclamation augured more impressments, word was that Napoleon planned energetic enforcement of the Berlin Decree—which would be ruinous to American shipping— and Washington had heard that the British intended more draconian steps against the French Empire's (and thus America's) seaborne trade.[24] What was to be done?

Congress on December 22, 1807, passed the classic Jeffersonian answer to war fever: the Embargo Act. Jefferson viewed this measure, which barred all foreign trade, as a kind of quarantine. Yes, his call for the Embargo Act was twinned with a proposal that Congress see to military preparedness—if of the peculiarly Jeffersonian ideological kind.[25]

At first the president said the embargo's "objects" were "keeping our ships and seamen out of harm's way." As the historian of Jefferson's policy toward Britain Burton Spivak explained, for Jefferson, "[t]he equation was quite simple. Trade now spelled certain captures, and for these, Jefferson feared, 'we must have gone to war to avenge the wrong.'" That inherently undesirable outcome would have been especially harmful because it came at a time when "defensive fortifications were painfully incomplete, state and national militias were undermanned and disorganized, [and] the amount of commercial wealth at sea and vulnerable to capture was still sizable." Putting off the day when America was drawn into European war would give time for growth of American population, payment of American debt, completion of American preparation, and perhaps even conclusion of a European peace, as Jefferson saw it.[26]

Yet in embargoing all the world the Republican high command doomed its strategy to defeat. Rather than targeting the British, and thus spurring development of alternative trading relationships while treating America's addiction to British products, this policy had neither of those effects. It also seriously damaged American agriculture, the mainstay of Republican political support. Most counterproductively, the embargo essentially handed over the role American shipping had played in the Western international economy to the British.[27]

Secretary Gallatin identified these drawbacks instantly, and so "considered from the first moment war as a necessary result."[28] He told Jefferson that the defensive embargo should have a six-month sunset. War would be preferable to a permanent embargo "in every point of view: privations, sufferings, revenue, effect on the enemy [and] politics at home." Unfortunately for the United States, Secretary Madison won this argument.[29]

Madison argued in a Republican-allied newspaper that the embargo would "have the collateral effect of making it the interest of all nations to change the system which has driven our commerce from the ocean." Both of the Great Powers stood to lose without the American trade, and it would not bring on war "if war be not predetermined on against us. Being a measure of peace and precaution; being universal, and therefore impartial; extending in reality as well as ostensibly to all nations, there is not a shadow of pretext to make it a cause of war." Oddly echoing John Winthrop's "City on a Hill" address, he summarized the Embargo Act's effect abroad by saying, "We shall be deprived of market for our superfluities. They will feel the want of necessaries."

So said the Master of Montpelier. The general historical appraisal of the embargo is that it hurt Napoleon's essentially self-sufficient empire not at all, and while Britain suffered slightly, the embargo's effect never approached the cataclysmic level that would have been required to make the United Kingdom abandon impressment and the Orders-in-Council. Whom it did hurt, and abundantly, were Americans.[30] So one irate constituent wrote to Jefferson:

I wish you would take this embargo off as soon as you possibly can, for damn my eyes if I can live as it is. I shall certainly cut my throat, and if I do you will lose one of the best seaman that ever sailed. I have a wife and four young one's to support, and it goes damn'd hard with me now. If I dont cut my *throat* I will go join the English and fight against you. I hope, honored Sir, you will forgive the abrupt manner in which this is wrote as I am damn'd mad. But still if ever I catch you over there, take care of your honored neck

He closed by giving his address in case "you want to see him, you damn'd rascal." (The weight of that last is lost today, but at the time, "damn'd rascal" was quite an insult.)

This attitude toward the president grew increasingly common—particularly in New England, where smuggling agricultural products to what is now Canada grew epidemic. Gallatin, charged along with his eighty-five customs collectors with enforcing the law, told his wife in mid-1808 that he expected the administration to be turned out at the next election. He repeatedly told Jefferson and their allies on Capitol Hill of the new enforcement powers he needed, and Congress passed four bills amending the law to placate him.[31]

It was futile in the end. Rather than admit as much, Jefferson essentially stepped aside in his administration's final days. Madison and Gallatin wrote to tell him that he must in the wake of an Annual Message admitting the embargo's failure to elicit a change of policy from either France or Britain decide on the policy America would now adopt.[32] The president remained silent. If his policy had failed to prevent war—and the reinflation of the national debt that would involve—he would not be responsible for the consequences. He had tried to avoid war so that his government could pay down its debt, but the attempt had failed. Let his successor face the consequences.[33]

Congress repealed the Embargo Act on March 1, 1809, three days before Thomas Jefferson's presidency ended, with an effective date of March 4th. Northern Republicans had flinched in the face of rising resistance in their region. The replacement Non-Intercourse Act excluded the British and the French from American ports, and at the same time, it provided new naval spending. Gallatin blamed this abandonment of his, and his friend the president's, priorities on Senators Smith, Nicholas, and Giles. With Jefferson essentially out of the way, the three of them were feeling their oats. The troubles they would cause had only just begun.[34]

PART II
THE NADIR

28

✢ ☼ ✢

By all accounts James Madison cut a weak figure at his inauguration. Mrs. Samuel Harrison Smith, wife of the publisher of the pro-Republican *National Intelligencer* and a friend of both the outgoing and the incoming president, said of his First Inaugural Address that "Mr. Madison was extremely pale and trembled excessively when he first began to speak." After a while, however, he "gained confidence and spoke audibly."[1]

She found herself overwhelmed with emotion as Jefferson, dear to her, left office. The peaceful transfer of power struck her too:

I have just returned from the solemn and affecting scenes of this day,—to many they were scenes of greatness, gaiety, and exultation. To me they were melancholy. My heart is oppressed . . . with a weight of sadness, and my eyes so blinded with tears that I can scarcely trace these lines. It is some pleasure to me to write to you who participate in my sentiments of affectionate veneration for this best of men. For the last time I have seen him in his own house. He is happy, he has enjoyed all his country can bestow of greatness and honor. . . . He goes to be *happy* without ceasing to be *great*.

She next recalled a brief conversation she had had with the new ex-president at the Madisons' Washington residence, in which they would stay for several more days while Jefferson prepared to depart the Executive Mansion: "'You have now resigned a heavy burden,' said I. 'Yes indeed' he replied 'and am much happier at this moment than my friend.'"

Conscious that after thirty-two years of close friendship and political alliance, Madison as of this day at last had become—at least for a time—the senior partner, Jefferson decided to show him deference. Thus, to the younger man's invitation to accompany him in his carriage to the Capitol for the inauguration, Jefferson said no. "I wished not to divide with him the honors of the day," he explained, "it pleased me better to see them all bestowed on him." One witness recalled that a "large procession of citizens, some in carriages, on horse back, and still larger on foot, followed Mr. Madison along Pennsylvania avenue to the Capitol, among those on horseback was Mr. Jefferson; unattended by even a servant, undistinguished in any way from his fellow citizens." More striking still was that when he arrived at the Capitol, the outgoing president "hitched his own horse to a post, and followed the multitude into the Hall of Representatives." Directed to a seat placed for him near Madison, he declined, saying, "This day I return to the people and my proper seat is among them."[2]

James Madison's First Inaugural Address reflected his personality.[3] Its first inaudible sentence, "Unwilling to depart from examples, of the most revered authority, I avail myself of the occasion now presented, to express the profound impression made on me, by the call of my Country to the station, to the duties of which I am about to pledge myself, by the most solemn of sanctions," would not have impressed his audience any more positively if they had heard it.[4] If it was at that point that the flush of nervousness passed and he warmed to the situation, Madison's audience heard him lay out a classic Jeffersonian summary of America's geostrategic situation.

America now faced a woeful foreign policy picture. This came upon it just as the right policy had yielded the greatest prosperity Americans had ever enjoyed. It had been "the true glory of the United States to cultivate peace by observing justice, and to entitle themselves to the respect of the nations at war, by fulfilling their neutral obligations, with the most scrupulous impartiality." The change owed not to an error in American councils, but to "the injustice and violence of the Belligerent powers. In their rage against each other, or impelled by more direct motives, principles of retaliation have been introduced, equally contrary to universal reason, and acknowledged law."

What the British minister thought of this passage, we cannot say. Surely at our remove it seems odd that Madison should have persisted in considering particular policies adopted by one or the other leading power in the struggle between Napoleon and Britain in relation to "universal reason, and acknowledged law"—and that, if he did, he should have concluded that either the emperor of the French or the United Kingdom would have thought the imperative to win their war ranked behind the less momentous concerns of the United States. That he persisted in falling back on this kind of disputation did not foreshadow success for his administration.

He next lamented that neither Britain or France gave any indication of intending to amend its "arbitrary edicts, . . . in spite of the demonstrations that not even a pretext for them has been given by the United States, and of the fair and liberal attempts to induce a revocation of them. . . ." As if that were not uninspiring enough, he segued directly into a recognition of his "deep conviction" of "my own inadequacy to" the presidency's "high duties."

Then came a list of the principles that would guide him. James Madison famously possessed an incisive analytical mind. He also had a tendency to produce turgid formulations. This longest paragraph in the address reflected that second quality. It made the fighting nostrums binding Republicans into a substantial majority dull enough to put the audience's minds to wandering. In succession he rattled off peace with nations that wanted it; neutrality toward belligerents; diplomacy instead of war when practicable; resistance to taking sides between foreign countries; political and sentimental independence; commitment to the Union "as the basis of [the states'] happiness"; support for the Constitution; devotion to the federal principle; support of the freedom of conscience; respect for other individual rights—particularly freedom of the press; economy; debt extinguishment; limitation on peacetime military spending/reliance on the militia; promotion of agriculture, manufactures, and commerce, science and education; and continued promotion of Indians' conversion from "savage" to "a civilized state" as principles to which he would be dedicated. As we shall see, Madison would indeed hew to these principles as president, for good and for ill.

In his last two paragraphs Madison first paid a high compliment to Jefferson, whose "exalted talents, zealously devoted, thro' a long career, to the advancement of [a beloved Country's] highest interest and happiness" had earned him a "rich reward": its "benediction." He then closed with an invocation of the citizenry's "intelligence and virtue" and "the guardianship and guidance of that Almighty Being whose power regulates the destiny of nations. . . ." In sum Madison had rhetorical gifts, and leadership aptitude generally, appropriate to a second-in-command, to the last aide who proofread a speech before the leader gave it. His fellow members of the Washington elite thought they knew this to be true in March 1809. By the time he left office, most would be sure of it.

The first practical task to which President Madison had to attend foreshadowed the difficulty he had throughout his presidency in dealing with congressmen of his own party, particularly when it came to the issue in which they were most interested: appointments. On the day before his inauguration, Madison received an anxious letter from Representative Wilson Cary Nicholas, Republican of Virginia.[5] "I have endeavoured to ascertain,"

Nicholas began, "how the votes wou'd be in the Senate upon the nomination of Mr. Gallatin."

Madison had in mind that his own ascent from the number-two job, secretary of state, to the top post would be followed by Gallatin's promotion from number three to number two. Gallatin's extremely able service in Congress and the Jefferson administration had earned him the promotion, and, nearly as importantly, Gallatin was a native Francophone European with important diplomatic experience. He had ideal qualifications at a time when relations with France would be a central concern of American diplomacy. Nicholas's intelligence, then, must have come as a shock.

"My information is that there are seventeen votes against him—ten gentn. will vote for him, some of them reluctantly, and that there are seven doubtful votes." Although some of this information came from people unfriendly to Gallatin, Nicholas said that he counted only "one person in that number about who I have much doubt. . . ." If that one voted for Gallatin's confirmation, Nicholas confided, "it will be out of respect to you." Nicholas concluded by urging Madison to nix the potential nomination soon if he intended not to make it, as he would thus avoid undercutting Gallatin and himself with "the responsibility of an unpopular appointment."

Not for the last time, Madison here ran up against the Senate "Invisibles," an unlikely quasi-opposition Republican alliance of Virginia's William Branch Giles, Pennsylvania's Michael Leib, and Marylander Samuel Smith. Giles, prominent despite not being overly bright, fancied himself as secretary of state—an office for which "nobody else seemed to think him qualified."[6] The acerbic John Randolph, hearing that Madison was mulling over a choice of Senator Smith's brother Robert for the top Cabinet post instead of the Virginia senator, is supposed to have quipped, "As he can spell he ought to be preferred to G[iles]."[7]

Giles had warned Madison not to settle on Gallatin.[8] He offered nine somewhat contradictory, in some cases nonsensical, reasons for opposing a Gallatin nomination, including among others that "I have no confidence in the sincerity of his professions either in favor of yourself or Mr. Jefferson"; "[h]is nomination . . . will disgust a very great portion of the Republican party, in my opinion the most respectable, and upon which alone you can rely for a support"; "[i]t will increase the shade of distrust now cast over the measures of the administration, respecting our foreign relations, at a time when not a doubt ought to exist upon that subject"; "[i]t will extend these distrusts even amongst the republicans, to every communication upon that subject during your whole administration . . ."; "[i]t will be considered as a part of Mr. Jefferson's arrangements, for the recommendation of his favorites, connected in his judgement no doubt, with the promotion of the public interests; but in which, others differ with him in opinion." Of this last consideration he added: "[t]his idea has more importance attached to it than you will readily believe."

How Madison appraised this memorandum from so prominent a member, beyond being annoyed at the insinuation that Gallatin's Swiss birth made him untrustworthy, we do not know. The president almost certainly considered that if Gallatin stayed at Treasury, he could be counted on to continue to do excellent service in that post, even as the president relied on him for foreign-policy advice just as during the Jefferson years, while if nominated for State and rejected by the Senate, he likely would resign. Historians have disagreed whether a Republican Senate majority would in the event have deferred to the first significant decision of the new Republican president. We cannot say. What we do know is that opting for Senator Smith's brother over Gallatin doomed the president to having an incompetent as his chief subordinate for years and helped set a pattern of lackluster-at-best Cabinet appointments that marred virtually the entire Madison presidency.

In quick succession Madison settled for the most part on essentially unqualified men—other than Gallatin at Treasury and Smith at State, he kept Jefferson's man Caesar Rodney as attorney general (which was then a part-time job, the Justice Department not yet having been created), and he put two utterly unfit men in charge of the War and Navy Departments. The former, William Eustis, came into a department without a general staff. Instead he found himself the leader of eleven clerks, none of whom had more than one year's experience.[9] Dr. Eustis was a physician and a notable Republican whose geographic background and family ties appealed to the president in a day when such considerations mattered. As one Madison biographer put it, however, "With these advantages he apparently did not need to have any particular talents or experience qualifying him for the War Department."[10] Dr. Eustis recognized that he was at sea in his important position, and so, as people in such positions commonly do, he fixated on picayune mundane administrative details. His incapacity would impose a crushing toll on the nation when the time for war came.[11]

A worse match for his position than Madison's War Department appointee was South Carolinian Paul Hamilton, the president's choice for the Navy Department. If Secretary Eustis had no pertinent qualifications, Hamilton by one account "was an alcoholic who fell asleep at his desk and made a spectacle of himself at social events." Madison eventually forced him out.

His successor, Pennsylvanian William Jones, proved to be a different kind of secretary entirely.[12]

Nearly a decade after the end of his administration, a younger Virginian of the prominent Lee family wrote to inquire of Madison about some events during his tenure. Having posed those questions, he concluded by saying, "The mention of the lake fleets, calls to my mind a reflection that frequently occurs to me[,] & never without giving me uneasiness. Nor can I without much [sensi]bility and deference mention it to you. I shall have frequently to advert to the Character & constitution of your cabinet—and I do not know in what way I shall account for the singular infelicity of many of your appointments."[13] Madison explained to him that, "Before I advert to your review of Cabinet appointments, I must allude to the field of choice *as narrowed* by considerations never to be wholly disregarded. Besides the more essential requisites in the candidate, an eye must be had to his political principles and connexions, his personal temper and habits, his relations of feelings towards those with whom he is to be associated; and the quarter of the Union to which he belongs."[14] After noting that both the Senate and the prospective appointee must approve the choice, he added, "You are probably very little aware of the *number of refusals* experienced during the period to which your observations apply."

In the course of this letter, Madison explained his selections of some dud generals and took up the causes of the Cabinet officers Lee had named. A typical defense, that of Dr. Eustis, began by referring to him as "an acceptable member of the Cabinet," whose experience during the Revolution had made him familiar with the army's life and organization and whose efforts would have been sufficient if Congress had satisfied the administration's request for assistants in his work. By 1827 a War Department staff with far fewer soldiers to attend to had been reorganized in a way that would have enabled Eustis to "satisf[y] public expectation" even in wartime.

That Madison took the time to answer Lee's questions at the length he did shows that he thought posterity deserved an explanation. We his intended audience need not be persuaded by it.

29

✦ ☼ ✦

U nlike previous presidents' wives Mrs. Madison would carve out a significant role in the capital during her husband's presidency.[1] While Gallatin's house on Capitol Hill, at the center of the congressional district, remained an important policy center for the Madison administration's first couple of years, Dolley's "squeezes"—jam-packed White House get-togethers with as many as three hundred people in attendance—came to be important social and political events in their own right.

Whether the Madisons envisioned them developing in this way, we do not know. What was clear was that the new president would not politic at the dinner table as his predecessor had done. Instead the Executive Mansion would host both sumptuous dinners and large public events, the latter with Mrs. Madison at center stage. These events allowed the president, not so magnetic as Jefferson, to yield the main social burden to his wife.

Contemporary scholarship highlights the formative role Dolley Madison played in making the District of Columbia into a national capital, besides her role in facilitating republican politics during her husband's administration. Where Jefferson had alternated between all-Republican and all-Federalist guest lists, Dolley Madison hosted whomever wanted to attend. Besides that, "The White House became a focus for visitors of all nationalities and all classes."[2]

Dolley Madison and architect Benjamin Henry Latrobe took Congress's $5,000 appropriation for Executive Mansion refurbishment (at a time when the president's salary was $25,000) and went to work. They soon put $3,150 into eight mirrors, and eventually they had expended $12,669.31 on furnishings. What was intended to pay for finishing the entire house covered only three rooms: the rooms in which Dolley Madison would entertain. Mirrors of size unrivalled in the United States, fabrics essentially unknown west of the Atlantic, and other expensive touches would make the White House a showcase for the president's wife. She lengthened the social season, formerly six weeks long, to ten—"from the first Wednesday in December until the middle of February." All indications are that while President Madison attended these events, Dolley stood at center stage. She wanted them to be overseen by the famous Gilbert Stuart portrait of President Washington, but Latrobe objected that the dining room ought to be the place for a gallery of presidential portraits. At last Dolley accepted his counsel—and opted to have her drawing room feature a portrait of her instead.[3]

Not only had she indulged herself (and spent beyond her husband's budget) on the house, but Dolley Madison assembled a phantasmagorical wardrobe. Colors, cloths, gems, garments, headdresses, and other touches generally unknown in the U.S.A. found their way onto her person. Her turbans became famous. The refreshments drew negative reviews from many attendees, but no one seems to have been put off by that factor.

Dolley Madison also made another significant change to the way the president conducted public business in his official residence. Jefferson, uncomfortable with slavery, had done what he could to keep his human chattels' household labors out of sight, in the White House as at Monticello.[4] Dolley, while still referring to herself as a Quaker[5] (which should have meant she opposed slavery), moved slavery out into the open in a way calculated to call it to guests' attention. At dinners each guest had an assigned slave at his beck and call,[6] and in the "squeezes" in the large drawing room, "black slaves and possibly white servants" walked around with trays of food and drink for guests' pleasure.[7]

James Madison theoretically could have vetoed these plans if he had been of a mind to. We cannot know how much he knew of Mrs. Madison's relationship to slavery. It seems unlikely that he knew some things, such as a story told by Sally Hemings's son James Madison, whom his family called "Jim-Mad." As Jim-Mad explained to an Ohio newspaper reporter in 1873, Dolley Madison encouraged the pregnant Sally Hemings to name her child "James Madison," in return for which she would give Sally (in his words) "a fine present." "She consented," he continued, "and Mrs. Madison dubbed me by the name I now acknowledge, but like many promises of white folks to the slaves she never gave my mother anything."[8]

Mrs. Madison starred at the first inaugural ball, which was "sponsored by the locals and held in her honor." She appeared in spectacular finery, with abundant pearls—which had just the right combination of intrinsic value and "republican" plainness (as distinguished from "undemocratic diamonds," which had earned Mrs. Merry a scalding rebuke at one public event).[9] Perhaps Dolley Madison was republican, but onlookers commonly referred to her as royalty. One biography describes her in the White House "[p]assing through crowded rooms, like a queen in satin and silk, displaying her pearls and silver, . . . asserting her and, by extension, her husband's right to their place as the nation's leaders."[10] No one ever referred to George and Martha Washington as "the nation's leaders."

James and Dolley surely must have seemed an incongruous pair in large social gatherings. As Paul Jennings, a longtime Madison slave who lived in the White House with them, described the president in his memoir of their time in Washington, "He was very neat, but never extravagant, in his clothes. He always dressed wholly in black—coat, breeches, and silk stockings, with buckles in his shoes and breeches. He never had but one suit at a time. He had some poor relatives that he had to help, and wished to set them an example of economy in the matter of dress." When Paul Jennings's memoir—"the first White House memoir"[11]—was published in 1865, powerful social taboos militated against forthright criticism of Dolley Madison by one of her family slaves. Yet one cannot help but note a certain undercurrent in this account given by the man who, as he went on to explain, "shaved [James Madison] every other day for sixteen years" down to his death.[12] Mrs. Madison's "flamboyant tastes" also extended to a "state carriage made in Philadelphia, a superb reddish brown vehicle trimmed inside with yellow lace, with an 'elegant Cypher' on the door," which "delighted" her.[13] Mrs. Madison made her social rounds in this style, certainly closer to Federalist style of old than to Jefferson's calculated, one might almost say "showy," plainness.

Like his predecessor's second term, most of Madison's presidency would be dominated by problems in foreign policy. Those problems would have beset him in any event, but his range of discretion would be tightly circumscribed by his and Gallatin's devotion to Republican orthodoxy. Maintaining Jefferson's position, Madison insisted on low government expenditures, thus on keeping only a small peacetime military establishment. When Madison's preferred response to difficulties with Britain and/or France, economic coercion, failed to alleviate America's diplomatic problems in the wake of the *Chesapeake-Leopard* Incident, he continued to insist on taking the same approach. The March 1, 1809 Non-Intercourse Act, which prohibited British and French public ships from entering American waters except when they were in extreme circumstances or on public business,[14] reflected Republican policy.

On March 17, 1809, Madison sent a lengthy letter to William Pinkney, his minister in Great Britain.[15] Describing the Non-Intercourse Act as "less operative than was at one time looked for," the president blamed Congress's hesitance to take sterner steps on "aversion to war, . . . inconveniences produced by or charged on the embargo, the hope of favorable changes [that is, French victories] in Europe, the dread of civil convulsions in [New England], and the policy of permitting the discontented to be reclaimed to their duty by losses at sea. . . ." No doubt shaking his head as he scratched out the words, Madison concluded, "Certain it is that no measure was ever adopted by so great a proportion of any public body, which had the hearty concurrence of so small a one. . . ." That it expired in May, just two months away, "must produce an apparent submission to the Foreign Edicts," he fumed, unless this law's operation were extended or something were devised to replace it.

The only alternative to new legislative action, Madison thought, was submission to the French and British decrees. Southerners in particular would be unlikely to tolerate this, though their exasperation with the legislatures of Massachusetts and Connecticut over first bewailing violations of sailors' rights, then alleging that defense of those rights amounted to hostility to New England could only with difficulty be exaggerated. Madison concluded that the New England governments really favored Britain over their own country in the controversy.[16] He surely did not imagine the lengths to which they would go ere his tenure ended.

Though President Madison disliked the Non-Intercourse Act in some of its particulars, he remained convinced that economic coercion could bring one or both of the major European powers to change its policies toward the United States. He therefore received quite unreservedly the news from the new British minister in Washington, David Erskine, that the U.K.'s government wanted to change its posture toward the United States.[17] In early April 1809, barely a month into Madison's tenure, Erskine received instructions that he should extend an offer to compensate the United States for the *Chesapeake-Leopard* Incident and inform Washington that the Cabinet would withdraw its offensive Orders-in-Council in exchange for American consent that the Royal Navy could stop and search American ships en route to France and for the automatic cessation of enforcement of the Non-Intercourse policy against the British Empire.

Madison convened his Cabinet at least once on this matter.[18] His treasury secretary characteristically gave him the best advice, asking whether the president's response should be silent about the fate of the British officer responsible for the attack on the American frigate or mention the matter in passing, and expressing his befuddlement at Erskine's offer to have the Orders-in-Council cease to be operative the following week—which, given the slowness of trans-Atlantic travel, the Briton could only have offered if he knew they were going to cease to be operative in any event. Perhaps, Gallatin guessed, Erskine meant that in case the Non-Intercourse Act ceased to be operative, American ships taken under the Orders-in-Council after that date would be returned.

Madison sloughed off the requirement that America consent to the searches, calling it "insulting," and agreed to the rest. The following Wednesday, April 19, 1809, Madison issued a triumphant proclamation saying that the British minister had informed the U.S. Government that the condition of the Non-Intercourse Act for the restoration of American commerce with Great Britain would be met through the termination of the British Orders-in-Council on June 10, 1809, and therefore American trade with the British Empire could resume on June 11th.[19]

So happy was the president that he had copies of the secretary of state's correspondence with Erskine and the presidential proclamation sent to the governors, among others.[20] He also wrote, on the day that he conceded to one correspondent his predecessor's superiority to himself by various measures, to Jefferson with an evaluation of British motives. For one thing he guessed that the U.K. hoped to entangle America in conflict with France—a goal he thought the Federalists would try to help the British achieve. Britain likely would sidestep this obstacle, he thought, particularly as Russia was suffering under Britain's maritime policy too; better relations with America had their appeal, but Britain needed alliance with Russia. Somehow Madison guessed that Napoleon might conclude that the Floridas ought to be turned over to the U.S.A., "which would present a dilemma not very pleasant."[21]

Jefferson answered that news of the Erskine agreement was "the source of very general joy" in and around Monticello.[22] Calling the Orders-in-Council Britain's "Algerine system" (that is, piracy), the former president held that not "any remaining morality" among Britons but "their unsteadiness under severe trial" had yielded the much-desired result, "But whencesover it comes, I rejoice in it as the triumph of our forbearing & yet persevering system."

Carried away with the country's good fortune, Jefferson told Madison his administration would now be entirely peaceful, and that Napoleon "ought the more to conciliate our good will, as we can be such an obstacle to the new career opening on him in the Spanish colonies. That he would give us the Floridas," he gushed, "to withhold intercourse with the residue of those colonies cannot be doubted." Even this amounted to nothing, because the United States could seize Spanish Gulf Coast colonies in the first moment of a war, and "until a war they are of no particular necessity to us." In order to ensure pacific relations with the Americans, he concluded, the French emperor surely would give up Cuba. Canada naturally falling into America's lap in time, "we should have such an empire for liberty as she has never surveyed since the creation. . . ." Fortunately, he continued breathlessly, "I am persuaded no constitution was ever before so well calculated as ours for extensive empire & self government." In case his fancy did not strike Madison as having overcome him powerfully enough, Jefferson asserted that the Cuban outer ring of the empire for liberty would provide no problem for Republican political economists at all, because "Cuba can be defended by us without a navy"!

Fearing a turn toward military conflict with Britain, the outgoing Congress had provided in January 1809 that the Eleventh Congress should meet for the first time not sometime between late October and early December of that year, but in late May.[23] Madison happily greeted it with the news of the Erskine agreement.[24] In the same vein as Jefferson had plumbed with him, President Madison began his special message to the federal legislature of May 23rd by saying that "it affords me much satisfaction to be able to communicate the commencement of a favorable change, in our foreign relations; the critical state of which induced a Session of Congress at this early period." The Non-Intercourse Act had been met by the British government, he said, with an avowal of intention to resolve the *Chesapeake* matter and to withdraw the offending Orders-in-Council, and so he had announced his intention to legalize commerce with Britain on June 10th. Madison also made clear that Republican policy and disposition had yielded this, the optimal outcome. In a foreshadowing of later policy nearly always overlooked by chroniclers of his administration, Madison told Congress that it should "make such further alterations in the laws, as will more especially protect and foster the several branches of manufacture, which have been recently instituted or extended, by the laudable exertions of our Citizens."

Somewhat startlingly in light of his lack of information about the British government's response to the Erskine agreement, Madison also announced that he had put such of the gunboats as he could in storage and moved to send home the one hundred thousand militiamen organized for federal service under the law of March 1808. He closed this portion of his message by hinting that Congress might move to decommission the four frigates that were to be ready for service by the end of July. The only prudent move he recommended was that Congress should provide funding for completion of the harbor fortification program the government had already undertaken—an easy task if, friction with the British really having ended, the government's books once again returned to balance.

Two and a half months into his first term, Madison had announced the Republican millennium. When next he wrote to Jefferson, it was to tell him that the Essex Junto (chief Federalist organization of Massachusetts, the leading Federalist state) had "[soured] towards England" and "As one proof of their present feelings . . . shew a marked alienation from Erskine," all of which left them "much less disposed than heretofore to render our interests subservient to hers [that is, Britain's]."[25] But the Bay State Federalists' discomfiture would be short-lived.

30

❖ ⚛ ❖

On June 19, Madison received information that Britain seemed to have reneged on its agreement.[1] To Jefferson he wrote of the strange circumstance that the government in Whitehall seemed to have gone back on Erskine's word by a new Order-in-Council dated April 26th, which made an odd picture when combined with Erskine's assurances that he had authority to enter into the agreement he had struck with the Madison administration. Startlingly, Madison remained confident that his diplomatic feat would stand. ("It may be expected, I think that the B. Govt. will fulfil what its Minister has Stipulated. . . .")

That the British foreign minister, George Canning, had rejected Minister Erskine's agreement with the U.S. Government became public knowledge in America by July 22.[2] Secretary of War William Eustis, encountering Erskine in Philadelphia, noted that he still insisted he had had authority to enter into the agreement.[3] President Madison, exposed to considerable embarrassment, found the entire matter no little bit infuriating, besides perplexing. "The conduct of the B. Govt. in protesting the arrangement of its Minister surprizes one in spite of all their examples of folly." Maybe their goal was to trick the Americans into allowing their merchant fleet to head out for Britain and British possessions, and thus avail themselves of American wares, he mused, before "adopt[ing] openly a system of monopoly & piracy"—reserving the European trade to themselves and licensing their ships to seize the cargoes of American ships violating their Rule of 1756. Perhaps, on the other hand, British smugglers had persuaded His Majesty's Government that if Americans continued to be denied access to Napoleon's ports, smuggling would return quite a handsome profit (and considerable tax revenues) to the United Kingdom. "Such an outrage on all decency," Madison fumed, "was never before heard of, even on the shores of Africa."[4]

There might, however, be a simpler explanation for Britain's inexcusable perfidy. Madison had made reference during the negotiations to the imperative that George III agree to punish the admiral responsible for the *Chesapeake-Leopard* Incident further, as "such an example . . . would best comport with what is due from His Brittanic Majesty to his own honor." Supposedly George III received the agreement Erskine had worked out positively—until he got to that.[5] If so, Madison's bold statement, uncharacteristic of him in its lack of political tact, would be among the most momentous errors ever made by a president of the United States.[6]

Madison found himself in a box. Canning's rejection of Erskine's agreement meant that Britain had not revoked its Orders-in-Council, and yet the president had exercised his power under the Non-Intercourse Act to waive its provisions concerning American trade with the British Empire. The obvious step was to impose the act's provisions anew by sending a circular letter to the American tax collectors, calculating on its becoming public. Yet he feared that his "power over the subject of it" ended with the revocation.[7]

He could call upon Congress to revivify the law. Yet the Legislative Branch was not in session. Seeing no alternative, Madison within a couple of weeks issued a proclamation resuscitating the Non-Intercourse Act's prohibition on trade with the British Empire.[8]

Meantime the British had recalled Erskine and sent a new minister to the United States: Francis James Jackson. This notorious figure bore the moral responsibility for the British bombardment of Copenhagen, the capital of neutral Denmark, which Jackson ordered to extort the surrender by that power of its entire navy to the British. In those pre–international law days, when realpolitik guided the major powers' behavior, this unblushing bit of criminality could be undertaken with sanguine impunity. The Madison administration, like the American public generally, could not but see replacement of Erskine for being too eager to reach an accommodation with the United States with Jackson, internationally notorious for having displayed the opposite disposition toward another neutral power, as a signal of the British Cabinet's actual attitude toward America.

With Madison away for the summer at the time Jackson arrived in the District of Columbia in July, Jackson fell into the British habit of hobnobbing with Federalists. This could not but turn out poorly, so far as his mission was concerned. He also seems to have misunderstood Madison's stay in the Piedmont as an incivility to him.[9] Madison rightly inferred that Jackson's standing on ceremony—his refusal to discuss diplomatic matters prior to his formal presentation to Madison—meant that his masters back in England had not charged him with any significant task to accomplish while in America.

Therefore the president decided not to press Jackson regarding his instructions. "From the character of the man, and the temper of his superiors," Madison counseled Secretary of State Smith, "any thing beyond that politeness which explains itself, and is due to ourselves, is more likely to foster insolence than to excite liberality or good will."[10]

The Madisons and the Jacksons became acquainted at last upon the president's return from his summer stay at Montpelier in October, at which time both of the Brits offered relatives back home biting appraisals of their opposite numbers. Minister Jackson judged the president "a plain and rather mean-looking little man," by which he meant that Madison was not up to much, while Mrs. Jackson, of noble Prussian origin, described Dolley in aristocratic French as "*une bonne grosse femme de la classe bourgeoise*" before adding that she was "without distinction either in manners or appearance." Even more cuttingly, Francis Jackson styled Dolley "fat and forty but not fair."[11]

If possible, the relationship went downhill from there.

When Madison returned to Washington, he immediately encountered difficulty with Jackson. Secretary of State Smith met with Jackson on October 4th and October 5th, and Madison concluded from those conversations that the British had sent an emissary without the requisite authority to resolve the outstanding issues. Although not yet sure of it, the president wrote that he expected Jackson to prove "deficient in the diplomatic . . . instructions."[12] (Attorney General Rodney drew the same inference.)[13] Madison therefore decided that further communication with Jackson would be conducted not by personal interviews followed by written messages, but exclusively via written messages. This decision was relayed to Jackson by Smith in a letter that expressed the administration's unhappiness that the U.K. had both disavowed Erskine's agreement and sent a new minister to Washington without an explanation of this decision.[14]

Jackson's manner turned offensive. Madison informed him that it was "more than merely inadmissible" for Jackson to accuse the Americans of having negotiated with Erskine in the knowledge that he was violating his instructions. On November 1st, Smith (or perhaps Madison) upbraided the Briton in writing, describing some of what Jackson had said as "irrelevant and improper allusions . . . inadmissible in the intercourse of a foreign minister with a Government that understands what it owes itself." Finally Jackson was told by a letter of November 8th that "no further communications will be received from you."[15]

On November 11th Smith sent the American minister to the Court of St.

James's, William Pinkney, an explanation of the president's decision to demand Jackson's recall.[16] The president informed the British ministry through his secretary that while Jackson's behavior in Washington had been insupportably insulting, the Americans remained open to "a friendly accommodation," which he said could be reached if Jackson's successor brought "all the authorities and instructions requisite for the complete success of his mission."

Congress turned to the task of adopting some kind of replacement for the Non-Intercourse Act. Speaker of the House Nathaniel Macon, a close friend of John Randolph as well as an ally of President Madison, submitted what came to be known as "Macon's Bill No. 1." It provided that although British and French ships could not come into American ports, British and French goods could. After amending it, the House on March 16, 1810, rejected it.[17] Secretary Smith asserted after he left the Cabinet in 1811 that Madison's ambiguous January 3, 1810, message to Congress, which pointed only to "the necessity of precautionary measures involving expense" in response to "the conduct of foreign Powers towards the United States," helped account for the defeat of Macon's Bill No. 1.[18]

Anyone who found that legislative effort lacking must have been completely unhappy with the follow-up, the so-called Macon's Bill No. 2 (which despite its name was not Macon's handiwork). Napoleon had responded to the Non-Intercourse Act by seizing American ships, and now America had adopted a policy of allowing American ships to carry the goods of both major powers while excluding both powers' ships. In case either France or Britain resumed open trade with the United States, at that point Madison was to cut off trade with the other.[19] As Madison described it, "it [put] our trade on the worst possible footing for France," which had been swept from the seas by the Royal Navy in 1805, "but at the same time, [put] it in the option of her, to revive Non-intercourse agst. England."[20]

Napoleon saw his chance to make sport of the United States. Through his foreign minister, the duc de Cadore, he seemed to make a great concession to the United States with what came to be known as the Cadore Letter. Just as Erskine had, so now Napoleon seemed to fulfill all of the Republicans' foreign policy hopes. He announced the repeal of the Berlin and Milan Decrees, which had excluded American shipping from the greater French Empire's ports, and said that he understood this would lead the British to renounce their Orders-in-Council restricting neutral—that is, chiefly American—shipping and negate their own blockade policy, or that the Americans would, as the American minister reported, "Cause their rights to be respected by the English."[21]

Secretary of the Navy Paul Hamilton sent Madison a New York newspaper including word of the Cadore Letter and the news that the British Cabinet would soon repeal its Orders-in-Council and send a new minister to Washington in late September.[22] Madison therefore rashly issued a proclamation on November 2nd, also signed by Smith, announcing that American trade with France would resume.[23] It seems that he felt sanguine in issuing this proclamation insofar as relations with Britain were concerned because of his ongoing annoyance with Jackson, who had dawdled for several weeks prior to departing, and with various British ministers' behavior toward Minister William Pinkney. "[E]verything," he told Pinkney, "was rendered as offensive as possible by evasions and delays. . . ."[24]

Madison also seems to have decided that in case war proved unavoidable, he preferred a British one to a French one.[25] Perhaps he thought self-respect required that His Majesty's Government's Rule of 1756 and the *Chesapeake-Leopard* Incident be avenged, maybe he had already decided on a military strategy for a British war, perhaps he still held out hope that the French would aid the United States in acquiring former Spanish territory in North America, or maybe, just maybe, the British were right that the president remained a Francophile at heart.[26]

Meanwhile, on October 10, 1810, Americans in Spanish West Florida seized Baton Rouge.[27] Napoleon's displacement of the Bourbon king of Spain, Fernando VII, and installation of his own older brother Joseph Bonaparte in his place touched off a wave of rebellions in Spain's enormous New World empire, where no one recognized Joseph as legitimate successor to the Spanish throne. In the coastal colony between the Mississippi and the Perdido, where Americans outnumbered Spaniards by four to one, Jefferson and Madison's long-standing expectation that the Gulf Coast region eventually would be America's seemed on the verge of fulfillment.

The Americans asked for West Florida to become "an integral and inalienable portion of the United States." When he got the news, Madison issued a proclamation.[28] In it he pointed to the American claim that West Florida was included in the territory obtained by the United States via the Louisiana Purchase. The government had been kept from acting on that claim by "conciliatory views, and by a confidence in the justice of their cause; and in the Success of candid discussion and amicable negotiation with a just and friendly power." Now, however, "a crisis ha[d] at length arrived subversive of the order of things under the Spanish Authorities whereby a failure of the United States to take the said Territory into its possession m[ight] lead to events ultimately contravening the views of both parties"—that is, British intervention.

Besides that worry Madison pointed to constitutional justification for what he was going to do: that "the tranquility and security" of America's adjacent lands were "endangered, and new facilities given to violations of our Revenue and Commercial laws, and of those prohibiting the introduction of Slaves" into the United States; and that in case America took possession of this territory, of which various acts of Congress had been written with possession in mind, America could still participate in "fair and friendly negotiation and adjustment" with Spain. Therefore he had directed Governor C. C. Claiborne of Orleans Territory to take possession of West Florida as part of his territory. The president privately instructed Claiborne not to use force against any Spanish force he might find still in possession of part of the colony, but instead to report the facts to Washington posthaste.[29] Meanwhile Secretary Smith made clear to the French minister in Washington that the U.S.A. would take whatever action was necessary to vindicate its purported right to West Florida.[30] Jefferson urged Representative Eppes that Congress grant Madison authority to seize East Florida as well, so that the British would not grab Pensacola and St. Augustine. Although Congress did indeed give him the authority in case of either a request from East Florida's inhabitants or intervention by a third power, Madison did not get to follow up on it. Americans hoping for Florida annexation would have to await unanticipated events in the Monroe administration.[31]

31

Even as this crisis was resolved to America's benefit, the administration suffered serious setbacks in Congress. Both centered on initiatives advocated by Treasury Secretary Albert Gallatin. First, although Gallatin had urged him to do so, President Madison did not publicly call upon Congress to recharter the Bank of the United States. Perhaps feeling himself to be in a sticky situation due to his having led the charge against the constitutionality of the bill chartering the bank both in the House and in private advice to President George Washington twenty years before, he instead let Gallatin advocate the new bill on Capitol Hill.[1] As historian Robert Rutland explains, Gallatin ". . . looked at the bank as a safe place to deposit government funds, an efficient clearinghouse for tax revenues from the several port collectors' receipts, and a ready source of capital when the government issued bonds to fill gaps between income and payments. . . . As usual, Gallatin was right on every count except the one that mattered most: the need for Republican support. Hard-core Republicans like Senator Smith of Maryland winced every time the Bank was mentioned. . . ."[2]

In the House, Speaker Macon held rumors of Madison's opposition to the bill responsible for the 65–64 vote to postpone a decision on the bank bill. In the Senate, Smith was not alone. Rather the other Invisibles, Leib and Giles, joined fourteen other Republican opponents in thwarting the ten Republicans and seven Federalists voting "aye." Vice President George Clinton explained his tie-breaking "nay" vote in February 20, 1811, remarks laying out the classic Jeffersonian position developed by Secretary of State Jefferson (in the mode of Representative Madison) in 1791: that power to charter a corporation "is a high attribute of sovereignty . . . not . . . derivative by implication, but primary and independent"—which is to say, it could not be teased out of the Necessary and Proper Clause or the General Welfare Clause, but would have been among the enumerated powers if it had been granted to Congress in the Constitution at all.[3] Congress also at about this time rejected Gallatin's request that import duties be raised to offset revenues lost due to the policy of nonintercourse with the British.

By this point the Smiths, senator and secretary of state, had rendered Madison's efforts to maintain an able, effective Cabinet impossible. The secretary's ineptitude posed the chief problem, but Senator Smith's intermittent efforts to thwart the administration's legislative initiatives, when considered in combination with Secretary Smith's sabotage of Madison's diplomatic efforts, had become insupportable. Top members of Congress, recognizing the problem, told Madison he had to be rid of Robert Smith. They included Speaker Macon and William Crawford, among others. To underscore the need for prompt action, Gallatin tendered his resignation.[4]

Essential to the Cabinet reorganization these men and Gallatin had in mind was that Madison's friendship with James Monroe had been reestablished.

Superior diplomat to his secretary of state, Madison thought to ease Smith out with an offer of the post of minister to Russia.[5] We have a detailed account from the president's perspective because upon seeing Smith's angry account in the press, the chief executive decided to write out a careful, detailed account of what had led them to that point. As Madison told it, he began by assuring Smith that he had let the intention simmer to ensure that his "communication might have the character of being not the result of any sudden impulse, but of a deliberate regard to public considerations, and official duty. . . ." He next told Smith, if his account is to be believed, that although Cabinet deliberations had been congenial, accounts of them heard out-of-doors often struck a different chord, and "this practice, as brought to my view, was exclusively chargeable on him." To Smith's denial Madison responded with reference to "facts and circumstances, brought to my knowledge, from so many sources and with so many corroborations, that it was impossible to shut my mind against them."

Madison went on to tell Smith that though the secretary had accepted Macon's Bill and the nonintercourse law in Cabinet discussion as the best likely to be obtained from Congress at a time when something must be done, "his conversations & conduct out of doors, had been entirely of a counteracting nature; that it was generally believed that he was in an unfriendly disposition personally and officially. . . ." To top it all off, "with those of a certain temper, . . . [he] had gone so far as to avow a disapprobation of the whole policy of commercial restrictions, from the Embargo throughout."

We ought not from the humiliating exchange to take the impression that the abashed secretary of state had been always in the wrong, as a policy matter, when he let people outside Madison's official circle know that he disapproved of administration policy. Thus, for example, one prominent newspaper editor had in January 1811 counseled Madison to await news that Napoleon actually had revoked his commercial decrees before the United States revoked its.[6] As we have seen, Madison's precipitation cost America many merchant ships, which were seized by France in Europe.

Along the way Madison also mentioned that he, the president, had given Smith aid in performing the duties of the secretarial office. In fact he told him that "it was an imperious consideration for a change in the Departmt. of State, that whatever talents he might possess, he did not as he must have found by experience, possess those adapted to his station; that this had thrown the business more into my hands than was proper," and that this added burden had become too much for the president to bear. To Smith's denial Madison responded with a harsher evaluation of his performance.

After a bit more of such back-and-forth, Madison at last told Smith that he wanted to make him minister to the Russian court. Smith answered that he would prefer the Court of St. James's, and when Madison swatted down that idea, he alluded to a likely pending opening on the Supreme Court. This hint too Madison rejected. The talk turned once again to Russia. In Madison's account his explanation to Smith of the grounds on which he favored this idea cannot have seemed to the secretary anything other than lukewarm. Now, however, Smith accepted. The two of them agreed on a date when the nomination was to be made public—before which Smith returned to Madison, accused him of leaking to the public the idea that this appointment was a palliative for being sacked as secretary of state, and said he no longer wanted the Russian post. Madison told Smith that one last point had occurred to him: while Smith's brother the senator had uniformly opposed the administration's foreign policy, thus leading the public to infer that the secretary of state must too, Madison had never ascribed any motive other than patriotism to the senator. Former secretary Smith left Washington on April 6, 1811, and a couple of days later, he wrote a friend a letter referring to "the enfeeble[d] mind of our panic-struck President." By the end of June, a pamphlet titled *Robert Smith's Address to the People of the United States* laid out his critique of Madison. None of this augured well for Madison's relations with Congress.

At last Madison could substantially upgrade his Cabinet by replacing a low-grade secretary of state. To do so he turned to his once and future friend James Monroe. Since playing the key role in the younger man's election by the General Assembly to the Virginia governorship and urging a reluctant

Jefferson to forgo seeking a constitutional amendment legitimating (if it had been illegitimate) Monroe and Livingston's Louisiana Purchase, Madison had, recall, played a part in President Jefferson's determination not to submit the Monroe-Pinkney Treaty to the Senate for ratification. Urged to do so by friends such as John Taylor of Caroline and John Randolph of Roanoke, Monroe took this as an affront—such an affront as to justify allowing the Old Republicans to put forward Monroe's candidacy in opposition to Madison's (spearheaded in Virginia by William Branch Giles, no less) for president in 1808.[7] He thought the Embargo Act debacle proved the wisdom of the Monroe-Pinkney Treaty, which he lamented that Jefferson (no doubt, he felt certain, at Madison's urging) had rejected.[8]

Jefferson lamented this all the while.[9] He wrote Monroe telling him to remember his old friends, as the disputants' coadjutors were likely to cause friction between them; he also assured him that Madison had ever borne him friendship.[10] Monroe, who had rejected the governorship of Louisiana Territory as beneath him, finally bowed to the will of the General Assembly, which made him governor again. It seems perhaps the president had intended this to happen, as he appointed Governor John Tyler to a federal judgeship, which cleared the way for Delegate Monroe.[11]

As these events occurred, a prominent member of the Virginia Senate, Chapman Johnson, wrote Monroe seeking reassurance. Though they knew Monroe as a devout Republican, the senators also knew he had allowed his name to be put forth as an alternative to Madison's in the 1808 presidential contest. Therefore, though he had no doubts, Johnson found that some friends of the Madison administration would like reassurances before they returned him to the chief executive's post.[12] A stickler for republican principle, Monroe replied that though happy with the "spirit of amity and conciliation" evident in his letter, and though he had no personal difficulties with the president, "a disposition" "to approve without examination and conviction every measure of any administration . . . cannot be indulged and acted on, without a surrender of the first principles of free government. . . ." "All that any administration can desire, of a free and rational people," he insisted, was "a rational and manly support of its conduct, when it bears the test of impartial investigation, by the standard of the constitution, and by its tendency to promote the public welfare." He would offer this to the United States Government, and he would expect no other type of support from Virginians.[13] As Monroe explained to a friend, by writing this letter he had "conceded nothing, in any one respect."[14]

These quasi-assurances marked a substantial break with his close ally of recent years, John Randolph of Roanoke—the leader of the Tertium Quids and chief instigator of Monroe's 1808 presidential candidacy. Not wanting to be seen in the company of the Madison administration's most vociferous critic, Monroe replied to a message from Randolph with a message of his own, then sent Monroe's son-in-law, John Hay, to speak to the congressman.[15]

Randolph, evidently irked that Monroe had not taken time to meet with him, essentially accused the governor of betraying him and their friends. Referring to "The habits of intimacy which have existed between us," the congressman mentioned rumors Monroe had sold out their principles in his quest to be elected governor of the Commonwealth. This had involved "unbecoming compliances with the Members of the Assembly, not excepting your bitterest personal enemies." Among expedients to which Monroe was supposed to have sunk, Randolph continued, were "explanations . . . of the differences heretofore subsisting between yourself & Administration, which amount to a dereliction of the ground which you took after your return from England, & even of your warmest personal friends." This, Randolph said, had made very bad impressions not only upon Randolph, but upon others Monroe had counted "among those most strongly attached to you."

Monroe's chief political confidant, his son-in-law George Hay, arrived at Randolph's lodgings just as Randolph finished reading two letters Monroe had sent to John Taylor of Caroline, another prominent 1808 backer of Monroe's. The first of them, which was quite lengthy, had two sections: the first and longer one, which described Monroe's reasons for being discontented with the Jefferson administration's foreign policy from the time Pinkney was sent to join him in negotiating with the British; and a briefer section explaining that although a minority grouping might occasionally arise in a majority party, the people's expectation that congressmen allied with the president would support him meant that in the end, they must return to routinely supporting the president. Those who had supported him in 1808 had the gratification of knowing that the embargo policy's failure had vindicated the Monroe-Pinkney Treaty, he continued. "To us who have suffered by unmerited suspicion and abuse," he concluded, "a fair opportunity is offer'd, to evince the purity and disinterestedness of our conduct." They should not gloat over their vindication, as their country had been injured in the process.

The second of the Monroe letters to Taylor that Randolph read dealt in part with a more historically significant matter. While the first of them showed that Monroe intended as a matter of principle—or so he cast it—to return to the Jeffersonian fold, this one found him considering the possibility of an America without political parties. He clearly thought this to be a worthy aim, though the ongoing existence of the Federalist Party, the continuing political activity of its leaders, meant that "keep[ing] the republican party in existence" remained necessary. With ongoing Federalist machinations, "there never was greater reason . . . for the preservation of the republican party, than at this time." The period of the embargo found New England Federalists so desperate that "had the federal party gained the complete ascendancy there, and had the government perserverd in its policy, . . . its leaders would have pushed their fortune to its greatest extremity." New Englanders thought economic coercion harmful to "their shipping, their fisheries, [and] their trade," and they did not "believe that they [would] ever thrive by systems of privation." Happily the perspective he had gained since had made clear to Monroe the necessity of relaxing the policy insofar as it affected New England.

In the wake of Hay's visit, Randolph wrote Monroe that he would always remember the personal kindness Monroe had done him by seeing to his handicapped nephew's British education and to insist that he would always "rejoice to hear of your personal prosperity." That he would no longer care for Monroe's political success went unspoken. Political Manichean that he was, Randolph that night jotted only four words in his diary: "Richmond, James Monroe, Traitor." The other leading Old Republicans, Taylor and Littleton Waller Tazewell, happily endeavored to escort their confreres into the Madison administration's good graces.[16] This was the ground on which Monroe entered upon his second stint as governor. He no doubt took it, as his friend Jefferson characterized it in a congratulatory letter, as "bearing testimony to the fidelity of [his] principles before the Republicans of the union generally."[17]

A few days later Madison asked Virginia (state) Senator Joseph Brent to sound out Governor Monroe regarding his willingness to become secretary of state. Brent told Monroe he had already relayed his belief that Monroe would be willing and that although he could not promise it, he was certain Monroe would be appointed as soon as his answer was given. Immediately upon receiving this news on March 13, 1811, Monroe wrote to Tazewell asking his advice. "The removal of the current incumbent, and the race of pigmy associates, who are combined with him, in a pestilent system of policy" was of course desirable, but Monroe worried that by entering the Cabinet, he would merely associate himself with a line of policy it was too late to change, thus damaging his own reputation without conferring any benefit upon the country. Too, he feared that leaving the governorship only a few days after accepting it would give the wrong impression. Therefore, he said, "The bias of my mind is against it."[18]

Tazewell hurried to write back that of course Monroe must accept the post. He likely thought it remarkable that so soon after the break with Randolph, thus Monroe's evident abandonment of the Tertium Quids, they were now to see their figurehead elevated to the second post in the government. He did say, however, that in case Monroe did accept the offer, he should condition his acceptance on the principles in foreign policy for which he was known to stand, which "are the result of much reflection & experience, and therefore will not probably be changed." Being known to have insisted on this condition would stand Monroe in good stead, Tazewell noted, whether he was taken into the Cabinet on that basis or not. If the measures Monroe favored were adopted, he would be directing the administration's chief policies—"in fact, altho' not in name, the President, & must hereafter inevitably succeed to the name also, provided the issues of your Counsels are prosperous." Tazewell hoped that the arrangement with Britain a Secretary Monroe could achieve would stand America in as good stead as if the Monroe-Pinkney Treaty had been ratified.

Perhaps such a British adjustment would lead to war with France, but Tazewell thought prudence could avert it. He also thought that the country had a right to expect Monroe to take this position, in which his weight on the side of good policy would help Madison, always disposed to do good, fend off the bad counsel by which he had sometimes been misled. To refuse the post would "give a death blow" to Monroe's career. Virginians, having put Monroe in the governor's mansion in anticipation of the good he could do there, surely would not resent his departing it in expectation of doing greater good in Washington.[19]

Monroe consulted other political allies as well. Besides Randolph, who criticized the idea, they sided with Tazewell.[20] He next drafted a letter accepting the offer, ran it by Tazewell, and sent it to Brent. It said essentially what Monroe and Tazewell had agreed it should: that Monroe recognized the crisis at which the nation's affairs had arrived, had always worked well with and respected Gallatin and Madison, and still held Madison in high esteem, and that he only thought he could enter upon this new role in case the government's policy was not already set in stone.[21]

Madison's response, dated two days later, said that Monroe's services would be needed for a short time starting in two weeks, after which he would be free to take a holiday.[22] Monroe answered that he would be happy to accept the post if Madison understood that he had thought in 1806 that America ought "to make an accomodation with England, the great maritime power, even on moderate terms, rather than hazard war, or any other alternative.

On that opinion," as Madison perfectly well knew, "I acted afterwards, while I remain'd in office, and I own that I have since seen no cause to doubt its soundness." Besides that, Madison could solve the ticklish problem Monroe faced in Richmond by sending Monroe a note explaining why his services were needed in Washington and in what capacity so that he could lay it before the General Assembly.[23] Madison answered that the general policy of trying to make peace with the great powers, "or with either, as leading to a settlement with the other; or that failing, as putting us on better ground against him," had been the general object of the U.S. Government since 1800. While there might be disagreement about specifics "even among those most agreed in the same general views," this would be the Executive's position going forward. The main bones of contention between America and Whitehall—"the *Chesapeake*, the orders in Council, and Blockades"—had all arisen since 1806, anyway.[24] Monroe then moved with his wife, Elizabeth, and daughter Maria to the District of Columbia, where he accepted a recess appointment on April 6th. Once Congress convened, the Senate, receiving a regular nomination on November 13th, confirmed the appointment (despite dilatory measures by Giles) unanimously (yes, including Giles) on November 25th.[25] (Perhaps worthy of note is that Virginia Council of State President George. W. Smith succeeded to the governorship upon Monroe's resignation. He was elected to a full term when Monroe's expired, was sworn in to that on December 5th, and so died in the great Richmond Theater Fire three weeks later.[26] Madison's appointment may have saved Monroe's life, then, although Elizabeth Monroe famously did not enjoy socializing, so it is possible the two of them would not have been at the theater that night even had James still been governor.)

⊹ ⌑ ⊹

While these events transpired, President Madison took the opportunity presented by two bills Congress presented for his signature to instruct the legislators and their constituents about the proper construction of the First Amendment's Establishment Clause.[1] By the first of the two bills, titled "An Act incorporating the protestant Episcopal Church in the Town of Alexandria in the District of Columbia" (Alexandria, recall, was originally part of the federal district), Congress had undertaken to incorporate into federal law various rules governing the parish thus created, "and," in Madison's words, "comprehending even the election and removal of the Minister of the same." The church in question "would be so far a religious establishment by law," particularly in light of the statute's making its "injunctions & prohibitions" subject to be "enforced by the penal consequences applicable to a violation of them according to the local law." Not only did it violate the Establishment Clause in this way, he concluded, but the bill's provision entrusting the church with power to support the poor and educate poor children "would be a precedent for giving to religious Societies as such, a legal agency in carrying into effect a public and civil duty." Presented with these objections, the House did not override Madison's veto.

The second of these veto messages concerned "An act for the relief of Richard Turvin, William Coleman, Edwin Lewis, Samuel Mims, Joseph Wilson, and the Baptist Church at Salem Meeting House, in the Mississippi Territory." Madison explained simply that in reserving public land for the Baptist Church at Salem Meeting House, "the Bill . . . comprises a principle and precedent for the appropriation of funds of the United States, for the use and support of Religious Societies" in violation of the Establishment Clause. Again the House did not override Madison's veto, but instead passed the bill again absent the offending section.

What Monroe may not have realized when he accepted the foreign minister's position was exactly how weak a position the United States was in. Treasury Secretary Albert Gallatin, realizing that military conflict likely would follow abandonment of the economic coercion policy, wrote to Representative John W. Eppes of Virginia, Chairman of the Committee on Ways and Means, on January 28, 1811, recommending that he see to a hike in the tariff. Eppes's committee reported a bill to do so, but the House never acted on it.[2]

Bereft of money, Congress cut military spending. It shaved the War Department's appropriations from $4.7 million in 1808 to "about $3,100,000" in 1809–1810, then to "barely $3,000,000" in 1811. Naval appropriations went from $3 million in 1809 to $1.86 million in 1811. As March 1811 dawned, the House considered a bill authored by Senator William Crawford, R-GA, authorizing the president to take fifty thousand volunteers. Henry Adams, after noting that "[t]he House, without a division, indefinitely postponed the bill," concludes his discussion of these matters this way: "and thus refusing to do more business of any kind, toward midnight of Sunday, March 3rd, the Eleventh Congress expired, leaving behind it, in the minds of many serious citizens, the repute of having brought Government to the last stage of imbecility before dissolution."

Meanwhile two Supreme Court seats had opened up. Here President Madison had the opportunity to steer the court, which had been entirely Federalist when Jefferson took office, but he made little of it. Quite the contrary, one of his appointments went on to dog Jeffersonian constitutionalism ever after.

First to go was Samuel Chase. Though a member of the court and not averse to dissenting, he had kept his politics private since his 1805 impeachment trial.[3] Yet, an uber Federalist to the end, he wrote admiring letters complaining of Jeffersonian political hegemony even to the ardent Timothy Pickering, the Hamiltonian secretary of state who had forced John Adams's hand rather than resign when exposed as a Hamiltonian taking Hamilton's advice behind the president's back.[4]

Madison's choice to succeed Chase, Gabriel Duvall, like Chase a Marylander, proved an eminently undistinguished justice. Apparently Duvall came to the Republican federal leadership's attention as "an early supporter of Jefferson," which is what—according to a leading authority—recommended him for the Supreme Court.[5] In nearly a quarter century as a justice, Duvall left "no evidence that [he] contributed intellectually to the Marshall Court," though he proved a reliable ally of Chief Justice John Marshall. Not for nothing is he considered to have been one "of the 'silent' Justices of the Marshall Court's cohesive years." "Even the few opinions he did write are not memorable: almost none involved major cases, and none was more than a few pages in length."[6]

If Supreme Court appointments' purpose is to ensure that the appointing president's and Senate's constitutional philosophy—in this case, James Madison's and congressional Republicans' constitutional philosophy—comes to be reflected in the work product of that court, Madison's other choice for a vacancy that arose in 1811 may have been the worst selection in history. Joseph Story proved not merely a reliable vote in John Marshall's pocket, but the other half of a Supreme Court partnership similar to—though opposed to—Madison's political partnership with Thomas Jefferson.

Madison faced difficult constraints in replacing Justice William Cushing. As justices in those days "rode circuit," he needed another Massachusettsian—a lawyer who knew Massachusetts law—for Cushing's seat. Republicans who fit the bill in the heart of Federalism were as rare as hen's teeth. One name that came up was that of Salem's Joseph Story, who had briefly been a congressman. Hearing of Story's candidacy, Jefferson wrote to persuade Madison to reject it. He referred to Story as "unquestionably a Tory."[7]

What had irked Jefferson so was Congressman Story's unwillingness to follow the administration line in the closing months of Jefferson's presidency. As Jefferson told it, repeal of the embargo had resulted from Representative Story's influence over fellow Republicans, which was enough to give the House's few Federalists an anti–Embargo Act majority. "I ascribe all to this one pseudo-republican, Story," Jefferson recalled. After hearing from Story, several Republicans were supposed to have decided the choice was "repeal or civil war" and so chosen "the fatal measure of repeal." Thus nonintercourse had come to be, which, fumed Jefferson, "has reduced us to a low standing in the eyes of the world." Back in Massachusetts, Story actually had vindicated the embargo against Federalist attacks, "eulogising Mr. Jefferson and his administration," but Jefferson did not know that. The leading Story biographer describes Story as having in the waning days of Jefferson's tenure "despaired that the whim and stubbornness of a president who refused to lead should have reduced foreign policy to a question of personal vanity, which the debate over the repeal date finally became." Like Jefferson, Story thought of the embargo as a temporary expedient—a means of coercing the great powers into treating America better or a shield behind which military preparations could be made—and he did not change his opinion when Jefferson, loath to go to war, decided to keep it longer than Story judged reasonable. Even then,

Story favored a June 1st repeal over the humiliating March 4th (final day of the president's term) Congress finally chose.[8]

More important than those facts by far is the effect his congressional experience had on Story. In short it persuaded him that republican politics did "bumbling work," and that "lawyers, judges, the courts, and the common law were a corrective to" "the pathology of party government." Story, in short, "chose the science of the law" over republicanism.[9]

The Story selection would be momentous. It is a clear example of the importance of chance in history, because Story was Madison's fourth choice for the post. Levi Lincoln did not want the job; the Senate rejected Alexander Wolcott's nomination; John Quincy Adams, who was in St. Petersburg at the time, said no even though the Senate had already confirmed his appointment; and at last came Story.[10] He eventually became the anti-Jeffersonians' second recourse, the right-hand man to John Marshall, whom he esteemed above all others. Story's enormously long tenure as a justice, from 1811 to 1845, was virtually the same length as Marshall's. While the important decisions he wrote were necessarily less numerous, Marshall taking virtually all of the key ones for himself, Story did write the pivotal nationalist opinion for the court in *Martin v. Hunter's Lessee* (1816), on which more below.

Also important, Story served as the first professor of law at Harvard University, where he trained numerous of the nineteenth century's most important lawyers and wrote several classic legal treatises. This meant that his views came to dominate the everyday work of attorneys all over the country. His treatise on the U.S. Constitution remains influential. Most important, Joseph Story's preference for judge-made law over legislation and his extreme nationalism could not have been more at odds with Republican dogma. He knew that and did not try to hide it.

The Congress that convened on November 4, 1811, marked a generational shift in the American republic's leadership. Notable additions to the House of Representatives included Tennessee's Felix Grundy, former senator Henry Clay of Kentucky, and South Carolina's Langdon Cheves and John C. Calhoun, among others. Though Republican, these men generally came into the House bent on confrontation with the British. Not for them further legislation like Macon's Bill No. 2. No more reductions in military expenditures. They would lead in shaping American policy for four decades to come. In their day as in this, Clay, Calhoun, and their colleague Daniel Webster generally were regarded as more significant historical figures than all but a couple of presidents between Monroe and Abraham Lincoln.

Clay set the new tone when, in response to a point of order, he ordered John Randolph to remove his hunting dogs from the House floor—a step no preceding speaker of the House had dared to take. Randolph tamely obliged. The Kentuckian would be a new kind of speaker: one who dominated the House's policy-making efforts. Three times—in 1850, in 1833, and, as we shall see, in 1819—Clay used his parliamentary expertise to cobble together compromises of major problems that had divided the Congress so severely as to seem irresoluble.

The general attitude of these young House upstarts was that the offenses the British had inflicted on the United States could no longer be tolerated. They were spoiling for a fight. The president, though perhaps not enthused about it, thought one likely in the offing. This explained his decision to call Congress back into session earlier than had been scheduled. By this point Madison had had enough of the absurd diplomatic situation in which the country found itself. Apparently his chief advisor, Gallatin, had to rein him in, else his State of the Union message would have been too strident.[11] On the other hand, even as war approached, Gallatin continued to insist on maintaining only a pared-back navy; after explaining that substantial expenditure in that area would result in the government's borrowing at 8 percent instead of 6 percent, he counseled that privateers be encouraged and that the government focus its efforts in the War Department. If reading this did not remind Madison of the feckless Smith, perhaps it should have.

Madison's State of the Union Address of November 5, 1811, made clear that the president had reached a breaking point. Years of patience with Britain and France had availed him naught. Instead a succession of legislative enactments intended to bring one or, optimally, both of the great powers to respect what he saw as America's basic rights, rights integral to the United States' independence, had failed to achieve their purpose. Madison's private secretary from White House days, Edward Coles, looking back on the years 1811 and 1812 many years later, told William Cabell Rives, a former U.S. senator and Madison biographer, that "it was congenial alike to the life and character of Mr. Madison that he should be reluctant to go to war . . . [a] savage and brutal manner of settling disputes among nations." However, he held that Britain's July 1811 decision not to rescind the Orders-in-Council unless America first made substantial concessions "closed the door to peace in Mr. Madison's opinion." Somewhat inconsistently Coles also blamed the War Hawks for both insisting on war without adequate preparation and denying the usefulness of new diplomatic initiatives.[12]

On April 5, 1811, both Houses of Congress heard President Madison's Annual Message.[13] Much of the address he devoted to a description of American foreign relations, particularly as they related to Great Britain. When last Congress met, he said, the evident withdrawal of the Berlin and Milan Decrees had given hope that the British too might establish a trading system more friendly to America. This hope, he said, had been disappointed. Instead "the orders were . . . put into more rigorous execution." Until France allowed neutral carriers to take British goods into territory it controlled, Britain would respond to America's Nonimportation Act with reciprocal exclusion. Besides that, "indemnity and redress for other wrongs, have continued to be withheld." Madison next conceded that contrary to expectation, France had not allowed America to trade freely with its territory either, nor had it shown any sign of intending "to restore the great amount of American property, seized and condemned, under Edicts; which, though not affecting our neutral relations, . . . were . . . founded in such unjust principles, that the reparation ought to have been prompt and ample." France's unexpected regulation of American trade might bring the administration to have to reciprocate toward her too. A minister plenipotentiary had been sent to France to sound the emperor's government out. Britain in particular, Madison said, had requited American attempts to move relations into a better track not with measures to resolve legitimate grievances, but with "war on our lawful commerce" on "the threshold of our Territory."

Then came the climax of the message. In light of these facts, Madison said, "Congress will feel the duty of putting the United States into an armour, and an attitude demanded by the crisis, and corresponding with the national spirit and expectations." Greater attention needed to be paid to smuggling, and something must be done to insure American manufactures' continued success once the present scenario of commercial restriction passed.

Madison noted that the government had paid down its debt substantially in the past year and urged Congress to prepare its fiscal house for whatever loans might prove necessary in the coming year. He closed with a prayer for "the blessing of Heaven on our beloved Country" in whatever measures might prove necessary.

Madison also referred in his annual message to ongoing developments in Spain's New World empire. By this point the U.S. Government had received communications from Venezuela asking that America recognize the government in Caracas. Madison told Congress it ought to look to all of "the great communities, which occupy the southern portion of our own hemisphere, and extend into our neighbourhood." America's "deep interest" should be prompted by "an enlarged philanthropy, and an enlightened forecast." In response a special congressional committee issued a statement that once they were independent, Congress and the Executive would establish "with them, as sovereign and independent States, such amicable relations and commercial intercourse as may require their Legislative authority."[14]

33

⊹ ⊛ ⊹

n November 7 Madison met with a delegate from Venezuela, Telesfora de Orea. Telesfora had given Monroe a copy of Venezuela's declaration of independence and asked for diplomatic recognition.[1] Soon after this Secretary of State Monroe wrote to the United States' ministers in Britain, France, Denmark, and Russia with a statement of the administration position regarding this matter.[2] He said that "A Revolution" had begun "in the Spanish provinces, South of the United States." Madison had proffered friendly sentiments to delegations from some of those provinces, though he had not recognized them as independent. Monroe's purpose, he concluded, was to instruct the ministers to endeavor to bring European countries to recognize these Spanish provinces as independent—both for their benefit and for America's. Perhaps surprisingly the French minister in Washington told Monroe that Napoleon's government would cooperate in this. The minister, Louis Sérurier, seems to have believed that Napoleon wanted American ships to be used to arm the Latin American revolutionaries—an odd deduction, as the reason they had moved toward independence was Napoleon's dominance of Spain.[3] Likely Napoleon judged that if not independent, the New World Spanish colonies' weight would be on the anti-French side in the Peninsular War.

As these events transpired, word had not yet arrived in Washington of extremely important developments in the Northwest (today's Midwest).[4] On November 7, 1811, the territorial governor of Indiana, William Henry Harrison, crushed a force of Indians in the Battle of Tippecanoe. Tecumseh, who, under the inspiration of his brother Tenskwatawa, aka the Prophet, had endeavored to unite Indians from Georgia to the Great Lakes against American expansion, was away trying to recruit Deep South Indian peoples into his pan-Indian resistance movement, but the Prophet was there. Sixty-eight of Harrison's frontiersmen died in the skirmish, and the governor's force took "90 fusees and rifles from the enemy, most of them new and of English manufacture." Americans generally, and their political leaders in Washington specifically, scented British policy in this.[5] Hostility among the Indians Tecumseh had recruited and was trying to recruit would be an important element of American foreign relations in the coming year.

Secretary Monroe confided to the American minister in Britain, Jonathan Russell, that the United States had been brought to a choice between "abandoning their Commerce" and "resorting to other means more likely to obtain a respect for their rights. Between these alternatives," he said, "there can be little cause for hesitation." The government, he said, was going to fill the ranks of the army, then recruit ten thousand more. It was also going to authorize American merchant ships to arm for their own defense—a step sure to lead to war with Britain. America still preferred to learn of a reversal of Britain's American policy, and Russell should call these facts to the British government's attention.[6]

Meanwhile Congress slowly turned in the direction the War Hawks urged. Henry Clay charged Representative John C. Calhoun with leadership of the Committee on Foreign Affairs, and the Carolinian intended to make a complete change. On November 29, 1811, the committee reported six resolutions to the House: that the Executive ought immediately to recruit as many soldiers as existing law contemplated, the bounty of pay and lands to be increased; that ten thousand more regulars ought to be recruited, again with a bounty of land; that the president be authorized to recruit fifty thousand volunteer reserves; that the president should be authorized to call out militia units as needed; that all of the navy's ships ought to be put in seagoing shape; and that merchantmen should be authorized to arm for self-defense.[7]

By this point in his young congressional career, Calhoun had already come to certain conclusions about the president. Although a brilliant and "amiable" man, Madison "has not I fear the commanding talents, which are necessary to command those about him. He permits division in his cabinet. He reluctantly gives up the system of peace." Yet perhaps the clear vector of developments would draw the chief executive along. "The Embargo is certainly a decisive stept. It is understood to be the prelude to war. I do not expect Congress will wait its termination to declare war."

Randolph of Roanoke intervened in the discussion to lay out his objections.[8] Here we have an illustration of the reasons why, on hearing Mr. Randolph was up, people rushed from all over the District of Columbia to hear. Along the way he pilloried the majority for its evident abandonment of the principles on which the Republican Party originally stood, saying:

I know not how gentlemen, calling themselves republicans, can advocate such a war. What was their doctrine in 1798–9, when the command of the army, that highest of all possible trusts in any government, be the form what it may, was reposed in the bosom of the Father of his country! the sanctuary of a nation's love! The only hope that never came in vain? When other worthies of the revolution, Hamilton, Pinckney, and the younger Washington, men of tried patriotism, of approved conduct and value, of untarnished honor, held subordinate command under him? Republicans were then unwilling to trust a standing army even to his hands who had given proof that he was above all human temptation. Where now is the revolutionary hero to whom you are about to confide this sacred trust?

Randolph thundered that James Wilkinson, the chief general in the American army, could not be compared to Washington; he called him "an acquitted felon." "What! *Then* you were unwilling to vote an army, when such men as have been named held high command! When Washington himself was at the head."

Randolph scoffed at the *causus belli* the Republican majority had in mind, demanding to know, "Will you say that your provocations were less then than now, when your direct commerce was interdicted, your ambassadors hooted with derision from the French court, tribute demanded, actual war waged upon you?" Then, in reference to his hearty few fellow Old Republicans, he noted that, "Those who opposed the army then, were, indeed, denounced as partisans of France, as the same men, some of them at least, are now held up as the advocates of England, those firm and undeviating republicans, who then dared, and now dare, to cling to the ark of the Constitution, to defend it even at the expense of their fame rather than surrender themselves to the wild projects of mad ambition!"

Insightful in his fury, Randolph turned to the psychology of power that had been preached by Jeffersonians when out of power in the 1790s. "There is a fatality, Sir," he insisted, "attending plenitude of power. Soon or late, some mania seizes upon its possessors; they fall from the dizzy height, through the giddiness of their own heads. Like a vast estate, heaped up by the labor and industry of one man which seldom survives the third generation, power gained by patient assiduity, by a faithful and regular discharge of its attendant duties, soon gets above its own origin. Intoxicated with their own greatness, the federal party fell. Will not the same causes produce the same effects now as then?"

Randolph would live to hear Federalists making the same prognostications and pleading the same moral case—but also to see fate treat Britain and America in the most surprising way. In 1812, however, unlike in days of old, few followed him.

Speaker Henry Clay took to the well of the House on December 31, 1811, and in a lengthy speech laid out for all the world to hear his understanding of the government's situation and the reasons why he thought the time had come for war.[9] This performance of the young speaker demonstrated the rhetorical ability and patriotic ardor that would help keep him at the very top of the American political elite for decades to come. He ranged across all of the outstanding issues, in the process knocking down objections to the Calhoun Committee's report raised mainly by John Randolph. The House had been discussing the question whether it ought to add fifteen or twenty-five thousand men to the army, and the speaker began by saying he favored the larger figure.

Clay reasoned that since one must in those days count on about one-third of total manpower to be unavailable due to "desertion, sickness, & other incidents to which raw troops are peculiarly exposed," since the likely American military objective, Quebec, probably would be defended by "between 7 and 8 thousand regular troops," and since the besieging force would need to be at least "double the force of the besieged," twenty-five thousand amounted to the minimum force to do the job.

Clay also pointed out to his countrymen the folly of "trusting too confidently on a calculation, the basis of which was treason." Absent Canadian assistance, for the army to proceed into Lower Canada would require garrisoning the conquered city first—which again would require manpower. American volunteers, he said, would not be fit "for the manning and garrisoning of forts." In short Clay gave the House multiple reasons to conclude that twenty-five thousand regular soldiers would be a bare minimum.

Clay noted that the purpose of these preparations was "war, and war with Great Britain. It had been supposed by some gentlemen," he continued, "improper to discuss publicly so delicate a question." As a newspaper reporter had Clay saying, "He did not feel the impropriety. It was a subject in its nature incapable of concealment." American war preparations could not be hidden anyway. What use could England make of its knowledge? "She may, indeed, anticipate us, and commence the war. But that is what she is in fact doing, and she can add but little to the injury which she is inflicting." He seemed to be warming to the idea of a declaration of war as he enumerated the losses America suffered: "commerce, character, a nation's best treasure, honor!"

America lost $10 million per year to the effects of the Orders-in-Council, Clay said. More onerously, he "could not . . . overlook the impressment of our seamen; an aggression upon which he never reflected without feelings of indignation. . . . The orders in council were pretended to have been reluctantly adopted as a measure of retaliation. The French decrees, their alleged basis, are revoked. England resorts to the expedient of denying the fact of the revocation. . . ." And now Augustus John Foster, the British minister to the U.S.A., demands that America secure passage of British manufactures into Europe.

Parrying one of Randolph's criticisms (which was also popular among Federalists), Clay noted that "England is said to be fighting for the world" before asking, "shall we, it is asked, attempt to weaken her exertions?" The British cause would indeed be admirable, he answered, if it were being pursued "[b]y scrupulous observance of the rights of others." It then would "command the sympathies of the world." Echoing Jefferson's reference to Napoleon as the dictator by land and John Bull (a popular metaphorical depiction of Great Britain) as the dictator of the seas, the Kentuckian said that Americans were asked "[t]o bear the actual cuffs of her arrogance, that we may escape a chimerical French subjugation! We are invited—conjured to drink the potion of British poison actually presented to our lips, that we may avoid the imperial dose prepared by perturbed imaginations. We are called upon [Hear him thunder!]—to submit to debasement, dishonor and disgrace—to bow the neck to royal insolence, as a course of preparation for manly resistance to gallic invasion!" "[I]t was not by submission that our fathers achieved our independence." Clay recalled that the Declaration of Independence rested its assertion of the necessity of independence on the "first appearance" of "encroachment." Now Britain had moved from denying America the indirect trade—the right to trade between the West Indies and Europe—to denial even of the direct trade—of trade between America and the Continent. "Yield this point, and tomorrow intercourse between . . . planters on James river and Richmond will be interdicted." The Royal Navy's bottling up of the United States' rivers amounted to invasion, he insisted.

Clay estimated that the fiscal advantage to Britain of this hostile policy toward America could not account for it. More likely the British hoped by closing off America's sea trade to draw American sailors, whom he estimated to number a hundred thousand, into the British merchant marine. He then insisted that talk of negative political consequences for the Republicans in case of war had to be mistaken. The people had seen this administration and the previous one endeavor to reach an honest accommodation with either or both of the great powers with "the utmost impartiality," and so would place the blame where it belonged. Anyway, duty called, and he would respond. "He concluded," the same newspaperman said, "by hoping that his remarks had tended to prove that the quantum of the force was not too great—that in its nature it was free from the objections urged against it, and that the object of its application was one imperiously called for by the crisis."

A few days later Chairman Calhoun reported on events in a letter to a friend in South Carolina. "Heretofore, the conductors of our affairs, have attempted to avoid and remove difficulties by a sort of political management. They thought, that national honor and interest could both be maintained and respected, not by war, or a preparation for it; but by commercial arrangements and negotiations. That might suit an inconsiderable nation," he fumed, "or one that had not such important rights at stake. Experience has proved it improper for us."[10]

The day Calhoun's committee reported, Secretary Monroe penned a lengthy letter to a British friend, Henry Vassall-Fox, Lord Holland.[11] Monroe had cultivated a good relationship with this correspondent while the two of them negotiated in London in 1806, and so this significant British statesman made a logical recipient of what amounted to a warning—a reluctant warning. After invoking "The danger of the present moment to the peace of our countries," Secretary Monroe described Britain's position as demanding "as a condition on which the orders in council are to be revoked, not that the UStates shall protect their neutral rights only, in a commerce with the British dominions, against French invasion, but that they shall open the continent to British manufactures & productions, and failing in that, repeal their non importation act, while G. Britain retains her orders in full force. This attitude, maintaind," he concluded, "must lead to war." The reason was obvious: "The UStates consider the orders in council, more especially since the revocation of the French decrees so far as they affected our neutral trade, as war on the part of G Britain, and you will be sensible that when one party wages war, the other cannot long remain in peace." Soon enough President Madison would issue a public statement echoing that last bit of plainspoken reasoning; we may suppose, then, that at least he had a hand in writing Monroe's letter.

Monroe continued by saying that these circumstances had filled American policy makers with substantial regret. The American leaders hoped a change of course on Britain's part would relieve them of the duty they otherwise would soon face. "If we go to war, we can, & shall, do each other much harm." And for what? Would Britain benefit? As Monroe saw things, Britain could, if it decided to, benefit for centuries from American growth and development; the British could (here he echoed Jefferson's *Notes on the State of Virginia*) "supply this country & this hemisphere" with manufactured goods. These developments "would, by the superior capital of G Britain, and her greater improvement in the useful arts . . . prove a source of prosperity & wealth to her as well as to themselves." "War," on the other hand, "will soon teach us to manufacture for ourselves. The restraints already laid on commerce have produc'd a wonderful effect in that respect." His warning went further, as he touched on the harm American privateers could do to British interests in both the Old World and the New. Yet none of this need happen. The Prince Regent still had time to spur his servants to conclude a mutually beneficial arrangement of their differences.

Congress, meanwhile, acted on the Calhoun Committee's recommendations. As President Madison explained to Thomas Jefferson on February 7, 1812, "With a view to enable the Executive to step at once into Canada they have provided after two months delay, for a regular force requiring 12 to raise it, and after 3 months for a volunteer force, on terms not likely to raise it at all for that object. The mixture of good & bad, avowed & disguised motives accounting for these things is curious eno', but not to be explained in the compass of a letter." Madison did in the end succeed in having the objectionable provisions of the legislation amended. The only happy news Madison had for Jefferson concerned Daniel Tompkins, the governor of New York, who at last had thrown in his lot with the mainline Republicans against the Clintonian faction otherwise ascendant in that state.[12] Time would tell that Tompkins had made a wise political wager.

About this time Madison gave lukewarm assent to a court-martial's acquittal of General James Wilkinson. He did this after noting that both Wilkinson and the court had behaved in ways "evidently and justly objectionable." With the return of his sword, Wilkinson again escaped the fate he so richly deserved—and would live to fight another day.[13]

Perhaps the most portentous decision made in Congress in those days concerned the president's proposal to prepare a significant naval force for the coming conflict. He asked Congress to fund twelve ships of the line and ten new frigates to add to the ten frigates the U.S. Navy already had, besides stockpiling various supplies essential in wartime. The proposal failed despite Federalist support, as Randolph highlighted New England Federalists' comparison of this measure to the Adams administration's shipbuilding project—opposition to which had been a key factor in Jeffersonians' ascent culminating in the Revolution of 1800. "The navy was sunk, 62 to 59," in "the most critical [vote] of the session," as a leading Madison scholar put it.[14] Not content with that, Congress also torpedoed the administration's proposal to create two new assistant war secretary positions even though Eustis struck one and all as "incapable of discharging the duties of [his] office," according to able Madison supporter Senator William Crawford, R-GA. Eustis's War Department staff continued to consist of eight clerks.[15] The Federalists, Invisibles, and Old Republicans were going to leave the United States bereft of a war machine even as it launched a war with the British Empire.

Secretary Gallatin continued to be of a divided mind in these matters. Although disappointed that "our hopes and endeavours to preserve peace during the present European contest have at last been frustrated," he counted himself "satisfied that domestic faction has prevented that happy result"— that is, that the administration had done its best. In the end he looked forward to the day when "our internal enemies, and the ambitious intriguers who still attempt[ed] to disunite" would "be equally disappointed."[16]

Though Gallatin believed that the administration's factious opponents would try to throw a wrench in the works, he expected to "rely with great confidence on the good sense of the mass of the people to support their own Government in an unavoidable war, and to check the disordinate ambition of individuals." He thought recent developments would "have a salutary effect in annihilating the Essex junto" (a prediction that would prove quite mistaken).[17] Pennsylvania, he averred, "never was more firm or united" behind the Republican banner. "The South & the West" could "not be shaken." If he had his way, America in the wake of the coming conflict would have "the smallest possible quantity of debt, perpetual taxation, military establishments and other corrupting or anti Republican habits or institutions." Even as the war came, in other words, the president's most trusted advisor remained committed to parsimony in military spending. In this he had substantial congressional support.

34

⊹ ⚛ ⊹

The recent developments to which Gallatin referred as likely to undercut domestic opposition related to one John Henry. This bit of skullduggery reduced whatever possibility of serious Republican opposition to the coming war still remained.[1] John Henry purported to have discussed their intention to betray the country with numerous New England Federalists. This series of disclosures he had captured in various documents. President Madison paid Henry $50,000 (at a time when, recall, the Federal Government's annual expenditures did not exceed $4 million) for the documents.

As Madison described the matter in his letter of March 9, 1812, to Congress covering Henry's documents:

> They prove[d] that at a recent period, whilst the United States, notwithstanding the wrongs sustained by them, ceased not to observe the laws of peace and neutrality towards Great Britain; and in the midst of amicable professions and negociations on the part of the British Government, through its public Minister here; a secret Agent of that Government was employed in certain States, more especially at the Seat of Government in Massachusetts, in fomenting disaffection to the constituted authorities of the nation; and in intrigues with the disaffected, for the purpose of bringing about resistance to the laws, and eventually, in concert with a British force, of destroying the Union and forming the Eastern part thereof, into a political connection with Great Britain.

He closed, after referring to "the effect which the discovery of such a procedure ought to have on the public Councils," by saying that this discovery ought to make the "happy Union of these States" "more dear to hearts of all good Citizens."

What the Henry letters purported to show was that northern Vermont had become home to so substantial an anti-administration sentiment that in case of resistance to the embargo by Massachusetts, the Green Mountain State would join in. Henry did report to his master, British Governor General of Canada Sir James Craig, that the Madison administration had grown "alarmed, at the menacing attitude of the Northern States," so that war was becoming less likely. A sterner British policy toward America could still push the Americans into war, but they would not undertake it on their own initiative. If war came, Henry counseled, the remaining Federalist states would convene a congress and form their own independent government. Such a government would likely enter into "a strict alliance" with the U.K. However, "[t]o bring about a separation of the States under distinct and independent Governments" seemed to Henry "an affair of . . . uncertainty" which "cannot be effected but by a series of acts and a long continued policy tending to irritate the Southern and conciliate the Northern people."

A House committee predictably concluded that Henry's papers showed the British had "been deliberately and perfidiously pursuing measures to divide these States, and to involve our citizens in all the guilt of treason, and the horrors of a civil war." The documents were published along with a letter from Henry to Secretary of State James Monroe explaining Henry's purpose.[2] Henry said that the great powers' abuse of the United States those last several years and "their present embarrassment" could be traced to the foreign governments' conviction that no matter what they did, the U.S. Government would be unable to rouse "a great majority of its citizens to concur." Henry added that he intended to do what he could to empower the government to do something about it—that is, to bring "unanimity among all parties in America." He informed Monroe that Governor General Sir James Craig had been behind his mission, adding that he thought perhaps this disclosure would persuade the British to elevate better men than Lords Castlereagh, Wellesley, and Liverpool to the top of their government. More important, he expected his revelations to assist Madison and Monroe in rallying America for more muscular measures.

Monroe verified from his files that the papers Henry sent did indeed bear authentic signatures of several top British officials. While Federalists in New England criticized Madison for the enormous amount he had expended to obtain this correspondence, Republicans outside the Federalist bastion took the news as the president had hoped.[3] Federalists, for their part, found the Madison administration's behavior in this matter absurd. Nothing in the documents exposed anyone as having done anything clandestine except for Henry himself. As Henry Adams summarized the entire affair, "After a night's reflection, the Federalists returned to the Capitol convinced that the President had done a foolish act in throwing away fifty thousand dollars for papers that proved the Federalist party to be ignorant of British intrigues that never existed. Fifty thousand dollars was a large sum; and having been spent without authority from Congress, it seemed to the Federalists chiefly their own money which had been unlawfully used by Madison for the purpose of publishing a spiteful libel on themselves." When the House moved to investigate the matter, it found that Henry had already fled for Europe.[4]

James Monroe told the House Armed Services Committee on March 31, 1812, that it should declare a two-month embargo before adjourning. (His war message appeared in the *National Intelligencer*. "The final step ought to be taken," it read. "Our wrongs have been great; our cause is just; and if we are decided and firm, success is inevitable. Let war therefore be forthwith proclaimed against England.") The next day President Madison's one-sentence note, marked "confidential," went up Capitol Hill: "Considering it as expedient," it said, "under existing circumstances and prospects, that a General Embargo be laid on all vessels now in port or hereafter arriving, for the period of sixty days, I recommend the immediate passage of a law to that effect." Thus encouraged, the House obliged—and the Senate, still hoping for an out, extended the sixty days to ninety. "The President was afraid," says his leading biographer, "this would be interpreted as weakness. . . ." British authorities in the end greeted America's decision with a mixture of annoyance and indignation, the latter a result of their calculation that in opposing Napoleon, they were on the side of the angels—as surely the Americans must realize. The British conclusion was underscored even as these events transpired by news that the emperor, determined to interdict transport of American grain to British armies in Iberia, had set French warships to destroying American merchant ships at sea. Monroe thundered at the French minister about the awkward position in which this put Madison, but to no avail.[5] In order to clarify America's situation in relation to France, the president and secretary of state published angry columns in the *National Intelligencer* explaining that in case the problems with Britain were resolved before the French ones were, "we should not be surprised to see the attitude of the United States change toward these powers."[6]

The two, no three, months should have given American civilian ships time to return to port before a declaration of war. Congress might have undertaken to undo its measures of the last eleven years stripping the Federal Government of fiscal resources, ships, and soldiers. Some insisted that the trade restrictions of the last five years ought at last to be ended. As one of them, New York's Representative Harmanus Bleecker, put it, "Where are your armies; your navy? Have you money? No, sir!"

Thus prompted, John Randolph rose to twist the knife:

> I am myself in a situation similar to what would have been that of one of the unfortunate people of Caracas, if preadvised of the danger which overhung his country. I know that we are on the brink of some dreadful scourge, some great desolation, some awful visitation from that Power whom, I am afraid, we have as yet in our national capacity taken no pains to conciliate. . . . Go to war without money, without men, without a navy! Go to war when we have not the courage, while your lips utter war, to lay war taxes! when your whole courage is exhibited in passing Resolutions! The people will not believe it!

The most fearsome debater of the lot, Calhoun, answered the Virginian in words that to our north still have not been forgotten. "So far from being unprepared, sir, I believe that in four weeks from the time that a declaration of war is heard on our frontiers the whole of Upper and a part of Lower Canada will be in our possession." No sooner had the Carolinian made this sorry prognostication about the course of military events than Tennessee's Felix Grundy, after Clay the most prominent western War Hawk, let slip an equally poor forecast concerning the political future. "It is only while the public mind is held in suspense, it is only while there is doubt as to what will be the result of our deliberations,—it is only while we linger in this Hall that any manifestations of uneasiness will show themselves. Whenever war is declared, the people will put forth their strength to support their rights."[7]

Meanwhile Republicans in Congress nominated Madison for another term. Despite the healing of the breach with Monroe and most of the Old Republicans and the president's incumbent status, the party once again supported Madison remarkably unenthusiastically. Vice President George Clinton died on April 20, 1812, and his political interest more or less fell in behind his nephew DeWitt Clinton.[8] Stealing a march on the DeWitt Clintonian faction, which was planning its own meeting for Albany, New York, about two-thirds of the Republican caucus voted to make Madison its candidate once again on May 18, 1812.[9] Gallatin, as clever a political gamesman as there was, confided to Representative Joseph Nicholson that he intended for John Langdon of New Hampshire to succeed George Clinton in the number-two job. Langdon did not want the post, and the Massachusetts Republicans favored Elbridge Gerry—recently defeated for reelection to their governorship. Langdon was "the most popular [candidate] we can get," he said, while Gerry's supporters insisted Gerry's candidacy would "unite." "But the fact that it would unite," Gallatin lamented, "is not true." In reality "[h]ow beloved [Langdon's] person by all who know him I need not tell you," he concluded, while "Gerry is, in both respects, the reverse; and I much fear that, if elected, he would give us as much trouble as our late Vice-President."[10] Yet vice president Gerry would be. Republicans would come to lament his defeat in Massachusetts, where his successor Federalist Caleb Strong used the office of governor to thwart Madison's war policy in myriad ingenious ways.[11]

Thus unimpressively fortified, Madison sent what is often called his "War Message" to Congress on June 1, 1812.[12] Some say that Madison "declared war" on Great Britain, but of course he did nothing of the kind. The power to declare war rested in the hands of Congress, as he well knew: he had been one of two Philadelphia Convention delegates who suggested the relevant constitutional wording.[13]

Madison included with his message the correspondence between Secretary Monroe and the British ministers, Jonathan Russell and the current one, Augustus John Foster. One letter concerned British impressment of sailors from American ships and American claims that some of those sailors were native Americans.[14] Foster requested that Monroe aid in capturing Royal Navy deserters resident in American territory. In return Foster said, "You need not I am sure, Sir, be reminded by me of the prompt attention which has invariably been given by His Majesty's Commanding Officer on the Halifax Station to the reclamations in similar cases which I have transmitted since my arrival in the United States to him in your name, nor of the readiness with which he has given directions when practicable for their being instantaneously discharged."[15] Foster was right: in all eight cases in which Monroe had asked that native American citizens who had been impressed be returned to the United States, Foster had arranged their release.[16]

At more or less the same time, Foster made a grave error: he disclosed to Monroe some of the contents of Lord Castlereagh's latest confidential instructions to Foster, which included that before the offending Orders-in-Council would be repealed, America must secure from France not only an end to exclusion of its ships from French-controlled ports, but an end to exclusion of any ships from French-controlled ports.[17] Although he had already decided to proceed with his message to Congress, President Madison must have been reassured by this news that he had made the only feasible decision.

So it finally was that on June 1, 1812, Madison laid out his reasoning to Congress.[18] The House clerk took three hours to read it. "I communicate to Congress certain documents," it began, "being a continuation of those heretofore laid before them, on the subject of our Affairs with Great Britain." One may be forgiven for doubting that, say, Abraham Lincoln on March 4, 1861, or Franklin Roosevelt on December 8, 1941, looked to Madison's composition for a model to emulate. It did not resemble one of his predecessor's written products, spangled as they tended to be with memorable formulations, either. Rather, as he had in his Publius essays a quarter of a century earlier, Madison wrote his message in tightly coherent paragraphs, which like a yarn sweater formed an interconnected whole. If not memorable for its poetry, Madison's War Message must be classified as a prime specimen of the slow burn.

35

＋ ⊛ ＋

I t laid out numerous grounds on which Americans had come to be righteously angry with His Majesty's Government through a succession of premierships. A kind of catalogue of offenses the United States had suffered, Madison's paper also described the many reasonable steps taken and arguments made to bring the British around to a position the United States could accept. He leads off with impressment, which he says is done "not in the exercise of a Belligerent right founded on the Law of Nations against an Enemy; but of a municipal prerogative over British subjects." This, he says, "is that substitution of force, for a resort to the responsible sovereign, which falls within the definition of War." Even if this were being done "within the exercise of a Belligerent right, the acknowledged laws of war . . . would imperiously demand the fairest trial, where the sacred rights of persons were at issue." Impressed Americans instead had their rights put under "the will of every petty commander."

"Thousands of American citizens," the president lamented, "have been dragged on board ships of war of a foreign nation; and exposed, under the siverities of their discipline, to be exiled to the most distant and deadly climes, to risk their lives in the battles of their oppressors, and to be the melancholy instruments of taking away those of their own brethren." Britain continued in this behavior despite American offers to help in "the recovery of British subjects." As if that were not bad enough, Britain had implemented the policy of stationing warships in American territorial waters, where "[t]hey hover and harrass our entering and departing Commerce." To American demands that the responsible officers be punished, they responded by "bestowin[g] on their commanders, additional marks of honor and confidence."

The Orders-in-Council too came in for detailed criticism from Madison. He described them as pretended blockades, which in their unreality violated the law of nations. He then reminded Congress that Britain's demand that

France's exclusion of American commerce must be lifted ere Britain's would be had been succeeded by a demand that France cease excluding Britain's commerce before Britain would cease to regulate American and, latterly, that America disavow France's "conditions and pretensions"—for which the United States bore no responsibility whatsoever. Madison could only conclude that all of this amounted to a ruse to cover a British "war against the lawful commerce of a friend, that she may the better carry on a commerce with an enemy." Even the American policy of denying Britain its American commerce until she fully resumed that trade, at which point America would deny its trade solely to Britain's French enemy, had not elicited a restoration of just intercourse between the British and the U.S.A. Britain remained committed to this stance even when it received word from the Madison administration that its resumption of trade with the United States would lead to war between the United States and France. Far from grasping so auspicious a prospect, the British ministry had disavowed Minister Erskine's agreement with the American government—even as Henry worked toward "a subversion of our Government, and a dismemberment of our happy union."

In addition to this précis of the recent history of British-American relations, Madison gave Congress reason to ponder the same period's deterioration of Indian relations. He said that "the warfare just renewed by the Savages, on one of our extensive frontiers"—"which [here he borrowed from the Declaration of Independence] is known to spare neither age nor sex, and to be distinguished by features particularly shocking to humanity"— seemed quite odd in its geographic reach unless coordinated by the British, with whose "traders and garrisons" the Indians were "in constant intercourse." Of course, Americans would recall "the authenticated examples of such interpositions, heretofore furnished by the officers and agents of that Government." "Such," he concluded his enumeration of American grievances, "is the spectacle of injuries and indignities which have been heaped on our Country: and such the crisis which its unexampled forbearance and conciliatory efforts have not been able to avert." "We behold, in fine," he summarized, "on the side of Great Britain a state of war against the United States; and on the side of the United States, a state of peace towards Great Britain." The author of the Helvidius essays of 1793, which argued against Treasury Secretary Alexander Hamilton's (Pacificus's) case for broad implied presidential powers under the Constitution, had no difficulty in asserting that the Constitution "wisely confide[d] to the Legislative Department of the Government" whether the obvious next step—a declaration of war—would be taken in relation to the United Kingdom.[1] The gloomy prospect held out by recent actions of France, whose government had in recent days "authorized illegal captures, by its privateers and public ships," would soon be clarified through ongoing discussions between French officials and the American minister.

On June 3, 1812, Calhoun's House select committee on foreign relations reported out an endorsement, at several points in more strident terms, of Madison's message.[2] That paper ended with an assertion that this would be a new war for independence. After presenting the report, Calhoun moved that it lie upon the table (that is, not be acted upon) and immediately presented a bill to declare war.[3]

The House voted for war, 79–49, on June 4th—three days after Madison's message. The outcome in the Senate remained in doubt. Some, including Monroe, wanted the war limited to naval affairs only, but that idea lost in the Senate on a 16–16 tie—six Republicans including Leib joining the Federalists in voting for it, but Smith of Maryland and Virginia's Giles coming down against it. Monroe's explanation of his position in favor of this policy and encouragement of Gallatin to lobby friendly senators in favor of it must, as Madison biographer Irving Brant noted, have meant that Madison did not advocate it.[4] Giles got the Senate to vote on a naval war against both Britain and France, but that failed by 14–18. The Senate at last voted for war, 19–13, on June 17th. Three Republicans—one each from New York, New Hampshire, and Ohio—stood with the Federalists against the declaration.[5] British minister Sir Augustus John Foster assigned an aide to keep Virginia Republican senator Richard Brent drunk, but Brent managed to make it to the Senate floor to cast his votes anyway.[6] Madison signed the bill on June 18th.[7]

The following day, June 19th, Madison and Monroe signed a proclamation that as Congress had declared war, such a state existed. It encouraged all Federal Government employees, civil and military, to "be vigilant and zealous in discharging their duties" and said the two high officials did

> exhort all the good people of the United States as they love their Country, as they value the precious heritage derived from the virtue and valour of their fathers, as they feel the Wrongs which have forced on them the last resort of injured Nations, and as they consult the best means, under the blessing of Divine Providence, of abridging its calamities, that they exert themselves in preserving order, in promoting Concord, in maintaining the

authority and the efficacy of the Laws; and in supporting . . . all the Measures which may be adopted by the constituted authorities for obtaining a speedy, a just and honorable peace.[8]

Then Madison, sporting "a little round hat [with] a huge cockade," visited the Navy and War Departments to firm their employees' resolve.[9]

Congressional Federalists responded with "An Address . . . to their Constituents on the subject of the war with Great Britain."[10] Thirty-five pages and eleven thousand words in length and signed by thirty-four House Federalists, it appeared in more than twenty thousand freestanding copies and in newspapers both Federalist and Republican—including the *National Intelligencer* and *Niles' Weekly Register*. This pamphlet amounted to a detailed refutation of the president's War Message. Beyond that, it committed its signatories to the claim that domestic dissension over the war flowed both "from a sense of the inadequacy of our means of success" and "from moral and political objections." It asked whether "[a] nation like the United States . . . happy in its local relations: removed from the bloody theater of Europe: with a maritime border, opening a vast field for enterprise: with territorial possessions exceeding every real want: its firesides safe: its altars undefiled: from invasion having nothing to fear; from acquisition nothing to hope; . . . [could] look to Heaven for its smiles, while throwing away, as though they were worthless, all the blessings and joys which peace and a distinguished lot include?" Here leading Federalists, generally sympathetic with the British, hostile to Napoleon, and disgusted with the Republicans, cast themselves as the peace party and Republicans' war policy as some mixture of foolhardy, ungrateful, and immoral.

At the state level Massachusetts Federalists as usual blazed a trail for their co-partisans. That state's House of Representatives adopted a resolution that "an offensive war against Great Britain" would be "impolitic, unnecessary, and ruinous." It would be foolhardy, according to that body, "to plunge into a war which desolates the European world, and from which it seems to have been the design of Almighty Providence to exempt us." Contra Republican references to the nation's honor, this document held that there would be no shame in America's "yielding to circumstances which it cannot control." Besides, martial success was highly unlikely. It was on these arguments that the representatives founded "this last respectful effort . . . to induce the National Government to pause" in light of their "attachment to the Union, . . . a persuasion of the invincible and growing opposition of the people to these measures, and . . . duty to themselves, to posterity, and to God."

The Boston Town Meeting said, "An immense majority of the people are invincibly averse from a conflict equally unnecessary and menacing ruin to themselves, and their posterity," and so it made this statement, which even if ignored might help "rescue the nation from ruin" when next Massachusetts citizens had resort to the "constitutional means of a change of men and measures." Harkening back to the Revolution, the town meeting even proposed that other northern cities embody committees "for corresponding or meeting with them." Thus prompted, the state's political leaders promulgated an "Address of the House of Representatives to the people of Massachusetts" in late June. Recent gerrymandering of the state Senate had denied Federalists what they deemed their rightful control of that body, and thus "exhibit[ed] you as a divided people." To their eyes the American declaration of war resulted from "the embarrassment arising from the precipitate declaration of the President . . . that the French decrees . . . were repealed," a desire "to aggrandize the Southern and Western States at the expence of the Eastern section of the Union," and a "spirit of jealousy, and competition with Great Britain"—which had led the American administration to the "mistaken belief that she would yield to the pressure of the continental system established by the Tyrant of Europe [the Emperor Napoleon]." Politically Madison could not retreat. However, the Massachusetts House suggested, he might still be denied reelection.

Further, Governor Caleb Strong appointed July 23rd a day of fasting. Connecticut joined in this rite, so that ministers across both states preached antiwar sermons that day. Numerous Massachusetts counties held large rallies in behalf of this cause, whether in the guise of opposition to the war or in the form of rallies against President Madison. Significant domestic antiwar activity would mark the rest of the War of 1812, and the most notable episode of antiwar activity helped doom the Federalist Party to extinction. But we get ahead of ourselves.

Unbeknownst to policy makers in Washington, Foreign Secretary Robert Stewart, Viscount Castlereagh announced in Parliament on June 16th the British Cabinet's intention to repeal the offending Orders-in-Council of 1807 and 1809 if America repealed its restrictions on British trade and warships. In reporting this event to Monroe, American minister to the Court of St. James's Jonathan Russell said, "I can but regret that in this document any reservation has been made of a power of restoring the orders . . . to their full affect, whenever it shall be judged expedient so to do, as such reservation manifests an intention to maintain the principle on which they were founded, and in which I conceive the United States can never acquiesce." Russell wrote

Castlereagh ten days later that he hoped this development would lead to a mutually satisfactory resolution.[11] In the interim Russell wrote Monroe describing a conversation in which Castlereagh told him that even if hostilities had already commenced in North America, "his government would be sincerely disposed to put and immediate end to all hostile proceedings and to cultivate peace & friendship with the United States." To Castlereagh's intimation that America ought to indulge Great Britain in light of "her present struggle for her rights & independence," Russell told Monroe, he "assured his lordship that we were fully aware of the peculiar nature of the times and ready to judge fairly, on the necessity to which he alluded, but that it ought never to be expected that the United States would submit to measures like the orders in council which mainly affected them and but feebly & incidentally injured the enemy of England."[12]

The administration hoped that Congress's declaration would not negatively affect American relations with other European countries. So Secretary Monroe wrote to John Quincy Adams, the American minister at St. Petersburg (then the Russian capital), that while America hoped the war would be "confined to [Great Britain] only," "[i]t is seen with much regret that the Emperor of Russia is also likely to be reduced to the necessity of becoming a party to the War, if he has not already done it," and that still "there is no reason why it should affect in the slightest degree the very friendly relations which now exist between the United States and Russia." He expressed similar hopes regarding the Portuguese government and the Spanish Regency at Cadiz (that is, the Spanish resistance): surely they would continue to rely on American supplies, and America would "continue to regard them as friends." Even an amicable arrangement between America and France did not seem likely to "produce any closer connection between the U.S. and that power," on the other hand.[13]

Although he favored war with Britain in the circumstances, then, James Monroe remained persuaded that normalcy meant having a modus vivendi with Britain—as it had in 1806. Unfortunately news of developments at Westminster arrived only in mid-August; by then, Madison decided, there could be no turning back.[14] More's the pity, as the United States military performed rather pitifully in the War of 1812. As J. C. A. Stagg, the editor of Madison's papers and leading historian of the War of 1812, put it, the "conflict was a ragged one, marked on the American side more by military fiascoes than successes on land and interspersed with occasional naval victories at sea that, though gratifying to the nation's tender sense of pride, were inconsequential in terms of larger outcomes." Only the wholly unanticipated—many

American clergymen said providential—downfall of Napoleon at exactly the time when America's military resources had been thoroughly spent enabled American negotiators to come away with a return to the *status quo antebellum* and the Madison administration shamelessly to declare victory.[15] Another fortuitous development at the end of the war made the claim seem plausible—but we will come to that.

36

⊹ ❁ ⊹

When Secretary Monroe wrote to Jonathan Russell with news of the declaration of war and instructions on the necessary provisions of a peace agreement, he added a caveat. All America wanted were revocation of the Orders-in-Council, an end to British impressments, and a cessation of illegal British blockades. If these were granted, America would adopt a law "to be reciprocal" that would "prohibit the employment of British Seamen in the public or commercial service of the United States." Alluding to past British skepticism about such an American law, Monroe hurried to note that "There can be no doubt that such an arrangement, would prove more efficacious, in securing to Great Britain her Seamen, than the practice, to which, it is proposed to be a substitute; independant of all the other objections to it." As a prod to the British, he confided, "It will, it is presumed, occur that a prosecution of the War for one Year, or even a few Months, if not for a shorter term, will present very serious obstacles on the part of the United States to an accommodation, which do not now exist." Specifically, in case of an American invasion of Canada, "the effect, which success, (which could not fail to attend it) might have on the public mind here, [would make] it difficult to relinquish Territory which had been conquered."[1] Such optimists sat atop the Executive Branch and in Congress.

As if this were not enough warning to the British of what the United States' military strategy would be, the *National Intelligencer* had spelled it out by early December 1811. "It would be the duty of the government of the United States," in case of a war with Britain, the administration organ said, "to lose no time in reducing the whole [of Canada] above [that is, west of] Quebec." To do so, editor Samuel Smith continued, "about 20,000 men would be proper, two thirds of whom might be volunteers and one third regulars." It then explained that there would be three American objectives: "the region of Montreal—the outlet of [Lake] Ontario—and across the Niagara river."[2]

One important obstacle to the American war effort made itself known by the end of June. It announced itself in the chief instrument of public relations of those days: a political pamphlet. Written by Massachusetts's and Congress's most eloquent Federalist, Representative Josiah Quincy, with help from Senator James Bayard, a Delaware Federalist, this lengthy statement reflected what would be the strong and persistent—eventually extreme, desperate, and in some cases unscrupulous—opposition of the signatories' party, now essentially reduced to a sectional party, to the American war effort. The argument it made had considerable force.[3]

The congressional debate on war resolutions occurred behind closed doors, these opponents lamented. "[T]he doors of Congress were shut upon the people." What reason Republicans had for going into executive session on so momentous an issue, the pamphleteers could not say: Madison's message to Congress conveyed no information not previously notorious. "The inadequacy of both our Army and Navy, for successful invasion, and the insufficiency of the fortifications for the security of our seaboard, were everywhere known." The reason for the secrecy must have been to "keep [the people] in ignorance of the progress of measures, until . . . the fate of the country [was] sealed." Lest they be thought to concur in such a stratagem, the signatories had they said sat silent through the entire closed-door discussions.

The signers drew the reader's attention to the "series of restrictions on commerce" opposed by them all along because "inefficient as respected foreign nations, and injurious chiefly to ourselves." Successive administrations' enforcement of them they explained by reference to the fact that "Success, in the system, had become identified with the pride, the character, and the hope of our Cabinet." Their failure to change directions owed to the fact that, "As is natural with men, who have a great stake depending on the success of a favorite theory, pertinacity seemed to increase as its hopelessness became apparent." The theory's failure "was carefully attributed to the influence of opposition." That factor, not "its intrinsic imbecility," received the blame whenever Republicans had to explain the situation to the people.

America did have real grievances, this congressional minority conceded. Yet, "although very grievous to our interests, and in many [aspects] humiliating to our pride, . . . [they] yet were of a nature which, in the present state of the world, either would not justify war, or which war would not remedy." So, for example, persistent British naval intrusions into American coastal waters called for improvement of coastal and harbor fortifications, "but, in no light can they be considered as making a resort to war, at the present time, on the part of the United States, either necessary or expedient." Too, some kind of accounting for the hostilities with the Indians in the Northwest in 1811 ought to be forthcoming from the Executive. Though Congress had been told that the British spurred Tecumseh and the Prophet into hostilities, Congress needed information about steps taken "to remove any cause of complaint, either real or imaginary, which the Indians might allege," and it seemed clear that declaring war on Britain had not heightened that region's safety.

Quincy and Bayard next turned to the obvious question of how a land war would resolve problems of "free trade and sailors' rights." "What balm," they asked, "has Canada for wounded honor? How are our mariners benefited by a war, which exposes those who are free, without promising release to those who are impressed?" Too, if American honor required war with Britain, what did honor urge in response to similar offenses by France?

"With a navy comparatively nominal," they concluded, "we are about to enter into the lists against the greatest marine on the globe. With a commerce unprotected and spread over every ocean, we propose to make profit by privateering, and for this endanger the wealth of which we are honest proprietors." The respective military assets of America and the United Kingdom made America's strategy of invasion foolish, and there was no need to enter into "that awful contest which is laying waste Europe" without substantial fortifications, men, or money. Perhaps worst, "It cannot be concealed, that to engage in the present war against England is to place ourselves on the side of France. . . ." The whole idea seemed immoral and imprudent—and thus drew the opposition of the country's conservative party, the party of Washington, Adams, and Hamilton.

In private some of them went further. Former secretary of state Timothy Pickering, highest of High Federalists, wrote that he had known directly from the French minister during the Washington administration of congressional Republicans bribed into taking a pro-French line. He could not, he said, "undertake to affirm that French money had been liberally distributed on this occasion," though he was certain of it. Fortunately the declaration of war had brought "all New England" around to opposing the Republicans, "nor can I doubt of it in New York." He said of Napoleon that "neither Jefferson nor Madison have dared resist [his] will; because I presume they stand committed to him, and dread an exposure."[4]

"I would preserve the Union of the States," Pickering continued, "if possible." "But I would not be deluded by a *word*. To my ears there is no magic in the sound of Union. If the great objects of union are utterly abandoned,—much more, if they are wantonly, corruptly, and treacherously sacrificed by the Southern and Western States,—let the Union be severed." He did not think it could happen, however, as the West would always need New Orleans as an emporium for its trade. "And peace with Britain we must have and will have. We cannot exist, but in poverty and contempt, without foreign commerce. And by a war of any continuance with Great Britain, that commerce will be annihilated." After expressing great confidence that out of self-interest, Britain would forgo "any destruction of our seaports," Pickering concluded that America "will have peace and commerce." He would do what he could to bring that into being.

Pickering also expressed confidence in the new governor of Massachusetts, Caleb Strong, and in the likelihood that Federalists would cement control of the Massachusetts General Court in the next election. Strong did not disappoint. Rather, almost immediately after Pickering's letter he gave Secretary of War William Eustis's request for "a detachment from the militia of Massachusetts for defence of the maritime frontier" the back of his hand. To Eustis's reminder that Madison had called on governors to get their militias ready, Strong replied that "The people of this State appear to be under no apprehension of an invasion. . . ." Although some coastal towns had requested resupply in light of the declaration of war, he said, "they expressed no desire that any part of the militia should be called out for their defence, and, in some cases, we were assured such a measure would be disagreeable to them."[5]

Strong next gave Eustis details of his reasoning in not providing the Federal Government the militiamen it had requested. He said that he inferred that Eustis did not believe the danger of a British invasion was "now very considerable," or else the plan would not have been to send Massachusetts units westward. Add to that the governor of Nova Scotia's proclamation "forbid[ding] any incursions or depredations upon our territories," and the U.S. Constitution's conditions on which the Federal Government could call militia units into its service had not been met. In general, then, he believed that Massachusetts men should remain in Massachusetts in preparedness for an enemy attack, as did his Council and Massachusetts's Supreme Court. (That court advised that only the governor could decide whether a call into federal service was constitutionally valid and that even if called into federal service, militia units must be commanded by state officers.)[6] Governor Strong would, he concluded, happily comply with federal orders in case the Constitution's conditions on which state units could be called into federal service were met in the future. Thus had the Federalists, heretofore the loose-construction and military-measures party, become the opposite. They would remain so through the balance of the war.

At the war's outset Secretary of War William Eustis's complete inadequacy to his role and General James Wilkinson's notoriety and general ineptitude posed substantial problems. In the last weeks before the declaration of war and the first weeks thereafter, a surprising answer to the Eustis problem percolated among the American elite. Richard Rush, son of signer of the Declaration of Independence Dr. Benjamin Rush and later a significant political figure in his own right, tried to persuade his acquaintances in the Madison administration's inner circle to shuffle the deck chairs to make room for Thomas Jefferson to resume his Washington administration position as secretary of state. James Monroe, meanwhile, would receive Washington's old military rank of lieutenant general.[7]

After sharing his idea with Jefferson in a letter that claimed Gallatin was on board ("tickled to the nines with the idea"), Rush concluded by saying, "[I]t is a little odd that I, who claim to be so retired, so falling back, at my onset here, should have begun in my [later?] moon with entirely new-modeling the cabinet!" And so that was that. Except that it wasn't.

Apparently Monroe took the notion of returning to the military life he had known in the Revolution seriously. He wrote to his chief political advisor, his son-in-law the prominent Virginia attorney George Hay, describing his thoughts about raising a force of Virginians and leading it north. Hay replied that he had spoken with Governor James Barbour, who sent Monroe a letter the same day agreeing that Monroe could raise a force in Virginia and assuring him that his great prestige in his home state meant probable success for his recruitment efforts. However, Barbour continued to say that news from Britain of the Orders-in-Council's repeal meant such efforts would likely be for naught, as the war now looked likely to be "evanescent."[8] Hay, on the other hand, said, "If the war continues, your Situation as Commander of a division of the army will be preferable to that which you now hold," but that the news from England seemed to indicate Monroe should remain in charge of the State Department.[9] He would, but the idea of a Canadian command continued to dance in his head.

Wade Hampton I, another of the brigadiers, loathed Wilkinson so intensely that he stayed on his South Carolina plantation rather than take up his position on the northern border. Similar problems beset the ranks of more junior officers. It would perhaps be the new recruits, then, who invaded Canada. Yet Madison and Gallatin's idea of putting Henry Clay in command of the fresh troops that he had just prodded Congress into empowering Madison to recruit, and even giving him George Washington's old rank of lieutenant general, ran aground on other Cabinet secretaries' insistence that the

Kentuckian could not be spared from Congress.[10] The incumbent military leadership would in the main have to do.

The westernmost American force was concentrated at Detroit, which is separated by only a narrow passage across the Detroit River from what then was Upper Canada (today's Ontario). As British troops in that entire extensive province numbered only around twelve hundred, it would have been an inviting target—if the president had had a way of knowing how minor its military resources were. Yet he could not know that Canada's total forces on hand numbered about six thousand British regulars, twenty-one hundred Canadian auxiliaries, and three thousand Indian allies because, as one historian put it, "the War Department had no intelligence information beyond vague rumors drifting across the Canadian border. Besides that, the generals had done no advance planning of potential operations against Canada."[11] Madison, Monroe, Gallatin, Eustis, and Hamilton did know that Canada was sparsely populated and Upper Canada had few troops on hand. They also knew that the United States' population of 7.7 million was counterposed to Canada's 500,000. Much of that Canadian population—about 60 percent—consisted of immigrants arrived from the United States since 1792 in quest of open land and the traditionally low British taxes. These "Late Loyalists," as they were known, seemed unlikely to be staunchly defensive of royal authority in the event of war. The local governor and military commander, Major General Isaac Brock, described them as "either indifferent to what is passing, or so completely American as to rejoice in the prospects of a change of Governments."[12]

Americans in government and outside it therefore felt an outsized optimism concerning their nation's military prospects. Former president Jefferson, for example, wrote William Duane, whom he had appointed a lieutenant colonel, thanking him for "the military Manuals you were so kind as to send me" and with some truly remarkable ruminations on the situation. "[T]his is the sort of book most needed in our country," he mused, "where even the elements of tactics are unknown. the young have never seen service; & the old are past it: and of those among them who are not superannuated themselves, their science is become so." Skipping past Duane's lamentations concerning the incompetence of Secretary Eustis, the effects of which Duane claimed to be able to detail at length, Jefferson admitted, "I see, as you do, the difficulties & defects we have to encounter in war, and should expect disasters, if we had an enemy on land capable of inflicting them." As it was, however, "the seeds of genius . . . which need only soil & season to germinate, will develop themselves among our military men. some of them will become prominent, and, seconded by the native energy of our citizens, will soon, I hope, to our force, add the benefits of skill. the acquisition of Canada this year, as far as the neighborhood of Quebec, will be a mere matter of marching; & will give us experience for the attack of Halifax the next, & the final expulsion of England from the American continent." The British "fleet will annihilate our public force on the water," he feared, "but our privateers will eat out the vitals of their commerce. perhaps they may burn New York or Boston," he warmed to his subject, but "if they do, we must burn the city of London, not by expensive fleets or Congreve rockets, but by employing an hundred or two Jack the painters, whom nakedness famine, desperation & hardened vice will abundantly furnish from among themselves."[13] Congressman John C. Calhoun put it more directly: "in four weeks from the time that a declaration of war is heard on our frontier, the whole of Upper and a part of Lower Canada will be in our possession."[14]

Madison opted then for both land campaigns and naval activity. The U.S. Navy would pose no threat to its British counterpart, but American warships and privateers (private vessels licensed by the Federal Government to conduct warlike measures against British ships, including taking them as prizes) could harass the Royal Navy while the main work was done on land. The U.S. Army, meanwhile, would head north from three staging areas: at Detroit, at Niagara, and farther east.[15]

The American strategy was to strike quickly before Britain could reinforce its North American troops. The invasion's objective was Montreal. The Northwest, Eustis believed, would not be a British target. Michigan Territory governor William Hull, a veteran of the Revolution, tried to persuade officials in Washington otherwise. Although Hull had earlier insisted that American control of Lake Erie must precede any significant incursion into Canada, he eventually abandoned that analysis in favor of the idea that a large American army's appearance at Detroit would intimidate the British into abandoning the region. Unfortunately for the American cause, the British captured Hull's papers, thus learning of Hull's plans. Major General Isaac Brock reported, "Till I read these letters, I had no idea General Hull was advancing with so large a force."[16]

37

Hull wrote very hopefully to Eustis on July 19:

The army is encamped directly opposite to Detroit. The camp is entrenched. I am mounting the 24-pounders and making every preparation for the siege of Malden. The British force, which in numbers was superior to the American, including militia and Indians, is daily diminishing. Fifty or sixty [of the militia] have deserted daily since the American standard was displayed, and taken protection. They are now reduced to less than one hundred. In a day or two I expect the whole will desert. The Indian force is diminishing in the same proportion. I have now a council of ten or twelve nations sitting at Brownstown, and I have no doubt but the result will be that they will remain neutral.

Then came the part of the letter on which the campaign would turn:

The brig "Adams" was launched on the 4th of July. I have removed her to Detroit under cover of the cannon, and shall have her finished and armed as soon as possible. We shall then have command of the upper lakes. If you have not a force at Niagara, the whole force of the province will be directed against this army. . . . It is all important that Niagara should be invested. All our success will depend upon it.[1]

The army's senior officer, Major General Henry Dearborn, made no urgent effort to invest Niagara with any alacrity. Then again, he was "an elderly man of sixty-one years who had grown enormously fat, and he could only move very slowly with great difficulty," which may help explain his hesitance before accepting his high command, so quickness could not be counted among his attributes.[2] Secretary of War Eustis gave no indication that he should hurry to Niagara. Having ordered Hull on June 24 to invade western Canada, Eustis two days later wrote Dearborn that it was uncertain when exactly Hull would invade Canada, and therefore Dearborn should "take [his] own time and give the necessary orders to officers on the sea-coast." Once he arrived at Albany, Dearborn would "be able to form an opinion of the time required to prepare the troops for action." Summing up Eustis's performance, Henry Adams judges, "Such orders as those of June 24 to Hull, and of June 26 to Dearborn, passed beyond bounds of ordinary incapacity. . . ."[3] Robert Allen Rutland, longtime editor of Madison's papers, does not excuse Eustis or Dearborn, but he puts ultimate responsibility where the Constitution does: with the commander-in-chief. "The early strategy of a three-pronged thrust into Canada," he says, "was based on the uninformed belief that British resistance might be little more than token. No timetable existed, which meant that the three efforts would be launched in helter-skelter fashion."[4]

Though he looked the part of a general, Hull combined the inapt character traits of "vacillation and stubborn pride,"[5] and his "qualities of indecision and inflexibility had possibly been reinforced by a stroke he had suffered about a year before his appointment to the army." One of his comrades later recalled that after that, "he never appeared to be the man he was before." His colonels agreed. Worse yet, his men saw him "in great embarrassment when, on parade before leaving for Detroit, the general lost control of his horse, his stirrups, his balance as well as his hat, and frantically clutched the mane of the frightened animal to save himself." Whatever prestige he had had in his army must have vanished after that.[6]

Hull crossed into Canada in the second week of July aiming to seize Fort Amherstburg. In an augury of things to come, two hundred Ohio militiamen refused to follow him. They claimed the Constitution required them to obey him only within the United States. Hull then issued a proclamation that defecting Canadians would be welcomed: "I come to *find* enemies," he said, "not to *make* them, I come to *protect*, not to *injure* you." He referred to his force as "an army of Friends." After warning, "If the barbarous and savage policy of Great Britain be pursued, and the savages are let loose to murder our citizens and butcher our women and children, this war, will be a war of extermination," Hull added, "The first stroke with the Tomahawk the first attempt with the scalping knife will be the signal for one indiscriminate scene of desolation. *No white man found fighting by the side of an Indian will be taken prisoner.*" Yet he concluded with an offer to accept into his force any Canadian who wanted to join it.[7] Though Hull's proclamation did not yield him significant additions to his force, it did persuade hundreds of Canadian militiamen to go home. In general things were going well.[8]

At this point Hull was spooked. A party he sent south to link up with a party of Ohio militiamen bringing supplies was thwarted by Indians led by Tecumseh and returned empty-handed. He next sent six hundred men, but they too were thwarted in the effort by Indians. Hull responded to news of the fall of Mackinac Island to a mixed force of "more than 1,000 British regulars, Canadian militia, and Indian warriors"[9] with retreat across the Detroit River back into Michigan—though he left three hundred men north of the border.[10] Brock followed him and laid siege to Detroit. He warned Hull, whose men had begun to grumble about his cowardice, that in case of an assault on the American position, the allied Indians under Brock's command might be impossible to restrain. Hull, despondent at the thought of what might befall the many civilians (some his own relatives) in his camp, exclaimed, "My God! What shall I do with these women and children?"[11] Now reduced to indistinct speech, constant dribbling, and crouching in corners of the fort, the general surrendered his command the next day, going so far as to surrender even those portions of it that had been detached and thus not encircled by the besieging British force. One of Hull's captains said, "Not an officer was consulted. Even the women was indignant at the Shameful degradation of the Americ[an] character."[12]

Madison remained in the dark about affairs in the Northwest for several days. On August 9th, he sent General Henry Dearborn salutations.[13] Dearborn's presence at Albany, the president thought, would "aid much in doing all that can be done for the reputation of the campaign." The awkwardness of the recruiting statutes "compel[led] us to moderate some of our expectations" concerning the war's progress. The plan had been for "invasions of Canada at several points" to "have secured the great object of bringing all Upper Canada, & the channels communicating with the Indians, under our Command; with ulterior prospects towards Quebec flattering to our arms." Now the United States must do as well as it could ere the campaign season had passed. Madison told Dearborn that fifteen hundred reinforcements had been sent to Hull to facilitate his movement east toward Niagara. Dearborn was to cooperate with New York's Governor Daniel D. Tompkins in defeating British forces at Niagara and establishing American control of Lake Ontario. Combined with Hull's success on Lake Erie, this would make possible future American operations on the two main towns in British North America. Dearborn was to endeavor to assemble such militia units as he could, in light of the Massachusetts and Connecticut governors' obstreperousness. In case he had enough men, he ought then to undertake "a demonstration towards Quebec . . . in aid of the measures agst. Montreal; which if we can take by means of any sort, we shall find the means of holding."

The president closed his missive by apologizing for the shortage of brigadier generals and telling Dearborn he was going to head to Montpelier on holiday; this last he put down to "the accumulating bile of which I am sensible, & which I never escaped in Augst. on tide water." Several days later Madison wrote to Gallatin, "The Command of the Lakes is obviously of the greatest importance & has always so appeared. I am glad to find it not too late to have that of Ontario. There must have been some mistake as to the effort to obtain it." He added in a postscript that, "We set off tomorrow morning early. . . ."[14] The clear impression these communications leave is that Madison had to this point failed to communicate, directly or through his military secretaries, even the rudiments of his war strategy to his commanders in the field. So unimportant did he find the results of this failure that he nonetheless absented himself from the capital for an extended period of time as the summer came to an end.

Dearborn meanwhile became bogged down in quarreling over not only strategic but command matters. He wrote to Eustis asking "who was to have the command in Upper Canada," which J. C. A. Stagg takes to have meant that he wanted to know who should command the invasion via the Niagara Peninsula. Characteristically, Eustis answered unclearly. Although at Albany, Dearborn remained distracted by the politics of New England military mobilization. He did at last take a significant step, agreeing to an armistice with the governor of Lower Canada on August 8th.[15]

Washington rejected this armistice on August 15th. Little did anyone know that as this burlesque of war proceeded on land, the picayune U.S. Navy was winning an epic victory at sea. Ironically the American commander who with his men made his frigate, U.S.S. *Constitution*, immortal was none other than Captain Isaac Hull, adopted son of General William Hull.[16]

We have a detailed account of the day's events from a member of U.S.S. *Constitution's* crew, Moses Smith. As he tells it, the American ship's pursuit of H.M.S. *Guerrière* came to a successful close on August 19, 1812. Steering southeast at 10:00 AM, "the lookout cried: 'Sail ho!' 'Where away?' inquired the lieutenant in command. 'Two points off the larboard bow, sir!' was the reply." Captain Hull ordered a man aloft, and when asked, the man reported seeing "a great vessel, sir! Tremendous sails." Before a subordinate could respond to Hull's command to call all hands on deck, the men appeared from below.

"The word had passed like lightning from man to man; and all who could be spared, came flocking up like pigeons from a net bed. From the spar deck to the gun deck, from that to the berth deck, every man was roused and on his feet."

Impressed with his own ship's speed, Moses Smith even at decades' remove remained impressed with its opposite number as well. "The stranger hauled his wind," he wrote, "and laid to for us. It was evident that he was an English man-of-war, of a large class, and all ready for action." Soon enough the American crewmen discerned emblazoned in one of the British ship's topsails the words "NOT THE LITTLE BELT"—a reference to British propaganda about an encounter in which an American frigate had had its way with a smaller British ship. (The British newspapers echoed *Little Belt*'s officers and crew in saying that the American ship had fired on her unprovoked and after she had surrendered—all of which was contrary to the sworn accounts of the American officers and crew.)[17] Soon enough, the Americans realized they faced the *Guerrière*.

"As we came up," Smith said, "she began to fire. They was evidently trying to rake us. But we continued on our course, tacking and half tacking, taking good care to avoid being raked. We came so near on one tack, that a 18 lb. shot came through us under the larboard knight-head, striking just abaft the breech of the gun to which I belonged. . . . We immediately picked up the shot, and put it in the mouth of long Tom, a large gun loose on deck—and sent it home again, with our respects."

Shortly Hull said, "Why don't you fire?" "We can't get our guns to bear," came the answer, "as she now lies." "'Never mind, my boys!' said he to the men. 'You shall have her as close as you please. Sailing master! lay her along side!' We came up into the wind," Smith said, "in gallant style. As we fell off a little the *Guerrière* ranged by us her whole length." Then: "'No firing at random!' cried Hull in a subdued tone of voice. 'Let every man look well to his aim.'" A shot from the enemy, and then, "'Now close with them!' cried Hull, raising his voice to its sternest note of command, so that it could be heard on the enemy's decks.

"Along side with her, sailing-master." A whole broadside from our guns followed this command. The Constitution shook from stem to stern. Every spar and yard in her was on a tremble. . . . We instantly followed the thunder of our cannon with three loud cheers, which rang along the ship like the roar of waters, and floated away to the ears of the enemy. This was a Yankee style which the British had not adopted. The English officers often spoke of it to ours, after the war was over. They said that they were astonished at the spirit of our men in the toil and heat of the battle. Amid the dying and the dead, . . . the American heart poured out its patriotism with long and loud cheers. The effect was always electrical, throughout all the struggle for our rights.

When the smoke cleared away after the first broadside, we saw that we had cut off the mizzen mast of the Guerriere, and that her main-yard had been shot from the slings. Her mast and rigging were hanging in great confusion over her sides. . . . This discovery was followed by cheers from the Constitution, and the cry; "Huzza, boys! We've made a brig of her! Next time we'll make her a sloop!"

A little later in the fight, Smith reported, "Several shot now entered [*Constitution's*] hull. One of the largest the enemy could command struck us, but the plank was so hard it fell out and sank in the waters. This was afterwards noticed, and the cry arose: 'Huzza! Her sides are made of iron! See where the shot fell out!' From that circumstance the name of the Constitution was garnished with the familiar title: 'OLD IRONSIDES.' By this title she is known around the world."

Still the *Constitution* continued to bombard the enemy vessel. "In a few moments the foremast was gone, and our prediction was fulfilled. The great Guerriere had become a sloop. Soon after the mainmast followed, rendering her a complete wreck." *Constitution* suffered very little in the fray. "As an intended insult, the English had hoisted a puncheon of molasses on their main stay, and sent out word: 'Do give the Yankees some switchel. They will need it, when they are our prisoners.'" To their surprise the Yankees soon shot the puncheon full of holes, thus bathing the deck of the British ship in the slippery stuff.

Then, out of the blue, the *Guerrière's* captain "appeared in one of our boats, and immediately surrendered himself as a prisoner of war. . . . The delivery of his sword to Hull by Dacres was a scene never to be forgotten by those who witnessed it. 'Captain Hull! what have you got for men?' 'O,' replied Hull, with a sly smile, 'only a parcel of green bush-whackers, Captain Dacres!' 'Bush-whackers! They are more like tigers than men. I never saw men fight so. They fairly drove us from our quarters.'" The American officers decided to blow up the defeated British ship, and the sight struck Smith as remarkable. "Thus ended the capture of the Guerriere."

This significant victory over a British ship, no less, made great impressions both in the United States and in the United Kingdom. People in both places found news of it remarkable, not to say unbelievable. America's naval forces would win other victories in the war, though in the end Britain's gargantuan advantage in number of ships assigned to New World stations meant that America's options in the area of naval strategy were tightly constrained.[18]

When General William Hull returned to the United States, he faced a court-martial. Despite his insistence that Dearborn's failure to mount an invasion to the east accounted for Brock's ability to concentrate two thousand troops around Detroit, he was found guilty. After noting that Hull's surrender entailed "the greatest loss of territory that ever before or since befell the United States," the historian Henry Adams counted this an absurd result: "The storm of public wrath which annihilated Hull and shook Eustis passed harmless over the head of Dearborn. No one knew that Dearborn was at fault, for he had done nothing; and a general who did nothing had that advantage over his rivals whose activity or situation caused them to act. Dearborn threw the whole responsibility on the War Department."[19]

The court sentenced Hull to death for cowardice and neglect of duty. President Madison accepted the court's recommendation that he pardon Hull in recognition of his record during the Revolution and in light of his age.[20]

38

✢ ❁ ✢

Madison understood the significance of these developments. On August 17th he wrote Jefferson that the New England governors', particularly Caleb Strong's, refusal to cooperate in war measures—specifically, in providing him with militia units for coastal defense so that he could use his regulars in Canada—likely would ruin his strategy.[1] Arguably the decisive event in the War of 1812 was Elbridge Gerry's electoral loss to Strong, whose leadership of the Bay State made him the most powerful man in New England. Before the war began Madison's plan was thwarted.

As Madison told it, "The seditious opposition in Mass. & Cont. with the intrigues elsewhere insidiously co-operating with it, have so clogged the wheels of the war, that I fear the campaign will not accomplish the object of it." Even universal cooperation in enlisting volunteers likely would have come up short, he said, but "the discouragements substituted and the little attraction contained in the volunteer act" meant the U.S. Army almost certainly would be inadequately manned. That would "leave us dependent, for every primary operation, on militia, either as volunteers or draughts for six months." Hull, it seemed, would be forced by the loss of Fort "Machilimackinac" either to join with the two thousand reinforcements Madison had ordered sent to him to take Malden, or to move to the other end of Lake Erie and join Generals Dearborn and Tompkins in occupying central Upper Canada.

Thus news of what had befallen Hull's force fell upon Washington like a thunderclap. It meant the conclusive disappointment of Americans' expectations for a quick, essentially costless victory in the war. As Secretary Monroe explained to Speaker Clay in a letter of August 28th,

We have just heard with equal astonishment & concern, that Genl. Hull, has surrendered by capitulation the army under his command at detroit, to the British force opposed to him. The circumstances attending this most mortifying & humiliating event are not known, but so far as we are inform'd on the subject, there appears to be no justification of it. I cannot suspect his integrity; I rather suppose that a panick had seized the whole force, & that he & they became victims, of his want of energy, promptitude of decision & those resources, the characteristic of great minds in difficult emergencies. we understand that after passing the river, he suffered his communication to be cut off with the states of Ohio & Kentucky, and without making any active movement in front to strike terror into the enemy, he remain'd tranquil, thereby evincing a want of confidence in his own means, and giving it time to collect its forces together. no intelligence justifies the belief that he gave battle in a single instance.

Both well informed about what had happened and clearly sick about it, Monroe concluded by saying he wished Madison would find some way to put him to use in the army, where "I wod in a very few days, join our forces assembling beyond the Ohio, & endeavor to recover the ground which we have lost."[2] Madison opted instead to elevate William Henry Harrison to command in that theater, where he made him a major general.[3] He could have used a competent general, and perhaps Monroe would have been one, but a competent secretary of state he already knew him to be. Madison had had enough experience with an incompetent foreign minister. A bird in the hand . . .

With Hull defeated and Dearborn dithering at Albany, the initiative (such as it was) among American commanders passed to the commander of the force on the Niagara River, Federalist patroon of Rensselaerswyck Stephen Van Rensselaer, commander of the New York militia. This land baron's chief qualification for the position was his political prominence, more particularly his position atop what remained of New York Federalism nearly a decade after the death of Alexander Hamilton and the retirement of John Jay. He had no military experience, but unlike Hull and Dearborn, Van Rensselaer demonstrated initiative. He was sent 1,650 U.S. Army regulars under the command of Virginian Brigadier General Alexander Smyth, the Inspector General, and 2,000 Pennsylvania militia volunteers to assist him, and he soon put them to use.[4]

Dearborn's omission to state clearly which of these two generals should be in command would haunt their forces. When Van Rensselaer ordered his men to attack Queenstown Heights on the Niagara Peninsula, they pushed the enemy back, killing General Brock in the process. American forces seized the heights across the river, but, as New York militiaman Lieutenant Jared Willson recalled, the Americans were captured by enemy forces "in fair view of two thousand militia on the opposite shore (poor dastardly wretches) who would not come to our assistance—had they come we might have held our ground untill this time. Oh! shame on them—there surely must be a severe punishment in reserve for these poor, ignoble, base-born wretches." Worst of all, "The indian war-hoop even echoed through their camp and still they could not be prevailed upon to mingle with their associates in arms to oppose the inhuman foe."[5]

One might have thought the Pennsylvanian militia to blame, yet that is not how this man saw it. "But I still think our commander in Chief [Van Rensselaer] is answerable for our ill success. He knew the militia would not all cross—He ought then to have ordered on Gen. Smyth's regulars in season to help us." The general's error supposedly lay in having taken the advice of his cousin, Lieutenant Colonel Solomon Van Rensselaer, "who, allured by the prospects of acquiring unfading Laurels, wished to make a firm stand in Canada with a few regulars and a few militia. This ambitious creature was to take the command, but in the first of the engagement, he was carried off the field severely wounded—Thus has the ambition of one man and the folly of another brought disgrace upon our country." General Van Rensselaer did not simply stand by and watch as the militiamen refused to join in the fighting, however: he later reported that "To my utter astonishment, I found that at the very moment when complete victory was in our hands, the Ardor of the unengaged Troops had entirely subsided. . . . I rode in all directions—urged men by every Consideration to pass over, but in vain." About nine hundred Americans were cut off and surrendered, among them Captain Winfield Scott. He did not assign blame as Lieutenant Willson did. "These vermin," he said of the New York militia, "who infest all republics, boastful enough at home, no sooner found themselves in sight of the enemy than they discovered that the militia of the United States could not be constitutionally marched into a foreign country." General Van Rensselaer, disgusted "with militia punctilios and the strutting General Alexander Smyth," resigned from the army.[6] Smyth succeeded him, "wasted his time composing bombastic proclamations that even the British found laughable," found that the Pennsylvania militiamen would not cross the border for him, and failed in his attack on Fort Erie. Mocked by his men and dropped from the list of American generals by Congress, he rode home to the Old Dominion, forgotten.[7]

In November Dearborn marched to Plattsburg. Apparently cowed by memories of the failed attempt to take Montreal in 1775, he opted to go into winter quarters rather than push an attack on the city and its five hundred defenders.[8] In his official report Dearborn said he had taken command at Plattsburg on November 19 and marched the army twenty miles to the Canadian border. The militia refusing to cross, he had then retreated to Plattsburg. "His campaign lasted four days," Henry Adams summarized, "and he did not enter Canada."

Learning of the other two American armies' situations, Dearborn at least had the good sense to offer his resignation. "I had anticipated disappointment and misfortune in the commencement of the war," he told the war secretary, "but I did by no means apprehend such a deficiency of regular troops and such a series of disasters as we have witnessed."[9] To the president he wrote that it would be necessary to expand the regular army if America were going to win the war.[10] "If an adequate force could be raised in season," he continued, "the latter part of February, or first of March, would be a favourable time to take possession of Montreal. . . ." The force that should be sent ought to be large enough not only to take the town, but to garrison it against the larger force sure to be en route from across the Atlantic. Madison must have been less than pleased with his top general's advice that "I think we ought not to attempt more than we can with certainty accomplish, delay would be a serious evil, but defeat would be a much greater misfortune. I should think it more advisable to act on the defensive the next campaign, than to attempt more than the strength of our regular force would be fully competent to. . . ."

Dearborn next agreed that he "expect[ed]" his "full share of [censure]" over the course of events. After referring Madison to his most recent letter to Eustis, Dearborn closed with, "It will be equally agreeable to me to employ such moderate talents as I possess in the service of my country, or to be permitted to retire to the shades of private life, and remain a mere but interested spectator of passing events."

With the exception of U.S.S. *Constitution,* the U.S. military had performed ineptly in 1812. However, Madison won reelection by a substantial majority. DeWitt Clinton's Republican splinter candidacy drew substantial Federalist support, and thus won all of the New England states other than Vermont. In New York, Clinton's Republican supporters joined with Federalists to give him the victory; not for the last time, Martin Van Buren pulled the wires to make that machine work. Other than that, Clinton and the Federalists also carried New Jersey, Delaware, and five of Maryland's eleven votes—the other six going to Madison. Thus Madison defeated Clinton 128 to 89, which was a narrower margin than 1808's 122 to 53 defeat of South Carolinian Philadelphia Convention Framer Charles Cotesworth Pinckney.[11]

The glaring inadequacy of the U.S. Army would be addressed immediately, starting at the top. As Gallatin explained to Jefferson,

> The series of misfortunes experienced this year in our military land operations exceeds all anticipations made even by those who had least confidence in our inexperienced officers and undisciplined men. I believe that General Dearborn has done all that was in his power. The conduct of Hull, Rensselaer, and Smyth cannot be accounted for on any rational principle. It is to be hoped that Mr. Eustis's resignation will open brighter prospects. For although those three disasters cannot with justice be assigned to him, yet his incapacity and the total want of confidence in him were felt through every ramification of the public service.

Alas, however, "To find a successor qualified, popular, and willing to accept is extremely difficult."[12]

Whether Madison had arrived by the end of 1812 at a similar appraisal of Eustis is a good question. In retirement, pressed on the subject of his high military appointments, he waxed defensive. Henry Lee, son of Madison's onetime friend General/Governor Henry "Light-Horse Harry" Lee, had begun to write about the War of 1812, and after receiving some encouragement in this project (as he had in previous projects) from Madison, he inquired about Madison's personnel decisions.[13]

> I shall have frequently to advert to the Character & constitution of your cabinet—and I do not know in what way I shall account for the singular infelicity of many of your appointments. I do not know that I shall go back as far as Robert Smith—But . . . Genl. Hull, Genl. Dearbourn, and Genl. Smyth—are probably phenomena, in the history of apparent and actual unfitness, that no other administration in any country can equal. I am at a loss to imagine & cannot presume to say, whether these men were recieved from the pressure of certain political causes, or owed their appointments to the erroneuous estimate of your own mind.[14]

Madison answered in detail:[15]

Selections for office always liable to error was particularly so for military command at the commencement of the late war. The survivors of the Revolutionary band who alone had been instructed by experience in the field were but few; and of those several of the most distinguished, were disqualified by age or infirmities, or precluded by foreknown objections in the advisory Branch of the appointing Department [i.e., the Senate]. This last cause deprived the army of services which would have been very acceptable to the nominating Branch.

He then got down to specifics.

That the appointment of Hull was unfortunate was but too soon made certain. Yet he was not only recommended from respectable quarters, but by his ostensible fitness also. He was a man of good understanding. He had served with reputation, and even some *eclât* in the Revolutionary Army; He had been the Govr. at Detroit, and could not but be acquainted with the population & localities on the hostile as well as on his own side of the boundary; And he had been the superintendent of our Affairs with the Indians, a knowledge which was of much importance. These advantages seemed to give him not only a preference, but an appropriateness for his trust.

Of course, he concluded, once Hull proved a spectacular failure in his role, "some who had been most warm in his recommendation, were most ready to condemn the confidence put in him."

As to Dearborn, "To say nothing of his acknowledged bravery & firmness, his military experience & local knowledge acquired during the Revolutionary war, had their value." Besides, he had for eight years served to President Jefferson's satisfaction as secretary of war, both in regard to his qualifications and in relation to "his sound and practical judgment." Dearborn also took to his post "a public standing calculated to repress jealousies in others, not easy to be guarded agst. in such cases."

On the other hand, Madison conceded, "The advanced position in the service, given to General Smyth was much to be regretted. Some of the circumstances which led to it were specious, and the scale & cultivation of his understanding very respectable, but his talent for military command was equally mistaken by himself, and by his friends."

"As you have made no reference to Docr. Eustis," he wrote, "I ought perhaps to observe a like silence. But having gone so far on the occasion, I am tempted to do him the justice of saying that he was an acceptable member of the Cabinet, that he possessed an accomplished mind, a useful knowledge on military subjects derived from his connexion with the Revolutionary army, and a vigilant superintendence of subordinate agents. . . ." Eustis's resignation, Madison offered, did not reflect on "these endowments." Rather the former secretary of war would have been regarded as a success in peacetime, and his failings in war resulted in the main from "the overload of duties required by military preparations on the great scale enjoined by law, and the refusal to him of assistants asked for who were ridiculed as crutches for official infirmity. . . ." Congress's postwar reorganization of the War Department "in a time of peace for an army reduced to so small an establishment," to Madison's eye, vindicated his defense of Eustis's performance.

39

A t the end of 1812, Madison shuffled his Cabinet. Secretary of War Eustis left, to be replaced on a temporary basis by James Monroe. That result could only follow once another possibility had been ruled out: that Monroe should take up a field command.

Monroe brought that matter up in a letter of September 2, 1812, advising the president that the administration certainly should not try to spare Hull the blame for the Detroit debacle, noting that, "If on further reflection you should be of opinion that my employment might be useful, I am inclind to undertake it."[1] "If I went," he said, "my wish would be to serve the active part of the campaign, & then return to my station here." In other words Monroe would lead an army only so long as was necessary to the conquest of Montreal, and then he would return to his post as the second-ranking civilian official in the government. "I think I might be back in Novr.," he concluded. If necessary, he said, "perhaps Mr Rush might act per interim, for me." On the other hand, he offered helpfully, someone might be appointed to serve in Monroe's absence, "with a view to keep it open to my renomination on my return, if you approved." He then named for Madison some of the officers who might accompany him, lamenting along the way that his absence "would I know lay new & heavy burthens on you."

Madison replied on September 5th that he thought this an excellent idea, if the secretary of war (Eustis) agreed, and he would leave it to Monroe and Eustis to decide whether the former should assume Hull's command or take up the more eastern command.[2] Madison saw two problems, however: first, that in light of logistical realities, it might be too late in the season for Monroe to undertake the western operation; and second, that Madison likely had already appointed the maximum number of generals that the law allowed. "Without some conspicuous effect, which might be found impossible," the president concluded, "the experiment might even have an injurious recoil."

After consulting with Eustis, Monroe advised the president of the secretary's endorsement of the plan.[3] He had in mind to go west, where even
if the "principal benefit would be the moral effect the measure might have
on the public mind," Monroe's presence with a substantial force would also
have a "salutary" "effect" "[o]n the operations under Genl. Dearborn . . . ,
as it would keep the whole force now in upper Canada still there." Monroe's
conclusion gave an indication of the nature of his relationship with Mrs.
Monroe. "In case I go," he said, "as is presumeable, I must get you to write
a letter to Mrs. Monroe apprizing her of the obligation I am under, & the
difficulty of my declining it. It would contribute to reconcile her to it." As
we shall see, Elizabeth Monroe was no Dolley Madison.

The next day Monroe wrote to the president again.[4] Although willing to
be sent west "to promote an organization of the forces, to digest their plan of
operations, & facilitate a concert between the generals," he had concluded
that "[t]he effect on public opinion would be greater, if indeed any useful effect might be expected from it, by appointing me to command, than merely
making a visit to the country." Eustis, said Monroe, thought that Monroe
ought to be made a major general, "in consideration of the large bodies of
volunteers collecting from the states contiguous to the scene of action." That
rank "would carry with it the command in that quarter." In light of his recent correspondence with James Barbour, Monroe told the president, "If
I take the command, I should write the Govr of Virga, by whose cooperation a considerable volunteer force of cavalry, may be procurd, as also of
infantry." Monroe told Madison that Eustis would be writing him with an
endorsement of Monroe's plan, and so he would no doubt have been disappointed to see that the secretary of war only advised, "Mr Munroe had
mentioned the subject and is willing, indeed he proposed to go out"—that
is, that he made no mention of rank at all.[5]

Monroe must have been happy to see Madison's missive to him of September 8th. However, it did again demonstrate, if additional proof were needed,
that Madison was out of his depth when it came to military matters. He did
not know, he said, what Dearborn had in mind—whether he intended to
head directly for Montreal, "or to draw away the force from above, in order
to strike at that at Niagara." Whatever he might do, Madison doubted it would
"heal the wound which Hull has given to the Campaign." "As men in abundance are already in motion," he continued, "or awaiting orders, nothing is
necessary but to give them a head that will inspire confidence, concentrate
their force, and direct the application of it. I am not without hopes that in
some way or other this critical service may proceed from you." After musing

a bit on various expedients that might be taken to get around the too-many-generals problem, Madison concluded that even if Monroe's presence did not yield sufficient enlistments to give him a force to command, he could carry "a blank commission of Majr. Genl. . . . in [his] pocket," and "in case of failure, [it wd] give the better gloss to your junction with the army, and guiding its councils if not commanding its operations."[6]

Monroe apparently decided he did not like the way this was going. Although he had sent him an announcement to be published in the *National Intelligencer* to the effect that he was going to Ohio to help organize a new levy of troops "to repell the invasion brought on the frontiers by the surrender of . . . Genl Hull, & to repair the losses of that unexpected disaster," and that he would have the rank of major general if the recruitment proved successful, he wrote the editor to hold back on publishing it until he received the final word from Madison.[7] Soon came word that the governor of Kentucky had appointed William Henry Harrison brevet major general of Kentucky's militia. Henry Clay said the appointment was provisional, but it seemed to cloud the waters in which Monroe was fishing.[8] By September 17th Madison had told Monroe that he preferred to keep Monroe right where he was, and Monroe insisted that "I had no opinion on the subject but was prepar'd, to act in any situation in which it might be thought I might be most useful."[9]

Monroe's closest political advisor, George Hay, best captured the situation Monroe found himself in.[10] First, he said that in case Monroe were offered "the Command of the army," he saw no reason he should not take it. Congress would have to pass a law empowering Madison to appoint a lieutenant general, and since the public was already aware that Monroe was being considered for the post, such a law would obviously be passed with Monroe in mind. Dearborn would have no valid complaint, as he had been appointed major general ahead of men who had outranked him during the Revolution. Anyway, Hay noted, the public did not hold Dearborn in very high regard.

"I take it for granted," Hay continued, "that you would not accept any Command, but that in chief." If he stayed in Washington, however, Monroe certainly should retain his present post. As the world would believe he had been consulted in the matter, Monroe could not possibly take Eustis's former job without seeming to have maneuvered himself into it. Even if Jefferson succeeded him at State, moving to War would still leave the impression that all of the changes had been intended to make room for Jefferson—and thus to demote Monroe. (Taking Jefferson into the Cabinet would be a bad idea in any event, as then three of the top officials would be Virginian.)

Hay also considered recent developments in Europe. They were auspicious for the United States. Napoleon's bad luck in Russia and faltering posture in Spain seemed to hint that moral objections to a war effectively on France's side no longer held any merit. From a practical point of view, this meant that American victory against Britain was not going to contribute to empowering Napoleon to invade the United States.

Hay closed with reference to Republicans' recent loss of the lower house of Maryland's legislature. "Was this change produced by the war," he asked, "or by the mob in Baltimore?" Here Hay referred to a notable episode of mass villainy: the Baltimore Riots of 1812.

The Baltimore Riots are recalled now, if at all, as the episode in which a hero of the Revolution, former Virginia governor and Revolutionary War general Henry "Light-Horse Harry" Lee, was beaten so severely as to be essentially disabled for the rest of his life. Lauded by General George Washington himself in a letter to Congress, Lee eventually became better known still as the father of the brilliant Confederate general Robert E. Lee.[11]

The riots pitted a Jeffersonian Republican mob against a highly Republican city's chief Federalist newspaper, the *Federal Republican*. The semiweekly paper's editor's mistake took the form of printing on June 20, 1812, a blast against the war as "unnecessary" and a vow to bring about its end using "every constitutional argument and every legal means." Two days later a mob assembled outside his place of business. Ultimately three separate nights saw huge crowds of hostiles converge on it, with the result that Lee was crippled, another veteran of the Revolution was killed, and five more Federalists were grievously wounded.[12]

The mobs of roving Republicans hurt various other Baltimore residents as well, among them "Briscoe, a free negro," who, because of his "expressions of affection for the British nation, had to deplore the sacrifice of his houses, (amounting to about eight hundred dollars,) by [the mob's] unfeeling agency." Recent immigrants to Baltimore, having brought their Old World animosities to the New World with them, gave vent to their passions under cover of the riot. "To this source may be traced," the legislative investigation concluded, "those convulsions of the city, where the United Irishmen and Orange-Men were the most prominent."

On July 27th a new number of the paper appeared. It "contained spirited strictures upon the lawless temper of the city, and the indisposition of the civil or military officers to discharge the respective duties of their offices; and upon the executive of Maryland." By "early candle light " a huge throng of men assembled outside the publisher's house. "Major Barney, with about thirty horsemen under his command, moved down between 1 and 3 o'clock to the house," but when his interposition proved ineffective, the mayor, the attorney-general, and the local militia commander escorted the publisher, Mr. Hanson, "and his friends, . . . to the gaol as a place of security." This hollow square's entire progress to the jail featured bombardment with rocks at times so heavy that the protected men feared for their lives, "notwithstanding it endangered the lives of the political favourites of the mob."

Meanwhile a Republican newspaper, the *Whig*, gave broad circulation to the charges that the men in the jail "were enemies to the country; that [Hanson's] visit to Baltimore was the consequence of an arrangement to insult and dragoon the citizens; that they were murderers; [and] that they would avail themselves of a constitutional right to change the *venue* to an adjoining county, and thus escape the punishment due to their crimes."

The mayor and the militia general on the scene refused to arm the men under their protection, and the general, John Stricker, was found by the legislative committee to have forbidden his subordinate colonel "to deliver out to the men under his command ball cartridges." When the militia infantry were called out, few answered—the committee said due "to the united causes of indisposition to protect the persons in the gaol, an apprehension of immediate danger, or future proscription, and to the inefficient preparation under which they were ordered to march."

The mob knew the militiamen had been removed from the scene. It also received a vow from the mayor that the men in the jail would not be relocated. Despite the mayor, the mob attacked the jail, and in the end it murdered General James Lingan, in days gone by recipient of accolades from George Washington himself. When the various malefactors came to trial, partisan Federalist juries acquitted even the most manifestly guilty of them—even the murderers of Lingan. This course of events led the committee to determine that Mayor Edward Johnson, Esq., displayed "indisposition to resort to the ordinary powers of coercion, with which he was invested, against the turbulent and wicked, . . . so distinguished as to encourage a belief that he connived at and approbated their excesses." He used "intemperate language against the *Federal Republican*, the inevitable effect of which was to sanction and excite . . . the popular excesses against the same." In short the mob took his and other officials' cues that it might have its way without interference from them. Stricker came in for similar legislative excoriation—in his case for ordering a subordinate not "to fire on any assailants." By merely rallying his troops in a display of force he could have overawed the mob. He could have, it said, but he never did. Finally the state's attorney general, by forgoing the option of moving the trials to a county not dominated by rabid Republicans, essentially made it impossible for "an impartial trial to be had." He too earned "from this house a severe animadversion"—for all the good it did.

In these events' aftermath, a handful of Republicans came to trial. A juror later said "that the affray originated with them tories [i.e., Federalists], and that they all ought to have been killed, and that he would rather starve than find a verdict of guilty against any of the rioters."[13] All were acquitted. The Federalist editor Hanson too, though he had been "severely beaten" repeatedly alongside General Lee, was brought to trial in the death of a man killed leading an assault upon the editor's house, and Maryland's leading Federalist attorneys—Luther Martin (long-time Maryland attorney general, he of Philadelphia Convention and Chase impeachment fame), Robert Goodloe Harper (hero of the XYZ Affair), and Philip Barton Key (also a Chase impeachment veteran, uncle of Francis Scott Key)—served him as defense counsel. Successful in their motion to relocate the trial to Federalist-dominated Annapolis, they persuaded a jury to acquit "without leaving its box."[14]

Federalists elsewhere expressed their outrage. The *Hartford Courant* thundered that the war's real purpose was to destroy the freedom of the press. Republican mobs' actions against the *American Patriot* in Savannah and the *Norristown Herald* in the Keystone State buttressed the allegation—as did local postmasters' actions against local papers in several places. Other states witnessed scenes of Republican political violence too.[15]

Republicans responded by hurling allegations of political machinations back at Federalists. The Baltimore government, apparently without any sense of shame, issued a report finding its own officials blameless.[16] Perhaps misled by the report, which came to him under cover of a letter from the Maryland attorney general explaining that the post office in Baltimore had never been in danger during the riots and averring that in case any effort were made against it, "it would be instantly put down by a Very large proportion of the people of Baltimore," President Madison characterized the city government's report as "a seasonable antidote to the misrepresentations propagated by" Federalists.[17]

40

✦ ❈ ✦

ongress turned to perfecting the military's organization at the end of 1812. A delegation demanded that Eustis be replaced, and he resigned.[1] This again brought up the question of what role Monroe would fill going forward. Senator William Crawford, R-GA, wrote that contenders for the War Department included Dearborn, Armstrong, Harrison, Tompkins, and Monroe.[2] Monroe and Dearborn having turned it down, Gallatin told Madison, "No person thinks [Tompkins] equal to the place at such time as this," then added, "The office requires first abilities & frightens those who know best its difficulties," so that Crawford likely would decline if offered too.[3] Crawford bowed out gracefully, telling Madison the day after receiving the offer, "I am not qualified to discharge the duties which would devolve upon me, by obeying your call, with reputation to myself, and with advantage to the Country." Guessing that Madison would see political calculation in this, the senator added that, "in the present Situation of the nation, nothing but a deep Sense of my incapacity to discharge the duties of the office . . . would induce me to decline the offer." Since DeWitt Clinton's stab at the presidency in 1812 ruled out a future party nomination for him, that left John Armstrong as Monroe's most likely rival in 1816. Yet his was the last candidacy standing for secretary of war.

The president received advice about Armstrong versus Tompkins from Gallatin. Perhaps Armstrong was indolent, he said, but taking Tompkins from the New York governorship would likely entail the loss of that position by the Republican Party at the next election. If Tompkins must be taken into the Cabinet, Gallatin would cede his position to the New Yorker and let him become treasury secretary. Besides, he insisted, "I feel no hesitation in saying that as respects talents & military knowledge, Gen. Armstrong is much superior to the Governor, who I fear would prove inadequate to the task of organizing the department & the army." Perhaps equally important,

"Public opinion has also assigned a standing to Gen. Armstrong both as a military man & as a man of talents, which will shield him & the administration from the attacks to which the other gentleman would be as much exposed as Dr. Eustis."[4]

Madison wrote Armstrong on January 14, 1813, asking him to relieve Monroe of having to do double duty *tout de suite* and enclosing his commission. Armstrong responded promptly that he would indeed accept the post, but that "an interview with Gen. Dearborn, preliminary to [his] entering on the duties of the War Department, would be so useful, if not indispensable to a prompt & regular discharge of [the duties of the War Department]" that he would set out for Albany immediately, and thence to Washington.[5] Madison could not have known that this minor instance of insubordination would come to be emblematic of Armstrong's tenure at the War Department. Due mainly to unhappiness with his performance in France and his role in the Newburgh Conspiracy, the Senate confirmed the new secretary's appointment by the narrow margin of 18–15.[6]

Navy secretary Paul Hamilton also left at last, to be succeeded by William Jones. The outgoing secretary responded to the idea of resigning by pointing to the U.S. Navy's several accomplishments in the war to this point, besides adding that the navy's ships had all been refurbished and the department's fiscal affairs carefully attended; but the president replied that Congress would make no further naval appropriations until Hamilton departed. Hamilton replied, "Sir, I understand your meaning, and here is my commission."[7]

The difference resembled that between night and day. Jones, a Pennsylvanian merchant and sea captain, had been considered for the post of secretary of the navy by Jefferson at the beginning of his administration. Madison would remember him as "the fittest minister who had ever been charged with the Navy Department," and although there had been only a handful by then, the former president meant that as a significant compliment.[8] No one knew when Jones assumed the post how straitened the navy's circumstances soon would be.

They also did not know—who could have dreamed?—that the geostrategic picture stood on the verge of a kaleidoscopic reorientation. Napoleon, successful in all of his wars from 1796 through 1809, decided in 1812 to attack his titular ally Alexander I, Emperor of All the Russias at the head of a 674,000-man army in the spring of 1812.[9] As the leading historian of Napoleon's warfare put it, "Time was to show that the decision to invade Russia constituted the irrevocable step which effectively compromised any remaining chance of survival for Napoleon and his Empire. From the time the first troops crossed the Niemen, the Emperor was committed to the path leading inexorably to St. Helena [the place of his ultimate exile], and although the next few years would hold several transient military successes for his arms, there could be no retracing his steps."[10]

The French emperor's army began to cross the Niemen, then the border between East Prussia and the Russian Empire, on June 23rd—five days after Congress declared war on Britain. The campaign's chief battle, which, though a victory, was not the climax Napoleon hoped it would be, occurred at Borodino on September 7, 1812, and a week after that, Napoleon marched into Moscow. He found that most of the city's three hundred thousand inhabitants had heeded their governor's order to abandon it.[11] Frustrated by his Russian counterpart's refusal to come to terms and immobilized by uncharacteristic indecision, Napoleon began the extremely long retreat back to France only after the Russian winter had begun to set in. By the time his *Grande Armée* crossed back out of Russian territory, it had dwindled to ninety-three thousand men. Napoleon had already reappeared in Paris to try to reconstitute his army; experienced soldiers and prime horses would prove impossible to replace.[12]

Ordinarily Americans of both parties would have rejoiced at the news of Napoleon's defeat. In 1812, however, it marked a significant strategic debacle for the United States. Having declared war on the chief power in a succession of anti-French coalitions, Great Britain, the Americans were left in a horrendously awkward position by Napoleon's shocking defeat. Soon, Britain might decide to redirect some more substantial share of its military power into the North American war. Given the Americans' poor performance in that war in 1812 and the Madison administration's relatively weak political position, any such shift could be a disaster.

However, Britain and America had a common friend: Emperor Alexander I. One need not accept Henry Adams's argument that his grandfather's skilled diplomacy accounted for Alexander's decision to stand up to Napoleon in 1812 rather than accept more severe enforcement of the Berlin and Milan Decrees, and thus for Napoleon's fateful decision to invade Russia, in order to believe that Adams did indeed stand close to the Russian autocrat. One need not accept it, but the French minister in St. Petersburg, Armand-Augustin-Louis, marquis de Caulaincourt, duc de Vicence, certainly did: "It seems you are great favorites here," he told the American, "you have found powerful protection."[13]

As Henry Adams put it, "Adams's diplomatic victory was Napoleonic in its magnitude and completeness." It marked a major turning point in European history—among other things, we can see it now as bringing on the end of a millennium in which France was the most important European power. It also provoked Alexander to take the next obvious step and try to patch things up between his two Anglophone friends.

The American minister kept a superb journal across his very long life from 1779, when he was aged twelve, until 1848, when he died three days after the last entry at age eighty. In that time he served in the highest governmental offices, including minister to Russia, member of the negotiating team at Ghent in 1815, United States representative, United States senator, secretary of state, and president of the United States. The diary is a priceless record of events only he could have described.

As Adams recounted it, he went to see Count Romanzoff, Alexander's chief minister, at 7:00 PM on September 21, 1812.[14] Alexander had told Romanzoff to discuss the new international situation with Adams. As Alexander saw it, the commercial benefit he had expected his people to reap from his having made peace with England—access to American goods—now stood to be lost because of the Anglo-American war. Alexander had thought both sides hesitant to engage in such a war, and so he intended to offer his mediation. Did Adams know of "any difficulty or obstacle on the part of the Government of the United States, if he should offer his mediation for the purpose of effecting a pacification?"

Adams replied that of course he could not at the moment know what his government was thinking, and in fact he had not even received official notice of the war's declaration,

> But that I well knew, it was with extreme reluctance they had engaged in the War; that I was very sure, whatever determination they might form upon the proposal of the Emperor's Mediation, they would receive . . . it as a new Evidence of His Majesty's regard and friendship for the United States; and that I was not aware of any obstacle or difficulty which could occasion them to decline accepting it—For myself, I so deeply lamented the very existence of the War, that I should welcome any facility for bringing it to a just and honourable termination—I lamented it, because I thought that the only Cause which made it absolutely unavoidable [the Orders-in-Council], was actually removed at the moment when the Declaration was made. . . .

According to Adams's account, he went on to add that he thought British policy had left America no alternative to declaring war. "The Declaration of the English Regent in April, and the letter which Mr. Foster had written to the American Secretary of State in communicating it, had as it appeared to me left the American Government no alternative, but an immediate appeal to arms, or a dishonourable abandonment of all the unquestionable rights for which they had contended, and even the essential characteristics of an independent Nation—The blame of the War," he concluded, "was therefore entirely on the English side; but the war itself was not the less disagreeable to me. . . ." In summation he insisted that "I lamented it particularly as occurring at a period when from my good wishes for Russia, and the Russian Cause, I should have rejoyced to see Friendship and Harmony taking place between America and England. . . . I knew the war would affect unfavourably the interests of Russia—I knew it must be highly injurious both to the United States and England—I could see no good result as likely to arise from it to any one. . . ."

The count replied that he and the emperor had come to the same conclusion. In fact the emperor had had this idea of offering his mediation. Perhaps having a friend to both parties aid in the negotiations would smooth the way to a resolution. Adams and the count went back and forth about details of arranging a mediation, and then the count offered that Alexander truly did admire America, adding that Alexander had insisted on hearing that the count had such a picture on seeing the count's picture of Monticello for himself.

When next Adams chatted with the count, the conversation turned to the American grievances that had prompted the declaration of war.[15] Yes, Adams told him, war might have been averted if the Orders-in-Council had been revoked sooner. Yet, war having begun, the U.S. Government almost certainly would insist on an end to impressment—a practice he went on to describe to the Russian. After telling him how it worked and why British sailors so strongly preferred service in American crews, for which the British government had "no other remedy . . . than that violent and tyrannical practice of their naval Officers of stealing men from our merchant vessels," Adams said to Romanzoff that he "hoped if we could not hit upon any expedient for arranging it, he, the Count would furnish us with one," and the Russian replied in the French that served as that era's diplomatic language, "il faudra travailler à cela" ("we'll have to work on that").

In the event the British rejected the mediation offer—Adams only learned of the British decision in November 1813, though Alexander, away at Bautzen in central Germany on campaign, received the news in July.[16] By then another year of war had gone by.

As Madison's first presidential term drew to an end, the personnel of his administration were being shuffled some more. Treasury Secretary Gallatin, his most trusted and ablest Cabinet member, so disliked dealing with Armstrong in the Cabinet that he accepted an appointment to the peace delegation intended to negotiate through the Russian emperor's mediation at St. Petersburg. Senator William Crawford, who accompanied Gallatin on the voyage to join Adams, advised Madison before he departed that General Wilkinson must not be left at New Orleans.[17] The general had grown to be so disliked there, he counseled, that his continued presence in Louisiana would mean that that state's senators would join the opposition in the next session of Congress—which would shift party control of the Senate into the hands of the Federalists. Rather than Wilkinson, Madison ought to send a general "whose character is above suspicion." "In the Western and Southern States," the Georgian senator said, Wilkinson "is generally believed to be one of the most abandoned and profligate of men. The Senators of these states with only two exceptions voted against him as major genl." (The inexhaustibly pestiferous William Branch Giles of Virginia was joined in this by a South Carolinian.) For Wilkinson to stay on would be "in opposition to the feelings & wishes of the great majority of the people." On March 10th Secretary Armstrong solved this problem: he ordered Wilkinson to report to General Dearborn, his new commanding officer, in the north.[18] Try as they might, scholars have been unable to say why Wilkinson was not simply cashiered from the service.

On March 4, 1813, Madison took the constitutional oath of office a second time and gave his Second Inaugural Address.[19] The *National Intelligencer* published the speech's text on the same day.[20] After a characteristically convoluted introductory section in which he said he would "be compelled to shrink" from his duty if not certain that the American people supported him and that the war was just—so just that "the smiles of heaven" must shine down "on the means of conducting it to a successful conclusion"—he laid out his understanding of the country's situation. As he told it, Great Britain "long" waged war upon the United States ere the United States, which forbore requiting that great power's hostility "until arguments and expostulations had been exhausted; until a positive declaration had been received, that the wrongs provoking it, would not be discontinued"; and until enduring unrequited war any longer risked "breaking down the Spirit of the nation, destroying all confidence in itself, and in its political Institutions," at last declared war on Great Britain. America had faced a choice between "perpetuating a State of disgraceful suffering" and "regaining, by more costly sacrifices and more severe struggles, our lost rank and respect."[21]

Madison next insisted that America's "equality with other powers" depended on vindicating its seamen's rights by putting a stop to British impressment of them.[22] "[T]he cruel sufferings of that portion of the American people," he said, "have found their way to every bosom, not dead to the sympathies of human nature." In its conduct during the war, America had followed every "usage of civilized nations" without violating any "precept of courtesy or humanity." Britain, for its part, had in this account transgressed those usages in numerous ways, notably by "retain[ing] as prisoners of war, citizens of the United States, not liable to be so considered," by refusing to recognize the American citizenship of British emigrés, and by taking Indian associates into battle with them "eager to glut their savage thirst, with the blood of the vanquished, and to finish the work of torture and death, on maimed and defenceless captives," besides "extort[ing] victory over the unconquerable valour of our troops, by presenting to the sympathy of their chief captives awaiting massacre from their savage associates." Everyone listening to or reading this address would have recognized Hull's fate in this passage.

After complaining that the United Kingdom had shown "further contempt for the modes of honorable warfare" by attempting to sow disunion sentiments in the United States, "and thus to dismember our confederated Republic," Madison underscored his claim about the morality of the American effort by invoking repeated attempts to end the war on "reasonable terms." These had been "received in a spirit, forbidding every reliance, not placed on the military resources of the nation." America's resources were so great that, while Britain's steps against American commerce "recoiled upon themselves," they also "have given to our national faculties a more rapid development; and draining or diverting the precious metals from British circulation & British vaults, have poured them into those of the United States."

"Already," he closed, "have the gallant exploits of our naval heroes, proved to the world our inherent capacity to maintain our rights on one element. If the reputation of our arms has been thrown under clouds on the other . . . [,] nothing is wanted to correspondent triumphs there also, but the discipline & habits which are in daily progress." So Madison, in this final great speech of his career in federal politics, focused almost exclusively on the ongoing military conflict. He said essentially nothing about what today would be called a "legislative program," or even about Republican principles. His points were that the war had been imposed upon the United States, whose leaders had declined it as long as self-respect allowed; that it had been fought morally and, so far as the United States Navy was concerned, well; that the dastardly enemy bore all the blame; that unanticipated economic development had been among its results; and that Americans had every right to expect their army to come up to their navy's level. Persevere was the lesson the president wanted his fellow citizens to draw from his address. Persevere.

41

+ ☼ +

ongress was to return in late May. In the interim financing the war effort
would be difficult because New England, particularly New England bankers, was becoming increasingly uncooperative. The British decision to
exempt New England ports from what otherwise was a blockade of the entire
American Atlantic coast undercut what in any event would have been a weak
pro-administration, pro-war impulse east of the Hudson.[1] Economic incentives too drew many New Englanders, but not only New Englanders, into
skirting the wartime ban on trade with the British.[2] Importation of contraband via New England ports meant that Boston bankers collected bank bills
issued by other states' banks. Bostonians' ability to redeem their notes for
specie whenever they wanted put other regions' banks at their mercy. They
could drain entire regions of specie (gold and silver)—or use the threat of it
to bend other regions' politicians in Washington to their will.[3]

To an increasing degree New England bankers expressed their growing
antipathy to the Madison administration, and to Mr. Madison's War, by a
more direct route: refusing to underwrite it. Secretary Gallatin's ingenuity,
which was considerable, met its match in this environment. As he confided
to Monroe early in 1813, "It is my opinion that . . . no limits should be volun-
tarily put to the national expenditure at this time; in other words that all the
resources which can be brought into action should be applied to the prosecution of the war in the most efficient manner."[4] Still, there were "natural
limits," he conceded, and he "doubt[ed] whether even a [F]ederalist having the confidence of money lenders would succeed." Even given $5 million
of plain money-printing, the military expenditures the administration contemplated would necessitate borrowing $26 million.

Gallatin mentioned a couple of expedients that might be adopted, then
concluded of the amount the administration would need that "It is six times
as much as the whole of what we could last year obtain from individuals; and

from Banks we can expect but a trifle more." To put this huge sum into perspective, he noted that, "It is equal to the whole domestic debt contracted by the U. States during the revolutionary war; and that debt was almost altogether the result of non-payment & not of voluntary loans." If that were not bad enough, he noted too that, "It is more than double the aggregate of all the loans (including that of 1812) obtained from individuals in America by the United States, since the establishment of this Government." Anyway, he concluded, asking for $18 million would be more likely to yield that amount than requesting $24 million would, because the latter figure would make the government appear desperate, thus not creditworthy. Whatever Monroe and his colleagues might think of that, Gallatin insisted that "all the resources which can be brought into action should be applied to the prosecution of the war."

In the early weeks of 1813, American forces in the Northwest took steps pregnant with negative consequences. Crossing the Canadian border into Upper Canada, an army under Brigadier General Zebulon Pike sailed to the provincial capital of York, which was thinly defended, and taking advantage of supporting fire from U.S. Navy schooners, the Americans took the town. The British commander on the scene ordered that the province's Government House be blown up, and Pike was killed when the British magazine exploded. The defending force of fewer than a thousand men escaped to fight another day, but the basis of the myth of wanton American destruction still central to Canada's national self-image had been established.[5]

The new Congress convened on May 24, 1813. Though still in control, Republicans commanded smaller majorities. Likely to Madison's relief, however, John Randolph of Roanoke had just suffered his first electoral loss. This left only one Tertium Quid in Congress, and the dissident Republican faction's longtime mouthpiece, *The Spirit of Seventy-Six,* closed up shop for lack of business the following spring.[6]

Madison's message to Congress, which was delivered on May 25th, concerned diplomatic and military matters alone.[7] As he explained, "Being aware of the inconveniences to which a protracted Session at this Season, would be liable [that is, exposure to the hot, humid Tidewater climate], I limit the present communication to objects of primary importance."

The president began by informing Congress of Alexander I's mediation offer and of his own decision to accept it. He explained that he had sent two negotiators to join Minister Adams in St. Petersburg for the purpose, adding that he had charged them to negotiate a trade treaty with Russia while they were at it. America could hope that Britain's desire for friendship with

Russia's ruler would lead her to negotiate in good faith, he insisted. So too Britain ought to prefer U.S. Government enforcement of the new American Seaman's Act of March 3, 1813, which established a substantial penalty for any American ship's captain who employed a sailor not either a native of the United States or having shown a certified copy of his naturalization papers to a customs collector, as well as a penalty for forging such papers, to impressment, "inasmuch as the latter, leaves the discrimination between the mariners of the two nations, to officers exposed, by unavoidable bias, as well as by a defect of evidence, to a wrong decision. . . ."[8]

Although he expressed hope that Britain would reason its way to the desired conclusion, he admitted that "vigorous employment of the resources of war" by Congress remained essential—particularly as the British, "uninfluenced by the unvaried examples of humanity set them, are adding to the savage fury of it, on one Frontier, a system of plunder and conflagration, on the other, equally forbidden by respect for national character, and by the established rules of civilized warfare."

Madison next described some of the previous year's successes of American arms—among which the story of the sloop *Hornet*'s victory over the sloop *Peacock* was to Madison emblematic. In the February 1813 contest between two twenty-gun ships off the coast of British Guiana,[9] Hornet made quick work of her enemy. As the American captain told the story, though the two ships fired broadsides at each other from fifteen yards' distance, *Hornet* suffered essentially no damage, but *Peacock* sank within minutes. "The British captain and four men were killed outright, thirty-three officers and men were wounded, and the brig was sunk in an action of less than fifteen minutes, while the '*Hornet*' lost one man killed and two wounded, all aloft, and not a shot penetrated her hull."[10] Madison was right to say that *Hornet*'s captain, James Lawrence, had won the battle "with a celerity so unexampled, and with a slaughter of the Enemy, so disproportionate to the loss in the *Hornet*, as to claim for the conquerors the highest praise," besides the cash award appropriated by Congress. American ships had thwarted British attempts to control American coastal waters too.

Madison was on less solid ground when he informed Congress, "On the Lakes our superiority is near at hand, where it is not already established," and had almost no ground for asserting that "the Army is destined to a glory not less brilliant, than that which already encircles the navy." Of particular note in this connection must be Madison's statement that "The attack and capture of York is, in that quarter, a presage of future and greater victories. . . ." It was a presage of something, Americans would learn soon enough. So too his calm reassurance that recent steps to enlist more soldiers and enlarge the army's staff promised success would seem fanciful soon enough.

Next came the passage in which Madison gave account of the government's finances. What either house of Congress thought as its clerk read his assurances that much of the money needed to fund the military during the following year would be obtained via issuance of treasury notes (that is, printing currency), and more would be obtained through sales of public lands, we can only speculate, but surely they cannot have found these expedients very hopeful. A loan of $1 million dollars from the Commonwealth of Pennsylvania for a government that had spent just over $15 million in the most recent six-month budgeting period made a rather pitiful resort. Madison came at last to the conclusion that "This view of our finances, whilst it shews that due provision has been made for the expenses of the Current year, shews at the same time, by the limited amount of the actual revenue, and the dependence on loans, the necessity of providing more adequately for the future supplies of the Treasury." With establishment of a system of internal taxes, the Federal Government could impress potential lenders as a better credit risk, and thus borrow money in the future at a lower interest rate than 7.5 percent—the rate it was paying on its most recent $16 million loan. If it put off that establishment, on the other hand, it would accrue additional high-interest loans, thus incurring unnecessary expense and undercutting its own creditworthiness.

Fortunately, he concluded, Americans were well situated to bear such a burden, which they would happily undertake in so good a cause as this war. Their motivations for doing so included "every motive that can animate an uncorrupted and enlightened people," including "an emulation of the glorious Founders of their independence" and "the sacred obligation of transmitting, entire, to future generations, that precious patrimony of national rights and independence, which is held in trust by the present, from the goodness of Divine Providence."

The president's allusion to the Tidewater climate's potential health effects—which had led him as a young man to opt for distant Princeton, New Jersey, instead of the Virginia squirearchy's customary choice, Williamsburg, as the place where he would obtain his college education[11]—proved well founded. Madison became so ill three weeks into the new session—with "bilious fever," in the vague medical terminology of the day—that talk of the presidential succession became widespread and "reports circulated that he was near death." As the commander-in-chief lay abed for five weeks, the warring republic lacked what little war leadership he had exercised when healthy.[12]

Despite the politicians' planning, military progress in the campaign of 1813 proved insufficient. On the offensive at Kingston and York and in the Niagara region, things generally went well, as Madison said, but midsummer passed without the United States securing control of Lake Ontario—its most important objective. Unfortunately Armstrong chose General Wilkinson to be the inept Dearborn's successor as theater commander—going from bad to worse. At the same time Armstrong dove into a new round of bickering with South Carolinian Wade Hampton, the other chief general in the theater. The sum of it is that the 1813 campaign season concluded without America's making significant strides toward the capture of Montreal[13]—which, recall, had been going to be easy pickings in 1812, according to Jefferson, Monroe, and other prominent Republicans. The entire American strategy, to seize Montreal quickly and use it as a bargaining chip with the British government, was no nearer to being implemented after two campaign seasons than it had been when the war began.

Meanwhile, on the Chesapeake, the war took an unexpected turn. As the historian of these events put it, "[S]ix hundred runaways stole boats and canoes to press themselves on the British, straining the capacity of the naval officers to feed the fugitives as well as their own crews." This gave the British not only a welcome augmentation of their manpower, but assistance in navigating a region with which they were unfamiliar.[14]

The British commander in the Chesapeake, Rear Admiral Sir George Cockburn, was able, experienced, and flamboyant. He had commanded a frigate at age twenty-three, and against The Netherlands in the 1790s he had commanded amphibious operations of just the type he would oversee in North America. Cultivating a reputation as an officer who, in a junior officer's words, "never spared himself, either night or day, but shared on every occasion, the same toil, danger, and privation" as his subordinate officers, Cockburn proved "a great wit."[15] Dolley Madison wrote to a relative in mid-1813 that Cockburn had "sent me word that he would make his bow at my drawing-room very soon." As Cockburn burned and pillaged along the Chesapeake coasts up to Havre de Grace, which he burned, Mrs. Madison saw fit to note that "though a Quaker, . . . [I] always have been an advocate for fighting when assailed."[16] We may infer that the idea of escaped slaves in Cockburn's force gave particular urgency to these ruminations.

The congressional elections had given the House of Representatives a new aspect, with not only Randolph of Roanoke but Josiah Quincy losing his seat, so that the opposition to Madison's war was bereft of its most powerful orators, Republican and Federalist. On the other hand both Pickering and Daniel Webster made their entrances. The former, a longtime fomenter of disunion, had not changed much, while the young Webster, a Massachusetts man educated at Dartmouth, would prove remarkably opportunistic. He in time put his oratorical powers, which in tandem with nationalist principles appealing to Chief Justice Marshall ultimately made him the leading Supreme Court advocate of his age, to work on both sides of nearly all of the major issues of the era. Perhaps most important, Philadelphia Convention Framer Rufus King, who, recall, had been the holdover minister to the Court of St. James's at the beginning of the Jefferson administration, took one of New York's seats in the Senate. Formerly a close ally of Alexander Hamilton and in the past a two-time Federalist nominee for vice president, King perhaps had his most important service ahead of him.

This Senate of the Thirteenth Congress appointed a committee to communicate with President Madison concerning the constitutionality of appointing Secretary of the Treasury Gallatin to serve concurrently on the peace commission in Europe. When the chairman of that committee visited the White House, Madison told him that as he did not understand the committee to be empowered by the Senate to consult with the president in person, he would not discuss the matter with them. If, however, the Senate rectified this defect in the committee's authority, Madison would speak with its members about the Gallatin issue. The Senate then perfected its orders to the committee members, who told Madison on behalf of the Senate that the two positions were so incompatible that Gallatin ought not to hold them both simultaneously. The committee's report back to the Senate made clear both that the committee had told the president his physical indisposition had kept the Senate from communicating its displeasure sooner and that Madison had proven uninterested in communicating to them anything further than that, in the committee's words, "he regretted that the measure had been taken under circumstances which deprived him of the aid or advice of the Senate"—which, too, was a reference to his life-threatening illness. The Senate rejected the Gallatin nomination by a vote of 17 ayes and 18 nays, with the Invisibles—Giles, Leib, and Smith—joining the Federalists, among others, in the majority. It then gave its consent to the appointments of John Quincy Adams and James Bayard by votes of 30–4 and 27–6. It next adopted a resolution objecting to the president's having purported to appoint Gallatin, Adams, and Bayard under his recess appointments power. That power applied only to openings arising in preexisting positions during Senate recesses, the Senate reasoned, and these positions had instead been created during a Senate recess. The Senate insisted it respected the president's authority, but added that it also had to insist on its own constitutional powers.[17]

Soon thereafter Madison and the Senate had a similar misunderstanding regarding the president's nomination of a minister plenipotentiary to Sweden. Madison nominated Jonathan Russell to the office, a senator proposed a motion that appointing anyone to that office would be inexpedient, and the Senate appointed a three-man committee including King and Giles, two devout oppositionists, to take it up with Madison.[18] Madison sent the Senate a memorandum explaining that in his understanding, the proper course of action for the Senate would have been to communicate with the head of the relevant department, in this case the secretary of state, about the matter. As the Senate and the president were "coordinate" when it came to appointments, "appointment of a Committee of the Senate to confer immediately with the Executive himself, appears to lose sight of the coordinate relation . . . which the Constitution has established, and which ought therefore to be maintained."[19] The three-man committee's composition hinted what the Senate felt disposed to do, and Madison's letter did not save Russell's nomination. The Senate did it without sending a delegation to consult with the secretary. Though they respected him, then, the senators did not defer to Madison as the "Father of the Constitution"—a title he anyway always rejected.

However unhappy these developments may have been, American arms enjoyed monumental success in the Erie theater during the 1813 season. Its genesis lay in Commodore Oliver Hazard Perry's shipbuilding program on Lake Erie. As the leading account says, "with this hastily constructed array of small brigs and schooners, he engaged and annihilated the British Lake Erie squadron on September 10." In the process the slogan on his flagship's battle flag, "Don't Give Up the Ship," won immortal fame. Having destroyed the enemy fleet, Perry dispatched to General William Henry Harrison a short note including another specimen of wordsmithing calculated to raise the hair on the nape of a reader's neck: "We have met the enemy and they are ours. . . ."[20] As Donald Hickey summarized matters, "The battle was the most important fought on the Great Lakes during the war. It changed the balance of power in the West and enabled the United States to recover all that it had lost in 1812."[21]

Perry's feat opened occupied Detroit to American attack. Tecumseh delivered an emphatic speech imploring the British not to retreat and reminding the commander at Fort Amherstburg of the promises that had persuaded the Indians to take up the hatchet against the United States. "Listen!" he said,

"You told us, at that time, to bring forward our families to this place; and we did so; and you promised to take care of them, and that they would want for nothing, while the men would go and fight the enemy." All the British promises never to withdraw from British land that had drawn the Indians into the war on their side, he lamented, were being abandoned. "We must compare our father's [King George's] conduct to a fat animal, that carries its tail upon its back, but when affrighted, he drops it between his legs and runs off."[22] British soldier John Richardson, a witness to Tecumseh's oration, later characterized him as having spoken "with powerful energy and gesticulation" and described him as one "whose gallant and impetuous spirit could ill brook retiring before his enemies." Perhaps recalling that British general Henry Procter had made a significant contrast, Richardson added that the American warrior's manner "could not fail to endear him to the soldier hearts of those who stood around, and inspire in them a veneration and esteem, not even surpassed by what they entertained for their own immediate leader."[23]

Tecumseh's eminence as an Indian warrior made General William Henry Harrison's victory in the Battle of the Thames, which proved pivotal in the history of the Northwest, even more significant. Fighting a battle somewhere on the Thames line northward represented a concession by Procter to Tecumseh.[24] Harrison, on the other hand, augmented his force with a levy of three thousand new Kentuckians, Governor Isaac Shelby among them, which gave him about fifty-five hundred men. (He had to turn away Ohioan volunteers for lack of supplies.)

Richard M. Johnson, in command of twelve hundred cavalrymen, led a charge against the British force of approximately six hundred British in two lines of battle, with five hundred or so Indians anchoring the British force next to the swamp on their right. The Americans made short work of the enemy force, though Procter did escape. Oddly the American horsemen relied on muskets rather than sabers. When the horsemen on the American right passed through the British lines, dismounted, and began to fire, the enemy was soon overcome. The battle lasted forty-five minutes at most, and British forces got off only one volley.[25]

Tecumseh died in this brief battle. Legend has it that Richard M. Johnson killed him. The notoriety accruing to Johnson as a result ultimately vaulted him to the vice presidency of the United States. Perhaps more remarkably Johnson eventually lived openly with a mixed-race slave woman, by whom he had several children, as his common-law wife, and his Kentucky constituents again elected him to high office.[26] Of more lasting moment,

Tecumseh's fighting death on October 15, 1813, meant that Indian power in the Old Northwest was gone for good.[27]

As these events transpired on the United States' northern flank, epic developments played out in Europe. By the middle of 1813, Napoleon had assembled a new army—though a smaller, less veteran one, and one plagued by lack of horses. The year's campaign came to a head in and around the beautiful old German city of Leipzig, where French forces found themselves faced by a numerically superior coalition of Russian, Austrian, Prussian, and Swedish ones. The diplomatic and military failures that had brought the armies of his former ally Alexander; his father-in-law Francis I of Austria; Frederick William III (the Prussian king he had treated disdainfully after Jena-Auerstadt in 1806); and former French marshal, now Crown Prince of Sweden Karl XIV Johan Bernadotte into coalition against his, left Napoleon at last with forces inferior to his adversaries'. Although Napoleon had won significant battles at Lutzen and Bautzen earlier in that year's campaign, the Battle of Nations was a full-fledged disaster. He had about two hundred thousand men at this great decision point, but his enemies massed three hundred thousand. In the words of its leading chronicler, "a combination of awakening Germanic nationalism and fast-exhausting French resources resulted in heavy defeat and the loss of almost all terrain lying to the east of the Rhine."[28] Any reasonable observer would have deduced that this must auger disaster for the fledgling North American republic, as Britain's military resources would be freed up for deployment against the United States.

42

✦ ❋ ✦

Madison's Annual Message was delivered to Capitol Hill on December 7, 1813.[1] He began by noting his disappointment that the British had rejected Alexander's offer of mediation. He asserted that this left America no alternative but to rely on her strength, which he illustrated by recounting a string of naval victories of which Perry's was the most notable and important. It had led to the success in the Battle of the Thames, "which quickly terminated in the capture of the British and dispersion of the savage force." Harrison, Johnson, and Governor Shelby—"whose heroism, signalized in the war which established the Independence of his Country, sought at an advanced age, a share in hardships and battles, for maintaining its rights and its safety"—drew particular praise. Progress on the banks of Lake Ontario, which like Lake Erie had come to be dominated by American arms, had been foiled in its beginnings by the weather, so that the planned campaign along the St. Lawrence had come to naught.

Madison lamented that the British, rather than emulating the Americans in not enlisting Indian nations into their forces, thus "mitigating [the war's] calamities," had instead employed them. "Wherever they could be turned against us, no exertions to effect it, have been spared." In the Southwest "a bloody fanaticism, recently propagated among them" had made it "necessary to crush such a war before it could spread among the contiguous tribes, and before it could favor enterprises of the Enemy into that vicinity." He then made reference to the American victories at Tallushatchee and Talladega only a few weeks earlier, where as many as five hundred Creek warriors met their ends. Here for the first time the name of Major General Andrew Jackson, "an Officer equally distinguished for his patriotism and his military talents," came to national attention.[2] Madison lamented that the British perseverance in recruiting Indian allies into their service had at last "forced upon us" a "departure from our protracted forbearance to accept the services tendered by them." Even in accepting groups of Indians into their ranks, he insisted, the Americans had not followed "the example of the enemy, who owe the advantages they have occasionally gained in battle, chiefly to the number of their savage associates; and who have not controuled them, either from their usual practice of indiscriminate massacre on defenseless inhabitants, or from scenes of carnage without a parallel, on prisoners to the British arms, guarded by all the laws . . . of honorable war."

Ruminating on this subject naturally led Madison into a lengthy passage on British treatment of American immigrants from Britain taken prisoner during the war. As they had been sent to Britain "for trial as criminals," "a like number of British prisoners of war were put into confinement, with a notification that they would experience whatever violence might be committed on the American prisoners of war, sent to Great Britain." When the British responded to this by putting twice as many Americans under close confinement and warning of the destruction they would mete out on American coastal towns in case the U.S. Government reciprocated for any executions the British might inflict, America had "immediately put into close confinement" an equal number of British prisoners and informed the enemy of this step. If the British continued on this path, America would reciprocate, Madison said, "any other proceedings against us, contrary to the legitimate modes of warfare."

In closing his address the president invoked the deity and foreshadowed the direction in which Republican statecraft would head in years to come. "If the war has increased the interruptions of our commerce," he mused, "it has at the same time cherished and multiplied our manufactures; so as to make us independent of all other countries for the more essential branches, for which we aught to be dependent on none. . . ." He added that the war's effect in eliciting and displaying America's military capacity and might ought to make foreign countries more respectful of Americans' rights in the future.

Just over three weeks after Madison sent out his Annual Message, important news arrived from Europe on a Royal Navy schooner. Napoleon had suffered a significant defeat at Leipzig, which might be expected to cut the legs out from under America's negotiating position, and Lord Castlereagh, the British secretary of state for foreign affairs, countered Madison's acceptance of Alexander's offer of mediation between the two warring parties with an offer of direct negotiations either in London or in Gothenburg, Sweden. Madison told Congress he had accepted Gothenburg. He hastened to add that "vigorous preparations for carrying on the war, can in no respect impede the progress to a favorable result; whilst a relaxation of such preparations, should the wishes of the United States for a speedy restoration of the blessings of peace be disappointed, would necessarily have the most injurious consequences."[3] (Here, as in his 1812 message hinting that the Congress should declare war, Madison avoided outright giving the Legislative Branch advice.) Within days the president nominated Henry Clay, James Bayard, and Jonathan Russell to join John Quincy Adams in Europe. The Senate ratified these appointments overwhelmingly.[4] While Castlereagh's answer had included a statement that he wanted an agreement "not inconsistent with the established maxims of public law, and with the maritime rights of the British empire," Clay at a public dinner for Commodore Perry before he departed toasted, "The policy which looks to peace as the end of war—and to the war as the means of peace." Perhaps the British intended to extract agreement that impressment and regulation of neutrals' seaborne trade were George III's rights, but Americans did not intend to agree to any such thing.[5]

The departures brought on yet another Cabinet shuffle. Gallatin's departure left Madison without his ablest subordinate and necessitated that he choose someone new for the most important post. Senator George W. Campbell of Tennessee, who had played a prominent role in Congress supporting the administration's financial measures, did not measure up. Next most notably, William Pinkney was out as attorney general. Though that was a part-time job in those days, his considerable legal ability and notable intelligence would be missed. As prominent Old Republican congressman and former speaker of the House Nathaniel Macon of North Carolina summarized these developments, "That Campbell and Rush [Pinkney's successor] are equal to Gallatin and Pinkney is not, I imagine, believed by anyone who knows them."[6] Of the adept Cabinet officers, only Monroe remained—and the worst stretch of Madison's administration was in the immediate offing.

When the two houses of Congress heard the president's message read, members can have been excused for taking its close somewhat sardonically. Whatever "daily testimonies of increasing harmony throughout the nation" the president might be hearing, sectional discord in the form of party conflict remained a prominent feature of the American scene. Congressman John C. Calhoun rose in the House a few days later to address this matter at length.[7]

The war's opponents, Calhoun began, insisted that the American effort was offensive. He would show the contrary. After defining an "offensive war" as a war that "has its origin in ambition, avarice or any of the like passions," he said that a defensive war is one "to repel insult, injury or oppression." This distinction made clear why Americans generally opposed offensive war: "the American sense of justice accounts for their feelings." The war's opponents on the other side of the House insisted "that if the repeal of the Berlin and Milan decrees had been communicated in time to the British government, the Orders in Council would have been repealed; and had the last event happened, the war would not have been declared." Here they have admitted, he continued, "that the Orders in Council, and not the conquest of Canada, as they now pretend, was the cause of the war; and it would be idle to enquire whether to resist them was in its nature offensive or defensive." "It would be equally so to examine whether the cause of continuing the war, to protect our seamen from impressment, is of an offensive or defensive character." If the war had originated and been continued with these goals, it would "not become offensive by being carried beyond the limits of our territory. The motive and cause will ever give character. . . ." The administration's opponents in the House admitted as much, he chortled, when they offered as an alternative to the current strategy that of pursuing the war at sea alone. "What! to the ocean! Carry the war beyond our territory! Make it offensive! The gentlemen surely do not intend to support an offensive war." "It is then admitted," the Carolinian said, "that it does not cease to be [defensive] by its being waged at sea. . . ."

Calhoun hurried to add that he "thought no effort ought to be wanting to reduce Canada. Should success accompany our arms," he reasoned, "we would be indemnified for the privations and expenses of the war, by the acquisition of an extensive and valuable territory." Besides that, offensive operations in Canada forced the enemy to deploy military assets there which he might otherwise set to ravaging the American coast. "Thus, even under the limited view of defence, the most effectual mode is that, which has been adopted. . . ."

These considerations led Calhoun into a larger topic of which he thought this one formed a part: that of the nature of congressional opposition to the American war effort. Though he conceded that opposition might legitimately arise out of differing evaluations of circumstances, he classified the bulk of antiwar agitation in America as "factious." "[H]ow much," he asked, "has it debilitated the energies of our country?" Even though men knew "of its pernicious effect," did they not agree that "every means that could excite opposition had . . . been unceasingly applied?" "In an unexampled state of national difficulties," he continued, "from the first belligerent decree against our neutral commerce down to this day, he would ask which one of all the measures of our government to resist this almost universal depredation, . . . has not, under one pretext or another, been opposed, ridiculed and weakened? Yes," he warmed to his argument, "opposed with a violence that would lead to a belief that the constituted authorities, instead of opposing the most gross and outrageous injustice, sought only the destruction of their country." By their arguments, it seemed to the committee chairman that opposition congressmen wanted people to "Withhold the laws; withhold the loans; withhold the men who are to fight our battles; or, in other words, to destroy the public faith, and deliver the country unarmed to the mercy of the enemy. Suppose all of their objects accomplished," he concluded, "and what would be the situation of the country?" It seemed that what had begun in this hall had "gone forth into the community, and wherever it has appeared, has exhibited the same dangerous appearances."

As he sat down, Calhoun said that he hoped his audience would consider what he had said. The Constitution did indeed protect men's right to criticize their government. A factious opposition, however, was beyond what the Constitution contemplated. "Universal experience and the history of all ages furnish ample testimony of its dangerous consequences, particularly in a state of war." Only "the good sense and the virtue of the people" could cure this contagion.

In Europe the first book of Napoleon's imperial story had reached its sad conclusion. On March 31, 1814, Marshal Michel Ney had led a mutiny of Napoleon's top subordinates, and when news arrived that Marshal Auguste F.L.V. de Marmont had deserted the French lines before Paris and handed his command over to the Allies, Napoleon saw that he must abdicate. He did so unconditionally by means of a statement he wrote on April 6th.[8]

Gallatin wrote to Clay about this immediately upon hearing of it.[9] The American position concerning the location at which negotiations with the British were to be conducted should be flexible now. Any neutral locale would do, Gallatin said, and America should accept it "on account of the late great changes in Europe & of the encreased difficulties thence arising in making any treaty. . . ." The end of the First French Empire meant a "total change in our affairs," he worried, as there had been a "restoration of universal peace in the European world, from which we alone are excluded."

Though not a military man, Gallatin did not miss the import of this development: "A well organised & large army," he scrawled, "is at once liberated from any European employment, and ready, together with a super abundant naval force, to act immediately against us. How ill prepared we are to meet it in a proper manner no one knows better than yourself, [sic] but above all our own divisions and the hostile attitude of the Eastern States give room to apprehend that a continuance of the war might prove vitally fatal to the United States."

What a diplomat posted abroad could see struck the eye of statesmen on this side of the Atlantic even more forcefully. The British delays in entering into negotiations clearly augured another all-out attempt to achieve victory over the North American republic that British elite and popular opinion alike saw as effectively if not forthrightly having been allied with Napoleon not only since the beginning of the war in 1812, but at least since the implementation of the embargo in 1807. In Canada, along the Atlantic coast, and in the Deep South, the next nine months would prove decisive. Along the way, whether Calhoun had been right in saying, "Mr. Madison is wholly unfit for the storms of war," would be decided once and for all.[10]

Gallatin and Calhoun were not alone in accusing Federalists, and particularly New England Federalists, of, as Tennessee congressman Felix Grundy put it, "moral treason" in relation to their opposition to the American war effort.[11] There was good reason for that conclusion. Madison's 1813 embargo, which "the New England states interpreted . . . as a declaration of war on them," led Massachusetts governor Caleb Strong to say that the mayhem and destruction resulting from the war were "chargeable upon that government which unreasonably begins the conflict." Each house of the Bay State's legislature issued a statement pledging not to support the war. "Forty Massachusetts town meetings sent petitions to the General Court" hostile to the war, Garry Wills notes, with Newbury's saying "we profess ourselves ready to resist unto blood." "Governor Strong," he concludes, "was already mulling over the idea of a separate peace."[12] As 1814 dawned, Strong remained unwilling to provide militia to the Federal Government when requested, and both New England's coast and its border with British North America were huge emporia for smuggling.

On Friday, June 3, 1814, Madison wrote Secretaries Armstrong, Jones, and Monroe that he wanted "a consultation with the Heads of Department on Tuesday next at Eleven OClock."[13] The subject of discussion on June 7th would be (as he told Armstrong) "the plan of campaign which our means, military & naval, render most eligible." Betwixt the two dates, Armstrong was to send him the numbers of soldiers at all American posts, "The numbers on the way thereto respectively," the number of other men enlisted at that time, the numbers of enemy men at various bases "in Canada or on the frontier of the U.S." and their locations, and the numbers expected both in Canada and on "our Atlantic frontier." Jones was to provide analogous data regarding enemy naval dispositions, and Monroe was to "cause to be made out & send over" any such information his department might have. Armstrong and Jones replied before the meeting, each providing the data regarding American forces Madison had required, though Armstrong noted that as the War Department had only military means of obtaining information on enemy forces, what he relayed "m[ight] be very erroneous."[14]

Armstrong's report to Madison, enclosed with his letter, put the army's strength at 31,503 men, of whom 27,010 were effective. Armstrong included an explanation that the report included recruits only for the Ninth Military District and an observation that "the difference between the effective and aggregate columns of these Regts. and particularly of those composing the Division of the right confirms Gen. Izard's representation of the wretched condition in which he found that command." Seemingly he also forwarded Madison the assistant inspector general's list showing recruitment of 9,588 men "for 5 years or during the war"—fruit of the January 27, 1814 law raising the enlistment bonus to $124.[15]

Secretary of the Navy Jones included eight documents with his response.[16] They showed that the odds were good for the U.S. Navy in the Great Lakes region, but that the many British seventy-four-gun ships in the Atlantic outclassed that service. Too, Jones said that sailors were difficult to recruit, and so he awaited American generals' loaning him army personnel. Finally, Captain Isaac Hull had relayed credible evidence that the Royal Navy planned to attack Portsmouth, New Hampshire.

According to Madison's notes, the Cabinet meeting of June 7th adopted a four-part plan for the campaign of 1814:

1. Eight hundred to a thousand soldiers on four or five naval vessels were to enter Lake Huron with the goal of occupying Machedash and St. Joseph's. About five hundred men were to occupy Machedash at least. All agreed.

2. If Commodore Chauncey could establish command of Lake Erie, General Brown's force was to move to Burlington Heights en route to advancing on York. Monroe expressed reservations, though he did not object.

3. "14 or 15. Armed Boats" were "to be built at Sacket's Harbour" to cut off British communication between Montreal and Kingston. All agreed.

4. General Izard's main force was "to make demonstrations towards Montreal" with the purposes of distracting the enemy

from American initiatives farther west "& affording a chance of compelling Prevost to fight disadvantageously." All agreed.[17]

The next day Jones wrote asking the president to name the three seventy-four-gun ships-of-the-line then being built. Madison scribbled "1. Independence / 2. Union / 3. Franklin (the Constitution wd. have been the name for the 3d. but for the Ship already of that name) / 4. Washington." Two of the four were launched by the war's end, and the Union never was.[18] Madison apparently did not know when he held the meeting that Secretary of War Armstrong and Major Generals Wilkinson and Hampton had already decided there should be another Niagara campaign in 1814.[19]

Opposition to the war continued to mount. Massachusetts's celebration of Napoleon's defeat was followed by word to Monroe from Representative Charles Jared Ingersoll that Pennsylvania Republicans wearied of fighting off criticism of the administration's half-hearted war.[20] No doubt the picture would have soured further if the public had seen Secretary Jones's prognostication of "a bloody and devastating summer and autumn."[21] Though Louis XVIII's government accepted Minister to France William Crawford's credentials, the Bourbons were highly unlikely to buck Britain in relation to the United States.[22] Having characteristically mulled the situation over some more, Madison met with his Cabinet to pose three questions:

1. "Shall the surrender by G.B. of the practice of impressment, in a treaty, limited to a certain period be an ultimation?" All but Attorney General Rush said no, and he leaned yes.
2. "Shall a treaty of peace, silent on the subject of Impressment be authorized?" The war and navy secretaries said yes, the others no.
3. "Shall a treaty be authorized comprizing an article referring the subject of impressment along with that of Commerce to a separate negotiation?" Four said yes, "Rush for awaiting further information from Europe."

The weak posture in which the Americans found themselves was recognized most clearly by the military secretaries, and the Cabinet in general had developed substantial flexibility on the issue Republican leaders had always said was a sine qua non of any peace treaty: British agreement not to impress Americans into the British navy. When Gallatin relayed news that fifteen to twenty thousand British veterans would soon be en route to North America and that the U.K. contemplated doing "very serious injury" to the United States, Madison responded by giving his commissions in Europe complete discretion regarding the impressment issue.[23] It seems that the Madison administration simply wanted a face-saving way out of its war.

In 1814 problems in Madison's war Cabinet dogged the government. Campbell was not up to the task of doing Gallatin's job, which during a war funded chiefly by borrowing required numerous new expedients. Monroe was competent, but jockeying for position between him and Armstrong, each of whom looked to succeed Madison as president, proved highly divisive. When Armstrong drove William Henry Harrison into resignation with inquiries into his private supply system for his army, then promoted Andrew Jackson to major general in his place, he and Madison butted heads.[24]

The summer's campaign began in earnest on the Lake Erie front, where Major General Jacob Brown's order to Brigadier General Winfield Scott— "company drills . . . in the morning, regimental drills in the afternoon and evening"—yielded a significant force of troops prepared to face British soldiers in combat.[25] Though disappointed by Commodore Chauncey's refusal to coordinate operations (he expected direct naval conflict with British forces, which would be his first priority)[26], Brown forged ahead.

Brown first faced British forces under Major General Phineas Riall at Chippewa on July 5th. Though outnumbered, Brown won the day.[27] Brown ordered Scott to attack, and as the two sides exchanged cannon fire, Scott's men coolly deployed under the barrage and exchanged several volleys. Assuming that Scott's men's gray uniforms marked them as militiamen, Riall exclaimed, "Why, these are regulars!"—still another statement the memory of which would long outlive this war. Seeing his right recoil before Scott's cool men, Riall retreated into Fort George. American losses were "325 killed, wounded, and missing, the British about 500." As the historian of the war Donald R. Hickey notes, this was "the first time that an American force had defeated a British force of equal strength on an open battlefield." In time the U.S. Military Academy at West Point picked up on Scott's mistaken notion that the Academy's cadets wore gray uniforms because his men had by saying that the color did indeed honor Scott's men.[28]

43

⁘ ☼ ⁘

Later that month British lieutenant general Gordon Drummond reinforced Fort George. He soon sent sixteen hundred men to Lundy's Lane. Seeing them, Brown ordered Scott to attack. At the head of twelve hundred men, Scott did as he had been told. Reinforcements came in on both sides, until the contending forces numbered around three thousand each. Seeing Scott's force under heavy cannon fire, Brown sent a detachment under Lieutenant Colonel James Miller to attack the British artillery. One British veteran of the Peninsular War said he had never seen the French—famous for fearlessness—do anything so intrepid. "The Americans charged to the very muzzles of our cannon and actually bayonetted the artillerymen who were at their guns," he recalled. After repeated British attacks, the two sides withdrew in exhaustion. Miller called the Battle of Lundy's Lane "one of the most desperately fought actions ever experienced in America." Hickey says it "was the bloodiest battle of the war." Brown, Scott, Drummond, and Riall were all wounded, and the casualties numbered 860 on the American side, 880 on the British. In a kind of summary of the war, this bloody conflict ended in a draw.[1] Though the British staged two ill-fated attacks on the Americans later on in the campaign, "The British retained possession of the Niagara peninsula, and . . . the front was quiet for the rest of the war."[2]

The overarching concept of the American campaign was to take one more shot at advancing down the St. Lawrence and Lake Champlain toward Montreal. In the end redeployment of ten thousand of Wellington's Peninsular veterans to North America and the U.S. Navy's failure to establish dominance of Lake Ontario meant that this plan never came to fruition. No significant strategic gain was achieved. Madison, learning that Armstrong had ordered the theater commanders to communicate with each other through him, blamed his war secretary.[3]

Meanwhile, in his usual not-very-insistent way, Madison had been trying to prod Armstrong into making provision for potential British attacks along the Atlantic coast. The difficulty of doing so, already great enough, loomed still larger after Vice Admiral Sir Alexander Cochrane's announcement of April 2, 1814, that "persons now resident in the UNITED STATES" desiring to "withdraw therefrom" could enlist in the British military or emigrate "as FREE Settlers to the British Possessions in North America or the West Indies, where they will meet with all due encouragement."[4] Madison learned of this by May 20th, when he told Armstrong that it "admonish[es] us to be prepared for the worst the Enemy may be able to effect agst. us. The date concurs with the measure proclaimed, to indicate the most inveterate spirit against the Southern States, and which may be expected to shew itself agst. every object within the reach of vindictive enterprise. Among these the Seat of Govt. can not fail to be a favorite one."[5]

No later than July 1st the issue of Washington, D.C.'s defense claimed the attention of the president and Cabinet.[6] Madison had just created a Tenth Military District including both Baltimore and Washington, putting Marylander Brigadier General William Winder, the Federalist governor's nephew, in command of it.[7] The president's "Memorandum on Defense of the City of Washington," compiled in a Cabinet meeting held on that day, includes figures for available cavalry, infantry, artillery, and marines from Washington and nearby and for Captain Joshua Barney's navy personnel, besides a fanciful figure of ten thousand "Militia to be designated & held in readiness."

Yet when Madison raised the issue of the capital's defense, no member of his Cabinet agreed with him.[8] Armstrong instead offered several considerations that indicated the British were unlikely to try to attack the capital and probably would fail in the attempt even if they did. They could have done so in 1813, he noted, and had not bothered. Far more sensible would be to attack one of America's seaside cities. If they opted to attack Washington, he insisted, they would have either to sail up the Potomac, which would be difficult for large ships, or to come via the Patuxent, from which they would have to march over easily defended terrain to reach the District of Columbia. Besides that, the British were unlikely to be able to land a force sufficient for the task.

Madison did not hear what Armstrong intended for him to hear. Instead he instructed Armstrong the next day to "digest & report to the President, corresponding precautionary means of defence, in reference to the other more important and exposed places along the Atlantic Frontier; particularly Boston, New York, Wilmington, Norfolk, Charlestown, Savanna, and N. Orleans." Besides providing ready caches of weapons, the relevant governors were also to provide "convenient designations of adequate portions of their Militia, with every other arrangement depending on the State Executives for having them in the best readiness for actual service in cases of emergency."[9] After this the process broke down. Armstrong sent the governors a letter telling them to prepare forces totaling 93,500 men, but he took no steps to ensure they knew where to concentrate them. He also did not coordinate defense of Washington with Winder. Madison assumed Armstrong would handle these details—without which the secretary's Cabinet observations about the difficulty of traveling up the Potomac and the ease with which the land between the Patuxent and Washington could be defended would be meaningless. Armstrong, on the other hand, let more than a month go by without doing much of anything about it at all, somehow assuming that the president, rather than he, would handle the details of coordinating what was clearly a War Department function.[10]

Not only did he not take the reins of preparing the town's defense, but Armstrong seems also to have omitted to impress on the president and Congress the urgency of providing him with funding to take the necessary steps to fortify the approaches to the capital. As William Tatham, described by Armstrong's biographer as "a consultant for the War Department's topographical branch who had studied the area about Washington," put it, "My belief is, we *cannot* defend Washington, because Congress have such a mistaken notion of *public* economy that they will not allow us the where-with-all!" In case the British navy sent a force to destroy the city, he predicted, "the result will be that, we shall fail; and popular clamour will shelter the real pitiful cause, by an abuse of John Armstrong, for being less than omnipotent."[11]

Meanwhile Secretary of State Monroe recounted in a manuscript letter a conversation with Secretary of the Treasury Campbell in which the latter responded to his draft letter to the editor of the *National Intelligencer* by saying that putting the situation in such dire terms as Monroe had might spoil Campbell's latest attempt to borrow money from the public. Monroe answered that to be less frank likely would bring down the public ire upon the administration if worse came to worst. Campbell assured Monroe that the British would not attack Washington, and so Monroe decided not to publish his letter.

Later Monroe wrote, "I have since reflected further on this subject, and am persuaded, that it would be safest to act on the presumption, that the dangers which are possible, will occur. I think I see manifest advantages resulting from it, without any real loss, under any circumstances that may occur." "The mov'ment on the other side," he fretted, "is active & vigorous, as we see by the proceedings Eastward. That movment has more effect, in consequence of our inactivity, even before the danger shews itself, and while there is a hope that we possess information of our security not known to the public. Even in this state the govt. shakes to the foundation. Let a strong force land any where, and what will be the effect?" As he reasoned, "We have a great majority of the nation with us. But to give energy to our cause, we must take the passions of the people with us also."

The chief Cabinet officer then turned to his policy prescriptions. "In looking to the worst my idea really is that the Congress shod. be conven'd for the purpose of providing more ample funds, preventing the exportation of specie from the country, establishing a national bank, and doing every thing that will give energy to the govt., & success to the war." If John Taylor and John Randolph could have seen their man now! What would the Frenchmen so enamored of their forthrightly Anglophobe American minister in the 1790s have thought to see the Republican secretary of state in 1814 committing to paper a program absolutely Hamiltonian in its contours? Alexander Hamilton could hardly have wished for a clearer vindication—though one was on the way. Monroe was driven to these conclusions by his estimate that Campbell's "little supply in view, on which every thing is suspended, is so temporary in its nature as to be comparatively a trifling object." In other words the Federal Government's great military weakness had pushed him in wartime to conclusions quite similar to those Treasury Secretary Alexander Hamilton and his Federalist supporters had reached in time of peace more than twenty years earlier.

Monroe was not alone in feeling the urgency of the situation. While Armstrong essentially treaded water, Major General Samuel Smith, Madison's former Senate irritant, pressed Armstrong for more manpower to defend Baltimore. Tidewater Virginians demanded aid in paying troops and funding fortifications in response to occasional British raids—not only to destroy farms and seize supplies, but to help slaves abscond. From New York, Philadelphia, and Baltimore, urgent requests for administration assistance poured in. Armstrong seems almost to have intended to make a show of nonchalance. One letter to Armstrong containing an urgent request that the Delmarva Peninsula be denominated its own military district was forwarded by him to Madison with the note "Submitted to the President" and returned with Madison's response, "What is the opinion of the Secretary of War as to the arrangement recommended herein?"[12] The secretary's constant omission to take matters obviously his responsibility in hand not only irked the president, but—more importantly—left the country's defenses unorganized.

Washington's aldermen and Common Council on July 18th sent Madison a resolution calling "their unprotected & defenceless state from menaced invasion" to his attention, asking him "to take such means for their early & effectual relief as in his judgement sh[ould] seem best."[13] Still Madison left matters to Armstrong, and still Armstrong did more or less nothing. The results would prove disastrous.

Responsibility ultimately lay with Madison. Not that Armstrong did not deserve blame.

In late July 1814 British troops came within twenty miles, and Mrs. Madison downplayed the danger. On August 20th, when others came up the Patuxent and disembarked at Benedict, only forty miles away, Madison was surprised the enemy were so near.[14] (The British had already decided by this point to attack Washington.[15]) Secretary of State James Monroe, who had quit William & Mary as a teenage freshman in 1776 to go join the Continental Army, now thirty-eight years later found himself—the national government's chief Cabinet officer—out scouting the countryside to ascertain the position, strength, and likely objective of the enemy. In a series of notes written every few hours on August 21st and 22nd between Monroe and the president, Monroe said he had sighted the British, denied they numbered three thousand, as Madison had been told, and at last said, "Our troops were on the march to meet them, but in too small a body to engage. General W[inder] proposes to retire, till he can collect them in a body. The enemy are in full march for Washington. Have the materials prepared to destroy the bridges." Below his signature he added, perhaps thinking what had happened during Jefferson's gubernatorial administration when a British force under Benedict Arnold took Richmond, "You had better remove the records."[16]

Meanwhile Winder agreed with Armstrong that it was unclear whether the British would attack Washington or Baltimore. He too failed to prepare Washington for attack—so much so that on August 22nd, Sérurier wrote to Talleyrand that the highest officials of the American government remained uncertain whether Washington would be attacked. As the Madison historian J. C. A. Stagg explains:

Before August 20, Winder had made no serious attempts to obstruct the gradual British advance by felling trees, destroying bridges, or harassing the enemy's flanks, and he was now accordingly compelled to improvise a desperate last-minute defense—the very thing that in early July he had declared he should avoid. He issued some final calls for volunteers, and, by the morning of August 24, he had been able to assemble a mixed force of regulars, volunteers, navy yard workers, artillerists, and militia from the District and Maryland. Altogether his forces totaled nearly 7,000 men, which numerically gave him an advantage over the British commanders, whose troops amounted to 4,500. These forces were arranged haphazardly on the field at Bladensburg by their commanders as they arrived.[17]

The American forces stood arrayed in three lines on the bank of the Potomac: the third line too distant to support the first two, of which Monroe (without authority to do so) redeployed the second line so that it was not in position to support the first. A Maryland militia general noticed Monroe's mistake, but thinking Monroe acted with Winder's authority, he did not countermand it. "The president and other civilian officials," Donald R. Hickey observes, "arrived on the scene just before the battle began and were on the verge of crossing the bridge into the approaching British columns when they were warned off by a War Department clerk who was serving as a volunteer scout."[18]

As James Scott, aide-de-camp to Royal Navy Rear Admiral George Cockburn, recalled the scene, "about noon we arrived at the heights above Bladensburg [a Maryland town less than ten miles from Washington], from which the whole American army were discovered drawn up strongly posted in two lines on the opposite side of the river, and their artillery so placed as to enfilade the bridge which we were obliged to cross before we could come to close quarters with them." In other words the American force had the defensive, on ground it had chosen, against a force inferior in numbers and to whom the ground was unfamiliar. "In addition to the heavy artillery on the upper height," Scott continued, "a block-house and field-pieces on the lower range defended the passage across."[19]

The American artillery, according to Scott, had spent "some hours the previous day" finding the range, so that when the British foot made its way to the bridge, "the American artillery now opened out upon the advanced guard, and caused a fearful destruction among our brave fellows. . . ." Seeing the Brits fall back, the Americans let loose "a deafening round of cheers . . . along their lines." Eventually, however, the British 85th Regiment, Colonel William Thornton commanding, headed out onto the bridge. A heavy fire of grapeshot, musket fire, and small shot commenced, the colonel's horse dying under him, yet he led on and his men followed. When the two forces met, the American "first line soon gave way at the point of the British bayonet, and retired in great confusion on their second; the action became general throughout the line."

As Scott tells the tale, the Congreve rockets the British fired into the American lines "create[ed] a fearful gap" in the American ranks, "and a much more fearful panic in the immediate vicinity."[20] Eventually "[o]ur gallant fellows had . . . got on the flanks of the enemy, and advancing in front at the same time with the bayonet, a general rout took place, the enemy abandoning great part of their artillery, every one appearing to think only of his own safety."

Soon after, Scott continues, "I stumbled upon an American officer among the bushes, close to their principal battery. He was severely wounded in the leg, and requested me to remain by him, announcing himself as Commodore Barney. I assured him," the captor says, "that he had nothing to fear in his state from our people, as he himself was, no doubt, aware." Barney apparently had offered an unknown British enlisted man "his watch and a well-lined purse" for safe passage, but the man had refused the offer: the Commodore's wounds would suffice. Still harder for Barney to believe was the British admiral's offer of parole to Barney and all the American officers with him. Commodore Barney's written account of these events to Navy Secretary William Jones tracked James Scott's in all of its essential features.

Scott's account of the Battle of Bladensburg ends with his observation that "[i]t seems that the President, 'whose martial appearance gladdened every countenance and encouraged every heart,' was on the field at the commencement of the action, but on the first shot had hastened back to Washington. . . ." A more direct American appraisal held that "Not all the allurements of fame, not all the obligations of duty, nor the solemn invocations of honour, could excite a spark of courage ******** [sic] and at the very first shot the trembling coward with a faltering voice exclaimed, 'Come, General Armstrong, come, Colonel Munro, let us go, and leave it to the commanding General.'"

The one component of the American force that had something good to say for its performance at Bladensburg was the small force of sailors under Barney. After the rout—which can be at least partly explained by unawareness on the part of the Maryland militia units in the first two American lines of Barney's men's arrival[21]—got under way, Barney positioned his men with their cannons to intercept the advancing British "just outside the District line."[22] In his soldiers' flight Winder made no attempt to command Barney, who as a Navy Department officer technically did not have to answer to him. With four hundred men these sailors would obstruct four thousand. As Barney told it:

> At length the enemy made his appearance on the main road in force and in front of my battery, and on seeing us made a halt. I reserved our fire. In a few

minutes the enemy again advanced, when I ordered an eighteen-pounder to be fired, which completely cleared the road; shortly after, a second and a third attempt was made by the enemy to come forward, but all were destroyed. They then crossed over into an open field, and attempted to flank our right. He was met there by three twelve-pounders, the marines under Captain Miller, and my men acting as infantry, and again was totally cut up. By this time not a vestige of the American army remained, except a body of five or six hundred posted on a height on my right, from which I expected much support from their fine situation.

Though disappointed, Barney's unit cannot have been much surprised when the vestige of the American army on its right fled, clearing the way for the British to flank his sailors and silence their guns. He commanded his subordinate officers to leave him wounded where he was—which is where the British found him. As in the case of Scott in the north, so here at the boundary of the District of Columbia. Barney had left the impression that things could have turned out differently if the Americans' able men had been in command. The British commander's official report said two hundred fifty of his fifteen hundred involved in the battle had been killed or wounded, but Lieutenant George Gleig of the Eighty-fifth, himself wounded on the field, doubled both of these numbers. Astoundingly the Americans abandoned the field and the route into their capital with it after losing only twenty-six killed and fifty-one wounded.[23] Not for nothing have the events that day in Maryland been known ever since as the "Bladensburg Races." For more than a generation Republicans had insisted little money or effort needed to be expended in maintaining America's defenses. The reckoning had come.

That night the British camped in sight of the U.S. Capitol. Fired upon from Gallatin's old house, General Ross ordered that it be burned. (Gallatin's partisan opponents could have found something poetic in this.) Ross then ordered the Capitol burned, after which he and Cockburn led a detachment to give the White House the same treatment. More than two centuries later, smoke stains are still in evidence inside the presidential mansion. On their arrival the British found "the place settings on the dinner table for the still-cooking meal."[1]

As the Madisons' slave Paul Jennings recounted events leading up to the invaders' arrival at the president's house, "I [had] set the table myself, and brought up the ale, cider, and wine, and placed them in the cooler." In the general pandemonium in the capital, Dolley Madison insisted that the White House not be vacated. Jennings recalled, "James Smith, a free colored man who had accompanied Mr. Madison to Bladensburg, galloped up to the house, waving his hat, and cried out, 'Clear out, clear out! General Armstrong had ordered a retreat!' All then was confusion." Mrs. Madison directed servants, Paul Jennings among them, to save the famous full-length Gilbert Stuart portrait of General Washington from within the house. "Jennings held the ladder," the editor of his memoir tells us, "and, after the enormous portrait, ninety-five inches high, had been freed from its frame, was undoubtedly one of the 'two colored boys' who helped a pair of 'gentlemen of New York' load the stretched canvas onto the cart they had managed to procure . . . [to be] ferried away to the safety of a barn in rural Maryland."[2]

The great artwork survived the British, but the sun did not rise on the White House the next morning. Nor did the nearby Navy Yard and naval vessels survive the night. As Henry Adams scornfully notes, "Before midnight the flames of three great conflagrations made the whole country light, and from the distant hills of Maryland and Virginia the flying President and

Cabinet caught glimpses of the ruin their incompetence had caused." No doubt Adams would have been more outraged had he known that Cockburn had first eaten the meal Jennings had laid out, then taken "the cushion of Dolley's chair, about which he 'added pleasantries too vulgar . . . to repeat.'"[3] The French minister, who had watched Madison mount his horse and ride out of town,[4] sent an emissary to ask a British officer that his residence, Virginia planter John Tayloe's famous Octagon building near the White House, be spared, and his wish was granted. The only government building spared by the marauding Redcoats was the U.S. Patent Office. Besides the Capitol and White House, the buildings housing the Cabinet departments went up in flames too. Adams summarizes their exploit by saying, "Ross and Cockburn alone among military officers, during more than twenty years of war, considered their duty to involve personal incendiarism. At the time and subsequently various motives were attributed to them,—such as the duty of retaliation,—none of which was alleged by either of them. . . ." Though lamenting that those officers seemed to have "assumed as a matter of course that the American government stood beyond the pale of civilization," he concluded that "in truth a government which showed so little capacity to defend its capital, could hardly wonder at whatever treatment it received." Fortunately a violent two-hour storm broke just then, so that the fires were put out without doing all of the damage they might have.[5]

These events led President Madison at last to take a step he seemingly had wanted to take months before: fire Secretary of War John Armstrong. Characteristically Madison took time to write long memoranda of his interactions with the secretary of war dated August 24th and August 29th. When read in combination with Monroe's memorandum of the events of August 24th to 28th, they tell a dreary tale.[6]

As Madison recounted the events of August 24th, he that morning received an urgent note from General Winder for Armstrong, who was not present. Accordingly, the president read the message and forwarded it to Armstrong.[7] Seeing that Winder requested (in the president's words) "the speediest Counsel," Madison then rushed to Winder's headquarters on horseback. Monroe, the attorney general, and the secretary of the navy soon arrived. Monroe, it was agreed, should head to Bladensburg. (Rushing to the battlefield, Monroe found that General Tobias Stansbury had disposed his men for battle. Monroe repositioned the infantry so that they were "both exposed and unable to support the artillery and rifle units posted in front of them, with deleterious consequences for the battle.")[8]

Winder was on his way, Barney about to follow with his men, when

Armstrong arrived. "On Genl. Armstrong's coming into the room," Madison said, "he was informed of the certain march of the Enemy for Bladensburg, and of what had passed before his arrival; and he was asked whether he had any arrangement or advice to offer in the emergency. He said that he had not, adding that as the battle would be between Militia & regular troops, the former would be beaten." Campbell, the secretary of the treasury, who boarded in the same house as Armstrong, confided in the president that he thought Armstrong's reserve could be explained by the fact that Armstrong thought Madison's having assigned command of the forces in Washington meant that he, the secretary of war, should not interfere. (We may note in light of the damage Monroe's interference wrought on the disposition of the American forces at Bladensburg that Armstrong's inclination made sense. The Cabinet politicians' legal superiority to the military officers did not reflect a congressional decision that they, not the generals, should command troops in the field.) Yet when Campbell conveyed to Madison his belief that the emergency situation meant that Armstrong's expertise ought to be employed, Madison "told him I could scarcely conceive it possible that Genl. Armstrong could have so misconstrued his functions and duty as Secretary of War" and added that any "suggestions or advice from him to Genl Winder would be duly attended to."

Madison then, apparently in Campbell's presence, turned his horse to Armstrong and told him that he was surprised by Armstrong's reserve in these circumstances. Armstrong's erring on the side of minding his own business probably owed at least in part to his recent dressing-down by Madison in writing, which had taken the form of a lengthy letter spelling out several classes of actions which the secretary of war must thenceforth only undertake with the president's prior approval.[9] Referring to that letter, Madison told Armstrong at this point that he "hoped he had not construed the paper of instructions given him some time before . . . so as to restrain him in any respect from the exercise of functions belonging to his office. . . ." Even if the recent slapping-down had not affected the prickly Armstrong's behavior in this circumstance, he seems at this remove to have been behaving just as a secretary of war ought insofar as the impending battle eight miles away was concerned. It was Madison who apparently had no clear conception of the proper distinction between the functions of civilian officials and those of military officers. (Madison at this point in his memorandum adds that, "I thought it proper particularly that he should proceed to Bladensburg, and give any aid to Genl. Winder that he could; observing that if any difficulty on the score of authority should arise, which was not likely, I should be near at hand to remove it," and, incredibly, that "it was my purpose in case there should be time, to have the members of the Cabinet together in Bladensburg, where it was expected Genl. Winder would be, and in consultation with him to decide on the arrangements suited to the posture of things." Armstrong closed the conversation by saying that he had not understood the letter from Madison in such a way and that he would head to Bladensburg directly.)

Madison noted that he relayed the gist of this conversation to Secretary Campbell immediately. This brings up the question of why Madison made these notes. Apparently he thought he would need to explain himself, but to whom? To the public, perhaps? This behavior was all quite peculiar. It would continue in the same vein. Riding on toward Bladensburg with the attorney general, he heard that the British were in Bladensburg, and, meeting Monroe and Armstrong, asked Armstrong whether he had interfered with Winder's disposition of the troops. Armstrong saying he had not, Madison told him he ought to and then accompanied him to where Winder was. His unruly horse kept Madison from participating in the ensuing "short conversation" between Armstrong and Winder. Madison recorded that Armstrong had refrained from making Winder reposition his forces—again, as if this were some kind of blamable omission on Armstrong's part. Thus Madison's memorandum of these pivotal events ended. According to Madison, "It had been previously settled that in the event of the Enemy's taking possession of the City," he and the Cabinet would reassemble in nearby Frederick, Maryland. No such meeting ever occurred.[10]

Madison arrived at the White House soon after Dolley departed around 3:00 PM on the day of the Bladensburg fiasco. He and Mrs. Madison traveled separately to numerous different locations in the District of Columbia, Maryland, and Virginia on August 24th to 26th. The editors of Madison's papers conclude that while Madison's perambulations could be seen as supporting either the popular account of a president driven by fear of capture or the alternative story highlighting his "calmness and resolution during the crisis," the most likely truth is that Madison reasonably left Washington ahead of the British forces' arrival in order to ensure "both the safety of his wife and the continuance of the U.S. government."

What remained, as Madison saw it, was to pin the blame where it properly lay. Madison prepared another lengthy memorandum describing the conversation between him and Armstrong on August 29th.[11] Washington remained on edge at the thought of a return of British forces, the president told Armstrong, and blame had landed on the two of them. "[T]he commanding General of the Militia" had told Madison "that every Officer would tear off his epaulets, if Genl. Armstrong was to have any thing to do with them," the president said, and Monroe had manifested a willingness, "though very reluctantly," to perform "the functions of Secretary of war," which "was very acceptable to them." Now that Armstrong had returned, the problem was what to do about this situation. (If the word of a District of Columbia militia adjutant is to be believed, there had indeed been a veritable mutiny, as upon Armstrong's appearing in their camp, one prominent Marylander and friend of both Madison and Monroe, "Charles Carroll of Bellevue . . . met him and denounced him, openly and vehemently, as the cause of all the disasters that had befallen the city—when, with one impulse, the officers said to General Smith, 'There, sir, are our swords; we will not employ them, if General Armstrong is to command us . . . but we will obey the orders of any other member of the Cabinet." Madison's response to this tale was supposedly, "Say to General Smith, *the contingency* (namely, that of any future orders being given by General Armstrong) *shall not happen*."[12]

In Madison's account Armstrong replied that "he had been aware of the excitement agst. him; that it was altogether artificial, and that he knew the sources of it, and the intrigues by which it had been effected, which this was not the proper time for examining; that the excitement was founded on the most palpable falsehoods, and was limited to this spot. . . ." He then offered his resignation, adding the option for the president of allowing Armstrong merely to "retire from the scene, by setting out immediately on a visit to his family in the State of N. York," as Madison recorded it. That Monroe had filled functions of the secretary of war with "unwillingness" may have seemed absurd to Armstrong, or perhaps he had an idea of his Cabinet colleague's backstage machinations. Perhaps he also knew of Carroll's role in the militia ultimatum. What "intrigues" the secretary had in mind, time would tell.

Madison scribbled that he had insisted of course that resignation "was an extent which had not been contemplated" and probably not the best option because "it might receive constructions which could not be desirable"; therefore, "a temporary retirement . . . was on the whole less objectionable. . . ." Armstrong insisted "that his conduct in relation to the defence of the City &c had proved that there had been no deficiency"—which betrayed his complete awareness that his nonfeasance over the course of several weeks had left the District of Columbia without the kinds of defenses that would soon prove impregnable elsewhere. Then followed a completely self-serving passage in which Madison said in his characteristic indirect way that Armstrong was indeed responsible for the absence of defenses around the capital. "I added," the president wrote, "that it would not be easy to satisfy the nation that the event was without blame somewhere, and I could not in candour say, that all that ought to have been done had been done & in proper time." Whether the author of these words recognized that, as one of his successors put it, the buck stopped with him is a good question.

Though Madison's characteristically oblique criticism of Armstrong might have stood there—particularly after the president conceded, "I well knew that some of the particular charges brought against him were destitute of foundation"—Armstrong pushed the issue. "He returned to an exculpation of himself," we learn, "and remarked that he had omitted no preparations or steps whatever for the safety of the place which had been enjoined on him." Then followed a lengthy paragraph in Madison's memorandum—the longest of eleven—in which Madison answered that Armstrong's duty as secretary of war was more than to take such measures as he was ordered to take, but that he was supposed "to devise and propose such as would in his opinion be necessary & proper," as indeed he had done in other regards so wantonly as to draw down upon himself the recent lengthy presidential letter listing various aspects of the business of the department under his charge that he must not exclude the president from supervising. Madison insisted that when it came to the likelihood events such as those of August 24, 1814, would occur, "it was due to truth & to myself, to say, that he had never appeared to enter into a just view either of the danger to the City wch. was to be apprehended, or of the consequences of its falling into the hands of the Enemy; that he had never himself proposed or suggested a single precaution or arrangement for its safety, every thing done on that subject having been brought forward by myself. . . ." Madison told the New Yorker he regretted having to speak thus, and had tried to remain on good terms with Armstrong all along, and the latter replied that "he was very sensible of my friendly conduct towards him, and always had, and always should respect me for it."

Madison suggested to Armstrong that he go visit his family in New York. The next morning he sent word that he would. When he reached Baltimore, he sent Madison a notice of his resignation.[13] The following day, September 5th, the *Baltimore Patriot & Evening Advertiser* included a September 3rd letter from Armstrong in which he described the conversation with Madison more or less as is seen in Madison's account, with the notable exception that he did not include the part in which the president upbraided him for not having prepared the capital's defenses. Armstrong also rejected the apparently popular rumors that he had ordered the retreat at Bladensburg and prevented Winder from defending Washington, adding that "if all the troops assembled at Bladensburgh, had been faithful to themselves and to their country, the enemy would have been beaten, and the Capital saved."[14] It is possible that Madison was right about Armstrong's performance and that Armstrong was right that it should not have mattered anyway, as either marginal intrepidity on the part of the Maryland militia or Monroe's deciding not to redeploy the Maryland troops would have won Americans the victory and spared the United States its greatest military humiliation. Whose fault was it, anyway, that the United States were reliant on militia units hastily called to the scene for the defense of their capital? (People in Washington seem to have decided: Armstrong's "effigy," one account has it, "was etched in the walls of the burnt Capitol building, where he was shown hanging from a gallows."[15] One newspaper said that Madison had cut ties with Armstrong because the president too had been "loudly threatened by the militia.")[16] Also on September 3rd Armstrong wrote that in the wake of his departure and by the demand of the same mutinous militiamen who had demanded the secretary's replacement, Monroe had been created "Major Gen. of the District & in this capacity, he commands in chief"—a result particularly objectionable because "It is a well-known fact that to this man's interference in the arrangements on the 24th Ult. much of our misfortune on that day was owing." "With men of such imbecility I cannot longer connect myself. I have therefore renewed my resignation by letter to the Presid[en]t & am therefore on my way home."[17]

Meanwhile Madison had issued a proclamation on September 1st.[18] Washington had been sacked by a force more numerous than its defenders, he claimed. During British control of the town "for a single day only, they [had] wantonly destroyed the public edifices having no relation in their structure to operations of war," some of them "edifices being also costly monuments of taste and of the arts, and others depositories of the public archives, not only precious to the nation as the memorials of its origin and its early transactions, but interesting to all nations, as contributions to the general stock of historical instruction and political science." They had also ransacked Alexandria despite its having been yielded to them peacefully, and all in furtherance of a stated policy of "destroying and laying waste such towns and districts upon the coast as may be found assailable." Madison mocked the claim that this constituted retaliation for American behavior in York, Upper Canada, a couple of martial seasons earlier, "when it is notorious, that no destruction has been committed, which, notwithstanding the multiplied outrages previously committed by the enemy, was not unauthorized, and promptly shown to be so. . . ."

Due to the enemy's apparent determination to ignore civilized rules of war even as the two sides had entered into negotiations for peace, Madison said, he called upon all officials concerned, throughout America, to fulfill their relevant duties, and particularly upon military officials "to be vigilant and alert in providing for the defence" of "the respective military districts." For this purpose he hereby authorized them to call on "portions of the militia most convenient" to them, even if those militia units had been called into federal service. They should follow the example of the fathers who had won American independence, "with the augmented strength and resources with which time and Heaven have blessed them."

Federalist newspapers, for their part, responded to Madison's proclamation by agreeing with the British: the burning of Washington was in retribution for American "conflagration and destruction of property" in Canada. The *Boston Spectator* persisted in referring to Madison's "WICKED, CAUSELESS WAR." "Not a finger will be raised in support of Mr. Madison's grounds of war, nor *his* honour," it continued. A Georgetown Federalist paper ran a bit of doggerel meant to be recited to the tune of "Yankee Doodle":

> *Since* Madison *has held the helm*
> *And steer'd by Jeff's old notions,*
> *Afflictions dire have spread the realm,*
> *Now goading to commotions.*

Reduced to moving in with his sister-in-law, the president had reached a low point.

Grim as the U.S. Government's fiscal situation had been throughout the war, the events of late August 1814 brought on financial calamity. Combined with the departure of Armstrong and a scandal involving longtime Postmaster General Gideon Granger, this made a good time for the departure of Treasury Secretary Campbell. He left soon after offering money-printing as the only fiscal expedient available. Granger had ignored Madison's wishes regarding a postmaster for Philadelphia, instead choosing a vehement opponent of Gallatin. One might have thought that a longtime high official would have at least some political sense, but Granger soon stooped to threatening to disclose sexual dirt about Dolley Madison and her sister. Apparently doubting that this would be pressure enough, Granger tried to blackmail former president Jefferson into interceding in his behalf by threatening to run the matter of Jefferson and Mrs. John Walker up the public flagpole one more time.[19] Campbell was succeeded in Gallatin's old seat by Gallatin's fellow

Pennsylvanian and longtime friend Alexander James Dallas, for whom the departure of Armstrong had been a sine qua non of accepting the position. Monroe stayed at State and added War to his portfolio when New York's Governor Daniel Tompkins refused the position.[20]

Having surprised Armstrong by attacking Washington, the British next headed where he had expected them to go in the first place: Baltimore. Here Samuel Smith, whom we have encountered as a Senate Invisible, in the role of militia major general proved quite competent, and indeed entirely successful. In organizing and leading his city's defense Smith "more often than not . . . defied rather than followed Monroe's directives."[21]

This is the incursion immortalized by Francis Scott Key in "The Star-Spangled Banner," an English drinking song with topical lyrics by Key which if anything underplays the spectacular American defensive success to which he was an eyewitness.

In the predawn hours of September 13, 1814, a Royal Navy flotilla under Admiral Cochrane set up five bomb vessels, eleven frigates, and a rocket ship in two rows two miles south of Fort McHenry, which dominated Baltimore Harbor. His hope was to enter Baltimore Harbor and fire upon the city's defenses, which the day before had thwarted an attempted attack by Colonel Arthur Brooke and more than four thousand troops. During the course of a bombardment lasting more than twenty-four hours, the British launched in excess of fifteen hundred rounds at Fort McHenry, which was defended by Major George Armistead and his one thousand. They scored approximately four hundred hits, but killed only four Americans and wounded only twenty-four more. (Included among the stricken defenders were all of the members of a twenty-four-pound cannon's crew, who received a direct hit.) Cochrane's plan of having barges carrying twelve hundred men bypass the fort and attack it from behind failed because of fire from American shore batteries. Realizing that the Americans' stratagem of filling the harbor with sunken ships probably meant that any support his ships could offer to the army would be paltry anyway, Cochrane abandoned his effort.[22]

"We were like pigeons tied by the legs to be shot at," recalled Joseph H. Nicholson, the former Republican congressman (at President Jefferson's suggestion, prime mover of the Chase impeachment), who commanded a Maryland artillery regiment during the attack. *Niles' Weekly Register* said the shells "flew like hail stones." Fifteen hundred rounds in twenty-four hours comes to more than one per minute, and one type of British mortar, the "carcass," weighed in excess of two hundred pounds and carried "a lethal mixture of incendiary materials." Marylander civilians of both sexes and all ages stood on Baltimore rooftops to watch the sickening spectacle.

At one point the British ships closed in upon the fort, but after incurring multiple hits, they recoiled to a distance out of American range and continued firing. During the British bombardment, a heavy rainstorm punctuated by nearby lightning flashes struck the city—without any noticeable effect on the Royal Navy gun crews' performance. Cochrane did at least realize that his and his men's efforts were all for naught. As day broke on September 14th, the firing stopped, and enemy sailing ships were seen departing from Baltimore Harbor for the last time.

Francis Scott Key, a Georgetown attorney prominent both in Federalist politics and in the Episcopal Church, witnessed all of these events from the deck of a British warship eight miles behind the thundering flotilla shelling Baltimore. On a mission to obtain release of his friend Dr. William Beanes, who was being held by the British, he had been told he would have to await this attack's conclusion before Beanes would be released. Key realized that the American defense of Fort McHenry had succeeded only when he witnessed the British squadron coming back down to the mouth of the Patapsco and saw that the ceremonial thirty-by-forty-two-foot American flag had been run up over the fort.[23]

Admiral Cochrane had told Key that in case it were conquered, Baltimore "must be burned," and, Key wrote to John Randolph soon after the event, "I was sure that if taken it would have been given up to plunder. . . ." He then added, "It was filled with women and children."

Inspired, Key—an inveterate lyricist—wrote down words on a scrap of paper he happened to have with him. Besides the famous first stanza's description of his relief at realizing the British attack had failed, Key wrote three more stanzas. Those familiar with his powerful religious faith were unsurprised by his concluding verse:

O thus be it ever when freemen shall stand
Between their lov'd home & the war's desolation!
Blest with vict'ry & peace, may the heav'n rescued land
Praise the power that hath made & preserv'd us a nation!
Then conquer we must when our cause it is just,
And this be our motto—"In God is Our Trust."
And the Star-Spangled Banner in triumph shall wave
O'er the land of the free & the home of the brave![24]

As Key told it, he completed his lyrics on September 14th and wrote out a fair copy in a hotel the following day. The next day, he gave it to his brother-in-law, Judge Nicholson. Within days, it appeared in a Baltimore newspaper, and within weeks, it had been published not only in Baltimore, but in Georgetown and Boston. It was given the now-familiar title when first published as sheet music.[25]

45

⊹ ⌖ ⊹

Rufus King, the leading congressional Federalist, lamented the dire state of things. He saw that in the administration and in Congress, "No plan for prosecuting the war, none for the restoration of the public credit are thought of or proposed. . . ." Congress was apt to let Madison and his men have their way in regard both to military personnel and to funding the war effort, he fumed, but, "Our rulers can neither make war, nor conclude Peace." When Campbell left the treasury, government expenditures for 1814 were only half-funded, and there was no clear idea how 1815's would be financed. Gouverneur Morris likened the Republicans' statesmanship to "the project of putting a world on an Elephant's Back to stand on a Tortoise and he on nothing."[1]

Soon thereafter terrible news arrived from Europe. Though Madison and Monroe on October 4th sent the peace commission instructions to reduce their demands to the *status quo antebellum*—the Great Powers' reciprocal trade restrictions and British impressment now being things of the past—word came to the Octagon House, the Madisons' new domicile, of draconian British terms. Britain wanted northern Maine, a buffer zone for its Indian allies in the Midwest, demilitarization of the Saint Lawrence River and Great Lakes, and the right to use the Mississippi at will. In addition Gallatin was certain that the British intended to seize New Orleans and use it as the center of a new sugar colony dominating western North America.[2]

Seeing how dire things had become, some prominent Federalists threw their support behind the administration war effort. King decided to play the part of the patriotic statesman. In September he publicly supported the Madison administration's war measures, and by year's end he backed a proposed $6 million direct tax to pay for the war. New England Federalists, whose region had benefited from exemption from the British blockade, were the last holdouts.[3] Timothy Pickering and Morris led them in obduracy.

In October 1814 Massachusetts's legislature invited other New England states to join the Bay State in sending delegates to what would come to be known as the Hartford Convention. Frustrated with Republican domination of the Federal Government and appalled by the effectively pro-French foreign policy vector on which Jefferson and Madison had launched the country, they thought they had spotted an opening. To their chagrin, however, only Connecticut and Rhode Island responded favorably to Massachusetts's call. Connecticut's legislature, in agreeing to add seven delegates of its own to the twelve Massachusetts would send, explained that the United States' inability to defend the Nutmeg State had forced that state to defend itself. It now would be happy to take this step "combining the wisdom of New-England, in devising . . . a proper course to be adopted, consistent with our obligations to the United States. . . ." Invoking "the pure principles" Connecticut citizens had "inherited from our fathers, conducive at once, to the preservation of liberty and order," that state's legislature did not echo its older brother's complaint that "the Constitution of the United States [had] failed to secure to this Commonwealth, and . . . to the eastern section of this union, those equal rights and benefits, which were the great objects of its formation." Rhode Island too issued a statement of its motivations in deciding to participate in the Hartford Convention. Rather than confrontation, Rhode Island said it was bent on cooperation—on joining with the other New England states in securing the mutual defense they were supposed to have reaped from the federal union "to restore and secure to the people [of the New England states], their rights and privileges under the constitution of the United States." New Hampshire's Federalist governor thought better of asking his state's legislature to send delegates, and the Vermont Legislature rebuffed Massachusetts's unanimously, but three counties in those two states sent their own delegates.[4]

Learning of these events left Madison down in the dumps. The French minister noted that "the great firmness of the President and the wisdom of the counsel he is given" were essential to the United States' ability to sustain a conflict with the United Kingdom "with so active a hostile faction at the heart of the nation." Madison and Monroe sent an army colonel on "recruiting duty" to New England with instructions to cooperate with Governor Tompkins of nearby New York in case of rebellion. For some reason Monroe expressed confidence that the citizenry would oppose "traitors" in New England if it came to that.[5] At just this time Madison's most prominent New England ally, Vice President Elbridge Gerry, died suddenly in November 1814. Thus did Madison, the only president with a former Antifederalist for a vice president (he had two), become the only president who had two vice presidents die in office.

The trouble with New England over foreign policy had been a serious issue since the Jefferson administration, of course. Yet the impending Hartford Convention seemed apt to make the theoretical a reality. Prominent Virginia politician Wilson Cary Nicholas, a former U.S. senator on the cusp of two terms as governor of the Old Dominion, wrote Madison about it in mid-November.[6] "When at war with the only nation that has the means of serious annoyance," Nicholas began, "to have the force of the nation impaired if not neutralized by faction, heaps upon the government difficulties that are almost insurmountable." So grievous was the domestic opposition from New England, he asserted, "that preparations shou'd be made to meet the event be it what it may." It seemed to Nicholas that there was "much reason to apprehend that one or other of" . . . "to sever the union or to resist the laws and produce by force a change in our government" was "contemplated." Whatever they were planning, "[t]here [was] no calculation to be made upon the patriotism, the interest or the loyalty of the men who direct[ed] the affairs of New England." Given the preparations they had made, it seemed to Nicholas that New England's top politicians faced a choice between "sacrific[ing] their country and their own degradation," and at such a juncture, people such as they would "never hesitate." Nicholas said that although he had no information not available to the general public, "It is the characteristic of treason to be secret." He could barely believe that "Pickering, Quincy, Oatis, Livermore and such men" had "infused into the majority of the people of that country [i.e., New England], the deadly and rancorous hatred they bear the southern people."

In estimating the detestation of New England for the South, Nicholas went so far as to say, "I do not believe national antipathy, was ever stronger in an Englishman towards a Frenchman, that that which is felt by these men towards us." Although "[t]heir conduct was atrocious in the early stages of the war," he fulminated, "they are now as dead to every feeling of interest, as they have long been to all regard to national character and honor." It was by this point not only the Northern extremists, but even the formerly moderate men of that region who had been carried away by party spirit. "It is almost as difficult," Nicholas thought, "to separate a man from his party as from his wife & children." If recent events had not rekindled patriotic feeling in the breasts of these people, he mused, nothing could do so. He could barely believe that rather than heed "their interest, their pride as Americans, their fidelity or their duty," "[a]ll these they disregard & go on heedless of the consequences, to the attainment of t[he]ir object." At this point, though Nicholas estimated that the Northern states were generally equally divided between pro- and anti-administration men, "The great weight of talents & wealth is admitted to be on the wrong side," and "with the command of the State governments [would] . . . soon silence all opposition, unless there shou'd be an immediate exertion of the force of the genl. Government." To head this off Nicholas counseled moving the contents of the Springfield Armory out of Federalist reach and convening a Republican regional convention analogous to what was going to happen at Hartford (although the latter would need to "appear to be their own act").[7] "If we are destined to have a civil war," he said, time to prepare was at hand.

As Nicholas understood the Federalist resisters to the Federal Government's war policy, they would not remain in the union unless the Republicans "submit[ted] to their dominion." They would not tolerate "their present constitutional weight" or "any other that is equitable." "In other words, they must govern the other States or they will separate. To such an union as this," he continued, "we cannot must not submit." After fulminating on Britain's manipulation of the rift between New England and the rest of the United States at Ghent, Nicholas asked Madison to excuse him for "the liberty I have taken in addressing you." He closed with (what may have been the purpose of this letter, given his and Madison's respective relations with the Smiths) assurances that as the Old Dominion's governor in case of election, he would make "every effort" to help bring the war "to an honorable termination."

By the time Madison answered now-Governor Nicholas, he had to plead indisposition as an excuse for not getting back to him sooner.[8] (It was during this period that Vice President Gerry died too.) Madison thought not only that New England opposition was the chief obstacle the administration faced in prosecuting the war, but that it was "the sole inducement with the Enemy to persevere in it." The New England "leaders" and "priests" had brought the region's general population "under a delusion scarcely exceeded by that recorded in the period of witchcraft. . . ." "Their object," as he said, "is power. If they could obtain it by menaces, their efforts would stop there," but otherwise, "they are ready to go every length for which they can train their followers." The government's options in case New England chose extreme measures would be complicated by "the pinch which exists in our fiscal affairs, & the lamentable tardiness of the Legislature in applying some relief."

As the year 1814 ended, word came that ten thousand veterans of Wellington's Peninsular War against several of Napoleon's marshals had arrived in the

Caribbean—evidently with the American Gulf Coast as their destination. Vice Admiral Cochrane, he of the Chesapeake expedition recently ended, decided on seizure of New Orleans as his strategic objective. Historians have floated various ideas concerning Cochrane's/Britain's plans for New Orleans once they obtained it, but "there is no evidence," the leading authority concludes, "to suggest that Cochrane's plans formed part of any larger scheme to extend British rule into the lower Mississippi Valley or to connect such conquests with the revised Canadian boundary and Indian buffer-state proposals that were being put forward at Ghent."[9]

Major General Andrew Jackson, in command of American forces in the South, understood that not New Orleans but Pensacola and Mobile would be Cochrane's first targets, so he seized them—without authorization from his superiors in Washington—and thus diverted the British from landing there. Jackson next went to see to the defense of New Orleans. One way to summarize Jackson's performance in Louisiana is by saying that he proved a kind of anti-Armstrong. Seeing that there were six potential approaches to the city—two from the south, two from the east, one from the west and one from the north—Jackson responded by preparing defensive obstructions of men and cannons on all six routes.

Not only that, but in an early display of his imperious nature, Jackson in December became the first American general to impose martial law on an American civilian population,[10] even going so far as to jail a judge for trying to stay the general's hand. Famously Jackson recruited local men to augment his forces, which ultimately included pirates commanded by Jean Lafitte and free blacks. Perhaps to the surprise of his British opposite number, Jackson took the initiative in the night of December 23, subjecting enemy forces who had advanced to within nine miles of the city to a night attack at the Villeré Plantation.

On Christmas, Lieutenant General Sir Edward Pakenham, the duke of Wellington's brother-in-law, assumed command of the invading forces. Neither pressing ahead through American defenses nor trying to find an alternative route to the city appealed to Pakenham, but he chose the former. On January 8th Pakenham sent his forces across a long, open field toward a fortified line at least five feet high at all points, behind which Jackson had carefully spaced his dozen cannons and "three thousand marksmen." On one end of his line, the American warship *Louisiana* had its cannon trained on the field, with "a strong battery on the opposite shore."[11] "The result," as J. C. A. Stagg puts it, "was a short and shocking slaughter of the British army. These veteran troops sustained more than two thousand casualties, including the loss of Pakenham and two of his generals." Perhaps even more stunning was that "American casualties, by contrast, amounted to seventy-one, only thirteen of which were deaths." As Jackson reported to Monroe the day after the battle, "I cannot speak sufficiently in praise of the firmness & deliberation with which my whole line received their approach:—more could not have been expected from veterans inured to war."[12]

One American soldier recalled:

> When the smoke had cleared away and we could obtain a fair view of the field, it looked, at the first glance, like a sea of blood. It was not blood itself which gave it this appearance but the red coats in which the British soldiers were dressed. Straight out before our position, for about the width of space which we supposed had been occupied by the British column, the field was entirely covered with prostrate bodies. In some places they were laying in piles of several, one on the top of the other. On either side, there was an interval more thinly sprinkled with the slain; and then two other dense rows, one near the levee and the other towards the swamp. About two hundred yards off, directly in front of our position, lay a dark dapple gray horse, which we understood had been Pakenham's.

(The general had ridden to the front in an attempt to urge his men on, had a horse shot out from under him, returned atop another one, and been "cut asunder by a cannon ball.")[13]

Meanwhile Federalist newspapers ran a series of open letters to the president. Signed "Refederator," they asserted that the federal union had reached an end and that this left the states free to reach separate peaces with the enemy. When they had concluded a peace with the United Kingdom, the states would be free to conclude a new federal agreement—an agreement from which the states beyond the Appalachians would be excluded. Those states, according to Refederator, "do not, ought not, and never can belong to the Union." The day the Hartford Convention opened, *The Boston Gazette* endorsed the original British peace proposal that had included substantial American territorial concessions. This seemed to reflect Massachusetts Federalists' considered views, as Governor Caleb Strong had responded to Madison's request for five thousand militiamen to be deployed in defense of Maine by refusing the call and broadcasting the story in the newspapers. Madison finally responded to this current in New England affairs by taking steps to put the Springfield Armory under the U.S. Army's ordnance department and giving Brigadier General Robert Swartwout $350,000 to recruit soldiers in New England in case that proved necessary to enforcement of the U.S. Government's authority there.[14]

The Hartford Convention concluded its business on January 3, 1815. "The commissioners appointed by the Massachusetts and Connecticut legislatures to press for the Hartford Convention's amendments to the Constitution and to arrange for New England's autonomy in defending itself," the historian of New England's opposition to the Madison administration says, "arrived in the nation's capital just as the first reports of Jackson's victory at New Orleans and news of the Treaty of Ghent restoring the prewar status quo, to which the prince regent had already affixed his signature, were received."[15] The American negotiators' success in obtaining British agreement to the *status quo antebellum* and Jackson's smashing success on the battlefield cut the legs out from under the marginally loyal New Englanders. Rather than getting the country off the hook, Federalists now seemed to have been engaged in undercutting Madison's administration in a time of desperate conflict with a power that had gratuitously burned down the national capital. Perhaps Madison's war aims—British agreement that "free ships make free goods" and a vow to cease impressing American sailors—had not been achieved, but the end of conflict with the French Empire rendered these issues moot. The people who had led the Hartford Convention had earned their party and their region ongoing suspicion and themselves obloquy. People outside New England understood that the Hartford Convention would be a secessionist cabal, and though it did not propose any such measures, it did leave the door open for future such conventions in case the Republicans did not agree to substantial constitutional changes to satisfy New Englanders' demands.

The report of the Hartford Convention proposed seven constitutional amendments. Their stated purpose was "to strengthen, and if possible to perpetuate, the union of the states," including by:

1. requiring a two-thirds vote of each house of Congress to declare war, cut off trade with any foreign country, or admit new states to the union;
2. limiting embargoes to sixty days;
3. eliminating the Three-Fifths Clause's application to apportionment of the House of Representatives, and thus the Electoral College;
4. disqualifying naturalized citizens from holding federal office; [and]

5. limiting presidents to one term and banning successive presidents from the same state.[16]

Far from spurring the end of the Virginia Dynasty, what this set of proposals did was signal the end of the Federalist Party as a national party. At the time, however, people welcomed the report with relief; Madison is supposed to have laughed when he read it. What an anticlimax these moderate proposals had turned out to be.[17] Though the Convention's proceedings had been conducted behind closed doors, moderation had been the word of the day. As John Armstrong put it, the New England Federalists seemed to have been up to "a game of bragge." Though Daniel Webster adjudged the proceedings "moderate, temperate & judicious,"[18] they would stain his and other New England Federalists' reputations for decades to come.

46

⊹ ⊛ ⊹

In February 4, 1815, Madison received the news from Ghent. The *status quo antebellum*—a return to the state of things as they had been before the war—was much better than had been feared just a few months earlier. All was jubilation. The president's special message to Congress of February 18, 1815,[1] summarized the stunning climax of fifteen years of foreign policy: Republicans had succeeded in spite of themselves. This outcome, Madison said, "terminates, with peculiar felicity, a campaign signalized by the most brilliant successes." Americans had not wanted the war, but it had become a necessary endeavor "to assert the rights and independence of the nation." Now "the causes of the war have ceased to operate," he noted, "the Government has demonstrated the efficiency of its powers of defence," and "the nation can review its conduct, without regret, and without reproach."

Historians traditionally have taken this statement as marking the end of the first phase of American history. Independence had at this point been secured in full and beyond doubt, and now there would come a turning. President Madison, however, did not understand the situation that way as he lived in it. He next noted that there would of course be an impulse in Congress and the country to pare back wartime military spending to traditional peacetime levels. He might have added, "as Republicans insisted should be done during the election campaign of 1800, and as President Jefferson said in his First Inaugural Address would be America's custom from that moment on." Although he traced American success in the war, such as it was, to "the public spirit of the militia, and . . . the valor of the military and Naval forces of the country," his experience at Bladensburg and in the Octagon House—his refuge from the charred remains of the Executive Mansion—made clear to the Father of the Republican Party that he and his friend from Monticello had been mistaken.

"Experience has taught us," he went on, "that neither the pacific dispositions of the American people, nor the pacific character of their political Institutions can altogether exempt them from that strife which appears, beyond the ordinary lot of nations, to be incident to the actual period of the world," so "a certain degree of preparation for war, is not only indispensable to avert disaster in the onset, but affords also the best security for the continuan[ce] of peace." Therefore Congress, he was sure, would "provide for the maintenance of an adequate regular force. . . ." He specified that the naval forces, the harbor defenses, militia training, and "cultivat[ion of] the military art" should receive Congress's attention on an ongoing basis.

Peace would bring an economic bonanza. The president forecast that America would enter into mutually beneficial trade relations with countries similarly disposed. He added the caveat, however, that "the constant guardianship of Congress" should be extended to "the manufactures which have sprung into existence . . . during the period of the European wars. This source of national independence & wealth," he concluded, "I anxiously recommend, to the prompt & constant guardianship of Congress." He closed his message with a wish that America and Great Britain might come to have ongoing friendly relations—a wish no one at the time could have imagined being so thoroughly and enduringly granted—and with an asseveration that the nation's highest officials should "never cease to inculcate obedience to the laws, and fidelity to the Union, as constituting the Palladium of the national independence and prosperity"—a statement that might as easily have been made by the Father of Our Country at the high tide of his alliance with Madison a quarter century earlier. Added to the complete success of American arms against the enemy's Creek allies in the South, the message marked the entire success of Republican policy.[2]

As soon as Congress ratified the Treaty of Ghent, President Madison asked for a declaration of war against the Barbary state of Algiers. That predatory power had resumed its old practice of preying on American Mediterranean shipping during the War of 1812, and now it would be taught the error of its ways. On May 20, 1815, a nine-ship U.S. Navy squadron under the command of Stephen Decatur set sail from New York. Decatur made quick work of that enemy, extracting a treaty from its dey by warning him that the American ships' guns would all fire on his city unless he conceded the error of his ways, released all Americans he was holding for ransom, and agreed never again to demand American tribute—an agreement more favorable, says Henry Adams, than he had ever signed with any other nation. This success achieved, Decatur imposed similar terms on Tunis and

Tripoli, which had even to pay American shipowners for their losses due to those states' piratical practices.[3]

If Andrew Jackson's victory at New Orleans made him the hero of a generation of Americans, the nineteenth-century American political figure most analogous to George Washington, Decatur, remains the country's preeminent naval hero. Not only his smashing successes at sea, but his toast at a banquet in his honor famously took patriotism about as far as it could be taken with its perhaps lamentable conclusion of "my country right or wrong."[4]

The president's annual message for 1815 capped off a year of spectacular achievement.[5] Madison began by describing Decatur's cruise, including his having captured the Algerine ruler's principal ship with his admiral aboard. Turning to the happy conclusion of the War of 1812, Madison said he hoped Congress would consider confining American navigation to American sailors—a measure which, he thought, would combine a "conciliatory tendency" with "increasing the independence of our navigation, and the sources for our maritime defence." The tribes that had taken Britain's side in the war, he advised, had with the exception of the more distant ones already been pacified, and he hoped those last would soon follow. There might still be further problems with the Creeks, he feared.

Unlike in times past Madison intended to act further on the path he and Congress had set off down when it came to the peacetime military establishment: a general staff was being organized. A thorough reform would come during the Monroe administration, as we shall see. The federal debt of various kinds he said had grown at least to $120 million. Assumption of the states' war-related debt (another jarring idea coming from James Madison and more vindication of Alexander Hamilton) would lead to a bit more. Fortunately various military expenditures (ships, harbor fortifications, etc.) would provide ongoing benefits. They likely should be maintained and manned evermore. He hoped the U.S. Military Academy could be enlarged and recommended "the establishment of others in other sections of the union," and he recommended that the state militias be reorganized uniformly via federal legislation. Too, the naval support facilities and the navy's ships would need to be maintained. Congress by the end of 1816 earmarked $8 million over eight years to build nine seventy-four-gun ships and twelve forty-four-gun ships, among other things, for the navy.[6]

If that were not enough, Madison now made public what in 1811 had been his private position: that Congress should charter a new bank to manage the public debt and provide a uniform national currency if the state banks could not. He next said that "[u]nder Circumstances giving a powerful impulse to manufacturing industry, it has made among us a progress, and exhibited an efficiency, which justify the beleif, that with a protection not more than is due to the enterprizing Citizens whose interests are now at stake, it will become, at an early day, not only safe against occasional competitions from abroad, but a source of domestic wealth, and even of external commerce." Congress also ought to take up the question of what tariff policy would insulate America from reliance on foreigners for military necessities or other necessary items. The proposals Secretary of the Treasury Dallas soon submitted to Congress did not prove so high-minded.[7]

Leading members of Congress paid particular attention to the following passage, in which the president told them he thought that institution ought to consider "the great importance of establishing throughout our country, the roads and Canals which can best be executed, under the national Authority." Not only would such projects have economic benefits, but they would have "the political effect of . . . bringing and binding more closely together, the various parts of our extended confederacy." The states had undertaken scattered projects of this kind, but the Federal Government might initiate "similar undertakings, requiring a national jurisdiction, and national means. . . ." In case the Old Republicans and committed Jeffersonians in Congress should balk at the idea, "it is a happy reflection," Madison blithely told them, "that any defect of constitutional authority, which may be encountered, can be supplied in a mode, which the constitution itself has providently pointed out." Surely no one could invoke the Constitution's amendment provisions with as much authority as the chief author both of the unamended Constitution and of its first ten amendments.[8] Unfortunately for all concerned, however, Madison's hint went unheeded in Congress.

As if a military buildup and construction of roads, canals, and bridges were not enough for Congress to finance, Madison came at the end of his address to an idea Jefferson and Washington had advocated unsuccessfully before him: "the establishment of a national seminary of learning within the District of Columbia." Such an institution would contribute to the "advancement of knowledge, without which the blessings of liberty cannot be fully enjoyed," and help both to inspire similar initiatives by the states and to diffuse culture.

Madison's address closed with a lengthy paragraph recognizing the "Superintending providence . . . to which [Americans] are indebted for . . . the happy lot of our country." Their institutions had proven well suited for war, through which they had earned "a growing respect abroad." Prospects seemed bright.

Bright from Madison's point of view, that is. John Randolph of Roanoke, on the other hand, back in the House after a one-term absence, spat out as the clerk finished reading the president's message that the Republican president "out-Hamiltons Alexander Hamilton."[9]

The brightness gained strength from the absence from Congress of Virginia's longtime senior senator, William Branch Giles. Though a prominent ally of Jefferson and Madison in the 1790s, Giles had been at odds with Jefferson regarding replacement of Federalist appointees in the Executive Branch at the beginning of the Jeffersonian era, and his disappointment with Madison's having overlooked him in repeated Cabinet shuffles left him as an odd kind of duck: a non-Quid dissident Republican, aka Invisible, who often opposed the administration.[10]

The new Congress saw Henry Clay back in the speaker's chair and South Carolinian John C. Calhoun taking a leadership role with him.[11] Both men favored the kind of active, nationalist program the president had recommended in his Annual Message, and Congress generally followed their, and Madison's, lead. So, on February 26, 1816, Calhoun as chairman of a special committee delivered in the Committee of the Whole a learned speech on introducing the Bank Bill.[12]

Those familiar with Calhoun only from his later Nullifier or Sectionalist phases will be surprised by the content of his Bank Bill speech.[13] He began by putting constitutional issues involved in legislating a new bank into creation aside as "an useless consumption of time. The constitutional question," he said, "had been already so freely and frequently discussed, that all had made up their minds on it." The question whether banks were congenial to "liberty and prosperity," he continued, had been rendered passé by "[t]he fact of the existence of banks." Only the practical questions involved in chartering a new federal bank remained to be answered. Obviously a bank would be useful in managing the federal finances, he insisted, so what he intended to do was to consider the nature of the disorders of the Federal Government's finances and "the question whether it was in the power of Congress, by establishing a National Bank, to remove those disorders."

As Calhoun spoke, he said, the one private bank in the United States at the time the Constitution was created had become two hundred sixty, and the $400,000 capital of the one had become two hundred times that much. "We have in lieu of gold and silver a paper medium, unequally but generally depreciated, which affects the trade and industry of the nation; which paralyzes the national arm, which sullies the faith, both public and private, of the United States. . . ." Passing this bill would restore these banks to their old function as "places of discount and deposit." "Resolve," the Carolinian insisted, "that every where there shall be an uniform value to the national currency; your constitutional control will then prevail." By refusing to receive the notes of banks that did not pay specie or to give them government business, the Federal Government could at once wring the inflation out of the economy. "The disease," he lectured, "arose in time of war—the war had subsided, but left the disease, which it was now in the power of Congress to eradicate. . . ." Omitting to do so would make Congress "abettors of a state of things which was of vital consequence to public morality. . . ."

Here Calhoun's position resembled the message Madison had issued in vetoing a bank bill in early 1814: that the bill "did not adequately invest the bank with the power to preserve a uniform (national) currency."[14] The bill passed the House 80–71 on March 13th, the Senate passed it with amendments on April 3rd, and the House accepted the Senate amendments on April 5th. Apparently satisfied that this new bill had no such flaw as that of 1814, Madison signed it into law on April 10th.[15]

Another hotly contested issue of this Congress, salaries for members of Congress, also drew Calhoun into leadership. He spoke in the House the day after Speaker Henry Clay told members that "although his compensation, whilst he had enjoyed the honor of presiding in this House, was double that of other members, he declared, with the utmost sincerity, that he had never been able to make both ends meet at the termination of Congress," even though he had in some instances attended Congress with only part of his family and sometimes without any of it.[16] To this point members had received only per diem allowances, but Calhoun thought salaries necessary. "Whenever this House is properly composed, when it contains a sufficient number of men of ability, experience and integrity," he held, "it of necessity will give direction to public affairs; but a weak and inexperienced House necessarily falls under executive control. The increased pay is calculated to draw men of abilities into this House; and, what is of equal importance, to keep them here till they are matured by experience." He said he had witnessed no shortage of talent in the House, but that a lack of experience had often made itself felt. One cost of a congressional career that members ought to bear in mind when they voted was that unless a member were significantly wealthy, he likely would not be able to afford to bring his wife and children to Washington with him—and thus would be separated from them. This reality prevented many able members from continuing their service. The bill passed that day by a vote of 81–67, and President Madison signed it into law on March 19, 1816.[17] Where formerly congressmen had received

$6 per day for their service, they now received $1,500 per session. So unpopular was this reform that two-thirds of its House supporters lost in that
year's elections, and even Calhoun had to face a former congressman at the
polls. Characteristically the young Carolinian rejected well-meaning counsel that he publicly apologize, but he yielded to the imperative to give public
speeches on the subject in the two main population centers of his district.
He was reelected.[18]

Besides the Bank Bill and the congressional salaries law, Congress also
enacted legislation in keeping with Madison's call in his annual message for
tariff protection and a buildup of the peacetime Department of War and Department of the Navy establishments. All this work done, President and
Mrs. Madison departed for Montpelier on June 5th, not to return until October 9th—their longest absence from the capital since they had traveled there
for James to take up the prime position in President Jefferson's Cabinet.[19]

47

✢ ✢ ⊛ ✢ ✢

hree other significant developments filled out the story of 1816. One
concerned the hitherto relatively obscure third branch of the Federal
Government, the federal courts. By a fluke of luck, the U.S. Supreme
Court on March 20, 1816 decided authoritatively for the first time the question of the relationship between federal and state courts when it came to
interpretation of federal law—specifically, when it came to appeals of questions of federal law from state supreme courts to the U.S. Supreme Court.[1]

The case, *Martin v. Hunter's Lessee,* concerned land titles in Virginia's
Northern Neck—a part of the Commonwealth that had once belonged
to Thomas, Lord Fairfax. Fairfax's estate comprised "about a third of the
populated area of Virginia," including the Northern Neck, and not wanting
to have his principality seized, Fairfax remained essentially neutral during
the Revolution. As he died intestate and without an heir in Virginia, some
Virginians assumed his land would simply escheat to the Commonwealth.
The Treaty of Paris, however, provided protection for British property in
the United States, and Antifederalists, including their leader Patrick Henry,
made an issue of the likely attitude of federal courts toward this provision in
case the Constitution were ratified.

Fairfax's British heir, Denny Martin Fairfax, retained as his counsel the
brothers James and John Marshall. The two of them anticipated being at
the front of the line of potential buyers in case Denny Fairfax decided to divest himself of his Virginian landholdings. John Marshall took point in the
legislative process giving effect to Denny Martin Fairfax's offer to deed his
undeveloped land in western Virginia to the Commonwealth in return for
clear title to his plantations in the settled part of the state. As the historian
of the litigation put it, the Marshall brothers' haul from this set of maneu-
vers amounted to "some of the choicest plantations in northern Virginia."
James Marshall tried to resuscitate the rents the lord had formerly collected

and lost in state court. The Marshalls won on appeal in 1805, however, with one caveat. Judge Spencer Roane, Patrick Henry's son-in-law and a devout Old Republican, pointed out in dissent that John Marshall had pledged to the Virginia Ratification Convention of 1788 that Fairfax quitrents would no longer be collected. Here the Marshalls themselves were collecting them. To Roane, as to Jeffersonians generally, the meaning of the Constitution depended on the explanation Federalists had provided to the ratification conventions—that is, on the Ratifiers' understanding of the document when they ratified it. Roane said the quitrents, or whatever they were now called, should be defunct. Learning of this passage of Roane's opinion, tenants on the Marshalls' lands remained recalcitrant in paying the Marshalls. This entailed years of additional litigation for the Marshalls.[2]

It was the Marshalls who kept what came to be known as *Martin v. Hunter's Lessee* (1816) going. In 1813 Justice Joseph Story for the Supreme Court said in *Fairfax's Devisee v. Hunter's Lessee* that the Marshall syndicate had had title to all of the Fairfax lands, thus, as the historian of Early Republic Virginia's legal system F. Thornton Miller notes, vindicating Patrick Henry's assertion that the federal courts contemplated by Article III of the Constitution would reestablish the entire Fairfax estate. (Yes, the Marshalls had surrendered some of it by 1813, but they had owned it in the first place.) Roane and his court called upon the Virginia bar to argue the question whether the Virginia Court of Appeals (now known as the Virginia Supreme Court) should respect the authority of the U.S. Supreme Court to overturn the Virginia court's decision in *Hunter v. Faifax's Devisee*. In other words, was Section 25 of the Judiciary Act of 1789, which granted the U.S. Supreme Court power to hear appeals from state supreme courts, constitutional? Did Congress have constitutional authority to make the highest federal court the ultimate appellate court not only in regard to cases arising in federal courts, but also in regard to matters of federal law arising in state courts?

Roane concluded for his court that though the Supremacy Clause required all American officials, federal and state, to treat the U.S. Constitution, besides treaties and statutes made in conformance with it, as the supreme law of the land, the First Congress, again in Miller's words, "had erred in establishing [a] procedure" "allowing the Supreme Court to act as the final court of appeals for each state." State and federal governments had parallel judicial systems, Roane insisted for Virginia's highest court.

Because the parties to the case included Chief Justice John Marshall, the Supreme Court's opinion in the case was said (though we may have our suspicions) to have been the work of Justice Joseph Story. Story, recall, had been appointed to the Supreme Court by President Madison over Thomas Jefferson's vehement opposition. In calling Story a "Tory" Jefferson had had in mind the congressman's role in the repeal of the Embargo Act, the centerpiece of the Virginian's foreign policy.

Jefferson likely would have opposed him even more strongly had he foreseen the justice's opinion in *Martin*. As Story's biographer R. Kent Newmyer put it, "*Martin* would be not only his first but his most important constitutional opinion. What Marshall did for judicial review in *Marbury*, Story would now do for the appellate power of the Court. The result was hardly less important." Perhaps overheatedly, Newmyer calls *Martin* "Virginia's Hartford Convention," adding that "The issue was . . . the constitutional foundations of the government itself." "The denial of the Court's jurisdiction under section 25 was the calculated decision by the states' rights forces of Virginia, not just Spencer Roane and the court of appeals but Thomas Ritchie of the *Richmond Enquirer*, the leaders of the Richmond Junto that controlled the state legislature, and Thomas Jefferson himself."[3]

As Story reasoned, since the Constitution left original jurisdiction over most suits in state courts, omission by Congress to adopt such legislation as Section 25, and thus to empower the Supreme Court to review state courts' decisions of federal questions, would mean that many questions of federal law could not be reached by the Supreme Court. Different states would resolve those questions differently. This must over time result in different regimes of federal law in different states. As Story reasoned, "From the very nature of things, the absolute right of decision, in the last resort, must rest somewhere. . . ."

Story claimed, contrary to Article VII of the Constitution (the ratification article), that "[t]he Constitution of the United States was ordained and established, not by the states in their sovereign capacities, but emphatically, as the preamble of the constitution declared, by 'the people of the United States.'" Story insisted that "where a power is expressly given in general terms, it is not to be restrained in particular cases," and Congress has the right "from time to time, to adopt its own means to effectuate legitimate objects, and to mold and model the exercise of its powers, as its own wisdom and public interest should require." Newmyer translates this as meaning that in regard to implied Article III powers, "the benefit of the doubt went to the national government."

Not only that, but for the Court Story claimed that this supervisory power "must therefore be vested in some court, by Congress: and to suppose that it was not an obligation binding on them, but might, at their pleasure, be omitted or declined, is to suppose that, under the sanction of the constitution they might defeat the constitution itself; a construction which would lead to such a result cannot be sound." However much the Congress or the people might dislike the Supreme Court's conclusion in *Martin,* in other words, passage of such a law as Section 25 was obligatory upon Congress. It could not be repealed.

Justice William Johnson, a Jefferson appointee, wrote a concurring opinion to say both that he lamented the heat of the Virginia court's opinion and that he did not think the Supreme Court was in *Martin* claiming any compulsory power over state supreme courts. In light of that fact, he said, he hoped a spirit of "comity" might come more clearly to mark the Old Dominion's judges' attitude toward the federal courts.[4] He must have been disappointed, then, that Judge Roane and company never responded to the Supreme Court's request that they forward the record of the case to Washington, D.C. In other words, though *Martin v. Hunter's Lessee* supposedly stands for the Supreme Court's power to review questions of federal law decided in state supreme courts, no such review occurred in that case.

The second remaining significant development of that year resulted from a volcanic eruption on the other side of the world—specifically, of Tambora in the Dutch East Indies (today's Indonesia).[5] That volcano's 1815 eruption was, one historian says, "ten times as powerful as the better-known Krakatoa in 1883, one hundred times the force of Mount St. Helens in 1980." This eruption released a huge amount of sulfur dioxide into the atmosphere of the Northern Hemisphere, and the effects on the United States were massive.

A summary of the Tambora eruption's effects on the United States must include the resulting European famine that spurred rapid migration from settled parts of the United States into the new territories of today's Midwest, where migrants purchased farmland on credit in hopes of capitalizing on significantly higher food prices in European markets resulting from food shortages.

Both Europe and the United States experienced extreme cold in 1816, a year New Englanders dubbed "eighteen hundred and froze to death." Americans who had lived through it generally called 1816 "the year without a summer." Boston had snow in the second week of June; New York City had a twenty-four-degree day that month; Pennsylvania's fruit was "chiefly destroyed by the late frosts"; Kentucky had freezing temperatures in August; Petersburg, Virginia, had frost that month; and Washington, D.C., that month had "a temperature, such as is generally experienced in the latter end of October." Similar reports exist from North Carolina. The problem did not end then. The *Richmond Enquirer* said in summer 1817 that the James River was lower than it had ever been since Jamestown's establishment in 1607, and the *American Beacon* said the Mississippi River stopped rising at New Orleans lower than anyone had ever seen there. At Pittsburgh the Ohio River—normally twenty-seven to thirty feet deep—was only three feet deep in 1819.

A result, predictably, was food shortage. The corn crop in New England for 1816 was very scant, and a bushel of wheat in New York rose in price from $1.41 in May 1816 to $2.50 by December. People responded by moving west and growing wheat on land they bought on credit. Western towns' populations grew quickly too—to some extent due to immigration from Europe.

Predictably, when the weather changed as time passed, production of foodstuffs rebounded in the older areas. Britain, which had put its Corn Laws (bans on importation of some crops) in abeyance in response to the poor domestic harvests resulting from the eruption, returned to enforcing them in autumn of 1818. As a result, recent migrants to the American West found that prices of their produce fell. This left them unable to service their land purchases. The BUS returned to enforcing its loans, and credit contracted throughout the economy. As one newspaper put it, "The [Bank of the] United States' branches are drawing the cord tighter and tighter; they are limiting the number of banks whose notes are receivable for lands." Besides that, Treasury Secretary William Crawford reported that "In the early part of 1819, the prices of all articles produced in the Western States fell so low as scarcely to defray the expense of transportation to the ports from whence they were usually exported to foreign markets."

The author of the most recent account of the Panic of 1819 says, "Three times before the Civil War the volume of public land sales reached its greatest heights: just before the Panics of 1819, 1837, and 1857. Each peak followed a rapid rise in commodity prices, and each downturn began soon after those prices fell." A faraway volcano caused a poor harvest in 1816, which led to a spike in grain prices and to a boom in land purchases. "More than seven million acres had been bought in the Northwest; most of it had been planted in wheat, corn, or rye, and by 1818 there was a glut." The bust was sure to follow.

48

The presidential contest of 1816 turned out to be no contest at all. The Federalists nominated for president Senator Rufus King of New York (by way of Massachusetts) to run against the Republicans' James Monroe. King, a Philadelphia Convention delegate who had been Monroe's friend in Congress, looked for his candidacy to help revivify his party in the Empire State. It was not to be: of 125,000 votes cast there, Monroe received 67,000. Perhaps, as King put it, the president-elect "had the zealous support of nobody," but being "exempt from the hostility of Everybody" proved sufficient—in New York and throughout the country. The Electoral College chose Monroe by 183 votes to 34, with only Massachusetts, Connecticut, and Delaware for the senator.[1]

Madison's Eighth Annual Message to Congress came before that body on December 3, 1816.[2] It was quite a lengthy one. Madison noted that while the peace between America and Britain and the cessation of the world war between France and her enemies had resulted in "a general invigoration of industry among us, and in the extension of our commerce," "particular branches of our manufactures" had suffered since importation of British goods became more or less free. Congress, he said, would want to remember that "manufacturing establishments, if suffered to sink too low or languish too long, may not revive" and take whatever steps might appear necessary to prevent recurrence of a situation "in which a dependence on foreign sources, for indispensable supplies, may be among the most serious embarrassments." So too would Congress want to consider establishing "navigation laws" reciprocating the exclusion from British ports of American ships carrying goods from British colonies. "The reasonableness of the rule of reciprocity" had been advocated by American diplomats to their British counterparts, but to no avail.

The president next discussed difficulties that had arisen in relations with

Spain and Algiers, neither of which seemed apt to develop into full-blown hostilities. "With the other Barbary States," he concluded, "our affairs have undergone no change." Indian affairs struck him as developing in a desirable way, as land purchases had smoothed the situation of frontier American citizens, and in some instances conflicting land claims among Indian tribes whose land the United States had wanted to purchase had been resolved by paying both tribes the going rate for the land. Here Madison invoked "the benevolent policy of the United States preferring the augmented expence, to the hazard of doing injustice; or to the enforcement of injustice, against a feeble and untutored people, by means involving or threatening an effusion of blood." Having restored peace among tribes and between Indians and Americans, he continued, "will favor the resumption of the work of civilization, which had made an encouraging progress among some. . . ." When America succeeded in "extending that divided and individual ownership, which exists now in moveable property only, to the Soil itself," he forecast, "the true foundation for a transit from the habits of the Savage, to the arts and comforts of social life" would have been laid.

Madison next recommended several types of legislation to Congress's attention. It ought to reorganize the militia in light of the experience of the recent war; it ought to establish "uniformity of Weights and measures"; it ought to create a national university within the District of Columbia; it ought "to effectuate a comprehensive system of roads and Canals; such as will have the effect of drawing more closely together every part of our Country"; and it should revise the federal criminal law. "The United States having been the first to abolish, within the extent of their authority, the transportation of the natives of Africa into slavery, by prohibiting the introduction of slaves, and by punishing their Citizens participating in the traffic, cannot but be gratified at the progress made by concurrent efforts of other nations, towards a general suppression of so great an evil." Congress, he suggested, ought to take steps "to give the fullest efficacy to their own regulations," whether by stopping American citizens who "mingle[d] in the slave trade under foreign flags" or by interdicting those who brought slaves into America through adjoining territories.

Madison called too for Congress to relieve Supreme Court justices of the rigors of riding circuit, which under the Federalists' hated Judiciary Act of 1801 had been abolished, but which Republicans' Judiciary Act of 1802 had restored. Congress did not act on this recommendation. Madison's recommendation that the office of attorney general be given "the usual appurtenances to a public office" also went unheeded. He next projected that the

Federal Government's revenue for the coming fiscal year would exceed expenditures by nearly 24 percent. In the management of the government's finances, he said, the new Bank of the United States would be quite helpful. Without naming him, Madison closed this portion of his address by saying that Gallatin deserved the credit for the healthy state of the government's finances.

"The period of my retiring from the public service being at a little distance," he said, he happily beheld America "blessed with tranquility and prosperity at home; and with peace and respect abroad." The success of its constitution pleased him. The Constitution's principles and operation struck him as right and proper. "These contemplations," he concluded, "sweetening the remnant of my days, will animate my prayers for the happiness of my beloved Country, and a perpetuity of the Institutions, under which it is enjoyed."

Madison's congressional allies, led by Henry Clay and John C. Calhoun, worked hard as his term drew to a close to smooth his way out of office with one last achievement: the Bonus Bill. Congress passed this legislation providing that the "bonus" the Federal Government reaped from its shares in the Second Bank of the United States would be spent on a national network of roads, canals, and bridges. As Calhoun's authorized 1843 campaign biography (of which he was a co-author) explains, the bill was thought to be consistent with the suggestion in Madison's Annual Message for 1815, which not only had called for such a program, but had said that in case "whatever constitutional power [Congress] might possess over the subject" should "prove inadequate," Congress ought to "apply for an amendment to the Constitution granting such additional powers as would be sufficient."[3] Calhoun thought a bill providing that the government's "share of its dividends" should be "set apart and pledge[d] . . . as a fund for internal improvement" and "ma[king] no appropriation" pending "the decision of Congress, in conformity with the president's views" would meet Madison's requirements. "He had not the least suspicion, in reporting and supporting the bill, that he went beyond the President's recommendation, or that he would have any difficulty approving it, till the bill had passed both Houses, and was sent to him for his signature."

The campaign biography says that knowing that Madison would soon depart, Calhoun

called to take his leave of him. After congratulating him on the success of his administration, and expressing the happiness he felt in having had the opportunity of co-operating with him in its most difficult period, that of the war, he took his leave. When he reached the door, Mr. Madison requested him to return. He did so, and took his seat; and for the first time Mr. M. disclosed to him his constitutional objections to the bill. Mr. Calhoun expressed his deep regret, first, that he should entertain them, and, next, that he had not intimated them to him in time, saying that if he had, he (Mr. Calhoun) would certainly not have subjected him to the unpleasant duty, at the very close of his administration, of vetoing a bill passed by the votes of his friends. . . .

Here we have a kind of summary of the detachment Madison maintained from his partisan allies in Congress. In this, of course, his style as chief executive was quite unlike that of his friend and predecessor.

So, on his last day in office, President James Madison issued his famous Bonus Bill Veto Message—but not before Henry Clay had tried to persuade him not to.[4] Leave it to your successor, Clay suggested. For all we know, the veto message had by then already been written.

Coming at the end of an administration that had featured the creation of a new federal bank and retention of tariff protection for some favored domestic industries, Madison's Bonus Bill Veto Message had the air of a throwback. Madison began by saying that he could not reconcile the bill with the constitution, and so he was returning it to the House (that is, vetoing it).

"The legislative powers vested in Congress," the author of *Federalist* #45[5] began, "are specified and enumerated" (as Publius thirty years earlier, he had said "few and defined") "in the 8th. Section of the 1st article of the constitution; and it does not appear that the powers proposed to be exercise[d] by the bill is among the enumerated powers; or that it falls by any just interpretation, within the power to make laws necessary and proper for carrying into execution those or other powers vested by the constitution in the government of the U. States."

He reached similar conclusions regarding Congress's powers to regulate interstate commerce and to tax to provide for the common defense and promote the general welfare. To read the relevant constitutional provisions as covering a power of Congress to build roads, canals, and bridges would "have the effect of giving to Congress, a general power of legislation, instead of the defined and limited one hitherto understood to belong to them; the terms 'common defence and general welfare' embracing every object and act within the purview of a legislative trust." In light of the Supremacy Clause of Article VI, reading the Constitution this way would empower Congress to supersede the powers of the states in all cases not expressly prohibited. "Such a view of the constitution, finally," the president concluded, "would have the effect of excluding the judicial authority of the U. States from its participation in guarding the boundary between the legislative powers of the general & State governments," because issues of "general welfare" are matters of "expediency & policy" not for judicial decision. Finally, if Congress did not have "a general power to construct roads & canals & to improve the navigation and water courses," Madison insisted, obtaining state assent on a case-by-case basis as the bill contemplated would not solve the constitutional problem.

In his last official communication as president, Madison said that he knew a power to construct roads and canals could be put to constructive use. However, he found no such power "expressly" granted and, believing a precedent for inferring it from some tangentially related provision would provide a precedent undermining the constitutional system generally, he had to veto the bill. By a vote of 60–56, the House failed to override his veto.[6]

Clay summed up this turn of events by saying, "No circumstance, not even an earthquake that should swallow up one half of this city, could have excited more surprise than when it was first communicated to the House that Mr. Madison had rejected his own bill. . . ." The speaker justified calling it Madison's bill by reference to the president's annual message, in which he had called for such legislation.[7] What Clay seems to have missed, however, is Madison's reference to "the expediency of [Congress's] exercising their existing powers, and, where necessary, of resorting to the prescribed method of enlarging them." Perhaps too he could have noted that although Representative Philip P. Barbour, an Old Republican who levelled a detailed constitutional objection to the Bonus Bill in the House, represented a Northern Virginia district, he had actually been born in Orange County, the president's home.[8] Philip Barbour and his brother James would be among Madison's pallbearers. That was nearly twenty years in the future. Between the Bonus Bill Veto and then, Barbour would become speaker of the House, then be appointed by a new kind of president, Andrew Jackson, to the Supreme Court. His rise to such august positions tells us a lot about the politics of the period.

PART III

THE ERA OF GOOD FEELINGS

⊹ ⊹ ❅ ⊹ ⊹

John Adams's administration famously ran aground on his decision to keep George Washington's Cabinet in place. The second president to succeed a same-party president, James Madison, did not make that mistake, retaining only the irreplaceable Treasury Secretary Albert Gallatin. James Monroe neither appointed an entirely new Cabinet nor kept on all of James Madison's secretaries. He would encounter significant difficulty with the one major Cabinet member he did retain, Treasury Secretary William Crawford of Georgia.

Monroe had in mind to smooth over old partisan divisions, and General Andrew Jackson urged him to follow that inclination.[1] As Jackson put it, "Every thing depends on the selection of your ministry. In every selection, party and party feelings should be avoided." Monroe, the general counseled, ought instead to choose men "most conspicuous for their probity, Virtue, capacity, and firmness," such as Jackson's favorite for secretary of war, South Carolina Federalist William Drayton.[2] Monroe considered this unadvisable and explained why.[3]

Doubtless calculating that Jackson would remain politically prominent for the foreseeable future, Monroe tried to ingratiate himself with the general. "It is very gratifying to me," he insisted, "to receive your opinions on all subjects on which you will have the goodness to communicate them, because I have the utmost confidence, in the soundness of your judgment, & purity of your intentions." Reading this, one cannot help but wonder whether Jackson took it at face value or received it, as we might, as a piece of attempted manipulation by a highly skilled politician. Monroe's assurance that "I will give you my sentiments on the interesting subject in question, likewise without reserve" could, depending on Jackson's disposition, have confirmed him in either approach.

"I agree with you decidedly," Monroe continued, "in the principle, that the ch: Magistrate of the country, ought not to be the head of a party, but of the nation itself. I am also of opinion, that the members of the federal party, who left it in the late war, and gallantly served their country in the field, have given proofs of patriotism & of attachment to free govt, that entitle them to the highest confidence." Some Federalists had been desirous during Washington's administration, Monroe continued, of changing our government to bring it into compliance with "principles . . . unfriendly to our system," in which Washington helped to thwart them—though they did make some progress "under handed, using his name and standing with the nation, as far as circumstances permitted, to serve their purposes." The Republicans "checked the career of this party, and kept it within moderate limits."

Monroe confided his belief that "[t]he conflict between parties never ceas'd, from its commenc'ment to the present time, nor do I think it can be said now to have ceased." Despite the national interest, he recalled, "You saw the height to which the opposition was carried in the late war; the embarrassment it gave to the govt; the aid it gave to the enemy." Jackson's and his men's victory at New Orleans and the Treaty of Ghent had "checked" party opposition—for the moment. The Hartford Convention, which "unfolded views, which had been, long before, entertaind, but never, so fully understood, contributed also in an eminent degree, to reduce the opposition, to its present state." Monroe's election had elevated one known to be devoted to the Republican cause. "How shall he act? How organize the admn . . . ? How fill the vacancies existing at the time?"

The nefarious purposes to which he referred, Monroe continued, had not been shared "by any large portion of the federal party," but instead had been "confined to certain leaders, and they principally to the Eastward." To incorporate people such as had held those views and undercut the war effort might be read by other Federalists as "an offer of compromise . . . which would lessen the ignominy, due to the councils, which produc'd the Hartford convention, and thereby, have a tendency, to revive that party, on its former principles?" He intended, therefore, to appoint Republicans in the main while "indulging toward" Federalists "a spirit of moderation, and evincing a desire to discriminate, between its members, & to bring the whole, into the republican fold, as quick as possible."

While his friend James Madison had written in *Federalist* #10 that party conflict was inevitable in developed societies, Monroe told Jackson that men of that opinion were mistaken. Yes, ancient republics and contemporary Britain had parties, but Monroe traced their origins not to "human nature," but to flaws in those polities' constitutions. "We have," he thought, "happily avoided those defects in our system." Even if his effort to amalgamate the two parties into one were to fail, he continued, he would blame his own faulty efforts rather than conclude his political science was mistaken. Most Federalists could be incorporated into the Republican Party. It was their chieftains who had caused the difficulty.

Monroe told Jackson that he intended in composing his Cabinet to appoint a man from each of the great geographic sections of the country: the East (meaning New England), the Mid-Atlantic, the South, and the West. Though this course would have both political and practical benefits, he would depart from it in case of necessity.

In the event Monroe did select a Cabinet more or less geographically diverse, with the exception that the West was excluded. To holdover Treasury Secretary William Crawford of Georgia and holdover New Englander Benjamin Crowninshield at Navy, he added prominent Supreme Court advocate William Wirt of Maryland in the attorney general's post and two truly brilliant choices: John C. Calhoun of South Carolina at War and, for the top job, secretary of state, John Adams's oldest son, John Quincy Adams.

Calhoun was not Monroe's first choice. The Carolinian's political allies were not enthusiastic about the possibility either. Secretary of war had in previous administrations been a second-tier Cabinet post, along with secretary of the navy and attorney general, and Calhoun seemed destined for greater things. He had, however, played a prominent role in the House of Representatives on behalf of war with Britain in the months before Congress's declaration in 1812, and once the war began, he had given it stalwart support. Besides that, Calhoun, a patriot, thought that substantial reform of the department needed to be undertaken before the next war, which he thought inevitable. Confident he could give the department an upgrade, Calhoun decided against his prominent ally William Lowndes's advice and took the job.[4]

To significant intellect Calhoun in high executive office added notable energy. Four years into Monroe's administration, John Quincy Adams said of his colleague, "Calhoun is a man of fair and candid mind, of honorable principles, of clear and quick understanding, of cool self-possession, of enlarged philosophical views, and of ardent patriotism. He is above all sectional and factious prejudices more than any other statesman of the Union with whom I have ever acted."[5] Calhoun proved the outstanding secretary of war in the period before the Civil War.

John Quincy Adams's diplomatic career had begun when, as a teenager, he accompanied his father the future president to various European courts, where he picked up several of the languages and got the lay of the land. During the Jefferson administration, then-Senator Adams decamped from the Federalist Party precisely because he was the type of patriot Monroe confided to Jackson that he took most Federalists to be: one who would not tolerate virtually treasonous behavior by other New England leaders of that party. After smoothing over the American relationship with Emperor Alexander in St. Petersburg during the War of 1812—not an easy task at a time when the United States was at war with Alexander's British allies—he had taken the lead in negotiating the Treaty of Ghent. An intellectually impressive if prickly man, John Quincy Adams remains today the most successful secretary of state in American history. That was all before him when, as one contemporary put it, appointment as secretary of state made him "according to the established order . . . the Heir Apparent to the government." The irony of that description lay in the fact that Monroe ultimately decided on Adams for secretary of state partly because he, unlike the alternatives, was unlikely ever to become president.[6]

Notably absent from Monroe's Cabinet was anyone from the West. Having expected to be offered the top job, Speaker of the House Henry Clay of Kentucky did not accept his exclusion gracefully. Besides Clay, his, Crawford's, and Calhoun's congressional allies, all Republicans, would persistently work to undercut other Cabinet members' proposals in order to ensure that none of them appeared too capable when the next presidential canvass arrived.

When Monroe took the oath of office on March 4, 1817, Washington still looked like a town that had recently been conquered. James and Dolley Madison had never moved back into the White House after the British burned it, and the Capitol remained unfinished. Worse, the two houses of Congress could not agree on protocol for the event, and so Monroe had to give his speech outdoors. As then-Speaker Clay recalled in a Senate speech twenty years later, the Senate had requested that the House chamber be the site of Monroe's address and that senators be permitted to bring their fancy chairs from the Senate chamber into the House. Instead of granting the point, the House had left it to the president to take his oath and give his address "outside, in the open air, in front of the Capitol."[7] One witness to Monroe's address wrote at the time that the president had been barely audible in reading his speech, which, to compound the effect, was written in pedestrian style.[8] It was not the last of Monroe's public papers to be written in pedestrian style.

He opened with expressions of gratitude for the honor that had been done him and a reference to "the distinguished men who have gone before me," whose example he would follow in explaining the principles that would guide him in the course of his term.[9] American republicanism, he continued, had been successful, and Americans had "flourished beyond example." New states had been added, and states had "improved their police" and "extended their settlements," all "under a mild parental system" which left to all "a just proportion of their sovereignty." "On whom," he asked, "has oppression fallen in any quarter of the Union? What has been deprived of any right of person or property? Who restrained from offering his vows, in the mode which he prefers, to the Divine Author of his being?" Besides enjoying "all these blessings . . . in their fullest extent,"[10] Americans also had seen "no example of a capital punishment inflicted on any one for the crime of high treason."

Perhaps in saying, "Other considerations of the highest importance admonish us to cherish our Union, and to cling to the Government which supports it," Monroe intended to call to mind the Federalists' disloyal behavior during the recent war. Happily situated as America was, only a decline in public virtue—"when the people become ignorant and corrupt"—could threaten America. "Usurpation," he held, "is then an easy attainment and an usurper soon found. The People themselves become the willing instruments of their own debasement and ruin. Let us then look to the great cause and endeavor to preserve it in full force. Let us, by all wise and constitutional measures, promote intelligence among the People, as the best means of preserving our liberties."

Next Monroe turned to the question of America's military defenses. He had seen during the late war, as during the war of his youth, how much more costly military conflict could be if the country entered into it unprepared. His solution would be to see that America never found herself in such a situation again. He said the coastal and inland defenses, the army, and the militia needed to be kept in fighting trim, with peacetime ground forces "constituting the elements of a greater force, to preserve the science as well as the necessary implements of war in a state to be brought into activity in the event of war" and sea forces able both to safeguard "the neutrality of the United States with dignity in the wars of other powers" and to be expanded in case of war.

Still, despite the experience of the recent war, including the Bladensburg debacle he had seen with his own two eyes, Monroe said the militia would have to contribute to America's defenses in case of invasion "too formidable to be resisted by any land and naval force which it would comport either with the principles of our Government or the circumstances of the United

States to maintain." "The great body of the People," then, must "be so organized and trained as to be prepared for any emergency."

The government could "bind the Union more closely together" through sponsorship of "roads and canals," the president went on to say, though officials must take care that they were "proceeding always with a constitutional sanction." So too ought it to give American "manufactures" its "systematic and fostering care." In light of the variety of America's raw materials, it "ought not to depend in the degree" to this point seen "on supplies from other countries." He reasoned, "While we are thus dependant, the sudden event of war, unsought and unexpected cannot fail to plunge us into the most serious difficulties." So too ought America to rely on its own capital rather than foreigners'. As Jefferson and Madison had done before him, Monroe held that Americans had a "duty to cultivate friendly relations and to act with kindness and liberality in all our transactions" with the Indians, all while continuing previous administrations' efforts "to extend to them the advantages of civilization." Privately Monroe told Madison, "The history of our settlements, from the first discovery of this country, is a practical illustration of the doctrine contain in my message respecting Indian titles, and I think that it is supported by natural law. My candid opinion is that the more we act on it, taking the Indians under our protection, compelling them to cultivate the earth, the better it will be for them."[11]

Though he had thus far given indications of changes of emphasis and of policy in the Republican administration of the Federal Government, Monroe's next paragraph—the twentieth of twenty-two—perhaps indicated the most significant change he looked for. As he had made clear in private correspondence with General Andrew Jackson, here he told the public that he thought it "gratifying . . . to witness the increased harmony of opinion which pervades our Union." Looking to the hoped-for disappearance of parties, the president said, "Discord does not belong to our system." Not for him Madison/Publius's idea that complex, modern societies will inevitably have a multiplicity of interests—and thus likely have party division. "The American people," Monroe counseled, have encountered great dangers, and sustained severe trials with success. They constitute one great family with a common interest." Harmony could be the result, he lectured, and, "To promote this harmony, in accord with the principles of our Republican Government, and in a manner to give them the most complete effect, and to advance in all other respects the best interests of our Union, will be the object of my constant and zealous attentions."

Fortunately, he concluded, the American nation continued in its unexampled territorial growth, improvement, and success. The government "has approached near to perfection," he rhapsodized, and "in respect to it, we have no essential improvement to make." A statesman's task could only be to "preserve it in the essential principles and features which characterize it . . . by preserving the virtue and enlightening the minds of the people." All this required was to continue in "the path already traced." He closed with plaudits to former president Madison, a vow to look to his predecessors' examples, and a prayer for the Almighty's continuing protection of the United States. (That single closing line dryly implicating God in America's story probably reflected political convention more than Monroe's personal faith. As David L. Holmes explains in an essay on the president's religious life, "Monroe seems to have been an Episcopalian of Deistic tendencies who valued civic virtues above religious doctrine" and "may have been the most skeptical of the early American presidents.")[12]

50

✦ ❀ ✦

The Republican *National Intelligencer* reported that "The ceremony and the spectacle were simple, but grand, animating and impressive. . . . The principles developed in his Inaugural Speech are . . . those of the honest Republican. . . . They afford us the highest presage of an upright and unsophisticated administration of the public affairs, on the solid principles of the constitution. . . ."[1]

Margaret Bayard Smith, longtime Washington dame, reported in 1817 that "People seem to think we shall have great changes in social intercourse and customs. Mr. and Mrs. Monroe's manners will give a tone to all the rest." What she had in mind was that Mrs. Elizabeth Kortright Monroe would in no sense try to perpetuate the Washington social whirl established by Dolley Madison. While Mrs. Madison's famous "squeezes" dominated Washington society, "Few persons are admitted to the great house and not a single lady has as yet seen Mrs. Monroe, Mrs. Cutts [Dolley Madison's sister] excepted. . . . Although they have lived 7 years in W[ashington] both Mr. and Mrs. Monroe are perfect strangers not only to me but all the citizens."

The new president did indeed make significant changes to Washington social etiquette. From now on, he early made clear, the president would only receive foreign diplomats for official functions, not socially. Considerations underlying this alteration included Monroe's impression that the Jeffersonian slackness had had a negative effect on European countries' appraisals of the United States (as, for example, in the Merry affair) and a desire not to seem to be favoring any particular minister.[2] Secretary Adams noted that this could cause trouble in particular with the Portuguese minister, who had been close with both Jefferson and Madison while president, as well as with Monroe prior to his becoming president.[3] Not only did it prove irksome to that official, the Abbé Corrêa da Serra, but it once led Monroe to cancel a planned visit to Madison's Montpelier due to the presence there of the British minister.[4]

Besides this, a particular hubbub was stirred up by Mrs. Monroe's adoption of a less public social persona than Mrs. Madison's. She announced that rather than making and returning calls, as Mrs. Madison had always done but Mrs. Monroe had not done even while James Monroe was a Cabinet officer, she would receive visitors in the morning. She generally passed off even this duty to the Monroes' daughter Eliza Hay, the wife of James's political advisor and confidant George Hay.

Monroe's leading biographer explains this change partly by reference to Mrs. Monroe's relatively poor health, which frequently confined her to her private quarters, and partly by the changing circumstances. Increased ease of travel and the growing population of the capital, he says, meant that the onerousness of a routine like Dolley Madison's would have been considerable—significantly greater even than in most of Dolley's day as the town's grande dame. Elizabeth Monroe's formal, reserved manners magnified the social consequences of these changes. Still, with the practical factors in mind, Secretary Adams's wife, Louisa, adopted the relatively restrictive rules Mrs. Monroe had followed while James was a secretary. The day of Dolley Madison had passed. Annoyed over the social repercussions of these changes, John Quincy Adams tried to get other Cabinet members to adopt a united front in this regard, but Treasury Secretary William Crawford refused.[5] It would not be the final time the Georgian opted to let his colleagues twist in the wind.

A month after Monroe's inauguration, the third president dashed off two letters to him from Monticello.[6] Much in the mode of James Madison maneuvering George Washington into attending the Philadelphia Convention so many years before, Jefferson began the first of them by saying, "The receipt of a commission as Visitor, will have informed you, if you did not know it before, that we have in contemplation to establish a college near Charlottesville." He then listed the other five other members of the incipient University of Virginia's first Board of Visitors, who included Madison and Jefferson. After telling Monroe that various arrangements remained to be made, among them the General Assembly's selection of a location, Jefferson informed Monroe that he preferred "your former residence above Charlottesville."[7]

Yes, this adroit politician did intend inclusion of himself and the other two living Virginia presidents on the Board of Visitors as a publicity stunt. As he explained, "[T]he attendance of yourself there, mr Madison and the others will be a spectacle which will vividly strike the public eye, and give preeminence to the place." It would give Albemarle the preference over a Tidewater location—and thereby ingratiate the president even further with his neighbors. In case this consideration did not suffice to draw the president into attending, his Monticello neighbor added that "a visit to your farm however short must be desirable to you." The other five visitors would be staying at Monticello, in case Monroe would like to see them the day before the meeting. A couple of days later, Jefferson wrote again to correct himself. The local court would meet "on the 5th instead of the 6th of May," and Madison would be there the day before.

On May 5, 1817, four of the six visitors—President Monroe, Jefferson, Madison, and the University's chief patron in the Virginia General Assembly, Senator Joseph Carrington Cabell—met formally for the first time. They decided to initiate a subscription campaign to raise private donations, with five of the six visitors pledging the large sum of $1,000 each and the sixth $200. Uncharacteristically Jefferson drafted a pseudonymous newspaper column to run in the *Richmond Enquirer,* the state's and perhaps the South's leading newspaper, in support of the fundraising effort. In it he boasted of Monroe's participation, along with the former presidents'. On October 6, 1817, the cornerstone of today's Pavilion VII "was laid with full Masonic honors," President Monroe participating.[8]

In the period between May 5 and October 6, 1817, Monroe undertook the first of his presidential tours of regions of the United States. Here as in other respects, Monroe had George Washington's example before him.[9] Though his chief intention was to inspect American military installations, he also hoped to achieve progress toward his goal of healing partisan divisions by appearing personally in various parts of the country recently on the verge of rebellion and even by June 1817 not supportive either of his administration or of the Republican Party. (He told Jefferson, though perhaps no one else, that he "hope[d] from it much advantage to [his] health" as well.)[10]

At least as early as March 25th, Monroe confided to the chief of army engineers, General Joseph G. Swift, that he intended to embark upon "a tour of inspection of the fortifications and navy yards of the Union," and Swift agreed by April 4th to meet Monroe in Baltimore "early in June" for this purpose. In days following Swift made some of the arrangements for Monroe's trip.[11]

If Swift responded enthusiastically to the concept of a tour of inspection, others told Monroe that his tour would have additional positive effects. For example, Nicholas Biddle, a friend who later became famous as Monroe's appointee for president of the Second Bank of the United States, enthused that "Ever since the time of Gen. Washington, the President has unfortunately appeared to the nation too much like the Chief Clerk of Congress, a cabinet man, stationary at his desk relying exclusively on Secretaries, & invisible except to those who seek him." Monroe's trip would correct this, and, "It will I am persuaded be highly gratifying to the community to see the Chief Magistrate examining for himself, & taking care that the great operations confided to him are not marred by the negligence or infidelity of Agents." After suggesting that Monroe visit "the route of the proposed canal to connect the Chesapeake & Delaware" in anticipation of the day when "any system of internal improvements is adopted" and make sure to see the "line of positions on the Brandywine" with military construction in mind, Biddle told Monroe that of course his "expedition" could be as public or as private as he preferred and laughed at himself for presuming to give the president this unsolicited advice.[12]

The newspapers began at about this time to run quite similar blurbs to the effect that the president would be visiting "most of the principal fortifications, and other establishments on the seaboard and the northern frontiers, and, should his health and time permit, will proceed eastward as far as Boston."[13] When word got out, prominent men began sending Monroe invitations to stay at their houses when he arrived in their cities—a type of invitation he had hoped for personal and political purposes to avoid, as he hoped his trip would have the benefit of smoothing ruffled feathers, not ruffle them further.[14] (Predictably, Monroe's wishes, not only about this but about public attention along his route, were routinely ignored by the people he encountered. One editor noted the apparent "rivalship in courtesy between the political parties" on this score.[15] That Monroe's wishes would be ignored was an open secret even before he set out.)[16]

The president, who was considerably less affluent than his three Virginia predecessors, decided to send Elizabeth and the children back to Virginia while he was away rather than have them stay in Washington or, even more improbably, take them along.[17] Joseph Gales's *National Intelligencer,* which since Samuel Harrison Smith's days as editor had been generally understood to be the Republican administrations' semi-official organ (Smith had been the one, remember, who greeted people departing the scene of Jefferson's First Inaugural Address with printed copies of that speech), ran a notice about Monroe's coming tour on April 23, 1817.[18] Besides noting what the official purposes of the trip were to be, this story said that the president would be traveling "as a private citizen" and that it would "not be in his power . . . to attend to those public or private invitations, which hospitality or respect for his public character might induce, if this intimation were not given." Gales closed by letting out that Monroe planned future tours of "the western and southern states."

Even this early in the enterprise, Monroe's first tour began to smooth over what had been truly dangerous partisan divisions during the War of 1812. The April 23rd Boston Federalist *Columbian Centinel* said that when Monroe arrived in the capital of Federalism, "no mark of attention and respect due to the Chief Magistrate of the Union will be omitted. . . ." Monroe would see that talk of Massachusetts disloyalty had been "slander," and "Mr. and Mrs. Monroe [were] intitled to the utmost courtesy for the illustrious example they have given of their desire to suppress party feelings; and for the polite attention they have paid to our fellow citizens who have visited Washington."

If at least some Boston Federalists were ready to pose as willing to let bygones be bygones, the Baltimore *Federal Republican* gave every indication that it had not forgotten being targeted in the infamous riots. Its attitude concerning Monroe's impending visit was captured in its statement that "To all his bluster it may [be] said that very few care whether the president does make the tour of the U. States or not; it will be a very expensive mode of ascertaining how little the good people of the U. States care about him."[19] From the surviving evidence this seems to have been an unusually jaundiced view.

More typical was a letter from David Humphreys, Monroe's Bostonian friend from Continental Army days. A prominent politician in his own right, Humphreys let Monroe know that his Connecticut connections "of every description" shared his enthusiasm at the thought of Monroe's impending visit to New England. He hoped the president's trip would "harmonise the public mind; &, as it were, . . . impart a national tone to it." It would "go far towards accomplishing the good work of uniting Parties." What with "Occasions for collision between the General & State Governments hav[ing] in a great measure ceased," Humphreys hoped that "asperity of Parties" would soon enough "be known only by the records of human frailties." Too, an enthusiastic welcome of Monroe in New England could be expected to impress Europeans with America's unity.[20]

All was not peaches and cream in New England, however. Some of the newspapers retained a notable partisan edge. From Justice Joseph Story's hometown of Salem came a mocking squib in the *Gazette* about the "Journey of the Royal Family" noting that "the President and the Presidentess" were making a tour of the "Eastern Dominions." The tour would end "about 'Lection time," the editor concluded, "when we shall probably become 'all Federalists, all Republicans.'"[21]

For their part Massachusetts Republicans had not entirely forgotten local Federalists' regrettable behavior during the war. The *Boston Patriot* began one account by saying that the *Centinel* promised no formality or sign of respect would be omitted during Monroe's approaching stay in Boston, then asked who could have decided that this would be so. "The *Centinel* says that 'slanderers' have long been 'using exertions' to degrade the reputation of Boston for urbanity, hospitality and patriotism," the editor continued, but, "We on the contrary assert that the Junto [the ruling clique of local Federalists] have by their exertions, degraded the reputation of this town. Who called the war, declared by the Representatives of the people and Congress, Madison's war? Who took sides with the 'lathing hatchet' mob at Baltimore? . . . Who have been endeavoring to affix to the word democracy and democrat, an odious meaning, as distinct from that of a republican? What city in the Union have cultivated a systematic discord like Boston?" More followed, reaching a climax with, "Had the Hartford Convention carried John Henry's plan into full operation, the high federalists of Boston would at this time boast of that which they are now ashamed of." "Their insolent and intolerant spirit has driven hundreds of our young men out of Boston," he continued, and they hoped by flattery to obscure what they had done.

This aggrieved Republican did hope that Boston would roll out a red carpet for the Jeffersonian president. If it did, "We shall feel pleased at seeing all ranks and all parties paying due honors to the Supreme Executive Officer of the Nation, because it is proper, while an attempt at an assimilation of political ideas and feelings would excite our laughter, and perhaps derision. If our domineering Juntomen are made to eat the bitter fruit of trees of their own planting, it is a food they ought to feed on until they repent and publicly confess their fault, and give signs of amendment."

Massachusetts Federalists had reason other than pride to try to make bygones be bygones. During the war Governor Strong had refused to make his state's militia available to the Madison administration—in the person of Secretary of War James Monroe—for the Bay State's defense, and so Monroe told Strong that the Federal Government would not reimburse Massachusetts the $800,000 in associated costs. Only at the end of his presidential tenure, it turns out, would Monroe urge Congress to reimburse Massachusetts.[22] Well might Monroe have taken his time about this issue, as not only had Bay State Federalists opposed Madison's and his war efforts in every manner that seemed opportune, but they had used the most scurrilous terms (including that he had introduced a French conscription plan) in describing Secretary Monroe.[23]

In the last days before he set out, Monroe dashed off a note to Andrew Jackson describing his impending voyage. He told Jackson that "Next year I propose to make a similar tour, should Congress adjourn in time, to the westward and southward, comprising in it the whole of the country in your division. I shall," he concluded, "then have the pleasure of seeing you."[24] Wise politico that he was, the president realized that establishing an in-person relationship with the Tennesseean might prevent difficulties in the future. He also took care to have military commanders along his route be informed that he wanted to minimize "military parade" and focus instead on the substance of his visits to the numerous installations he would see—though Secretary of the Treasury Crawford made sure revenue cutters would be available for the president's transportation in case it proved convenient for him to use them.[25]

⤙ ❁ ⤚

After being detained some few days by a malady, Monroe left Washington with his party on May 31, 1817. The Georgetown newspaper noted that despite his wishes, preparations had already begun along his route "to receive him with those open marks of respect, which a free people may properly testify towards a chief magistrate whom they have chosen for his talents and his virtues." According to the *National Intelligencer,* the parties stood poised to compete in their displays.[1] The Old Republican *Richmond Enquirer,* meanwhile, harrumphed about the inappropriateness of treating an American president as head of "a triumphal procession."[2]

As he approached the first city on his route, Baltimore, Monroe encountered the First Baltimore Hussars, who with "a large concourse of citizens on horseback" escorted him into town. (A newspaper in distant Springfield, Massachusetts, reported angrily that Monroe had "entered Baltimore on Sunday, escorted by the civil and military, and a large cavalcade of citizens, amidst the playing of fifes and the rattling of drums"— all in violation of the injunction to "Remember the Sabbath Day to keep it holy.")[3] Local dignitaries had scheduled a review of local troops for June 1st. A local paper somewhat naughtily said that, "the people cannot permit [Monroe] to pass among them without evidencing to him those marks of gratitude and esteem, which are due, not more to his station as chief magistrate of the only really independent republic on earth, than to the important benefits he has rendered his country." In addition Monroe called on the chief local dignitary, Declaration of Independence signer Charles Carrol of Carrolton.[4]

Before leaving the city Monroe was taken to Fort McHenry, already famous as the site where "the honor of the Star-spangled Banner was bravely maintained." Having visited some local monuments (one to Washington), the president "expressed his entire approbation of the public spirit of the

Citizens of Baltimore."[5] After being presented an address by the mayor and city council, Monroe gave a lengthy response. He then heard a Latin address from an official of what is now the University of Maryland, Baltimore. On June 3rd he departed for Philadelphia on a steamboat.[6]

Thus it went, as Monroe visited New Castle (June 3 to 5), Philadelphia (June 6 to 7), and on, and on. Though Monroe did take in a myriad of present and potential military sights, he also constantly had to deal with the various signs of respect (and self-indulgence) his fellow Americans provided (or, as he may have thought, inflicted upon) him along the way.

From Philadelphia, Caesar Rodney wrote Monroe with advice on a touchy constitutional issue.[7] Rodney, attorney general under Jefferson and Madison, was Monroe's choice for some diplomatic matters involving the new republic of Argentina.[8] He told the president of a Supreme Court case "in which the question, whether St. Domingo was independent of France, was argued at great length" before "the court observed, it was for government to decide that point, and not the judiciary. That the Island must be considered a dependent colony, and not a sovereign state, by courts of justice, until its independence was recognized by competent authority under our constitution." When it came time for his opinion, Rodney said, "I should consider congress vested with the powers of government, for this purpose. I should doubt the authority of the Executive, singly, to perform the duty, more especially in a case, which according to received principles, would furnish direct cause of war, and produce, in all human probability, immediate hostilities."

Of particular note is Monroe's June 7th return to Trenton, New Jersey, the site of his heroic feats in the battle fought there during the Revolution. Arriving in the evening, Monroe and his traveling companions were met by civil and military leaders of the town. A cannon announced his arrival, after which bells rang, and when he reached Anderson's tavern, "a feu-de-joie was fired" and he was welcomed by the town recorder, who read him an address. Among other things, the address referred to Trenton as "the scene, Sir, of some of the services you have rendered our country. We most sincerely wish you the enjoyment of health, long life, and a prosperous administration." Monroe extemporaneously replied, in part:

> I feel very sensibly this kind attention on the part of the authorities of the city of Trenton—the place where the hopes of the country were revived in the war of the revolution by a signal victory obtained by the troops under the command of General Washington, after a severe and disastrous campaign. I am well acquainted with the patriotism of the citizens of Trenton, and,

indeed, of Jersey; for none suffered more, or displayed greater patriotism in our revolutionary contest.

The *National Intelligencer* closed its account of the exchange with the observation that "in the battle of Trenton which terminated in the capture of the Hessians, in the revolutionary war, Mr. Monroe received a wound, which confined him nearly nine weeks at the house of Judge Wynkoop, of Buck county." The informed public knew of this at the time, though perhaps some readers did not.[9]

Among the news accounts of his other stops on the journey north, one describing Monroe's visit to Elizabethtown deserves attention. It drew a contrast between the American president's mode of travel—"Unarmed, unguarded, he can traverse the Union without personal injury, cheered by the plaudits and good wishes of almost innumerable freemen"—and that of the British prince regent, who could "barely stick his nose out of the door without being 'stoned or fired upon.' And as for traveling, [the prince regent] would as soon be hung as venture his precious carcase in Ireland, or many other parts of his kingdom, without a guard of soldiers equal to our peace establishment!"[10] The safety in which a republican society's elected chief executive could travel at large among his constituents made a happy contrast with the strict safety protocols even a British monarch had to observe.

Another contrast would be evident when Monroe arrived in New York: one between the bowing and scraping, the "excess of ceremony" and the extreme splendor with which a European king was received and the simple republicanism marking the reception of the American president. He should be "offered" "every thing that politeness or civility can dictate," certainly, but that was all.[11]

Predictably Monroe's sojourn in New York left a substantial documentary trail. In general his visit resembled those earlier on his way, except that there was more magnificence in every particular. Perhaps most interesting is a letter to former senator from Massachusetts Christopher Gore from Rufus King, a Philadelphia Convention Framer and holdover minister to the Court of St. James's at the beginning of the Jefferson administration who had lost the 1816 presidential election to Monroe.[12] King reported interacting with Monroe at the public reception in City Hall, where Monroe "recd. me as he has been accustomed to do with Expressions of consideration." The pro forma interaction with various other people having come to an end, "he came up to me, and made the usual Enquiries of Civility—this afforded me an opportunity of requesting him to come and pass a Day with me here. He civilly intimated the Pressure of his Engagements [that is, that his schedule was more than full], and would if he could." In summing up what Monroe had said to him, King noted that "[m]en in pub. places speak in generals, and so, whether in earnest or otherwise, that nothing of particularity can or ought to be inferred from the Conversations of this sort."

King told Gore what we have already seen about the aims of Monroe's trip. Catching the point about tamping down party passion, King said:

> that in the Principles of our Constitutions and Laws, in our manners and language, as well as in our occupations and Enterprize there was more of Identity, than existed perhaps, on these Particulars, in any other country. That our People were susceptible of great animation & of Enthusiasm, and were devoted to the free Institutions of other [their?] General & State Govts—that such a people had the strongest Claims on their Govt. which owed them in return, confidence, affection and the most impartial and faithful execution of its Duties. To all this the Pr. assented—to this purpose the conversation continued for some time & until the dinner was announced.

King closed his communication with a list of upcoming stops on Monroe's trip—West Point, the Narrows, Sandy Hook, New London, Newport, Providence, Boston. . . . "The Reception wh. the Pr. has received at N.Y. has been a flattering one and I have no doubt that he has been pleased with it—that wh. awaits him in Mass. will probably be still more gratifying, as he might not have anticipated it."

When he arrived at West Point, Monroe wrote to a friend updating him on the progress of his trip.[13] It had been a taxing task. "You can form no idea," the president confided, "of the exertion I have been called on to make, and which it has been impossible to avoid. My progress has in consequence been pretty rapid."

King wrote Gore again when Monroe had been in New York for ten days and departed for New Haven.[14] "Shew[ing] himself to, & be[ing] seen, and approached by, all the world . . . has as I think been favorable to him," King conceded. Monroe's "Expenses of every kind have, as I have heard, been defrayed by the City Corporation," he continued, and "the same course will probably be followed by your metropolis," and soon enough, the president would appear in "*the Head Quarters of good principles*." His plan was still "going across the Country from Portsmouth to Plattsburg; then along Lake Ontario to Niagara, when he will proceed to Detroit, return thro' the State of Ohio, and cross the mountains homeward on horse back." Since

King did not believe Monroe had fully recovered from "the attack of Fever which he suffered at Washington," King looked for the environment of the Great Lakes to pose a hazard. King closed by telling Gore that Monroe had inquired after the latter's health, that he expected Gore to receive a presidential visit, and that while "I wd. show no solicitude to manifest any zeal on this occasion; I would avoid the appearance either of dissatisfaction, or of the want of Respect for the first Magistrate of the nation."

From Boston, Monroe received a request that he reconsider his stated "intention of declining attentions." "This will probably be the only occasion when the citizens of this State will ever see you," a correspondent reasoned, and, "I believe that in a *national* point of view, it will be productive of good consequences if the people here of every class can have a chance of seeing you and that you yourself will be gratified in seeing what are the feelings of our citizens, when free from the temporary excitement of party, and showing spontaneously their natural character." Despite the intense party friction of prior administrations, it seems, Monroe's appraisal of the matter was not his alone. Perhaps Jefferson's famous characterization of the relationship between Republicans and Federalists was accurate.

Former president John Adams, for his part, asked a Harvard professor, "Have you adjusted your Bib & Tucker to visit the President? There is no other theme of conversation at present. It is kind in him at this pressing time to give the Nation something to talk about. His plain manner will please in general. Tranquillity & prosperity to his Administration. Amen."[15] He invited Monroe and his traveling companions to dine with him in his "cottage."[16]

Boston, perhaps to highlight the "tranquillity" to come, had appointed "Mr. Otis, the celebrated Conventionist," head of its committee to organize Monroe's reception. "The time has happily come," as one observer had it, "when the Lamb may safely lie down with the Lion—when the Republican and the Federalist cordially join, heart and hand, in rendering all due honor to the Chief Magistrate of the Union!"[17]

En route to Boston, Monroe encountered New England's Second City, Hartford, Connecticut. In light of Hartford Federalists' quite recent opposition "not only to the administration of the Government, but to the constitution and the Government itself," a local Republican newspaper found the Hartford Corporation's elaborate ceremonial in welcoming the president to town quite extraordinary.[18] Here "the men who, two years since, were in the steady habit of reviling Mr. Monroe (who by the by has undergone no change) with every epithet of abuse which a scholarship of twenty years in the school of political billingsgate could supply" were "anxious to [render] him homage—esteeming it an honor 'to touch the hem of his garments,' and even to be smothered in the dust which his horse kicked up in the streets." "The conversion of great sinners," the chronicler said, "generally affords something interesting. That of St. Paul required miraculous power. If they have become friendly to the Administration, and honestly disposed to pay a tribute of respect to the members of it, why not unite upon equitable principles with the republicans on such occasions." In endeavoring to arrive at an explanation of this sudden volte-face, he concluded that "perhaps their zeal, like that of new converts, was so intemperate as to have deprived them of their discretion in the manifestation of their 'newly awakened love.'"

Connecticut Federalists' leading newspaper replied,

> What, shall it be permitted in this country, that the same men who have opposed dragging the militia like conscripts to Canada, and who did not believe in the necessity of the war, shall now be permitted to speak of the victories gained by our navy and army, or to enlarge upon the blessings of peace? . . . Shall they be suffered to hope that wisdom may be gained from the experience of the past, or to anticipate that the government may be administered upon correct principles—especially when they are daily told that the administration have adopted the old federal principles!

It was odd to read such criticism "by the men who want to see party spirit buried—by the men who talk of Connecticut as having estranged herself from the Union, and who wish to see her restored." Federalists would, it said, support or oppose the Monroe administration as its measures merited.[19]

For his part, when the president had the opportunity at New London to address the assembled officials and a large part of the citizenry of the town, he ignored the origin of the term "blue light Federalists." (As the story goes, opponents of the American war effort in New London had during the war signaled the Royal Navy to be on the lookout for American blockade runners by hanging out blue lights. New England Federalists were tarred with this image for decades after the war.) He instead emphasized that "In the pursuit of great national objects, it is equally the interest and the duty of the whole American people to unite. Happy in a government, which secures to us the full enjoyment of all our civil and religious rights, we have every inducement to unite in its support. With such union, we have nothing to dread from foreign powers."[20]

Later at nearby Groton he was introduced to two veterans of the cruel injuries the British inflicted on surrendered soldiers of the garrison of Fort Griswold on September 6, 1780. Not since Washington's day had the chief executive been a veteran, and no other ever was a veteran grievously wounded during the Revolution, so it was particularly striking that "Their scars were too conspicuous to permit them to escape the particular notice, and kind attention of President Monroe. Past scenes crouded on his recollection, and when, under the impulse of the moment, he laid his hands on the traces of their wounds, these venerable patriots realized that their country blessed them, while her chief gratefully noticed the scars which bore honourable testimony to their valour, and their sufferings in her defence."

On Monroe went, visiting military facilities, hearing from elected leaders, and being joined en route into towns large and small by significant concourses of local people. A particularly notable mishap marred the military ceremony prepared for the president as he approached Salem, Massachusetts. A Matthew Slocum of Patuxent was ramming down the charge in a cannon that was to be fired in the president's honor when, the gun "not having been properly spunged," the weapon exploded. Both of his arms were so severely injured that they had to be amputated above the elbows. "He was," the *Salem Gazette* concluded, "otherwise considerably burnt and bruised, but his situation is a comfortable as the painful circumstances of his case will admit." Slocum and his young family became the objects of attempts to arrange monetary relief, which the *Rhode Island Republican* encouraged.[21] Whether Monroe knew of these events, we do not know.[22]

52

⧖ ✦ ⧗

Farther on the road between Providence and Boston, Monroe's carriage was hailed by a man who offered him strawberries. "Thank you," replied Monroe, doffing his hat, "pour them into my hat." The man replied that Monroe must take the berries and the box alike, which Monroe did, immediately enjoying the berries.[1] Monroe's plain manners typified an era in which his predecessor had routinely been addressed in conversation as "Mr. Madison."[2]

Watching events from afar, some decided party rancor had disappeared, others that Federalists had lit upon disingenuousness as their most promising approach to regaining power. The *Lexington Gazette* noted that no Republican had been more reviled by the Federalists from 1796 until the end of the War of 1812, with Harrison Gray Otis, Josiah Quincy, and the rest of their Essex Junto leading the way—but now the Federalist Massachusetts Senate, led by the same Otis and Quincy, had appointed a committee to propose measures for welcoming Monroe to the state, and Otis chaired a separate committee with a similar purpose. Federalists must have their eye on appointed office.[3] Other Republicans, however, saw this domestic political tranquility as of a kind with the perfect peace America enjoyed at this time with every nation in the world.[4]

After a grand procession of Monroe's party and Boston's carriage-bound elite, Monroe was escorted into the Exchange Coffee-House, where he was to stay, by Colonel Rogers and the Independent Cadets. A lengthy address was read to him on behalf of the local Committee of Arrangements by attorney Charles Bulfinch, whom Monroe would soon appoint Benjamin Henry Latrobe's successor as architect of the U.S. Capitol.[5] Bulfinch invoked George Washington's visit to the Massachusetts capital as precedent for Monroe's, as well as bringing up the "principles of an elevated and impartial policy" which Monroe had "been pleased to promulgate." So too did he mention

Monroe's service during the Revolution, in which Monroe had been "distinguished."[6]

Monroe developed Bulfinch's reference to Washington, rejoiced that the new government had been successful through nearly three decades, and closed by saying, "Let us, then, unite in grateful acknowledgements to the Supreme Author of all good for extending to us so great a blessing. Let us unite in fervent prayers that He will be graciously pleased to continue that blessing to us, and our latest posterity." He expressed "confidence" in "the firm and generous support of [his] fellow citizens throughout" the United States.[7]

Bostonians took Monroe on tours of numerous military and other sites, treated him to several public meals, presented numerous addresses, and heard his answers to those speeches. On Independence Day the president was taken to the Old South Meeting House to hear the annual address marking the occasion. Although the state legislature had adjourned, a number of legislators tendered an appreciative message, which included both plaudits for his past services and what had by this point on his trip become the obligatory observation that unlike that of a European monarch, "the personal safety of the Chief Magistrate of a Republican Government requires no other protection than what arises from the affections of his fellow citizens."[8] He then feasted with some six hundred locals, and when it came his turn to offer a toast, Monroe said, "The Commonwealth of Massachusetts—Whose Sons so eminently contributed to the Independence we this day celebrate." As Monroe retired, the governor led the assemblage in nine cheers.[9] Before going to bed Monroe sent a letter to John Adams accepting his invitation to dinner.[10] As Christopher Gore summarized the situation, "The President is here, he rides hard, visits everything, and in so rapid a manner that it is utterly impossible he should burden his mind with any superfluous knowledge." As for the president's remaining Boston itinerary, Gore said, "To-morrow he visits the Navy yard, seventy-four gun ship, reviews Middlesex militia, dines with the Governor, and spends the evening with Senator Otis. So we go, and the sooner he goes the sooner will the town and its neighborhood be at rest."[11] As for Monroe himself, he answered a query whether "he was not completely worn out" by saying, "o no—a little flattery will support a man through great fatigue. . . ."[12]

The next day, pioneering nurseryman John Kenrick of Newton wrote Monroe enclosing a pamphlet he had recently written, *The Horrors of Slavery*. Kenrick lamented to Monroe that "*the unhappy system of Slavery . . .*

still exist[ed] in this land of freedom." The pamphlet, Kenrick said, had been "lately compiled with a view to awaken public attention to an evil so obviously inconsistent with moral right, and our professed attachment to equal liberty." The author would "be unspeakably happy" in case his correspondent used his "influence in favour of any judicious & honorable plan for restoring the degraded African slaves of [America] to those natural & civil rights we all so dearly prize." As we have seen, then-Governor Monroe had determined that slavery in Virginia must end, and as will be detailed hereafter, President Monroe took steps that set American slavery on a course to extinction—steps Mr. Kenrick lived to see.[13] The day after Kenrick wrote his letter, the president received communion at Christ's Church in Boston, which had been the site of Paul Revere's famous signal of two lit lanterns for under a minute on the night of April 18, 1775.[14] The following day Monroe sat for a portrait by Gilbert Stuart, went to Harvard College to receive an honorary LLD, and reviewed two thousand militiamen on Boston Common.[15] Afterward he dined with John Adams in Quincy.[16] It was in its account of the dinner that the Boston *Columbian Centinel* coined the term "Era of Good Feelings," which has ever since been used in reference to the Monroe administration.[17] The sentiment of universal fellow feeling was promoted by Monroe in his evenhanded dealings with all whom he encountered on his trip, perhaps particularly in response to a communication from Republicans in the Massachusetts legislature. "[P]resented an address" by two of them on behalf of their caucus, "[h]e instantly replied (as is said) that He knew no Party. They then said it was from the Minority of the Legislature."[18] Monroe wrote them a note saying he looked for what we now would call bipartisan cooperation, or even the disappearance of partisanship, in pursuit of measures all knew to be desirable. As "our principal dangers and difficulties have passed," he hoped "that the character of the deliberations, and the course of the government itself, will become more harmonious and happy, than it has heretofore been. Satisfied, as I am, that the union of the whole community in support of our republican government, by all wise and proper measures, will effectually secure it from danger, that union is an object, to which I look with the utmost solicitude." He, for his part, would work in "support of our republican government" as his "sole object"—which is to say, he would not act for party purposes.[19]

Monroe's attempt to prevent this address, coupled with his tepid response, seemed to some to have "mortified, if not offended, the democracy of N. England."[20] As he told Jefferson later in his tour, "In all the towns thro' which I passed there was an union between the parties, except in the case of Boston. I had suppos'd that that union was particularly to be desir'd by the republican party, since as it would be founded exclusively on their own principles, every thing would be gain'd by them." Some Republicans disagreed, and even presented their own address. "This form'd the principal difficulty, that I have had to meet to guard against any injury arising from the step taken to the republican cause, to the republican party, or the persons individually." Having seen the address and Monroe's response, Jefferson would understand.[21]

The Republican *Boston Patriot* expressed unease over the evident disappearance of parties. It conceded that "appearance of concord is valuable," adding that "Little more is required to remove the prejudices against each other entertained by partisans of opposite sides than free, social and personal intercourse. It is soon found that there is about an equal share of talents, virtue and good fellowship on both sides—in comparison with which difficulties of opinion are of minor importance and even these will generally in such cases be found to be much less than was before supposed." On the other hand, however, what was happening in America went beyond this. "I have heard it suggested," the editor continued, "that the federalists have consented to suspend hostilities against the republicans, because the republicans have adopted the federal creed—'You come over,' say they, 'to our measures—we go over to your men.' I am not able to say how general this opinion is, but as I have heard it myself from two or three persons, it appears to me entitled to a little attention." He went on to say that the chief difference between the parties was that between aristocrats (the Federalists having, for example, always preferred the British to the American constitution) and proponents of "a purely popular government." If the two sides had converged, he insisted it was the Federalists who had changed. He reasoned similarly in regard to the need for some kind of permanent military establishment, and he denied that favoring a federally chartered bank amounted to Republicans' having abandoned their position regarding "too great license . . . in interpreting the general phrases used in the Constitution in favor of the government." "The truth is," he concluded, "the parties are founded on the natural division of Aristocracy and Democracy—a division which . . . nothing can ever thoroughly reconcile."[22]

Besides ignoring the impulse of partisanship, Monroe also resisted the temptation to allow the various parades, musters, addresses, and displays of pomp to which he was subjected along his way to affect his ego. So when on July 12th he received a laudatory address from a town elder in Portsmouth, New Hampshire, the president replied, in part, "Fellow citizens—Accept my best thanks for your kind reception, which is characterized by so many interesting circumstances. This general movement of my fellow-citizens, and the expression of their regard, for the Chief Magistrate of the Nation, is not directed to me personally. My humble services give me no such claim. I see in it the strongest evidence of their attachment to the free government under which we live, and of an enlightened and expanded patriotism. . . ." He would respond similarly to other such addresses, on this trip and in the future, and he knew that his fellow Americans could only come to fair conclusions concerning his merits "when [he] retired from public life."[23]

Monroe, on stage all the while, said this politely. On the other hand the *Richmond Enquirer* found the whole spectacle disgusting:

> So much parade—such bombastic accounts of who he breakfasted or dined with; his cortege, and coteries, and collations, and balls; mixed up with such ridiculous and parasitical accounts of "Mrs. Harrison Gray Otis's mansion," "The splendid mansion of Mr. Speaker Bigelow," &c. &c. that we turn away with disgust and ask ourselves: Is this America? Are these the manners of republican citizens? Is this the description of the trip of an American officer in the discharge of his Executive duties? Or are we in England, where 'the great man' scarcely moves without a herald at his heels? James Monroe is an honest man . . . one of the plainest men that ever sat in the chair of any state. But these descriptions suit not him, nor the office which he fills, nor the people, whose agent he is.[24]

At Kennebunk, Maine District, Massachusetts, Monroe explained that he had intended on his journey "to have devoted my attention exclusively to . . . public and national objects," but "when I found a disposition so generally manifesting itself, to improve the occasion for a personal interview of the people with the Citizen whom their voluntary suffrages had elevated to the highest office in their gift, and the high value which they entertain for its republican form, I cheerfully yielded to their wishes." Having accepted the modification, he learned "how much we are one people; how strongly the ties, by which we are united, do in fact bind us together; how much we possess, in reality, a community, not only of interest, but of sympathy and affection." He told the Kennebunkers how happy he was to see that "you are pleased to express a confident hope that a spirit of mutual conciliation may be one of the blessings which may result from my administration. This, indeed," he continued, "would be an eminent blessing, and I pray it may be realized." He thought that

Nothing but union is wanting to make us a great people. The present time affords the happiest presages that this union is fast consummating. It cannot be otherwise. I daily see greater proofs of it. The further I advance in my progress through the country, the more I perceive that we are all Americans. . . . Nothing could give me greater satisfaction than to behold a perfect union among ourselves—an union which, as I before observed, is all we can want to make us powerful and respected—an union, also, which is necessary to restore to social intercourse its former charms and to render our happiness, as a nation, unmixed and complete.

Lest his audience think that Monroe intended simply that his past political foes should accept the rightness of Republicans' program, he hastened to correct them. "To promote this desirable result," he instructed, "requires no compromise of principles; and I promise to give to it my continued attention. . . ."[25]

As in previous stages of his trip, Monroe in Maine encountered official welcomes in each town he entered. One typical specimen is the brief message from Biddeford, whose leading men said that although their town included neither natural nor artificial attractions worth his time, yet its citizenry wanted to express its respect and pleasure at his visit.[26] To similar sentiments the residents of neighboring Saco added praise for his role in the Madison administration and hope that he would support Maine's statehood movement.[27] In planning their visit Portlanders held that even if they could not "give him a reception of such gorgeous show and imposing splendor as he found in New York and as he is likely to meet at Boston—we are sure that it will not be less cordial."[28] Afterward a local woman wrote of her town's experience with Monroe that, "There appeared to be an entire oblivion of party spirit, and all hearts seem'd to harmonize in the honours paid to the President."[29]

As Monroe made his way from one little New Hampshire town to another, he received a notice from Governor William Plumer, the former U.S. senator, that the two would not be able to meet. "I am still confined to my chamber & bed," Plumer wrote, "by a severe attack of the typhus fever, which has not yet, I fear, reached its crisis." Though no longer a Federalist, this official was not one on whose support Monroe could confidently count—as we shall see.[30] Plumer's omission to prepare a fancy reception for the president elicited public criticism of him, whatever his state of health.[31]

Meanwhile, in describing the popular turnout for the president's passing, the Concord *New Hampshire Patriot* picked up on the by now common metaphor of "the red rose and white" being "literally united—party considerations were buried"—denoting a surprisingly peaceful outcome, as the Wars of the Roses had ended only in the destruction of both the House of York and the House of Lancaster, respectively the House of the White Rose and the House of the Red Rose. (This heraldic imagery was known to Americans of the Jeffersonian era from David Hume's famous *The History of England.*) This paper too invoked a bipartisan "era of good feelings" coincident with Monroe's administration.[32] The Charleston, South Carolina, *Southern Patriot,* which struck a Madisonian note in insisting that parties would always exist where there were "free institutions" alongside "occasions that nourish party agitations" and that it was undesirable party should pass away, because "our government is upheld by these checks and jealousies of party, which eminently characterize free commonwealths," seems to have been decidedly in the minority in looking upon President Monroe's efforts to tamp down party disputation skeptically.[33]

We have, unfortunately, no word from Monroe about his reaction to visiting the most famous denizens of Enfield, New Hampshire, in the "Habitation of the Shaken community": the Shakers. This celibate religious sect, whose name recognized that dancing was part of their religious practice, had attained a position of considerable notoriety, not only for its unusual religion, but for its fine woodworking. A newspaper account said of the visit that "[Monroe] was received with the simplicity which distinguishes the sect." After a stilted welcome from the group's elder, "The President examined the institution and their manufactures, was also welcomed by the women, and having remained about an hour, he retired very much pleased with his visit."[1] How exactly this attraction made its way onto Monroe's itinerary is unclear.

Monroe's impression of Hanover, New Hampshire, may have been expected by one and all to be dominated by the local Dartmouth University, whose trustees unanimously voted to confer the degree of Doctor of Laws (LLD) upon the president,[2] but things did not turn out that way. Rather, one evening at a social gathering, "A most interesting interview between the President and Mrs. Wheelock, widow of the late [Dartmouth] President Wheelock, was witnessed with great pleasure. Mrs. W.," the *Concord* (N.H.) *Gazette* account said, "had officiated as nurse to Lt. Monroe when he was wounded at Trenton, during the revolution, and thrown into the house where she then resided. A recollection of the fact, and rehearsal of the circumstance, made a great impression on the assemblage, and the sentiments expressed on the occasion cannot be forgotten by any who were present."[3]

In fifteen days in New York, Monroe visited places in or associated with over a dozen towns. He was fêted in each, besides which special mention was made by the locals in their formal addresses to him of nearby sites of military events in the recent war (for example, Sacketts Harbor). As in other places on his tour, Monroe attended church services when convenient.[4]

At Ogdensburg in northernmost New York on August 1st, a local eminence was chosen to deliver Monroe an address in which he said that people in that part of the country had special reason to endorse the president's mission, as they had before found themselves under attack from the powerful enemy to the north and could expect in case of future hostilities to endure the same problem again. In his response the president said that "[h]e perfectly agreed that a time of peace was the best time to prepare for defence," but he observed that he "had much pleasure in stating that the best understanding prevailed between our government and that of Great Britain, and was persuaded we had every reason to look for a permanent peace."[5] The accuracy of Monroe's appraisal of the situation was reflected in a polite letter from Colonel Lewis Grant, commander of His Britannick Majesty's Troops on the Niagara Frontier, inviting the president to cross over into Canada and either be officially welcomed or not, whichever he might prefer.[6] The British minister to the United States forwarded to Foreign Secretary Viscount Castlereagh Grant's subsequent letter explaining that Grant's invitation to the president had arrived too late, Monroe already having boarded a ship to continue his trip when he received it.[7]

At about the same time, Acting Secretary of State Richard Rush wrote to Monroe from Washington that John Quincy Adams was expected any day, that the great enthusiasm for Monroe throughout his tour ought to redound to America's diplomatic benefit in Europe, and that Albert Gallatin's endeavors to obtain reparations from the French for American ships wrecked by them during the First Empire seemed apt to come to naught. Rush said he hoped that "in the midst of so many and unusual fatigues," the president would "escape with [his] health."[8]

Monroe lamented that Rush

. . . can hardly form a judgment from the papers, tho' they give many details, of the obstacles I have had to encounter & surmount in my tour. They have been very great. It has been my constant effort to press forward, well knowing that delay at any place would produce it elsewhere, & thus retard, far beyond my wish, my mov'ment, and even beyond what would be proper. It has been impossible to get forward faster than I have done. My difficulties have proceeded from many causes. The solicitude of the people to manifest respect for their govt has been a principal one. I have been forc'd either to repell the measures taken by them for the purpose, and thereby give serious offense, or to yield to it, and I thought it best to take the latter course. The replies which it has been necessary to give to addresses have also consum'd time & increased my difficulties.[9]

As to the effect of the tour and popular response to it upon European (and particularly elite European) opinion, the first signs—unbeknownst to the American government—were not good. For example, Bagot wrote to Castlereagh that

> It is well understood that the President himself has long become sensible of the various evils to which the Executive Government of the Country has been exposed by the license of Democratic principles; and, difficult as it may be, (for him especially) to work the change, there is no doubt that he is labouring to put the whole system of the Government upon a different, and higher footing than that upon which it has long been placed, and to restore it, as far as he can, to that strength and dignity of which it was so entirely divested by the doctrines and examples of Mr. Jefferson, and his Successor.

He knew, he said, that the Federalists had assured Monroe they would support a change "so congenial to their own principles." On the other hand he thought Clay and Crawford were prepared to use any such change to their own political benefit, particularly in the West.[10]

Upon his arrival at Detroit, Monroe responded to a welcoming committee's by-now-routine welcoming address with a speech of his own. It was not routine. For one thing, after noting that this would be the most distant point on his trip, he said that Detroit had had an "establishment . . . in its origin, colonial: but on a new principle." "Your commencement," he continued, "is founded in rights, not of a personal nature only, but on incipient sovereignty, never to be shaken." When the time comes, he lectured, "you will become a member of the Union, with all the rights of the original states." Though they could not have recognized it as such, his Michigander audience had just heard its guest lay out the Jeffersonian view of the rights of the states in the American union—a position that would be at the center of the chief dispute in American politics during the Monroe administration. As the president closed his little talk with invocation of "the termination of party divisions, and the union of all our citizens in the support of our republican government and institutions," neither he nor they knew that it was not to be.[11]

As Monroe wrote to Rush on August 16th, he and his suite would two days later head to Sandusky, go through Ohio via the Cumberland Road, and from there proceed to Washington.[12] Perhaps most notable among the various events and addresses held and exchanged along the way was that of the welcoming committee at Delaware, Ohio, which said in part that "The professions and conduct of the citizens of Ohio have already evinced an attachment to the political principles and conduct of Mr. Monroe. . . . It will not then be expected that we should make any extraordinary display of our devotion to convince him we are his friends, that we sincerely wish him happiness in his public and private course. Let us then disdain to use the language of adulation, but receive him with that respect and gratitude, which can only do ourselves honor, and confer honor on the President."[13] In a day when newspapers relayed partisan positions and transmitted party culture across the American landscape, it seems some men of northern Ohio had come to agree with Republicans elsewhere that the fawning and show of the leaders of some of America's largest urban areas were indeed inappropriate responses to a visit among republican citizens by a republican official. On the other hand a few weeks later a local newspaper carried a notice that a new Ohio town, Monroe, had been laid out, and that the first lots would be auctioned on October 9th.[14]

When finally, on September 17th, the president returned to Washington, he was met on the approach by Captain William F. Thornton and his Alexandria cavalry—the same unit that had accompanied Secretary Monroe out into the Maryland countryside to locate approaching British forces in 1814. The president and the large body of townsmen escorting him found that the White House was in an adequate state of repair from the damage done to it during the war for him and the rest of the Monroe family to take up residence in it.[15] From his departure on May 31st to his return on September 17th had been a period of 109 days. He entered the White House, the *National Intelligencer* reported, "in the midst of the hearty cheers of the spectators." "Salutes" had been "fired from the public works in the city on the President's approach, and in the evening a number of Sky-rockets were discharged in honor of the occasion."[16] One last time a mayor presented an address to the itinerant president, and one more time Monroe requited the effort.

The trip had been well worth his time and effort, Monroe told the Washington mayor, Board of Aldermen, and Board of Common Council. He had come to have a clear understanding of the military preparedness of the portion of the country he had seen, and he had "seen, with delight, proofs the most conclusive, of the devotion of our fellow-citizens to the principles of our free republican government, and to our happy union." In the end he "rejoice[d] to find the public building intended for the accommodation of the Chief Magistrate in a state to receive" him.[17]

Monroe's progress and the reception given to him by Federalists in the North left loyal Republicans anxious lest the president be duped into dividing the "loaves and fishes" with apparently mollified (but in fact, as many Republicans saw it, dyed-in-the-wool) Federalists. As in the earliest days of the Jefferson administration William Branch Giles warned the president he must not fail to ensure that his steadfast supporters have their share of federal offices, so now newspapermen such as the editor of the Lexington *Kentucky Gazette* believed completely that there were

> in [F]ederalism, not so much in the great mass of that party, as in its leaders, two or three traits of character, which forbid any just hope of a change in its conduct, and which therefore render it inexpedient to trust any of that party with any influential station. Federalism has ever been insatiably ambitious and boldly aristocratic; it has pretended to the possession of all the talents and all the respectability in the nation, and to a sort of patent right to the monopoly of the powers and rewards of public office; it has affected to look upon the republican party as a 'swinish multitude,' and to treat them with the malignity and disdain which all aristocrats have in all ages shown towards those who in their opinion, could boast of no 'noble blood.'[18]

To reach an accommodation with such people would be unwise, because a leopard could not change his spots. (Monroe's son-in-law and confidant George Hay had expressed the same sentiment in virtually identical terms a few days earlier.)[19] However, whatever this outback paper may have said, the *National Intelligencer* stressed the benefits of an end to party disputation. "[L]et those who are so precipitate in condemning [New England Federalists] as traitors remember the fallibility of our nature, and how liable we all are to be diverted from the course of rectitude," it said. "We rejoice that the tour of the President has elicited the latent sentiments of New England patriotism. . . ."[20] This likely reflected the administration's view.

Monroe a few days after arriving in Washington returned to his farm in Albemarle County, where his family awaited. Among the first tasks he took up there was to write General Andrew Jackson to say that though he had been pressed for time, "Your case shall receive my earliest attention, & in the spirit mentioned in my last, for be assur'd that I take a deep interest in whatever concerns your interest or honor."[21]

Monroe prepared a memorandum for his Cabinet members—all but Calhoun, who would not assume his post until December—laying out the agenda in their first meeting.[22] The eight questions of which it was composed concerned potential American responses to revolutionary events in Spanish colonies south of the United States, relations with Spain, and nascent efforts by French emigrants to establish Joseph Bonaparte, Napoleon's older brother, whose installation as king of Spain by him had precipitated those revolutionary events in Spanish New World colonies, in Mexico. Had the memorandum been made public, it surely would have reminded at least some readers of the newspaper dispute between Treasury Secretary Alexander Hamilton and Representative James Madison over President George Washington's Neutrality Proclamation.

Monroe asked his advisors whether the president had authority to recognize the independence of new states not recognized as independent by their parent country, with whom that new state was at war; whether sending a minister (we would say "ambassador") to such a new state would be seen as acknowledging its independence; whether such acknowledgement justified war by the mother country or "complaint" by another; whether the United States ought to recognize "Buenos Ayres" or any other Spanish territory as independent; and so on.

These matters ended up being discussed in three meetings—of four hours on October 25th, four and a half hours on October 28th, and many hours on October 30th. The army was ordered to break up marauders' bases at Galveston and St. Mary's Island (the latter on the Florida/Georgia border), and a fact-finding voyage to Buenos Aires was to be organized. Due to Adams's opposition, the president decided not to recognize Buenos Aires yet.[23]

On November 28th Monroe presented his draft Annual Message orally to the Cabinet, which then took it up paragraph by paragraph. Adams recorded that the whole Cabinet was present except for Calhoun, whose role was filled by Acting Secretary of War George Graham. "There was a variety of discussion on certain passages," he noted, "and good alterations made."[24]

54

⊹ ❀ ⊹

When on December 2nd Monroe submitted his Annual Message to Congress, he believed that "some of the ideas were strengthened, if not deriv'd from my late tour."[1] The strongly positive tone definitely reflected the mood that had characterized the tour.[2] "At no period of our political existence," he began, "had we so much cause to felicitate ourselves at the prosperous and happy condition of our country." American agriculture and commerce thrived. Defense preparations continued apace, as "we ought not to expect to be exempted" from "future wars" (though the Jeffersonian hope to be exempted from them would crop up again periodically in American history). "The public credit," he boasted, "has attained an extraordinary elevation." "Local jealousies," so recently so powerful, "are rapidly yielding to more generous, enlarged, and enlightened views of national policy." "Advantages so numerous and highly important" must be gifts of the "Omnipotent Being," and thus "unceasing prayer" that He "endow us with virtue and strength to maintain and hand them down in their utmost purity to our latest posterity" was "our [that is, the president's and Congress's] duty."

Monroe next announced the second most important result of the War of 1812: an agreement between the United States and Great Britain that each side's armament on the Great Lakes would be limited to one ship on Lake Champlain, one on Lake Ontario, and two on the upper lakes, with none of those ships to be armed with more than one cannon. In case either side wanted to terminate the agreement, it would have to give six months' notice. In this way, needless expenditure resulting from accidental conflict between the two parties was to be prevented.

Monroe next devoted several paragraphs to the situation in Spain's New World empire, concerning which Americans of course felt a keen interest, but in which the United States Government scrupulously avoided meddling. Rather, America would be neutral between Spain and each colony. A major problem had arisen, he explained, in relation to Amelia Island, which lay "near the boundary of the State of Georgia." Spanish colonists took possession of the island, and this complicated ongoing attempts by the United States to obtain the island, "bounded by the United States and the ocean on every side," in exchange for spoliations or for "territory of equal value westward of the Mississippi." "Projected and commenced with an incompetent force," the occupation apparently was to be strengthened by manpower attracted from within the United States. That failing, "it has assumed a more marked character of unfriendliness to us, the island being made a channel for the illicit introduction of slaves from Africa into the United States, an asylum for fugitive slaves from the neighboring states, and a port for smuggling of every kind."

Unfortunately a similar situation had developed in "Galvezton," which Monroe hastened to add was "within the limits of the United States, as we contend, under the cession of Louisiana"—and who knew better than he? This Gulf Coast situation had "been marked in a more signal manner by all the objectionable circumstances which characterized the other, and more particularly by the equipment of privateers which have annoyed our commerce, and by smuggling." Therefore Monroe had ordered that "[t]hese establishments . . . be suppressed." To ensure that no such situation would develop there again, Monroe had "thought proper to send a ship of war with three distinguished citizens along the southern coast" to take the matter up with "those in possession of and exercising the sovereignty"—which, note, might well not be the titular Spanish authorities.

Relations with "the other powers of Europe," the Barbary states, and "the Indian tribes" remained "pacific." In case peace continued, the Louisiana Purchase would be paid off in 1819 and the $26 million of annual revenue after 1819 would leave an annual surplus of $4 million. Though nominally the states' militia forces totaled eight hundred thousand men, "the organization and discipline of the militia is," Monroe continued, "one of the great objects which claims the unremitted attention of Congress." If Republican dogma was to continue to be preached, militia must be prepared to perform better than in the recent war.

Various purchases of Indian lands had opened all of Ohio and some of Michigan Territory to American settlement. "In this progress, which the rights of nature demand and nothing can prevent, marking a growth rapid and gigantic," he said, "it is our duty to make new efforts for the preservation, improvement, and civilization of the native inhabitants." He went on to explain, in terms familiar to the public since Jefferson's day, "The hunter state can exist only in the vast uncultivated desert. It yields to the more dense and compact form and greater force of civilized population; and of right it ought to yield, for the earth was given to mankind to support the greatest number of which it is capable, and no tribe or people have a right to withhold from the wants of others more than is necessary for their own support and comfort."[3] He explained that "the reservations of land made by the treaties with the tribes on Lake Erie were made with a view to individual owner-ship among them and to the cultivation of the soil by all," with "an annual stipend . . . to supply their other wants." The pacification resulting from conversion of Indians to agriculture would mean ongoing peace with the Indian tribes in those areas.

Having repeatedly mentioned America's fabulous extent, its great pro-ductions of every kind, etc., Monroe turned to the issue on which Madison's presidency had closed. "When we consider the vast extent of territory within the United States," he wrote, "the great amount and value of its produc-tions, the connection of its parts, and other circumstances on which their prosperity and happiness depend, we can not fail to entertain a high sense of the advantage to be derived from the facility which may be afforded in the intercourse between them by means of good roads and canals. Never did a country of such vast extent offer equal inducements to improvements of this kind. . . ." He had brought this matter up, he said, to highlight the "dif-ference of opinion . . . respecting the right of Congress to establish such a system of improvement." In light of his high office and the past disagree-ments, he felt bound to inform Congress that after extensive consideration of the subject, he had reached "a settled conviction . . . that Congress do not possess the right. It is not contained in any of the specified powers granted to Congress, nor can I consider it incidental to or a necessary means . . . for carrying into effect any of the powers which are specifically granted." Duty therefore impelled him to recommend that Congress propose an appropri-ate amendment to the states.

Such an effort would not be for naught, the president thought, because "the benign spirit of conciliation and harmony which now manifests itself throughout the Union promises to such a recommendation the most prompt and favorable result." While Congress was at it, he hoped it would include a provision empowering Congress "to institute likewise seminaries of learn-ing, for the all-important purpose of diffusing knowledge among our fellow citizens throughout the United States." So too Congress must concern itself with "preservation" of "our manufactories," which depended on "due en-couragement" and were "connected with the high interests of the nation."

While the Capitol had not yet been completed, the wings likely would be ready for the two houses' use at the next congressional session. The various executive departments' buildings were in many cases entirely insufficient, so that some of the Executive Branch found itself "subjected to the necessity of obtaining [space] in private buildings at some distance from the head of the department." Congress ought to solve this problem too. So too ought it to provide "convenient accommodation" for the heads of departments and the attorney general. In their waning days the few surviving veterans of the Revolution who were "reduced to indigence and even to real distress" had a moral claim to the public's aid as well.

Monroe saved the best for last. As tariffs and tonnage taxes, in combination with revenue from sale of public lands, would cover all of the government's expenses, including the navy's shipbuilding program, he called for Congress to repeal the internal taxes. Imposing taxes when necessary was an important duty, he said, and so was their repeal "when it may be done with perfect safety."

President Monroe did not say, though doubtless everyone realized, that Thomas Jefferson and the Republican majorities elected in 1800 had eliminated the internal taxes too—nor did he need to note that for the first Republican treasury secretary, Albert Gallatin, shipbuilding was the paradigmatic Federalist program that had to go. Unlike the Bourbons of 1815 and after, then, Republicans by 1817 had learned at least a thing or two. What Monroe did note about his predecessors' policy was that when they imposed internal taxes, "the demand was imperious," and he hastened to add that unlike Federalists' taxes, they had "been sustained [by the people] with exemplary fidelity." If a new need should arise, "should any future emergency occur," he would "be not less prompt to suggest such measures and burdens as may then be requisite and proper."

Opinion about that last matter was decidedly mixed. Representative Hugh Nelson, R-VA, for example, said the address would be welcomed on account of its recommendation that the internal taxes be repealed. Senator Jeremiah Mason, F-NH, on the other hand, called this idea "what I least expected and dislike most. . . . This is the only tax which tends to an equalization of burdens between the sea-board and interior states."[4]

This was not the only controversy spurred by what to that point was the longest of Annual Messages. Former president James Madison wrote Monroe a week later with interesting observations.[5] After holding that "[i]t is a fine landscape of our situation, and can not fail to give pleasure at home, and command respect abroad" and observing that "[t]he recommendation of the repeal of taxes is happily shaped," he came to his problems with it. First, he could not tell whether "the proposed suppression of the establishment at Amelia Island" was intended to be "effected by a military force employed out of our territorial claims." More intriguingly, he took gentle exception to Monroe's "principle on which the right of a civilized people is asserted over the lands of a savage one." Here legal layman Madison had the better of his legal argument with former attorney Monroe. European law had from the beginning of the Age of Discovery held that while the first European power to discover part of the New World thereby acquired a claim on it good against all other European nations, the local aborigines (if any) retained their rights in that land until/unless they alienated it to the discovering power.[6] Unfortunately Madison did not suggest to his successor that he somehow correct the public record, thus possibly preventing fellow citizens from being misled into acting on Monroe's mistaken principle. (Perhaps the oddest thing about this exchange is that at virtually the same time, Monroe wrote to Lieutenant General Andrew Jackson explaining the law of Indian land rights exactly as Madison had tried to persuade him to understand it.)[7]

Monroe wrote back "correcting" Madison. "The history of our settlements, from the first discovery of this country, is a practical illustration, of the doctrine contain in the message respecting Indian titles," the president insisted, "and I think it is supported by natural law. My candid opinion is that the more we act on it, taking the Indians under our protection, compelling them to cultivate the earth, the better it will be for them." Here Monroe elided the principle of discovery that actually underlay the law of such questions. We have no evidence concerning Madison's response to this argument.[8]

Madison also said, "You say nothing, I observe, of remodelling the Judiciary. Perhaps you may have in reserve a special message, or may think it best to let the subject originate in Congress; or it may not appear to you in the light it does to me. I have long thought a systematic change in that department proper, and should have pressed it more when in office, but for the circumstance of its involving a personal accommodation. . . ." Still, "The extension given to the Judiciary sphere by new States & territories, will require at least some further provisions of law." (The matter of personal delicacy at which Madison hinted was that Justice Thomas Todd was his sister-in-law's husband, and thus any reform of federal judges' compensation, elimination of the requirement that justices ride circuit, establishment of a new circuit or circuits, or other legal change benefiting federal judges during his administration might have seemed inappropriately self-interested—and in fact Justice Todd had recently brought this urgent matter to Madison's attention.)⁹ Monroe answered, "I think with you, that the Judiciary should be arrangd, in the manner suggested in your message, & that a new dept. should be instituted, & should have stated it, but was advisd, not to load the message with too many subjects. I shall see what is done, in the progress of the session," he concluded, "& how far, a special interference, may be useful."

Monroe closed his communication to Madison with a thorny problem concerning Congress's power to fund roads. "The subject of an amendment to the Constitution, as brought before Congress, in the message, is opposed by a report from Mr. Tucker [a representative from Virginia]. . . . I understand that it criticises with severity, the doctrine containd in the message, & endeavours to invalidate it, by the measures already sanctiond by Mr. Jefferson yourself, & in part by me, in ordering a fatigue party, to improve the road between Plattsburg & Hamilton." Madison must have winced in anticipation of the kicker: "Be so good as give me in detail the reasons which justify the Cumberland road[,] which presents the greatest difficulty."¹⁰

Madison had already seen the report, as Tucker had sent him a copy.¹¹ Deferential to Madison in constitutional matters, Tucker said this issue "has fallen to my duty to draw up," excused the essay's brevity, and guessed that and "the pressure of circumstances" might have resulted in error. Since "I am indebted to yourself for every principle of Constitutional law which in early life was impressed upon my mind," he continued, "I am anxious to avail myself of an occasion of acknowledging the great advantages I have derived in common with the rest of my Countrymen from your profound Speculations on the Charter of the Government." He hoped his comments on Madison and his administration would not strike Madison as "unfair."

While Madison took no personal exception to Tucker's pamphlet, he immediately rejected its argument *tout court*.¹² His respect for the House's right and duty to investigate such questions and consciousness of his own fallibility kept him from viewing even "the most rigid and critical examination of the particular question" at hand "with any other feeling, than a solicitude for . . . truth and the public good." "I am not unaware," he invoked his authority as a Framer and Ratifier of the Constitution, "that my belief, not to say knowledge of the views of those who proposed the Constitution, and what is of more importance, my deep impression of the views of those who bestowed on it the stamp of authority, may influence my interpretation of the Instrument." Still, "those who consult the Instrument without a danger of that bias [might] be exposed to an equal one, in the anxiety to find in its text an authority for a particular measure of great apparent utility." He yet hoped Tucker would "be assured that altho' I can not concur in the latitude of Construction taken in the report, or in the principle that the consent of States even of a single one can enlarge the jurisdiction of the General Govt: or in the force & extent allowed to precedents & analogies introduced into the report," yet that did not lessen his "esteem for the talents" of Tucker, its author. Rather he was grateful for the gift of the report and the kindness of Tucker's cover letter. What Madison was saying, then, was that though knowledge of the framing of the Constitution could be an important aid in proper interpretation, "what is of more importance" is knowledge of the ratifiers' views, and "anxiety to find in [the Constitution's] text an authority for a particular measure of great apparent utility" is apt to lead people to mistaken interpretations. Besides, one state's or several states' readings could not change the Constitution's meaning, and "precedents and analogies" must be handled with extreme care where the question was whether the Federal Government had powers under the Constitution not previously recognized. Here, nearly three years after his Bonus Bill Veto Message, this prominent actor in the making of the United States Constitution underscored his argument in that famous message.

Four days later Madison addressed Monroe's claims.[13] Beginning by saying he understood that the crush of work would not leave the president time to reply to Madison's letters simply to be polite, and therefore he hoped Monroe would not do so, Madison got right to the point. First he said his question about the Amelia Island expedition had related only to the Executive's power in that connection. Next he clarified his objection to Monroe's statement about Indian lands. Madison had based his assertion on "the principle which has limited the claim of the U.S. to a right of pre-emption." Besides, Madison observed,

> an *unqualified* right of a civilized people to land used by people in the Hunter State, on the principle that the Earth was intended for those who would make it most conducive to the sustenance and increase of the human race, might imply a right in a people cultivating it with the spade, to say to one using the plow, either adopt our mode, or let us substitute it ourselves. It might also not be easy to repell the claims of those without land, in other Countries, if not in our own, to vacant lands within the U.S. likely to remain for a *long* period of years, unproductive of human food.

In relation to the still more ticklish issue of federal funding of the Cumberland Road, Madison noted that it had occurred during the Jefferson administration, that it was "as far as I recollect not then brought to my particular attention," that he did not know on what grounds Jefferson or Congress had adjudged it constitutional, and that "I suspect that the question of Constitutionality was but slightly if at all examined by the former, and that the Executive assent was doubtingly or hastily given." Once it had "become a law, and being a measure of singular utility, additional appropriations took place of course under the same administration: and with the accumulated impulse thence derived, were continued under the succeeding one, with less of critical investigation perhaps than was due to the case." Anyway, he continued, the Cumberland Road funding differed from what Congress was now considering "by the circumstances 1. that the road was undertaken especially for the accommodation of a portion of the Country, with respect to which Congress have a general power not applicable to other portions. 2. that the funds appropriated and which alone have been applied, were also under a general power of Congress, not applicable to other funds."

The former president continued that whatever one might think of the Cumberland Road project, "the case is evidently without the weight allowed to that of the National Bank, which had been often a subject of solemn discussion and had recd. reiterated and deliberate sanctions of *every* branch of the Govt: to all which had been superadded many positive concurrencies of the State Govts and implied ones by the people at large." "As to the case of post roads and military roads; instead of implying a general power to make roads, the constitutionality of them must be tested by the bona fide object of the particular roads. The Post cannot travel, nor troops march without a road. If the necessary roads can not be found, they must of course be provided." Not only did "unwarrantable latitude of construction" threaten "the genuine sense of the Constitution," but so did precedents established by congressional or presidential "inadvertence," perhaps "in the midst of a group scarcely admitting perusal, and under a weariness of mind as little admitting a vigilant attention." Another factor threatening to lead to establishment of mistaken constitutional precedents was "the usefulness & popularity of measures"—which to Madison accounted for Congress's passage of the Bonus Bill he had had to veto.

Historian David P. Currie summarizes Madison's overall argument here as having three parts: that "[t]he Cumberland Road was an isolated, ill-considered mistake that ought not to be repeated"; that "[i]t was justified, if at all, by Congress's plenary powers over the territory and property of the

United States"; and that "Congress *did* have authority to build military and post roads—but . . . not a general system of commercial highways when the country was at peace." Currie considers the first and last of these points convincing, but says of the other that "even if the [Territories Clause] power to adopt regulations 'respecting' the territories included the right to build roads elsewhere to reach them—a concession with somewhat frightening implications—Ohio had ceased to be a territory before the road was begun." Most interesting, perhaps, is Currie's observation that the point about military and post roads indicates Madison "had not been entirely candid in failing to discuss the postal and war powers when he vetoed the Bonus Bill"—though one might explain this omission from a veto message issued on Madison's last day in office too as resulting from the press of business.[14]

❈

Secretary Adams met on December 31st with a Mme. Plantou, who had come to show him her allegorical painting of the Peace of Ghent. Unhappily Adams wrote in his diary that "she laid me under a contribution." He continued:

> It was a bombastic and foolish thing, but Madame Plantou gives herself out for a native of Philadelphia, and is a Painter. . . . There is an America in a triumphal Car, and a Britannia, upon her knees, submitting to terms of Peace dictated by Minerva and Hercules—Oh! the voracious maw, and the bloated visage of national vanity—If it were true that we had vanquished or humbled Britannia it would be base to exult over her, but when it is so notorious that the issue of our late War with her was at best a drawn game, there is nothing but the most egregious National vanity that can turn it to a triumph.[1]

On January 5th, after Mrs. Adams was bled by a doctor, Adams went to "the President's" and found that both Crowninshield and Calhoun had brought dispatches concerning the surrender of Amelia Island. Monroe called a Cabinet meeting for the next day to discuss it.[2]

Sir Gregor McGregor and his one hundred fifty men of various origins had taken the island on June 29, 1817. Essentially pirates, they immediately began attacking ships that ventured too near the Florida coast. McGregor's term "blockade," which he intended to indicate he would target only Spanish vessels, fooled no one. By the fall Spanish attention had been completely diverted by revolutions elsewhere in the New World, even as "brigands and pirates flocked to Amelia Island, much to Gregor McGregor's dismay." He left on September 4th, soon to be succeeded by Luis Aury, whose goals were reflective more of Venezuelan patriotism than of raw avarice.[3] America's problem with Amelia Island related to the pirates' failure to draw the line between attacks on enemy Spaniards and "freebooting against the commerce of neutral nations, including that of the United States."[4]

In the Cabinet meeting of January 6, 1818, the seizure of Amelia Island—already accomplished—was discussed. Monroe had ordered that no Spanish property should be allowed to be taken by the island's occupants, which left the complication of what to do with the "two or four Cannon" that had thus fallen into American possession. "The President," said Adams, "is apparently determined, to withdraw the troops from the Island, but he asks the opinions of the Cabinet. . . ." Crawford, Crowninshield, and Wirt agreed with Monroe that the troops ought to be withdrawn, while Adams and Calhoun thought the island ought to be held for use as a bargaining chip with Spain. Adams's diary entry for the day closes with astute, characteristically unsparing, appraisals of his colleagues' personalities. "If I understand the characters of my Colleagues," he says, "Crawford's point d'honneur is to differ from me, and to find no weight in any reason assigned by me. Wirt and Crowninshield will always be of the President's opinion—Calhoun thinks for himself, independently of all the rest, with sound judgment, quick discrimination and keen observation. He supports his opinions too with powerful eloquence." Adams did indeed "understand the characters of [his] Colleagues."[5]

After the meeting Monroe drafted a special message to Congress.[6] Though Monroe had to make clear that he had not exceeded the Executive's unilateral authority in foreign relations, it reads as a kind of press release for the perusal of the Spanish authorities. The enterprises at Amelia Island and "Galveztown" had been suppressed, he said. McGregor's announced purpose, particularly as it affected "that part of West Florida which is incorporated into the State of Louisiana," besides the occupants' "conduct while in the possession of the island making it instrumental to every species of contraband, and, in regard to slaves, of the most odious and dangerous character," meant the U.S. Government had to intervene. As the authorities in those outposts had purported to be sovereign, Monroe had to decide whether to extend to them "that neutrality which the United States had proclaimed, and . . . observed in favor of the colonies of Spain" which "had declared their independence and were affording strong proof of their ability to maintain it" or to suppress them.

To have recognized Amelia Island and Galveztown as independent would in some sense "have sanctioned all the unlawful claims and practices of this pretended Government in regard to the United States," besides "countenanc[ing] a system of privateering in the Gulf of Mexico and else-where the ill effects of which might . . . have been deeply and very extensively felt." Besides, the president explained, the 1811 congressional No-Transfer Resolution and accompanying law were immediately seen as being applicable when the Executive saw McGregor's proclamation. The operative part of the No-Transfer Resolution said that the United States "could not without serious inquietude see any part of" "the territory adjoining the southern boundary of the United States" pass "into the hands of any foreign Power" and might "under certain contingencies" occupy that territory temporarily itself. In case it did, that territory would "remain subject to a future negotiation."[7] Monroe said that "Early intimation having been received of the dangerous purposes of these adventurers, timely precautions were taken by the establishment of a force near the St. Marys to prevent their effect, or it is probable that it would have been more sensibly felt."

After saying that the Spanish colonial governments had been unaware of, and not responsible for, these developments, Monroe expressed confidence that they would "prevent the abuse of their authority in all cases to the injury of the United States." In case they were unable to do so, "The territory of Spain will nevertheless be respected so far as it may be done consistently with the essential interests and safety of the United States." The United States had not intended in expelling the adventurers from Spanish territory to injure either Spain or her colonies. That injuries such as those recently suffered should not recur, and no foreign government occupy those territories, he concluded, "will be provided for . . . in a spirit of amity in the negotiation now depending with the Government of Spain."

Secretary Adams and Spanish Minister Luis de Onís y Gonzales had a lot of work to do.

Their work would be complicated in 1818 by the human analogue of a loose cannon: Battle of New Orleans—and Horseshoe Bend—victor Major General Andrew Jackson. Ordered to pursue the Seminoles to Spain's chief posts in the Floridas, Jackson went farther. Long having believed that America should seize West and East Florida from the decrepit Spanish administrations there, he seized Pensacola and St. Marks, the colonial capitals, arrested two British subjects he thought had been encouraging the Indians in marauding raids against Americans in Georgia and Alabama Territory, and put the Brits on trial. One, the Scottish trader Alexander Arbuthnot, was hurriedly convicted and sentenced to death, at which point Jackson had him hanged from his ship's yardarm. The other, former Royal Marine Robert Ambrister, was convicted but not sentenced to capital punishment by the court. Jackson overrode the court's decision, though in a bow to Ambrister's military record he sentenced him to a more respectable death by firing squad.[8]

Jackson's attitude concerning his own authority was seen by many in his own day as similar to that of a Caesar. For example, on April 22, 1817, he told his officers that they should not obey orders coming directly from the War Department, but instead should do as the civilians said only if such orders had passed through Jackson. Any other course, he said, "would be a tame surrender of military rights and etiquette." If George Washington had thought of "the tame surrender of military rights to civil authority as the principal bulwark of republican liberty," George Washington was no Andrew Jackson.[9] Given the slowness of communications between the Florida frontier and Washington, D.C., it took six months for President Monroe to be informed of this, run it past his Cabinet, and send Jackson a correction. Characteristically indirect as Jackson was nearly the opposite, Monroe told his constitutional subordinate that he did not know how Jackson's directive could be acceptable. He closed his letter by saying that of course he hoped Jackson would stay in service.[10]

On December 26, 1817, John Quincy Adams noted that he "[r]eceived a Note from the President, asking me to call at his house at twelve O'Clock, to meet the other Heads of Departments, and consult upon the War, with a Southern tribe of Indians; the Seminoles."[11] Monroe told Adams, who arrived an hour early, that he should consult freely with the chairman of the House Committee on Foreign Relations, saying, "This had heretofore been the practice and had been found very useful to the Government," and that Representative John Forsyth, R-GA, was friendly to the administration. At noon Crawford, Calhoun, and Crowninshield arrived and the discussion began. "The Seminole Indians," Adams wrote, "have commenced actual hostilities; and cut off a detachment of fifty men going with a boat and provisions for a part of the troops under General Gaines." In response Monroe and his advisors decided Jackson was to be sent to take command, while Gaines was to concentrate all of his men, "with the Addition of Militia from the State of Georgia, and to reduce them by force, pursuing them into East Florida, if they should retreat for refuge there. . . ."

Calhoun had told General Edmund Pendleton Gaines ten days before to feel free to march into Florida and attack the Seminoles "unless they should shelter themselves under a Spanish post." When he learned of this, Jackson fired off a letter to Monroe insisting on a different plan. The Seminoles, he counseled, must be pursued even into Spanish posts "where an enemy is

permitted and protected or disgrace attends." He insisted that seizing East
Florida was the best strategy and that he'd implement it if signaled. Rather
than wait for his message to make its long way to Monroe and for Monroe to
send a response the long way back, Jackson grasped the reins of the situation, raising forces and hitting the road on January 22nd. Asked by Representative John Forsyth about Monroe's orders to Jackson, the administration
answered that since Spain could not stop the Seminoles' incursions into the
U.S.A., his administration would do so. General Jackson, he said, had been
told not to enter Florida unless pursuing Seminoles. On this basis, he seized
St. Mark's on April 7th.[12]

President Monroe started on his second American tour—this one of the
Chesapeake Bay region—on May 28, 1818. At three weeks' length, it would
be far briefer than his northern tour.

The Chesapeake Bay tour, confined as it was to towns of military significance in the president's home region, concerned itself, as Monroe had
intended the previous one to do, with inspections of the nation's military defenses. It included no grand patriotic spectacles such as had greeted Monroe
in New York and Boston. No prominent men's guilty consciences, it seems,
prodded them to flaunt their love of country along the way this time.

Monroe initially envisioned a trip "to examine the Chesapeake" for
the purpose of ensuring the fitness of the region's fortifications, with his
youngest brother, Joseph, and son-in-law George Hay accompanying him.
Hay in the event did not make it, but Joseph went along as the president's
secretary. The plan was to set out from Washington for Baltimore, then
take a steamboat to Annapolis. From Annapolis, the president and his
Cabinet secretaries would travel via a U.S. Navy schooner. Secretary of
the Navy Benjamin Crowninshield provided sumptuous food for Monroe
and his traveling companions aboard their ship.[13]

The popular press explained to the public that Monroe had intended
to inspect the Chesapeake defenses the year before, but that his unantici-
patedly time-consuming tour of the North had kept him from it.[14] The first
stop on the trip, Annapolis, was void of "an affectation of pomp or parade,"
as the *Baltimore American* noted. "Immediately on [Monroe's] arrival the
flag of the Union was displayed from the spire of the State-house," added
the (Annapolis) *Maryland Gazette*. The following morning, however, Bali-
moreans woke to a twenty-one-gun salute (what was a little "pomp or parade" among friends?), and Monroe was read an address by the local mayor.
His main point was that many of his constituents remembered Monroe's
having been in Baltimore while a congressman in 1783. The president re-

plied that he recalled those days and was happy to see people familiar from that time, when he in entering upon a public career had been a witness as "the illustrious commander of our revolutionary armies, after performing services, which a grateful country can never forget, nor time obliterate, restored his commission to the authority from whom he had received it" (that is, resigned his commission and returned it to Congress). The dinner party drank thirteen toasts, including "The memory of Washington," "The survivors of the Revolutionary Army," "Jefferson and Madison," "The freedom of the Press," "The militia of the U. States," and "The improvement of our docks and harbours." One could almost have concluded that it was a partisan event.[15]

The party left Baltimore headed down the Chesapeake on May 30th. "It is understood," a local paper noted, "that St. Mary's, York, James, and Elizabeth Rivers [the first in Maryland, the other three in Virginia], will severally be visited and probably Albemarle [in North Carolina], when the Secretary of War will proceed to his residence in South Carolina."[16] On June 5th the president and his party arrived at Yorktown, where, according to Chief of (Army) Engineers Joseph G. Swift, Monroe, Calhoun, Crowninshield, and Monroe's private secretary "visited the site of the marquees of Washington and Rochambeau on the field of 1781." The day after that, they "looked over the positions that the board had surveyed near York. . . ."[17] On June 8th Swift, apparently weary of the folderol, recorded only that the party had "examined the navy yard and forts" at Norfolk.[18] The (Norfolk) *American Beacon,* on the other hand, named everyone in the presidential retinue, described four different military posts' ceremonial cannon fire as the president's ship passed them, and gave the particulars of Monroe's landing. "As might have been expected," it continued, "such was the curiosity to behold the man in whom the confidence and affections of a nation of freemen are concentered, that we never have witnessed such an indiscriminate assemblage on any occasion in our town." Perhaps recalling the un-Virginian ceremonial that had met Monroe in the North, it observed that, "It might indeed be said, that the reception was in a style of genuine Republican simplicity." Local military units, adult and junior, performed "the usual evolutions of the countermarch," and otherwise attempted to display their martial skill for the president, whose "generous smile of approbation, which beamed in the countenance of this Veteran of the Revolution, as he moved down the line, surveying all their movements with the eye of a soldier, was animating beyond description. . . ." The presidential party visited three neighborhood military installations, was treated to more military ceremonial, and retired for the night.[19]

The southern terminus of the tour, Elizabeth City, proved an enjoyable place to visit. Lemuel Sawyer, the brother of Monroe's host, recorded that "We heard of their approach; and in the afternoon I rode a few miles out to meet the cortege, the dust of which, for near a mile off, gave signs of their approach. The President's carriage, surrounded by a dozen attendants on horseback, was in the van, and Mr. Crowninshield and Calhoun followed, and I fell into the rear. . . ." Monroe was easily persuaded to stay the night, and the locals prepared to give him "the hospitalities of the town." "A fine green turtle" was the centerpiece of the dinner the Monroe party enjoyed. A prominent local, Lemuel Sawyer, took Calhoun in his "barouche" to the home of his brother Enoch Sawyer, appointed by Washington Collector of Customs for Camden, North Carolina, who put up the president's party in a house spacious enough for "Lear with his hundred knights." "My niece Mary," Lemuel Sawyer wrote, "a beautiful and accomplished young maiden, entertained the party . . . by some of her best airs on the harp, an instrument on which she excelled, accompanied by a sweet well-trained voice."[20]

At Norfolk the president heard from the mayor an address about the blessing of America's republican institutions in lieu of Europeans' "obsequious homage to the arbitrary distinctions of hereditary, rank, and adventitious birth." Fortunately they had him for their chief magistrate as a result of "the unbiassed and unerring verdict of the public will." The rest of the address was along the same lines—recalling Monroe's long record of public service, his martial exploits, and his creditable principles before saluting his decision to inspect America's defensive installations. All would be well, and in time Monroe would retire with "the most precious of all earthly consolations— that of having done your duty." Monroe's response was equally routine for him by this point. Then followed another public dinner, after which came the usual routine of numerous toasts.[21]

Arriving at Hampton, Virginia, on June 13th, the president's ship was intercepted by a boat bearing prominent local citizens. Monroe accepted their invitation to a public dinner, and he and his party went ashore to the sound of ceremonial cannon fire. Having dined with local people, Monroe returned to his ship and went to Old Point Comfort, "from whence at 8 o'clock in the evening, he took his departure for Washington."[22] The *National Intelligencer* of June 18th reported that Monroe the morning before had left the *Nonsuch* and been rowed up the Potomac to Washington. "Thus," it concluded, "has the President terminated the tour of observation of the waters of the Chesapeake, which his official duty devolved upon him."[23]

56

❖

Back in Washington on July 15, 1818, the Cabinet discussed General Jackson's actions for five hours.[1] He had taken Pensacola, the capital of West Florida. "The President and all the members of the Cabinet except myself," Adams wrote, "are of opinion that Jackson acted not only without, but against his Instructions—that he has committed War upon Spain, which cannot be justified, and in which if not disavowed by the Administration, they will be abandoned by the Country. My opinion is that there was no real though an apparent violation of his instruction; that his proceedings were justified by the necessity of the case, and by the misconduct of the Spanish commanding Officers in Florida." As the secretary of state reasoned, "The question is embarrassing and complicated, not only as involving that of an actual war with Spain; but that of the Executive power, to authorize hostilities without a declaration of War by Congress." Jackson, he continued, had been authorized to pursue hostile Indians across the Florida border. The constitutional issue arose when his actions passed from defensive—"There is no doubt that *defensive* acts of hostility may be authorized by the Executive"—to offensive.

As Adams understood matters, everything Jackson had done, including even "the order for taking the fort of Barrancas [at Pensacola] by storm," had been "incidental" to "the object" of "the termination of the Indian War." Jackson said as much, and the general denied that merely crossing a line of latitude could shield the hostiles from American military action. On the other hand, Calhoun, "generally of sound, judicious and comprehensive mind, seems in this case to be personally offended, with the idea, that Jackson has set at nought the Instructions of the Department." Unbeknownst to Adams, Calhoun's initial instructions to Jackson had told him to "concentrate your forces and to adopt the necessary measures to terminate a conflict which it has ever been the desire of the President . . . to avoid. . . ." In other words Calhoun had (perhaps unintentionally) given Jackson orders seemingly conferring very broad discretion.[2] Monroe conceded in theory that Jackson's measures could have been justified, but he thought "that he has not made out his case." After dinner with the president and his colleagues, Adams discovered upon walking home that the French minister awaited him there—quite concerned to maintain peace between America and Spain.

The following day, July 16th, Adams found himself alone in the Cabinet in defending Jackson.[3] The issue now was "the degree to which his acts are to be disavowed." Crawford, who was angling for Virginian support in the presidential succession, insisted the administration must disavow Jackson and return Pensacola. It seemed to Wirt that Judge Spencer Roane—son-in-law of Patrick Henry, chief judge of the Virginia Court of Appeals, leader of that court in opposing John Marshall's Supreme Court in *Martin v. Hunter's Lessee,* and intellectual eminence of the fabled Richmond Junto—had launched a series of anti-Jackson editorials in the *Richmond Enquirer.* Roane considered Jackson's invasion unconstitutional, yes, but he had mixed feelings about the victor of New Orleans. He urged his "readers to 'divest . . . of the irritated feelings about Indian cruelties, united to Spanish insults' and submit Jackson's conduct 'to the tribunal of reason.'" Virginians should join Roane in "grief[,] . . . shame and abhorrence" in considering "the bloody massacre" of the friendly Creeks, besides the general's "imprudence . . . [and] contempt of the laws."[4] Adams stood firm, however: to fire Jackson would be to turn him loose to attack the Monroe administration, which he would do with great vigor. On the other hand, if Jackson were not relieved, "Pensacola might be restored, and its capture by him still justified." When, during a break in the meeting, Adams found the French diplomat Hyde de Neuville in his office, he responded to his offer to mediate between the Americans and Onís by saying he should be told that Pensacola could be returned, its capture should be understood as undertaken by Jackson without orders, "no blame could be admitted as attaching to General Jackson," and blame should be attached to both the governor of Pensacola and the commandant of St. Marks. Monroe agreed to this. Adams walked home with Calhoun.

In the end, after six Cabinet meetings in seven days, the American government decided that Pensacola could not be kept by the Americans without congressional authorization. The *National Intelligencer* ran a column (apparently written by Attorney General Wirt) that, besides this, also told the public that "the King of Spain shall, hereafter, keep such a force in those colonies, as shall enable him to execute, with fidelity, the fifth article of the treaty between the United States and Spain"—that is, to keep Florida Indians from raiding American territory or attacking Americans.[5]

On July 19th Monroe wrote to Jackson to inform him of the administration's decisions and explain the reasoning underlying them.[6] He began by telling the general he would observe in this letter the "freedom and candor" that had "invariably" characterized his communication with the general. First, Monroe said, "the view and intentions of the Government were fully disclosed in respect to the operations in Florida" when Jackson was called "into active service against the Seminoles." "In transcending the limit prescribed by those orders," he continued, "you acted on your own responsibility, on facts and circumstances which were unknown to the Government when the orders were given, many of which, indeed, occurred afterward, and which you thought imposed on you the measure, as an act of patriotism, essential to the honor and interests of your country."

Seeming very much to be writing for another audience—for the public, perhaps, or for a congressional committee—Monroe continued that "The United States stand justified in ordering their troops into Florida in pursuit of their enemy. They have this right by the law of nations, if the Seminoles were inhabitants of another country and had entered Florida to elude pursuit." Our order "is not an act of hostility to Spain"—particularly as "her government is bound by treaty to restrain . . . the Indians there from committing hostilities against the United States."

On the other hand, the president continued, an order to attack a Spanish post would be a different matter. "It would authorize war, to which, by the principles of our Constitution, the Executive is incompetent. Congress alone possesses the power." Hypothetically, Monroe continued, a general might find himself authorized by circumstances to attack a foreign country. He then laid out a scenario indistinguishable from the one Jackson had encountered: the neutral power's forces "forget the obligations incident to their neutral character; they stimulate the enemy to make war; they furnish them with arms and munitions of war to carry it on; they take an active part in their favor; they afford them an asylum in their retreat. The general obtaining victory pursues them to their post, the gates of which are shut against him; he attacks and carries it. . . ."

When the foreign power demands an account of what has happened—"was this your act? or did you authorize it?"—the general's government replies, "I did not: it was the act of the general. He performed it for reasons deemed sufficient himself, and on his own responsibility." The offended country insists, "I demand, then, the surrender of the post, and his punishment." The general's government provides the grounds on which the general was justified, "and prov[es] the misconduct of . . . officers" of the aggrieved country so that their government may punish them. Monroe says he has charged the Spanish officers with misbehavior, and—here is the key—tells Jackson to provide him with a clearer statement of the situation he faced so that the U.S. Government can "take the ground which you have presented." However, America could not hold the posts Jackson had seized without effectively declaring war on Spain, which only Congress could do.

Taking the general fully into his confidence, Monroe told him that the "consequences" of "hold[ing] the posts" would be "impossible to calculate." Britain likely could be found on the opposing side, various countries' privateers would begin to prey on America's lucrative seaborne commerce, and "we do not foresee that we should have a single power in Europe on our side." Why bother, he asked, in light of the fact that Spain's preoccupation with her New World colonies' rebellions likely would eventually lead her "to cede the territory" of Florida anyway? Holding the posts would prevent Spain from taking such a step. Thus withdrawing from the posts seemed the best alternative, and it seemed bound to yield the results Jackson wanted.

Also making this course appear attractive was the calculation that if the United States returned control of Spain's territory to that power, neither Jackson nor the Monroe administration would have even arguably violated the Constitution—"the last imputation," Monroe insisted, "to which I would consent justly to expose myself." To the contrary, he insisted, "my public life has been devoted" "to the support of" it, "on pure principles." Perhaps most remarkably, Monroe closed this lengthy letter by offering Jackson the opportunity to "correct" his wartime letters to the War Department, which Monroe was willing to say had been "written in haste, under the pressure of fatigue and infirmity." The passage in which Jackson mentioned "the incompetency of an imaginary boundary to protect us against the enemy," in particular, as "the ground on which you bottom all your measures," as "liable to the imputation that you took the Spanish posts . . . as a measure of expediency, and not on account of the misconduct of the Spanish officers" might be corrected. If Jackson wanted to send corrected copies to Monroe or Calhoun, that would be best, but one of them could correct the ones already in their possession if that were Jackson's preference.

Monroe closed by observing that the great European powers were in the process of deciding what to do about the Spanish and Portuguese New World empires. "England proposes to restore the colonies to Spain with free trade and colonial governments," but other European powers are "less favorable." If war must come to make the Floridas, etc., American, popular unity will be essential, and that will require that Spain initiate the conflict "and, above all, that the government be free from the charge of committing a breach of the Constitution."

Reading this letter from President Monroe to his theater commander, one cannot help but conclude that Jackson's conduct in relation to the Ambrister trial was characteristic of the U.S. Government after all. It calls to mind later presidencies' handling of records of private communications, besides their manipulation of popular opinion in steering America into war. What perhaps differentiated this situation from later ones is that the general was having none of it.

In his response to Monroe, Jackson said that although he would at a later date take up the other issues Monroe had raised, he would at this point merely refute the claims "that I *transcended the limits of my order*, and that I *acted on my own responsibility*."[7] "The requisitions of the order," he said, "are, for the comdg. Genl to assume the immediate command at Fort Scott—to concentrate all the contiguous and disposable force of the Division on that quarter, to call on the executives of adjacent states for an auxiliary militia force, and concludes with this general, comprehensive command—'with this view, you may be prepared to concentrate your forces, and adopt the necessary measures to terminate a conflict which it has ever been the desire of the President, from motives of humanity, to avoid, but which is now made necessary by their settled hostility.'" "For as long as the main legitimate design is kept in view the policy of the measures, adopted, to accomplish it, is alone to be considered." As he understood it, Jackson had in the First Seminole War (as it is now known) always kept "the main legitimate design . . . in view," and so the general had not "transcend[ed] the limit prescribed by those orders" at all.

Meanwhile Monroe wrote to his son-in-law and advisor George Hay. Jackson's success in Florida had shown that Spain could neither defend her bases in the Floridas nor "fulfill her duties towards us." What was to be hoped was that the ease of Jackson's success "may produce a good effect in promoting a cession, which the restoration of the posts enables her to do with honor." Turning on Jackson would have led to "internal feuds, of the most pernicious character, and told Spain that she had nothing to fear from us." As it was, Spain now could see that she could do what America wanted "with honor" and would risk much in resisting the outcome the Monroe administration sought. Soon after this, the president told Jackson he regretted that Jackson had understood his instructions differently from the way the president intended, but since Jackson had acted according to his reasonable interpretation, Monroe "was satisfied . . . that you had good reason for your conduct and have acted in all things on that principle."[8]

As everyone in Washington knew, Secretary of State Adams had been working with Minister Onís on a treaty to obtain these territories, in which Spain maintained only nominal military presence and which were so essential to the United States from a geostrategic point of view. Everyone also knew that Speaker Henry Clay stood for American endorsement of the independence of Spain's rebellious New World possessions. Jackson's actions, in response to which Secretary of War Calhoun insisted in multiple Cabinet meetings that Jackson had contravened his civilian superiors' express orders, could not but complicate Adams's task.

57

When President Monroe presented these matters to the House for its consideration, Clay delivered the first of the speeches that made him famous. As historian Merrill Peterson put it, it was "the first of the great oratorical displays in the capital that captivated the age." (Somewhere the shade of John Randolph of Roanoke is taking exception to that.) All of Monroe's secretaries but Adams having criticized Jackson in the Cabinet, yet all having defended him in public, Clay became the chief figure openly criticizing Jackson (whose ambition he compared to Caesar's). Nothing personal, Old Chap, Clay assured Jackson. Jackson, for his part, never forgot a slight, let alone a public insult: for him, politics was deeply personal. Their mutual enmity was destined to become the hard core of the Second Party System as Monroe's administration came to an end in 1825.[1]

Meanwhile Onís demanded that Jackson receive "lawful punishment."[2] Spain's foreign minister in Madrid broke off talks with the American minister in Madrid, but he told Onís to keep making territorial concessions in his negotiations with Adams. The Spaniard pushed Adams to divulge his ultimate position; the Yankee replied only that if the Floridas were yielded, perhaps the western boundary could wait. His Catholic Majesty's real aim in negotiating the loss of indefensible East and West Florida was to agree to a permanent western border, so surrendering them without obtaining that was not an option. Okay, Adams said, "we can take the Rio Bravo del Norte [aka, the Rio Grande] for a frontier." "Better still the Mississippi," replied Onís. To the Spaniard's claim that Juan de Fuca had established Spain's claim to North America north to the fifty-sixth parallel, which would have given Spain a claim to southernmost Alaska, Adams replied, "Nonsense. The English pretend the Columbia River is theirs. The Russians have possessions north of it which you have never disputed, and we have more right than anybody else to the River Columbia [thanks to Lewis and Clark]. We have establishments on its banks, and we need it to keep open our communications with the interior." Onís reported home that this was the Americans' true position and urged his foreign minister to cut a deal, "seeing that things certainly won't be better for a long time." Lest he receive instructions to make a counteroffer, he added that Spain could not keep the Americans from recognizing the colonial rebels' independence.

The two negotiators disagreed at this early stage about a boundary between their territories in the east—Onís pointing to the Missouri, Adams liking the Arkansas—but Adams's real goal was to secure the Columbia in the northwest all the way to the ocean. The president, for his part, was fixated on the Floridas, considering more westerly lands to be bargaining chips of distinctly secondary interest, though he proved amenable to Adams's persuasion as the negotiations proceeded. On August 10th Monroe wrote to Adams that Onís ought to recognize that the United States Government was being quite generous in leaving to Spain "all the country between the Rio Bravo and the Sabine" (more or less the territory of today's Texas). If Spain did not accept this position, likely Congress at its next session would endorse seizure of the Floridas, and if Spain tried to resist, "we shall expell Spain from this hemisphere."

Monroe's Second Annual Message, delivered on November 16, 1818, focused largely on relations with Spain.[3] The Convention of 1802 "providing for the adjustment of a certain portion of the claims of our citizens for injuries sustained by spoliation," Monroe said, had at last been ratified by Spain. This left other American claims unaddressed, and it did nothing about the matter of boundaries.

Turning to the Floridas, Monroe said that in those huge territories, the king's authority had "been confined almost exclusively to the walls of Pensacola and St. Augustine," and even there "only small garrisons have been maintained." As a result, "[a]dventurers from every country, fugitives from justice, and absconding slaves" had appeared there, joining "Indians, strong in the # of their warriors, remarkable for their ferocity, and whose settlements extend to our limits." Here had developed a field for people to flout "our laws prohibiting the introduction of slaves," besides dodging American tax laws and "commit[ing] every kind of outrage on our peaceable citizens which their proximity to us enabled them to perpetrate." Spain's inability to suppress the Amelia Island invaders, their numbers "not exceeding 150," "clearly proves how completely extinct the Spanish authority had become." "A system of buccaneering was rapidly organizing over it which menaced in its consequences the lawful commerce of every nation, and particularly the United States. . . ."

Monroe next made the striking assertion that "the Indian tribes have constituted the effective force in Florida. The Seminole War owed its genesis to the manipulation of the Indians in connection with their land claims, besides "practicing on their savage propensities." Men who manipulate Indians into war, "which is always attended on their part with acts of barbarity the most shocking, deserve to be viewed in a worse light than the savages." They deserved the punishment that "might be justly inflicted on the savages themselves."

The American attack on Amelia Island was justified by "the right of self defense," which "never ceases." The Amelia Island projectors' "unlawful purposes," their various actions in furtherance of those purposes, "and, above all, their incitement of the Indians to massacre our fellow citizens of every age and of both sexes, merited a like treatment and received it." (Note Monroe's echo of the famous characterization of Indians' mode of warfare in the Declaration of Independence.) Spain's inability to exert control over its Florida colonies had required the United States to intervene. This American action reflected "no unfriendliness . . . toward Spain," as she had lost Amelia Island before. The same went for authorizing General Jackson "to enter Florida in pursuit of the Seminoles." Monroe lamented that in the course of the incursion, Jackson discovered that Spanish officers had played a role "in encouraging the war, furnishing munitions of war . . . , and in other acts not less marked which evinced their participation in the hostile purposes of that combination"—all of which made clear to "the savages that by those officers they would be protected." Here Spain violated Article V of the treaty of 1795, which bound her to "restrain" the Indians "even by force."

Yet Monroe had not concluded that the Spanish government bore blame for its local commanders' behavior. He had therefore ordered the major posts' return to Spanish control—and thus maintained America's "amicable relations" with Spain. Only Congress could change them.

The ongoing war between Spain and some of its New World provinces continued. When it would end was not yet clear. European powers were in the process of mediating between the parties. American relations with the major European powers continued to be friendly.

Monroe looked forward to a $2 million annual surplus from federal revenue of over $26 million. More federal land had been sold at high prices than ever before, and Monroe looked to "a progressive improvement in that source of revenue." Protective tariffs had had positive effects, and "the expediency of granting further protection is submitted to your consideration." He listed several Indian tribes in numerous states with whom treaties had been made, one result of which was transfer of considerable lands to the United States. More would come. Secretary Calhoun had established significant military posts at three river sites "at no great distance from our northern boundaries." It was thought that this would help to maintain peaceful relations with various western Indian tribes, besides helping speed "the great object of their civilization."

Turning to a topic that had been dear to Jefferson's heart and which he had discussed with Madison, the president said, "Experience has clearly demonstrated that independent savage communities can not long exist within the limits of a civilized population." Progress of the civilized had repeatedly led to "the extinction" of the Indians. "To civilize them," then, "and even to prevent their extinction, it seems to be indispensable that their independence as communities should cease, and that the control of the United States over them should be complete and undisputed. The hunter state will then be more easily abandoned," and sedentary ways akin to Europeans' taken up—thus dissolving the old Indian identities. Monroe closed these ruminations with a hint that Congress should take up "some benevolent provisions" to speed the process.

Monroe cheered Illinois's accession to statehood as the twenty-first state earlier that year. Increasing the number of states tended, he thought, to make existing states feel more secure in relation to the "National Government." The federal principle's necessity—the requirement that most authority be exercised at the state level, with only a few powers delegated to the center—would be "universally admitted" as the process continued, and "the General Government will no longer be dreaded." A more variegated, larger national economy would tie distant parts of the country more powerfully together too. Yet as the country grew Congress had less time for exercise of its exclusive power over the District of Columbia—which was a problem it could address. He closed by recommending his countrymen thank "the Divine Author of All Good" for America's great and growing blessings.

So that the British public might understand America's position, Adams on November 28, 1818, sent U.S. Minister to Spain George W. Erving new instructions. He made them public via the American press long before they could have reached Erving. Their gravamen was that Spain's inadequate rule in the Floridas left open the probability of future "Indian and Negro" attacks on Americans. Jackson had been right to seize St. Marks and Pensacola in his mission to head off further such attacks, Adams insisted, and the Spanish authorities ought to answer for their own behavior. If Spain's governors had had no choice in the face of Indian power but to aid the Indians in attacking the United States, "it must carry demonstration irresistible to the Spanish Government, that *the right of the United States can as little compound with impotence as with perfidy,* and that Spain must immediately make her election, either to place a force in Florida adequate at once to the protection of her territory and to the fulfillment of her engagements, or cede to the United States a province, of which she retains nothing but the nominal possession. . . ."

Monroe sent Thomas Jefferson copies of the papers he submitted to Congress on this subject. Jefferson replied thankfully, adding that Monroe ought to seek publication of Adams's efforts in the *Leyden Gazette,* "from which it would go into the other leading gazettes of Europe. it is of great consequence to us," the former president explained,

> . . . & merits every possible endeavor, to maintain in Europe a correct opinion of our political morality. these papers will place us erect with the world in the important cases of our Western boundary, of our military entrance into Florida, & of the execution of Arbuthnot and Ambrister. on the two first subjects it is very natural for an European to go wrong, and to give in to the charge of ambition, which the English papers (read every where) endeavor to fix on us. if the European mind is once set right on these points, they will go with us in all the subsequent proceedings, without further enquiry.

Jefferson closed by urging Monroe to have Adams return any letter in which the American president was referred to by Onís as "his Excellency," which put him on a par with "mr Onis himself, with the Governors of provinces, and even of every petty fort in Europe, or the colonies." Absent such foppery, Jefferson mused, "an American gentleman in Europe can rank with the first nobility because we have no titles which stick him at any particular place in their line." In his old age Jefferson's mind carried him back to the Senate debate over Vice President John Adams's proposal to address President George Washington using a fancy honorific.[4]

Not only did Adams's papers undercut congressional criticism of Jackson and the administration, but they persuaded His Majesty's Government that Arbuthnot and Ambrister had gotten what was coming to them. As Lord Castlereagh told Minister Richard Rush, popular anger had first been so great that war would have been the result if only the ministry had "held up a finger." Having read Adams's arguments, however, Castlereagh decided the two had gotten what they deserved. The spectacle of British swords remaining sheathed after Jackson's summary treatment of two of King George's subjects made a mighty impression on European opinion as well. America, it seemed, really was the master of its own continent.

Most important, as the historian of Adams's foreign policy statesmanship put it, "It settled the Florida Question." At the same time Spain's Foreign Minister Pizarro yielded his office to the same marquis de Casa Yrujo who had held office in the District of Columbia in Jefferson's day. Yrujo told Onís to make the best deal he could—preferably with a boundary at the Sabine, but definitely with a western boundary "as far north as possible"—which was the first indication that Madrid would accept a transcontinental treaty.[5]

On January 30, 1819, the U.S.A. exchanged ratifications of an agreement with the U.K. recognizing the forty-ninth parallel as the boundary between America and Canada all the way to the Rocky Mountains. As a complement, Adams wanted Spain to concede American control of the whole Columbia River basin. What he did not know was that Onís stood ready to cede all of Texas to the United States if that was what it took to end this squabble, and thus free Spain up to try to reestablish control of its South American colonies.

President Monroe, a bit less confident of America's position, intervened. At the White House on February 18, 1819, he told Onís, "I will do anything you want. I have had a great personal esteem for you ever since the first day I dealt with you. Have a glass of wine with me." When next the two met privately, however, Adams told Hyde de Neuville that he was the American officer conducting the negotiation and that taking it up with the president was "improper." Monroe would be "much and justly displeased if he ha[d] reason to think that a complimentary expression of politeness used by him in answer to a remark made to him by a foreign minister at the drawing-room were to be construed into an abandonment of an important principle in a pending negotiation." "That is perfectly just," the French minister/intermediary in the negotiation agreed.

The Transcontinental Treaty was signed on Washington's birthday, two days after it was agreed. Onís went to Adams's office for the signing of the two versions—Spanish and English.[6] Adams then took his to the White House, where Monroe's transmittal message for the Senate was prepared. It was read in the Senate that day, with, as a senator reported to Adams, "universal satisfaction." After a dinner party Adams arrived home late—"near one in the Morning"—and "closed the day; with ejaculations of fervent gratitude to the giver of all good—It was," he said, "perhaps the most important day of my life."

The chain of events culminating in America's acquisition of a huge share of Spain's North American empire, including both Florida and territory connecting the Mississippi River Basin to the Pacific Ocean, had been "brought about in a manner utterly unexpected" through the agency of "the all-wise, and all beneficent disposer of Events . . . by means the most extraordinary and unforeseen." Adams exulted, "Its prospects are propitious and flattering in an eminent degree—May they be realized by the same superintending bounty that produced them!" He tried to persuade himself not to "ascribe to [his] own foresight or exertions any portion of the Event," but could not help gushing over "acquisition of the Florida's"—"long an object of earnest desire to this Country"—and "acknowledgement of a definite line of boundary to the South Sea" [the Pacific Ocean], which together made this Transcontinental Treaty "a great Epocha in our History." (Like John Quincy Adams, we recognize this as a phrase his father used, e.g., in the diary entry he wrote the day after the Boston Tea Party.[7]) "The first proposal of it in this Negotiation," he continued, "was my own," and it had never even been hinted at in previous American negotiations. Besides, the American-Spanish relationship would be transformed by the treaty from a state of expectation of war to one centered on "a fair prospect of tranquility and of secure peace."

This momentous time in Adams's superb diplomatic career was not one of unalloyed satisfaction, however. "My Mother," the secretary of state mused in his diary,

> was an Angel upon Earth—She was a Minister of blessing to all human beings within her sphere of action. Her heart was the abode of heavenly purity. She had no feelings but of kindness and beneficence. . . . She was the real personification of female virtue—of piety—of charity, of ever active, and never intermitting benevolence—Oh! God! could she have been spared yet a little long! . . . I have enjoyed but for short seasons and at long distant intervals the happiness of her Society—Yet she has been to me more than a Mother. . . . without her the world feels to me like a solitude—Oh! what must it be to my father. . . . —Not my will, heavenly father, but thine be done![8]

And:

> The mail had brought me too fatal a confirmation of my apprehensions, in a Letter from my Son John . . . informing me that . . . my Mother, beloved and lamented more than language can express, yielded up her pure and gentle Spirit to its Creator! . . . Had she lived to the age of the Patriarchs,

every day of her life would have been filled with deeds of goodness and of love. There is not a virtue that can abide in the female heart, but it was the ornament of hers. She had been fifty-four years the delight of my father's heart; the sweetener of all his toils—the comforter of all his sorrows; the sharer and heightener of all his joys—It was but the last time when I saw my father that he told me, with an ejaculation of gratitude to the giver of every good and perfect gift, that in all the vicissitudes of his fortunes, through all the good Report, and evil Report of the World; in all his struggles, and in all his sorrows the affectionate participation, and cheering encouragement of his wife, had been his never failing support. . . .[9]

58

✦

T he night he signed the Transcontinental Treaty, Adams had dinner at a congressional boardinghouse, where he found that conversation focused on the treaty and "the arguments now delivering before the Supreme Court of the United States."[1] The case at hand in the high court, *McCulloch v. Maryland,* concerned the new Bank of the United States Congress had created in 1816, and Adams's use of the present tense refers to the Supreme Court's practice at the time, according to which arguments "invariably lasted longer than a day."[2] Although President Madison had convinced himself to sign the legislation creating this bank into law, many Republicans outside Washington, D.C., remained unconvinced, even passionately opposed.

Americans had experienced a substantial economic downturn in 1818. European economies, at last having recovered from the wars of the French Revolution and Napoleon, returned to full-scale peacetime production— thus Europeans desired fewer products from the United States. This decline in demand led to declines in prices. For example, where Southern cotton had topped a price of $.30 per pound through virtually all of 1818, it fell to $.015 in 1819. So people cast about for an explanation.[3] Many settled on the operations of the Bank of the United States (BUS).

This was a fair conclusion. After all, the BUS engaged in an unprecedented monetary contraction beginning in December 1817, besides ceasing its policy of ready lending, because both its easy money policy and its readiness to keep other banks' notes instead of specie on hand threatened to leave the bank without the requisite specie to finance the first payment to France on the Louisiana Purchase, which would come due on October 21, 1818. "As soon as the policy of contraction was announced," one expert says, "the Bank and its president became the scapegoats for the hard times the nation experienced."[4]

The Bank's esteem with the public also was not helped by the fact that it had been run corruptly for years. A special House committee to investigate its operations reported in late 1818 that it "had violated its charter by failing to require the payment of specie for its stock, by paying dividends to stockholders who had not completed the purchase of their stock, by allowing numerous irregularities to take place during the election of its board of directors, by making questionable loans, by generally poor management, and by not paying sufficient attention to its public responsibilities."[5]

Several states had adopted anti-BUS measures by 1819. The Indiana Constitution of 1816 and Illinois Constitution of 1818, for example, disallowed establishment within those states' borders of any bank not chartered therein. Georgia, Tennessee, and North Carolina imposed taxes on out-of-state banks, and Kentucky and Ohio targeted BUS branches specifically. Five states supported a constitutional amendment limiting BUS operations to the District of Columbia. The leading historian of the litigation argues persuasively that these measures were not all motivated by hostility to the BUS. For example, Maryland, North Carolina, and Georgia intended their tax measures to raise revenue. Maryland's members of Congress, he notes, did not support congressional efforts to strip the BUS of its charter.[6] (This of course is not dispositive evidence, as state legislators and members of Congress are elected independently.)

Six highly esteemed lawyers argued before the Supreme Court in *McCulloch v. Maryland,* among them the Maryland Philadelphia Convention delegate Luther Martin and an up-and-comer from New Hampshire by way of Massachusetts, Daniel Webster. Yet it seems one attorney had by far the most impact on the case's outcome, as Justice Joseph Story described Marylander (and former Madison administration attorney general) William Pinkney's argument in *McCulloch* by saying, "I never, in my whole life, heard a greater speech; it was worth a journey from Salem to hear it; his elocution was excessively vehement, but his eloquence was overwhelming. . . . All the cobwebs of sophistry and metaphysics about state rights and state sovereignty he brushed away with a mighty besom."[7]

That the Court adopted Pinkney's argument as its own, more or less, would not have shocked any careful watcher of Marshall and his colleagues. In fact Webster claimed that Marshall's opinion in a famous case still taught in constitutional law courses was "little else than a recital of my argument"—a claim he would not have made if false, as others in the small world of Supreme Court advocates would have recognized it as such. The Supreme Court reporter's version of Pinkney's argument shows that Marshall's opinion for the court in *McCulloch* included several passages closely imitative of what Pinkney said.[8]

Chief Justice Marshall worked backstage before oral argument to ensure that the disputants discussed the issues he wanted them to, as William Pinkney wrote Webster that "I now suppose it will not be necessary [to discuss the shape their presentations would take beforehand], since it is said that little else than the thread bare topics connected with the constitutionality of the Bank will be introduced into the argument. . . ."[9]

Webster kicked off the argument for McCulloch. He said the case presented two issues: whether the BUS's chartering legislation was constitutional and whether Maryland had a right to tax the Bank. In relation to the former, he relied on Alexander Hamilton's 1791 argument in President Washington's Cabinet in favor of the First Bank of the United States.[10] All three branches of the Federal Government had acted on the basis of accepting the bank laws' constitutionality for nearly thirty years, he said, which made it a settled question. His Hamiltonian argument rested on the Necessary and Proper Clause—which he said meant a law must in Congress's appraisal be "*Best* and *most useful*," not "*absolutely* indispensable." This test could only be applied by Congress, not by a court.

Webster made quick work of the taxation question. If a state could tax a federal instrumentality, he said, it could keep the Federal Government from exercising a constitutional power. Soon after his argument, Webster wrote a friend that "of the decision I have no doubt."

Counsel for Maryland replied that while Hamilton's First Bank of the United States had been necessary and proper, the new Bank was not. Certainly, he said, the power to establish branches all over the country at the will of the Bank's officers was not needed for the BUS to perform the functions the Federal Government needed it to perform. As to the power of this private corporation to enter a state and exercise powers "and privileges possessed by no other *persons, corporations* or *property* in the State," this again seemed an easy question. Maryland's power to tax was the "highest attribute of sovereignty," and Maryland was exercising it to raise revenue, not to restrict the BUS's operations. Too, this bank did not possess any attribute of sovereignty, but was merely a private corporation in business to make money. The United States merely owned shares. Maryland had done nothing that hinted at destroying the BUS branch by taxing it. William Wirt answered for McCulloch that a power to tax could be used to destroy, "and nothing but their own discretion can impose a limit upon this exercise of their authority."

Luther Martin, the attorney general of Maryland and an effective delegate to the Philadelphia Convention, closed for Maryland. An Antifederalist then and a Federalist now, Martin harkened back to ratification days, when he and his then-fellows had warned that the new government's powers would be broadened by construction—when "this apprehension was treated as a dream of distempered jealousy" by Federalists. "We are now called upon," he said, "to apply that theory of interpretation which was then rejected by the friends of the new constitution, and we are asked to engraft upon it powers of vast extent, which were disclaimed by them, and which, if they had been fairly avowed at the time, would have prevented its adoption." "The power of establishing corporations," he concluded matter-of-factly, "is not delegated to the United States."[11] So too with regard to the power of taxation, he recalled that states' power had only been limited in connection with imports and exports, and that "[t]he states would not have adopted the Constitution upon any other understanding."[12]

At last came Pinkney and the speech Justice Story so admired. He began by saying the people, not the states had created the Federal Government. "No state, in its corporate capacity ratified it; but it was proposed for adoption to popular conventions. It springs from the people. . . . The state sovereignties are not the authors of the Constitution of the United States."[13] Unfortunately we have no surviving commentary of any of the counsel for Maryland or the Supreme Court justices on this howler of a claim. Surely all of them knew that Article VII of the Constitution says that "[t]he Ratification of the Conventions of nine States, shall be sufficient for the Establishment of this Constitution between the States so ratifying the Same." If "the States so ratifying the Same" were not "state[s] . . . in their corporate capacit[ies]"—if ratification conventions are not in the federal system standins for the states "in their corporate capacit[ies]"—one could wish we had Pinkney's explanation of what they are. Certainly Luther Martin, the Maryland counsel whose argument he was answering, understood what a ratification convention was in the Constitution's system: it was the sovereign people of its state incarnate. That was why it had power to delegate a state's authority to the new government and to adopt the federal charter's new limitations on state power for its state. Pinkney concluded by reasserting that a state power to tax a federal instrumentality must be disallowed, as it was "a direct interference with the legislative faculty of Congress."

Less than three days after oral argument, Chief Justice Marshall read from the bench his court's explanatory opinion in favor of McCulloch/the Bank of the United States on both of the questions at issue. As R. Kent Newmyer, biographer of both Marshall and Story, described it, Marshall's opinion took as its "foundational proposition . . . that the Constitution was created by the American people and was intended to govern a great nation." He answered Martin and company on the issue of enumeration of powers by saying that, in Newmyer's words, "it was not a legal code encumbered with a 'prolixity' of details that 'could scarcely be embraced by the human mind' and that 'would probably never be understood by the public.'" What powers the Federal Government had would be "deduced from the nature of the objects themselves." Somewhat mischievously he said that "We admit, as all must admit, that the powers of the government are limited, and that its limits are not to be transcended. But we think the sound construction of the constitution must allow to the national legislature that discretion, with respect to the means by which the power it confers are to be carried into execution, which will enable that body to perform the high duties assigned to it, in the manner most beneficial to the people."[14]

In regard to the taxation question, the answer followed naturally: the states might tax their own citizens, but "the only security against the abuse of this power, is found in the structure of the government itself." As Newmyer put it, "[T]he state legislature may tax only its own constituents, and by the same principle is prohibited from taxing citizens of other states and citizens of the United States. . . . the legislature of Maryland could not tax the Bank of the United States because the bank was created by Congress, which represented all the people of all the states."

Perhaps, as John Marshall said in *McCulloch*, the American people "did not design to make their government dependent on the states," but from Virginia would come the argument that they did not design to make the states dependent on the Federal Government either. Judge Spencer Roane told a friend that because Alexander Hamilton's bank had existed for twenty years, "*factum valet fiery non debet* [that thing that should not be done, but is done, is valid] forcibly applies." (According to President Monroe, this was Jefferson's and Madison's position as well.)[15] Marshall went much further than that, however, laying out a very broad justification of claims of implied powers of Congress. The ascendant clique in Richmond, Judge Spencer Roane at its head, would not let that pass.[16]

59

✢ ⊛ ✢

Within months the Virginia General Assembly protested the Supreme Court's performance, insisting that the court's broad reading of congressional powers was "eminently calculated to undermine the pillars of the Constitution itself, and to sap the foundations and rights of the State Governments," and once-and-future senator John Taylor of Caroline began work on his topical book *Construction Construed, and Constitutions Vindicated.*[1] Taylor, the chief Jeffersonian penman/theorist of the 1790s, castigated the Supreme Court for its opinion in *McCulloch v. Maryland.* Since the Supreme Court had allowed the Federal Government unlimited means, Taylor said, the Federal Government would soon be able to pursue whatever ends it wished—thus essentially destroying "the equalities of ends plainly established by the constitution." Taylor saw "an emerging capitalist class gaining special privileges for itself from the central government." He also insisted, as his foremost biographer explains, that "the 'new notion of a constitution by implication' was 'exactly like no constitution at all.'" The gist of Taylor's quarrel with John Marshall (and Joseph Story) was to be found in Taylor's objection to the Supreme Court's idea of the "convenience or necessity of uniformity," the advocacy of which by the judges Taylor analogized to Archbishop Laud's endeavor to impose religious uniformity in England during the reign of Charles I. (Taylor's readers would have known that this precipitated the English Civil War.) In other words, as the Supreme Court worked to homogenize the United States, Taylor stood athwart history, yelling, "Stop!"

Perhaps the most significant immediate Virginian response to *McCulloch,* however, was that the first of two series of anti-*McCulloch* essays began appearing in the *Richmond Enquirer.* That series, under the pen name "Amphictyon," was in the making when, a week after his court issued its opinion, the chief justice got home to Richmond. He soon wrote to brother

Justice Story, "Our opinion in the Bank has roused the sleeping spirit of Virginia—if indeed it ever sleeps." The attack would be characterized by "asperity."[2] To Justice Bushrod Washington, nephew of the general, Marshall confided that "We shall be denounced bitterly in the papers, & as not a word will be said on the other side we shall undoubtedly be condemned as a pack of consolidating aristocratics." Not the case's result but the judges' latitudinarian reasoning would be the target, as the Richmond Junto generally supported the case's outcome. The judges were to be castigated for "our heretical reasoning," which "is pronounced most damnable." The Supreme Court alone would be the target, not the president or Congress, as the latter "have power & places to bestow," and thus "will escape with impunity." The justices, on the other hand, "have nothing to give & . . . nobody is afraid" of them, so they alone would have to absorb the criticism.[3]

Editor Thomas Ritchie's introduction to the first Amphictyon essay included a vow that "Whenever state rights are threatened or invaded, Virginia will not be the last to sound the tocsin" and the statement that "We cannot too earnestly press upon our readers, the following exposition of the alarming errors of the Supreme Court of the United States in their late interpretation of the Constitution." The essay by Virginia General Court Judge William Brockenbrough, another connection of Judge Roane and editor Ritchie, begins with lamentation of the judges' having joined in one opinion without saying whether they all agreed in every bit of its reasoning. It then avers that "[t]here are two principles advocated and decided on by the supreme court, which appear to me to endanger the very existence of state rights. The first is the denial that the powers of the federal government were delegated by the states; and the second is, that the grant of powers to that government, and particularly the grant of powers 'necessary and proper' to carry the other powers into effect, ought to be construed in a liberal, rather than a restricted sense. Both of these principles," Amphyictyon concludes, "tend directly to consolidation of the states. . . ." If Congress exercised all of the power thus granted it, "it is difficult to say how small would be the remnant of power left in the hands of the state authorities."

Amphictyon makes short work of Marshall's claim that the states did not delegate the Federal Government its powers, first noting that answering this question was not necessary to the resolution of the case, so that the court's answer is "not more binding or obligatory than the opinion of any other six intelligent members of the community," then adding that "[t]he opinion is erroneous. The several states did delegate to the federal government its powers, and they are parties to the compact." If the powers of the government came from "the people," then the whole people would have been bound as soon as a majority had consented. Everyone knew that "[t]he constitution was not binding on any state, even the smallest, without its own free and voluntary consent." The states' ongoing existence of course was also the basis, for example, of elections to the House of Representatives. For good measure, he cited (Hamilton's) *Federalist* #28 and the *Virginia Report* of 1798 (aka "Madison's Report").

Amphictyon's second letter discussed the hermeneutical approach the Supreme Court said it would follow.[4] The essay's key point is that "[t]he consequences of giving an enlarged, or what is called a liberal construction to the grant of powers, are alarming to the states and the people." That the Necessary and Proper Clause would be abused in this way—"construed into an unlimited commission to exercise every power, which might be alleged to be necessary to the general welfare"—"its opponents foretold" "whilst the constitution was under discussion." The result would be essentially limitless power in Congress. As we shall see, former president James Madison's evaluation of Marshall's opinion was very similar on this last point.

Chief Judge Roane wrote four *Richmond Enquirer* essays about *McCulloch v. Maryland* under the penname "Hampden"—a name recalling one of the foremost Parliamentary leaders in the English Civil War. Roane said in his first essay, "It has been the happiness of the American people to be connected together in a confederated republic" in which the government "possessed only such [powers] as were expressly granted, or passed therewith as necessary incidents" and the states retained "all the residuary powers."[5] Here Roane brandished his familiarity with the record of the Virginian Ratification Convention of 1788, in which Governor Edmund Randolph, a prominent Philadelphia Convention Framer and Virginia Ratification Convention Federalist, repeatedly responded to Patrick Henry's forecasts that the Necessary and Proper Clause would be read by federal officials as the Supreme Court in the event had read it in *McCulloch* by saying the new government would have only the powers "expressly granted." To be doubly certain the constitution was understood this way, Roane continued, the Tenth Amendment reiterated the point.[6]

Roane next made the 1816 Bank Bill and the 1798 Sedition Act fellow manifestations of the "proneness of all men . . . to feel power and forget right." Marshall's court, unlike Congress, had to answer to no one, and so had undertaken in *McCulloch* to give Congress unlimited means to exercise limited powers. "That man must be a deplorable idiot who does not see that there is no earthly difference between an *unlimited* grant of power," he wrote, "and a grant limited in its terms, but accompanied with *unlimited* means of carrying it into execution." While the Necessary and Proper Clause seemed to Roane to be a limitation of Congress's power, the justices had "expunged those words from the Constitution . . . [by] reading them in a sense entirely arbitrary with the reader." Again alluding to history familiar to all learned Americans—certainly all learned Virginians—of his day, Roane said that if this constitutional language were read as Marshall's court here construed it, "[i]f the limits imposed on the general government . . . are stricken off, they have, *literally*, the power to legislate for us in all cases whatsoever." Here Roane echoed the British Parliament's Declaratory Act of 1766, in which it claimed power to legislate for the colonists "in all cases whatsoever"—which was the very definition of despotism. Once Parliament had responded to the Virginia legislative resolutions of 1765 that made Patrick Henry famous by claiming a right to legislate for the Old Dominion "in all cases whatsoever," all that stood between the colonists and declaring independence was time.

In the balance of his performance as Hampden, Roane showed that Marshall and company were turning the U.S. Constitution into "a nose of wax . . . stretched and contradicted at the arbitrary will and pleasure of those who are entrusted to administer it." In the end this would mean interpretations "by those who, possessing power, will not fail to 'feel it, and forget right.'" He then, as his biographer put it, "cited Madison, Edmund Randolph, Richard Henry Lee, the *Federalist Papers,* the Virginia Resolution of 1799, and his own opinion in *Hunter v. Fairfax* in support of the proposition 'that in the case of an infraction of the constitution, the *states* have a right to interpose and arrest the progress of the evil.' If that right was ever denied, 'the principle on which our independence was established would be violated.'"

Roane sent a copy of his essays to Thomas Jefferson with a letter saying, "The friends of liberty in our Country continue to regard you with veneration and gratitude, for your great & Eminent services:—and your opinion on such a question as this, would be considered as a great authority."[7] The Sage of Monticello, never averse to being complimented, sent the judge a lengthy letter of praise in response—one in which he coined a memorable Jeffersonian phrase.[8]

"I had read in the Enquirer," he began, "and with great approbation the pieces signed Hampden, and have read them again with redoubled approbation in the copies you have been so kind as to send me. I subscribe to every tittle of them. they contain the true principles of the revolution of 1800. for that was as real a revolution in the principles of our government as that of 76. was in it's form; not effected indeed by the sword, as that, but by the rational and peaceable instrument of reform, the suffrage of the people."

However, Jefferson thought he saw that the Federalists perhaps had not been vanquished permanently. "[T]he nation declared it's will," he continued, "by dismissing functionaries of one principle, and electing those of another, in the two branches, executive and legislative, submitted to their election. over the judiciary department," alas, "the constitution had deprived them of their controul. that therefore has continued the reprobated system. . . ." One might have thought that new Supreme Court appointments would have transformed the high tribunal, but no: "altho' new matter has been occasionally incorporated into the old, yet the leaven of the old mass seems to assimilate itself to the new; and after 20. years confirmation of the federated system by the voice of the nation, declared thro' the medium of elections, we find the judiciary o[n] [e]v[ery] occasion, still driving us into consolidation."

The Republicans' guiding light did not agree with Roane's essays completely, he hastened to add. "[I]n denying the right they usurp of exclusively explaining the consti[tu]tion[,] I go further than you do, if I understand rightly your quotation . . . of an opinion that 'the judiciary is the last resort in relation *to the other depart[ments]* of the government, but not in relation to the rights of the parties to the compact under which the judiciary is derived.'" (Here Jefferson referred to the U.S. Constitution.) If that principle were granted, "then indeed is our constitution a complete felo de se. for intending to establish three departments, coordinate and independant, that they might check and balance one another, it has given, according to this opinion, to one of them alone the right to prescribe rules for the government of the others; and to that one too which is unelected by, and independent of, the nation. for experience [(the Chase impeachment acquittal)] has already shown that the impeachment it has provided is not even a scare-crow. . . ." Marshall and his colleagues, Jefferson noted, had come into the habit of casting out theoretical opinions such as *McCulloch* "not belonging to the case often, but sought for out of it, as if to rally the public opinion beforehand to their views, and to indicate the line they are to walk in," without drawing any criticism at all in the House of Representatives—the body with impeachment power. As a result, "the constitution, on this hypothesis, is a mere thing of wax in the hands of the judiciary which they may twist and shape into any form they please." He added that any independent power was absolute.

Jefferson closed by insisting that "each department is truly independent of the others" in interpreting the constitution in cases properly before it, "and especially where it is to act ultimately and without appeal." He gave the examples of his pardons of Sedition Act convicts, his withholding of Marbury's commission—which despite the Supreme Court's decision he deemed incomplete because delivery was "essential to compleat a deed"— and his decision not to submit the Monroe-Pinkney Treaty to the Senate for its ratification, as he thought he could decide not to "confirm" a treaty without involving the Senate. There were also the (perhaps partisan) decisions of a federal judge and the U.S. House of Representatives about the citizenship status of a Republican (judged not a citizen) and a Federalist (deemed a citizen) in similar circumstances "during the federal ascendancy."

As for Roane's implication that Jefferson should take a public stand concerning *McCulloch*, Jefferson said no, he wanted to avoid that. Doing so might undercut support for his ongoing attempt to establish a new public university in the Old Dominion. He did, however, close by saying, "I hope your labors will be long continued . . . , in maintenance of those principles on which I verily believe the future happiness of our country essentially depends," followed by conveyance of "affectionate and great respect."[9]

The letter covering the set of the Hampden essays Roane sent the other Virginian ex-president included the observation that "[n]o man in our Country has done so much as you, in Establishing our present happy system of government, or can feel greater interest in preserving it."[10] The judge knew his mark, and soon enough, a lengthy, thoughtful answer made its way to him from Orange County.[11]

As Madison had called on Congress to create the Second Bank of the United States and signed the legislation doing so into law, Chief Justice Marshall might have thought the Virginian Publius would sympathize with his effort. He would have been mistaken. Referring to Marshall's reading as "latitudinary," Madison said, "It appears to me as it does to you, that the occasion did not call for the general & abstract doctrine interwoven with the decision on the particular case." Like his friend in Albemarle, the fourth president said that rather than laying out a general theory of constitutional legislation under the Necessary and Proper Clause, Marshall ought to have confined himself to the facts at hand. "I have always supposed," Madison said, "that the meaning of a law, and for a like reason, of a Constitution, so far as it depends on Judicial interpretation, was to result from a course of particular decisions, and not these, from a previous and abstract comment on the subject." Marshall had instead "reverse[d] the rule, and . . . forego[ne] the illustration to be derived from a series of cases actually occurring for adjudication." Madison also would have preferred seriatim opinions instead of all of the other justices' silently joining in Marshall's, as the latter meant the public did not know how much force to allow the opinion.

"But what is of most importance," he continued, "is the high sanction given to a latitude in expounding the Constitution, which seems to break down the landmarks intended by a specification of the powers of Congress; and to substitute for a definite connection between means and ends, a legislative discretion as to the former, to which no practical limit can be assigned." Exasperated, he asked, "Is there a Legislative power, in fact, not expressly prohibited by the Constitution, which might not, according to the doctrine of the Court, be exercised as a means of carrying into effect some specified power[?]" In fact, "Does not the Court also relinquish, by their doctrine, all controul on the Legislative exercise of unconstitutional powers? According to that doctrine, the expediency & constitutionality of means for carrying into effect a specified power, are convertible terms; and Congress are admitted to be the judges of the expediency. The Court certainly can not be so; a question, the moment it assumes the character of mere expediency or policy, being evidently beyond the reach of Judicial cognizance." He then gave as a hypothetical example the practice under the French ancien régime of granting monopolies to particular favorites. Doing that would be unconstitutional, Madison reasoned, but now Congress could say this was a means to the end of borrowing money, and voilà! It would be constitutional under the reasoning in *McCulloch*.

Having lodged one apparently fatal practical objection to Chief Justice Marshall's opinion, Madison now reached the most powerful objection to it. "Those who recollect, and still more, those who shared in what passed in the State Conventions, thro' which the people ratified the Constitution, with respect to the extent of the powers vested in Congress, can not easily be persuaded that the avowal of such a rule would not have prevented its ratification." America was unique, Madison said, in that its government had been created popularly and that only the people could alter it, for which provision had been made in the constitution. "It is anxiously to be wished therefore," he concluded, "that no innovations may take place in other modes; one of which would be a constructive assumption of powers never meant to be granted. If the powers granted be deficient, the legitimate source of additional ones is always open, and ought to be resorted to." Thus wrote the author of the Bonus Bill Veto Message—and the man who had signed the bank into being.

Madison added one last federalism-related point before concluding his little treatise on popular constitutionalism. The typical sovereign government must be understood as having all of the powers "necessary or useful," lest the people suffer from its absence. In America, however, though the general government's powers were limited, the state governments' were not, and in fact, "the exercise of [a power] elsewhere [than by the general government] might be preferred by those who alone had a right to make the distribution." The presumption should be that if the people wanted the distribution of powers altered, they would make the alteration by constitutional amendment. Roane agreed, and the dispute between Chief Justice Marshall and his Virginia countrymen had not ended.

I f the Transcontinental Treaty and *McCulloch v. Maryland* were not enough momentous developments for one congressional session, the first weeks of 1819 also saw the beginning of what then and since has been recognized as the first great sectional crisis of the United States. The animating factors are hard to disentangle, but the chronology was simple enough.

House Speaker Henry Clay, receiving a petition for statehood from citizens of the Missouri Territory, referred the petition to a committee. Doubtless he expected this to lead to a pro forma process of acceptance of the newest state into the federal union without any difficulty.

Master of the House though he was, Clay miscalculated. In fairness to Clay, it is hard to see how he could have expected James Tallmadge Jr., then serving what proved to be his only term in the House, to gum up the works in this circumstance. Those who knew Tallmadge from New York were unsurprised, however: though a Republican, Tallmadge had gravitated to Governor DeWitt Clinton's faction of the Republican Party, which generally resented Southern domination of the party and the Federal Government, rather than the opposition "Bucktails," which took the opposite position. That he would propose an end to expansion of slavery across the North American landscape, beginning with Missouri in February 1819, did not surprise them at all.[1]

Tallmadge's proposal had two parts: prohibition of importation of any more slaves into Missouri and emancipation at age twenty-five of any slave born in Missouri after his proposal's adoption. As historian Merrill D. Peterson put it, the Tallmadge amendment "raised serious questions about the constitutional authority of Congress, the nature of the Union, the future of the West, the morality of slavery, and the sectional balance of power."[2]

That the "anti-Missouri" impulse in Congress rested on political considerations came to be a common impression among Southern Republicans. That impression gained strength from the energetic part played in it by Senator Rufus King, F-NY, who had twice been his party's nominee for vice president and once been its presidential candidate. Though King seems to have been authentically opposed to slavery, his biographer concedes in discussing his role in the Missouri controversy that "King's interest in slavery was primarily political." In fact, King had a record of objecting to extension of slavery into new territories in part because of opposition to, as he put it, "the present inequality, arising from the Representation of Slaves."[3]

Speaker Henry Clay shared this sentiment. He even said that he would be happy to see Congress bar slavery and would endorse freeing slaves who entered Missouri—if only Congress had constitutional authority to make such a policy. He denied that it did, however.[4]

The House at first disagreed with the speaker. On February 16, 1819, it passed the part of Tallmadge's amendment banning taking slaves into Missouri, 87–76; congressmen from the North favored the proposal by 86–10, while those from the South opposed it 66–1. Tallmadge's other proposal, that slaves born in Missouri after statehood become free at age twenty-five, passed the House by only 82–78, with Northern congressmen supporting it by 80–14 and Southern ones opposing it 62–2. The Senate ultimately blocked both parts, the first by 22–16 and the second by 31–7. Of particular note is that the ban on introduction of new slaves into Missouri failed by the margin of five Northern senators', including both Illinois senators', votes against their section. When March 4, 1819, came, Tallmadge's House career ended. So too did Missouri's chance of joining the union as a state that year.[5]

That day Representative Ephraim Bateman of New Jersey sent a circular letter—nineteenth-century analogue of congressional junk mail—to his constituents.[6] After describing the Tallmadge Amendment and explaining that the Senate had struck it out, following which the bill had failed in the House, Bateman said he wanted to hear the public's opinion of the matter. As for himself, he said he had thought "that a spirit of gradual emancipation had gone forth" and so was surprised to see extension of slavery into Missouri so vigorously advocated.

Bateman told his constituents that he thought the answer to the question whether Missouri would have slavery would decide the issue for "the whole range of country west of the Mississippi," so that "I cannot but consider it as a question of the greatest magnitude to the interest of humanity that was ever debated in the Congress of the United States." He next explained that he did not see that the treaty with France guaranteeing to people in the Louisiana Territory the rights of other Americans barred Congress from excluding slavery from that territory, as a state would be able to do, and as indeed Congress had banned slavery from the Old Northwest. The popular Southern argument that diffusing slavery across the continent would ameliorate the condition of the slaves and make abolition of slavery in East Coast states more likely, Bateman wrote, "has little force in my mind." Slavery already was legal in the region bounded by Pennsylvania, the Gulf of Mexico, the Atlantic Ocean, and the Ohio and Mississippi Rivers, he noted, adding that this huge space was "surely sufficiently ample for every such purpose." More land for slavery seemed certain to "increase the demand for, and raise the price of slaves," strengthen incentives for smuggling slaves into the United States, "and blight all the hopes of an ultimate final emancipation of that unfortunate race of beings." He concluded by observing that he was "compelled to believe, that the principle of slavery has of late taken still deeper root in some portions of our country" due to the high profits from Southern agricultural products.

During the months between congressional sessions, antislavery organizations trumpeted the success in blocking Missouri statehood and worked to drum up opposition to Missouri statehood, with "innumerable public meetings organized in the Northern states by antislavery groups." Southerners organized their own pro-Missouri gatherings once they realized what their opponents were doing. The December 1819 congressional session, with a narrow House anti-Missouri majority and a substantial pro-Missouri one in the Senate, would belabor the Missouri issue for three months.[7]

President Monroe used the congressional recess to undertake another tour, this time of the South. He had begun preparing for this four-month sojourn at the end of November 1818, when he wrote a friend that "I contemplate a journey in the spring to the [South], as far as Georgia, & thence westward to the Missouri territory, back home thro' Kentucky. I should be happy to descend the Miss[issippi], but fear that it will be too late in the season to admit of it."[8] He could combine his stated military and administrative aims with some matters of personal finance and electoral politics by going to Louisville during this journey, a Kentucky attorney explained to him at the beginning of March.[9] Apparently Monroe at first contemplated following the coast from Washington all the way to New Orleans, but he changed his mind "under the apprehension that the season [would] not permit him to proceed so far along the coast." He and Secretary Calhoun decided to depart on March 29th for Charleston, with Monroe to continue to Georgia before heading west as far as he could, and he expected to return to Washington by July 4th.[10]

Monroe, Calhoun, and the Monroe family set out by steamship on March 30th. "A very heavy gale," thunder, and lightning bade them godspeed.[11] The *City of Washington Gazette* took a sardonic view, however. If Monroe did actually proceed all the way to St. Louis, on "a route of near 3,000 miles," he would hardly have time to take in all of the fortifications, inlets, Indian settlements, military dispositions, and other such sights that it was his stated aim to see. Besides, "he could as well ascertain [what he needed to know about them] by a call on the respective departments, and investigate these various subjects, comfortably seated at his own fire side. . . . [T]he people do not expect or desire such a sacrifice of bodily fatigue from its venerable and respected chief magistrate. We see no national necessity for it."[12]

At Norfolk the presidential party received the same type of welcome as in most places along Monroe's earlier tours. Monroe inspected the intended site of a new naval depot and witnessed the laying of the cornerstone of a new custom house, which culminated in the by-now-customary procession of a band and some musicians and signs of adoration from a large crowd. What made this particular event distinctive was the participation in the procession of the local Masons.[13]

At Roanoke Island, Plymouth, Washington, and other stops in North Carolina, Monroe, Calhoun, and their companions made a good impression on those who came out to see the president. Bands played, politicians read messages of greeting, and the federal officials examined actual or potential military sites. In several places newspapers, diarists, and correspondents commented on "the manners of the President—unostentatious, mild and affable, he unites in his deportment the frank simplicity of a Republican citizen with the dignity which becomes the Chief of a great nation. His manners," the *Edenton Gazette* concluded, "are as well fitted to win affection as his talents to command respect."[14] Monroe had found the sweet spot, it seems, between George Washington's stilted *levées* and the extreme informality with which Thomas Jefferson had offended Minister Merry. As had people he encountered on his northern tour, Southerners saw in Monroe a last living embodiment of the Revolution, as welcoming committees repeatedly mentioned in their oral messages. For his part, the president happily indulged them in recalling those days of what the Plymouth, North Carolina, welcoming committee called "the first dawnings of your manhood." He said to the Carolinians, "The zeal which animated me in that cause, of which you have generously expressed a favorable sentiment, was common to our fellow-citizens," thereby at once denying that he had been anyone special among Continental Army soldiers and subtly underscoring his life-long commitment to the republican cause.[15]

By this point the form of reception of the president and his party into each town he entered had become standard. Monroe's off-the-cuff responses to the addresses he received were similar as well. So, for example, William Alston, South Carolina's largest landowner, lent the president his "elegant barge, which was rowed and steered by a competent number of respect-able masters of vessels (who had volunteered their services) and over which proudly waved the star-spangled banner. As soon as the barge and boat ac-companying it, made their appearance at the entrance of Sampit river [outside coastal Georgetown], a federal salute was fired from field pieces, manned by volunteer citizens." Former congressman Benjamin Huger read Monroe a substantial address at "the house prepared for the President and his suite," in which the most striking passage said:

> The arrival of the fifth President of the United States very naturally recalls to our recollection, a similar visit paid us some twenty years since, by the Father of his country, our beloved and never to be forgotten Washington. At that time the Constitution under which we live was in its infancy. It was his object to conciliate the feelings and reconcile the minds of the citizens to the new Federal Compact just brought into operation under his auspices. His success was complete. . . . You alone of his successors have judged it proper . . . to follow the example, and we fondly anticipate consequences equally beneficial to the community and gratifying to yourself.

A florid account of America's current situation and equally positive words about Monroe's record as soldier, secretary, and president, as well as about his personality, followed. Monroe answered, "I concur in the sentiment which you have expressed, that the example of those to whose virtue and talents we are so much indebted should be the object of our constant atten-tion, and that the very extraordinary services of him, who has been emphati-cally called the father of his country, give him a just claim to that venerated title." He said that he had done his duty under a quite able predecessor and that though of course he admired those who had gone before, America's liberty and prosperity owed most of all to the American people. A feast and toasts followed.[16]

The president may have enjoyed or found some satisfaction in seeing the various elements of the southland's geography. If so, that might have made up for the monotony of one florid address with the same elements as all the rest, to which he felt bound to respond, followed by dinner with various local potentates and, of a Sunday, religious services one after another. One development that may have stood out in his memory was the Charleston, South Carolina City Council's decision to ask that President Monroe sit for a portrait by Samuel F. B. Morse, a prominent portraitist now better known to us as inventor of the telegraph and the eponymous code. Morse brought that request to the president's attention, promising to take no more of his time than was necessary, when the latter had returned to Washington, and the president agreed to see Morse on December 11, 1819. In the end, however, it took Morse several White House visits to complete his work. As he explained to his mother, "He cannot sit more than ten or twenty minutes at a time, so that the moment I feel engaged he is called away again. I set my palette today at ten o'clock and waited until four in the afternoon before he came in. He then sat for ten minutes, and we were called to dinner." Nonetheless the resulting portrait is now in the White House Collection.[17]

Despite his absence from the Old Dominion and the federal capital, Monroe kept tabs on developments in them. His chief agent for this purpose, George Hay, he instructed, "You will . . . attend to the movement of parties, and likewise to public opinion, so as to be able to give me the best advice when we meet." He complained that the Charleston locals' expectations had made it "impossible to quit this place, without offending public opinion, & evidently slighting some objects meriting attention, without devoting to it a full week." Whatever he might think, "The solicitude of the inhabitants to become acquainted with the Ch. Magistrate equalls what I experienced to the Eastward."[18]

Monroe took advantage of a prime opportunity for tamping down party animosity while in Charleston. There General Charles Cotesworth Pinckney, a Philadelphia Convention delegate and past Federalist presidential nominee, besides being a member of one of South Carolina's two leading political dynasties, helped him negotiate the Charleston social scene. "Genl. P.," the president wrote, "participates in the fatigues, which is the more honorable on his part, and friendly to me, as his career is finish'd, being 68 years of age, & having no view to public life." After describing his connections to a number of prominent Pinckneys during and since the Revolution, Monroe noted of General Thomas Pinckney—like nearly all other Pinckneys, a Federalist—that "[h]is services in the late war, while party spirit ran so high, was a proof of the confidence of the govt. & of his patriotism." Monroe thought it would do good for Hay to put "a paragraph" in a newspaper about Monroe's good relations with the Pinckneys. Whatever others might think of it, he explained, "It is an illustration of the principles on which I act." He was "inclined," he said, "to think that such a paragh. would have conciliatory effect, in drawing the country together, shaking the foundation of party animosities, on just principles." "My great object," he closed, "is to bring the country together on just principles. . . ."

The *Charleston Courier* said as the president left town that "We rejoice in the opportunity which has been afforded us, of an interview with the Chief of our Republic; whose modest greatness reminds us of the heroism and the humility of the Ancient Patriots of Rome."[19] As we have seen, the president's manner commonly made this impression on people. A contemporary stranger's physical description of him said, "[T]he present President of the United States is a large and tall man of dark Complexion & blue eyes & a very grave countenance—and in no wise [foppish] but plane. . . . His dress was blue Broadcloth coat & pantaloons, a light coloured waist coat and a common beaver Hat &c."[20]

We may guess that if Monroe had a more impressive hat with him, he wore it in Charleston. Yet the president was at pains to ensure that all had access to him. From the prosperous port town Salem, Massachusetts, came an account of his visit to Charleston saying that

> The reception he has met with, though unostentatious, and conducted in a style far below that of many of our Eastern [meaning northeastern] cities, in point of pomp and magnificence, has given the most ample satisfaction, The Chief Magistrate of the Union has been greeted by his fellow citizens as a man—as a man he has received their civilities. [That is, the president had not been treated as a quasi-deity in the mode of a Turkish sultan, a Russian emperor, or any other such potentate.] Every decent member of society has had, (or could have had) access to him. The rich and poor alike proffered their congratulations, and all were received with the most unaffected simplicity and republicanism of manner.[21]

People in several towns on this tour, as on his prior ones, came away with similar impressions.

61

◦╪◦ ◈ ◦╪◦

T he wide distribution of newspapers such as the *National Intelligencer* led to pervasive knowledge of the major outlines of political debate in Washington during the Monroe administration. One aspect of common knowledge was awareness throughout the country of the form that welcomes of the president to new towns on his way took during his initial tour through the northern United States. This must account for appointment in virtually every town he visited of a local committee to handle his accommodations and organize local activities, presentation of a formal welcome message by some local leader(s), provision of one of the nicest houses in town for Monroe to stay in by one of the town's leading citizens, etc.—just as in Baltimore, Philadelphia, New York, and Boston. That the pattern, once established, was followed virtually everywhere did not mean that everyone liked it. One Lexington, Kentucky, citizen put it this way:

> Indeed we should feel mortified were he to pass through without respectful notice. But we do not think it will add to his happiness—nor reflect any peculiar credit on the town—to make a military parade—and march out to escort him to the lodgings provided for him. If any escort were necessary, a few citizens could meet and welcome him. It ought to be remembered that Lexington was not silent on the subject of the pomp displayed, when Mr. Monroe made his eastern tour. If all the arrangements of the committee are executed, our citizens will hereafter be compelled to seal their lips, with regard to show and ostentation.[1]

"Republican" of Savannah took exception to some of the festivities associated with the president's progress.[2] "I regret very much," he said, "both for [the president's] own sake and for the republican character of the country, that he deviated from his first resolution of receiving no attentions during his military survey." Because "[i]t is usually the case that when great men visit cities, the rich encircle them so closely and attentively, that the rest of the community are kept off," it ought to be understood as "the duty of our public functionaries to prevent this in the present case, and shew that we have some republican ideas among us." When the public meeting to plan the visit resolved that "inasmuch as the public squares form a conspicuous part in the ornament of our city, that it be recommended to council to have the work shops erected thereon removed, and the rubbish taken away previous to the arrival of the president,"[3] "An Observer" (sounding very much like "Republican") objected in the same newspaper, "That part of the report of the committee of the citizens . . . wherein it is recommended to remove the workshops erected on the squares, seems particularly injudicious. Will it offend the eyes of the President to see the shops of busy artificers even in the heart of our city, or will it not afford an occasion rather to remind him that it is an evidence of our thriving condition?" If he were a king, clearing the way of whatever might "offend the fastidious eye of royalty" might be appropriate, but it was entirely inapt to do so in preparation for the visit of a republican chief executive.[4] The following week the same paper carried an essay by "Americanus" saying, among other things, that, as the city's preparations proceeded, "There is something republican in the stile [sic] of the bower, and I am satisfied that it will be more pleasing to him than the gaudy expensive frippery which has been exhibited to him in many of the cities through which he has passed."[5] In the event these pseudonymous penmen had their expectations concerning Monroe's tastes borne out when he rejected the offer of "a superb barouche" to carry him from the wharf to his assigned lodgings, opting instead to ride atop a horse.[6] At the public dinner held for him in Savannah, Monroe gave a short talk in which the central point was the significance of the services given to the country by his predecessors, three of them still living and rightly following the example "of him, who was, deservedly, first called to this high station." His audience must have noticed that he made no party distinction among the four, which clearly reflected Monroe's desire to see party distinctions fade away.[7] People noticed once again that "[t]he rich and the poor alike proffered their congratulations, and all were received with the most unaffected simplicity and republicanism of manner."[8]

Monroe went further than merely mixing comfortably with both rich and poor. On May 25, 1819, and a few nights before, the president stayed in houses between Athens and Spring Place, Georgia, owned by Cherokee chief Joseph Vann—the second night with Vann. Apparently this was an unplanned result of very bad weather en route.[9] At Brainerd Mission, Tennessee, Monroe expressed his strong endorsement of the Indian school in this Cherokee Nation location. "He looked at the buildings & farm," the American Board of Commissioners for Foreign Missions' *Brainerd Journal* says, "visited the school, & asked questions in the most unaffected & familliar manner: & was pleased to express his approbation of the plan of instruction; particularly as the children were taken into the family, taught to work &c. He thought this the best, & perhaps the only way to civilise & christianise the Indians: and assured us he was well pleased with the conduct & improvement of the children."[10] Soon after this Monroe wrote to Cherokee agent Return J. Meigs, "I am much pleased with the progress made in instructing the Indian youth, & have no doubt that in this mode, that is, by acting on the youthful mind, the nation, & other nations, may be civilized." He instructed Meigs to forward considerable money for construction of new buildings at the school, and Chief John Ross noted happily that Monroe's endorsement "was highly gratifying to the Mission Family as well as to the Nation."[11]

The hard weather having slowed his progress considerably, particularly in Cherokee country, Monroe decided by mid-June not to go as far west as Missouri, but rather to turn back toward Washington at Nashville. He hoped this was necessary because the Spanish treaty should have arrived at the capital by the time he got there, even after a truncated trip.[12] He wrote to Secretary Adams on July 5th that he would set out from Lexington for his Albemarle County, Virginia home, where he hoped to find his wife and daughters, the next day, and so Adams should have the rest of the Cabinet ready for the president's return.[13]

A week after that Monroe sat for yet another portrait in Danville, Kentucky. The portraitist, Asa Park, did that kind of work in central Kentucky. According to the local newspaper, Monroe dubbed this painting, in the journalist's words, "the most admirable likeness ever taken of him."[14] As the portrait is lost, we are left to decide whether the president was more likely being candid in his appraisal or being congenial in his flattery.

Throughout the trip Monroe made a point of attending religious services—sometimes twice—on Sundays.[15] He also repeatedly encountered Masonic groups anxious to make a public show of welcoming him as a brother Mason. Of course Monroe had made no secret of his membership, but instead had, for example, publicly participated in Masonic ceremony at the groundbreaking for the first building on the grounds of the University of Virginia. Still, southern Masons wanted this point called to countrymen's attention.[16]

When Monroe got back to Washington, D.C., a local paper calculated that he had been gone for "upwards of nineteen weeks."[17] Adams said Calhoun had come to his house after dinner, at which point they "rode to the president's house. We found him returned from his Journey," the secretary continued. "He is in good health, though much exhausted by a journey of 5000 Miles all South of this Latitude, and almost all in Summer."[18]

What awaited Monroe upon his return to Washington, besides his two chief Cabinet advisors, was yet another welcoming committee prepared to present a lengthy address. (Imagine his delight.) It praised the president for the "personal intercourse with your fellow citizens, and interchange of sentiments, which has marked your course through the country." Together they had fostered greater popular confidence in the government and unity "in feelings and opinions" than ever before. Too, "[h]aving passed through a populous portion of the Indian country, to which civilization and letters have, by the humane policy of our government, in some degree, extended their blessings, as well as amongst other tribes yet enveloped in the wretchedness of their primitive barbarism," Monroe was "enabled to appreciate the value of what has been done, and to apply, with an enlightened judgment, the means which are, or may be, placed in your hands by the public liberality. We are called upon by all the considerations of humanity and justice to cherish and to protect, not to annihilate, those untutored and suffering, but high-minded wanderers of the forest, once lords of the fair land which we now enjoy." Besides that, the committee concluded, "It is now . . . a settled conviction with all reflecting men, that the immovability of the seat of government is closely connected with the integrity of our Union." Monroe replied that he would happily enforce Congress's laws for the promotion of Indians' "civilization and happiness" and that there was but one opinion concerning the future of Washington, D.C., as America's capital.[19]

James Monroe's Third Annual Message went to Capitol Hill on December 7, 1819.[20] He began by saluting Congress for its return to conducting business in the Capitol—more than five years since the invaders departed. He then launched into a lengthy discussion of His Catholic Majesty's omission to ratify the Transcontinental Treaty agreed by Adams and Onís, which he described as giving Spain significant benefits in exchange for title to lands it no longer effectively controlled anyway, concluding in an intimation that America would be justified in unilaterally putting the treaty into operation— that is, among other things, in proceeding to take possession of the territories America was to gain by operation of the treaty. America, Monroe said (indirectly but clearly), could seize substantial property from Spain. "An ample field for ambition is open before [the United States], but such a career is not consistent with the principles of their Government nor the interests of the nation." As Spain "was bound to ratify" the treaty, "it is submitted to the consideration of Congress whether it will not be proper for the United States to carry the conditions of the treaty into effect in the same manner as if it had been ratified by Spain." "We must," the president insisted, "have peace on a frontier where we have been so long disturbed; our citizens must be indemnified for losses so long since sustained, and for which indemnity has been so unjustly withheld from them." Still he recommended that Congress empower the president to put the treaty into effect as soon as Spain's delegate explaining the holdup arrived. He communicated the treaty and supporting documents to Congress, saying that while the United States had remained neutral toward the revolutions in various Spanish New World colonies, it seemed obvious that Spain eventually would have to concede their independence.

Next, in the economic section of the address, Monroe explained diminution of American trade by reference to American banks' having to call in their loans due to lack of specie. He also thought that American manufactures should be encouraged by continued tariff protection. Despite these problems progress in construction of naval fortifications continued. In closing the president lamented the recent passing of Commodore Oliver H. Perry, naval hero of the Battle of Lake Erie in 1813, who had coined the immortal rallying cry "Don't Give Up the Ship!" Any such reminder of American military glory during the Jeffersonian era would of course tend to redound to the political benefit of President Monroe, the one Jeffersonian president who had been a soldier—and an authentic war hero besides.

Adams described a development that provides us some insight into Monroe's political skills. The new Congress that met in December 1819 would have to organize itself, which would involve first of all the selection of a House speaker. Several congressmen sounded out the president on the idea of replacing Clay. Monroe could be expected to support this move, as Clay had made a point of making himself an impediment to several of the administration's leading initiatives. Too, Clay's "inability" to rendezvous with Monroe during his trip through Kentucky had struck one and all as a public snub. Monroe refused to assist in this replacement effort, however, saying, "First, it would be giving Mr. Clay more consequence than belongs to him." Next, Clay's obstructionism actually had damaged Clay's public image. "If it should be necessary to put him down," Monroe continued, "let it be done by his constituents." Besides, as the Cabinet included no one from the West, it would be bad politics for the president to be seen to thwart Clay. "It would be best," then, Monroe concluded, "to leave him in his chair." Adams was persuaded.[21]

President Monroe from an early point in this session decided he would insist on what now is called the "Equal Footing Doctrine" in the ongoing Missouri dispute: that Missouri, like all of the other states before it, must be admitted to the Union "on an equal footing with the original States in all respects whatever,"[22] and thus left to decide for itself the question of slavery within its own borders, as all the states before it had been. The draft veto message the president prepared in case the Tallmadge Amendment were passed relied chiefly on this principle. He also asked what would happen in case the slave population were confined to the states in which slavery already existed, leading white population to flee them. He averred that "diffusion"— spreading the slave population of the country across more of its territory— would not only ameliorate slaves' condition but also facilitate abolition.[23]

Meanwhile Monroe's confidential advisor and son-in-law George Hay took up his pen in behalf of the administration's cause. Hay took an opportunity presented by an attack on American slaveholders by the *Edinburgh Review,* published in Scotland but widely read among American men of letters, for some sectional self-absolution. It took some gall for Scots to blame Americans for slavery, said Hay, when in reality, "[s]lavery was introduced into America, our America, by you; by the merchants and traders of Great Britain." Not only that, but "the people of Virginia . . . claim the merit of having done their best to oppose it." (Virginians reading this, at least, would have recalled repeated colonial efforts during the Imperial Crisis to impose taxes on slave imports so onerous as virtually to prohibit them— which Jefferson had made famous in "A Summary View of the Rights of British America.")[24]

The president asked Hay to take up his pen again. "A paper showing that Congress have no right to admit into the union any new state on a different footing from the old, written with ability and moderation, would be eminently useful, if published immediately," he counseled. Hay replied that he expected his two essays on the subject to appear in Ritchie's *Richmond Enquirer* soon. Monroe confided that he hoped the opponents of Missouri statehood in Congress would indulge the South a bit. During the Revolution and after, Southerners had gone "the full length with our northern brethren" in relation to slavery's confinement, Monroe said in recollection of Virginians' leading role in adopting the Northwest Ordinance, but "[w]e have since had experience, and we expect, as we are equally attached to liberty with them, of which that fact is proof, that they will show some regard for our peculiar situation."[25]

Likely unaware that Monroe was coaching Hay concerning what to include in a sequence of *Richmond Enquirer* essays on the Missouri Crisis, Secretary Adams on January 8, 1820, made a lengthy, gloomy entry in his diary.[26] After going through the reasons why he judged the United States' foreign relations to one degree or another unsatisfactory with every country, New World and Old, that came to mind, the secretary of state mentioned various domestic matters that also were contributing to his state of disquietude. Did the president share his appraisal of things—which seemed to augur that his unprecedentedly placid first term would be succeeded by a stormy second one?

Adams wrote that in response to his reference to "the Missouri Slave Question," Monroe said "he apprehended no great danger from that—He believed a compromise would be found and agreed to, which would be satisfactory to all parties." Characteristically the secretary "did not enquire further, though I was much surprized at this remark—All the public appearances are directly the reverse," he continued, "and either there is an underplot in operation upon this subject of which I had no suspicion, or the President has a very inadequate idea of the real state of that controversy." His suspicious character led him to add "or he assumed an air of tranquility concerning it in which there was more caution than candour, more reserve than sincerity."

62

✦ ⊛ ✦

Two days later Monroe wrote to his son-in-law explaining his own views on the ongoing Missouri dispute. For his part, he held to the Equal Footing Doctrine. "The Eastern people [meaning New England congressmen], who are so much pressed by their constituents, who have been moved by political men, for purposes of personal aggrandizement, want some ground on which to justify them in a measure of accommodation, to their constituents." (Note Monroe's idea that New England congressmen were being pressed by their constituents, that is, would not otherwise so stoutly have pushed the position they were taking.) These congressmen, he explained, went on the theory that the Equal Footing Doctrine came into force only when a territory became a state. Prior to that, Congress could, for example, exclude slavery, "leaving the state free, to admit it, after it becomes one." Such members were ready, "as I am told," to admit Missouri to the Union with slavery while preparing to take antislavery steps in regard to the remainder of the Louisiana Territory north of "the northern boundary of that state." Monroe asserted to Hay that he took "of course no part in these concerns," of which we can be skeptical, but added that he was "inclined to think that a difference exists in the two cases" (meaning between Congress's power in relation to a territory and Congress's power in relation to a state). In closing Monroe praised Hay's pro-Southern columns in the *Enquirer,* which Monroe believed had clarified things for "the south and west, by arguments which have been much felt to the East and North, without producing any irritation."[1]

Secretary Adams must be counted among those whose sentiments were severely shaken by the Missouri Crisis. His subsequent career would be notably shaped by it. He lamented that "the superior ability of the Slavery party" was apt to carry its preferred policies through Congress. "With the exception of Rufus King," he wrote, "there is not in either house of Congress a member from the free States, able to cope in powers of the mind, with

William Pinkney or James Barbour—In the House of Representatives the freemen have none to contend on equal terms either with John Randolph or Clay. . . ." Besides that, he continued, "The slave men have indeed a deeper immediate stake in the issue," while "their antagonists['] . . . only individual interest in this case arises from its bearing on the balance of political power, between North and South." One sees here that Adams's account provides ammunition neither to the "it was about principle" nor to the "it was about political power" side of the historians' argument, as he says it was both.[2] On February 6, 1820, Senator Barbour wrote an important figure in the Virginia General Assembly, Charles Yancey, informing him that he and Virginia's other U.S. senator, James Pleasants, intended to support the Thomas Amendment, which would prohibit slavery from the rest of the Louisiana Territory north of 36° 30′ latitude. Monroe and his Cabinet were also going to opt for this rather than endanger the Union.[3]

No doubt to the surprise of President Monroe and Senator Barbour, Yancey replied that his passing Barbour's letter around among fellow state legislators on the day before the scheduled Virginia presidential caucus "caused a high excitement here," as a large House of Delegates majority was "for risking consequences" rather than accepting Thomas's compromise proposal. Yancey wrote back telling Barbour that he should oppose the compromise "if you wish to speak the voice of our present legislature" (which, remember, in those pre–Seventeenth Amendment days elected Virginia's U.S. senators) and that the presidential caucus scheduled for that evening would likely be postponed. "It is said by many," he wrote, "that the President and others in power think more of their *situations,* than the best interest of the people whose rights are involved in the Missouri questions—harsh expressions are used in relation to you all." When the caucus met on February 9th, it adjourned until February 17th, and Yancey said that if Monroe advocated the compromise, "we will show him that we are for principles and not men." The next issue of the *Richmond Enquirer* held secession preferable to capitulation on what the editor called this point of principle.[4]

Barbour, for one, had his "principles" too, and one of them was fidelity to the Union—which he believed could well fall apart if a compromise was not reached.[5] As he wrote to James Madison on February 10th, "The Missouri question in its consequences threatens the tranquility if not the dissolution of the Union. Altho in the Senate we have a large majority against restriction yet in the House of Representatives the majority is decidedly the other way. And upon the exclusion of Slavery from the territories there is a Majority in both Houses." After describing the Thomas Amendment, the senator said "every Member of the administration" supported it, as did Clay, but "King & Otis" (he of Hartford Convention fame) wished "to keep open the question for purposes it is unnecessary to State," and "many also of our Southern Brethren," including in the Virginia legislature, seemed apt to oppose any compromise. Barbour feared failure to resolve this question along compromise lines would mean Maine statehood, exclusion of Missouri and the rest of the Louisiana Territory, and election of Rufus King or DeWitt Clinton as the next president. He prayed Madison give him advice. Oddly Madison replied that in case there was to be a partition of the remaining Louisiana Territory lands, it ought to depend on "the estimated proportions in which the common property was paid for by the two descriptions of owners" (slaveholding and non-slaveholding).[6]

Six days later the Senate voted 23–21 to join the Maine and Missouri statehood bills. The day after that Thomas's amendment passed the Senate 34–10, and the Maine-Missouri bill, with the 36° 30′ provision, passed 24–20. Slave state senators supported both bills strongly.[7] When the issue got to the House, Clay separated the bill into three parts: Missouri with slavery, Maine statehood, and a 36° 30′ line. One authority notes that although most of what was left of the Louisiana Purchase Territory looked uncongenial to slavery anyway, this agreement made annexation of Texas more likely—even if it required a war to obtain it. He also notes that the lingering memory of the Missouri Crisis likely undercut prospects for congressional support for Clay's active-government program of a national bank, protective tariffs, and internal improvements—which he ultimately dubbed "The American System"—among Virginians now more apt to sympathize with the Old Republican constitutional position.[8]

The Missouri Crisis had other significant fallout. For example, John Quincy Adams recorded in his diary a momentous conversation with John C. Calhoun on the general question of the likely outcome should Congress reject Missouri's application for statehood with a pro-slavery constitution.[9] Calhoun told him that

he did not think it would produce a dissolution of the Union, but if it should the South would be from necessity compelled to form an Alliance Offensive and Defensive with Great Britain. . . . I asked him whether he thought, if by the effect of this alliance offensive and defensive, the population of the North should be cut off from its natural outlet upon the Ocean, it would fall back upon its rocks bound hand and foot to starve, or whether it would not retain its powers of locomotion, to move Southward by Land. Then he said they would find it necessary to make their communities all military. I pressed the conversation no farther, but if the dissolution of the Union should result from the Slave question, it is as obvious as any thing that can be foreseen of futurity, that it must shortly afterwards be followed by the universal emancipation of the Slaves.

In the full flush of his foreign ministry's enormous success, Adams ruminated that in this case, "[a] dissolution at least temporary of the Union as now constituted would be certainly necessary. . . . The union might then be reorganized, on the fundamental principle of emancipation." Perhaps envisioning the career in which his life would end, he concluded, "This object is vast in its compass—awful in its prospects, sublime and beautiful in its issue. A life devoted to it would be nobly spent or sacrificed."

Meanwhile Monroe confided to former president Jefferson, "I have never known a question so menacing to the tranquility and even the continuance of our Union as [the Missouri issue]. All other subjects have given way to it, & appear to be almost forgotten." It seemed likely, however, that slavery would be prohibited north of 36° 30´ latitude and permitted south of it, "Missouri & Arkansas, as is presum'd, to be admitted, without restraint." Congress seemed about to ban slavery in those territories after statehood as well as before, concerning which he told his friend, "Many think that the right [of Congress] exists in one instance & not in the other"—that is, that Congress could ban slavery in a territory, but not in a state.[10] As we have seen, this was the president's position.

John Randolph of Roanoke voted with the majority on March 2nd so that he could make a motion to reconsider. When he made that motion, Speaker Clay twice ruled him out of order. At last Clay announced that he did not have the bill, which had already been signed by him and taken to the Senate by the House clerk. This underhanded maneuver was referred to by Adams as "an outrage" and "an unprincipled artifice." From that point the rancor between the speaker and the Virginian would build and build.[11]

It was in the wake of the final Missouri vote that Randolph sneeringly described Northern congressmen supportive of the Southern position on Missouri as "scared of their own doe faces—yes, they were scared at their own doe faces! We had *them*," he said, "and if we had wanted *three* more, we could have had them: yes, and if *these had failed, we could have three more of these men, whose conscience, and morality, and religion, extend to 'thirty-six degrees and thirty minutes north latitude.'* Thus were "Northern men with Southern principles" branded with the sobriquet by which they have been known ever since (though the spelling changed in the retelling).[12]

Monroe signed the Missouri Compromise into law on March 6th.[13] Ever careful, Monroe before signing it exercised for the first time his constitutional power to require written opinions of his Cabinet officers, and on two questions: whether Congress could ban slavery from a territory, and whether the Thomas Amendment (establishing the 36° 30′ line) would apply once all or part of the region in question became a state. All agreed that the answer to the first question was yes, though Adams took some pleasure in observing that Crawford, Calhoun, and Wirt (all Southerners) had been unable to locate any "express power to that effect given in the Constitution, and Wirt declared himself very decidedly against the admission of any implied powers." Thus, he said, had "[t]he progress of this discussion . . . totally merged in passion all the reasoning faculties of these Slave-holders, that these Gentlemen in the simplicity of their hearts had come to a conclusion in direct opposition to their premises, without being aware or conscious of inconsistency." John Randolph of Roanoke had highlighted this objection in the House, but the Southern Cabinet members' "compromise measured by their own principles is a sacrifice of what they hold to be the Constitution."[14]

Adams angrily described his own reading of the Constitution, which most certainly did include taking the Territories Clause to mean that Congress could exclude slavery. "What can be more needful [in that clause's terms] to the establishment of Justice [he here refers to the Constitution's Preamble], than the interdiction of Slavery where it does not exist." He also thought the answer to Monroe's second question was yes, ". . . because by its interdiction in the Territory, the People when they come to form a Constitution, would have no right to sanction Slavery." To Crawford's assertion in Cabinet discussion that a state's legislature might, whatever had been its law during the territorial stage, pass a law establishing slavery, Adams replied that "The Declaration of Independence, not only asserts the natural liberty of all men, and their unalienable right to Liberty; but that the only *just* powers of government are derived from the consent of the governed. A power for one part of the people to make slaves of the other can never be derived from consent," he concluded, "and is therefore not a just power." To Crawford's observation that this was Senator King's position, Adams replied that it was King's and his, and "was an opinion universal in the States where there are no Slaves." One supposes that Adams thought of both his father's and Samuel Adams's roles in creating the Declaration of Independence and of their roles in abolition of slavery in Massachusetts as he made these arguments. Perhaps Calhoun, educated at Tapping Reeve's Litchfield Law School after graduating from Yale, thought of them as well.

Adams's diary entry for this day makes clear that the Equal Footing Doctrine seemed, as it applied to new states' legislative power in relation to slavery, morally unacceptable. He therefore concluded it was invalid. In response to Crawford's assertion that, for example, the Northwest Ordinance did not bind the states it had governed while territories, he wrote, "It was sickening to my Soul to hear the assertion," but he decided not to argue the point in the Cabinet, as doing so would only have divided that body as the two houses of Congress had been divided over Missouri. Doing so was not pertinent to consideration of the questions the president had asked. After another round of observations along these lines, Monroe interceded to say that he agreed with Adams "that the Rules and Regulations, which Congress were authorised to make for the territories, must be understood as extending to their inhabitants—And he recurred to the history of the Northwest Territory." We know that Adams put his diary to no contemporary political use on this point—which seems to make his account trustworthy.

At the conclusion of this discussion, Adams told Monroe that although he wanted brief opinions, Adams's isolation in regard to the second question meant he would have to explain his reasoning in his written opinion. Calhoun said he "thought it exceedingly desirable that no such argument should be drawn up and deposited." He asked Monroe whether Question 2 could be changed to, "whether the 8th Section of the Bill was consistent with the Constitution?" The other members of the Cabinet could answer in the affirmative on the ground that it only applied during the territorial phase, while Adams could answer in the affirmative without thinking the section's import so circumscribed. Monroe agreed, and so did Adams. Adams said that Crawford's ceaseless maneuvering for the presidency had led him to support parties in Indiana, Ohio, and Illinois pushing to open those states to slavery.

As if this were not significant enough activity for one day, Adams on departing from the Cabinet meeting fell into walking home with Calhoun. Recall that on meeting Calhoun when he first arrived in America upon returning from Russia, Adams had found the Carolinian the most clearheaded, capable, and frank of his colleagues by far and that he expressed similar assessments thereafter. This stroll would perhaps influence American history as much as the months of debate in Congress over Missouri that had led to the Cabinet meeting. On their way Calhoun told Adams that "the principles, which I had avowed were just and noble; but that in the Southern Country, whenever they were mentioned, they were always understood as applying only to white men."[15] According to Adams, Calhoun went on to explain that "[d]omestic labour was confined to the blacks, though other types of labor were open to whites as well." "He himself," Adams wrote, "had often held the plough—So had his father—Manufacturing and mechanical labour, was not degrading—It was only manual labour—the proper work of slaves—No white person could descend to that—And it was the best guarantee to equality among the whites."

Adams said he told Calhoun, "I could not see things in the same light—It is in truth all perverted sentiment—mistaking labour for Slavery, and dominion for Freedom—The discussion of this Missouri question has betrayed the secret of their Souls—In the abstract they admit that slavery is an evil. . . . But when probed to the quick upon it they show at the bottom of their Souls, pride and vain-glory in their very condition of masterdom. . . ." Among the absurdities Adams identified as flowing from slave-owning were that "[t]hey fancy themselves more generous and noble hearted than the plain freemen who labour for subsistence—They look down upon the simplicity of a yankey's manners because he has no habits of overbearing like theirs, and cannot treat negroes like dogs." Slave masters' reason, their logic, their very Christianity were perverted by the institution, he held, and even as they blamed Britain for inflicting slavery upon them, they "at the same time . . . burn at the Stake, negroe's convicted of crimes. . . ." In short this discussion led Adams to conclude that "the bargain between Freedom and Slavery contained in the Constitution of the United States is morally and politically vicious—Inconsistent with the principles upon which alone our revolution can be justified. . . . The consequence has been that this Slave representation has governed the Union." Perhaps, he concluded, it would have been wiser "to have persisted in the restriction upon Missouri, till it should have terminated in a Convention of the States to revise and amend the Constitution. This would have produced a new Union of thirteen or fourteen States, unpolluted with Slavery. . . . If the Union must be dissolved, Slavery is precisely the question upon which it ought to break."

63

✦ ❀ ✦

As it turned out, the political establishment had not heard the last of Missouri. As soon as it had the chance, Missouri adopted a constitution banning immigration of blacks into the state and denying the state legislature the power to free slaves without masters' consent.[1] Henry Clay in the House appointed a committee that proposed a resolution for Missouri's admission to the Union with the requirement "that the said state shall never pass any law preventing any description of persons from coming to or settling in the said state, who are now or may hereafter become citizens of any of the states of this union," which the territorial legislature of Missouri would have to assent to before statehood. A Connecticut representative observed that this meant Missouri's legislature was agreeing not to do something its constitution required it to do. The resolution failed 80–83 on the third reading, with John Randolph of Roanoke and two other Southerners joining the Northern majority. Reintroduced by Clay the next day, the bill failed of approval again, 82–88.[2]

The presidential election of 1820, meanwhile, proved to be the least divisive, indeed virtually the least popular, in American history. Incumbent James Monroe received all but one electoral vote, including even that of Massachusetts elector John Adams. The one dissident, New Hampshire's William Plumer, who had been too ill to meet with Monroe on the president's trip through New England, explained that Monroe's economic policies displeased him, Monroe had "conducted, as president, very improperly," and the president had "not that weight of character which his office requires."[3] Turnout was a mere 10.1 percent, second lowest in American history behind only the election of 1792 (when George Washington too had run without major opposition).[4]

On February 14, 1821, the House and Senate met to count electoral votes. The Senate considered Missouri as already a state, while the House did not.

Unable to work out a common approach, a joint committee decided that each would read its set of electoral votes. "The President of the Senate then proceeded to make proclamation of the election of Mr Monroe & Tompkins, when he was interrupted by Floyd and Randolph, who enquired whether the votes of Missouri had been counted. . . . He however at length said that he could answer no questions, & had nothing to do but declare the election. . . ." This repeated itself, there were cries of "order," Clay ordered them to be seated, and eventually the Senate retired from the House chamber. Historian Robert Pierce Forbes finds this odd, as, though Virginians, Floyd and Randolph had been vociferous opponents of the Thomas Amendment, and Randolph in particular had long been a loud critic of slavery. Devotion to states' rights, Forbes says, cannot explain this; rather he attributes it to "a refusal to countenance official sanction of slavery combined with a deep-seated fear of the consequences of tampering with it." Congress should, in this view, not discuss the issue at all.[5]

Congress resolved the new Missouri issue—reached a "second Missouri Compromise"—by agreeing to Clay's new language that the Missouri Constitution's provision for laws barring entry of free blacks "shall never be construed to authorize the passage of any law . . . by which any citizen, of either of the states in this Union, shall be excluded from the enjoyment of any of the privileges and immunities to which such citizen is entitled under the constitution of the United States." Each side could read this as giving it what it wanted, and so on February 26, 1821, the House voted to remove the restriction on Missouri's admission to the union.[6]

If Secretary of State Adams's thinking had been powerfully altered—his attention forevermore drawn to the slavery issue, and his impression of the South and Southerners changed permanently—in the course of the Missouri Crisis, his response to these momentous events was not shared by all. Secretary of War John C. Calhoun thought the idea that a contest for mastery between the North and the South had commenced with the Missouri Crisis mistaken, except for a few Northerners "found almost wholly in New York, and the mid[d]le States." Most proponents of slavery restriction he found "actuated by a variety of motives." "Very few indeed look to emancipation," he thought. Southerners needed to resist the idea of "a conspiracy either against our property, or just weight in the Union. A belief of the former might, and probably would, lead to the most disastrous consequence. Nothing would lead more directly to disunion with all of its horrors. That of the latter, would coöperate, as it appears to me, directly with the scheme of the few designing men of the North, who think they see their interest

in exciting a struggle between the two portions of our country." Southerners must not succumb to this temptation. Systematic Southern opposition
to the North would lead "to a similar opposition to us. Our true system,"
he concluded, "is to look to the country; and to support such measures and
such men, without regard to sections, as are best calculated to advance the
general interest." If there be virtue and intelligence enough in the populace,
"those individuals and sections of the country, who have the most enlightened and devoted zeal to the common interest must have also the greatest
influence." Emancipation would be resisted then, he said, but let us not
jump to hasty conclusions about others' goals. Calhoun wanted to hold
off on "resist[ance]," he wrote a Georgia U.S. senator, until emancipation
clearly had become the goal sought "not by a few, but of a large portion of
the non slave holding States."[7] As his most recent biographer summarizes
Calhoun's thinking at this time, "his description of the way politics should
work and his faith that the American people could get it right despite a few
designing politicians are strikingly idealistic."[8]

Not all Southerners were so sanguine. Perhaps the most famous response
to the unexpected sectional confrontation over slavery in Missouri came
from that greatest of Republican penmen, former president Thomas Jefferson. To the leading Maine District politician of the era, Jefferson wrote of
the ongoing crisis:

> I had for a long time ceased to read newspapers or pay any attention to pub-
> lic affairs, confident they were in good hands, and content to be a passenger
> in our bark to the shore from which I am not distant. but this momentous
> question, like a fire bell in the night, awakened and filled me with terror. I
> considered it at once as the knell of the Union. it is hushed indeed for the
> moment. but this is a reprieve only, not a final sentence. a geographical line,
> coinciding with a marked principle, moral and political, once conceived and
> held up to the angry passions of men, will never be obliterated; and every
> new irritation will mark it deeper and deeper.

Having thus introduced the general subject, he turned to the obvious
question of his own ownership of slaves—and his yearning to be relieved of it:

> I can say with conscious truth that there is not a man on earth who would
> sacrifice more than I would, to relieve us from this heavy reproach, in any
> *practicable* way. the cession of that kind of property, for so it is misnamed,
> is a bagatelle which would not cost me a second thought, if, in that way, a

general emancipation and *expatriation* could be effected: and, gradually, and with due sacrifices, I think it might be.

Then came the climax:

but, as it is, we have the wolf by the ear, and we can neither hold him, nor safely let him go. justice is in one scale, and self-preservation in the other. of one thing I am certain, that as the passage of slaves from one state to another would not make a slave of a single human being who would not be so without it, so their diffusion over a greater surface would make them individually happier and proportionally facilitate the accomplishment of their emancipation; by dividing the burthen on a greater number of co-adjutors.

At last, Jefferson offered a prescription:

an abstinence too from this act of power would remove the jealousy excited by the undertaking of Congress; to regulate the condition of the different descriptions of men composing a state. this certainly is the exclusive right of every state, which nothing in the constitution has taken from them and given to the general government.

Having considered this issue, Jefferson thought of the larger implications before concluding, characteristically, that all would turn out as he preferred even if nothing were done about it now:

I regret that I am now to die in the belief that the useless sacrifice of themselves, by the generation of '76. to acquire self government and happiness to their country, is to be thrown away by the unwise and unworthy passions of their sons, and that my only consolation is to be that I live not to weep over it. if they would but dispassionately weigh the blessings they would throw away against an abstract principle more likely to be effected by union than by scission, they would pause before they would perpetrate this act of suicide on themselves and of treason against the hopes of the world.

We know that Rufus King was not a "son" of "the generation of '76," but an actual Philadelphia Convention Framer, and that the intense passion evoked in John Quincy Adams by the Missouri debates was not "unworthy" of his illustrious father. What Jefferson had in mind, however, was not righteous disgust with slavery, but manipulative endangerment of the American Union.

The year 1819 saw the beginning not only of the Missouri Crisis, but of a series of the most cited decisions of the United States Supreme Court.[9] John Marshall's—the Court's—performance in *McCulloch v. Maryland* would in itself have provoked significant response, going as it did against the mainline Republican Party reading of the U.S. Constitution. In 1819, however, there was far more to provoke a Jeffersonian backlash: both the economic downturn and the Missouri Crisis.

Shortly before *McCulloch,* the Court handed down its decision in *Dartmouth College v. Woodward,*[10] in which it accepted Dartmouth alumnus Daniel Webster's argument that Dartmouth College's corporate charter was a contract, and so the state of New Hampshire could not revoke or alter it. Therefore Dartmouth must be left in control of its Federalist board of regents—that is, a New Hampshire law remaking Dartmouth College into Dartmouth University was unconstitutional. Republicans' newfound ascendancy in New Hampshire's government had made reorganization of the college virtually inevitable once the school's president requested it, but Marshall's Supreme Court would not allow the reorganization to stand.[11]

The New Hampshire Supreme Court of Judicature unanimously ruled in *Dartmouth College v. Woodward* that the Contracts Clause applied only to corporations whose purpose was to further private individuals' property interests. Dartmouth's founding as a school to Christianize Indians put it outside that class of corporations, thus beyond the reach of the Contracts Clause.

The Marshall Court disagreed, ruling that Dartmouth College was not a public but a private institution, and thus that New Hampshire had no right to remake it. The college's charter was a contract coming under the Contracts Clause, Marshall said—despite the fact that there had been no consideration given for the charter by the regents (which is necessary for the existence of a contract). Over time this precedent would lead to later Supreme Court majorities' using the Contracts Clause to insulate much of American business from democratic majorities' power—even though, as Marshall conceded, no one is known to have intended or expected in creating the Contracts Clause for it to be used to protect corporate rights.[12]

Two years later the Supreme Court by chance found itself deciding another important case in which the Commonwealth of Virginia was a party. Once again, to the Old Republican Richmond Junto's dismay, Virginia lost. The case was *Cohens v. Virginia.*[13]

Congress had empowered the District of Columbia to set up the Grand National Lottery to fund a new United States Capitol.[14] Maryland, D.C., and Virginia were the anticipated markets for lottery tickets, but the Virginia

General Assembly passed a law banning sale in Virginia of lottery tickets not authorized by the Virginia legislature. Philip and Mendes Cohen were convicted in Norfolk of selling District of Columbia lottery tickets in Virginia and fined $100.

The Cohens retained William Pinkney, winning counsel in *McCulloch v. Maryland* and onetime colleague of James Monroe in negotiating the Monroe-Pinkney Treaty, to represent them. Rather than appeal in Virginia court, Pinkney appealed in federal court. As Congress had empowered the District of Columbia to establish the lottery, he argued, the Cohens' appeal came under federal courts' "arising under" jurisdiction. The case presented two questions: whether Virginia could constitutionally ban sale of lottery tickets authorized by federal law, and whether a state supreme court's decision could be appealed to a federal court.[15]

Judge Spencer Roane coaxed the General Assembly along in this matter. It resolved that federal courts had "no rightful authority under the Constitution to examine and correct the judgment" of the Virginia court. As one vociferously pro-Marshall authority put it, "That Virginia should be cited to appear at the bar of the Supreme Court to defend its right to enforce its own penal laws was regarded as a monstrous invasion of state sovereignty and independence. Before the case was argued, the state legislature issued a report and resolutions denying the Supreme Court's jurisdiction. Another resolution instructed the lawyers appearing for the commonwealth to argue only the question of jurisdiction, and if that should be sustained, they should 'consider their duties at an end.'"[16] Virginia's governor, Jefferson's son-in-law Thomas Mann Randolph, appointed U.S. Representatives Alexander Smyth and Old Republican Philip P. Barbour to serve as counsel for the Commonwealth. Smyth told the Supreme Court that "To confer the jurisdiction claimed, the constitution should have said that the judicial power of the United States shall have appellate jurisdiction over the judicial power of the several States. . . . There is not a word in the constitution that goes to set up the federal judiciary above the state judiciary."

Marshall, for the court, had no trouble finding that the federal courts' "arising under" jurisdiction extended even to cases in which a state was properly a party. Marshall said that in creating a constitution "for ages to come," the framers must have intended to give the government "the means of self-preservation from the perils it may be destined to encounter." One of the chief shortcomings of the Articles of Confederation during the Critical Period had been the lack of a method of bringing the states to comply with Congress's laws. The general language in which federal courts had been given "arising under" jurisdiction had been intended to remedy this problem.

Counsel for Virginia noted that the Constitution gave federal courts appellate jurisdiction where a state was a party and original jurisdiction under the "arising under" language. What if both applied? Marshall reasoned that federal courts must have original jurisdiction in "arising under" cases even when a state was a party, because otherwise federal courts would not have either kind of jurisdiction in such cases. A more difficult question concerned the Eleventh Amendment, which denies federal courts jurisdiction over a case between a state and a citizen of another state. Marshall held that this only applied to suits in which a creditor sued a state, and not to writs of error filed to force a state to appear in a federal appeal (thus rendering the amendment nearly ineffectual).

This brought Marshall to the Virginian claim that the Supreme Court did not have appellate authority over state courts' decisions—that the federal and state court systems were separate, independent systems. Marshall said that *au contraire,* the U.S. Supreme Court had authority to review all decisions based on federal law. "[T]he necessity of uniformity as well as correctness in expounding the constitution and laws of the United States," he argued, "would itself suggest the propriety of vesting in some single tribunal the power of deciding, in the last resort, all cases in which they are involved." The texts of *The Federalist* and the Judiciary Act of 1789, he said, showed that this had been the contemporary understanding of the matter.[17] After this, Marshall had no trouble with the argument of counsel for Virginia that in legislating for the District of Columbia, Congress acted not as the federal legislature, but as the local legislature of that district—and thus could not bind the states. Marshall held the contrary, but the whole court decided in the end that in creating the District of Columbia's government, Congress had not intended it to have any power beyond the District's limits— "and certainly not," according to Marshall papers editor and Marshall biographer Charles Hobson, "to interfere with a state's police powers." So, though they had won on the jurisdictional question, the Cohens lost on the merits. The greatest of Jefferson scholars captured these events perfectly in saying Marshall and his court had in "a petty case . . . assert[ed] vast authority."[18]

pencer Roane, as these events took place, asked Thomas Jefferson to speak out in response.[1] Jefferson answered that he paid little attention to public affairs, and thus "kn[e]w little about them." He went on to say, however, that he was

> sensible of the inroads daily making by the federal, into the jurisdiction of it's co-ordinate associates the state-governments. the legislative and executive branches may sometimes err, but elections and dependance will bring them to rights. the judiciary branch is the instrument which working, like gravity, without intermission is to press us at last into one consolidated mass. against this I know no one who, equally with Judge Roane himself, possesses the power & the courage, to make resistance; and to him I look, and have long looked, as our strongest bulwark.

If Congress would not address the problem, "the states must shield themselves *and meet the invader foot to foot* [emphasis added]." He closed by asserting that John Taylor of Caroline's recent book *Construction Construed, and Constitutions Vindicated*[2] was "the most effectual retraction of our government to it's original principles which has ever yet been sent by heaven to our aid" and saying the state legislatures ought all to give copies to all of their congressmen.

Soon enough Roane wrote Jefferson responding to his wish to remain retired from politics, "[A]lmost thou persuadest me to be a christian." He thought "in losing our Leader, we run the risk of losing our all," but he informed Jefferson that he had forwarded Jefferson's letter with the encomium to Taylor's book to Taylor. Roane added, "To that work may, already, in a measure, be ascribed, the revival which has taken place, on the subject of state-rights."

Jefferson answered, "I should not shrink from the post of duty, had not the decays of nature withdrawn me from the list of combatants."[3] While he thought the problem of government prodigality would be attended to, he hurried to add that "The great object of my fear is the federal judiciary. that body, like Gravity, ever acting, *with* noiseless foot, & unalarming advance, gaining ground step by step, and holding what it gains, is ingulphing insidiously the special [that is, state] governments into the jaws of that which feeds them." He hoped, however, that Taylor, Roane, and Smyth would "be heard, & obeyed, & that a temporary check will be effected. yet," he said, "be not weary of welldoing. let the eye of vigilance never be closed."

This general line of thought led the former president to add, "Last and most portentous of all is the Missouri question. it is smeared over for the present: but it's geographical demarcation is indelible. what it is to become I see not; and leave to those who will live to see it."

James Madison's take on *Cohens v. Virginia* was characteristically different. Roane wrote to Madison addressing him as author of "the celebrated report, that produced the glorious revolution of 1799. In fact it is believed," he said, "that this decision has entirely subverted the principles of that revolution." Republicans generally, Roane insisted, saw "in your pen, which has so often charmed them, and saved the liberties of our country, the only certain antidote, to the ingenious and fatal Sophistries of Marshall." If he opted not to take up his pen against Marshall's opinion in *Cohens*, Madison ought at least to advise Roane on what course to take.[4]

Madison answered at some length.[5] He began by referring to the "technical points of law" underlying the Supreme Court's recent opinions as "foreign to my studies," and "familiar to yours," on which ground he ordinarily would "be disposed rather to put such a subject . . . into your hands, than to take it out of them." Getting to the point, however, he said, "It is to be regretted that the Court is so much in the practice of mingling with the Judgments pronounced, comments & reasonings of a scope beyond them; and that in these there is often an apparent disposition to amplify the authorities of the Union, at the expence of those of the States." Sounding very much like Roane, the Richmond Junto, and the General Assembly, he said, "It is of great importance, as well as of indispensable obligation, that the constitutional boundary between them should be impartially maintained. Every deviation in practice detracts from the superiority of a chartered [that is, a constitutional] over a traditional Government, and marrs the experiment which is to determine the interesting problem, whether the organization of the political System of the U.S. establishes a just equilibrium, or tends to a preponderance of the national or of the local powers. . . ."

Though judicial usurpation could theoretically become problematic, Madison said, "it is less formidable to the reserved sovereignty of the States, than the latitude of power which [the Judicial power of the U.S.] has assigned to the Legislature," and the threat from the Congress is animated mainly "by a majority of the States seduced by expected advantages." Because of Congress's power of impeachment (here he disagreed with Jefferson), "It is not probable that the Supreme Court would be long indulged in a career of usurpation opposed to the decided opinions & policy of the Legislature."

As to congressional usurpation, Madison hazarded that the modes of election of members of the two houses "seem to be, in the present stage at least of our political history, an adequate barrier." He pointed to the states' success in having "crushed at once" the Alien and Sedition Acts, "notwithstanding the co-operation of the federal Judges with the federal laws."

What if Congress, backed by majorities of their constituents, acted as in the recent Missouri controversy or, "as may happen, on the constructive power relating to Roads & Canals?" Only "sound arguments" directed to both their constituents and the members could prevent such behavior "within the pale of the Constitution." Alluding perhaps to Marshall's invocation of *The Federalist* in *Cohens v. Virginia,* he added, "In expounding the Constitution, the Court seems not insensible that the intention of the parties to it ought to be kept in view; and that as far as the language of the Instrument will permit, this intention ought to be traced in the contemporaneous expositions. But is the Court as prompt and as careful in citing & following this evidence when against the federal authority, as when agst. that of the States?" He also thought it "a peculiar impropriety" to make of "the exclusive jurisdiction over the ten miles square," which he considered "an anomaly in our representative System . . . the fulcrum for a Lever stretching into the most distant parts of the Union, and overruling the municipal policy of the States." So much for *Cohens,* and for using Publius as authority for *Cohens.* Congress ought, he said, to exercise its exclusive jurisdiction over Washington and military bases "in the ways as little intrusive as possible on the powers & police of the States." He also thought it important to distinguish between "legal precedents . . . such as take place under transitory impressions," and those "as pass with solemnities & repetitions" seeming to carry public approval. He did not disapprove of all recourse to invocation of constitutional precedents, but he thought legislative ones—especially those from the rushed last hours of congressional sessions—particularly dubious. (Here he no doubt had in mind his communication with President Monroe about congressional funding of road projects.)

On the matter actually at issue in *Cohens,* "involuntary submission of the States to the Tribunal of the supreme Court," he regretted that "the Court seems not to have adverted at all to the expository language held when the Constitution was adopted; nor to that of the 11th amendment which may as well import that it was declaratory, as that it was restrictive of the meaning of the original text." He thought it too an odd judicial discovery that states had "less of sovereignty" in controversies with their own citizens "than in controversies with foreign individuals." He mused that "prudence" should lead federal courts to forebear "taking cognizance of cases arising under the Constitution, and in which the laws or rights of the States may be involved . . . in consideration of the impracticability of applying coercion to States."

A few weeks after this exchange, Roane took up his pen for the *Richmond Enquirer* and drafted five "Algernon Sidney" essays against Marshall's work in *Cohens.* Marshall described these essays to Justice Story as displaying "a degree of virulence transcending what has appeared on any former occasion." Roane's biographer calls these essays "eloquent and violent, reasonable and vehement, authoritative and hectoring." Roane's goal, he says, was "less to win the legal argument and more to spur a people to action."[6]

"I address you under a solemn conviction that the liberties and constitution of our country are endangered, deeply and vitally endangered, by the fatal effects of that decision," Roane began, because it "negatives the idea that the American states have a real existence" and finds power in the Supreme Court "to amend the federal constitution at [its] mere will and pleasure." Though "our general government is a national one as to some purposes, it is a federal one as to others," and yet the Supreme Court had moved America far down the road toward complete consolidation.

Roane found Marshall's focus on the general government's "supremacy" particularly irksome because wholly false. "A government which is only entrusted with a few powers," he said, "and is limited in acting upon those powers by the expression of the Constitution . . . can scarcely be said to be supreme." He held that "the whole government" and "the people themselves" were not supreme either, as "those great principles which soar above all constitutions and are paramount to the rightful power of the people themselves" bound them.[7] Roane concluded by pointing back to the Virginia Ratification Convention, in which his father-in-law's coadjutor George Mason foretold that the "Ten Miles Square" "might be 'unquestionably extended by *implication to overthrow the rights of the states.*'"

Madison's response to these essays must have shocked Roane.[8] "The Gordian Knot of the Constitution," he held, "seems to lie in the problem of collisions between the federal & State powers, especially as eventually exercised by their respective tribunals." While he had always held that the Constitution ought to be read to avoid such problems, "on the abstract question whether the federal, or the State decisions ought to prevail, the sounder policy would yield to the claims of the former." The Constitution, he reasoned, had been created "by a compact, not between the Government of the U. States, and the State Governments; but between the States as sovereign communities," with each agreeing some powers would be exercised in common and "all their other authorities" retained by them. "The possibility of disagreements concerning the line of division" between state and federal power "could not escape attention." If the individual states decided this question each for itself, "the Constitution of the U. States might become different in every State, . . . and the vital principle of equality which cements their Union, might thus gradually be deprived of its virtue." If the central government decided this question for all, the problem of equal application would not arise, and the states would maintain control due to their control over "the Trustees" "directly or indirectly."

Over time, Madison thought, "successive decisions sanctioned by the public concurrence" would narrow "the room for jarring opinions between the national & State Tribunals," while selection of better state judges would give state tribunals' decisions more weight. (Roane must have blanched at this idea.) Already, Madison said, the improvement in the quality of state judiciaries gave them more weight than they had when the Constitution was written. Madison asked rhetorically whether it was too much to expect that as federal and state judges approached each other in talents, integrity, and impartiality they would "vary less & less also in their reasonings and opinions on all Judicial subjects," so that in the end they would agree where the federal/state line ought to be drawn.

By the time *Cohens* was decided, the all-Federalist Supreme Court of 1801 had come to have only two Federalist members: John Marshall and Bushrod Washington, both John Adams appointees. Yet the Court in cases like *Martin, McCulloch,* and *Cohens*—not only the holdings but the opinions—continued to dismay leading Republicans with the direction the country's constitutional law was headed.

Former president Jefferson at last decided to take an unusual step: he wrote a lengthy letter to his first Supreme Court appointee, Justice William Johnson of South Carolina, on the issue of the Marshall Court's practice of delivering (usually through the chief justice) one opinion of the court rather than having each judge present his views seriatim (that is, in turn).[9] Seriatim opinions had been the custom in England for quite a long time, except in the day of Lord Mansfield, and they had at first been the practice of the U.S. Supreme Court. Jefferson's complaint was that when the court presented only one opinion, no one could tell whether and on what issues there had been disagreement among the judges. "[S]ome of these cases too," he explained, "have been of such importance, of such difficulty, and the decisions so grating to a portion of the public, as to have merited the fullest explanation from every judge seriatim, of the reasons which had produced such convictions on his mind."

Jefferson reasoned that the Constitution's grant of "good behaviour" tenure left the judges accountable in only two ways: via impeachment, and before the bar of public opinion. Hiding the extent to which a particular judge shared in the opinion of the whole court meant shielding a particular member of the Supreme Court from both kinds of accountability for his performance in a particular case. Jefferson asserted that Attorney General Edmund Randolph had proposed to Congress during the Washington administration to begin publishing individual justices' seriatim opinions. Congress had not had time to take this up, to Jefferson's disappointment.

Jefferson concluded by asking Justice Johnson what he thought of the state of parties. "[A]n opinion prevails that there is no longer any distinction," he said, but it was not true. Seeing that the Battle of New Orleans had destroyed the "Federalist" label and having found monarchy a forlorn hope in the United States, Federalists now worked under the Republican name for the next best thing: to amalgamate the states. "[T]heir aim is now therefore to break down the rights reserved, by the constitution, to the states as a bulwark against that consolidation, the fear of which produced the whole of the opposition to the consititution at it's birth." He expressed confidence that this new gambit would fail as the old approach had.

Johnson responded, perhaps surprisingly, quite ingenuously:[10]

> With regard to the Subject of the Supreme Court, I really am happy to be favoured with an Excuse for expressing myself freely and confidentially to you. Be assured that my Situation there has not been 'a Bed of Roses.' But it partakes in so many Respects of the Nature of a Cabinet that a Degree of Circumspection is indispensable in lifting the Curtain; and often, very often, have I wishd for some one whom I could consult on the Course proper to be pursued in discharging the Duties which devolved upon me there. But unfortunately I have never had a single Individual on the Bench with whom I could confer with unlimited Confidence."

While a South Carolina appellate judge, Johnson had been used to delivering seriatim opinions. He found early in his federal tenure, however, that his colleagues refused to do this, instead allowing Marshall to deliver all of the opinions—even in some instances when the court decided against his vote. Told this practice reflected the other justices' respect for Marshall, "I soon . . . found out the real Cause. Cushing was incompetent, Chase could not be got to think or write—Patterson was a slow man & willingly declined the Trouble, & the other two Judges you know are commonly estimated as one Judge." Though he tried dissenting once early in his tenure, "[a]t length I found that I must either submit to Circumstances or become such a Cypher in our Consultations as to effect no good at all. I therefore bent to the current," though he did persuade the others to appoint an author for the majority and allow the others "to record their Opinions or not ad Libitum." Trying to change things now would have the same negative consequences, and it would not lead incompetent justices to resign—only to give their votes over to others who would write on their behalf.

Jefferson persisted.[11] After encouraging Johnson to complete a history of parties on which he was launched (a project Jefferson had tried to recruit other people to undertake),[12] he devoted the last part of another letter to the task of persuading the justice to write separate opinions more often. If Johnson did and others did not, their continuing "consolidation of our government by the noiseless, and therefore unalarming instrumentality of the Supreme court" would beget "suspicion that something passes which fears the public ear, and this spreading by degrees must produce at some time abridgement of tenure, facility of removal, or some other modification which may promise a remady. for in truth there is at this time more hostility to the federal judiciary than to any other organ of the government." So Johnson at last agreed to write separate opinions in regard to "all Subjects of general Interest; particularly constitutional questions."

In return he asked Jefferson to let him know ". . . how far the Supreme Court has yet trespassd upon their Neighbours Territory, or advanced beyond their own constitutional Limits." "I will not pretend that I have no View," he continued,

> to bringing about a Change of your Opinions on the Subject, not for the Triumph, but for the Support it would afford me; but to have my own fairly & fully tried, believe me is my leading Motive. I cannot I acknowledge but flatter myself that in the main the Country is satisfied with our Decisions; and I urged our Friend Stevenson to bring forward his Motion on the 25th

section of the Judiciary-act, in the Hope that there would be some Expression of public Sentiment upon the Subject. The Resolution unfortunately could not be taken up at the late session, and we are still left to conjecture. I acknowledge that some things have fallen from particular Judges which are exceptionable, and I exceedingly regret their Publication. But when the Decisions are examined upon their own Merits independently of the bad or defective Reasons of the Judge who delivers them, I do flatter myself that all in which I ever concurred will stand constitutional scrutiny.[13]

Jefferson answered the question whether the Supreme Court had gone against the Constitution in his next letter[14] by pointing to Roane's "Algernon Sidney" essays, which "appeared to me to pulverise every word which had been delivered by Judge Marshall of the extrajudicial part of his opinion but, unable to claim that case, he could not let it go entirely, but went on gratuitously to prove that; notwithstanding the X[I]th amendment, of the constitution a state *could* be brought, as a defendant, to the bar of his court. and, again, that Congress might authorise a corporation of it's territory to exercise legislation within a state, and paramount to the laws of that state." There had been several decisions of the Supreme Court cutting into the reserved powers of the states, Jefferson insisted, and this reflected what he called the new program of the Federalists. Having failed to install a monarchy in the United States, they had decided to amalgamate the states into one political body, and the Supreme Court under John Marshall was leading the way.

What galled Jefferson most about Marshall's performances, here and in other cases, was his habit "of travelling out of his case to prescribe what the law would be in a moot case not before the court," which Jefferson called "very irregular and very censurable." The example that came to mind was *Marbury v. Madison,* in which, as the former president recalled, the Court had decided it had no authority to decide such a case, "but the Chief Justice went on to lay down what the law would be, had they jurisdiction of the case: to wit, that they should command the delivery."

Warming to his subject, Jefferson continued that

the object was clearly to instruct any other court having the jurisdiction, what they should do, if Marbury should apply to them. besides, the impropriety of this gratuitous interference, could any thing exceed the perversion of law? for if there is any principle of law never yet contradicted it is that delivery is one of the essentials to the validity of a deed. altho' signed and sealed, yet as long as it remains in the hands of the party himself, it is in fieri only, it is not a deed, and can be made so only by his delivery. in the hands of a third person it may be made an escrow, but whatever is in the executive offices is certainly deemed to be in the hands of the President; and in this case was actually in my hands, because when I countermanded them there was as yet no Secretary of state. yet this case of Marbury and Madison is continually cited by bench and bar, as if it were settled law, without any animadversion on it's being merely an obiter dissertation of the Chief Justice.

So it is now, more than ten generations later. In the meantime, after the exchange with Jefferson, Justice Johnson did file notably more dissenting and separate concurring opinions than any other justice, and more majority opinions than any but Marshall and Story, but it is not clear that the pattern of his doing so changed much.[15]

65

The final "great" Supreme Court decision of the Jeffersonian era came in the case of *Gibbons v. Ogden,* the famous Steamboat Case.[1] New York had granted Robert Fulton and Robert Livingston a monopoly of the steamboat business in New York waters. When New Jersey and Connecticut responded by authorizing seizure of New York–licensed steamboats, animosity reached a high pitch.

Livingston and Fulton licensed Aaron Ogden to run a ferry line between New York City and New Jersey, and in 1818 Thomas Gibbons began running a competing business—authorized by the federal coasting act—on the same line. Ogden secured a New York judge's restraining order against Gibbons, who appealed to the U.S. Supreme Court. Under the Supremacy Clause, he claimed, the federal coasting act validly authorized him to run his business, whatever the New York statute might say. As one scholar notes, the implications were enormous, for a decision recognizing New York's power to grant an exclusive license to the New York–New Jersey shipping business could lead other states to grant exclusive rights to portions of other American lakes and rivers adjoining their territory.

Daniel Webster and William Wirt, two of the advocates who won *McCulloch v. Maryland,* signed on for Gibbons, while William Pinkney took Ogden's side. This seemingly set the stage for their first courtroom contest—but then Pinkney died in February 1822.[2] The issue in the case was whether Congress's Commerce Clause power was exclusive or states could regulate interstate commerce insofar as Congress had not done so. Webster, for Gibbons, said it was exclusive, while counsel for Ogden argued that states could regulate commerce "until," as one authority puts it, "Congress ha[s] acted so as to collide with state power and thereby occupy the field." Counsel for Ogden provided several examples of states' ongoing commercial regulations. This raised the question of whether navigation on inland waterways was even "commerce" in the constitutional sense at all. If it was, perhaps both Congress's Commerce Clause power and its power to grant federal courts admiralty jurisdiction applied.

Gibbons marked a watershed in disputation about sovereignty in the federal system. If Marshall and his colleagues in *Martin, McCulloch,* and *Cohens* had rejected compact "theory" in favor of a not-quite-historical account of the Constitution while asserting broad understandings of federal power under Article III and Article I, *Gibbons v. Ogden* marked the genesis of a new theory among the justices: "concurrent power theory."

Marshall's opinion began by saying that a term of the Constitution must be understood in its natural sense, and a power must be seen in relation to "the objects for which it was given." So, what was the meaning of "commerce," and why was the power to regulate interstate commerce given? Marshall easily determined navigation to be commerce, saying, "Commerce, undoubtedly, is traffic, but it is something more: it is intercourse." (A wag who witnessed Marshall reading his opinion from the bench wrote a friend immediately thereafter that, "I shall soon expect to learn that our fornication laws are unconstitutional.") He then held that New York's licensing act and the federal law at issue were in "direct collision." The concurrent sovereignty theory held that where Congress had not acted, a state could—and thus that if Congress had not adopted a coastal regulation, a state would have retained power to do so. Yet Marshall had not used the term "concurrent power," and so the holding in this respect remained somewhat opaque. Despite the case's fame, then, Marshall Court historian G. Edward White concludes, "It remained unclear what 'principles' had actually been enunciated in *Gibbons,* and what 'tests' would be used for future Commerce Clause cases."

These precedents are treated as seminal even now. In one sense, while the Jeffersonians were winning all of the electoral battles, John Marshall, Joseph Story, and their colleagues were winning the jurisprudential, meaning eventually the constitutional, and ultimately the political war. "Ultimately" is the key word here, however, because as Michael J. Klarman put it, "it is clear that nationalist decisions such as *McCulloch* and *Gibbons* had little [short-term] concrete effect, given that Congress did not take up the Court's broad invitation to exercise national power until well after the Civil War, at which point the invitation was partially withdrawn." He wonders whether it might be more accurate than the reigning triumphalism about these cases to say that "rulings like *McCulloch* were more important for mobilizing states' rights opposition to the Marshall Court than for educating public opinion in support of the Court's nationalism."[3] In considering that question, one should remember that the private political correspondence of Jefferson, Madison, and other critics of the Marshall Court would be published while Marshall was still chief justice.

John Quincy Adams summarized the state of affairs in a focused diary entry for March 3, 1821, the last day of the outgoing Congress and of James Monroe's first presidential term.[4] His chief political opponent, driven out of office by his constituents because of his role in the Missouri Crisis, approved of his management of the State Department. Henry Clay gave a poor speech in support of a vote of thanks for the outgoing speaker of the House. After 12:00 AM on March 4th, the Congress finished its business, and the president signed its last two bills thirty minutes later, of which he notified the two houses. A joint committee told Monroe they were ready to adjourn, unless he had reason why they should not. He said he did not, and the Congress adjourned around 1:00 AM.

Adams walked home with John Calhoun, as was his wont, and "found him in some degree dispirited by the results of the attacks systematically carried on through this whole Congress but especially through the Session just expired, against his management of the War Department." Calhoun thought Congress's repeal of the internal taxes and "profuse pension Act" (as Adams put it) had led to the current substantial revenue shortfall, which (per Calhoun, but in Adams's words) "ought to have been foreseen." Once that had happened, the War Department was bound to be the one cut.

Calhoun had proposed reducing U.S. Army manpower chiefly by cutting the number of enlisted men in the force during peacetime. He reasoned that it thus could be quickly expanded in the event of war. The relevant House committee rejected his idea, however, opting instead to cut the force generally. The Senate substituted a midway program of cutting army manpower by 40 percent and giving the secretary authority to reduce ranks of some officers in peacetime. Calhoun saw this as progress, though not optimal. Congress also cut appropriations for defensive construction from $800,000 to $202,000. As this spending was known to be among Monroe's top priorities, it was "a humiliating close to his first term."[5] It could have been worse if some hostile congressmen had succeeded in their efforts to abolish the United States Military Academy.[6]

Calhoun and Adams agreed that "the Coalition of Crawford's, Clinton's, and Clay's partizans, though with views quite hostile to each other," had been steadfast "in the assaults of this Session, against the administration." Speaker Taylor had appointed "the most violent opponents to the Administration upon Committees." Besides, "the Georgia, Tennessee, Kentucky, New-York and Vermont members, devoted to their respective leaders," had all been seen "joining their forces against the Administration." "All this," Adams noted of Calhoun's observations, "is unquestionably true." In addition, "There have . . . been transactions in the War Department, in the Post-Office, and in the Bank of the United States, which have unfortunately given handle to every class of disaffection." In foreign policy too the opponents of the Monroe administration had found grist for their mill. "Jackson's Seminole Campaign, the Florida Treaty, and the South-American insurgents have all been used in turn as weapons of annoyance." As Adams understood it, "By the practical operation of our Government, the whole system of our Politics is inseparably linked with the views of aspirants to the Presidential succession; and by the peculiarity of our present position, the prospects of *all* the candidates in reserve for the next Presidency, excepting the Vice-President, and setting aside the Secretary of State depend upon the *failure* of the present Administration for their success." (It is unclear whether Adams intended Calhoun too to be included among those seeking the Monroe administration's failure. This passage was followed by a lengthy exploration of the energetic efforts of Secretary Crawford to thwart the administration at every turn. "Crawford," Adams said, "has been a worm preying upon the vitals of the Administration within its own body.")

Monroe's second term began on Sunday, March 4, 1821. Yet, Secretary Adams observed, "the Administration of the Official Oath, which the Constitution prescribes that he shall take *before* he enter on the Execution of his Office, being postponed till to-morrow this day was a sort of interregnum, during which there was no person qualified to act as President; an event of no importance now, but which might be far otherwise under supposable circumstances."[7]

Besides putting off taking his oath, Monroe had recently come under pressure from "his Virginia friends" to forgo the opportunity to give an address. Raising this idea with Adams, he received the response that if he decided not to speak, he had better make his intention known ahead of time, lest the large assemblage come to hear him be disappointed. Monroe said he would bring it up at the next Cabinet meeting, which he did. Navy Secretary Smith Thompson took the nay side, noting that the Constitution did not call for an address and saying that if the question were a new one, he would oppose giving one. Adams replied that "there was a propriety in the thing itself," indeed the only one like it under our system, that it had been uniformly done, and that it ought to be done again. The other members agreed there was no adequate reason to discontinue the practice.[8]

As Clay was no longer speaker, this inauguration ceremony could take place in the House of Representatives chamber. The president asked the secretaries to meet at his house to travel with him. As the secretary of state described the scene:

> The President attired in a full suit of black broad cloth, of somewhat anti-quated fashion, with shoe and knee buckles rode in a plain Carriage with four horses, and a single coloured footman. The secretaries of State, the Treasury, War and the Navy, followed, each in a Carriage and pair—There was no escort nor any concourse of people on the way—But on alighting at the Capitol, a great crowd of people were assembled, and the avenues to the Hall of the House were so choaked up with persons pressing for admittance, that it was with the utmost difficulty that the President made his way through them into the House."[9]

The chamber was crowded, as it usually was when something impor-tant was happening, and "the British Minister had to push his way through a horde of 'sturdy and ragged citizens.'" (His annoyance declined when he saw the president having to do the same.)[10]

In a chamber "as thronged as possible," with "loud talking, and agita-tion in Gallery; not altogether ceasing even while the President was reading his Address," Monroe took the oath from Chief Justice Marshall and gave his speech "in a suitably grave, and rather low tone of voice." People rushed afterward to shake his hand, and "At his departure from the House, there was a cheering shout from the people in the Galleries, and the Music of the Marine Band played both at his entrance and his departure."

The speech was not remarkable. Monroe began by noting the resound-ing victory he had won in the election and saying that this endorsement of his performance in this office thus far "affords me a consolation which I shall profoundly feel through life." His aim in this second term would be "[t]o merit the continuance of this good opinion."[11]

As he had done numerous times on his presidential tours, Monroe in-voked his presidential predecessors in order to distinguish himself from them. "Having no pretensions to the high and commanding claims of my predecessors, whose names are so much more conspicuously identified with our Revolution, and who contributed so pre-eminently to promote its suc-cess" he said, "I consider myself rather as the instrument than the cause of the union which has prevailed in the late election." It was attributes of the Union, not "my humble pretensions," that had yielded consensus in the election (one candidate receiving all but one vote), and he expected the Union's strength to continue to draw Americans together even in circumstances, such as an election campaign, in which one might have expected division to rear its head.

Congress responded to the War of 1812 by providing for naval spending and construction of coastal fortifications, he went on, and he calculated that those expenditures would be recouped in the first six months of any future invasion by a force of twenty thousand men; they were placed to concentrate the military effort of a war's early months, during which militia might be mobilized against incursions at a few particular points—instead of all along the American coast, as in the War of 1812. In other words "an armed front from St. Croix to Sabine . . . would protect in the event of war our whole coast and interior from invasion. . . ." "It is believed," he continued, "and experience has shown, that such a preparation is the best expedient that can be resorted to to prevent war." This American expenditure must not be understood as indicating hostility to any other country, and "these measures of defense . . . will be completed in a few years. . . ."

Turning to foreign policy, the president described the punctiliously neutral posture his administration had maintained in relation to the rebellions in Spain's New World colonies and vowed it would continue, explained that he had put down the Amelia Island piracy and imposed condign punishment on the participants, and said he had resolved the boundary dispute with Spain through a treaty that "has placed the relations of the two countries on a basis of permanent friendship." "But to the acquisition of Florida too much importance can not be attached," he pointed out, not only because the territory was valuable in itself, but because it provided water access to the Gulf of Mexico for much of the South, "secure[d] us against all future annoyance from powerful Indian tribes," and provided several potential naval bases for even the largest warships. Both in the Mediterranean and in the Pacific, America maintained a naval presence to protect its commercial fleet—besides to suppress the Atlantic slave trade.

Taxes of various kinds had been eliminated, and still the government took in substantially more money than it spent each year. That was applied to the federal debt. Loans were taken out to pay the government's expenses for 1820, but Monroe thought this would be unnecessary once the ongoing price depression ceased. In general he favored pay-as-you-go budgeting. He did favor imposts on various goods in order to "enhance the price of produce, promote our manufactures, and augment the revenue, at the same time that they made it more secure and permanent."

The next passage of his address turned to a topic that had long played on Monroe's mind: the situation of American Indians. "The progress of our settlements westward, supported as they are by a dense population," he noted, "has constantly driven them back, with almost the total sacrifice of the lands which they have been compelled to abandon." Here he located a failure of American policy, as "The care of the Indian tribes within our limits has long been an essential part of our system, but, unfortunately, it has not been executed in a manner to accomplish all the objects intended by it."

President Monroe called for abandonment of the long-standing policy of "treat[ing] them as independent nations, without their having any substantial pretension to that rank. The distinction," he said, "has flattered their pride, retarded their improvement, and in many instances paved the way to their destruction." The attentive would here have recalled his similar statements four years earlier, and perhaps thought of Secretary Calhoun's Indian policy at the War Department. Calhoun had in an official report of December 5, 1818, written that, in part as a result of extensive trade with the United States through his department, "the neighboring tribes are becoming daily less warlike, and more helpless and dependent on us, through their numerous wants; and they are rendered still more pacific by the fear of forfeiting their lands and annuities. They have, in a great measure, ceased to be an object of terror, and have become that of commiseration." He concluded that "[t]hey neither are, in fact, nor ought to be, considered as independent nations." "By a proper combination of force and persuasion," then, "they ought to be brought within the pales of law and civilization. Left to themselves, they will never reach that desirable condition." The wave of American migration westward would "overwhelm" them, and so the question of how their current situation could be accommodated to mutual advantage must be answered. Calhoun, likely for Monroe, had replied, "Such small bodies, with savage customs and character cannot, and ought not, to be permitted to exist in an independent condition in the midst of civilized society. Our laws and manners," he concluded, "ought to supersede their present savage manners and customs." The government should make them "contract their settlements within reasonable bounds" and guarantee their remaining lands "for their permanent home."[12] Though he had made no such detailed statement, Monroe's address at the Brainerd Mission Cherokee school was consistent with his war secretary's position: American Indians in the United States should be assimilated, beginning with education of the young.

66

✦ ◌ ✦

Irving Bartlett, author of the best Calhoun biography, makes an important point about Calhoun's—and, by implication, Monroe's—Indian policy. "Although Calhoun's ideas may seem hopelessly culture-bound to the modern mind," he says, "they marked him as a reformer in 1818." He contrasts Calhoun to General E. P. Gaines, who told the war secretary that "The Savage must be taught and compelled to do that which is right and to abstain from doing that which is radically wrong. The poisonous cup of barbarism cannot be taken from the savage by the mild voice of reason alone." Bartlett speculates that Calhoun's experience of Indian leaders while secretary of war may account for his enlightenment in this regard.[1]

In his inaugural address the president declared that the Indians "have claims to the magnanimity and, I may add, on the justice of this nation which we must all feel. We should become their real benefactors. . . ." Instead of gigantic swaths of land nominally held in common but which they could not defend, "the right of soil should be secured to each individual and his posterity in competent portions," besides which the government should set aside some sum "to be vested in permanent funds for the support of civil government over them and for the education of their children. . . ." Congress should legislate on this matter.

Europe seemed to be on the verge of yet more war. America should prepare now, as peacetime was the best time to make ready. With the customary recap of America's constitutional and geostrategic success of the preceding forty-five years and a nod to the expected collaboration of officials in the other branches of the government, Monroe closed this final inaugural address of a Patriot of the Revolution with an invocation of "the protection of Almighty God."

In preparing South Carolina planter Henry Middleton to be American Minister to Russia in 1820, John Quincy Adams provided him with a lengthy memorandum on the European diplomatic scene and America's place in it.[2] Russia was the mightiest European power, he said, and Emperor Alexander I was dedicated to peace. The United States he classified as an "Extra-European" power, like Turkey and Persia. "To stand in firm and cautious independence of all entanglement in the European system, has been a cardinal point of their policy under every administration of their Government from the peace of 1783 to this day." "Every year's experience rivets it more deeply in the principles and opinions of the nation." That Adams knew Alexander well could be seen in his telling Middleton that America would stay outside the Holy Alliance (of Russia, Austria, and Prussia) while respecting "the peculiarly Christian maxims of mutual benevolence and brotherly love" for which it stood. Middleton was not to agree to join the alliance, though he was not to give an "explicit refusal."

These calculations were all thrown up in the air by France's invasion of Spain to restore the ousted Bourbon king Fernando VII in 1823. Monroe wrote to Jefferson, "If the spirit of the [French] revolution, & of liberty, is not extinct, in France & throughout Europe, the passage of the Pyrenees by the French armies promises to be a signal for great events. That [Emperor] Alexander will profit, of the state of things, west and south of him, is probable; what Britain will do is uncertain." Of the British foreign minister the president said, "[George] Canning has more talents, & a better heart than his predecessor [Lord Castlereagh], but yet, I fear that he has not those fixed principles, which distinguished Fox among modern English Statesmen, and cannot therefore be thoroughly relied on, for a persevering effort against the course, and in support of the right cause."[3]

To Richard Rush, Minister to the Court of St. James's, Adams on July 22, 1823, wrote that, among other things:

> The exclusive rights of Spain to any part of the American Continents have ceased. That portion of the Convention which recognizes the exclusive colonial rights of Spain on these Continents, though confirmed as between Great Britain and Spain by the first additional Article to the Treaty of the 5th of July 1814 has been extinguished by the fact of the Independence of the South American Nations and of Mexico. . . . A necessary consequence of this state of things will be that the American Continents henceforth will no longer be subjects of *colonization*. Occupied by civilized Independent Nations, they will be accessible to Europeans and to each other on that footing alone, and the Pacific Ocean in every part of it will remain open to the Navigation of all nations in like manner with the Atlantic. . . .

Six days later he further instructed him that the influence of Christianity had wrought "[t]hese great and cheering indications of progressive amelioration in the condition of man" and that "the feelings in which these improvements upon the ancient law of nations originated are strong in the breasts of [Great Britain's] statesmen of the present age," as was "proved, not only by the spirit and perseverance with which they are pursuing the abolition of the African slave trade," but by other evidence, and that the same principles could underlie agreement on the proposals Rush was to make.[4]

Adams continued that while Britain's national interests were formerly belligerent, they were now neutral. The Rule of 1756 would not again be an issue, as "all the ex-colonies of Europe, and the colonies yet existing, her own included, [were] open to foreign commerce and shipping *in time of peace*," so that neutral shipping cannot be seized by her during the next war on the grounds that such commerce was banned in time of peace. The two could cooperate as "nations intent . . . upon the final and total suppression of the slave trade."

Rush told Adams in a letter of August 19, 1823, that he having brought up the subject of a British diplomatic note of March 31st saying that Britain would not try to seize any former Spanish New World colonies and that France would not either, Foreign Minister Canning asked "what I thought my government would say to going hand in hand with this, in the same sentiment."[5] Canning said he did not intend for either country to commit to "any concert in action under it," but that he thought in light of their combined share of the world's maritime power, a joint statement would influence "the rest of the world." Rush answered by asking Canning what Britain's position concerning the new states' independence was, to which Canning answered that Britain would not mediate between Spain and her colonies, but she would not prevent their reaching some kind of resolution either.

Canning sent Rush a note the next day laying out Britain's position regarding the New World Spanish colonies in five points:

1. We conceive the recovery of the Colonies by Spain to be hopeless.
2. We conceive the question of the Recognition of them, as Independent States, to be one of time and circumstances.
3. We are, however, by no means disposed to throw any impediment in the way of an arrangement between them and the mother country by amicable negotiation.
4. We aim not at the possession of any portion of them ourselves.

5. We could not see any portion of them transferred to any other
   Power with indifference.

He said Britain and America ought to declare these principles jointly to
each other and the world, which would likely short-circuit other powers'
planning to intervene in internal broils in the colonies, if there were any,
besides "put[ting] an end to all the jealousies of Spain with respect to her
remaining colonies."

The most important part came at the end, where Canning asked Rush
whether he was empowered "to enter into negotiation, and to sign any Convention upon this subject." If not, Canning wondered whether Rush could
"exchange with me ministerial notes upon it." Canning thought "there has
seldom, in the history of the world, occurred an opportunity, when so small
an effort, of two friendly Governments, might produce so unequivocal a
good and prevent such extensive calamities."[6]

In the middle of October, Monroe forwarded these two letters to Thomas
Jefferson.[7] Monroe said Canning had suggested "designs of the holy alliance,
against the Independence of So. America, & propos[ed] a co-opration, between G. Britain & the UStates, in support of it, against the members of that
alliance," adding that Canning expected this project to have a significant
diplomatic effect—perhaps "by defeating the combination." Monroe asked
Jefferson for his opinion. Jefferson's response[8] began by saying, "The question presented by the letters you have sent me, is the most momentous which
has ever been offered to my contemplation since that of Independence. That
made us a nation, this sets our compass and points the course which we are
to steer through the ocean of time opening on us."

America, Monroe's old tutor insisted, should have two rules: "never to
entangle ourselves in the broils of Europe" and "never to suffer Europe
to intermeddle with cis-Atlantic affairs." Mirabile dictu, the one nation that
"could disturb us in this pursuit" instead "now offers to lead, aid, and accompany us in it." To accept Canning's offer would be to "bring her mighty
weight into the scale of free government, and emancipate a continent at one
stroke, which might otherwise linger long in doubt and difficulty." To him
the correct response was obvious. "Great Britain is the nation which can do
us the most harm of any one, or all on earth; and with her on our side we need
not fear the whole world. with her then, we should most sedulously cherish a
cordial friendship; and nothing would tend more to knit our affections than
to be fighting once more, side by side, in the same cause."

Musing on these matters a bit, Jefferson saw a problem. "But we have first to ask ourselves a question," he continued. "Do we wish to acquire to our own confederacy any one or more of the Spanish provinces? I candidly confess, that I have ever looked on Cuba as the most interesting addition which could ever be made to our system of States." Quickly sketching the geostrategic advantages of adding that territory to the Union, he concluded that now was not the time to annex it, and so Monroe should pledge to Britain that America did not intend to add any of Spain's former (or, in Cuba's case, remaining) colonial possessions to its own territory.

Jefferson forwarded Monroe's cover letter and the Canning-Rush papers to James Madison on behalf of Monroe. Madison's response to Monroe's query differed from Jefferson's as the two men's personalities differed.[9] Madison thought it certain that Canning intended to do what he proposed to Rush that Britain and America do in tandem, whatever the American response to his feelers might be. Should Monroe not accept Canning's offer, Britain in case of war must "either leave us as neutrals to extend our commerce & navigation at the expense of hers" or bring its "paper blockades" back into action for the purpose of coercing her European enemies by restricting America's trade. "It may be hoped," Madison said, "that such a dilemma will not be without a permanent tendency to check her proneness to unnecessary wars." While Jefferson was clear in insisting America not follow this train of policies into European broils, Madison thought the moment was propitious for trying to elicit from England a condemnation of France's Spanish invasion and even a "declaratory act in behalf of the Greeks"—that is, endorsement of Spanish and Greek claims to self-government. In any event, Madison calculated, adding the British and American fleets meant "we should be safe against the rest of the world."

Back in England, Rush had told Canning he agreed with his argument but would have to contact Washington for instructions on how to reply.[10] He then wrote Adams, describing his communication with Canning and adding that he inferred something untoward must be in the offing that had precipitated Canning's actions.[11] That same day, Canning wrote Rush again, this time telling him about intelligence that as soon as France's invasion of Spain had had its desired result ("of which the French expect, how justly I know not, a very speedy achievement"), a European congress was to be held to address "the affairs of Spanish America." "I need not point out to you," he concluded, "all the complications to which this proposal, however dealt with by us, may lead."[12] Rush told Canning that if Britain recognized the Spanish colonies' independence right away," he was certain "that it would accelerate the steps of [the United States Government] in a course of policy intimated as being common to this government, for the welfare of those states."[13]

Rush wrote to Adams in a state of high excitement saying that "if the recognition be made by Great Britain without more delay," Rush was ready to vow of his government "that it will not remain inactive under an attack upon the independence of [the former Spanish New World colonies] by the Holy Alliance." He knew he would bear full responsibility for this unauthorized act, but his certainty that it "would prove at least a probable means of warding off the attack" made it seem worthwhile. Of course the administration could disavow his act.[14] Canning predictably rejected the idea of a British announcement unaccompanied for the moment by any public statement from the United States.[15] On September 8th, having just received Canning's message, Rush wrote to Adams that he would take no action until he received new instructions.[16]

A week later Rush sent a lengthy private communication to Monroe.[17] He made clear that he did not believe America was "likely to witness any very material changes in the part which Britain has acted in the world for the past fifty years, when the cause of freedom has been at stake; the part which she acted in 1774 in America, which she has since acted in Europe, and is now acting in Ireland." He thought the Parliament's leaders "anxious apparently only about monarchs and thrones," which explained why Britain now stood as "in effect a member of the Holy Alliance," ready to intervene in the affairs of Naples "not on any new extremity of wrong or oppression to the *people* of Naples, but on any molestation to the royal family." At the time Britain was standing by as France levied a war "upon the independence of Spain, as unjust, as nefarious, and as cruel, as the annals of mankind can recount." Any cooperation with America in relation to former New World Spanish colonies, then, must result from British calculations about British interests. Still "whatever may be the *motive* of these approaches, if they give promise of leading to good *effects,* effects which the United States from principle and policy would delight to hail, I grant that a dispassionate and friendly ear should be turned to them."

Monroe and his Cabinet discussed these matters in several meetings beginning on November 7, 1823.[18] The first meeting, attended by the president, Adams, Calhoun, and Navy Secretary Samuel L. Southard, lasted two and a half hours in the afternoon of a rainy day. As Adams understood the matter, Canning had approached Rush in relation to "the projects of the holy alliance upon South-America." Canning wanted a "public pledge from the

Government of the United States, ostensibly against the forcible interference of the Holy Alliance between Spain and South-America; but really or especially against the acquisition to the United States themselves of any part of the Spanish American Possessions."

Adams came into disagreement with Calhoun about this. The war secretary wanted to give Rush discretionary authority to enter into such a joint pledge with the British, "if necessary even if it should pledge us not to take Cuba, or the Province of Texas." This, Calhoun reasoned, would be to trade nothing for something, as America did not at the moment have means to seize either of those possessions, while the British did. Adams thought that since America had no present intentions in relation to those territories, though their residents were always at liberty to ask to join the United States, while they would never ask to join the Britain Empire, a joint vow not to seize any such territory amounted to obtaining a worthless vow for one that could affect future policy. Adams insisted America should keep its options open.

It was President Monroe who, according to Secretary Adams, "was averse to any course which should have the appearance of taking a position subordinate to that of Great Britain." Monroe also broached the idea of sending a special delegate to Europe "to *protest* against the interposition of the Holy Alliance." Adams's position was that rather "than to come in as a Cock-boat in the wake of the British man of War," the administration should "take our stand against the Holy Alliance, and at the same time . . . decline the overture of Great-Britain." All agreed.

67

✢ ☼ ✢

When Adams visited Monroe about the upcoming Annual Message six days later, Monroe seemed "altogether settled in his own mind, as to the answer to be given to Mr. Canning's proposals." Besides this, the secretary was surprised to find the president "alarmed far beyond any thing that I could have conceived possible, with the fear that the Holy Alliance are about to restore immediately all South-America to Spain." Adams blamed the secretary of war for the president's state of mind, "and the news that Cadiz has surrendered to the French, has so affected the President that he appeared entirely to despair of the cause of South-America." Adams concluded that Monroe would snap out of it, though only "in a few days." Asked by Adams for guidance whether to draft a note accepting or a note dismissing Canning's proposals, Monroe said only that they would discuss the matter the next day.

The November 21st meeting centered on Adams's draft response to Minister Rush lasted four hours.[1] Adams took to the meeting his draft of an answer to Rush regarding Canning's proposals. Monroe proposed several amendments to Adams's draft, to virtually all of which both Adams and Calhoun strenuously objected. The most notable argument concerned the Adams draft's statement that America would expect most favored nation trade status in all of the newly independent former Spanish colonies, which Monroe wanted to amend to concede that, in Adams's words, "special favours or even a restoration of authority might be conceded to Spain." Adams and Calhoun won this dispute on the substance, though not before—as Adams recalled grumpily—"[t]he President . . . finally required that the phraseology of it should be varied." Adams said he also received Monroe's approval of his plan to give the Russian minister a note "declar[ing] our expectation and hope that the European Powers will equally abstain from the attempt to spread their principles [meaning some form of authoritarian monarchy] in the American Hemisphere, or to subjugate by force any part of these Continents to their will."

Next the Cabinet took up Monroe's draft of his Seventh Annual Message. Adams found Monroe's "tone of deep solemnity . . . and of high alarm" inappropriate. As Monroe had it, America was (in Adams's account) "menaced by imminent and formidable dangers, such as would probably soon call for their most vigorous energies, and the closest union." The draft's account of America's foreign relations used "terms of the most pointed reprobation" in relation to Iberian developments, besides treating the Greeks as independent and calling on Congress to fund an American minister (we would say "ambassador") to be sent to them. "Of all this," Adams noted, "Mr. Calhoun declared his approbation."

The secretary of state called on Monroe to "reconsider the whole subject." The introduction would shock the country, he said, and it seemed odd coming in "a period of so deep calm and tranquility as we now enjoyed. We never were upon the whole in a state of peace so profound and secure with all foreign Nations as at this time." Yet "[t]his Message would be a summons to arms—To arms against all Europe; and for objects of policy exclusively European, Greece and Spain." (Adams clearly had not read Madison's letter to Monroe of October 30th, in which the former president had recommended the United States take the positions Monroe here was taking in regard to Greece and Spain.)

Adams pointed out to the president that his message in its present form would work a revolution in American foreign policy, which through three decades had been one of studied aloofness as virtually every country in Europe had been "alternately invading and invaded—Empires, Kingdoms, Principalities, had been overthrown, Revolutionised and counter-revolutionised; and we had looked on, safe in our distance beyond an intervening Ocean, and avowing a total forbearance to interfere. . . ." Here America would at least seem to be declaring her intention to participate in Europe's broils, "and I should not be surprised if the first answer to it from Spain, and France, and even Russia, should be to break off their diplomatic intercourse with us. . . ." If Adams had his way, America would remain above it all as long as feasible.

Calhoun, Adams said, interjected at this point to say that his Massachusetts colleague had it all wrong. "[T]here was great anxiety in the thinking part of the Nation" and "a general expectation that the Holy Alliance would employ force against South-America," which meant "it would be proper that the President should sound the alarm to the Nation." Southard said little in this discussion, according to Adams, though he did generally prefer Adams's argument to Calhoun's. Monroe and Calhoun both replied to Adams, saying that the recent French intervention in Spain was different in kind from the wars of the French Revolution and Napoleon. France in Spain had acted directly against "the popular principle." Thus it could be right for Monroe to break with past practice and decry this latest European act of conquest. (Albert Gallatin, freshly returned from a tour as American minister to France, had urged Monroe to speak out about the French invasion only a month earlier, though he had rightly observed at the same time that America had actually been silent in the past about monarchist attacks on republics, notably during the wars of the French Revolution and Napoleon.[2] What neither Gallatin nor Monroe knew was that even before Rush's letters reached the White House, Canning had persuaded the French ambassador to the Court of St. James's, the prince de Polignac, to give him a memorandum vowing that France had no intention to intervene in Spanish America—thus rendering Canning's initiative with Rush moot.)[3]

The next day Adams stopped by to discuss this matter with Monroe one more time. If he could finish his term "at peace and amity with all the world," Adams said, the president's administration would be recalled "as the golden age of this republic." What Adams wanted was "earnest remonstrance against the interference of the European powers by force with South America, but to disclaim all interference on our part with Europe; to take an American cause, and adhere inflexibly to that."[4]

Though responsible for enormous American territorial expansion, James Monroe is most remembered today for parts of his Seventh Annual Message.[5] That is where he laid out the point of policy on which he, Adams, Calhoun, and Southard, with the input of Rush, Jefferson, and Madison, had worked so doggedly—the foreign policy principle now known as the Monroe Doctrine. The famous pronouncement about foreign policy is found in the main at the end of a string of rather tedious sections telling what the Executive has spent money on in the last year, an account which reminds one of Francis Walker Gilmer's appraisal of the third, fourth, and fifth presidents' intellects. A son of Jefferson's Albemarle County friend and neighbor Dr. George Gilmer and brother-in-law of Attorney General William Wirt, Francis Gilmer was chosen by Jefferson to go to Europe and recruit faculty members for the University of Virginia. After that a grateful Master of Monticello tapped him to be the new university's first law professor (though he would die before teaching law). Francis thus knew whereof he spake when he told one of Jefferson's nephews concerning Jefferson and Madison that "[t]here is no comparison between the two men. Madison I hear was logical in debate. But in every thing I have seen from him, his logic is artificial & shallow. In conversation he is a disputatious polemic; but I think by no means a powerful adversary. He is however as much superior to his successor as he is inferior to his predecessor."[6] (In correspondence with his own brother, Gilmer, after having been to dinner at Monticello with Monroe present, evaluated Monroe even more harshly.)

On the other hand John C. Calhoun, who had worked closely with Monroe for eight years and whose intellectual star far outshone Gilmer's, remembered his former chief more positively at the time of his death. "Tho' not brilliant," he wrote, "few men were his equals in wisdom, firmness and devotion to the country. He had a wonderful intellectual patience; and could above all men, that I ever knew, when called on to decide an important point, hold the subject immovably fixed under his attention, until he had mastered it in all its relations. It was mainly to this admirable quality that he owed his highly accurate judgment. I have known many much more rapid in reaching a conclusion, but few with a certainty so unerring."[7]

While toned down enough to placate the secretary of state, the message's opening paragraph still said that "there never was a period since the establishment of our Revolution when, regarding the condition of the civilized world and its bearing on us, there was greater necessity for devotion in the public servants to their respective duties, or for virtue, patriotism, and union in our constituents." After some matters of routine or passing interest, in the seventh paragraph of his message Monroe got to the Russian minister's invitation to negotiate each party's rights in northwestern North America. In this context, he said, "the occasion has been judged proper for asserting, as a principle in which the rights and interests of the United States are involved, that the American continents, by the free and independent condition which they have assumed and maintain, are henceforth not to be considered as subjects for future colonization by any European powers." Two paragraphs farther down, he said American ministers had been instructed to implement the House of Representatives' resolution that American ministers in Europe and America propose proscription of the slave trade, which Monroe called an "odious and criminal practice," by having it classified as piracy and those who engaged in it punished as for piracy. The president also said that America was seeking to have the European powers adopt as their rules the rules France imposed on itself in its current war with Spain: no privateering and no interference with enemy or neutral commerce at sea unless it was "in the breach of a lawful blockade." These policies, for which America had contended in the War of 1812, would yield an "essential amelioration to the condition of the human race" with only "the consent of a few sovereigns," which "the friends of humanity" must hope would be forthcoming.

The process of recognizing the newly established Hispano-American republics continued apace, as did the exchange of diplomats. So too did the speedy extinguishment of the public debt. Without mentioning Calhoun, Monroe boasted of the remarkable improvement of the state of the army and its supply system. Three significant military posts would be completed in the coming year. An act of 1820, Monroe continued, "provides that the system of tactics and regulations of the various corps of the Regular Army shall be extended to the militia. This act has been very imperfectly executed from the want of uniformity in the organization of the militia. . . ." Averse to Calhoun's innovative organizational initiatives relating to the U.S. Army, Congress would not have welcomed more significant steps in relation to the militia, even though it had proven an inapt instrument—and the Executive would continue to find it inapt—as Monroe knew all too well it had been during the War of 1812.

Meanwhile orders had gone out for American-flagged ships engaged in the slave trade to be arrested and brought to port. "I have the gratification to state," the president said, "that not one so employed has been discovered, and there is good reason to believe that our flag is now seldom, if at all, disgraced by that traffic."

Monroe reminded Congress that in his previous annual message he had explained his understanding of "the encouragement which ought to be given to our manufactures and the principle on which it should be founded." His understanding remained unchanged. He therefore again called on Congress to provide tariff protection for "those articles which we are prepared to manufacture, or which are more immediately connected with the defense and independence of the country." So too he reported that the last congressional session's appropriations for repairs of the Cumberland Road had been spent for that purpose. On the related subject of a canal connecting the Chesapeake Bay to the Ohio River, Monroe said that he believed "Congress possess the right to appropriate money for such a national object (the jurisdiction remaining to the State through which the canal would pass)," so Congress ought to consider whether the Army Corps of Engineers should research the project's feasibility. Too, he recommended that the Corps investigate the feasibility of connecting the Ohio River to Lake Erie. His final proposal along this line was that in light of Congress's omission to propose an internal improvements amendment to the states, the Executive might be authorized to inquire of governors through whose states the Cumberland Road passed about being allowed to set up tolls to fund ongoing repairs to the road.

Monroe next explained why Americans hoped for success in "the heroic struggle of the Greeks, that they would succeed in their contest and resume their equal station among the nations of the earth. It is believed," he hazarded, "that the whole civilized world take a deep interest in their welfare." This logically led him into two lengthy paragraphs—the last two before his message's conclusion—enunciating the Monroe Doctrine. "[W]e should consider," the president said, "any attempt on [the allied powers'] part to extend their system to any portion of this hemisphere as dangerous to our peace and safety." America had not interfered and would not interfere with European colonies, and "with the Governments who have declared their independence we have, on great consideration and on just principles, acknowledged, we could not view any interposition for the purpose of oppressing them, or controlling in any other manner their destiny, by any European power in any other light than as the manifestation of an unfriendly disposition toward the United States." Further, America would continue to refrain from interfering in the internal affairs of any European power, "to consider the government de facto as the legitimate government for us," and "to cultivate friendly relations," "meeting in all instances the just claims of every power, submitting to injuries from none." Spain obviously could not subdue her former colonies, but America's policy was not to interfere.

68

⊹ ⊛ ⊹

James Monroe's Seventh Annual Message was an immediate success. Members of Congress endorsed it (though Daniel Webster wished Monroe had proposed concrete action on behalf of the Greeks), and the U.K.'s minister in Washington said Madison's position on European interference in former Spanish colonies "has evidently found in every bosom a chord which vibrates in strict unison with the sentiments so conveyed." The General Assembly of Pennsylvania adopted a resolution that Monroe's statement about "defence of the cause of Liberty in this Western Hemisphere" had earned "the entire approbation of the General Assembly of this Commonwealth." The British press liked that too, though Canning felt compelled to disclose the Polignac letter. In France liberals like Lafayette were pleased, while the government was not. It was also generally well received in South America.[1]

Though this annual message was the highlight of Monroe's second term, other matters drew his attention as well. For example, in February 1824 he addressed the long-standing claim of the government of Massachusetts for federal reimbursement of some of the expenses the Commonwealth had incurred in mobilizing its militia during the War of 1812.[2] Recall that Massachusetts had taken the lead among New England states in being uncooperative with the Federal Government's military effort, among other ways by refusing to make the state's militia available when properly requested. Monroe's official memorandum to Congress explained the lengthy delay in addressing this matter by saying, "It affords me great pleasure to state that the present executive of Massachusetts has disclaimed the principle which was maintained by the former executive, and that in this disclaimer both branches of the legislature have concurred." He went on to recommend to Congress that Massachusetts militiamen who had served during the war be fully compensated as those from other states had been—even though Governor Strong had refused to put the Bay State's militia under federal command.

During the war, the war secretary had told Massachusetts authorities that this would mean the state would not receive compensation, yet its governor had continued to refuse full cooperation. Here Monroe held out an olive branch to citizens of Massachusetts, saying that "even those who now survive who were then in error can not fail to see with interest and satisfaction this distressing occurrence thus happily terminated."[3]

Another significant issue that came up repeatedly across the eight years of Monroe's presidency was government spending on roads, canals, and bridges—what in those days were called "internal improvements." Monroe entered into the presidency as his immediate predecessor, the constitutional authority, had just issued a thundering veto of Representatives Clay and Calhoun's Bonus Bill. He followed in James Madison's footsteps in this regard, after a fashion. He mentioned internal improvements in his First Inaugural Address, his First Annual Message, and elsewhere, urging Congress to propose a constitutional amendment to address the problems Madison's Bonus Bill Veto Message had identified. Congress did not do so, as proponents of this policy commonly insisted Madison had been mistaken in vetoing the Bonus Bill. Monroe's position was somewhat opaque.

So, for example, midway through his second term Monroe vetoed a bill "for the preservation and repair of the Cumberland Road" from Cumberland, Maryland, to Wheeling, Virginia.[4] He did so "with deep regret, approving as I do the policy," he said. Then followed six paragraphs explaining how he had come to the conclusion that the bill was unconstitutional.

He conceded that Congress had a constitutional "right of applying money under the power vested in Congress to make appropriations, under which power, with the consent of the States through which this road passes, the work was originally commenced." This right was, however, not to be confused with the idea underlying the bill: that Congress had "a power to establish turnpikes with gates and tolls, and to enforce the collection of tolls by penalties." If Congress had that power, it would have "the right to take the land from the proprietor on a valuation and to pass laws for the protection of the road from injuries, and if it exist as to one road it exists as to any other, and to as many roads as Congress may think proper to establish." This would be nothing less than "a complete right of jurisdiction and sovereignty for all the purposes of internal improvement, and not merely the right of applying money under the power vested in Congress to make appropriations, under which power, with the consent of the States through which this road passes, the work was originally commenced, and has been so far executed." Lest one infer that a state could consent to Congress's exercise of the power he was saying it lacked, Monroe added that although the states could agree for Congress to spend money "within their limits for such purposes, they [could] grant no power of jurisdiction or sovereignty by special compacts with the United States."

Considering the Constitution's text, Monroe said he neither found such a congressional power enumerated therein nor thought such a power "incidental to some power which has been specifically granted," including the power to establish post offices and post roads, the power to declare war, and the power to regulate interstate commerce. He also did not think it incidental to the General Welfare Clause, the Necessary and Proper Clause, the Preamble's reference to "provid[ing] for the common defense," or the Territories Clause. Only a constitutional amendment could give Congress that power. He closed by saying he would relay a lengthy explanation of his views on this subject soon.

Organized more or less as the veto message was, Monroe's pamphlet, "Views on the Subject of Internal Improvements," considered each of the clauses there mentioned one at a time and concluded that it did not give Congress power to do what the bill would have done. Monroe circulated the pamphlet among his acquaintances and sent copies of it to the members of the Supreme Court. He received three answers. Justice Joseph Story told him that as the question might come before the Court, he could not express an opinion on it. Chief Justice John Marshall, on the other hand, told the president of his views that "To me they appear to be generally just" before saying that, "I despair however of the adoption of such a measure"—which seems to leave unclear whether the element of Monroe's argument he found "generally just" was his argument for Congress to exercise the power he already thought it had or his call for an amendment.[5]

However, Justice William Johnson, Thomas Jefferson's sometime correspondent, wrote Monroe that

> Judge Johnson has had the honour to submit the President's argument on the subject of internal improvements to his brother-judges and is instructed to make the following report.
>
> The judges are deeply sensible of the mark of confidence bestowed on them in this instance and should be unworthy of that confidence did they attempt to conceal their real opinion. Indeed to conceal or disavow it would be now impossible as they are all of opinion that the decision on the bank question [*McCulloch v. Maryland*] completely commits them on the subject of internal improvements as applied to post-roads and military roads. On

the other points it is impossible to resist the lucid and conclusive reasoning contained in the argument.

The principle assumed in the case of the Bank is that the grant of the principal power carries with it the grant of all adequate and appropriate means of executing it. That the selection of those means must rest with the general government and as to that power and those means the Constitution makes the government of the U.S. supreme.

Johnson then suggested that the secretary of state circulate copies of *McCulloch v. Maryland* throughout the country. The justice's biographer is right to call this "virtually an advisory opinion" and to say that it "today would be deemed highly exceptionable."[6]

Another subject that occupied the attention of Monroe, Calhoun, and the administration generally during Monroe's tenure was the future of American Indians. As we have seen, both Monroe and Calhoun hoped that the Indians could be assimilated into American society—on which indeed some particular local groups were making progress. However, by 1824 Georgians were increasingly insistent that the Federal Government must keep its end of the bargain it had reached with Georgia over the Indians' relocation in 1802. Monroe sent a message to Congress on March 30, 1824, explaining where things stood.[7]

"By the fourth article of that compact," Monroe said, "it was stipulated that the United States should at their own expense extinguish for the use of Georgia the Indian title to all the lands within the State as soon as it might be done *peaceably* and on *reasonable* conditions." Although the documents he relayed to Congress explained what the Executive had done in fulfillment of the compact, including how much money had been paid for how many acres, matters had reached a point at which the Executive could not "make any further movement with this tribe [the Cherokees] without the special sanction of Congress."

Monroe said the records testified to Jefferson and Madison's efforts in this connection, adding, "I have also been animated since I came into this office with the same zeal, from an anxious desire to meet the wishes of the State, and in the hope that by the establishment of these tribes beyond the Mississippi their improvement in civilization, their security and happiness would be promoted." He pointed out that he had explained in recent discussions with the Cherokee "the incompatibility with our system of their existence as a distinct community within any State," besides offering to trade them trans-Mississippi land of equal value for their land in Georgia or to pay them for their Georgia lands. Their "unqualified refusal" meant they could only be removed by force, "to which . . . the Executive is incompetent."

Monroe went on to add what Georgia congressmen, at least, did not want to read: that as the compact said (in Monroe's words) "that their title should be extinguished at the expense of the United States when it may be done *peaceably* and on *reasonable* conditions," the Indians were understood by both parties to the compact to be "free agents. An attempt to remove them by force would, in my opinion, be unjust." He observed that "In the future measures to be adopted in regard to the Indians within our limits, . . . the United States have duties to perform and a character to sustain. . . ." The Federal Government's long-standing concern with "their improvement in the arts of civilized life," "dictated by motives of humanity," applied to "all the tribes within our limits."

Monroe remained convinced that it would be in the tribes' best interest "to retire west and north of our States and Territories on lands to be procured for them by the United States, in exchange for those on which they now reside," as the flood of white population into lands around the Indians' would make it "difficult if not impossible . . . with their kind of government, to sustain order among them." This would mean increasingly frequent U.S. Government interference in their lives, "and thus their government will gradually lose its authority until it is annihilated." He hoped Congress would find a solution satisfactory to both Georgia and the Cherokee, while remaining careful not "to commit any breach of right or of humanity in regard to the Indians." Congress did not act on this matter during Monroe's tenure—much to the Indians' eventual detriment.

69

⸬

That same day, March 30, 1824, Henry Clay stood up in the House of Representatives to deliver the most important speech of his long political career. Already famous for his oratory, most notably in support of the Spanish colonies' independence, Clay for the balance of that day and much of the next would detail what he called his "American System." With John Randolph of Roanoke and Daniel Webster, Clay was one of the outstanding congressional orators of the age, besides one of the outstanding politicians of the era, and the program he developed on those two March days in 1824 eventually would form the keystone to the Whigs', and later the antebellum Republicans', political appeal.

Clay did not speak only to advocate a program. Treasury Secretary William Crawford of Georgia, known since 1822 to be intent on winning that year's election, had been nominated for president on February 14, 1824, by a caucus of a minority of Republican congressmen.[1] Besides, War Secretary John C. Calhoun was known to be in the field, and Clay was kicking off his candidacy in earnest. For several election cycles the Republican candidate had been selected by a caucus of Republican congressmen, but both democratic principle and cold, hard calculation that Crawford likely would be the caucus nominee led to growing criticism of the caucus procedure. Secretary of State Adams, one historian concludes, "was unequivocally opposed to his being nominated by a caucus, while Clay felt he had nothing to fear from a caucus of all Republican congressmen." Calhoun stood somewhere between them. (The relatively paltry attendance meant it would be the last such caucus. This cycle marked the permanent transition from caucuses so conventions. So too for the first time the major candidates established connections to newspapers supportive of their candidacies.)[2] Hugh Lawson White, a Jackson supporter, responded to news that his man had been nominated by the Tennessee Legislature by calling that method "highly improper"—even "dangerous in the extreme."

The South Carolina Legislature's very early (1821) endorsement of a favorite son other than Calhoun, William Lowndes, had weakened Calhoun's candidacy, though when Lowndes died a few months later, the Legislature corrected its error. The Tennessee Legislature adopted a resolution against congressional caucuses to choose presidential candidates (because, the 1824 election's leading historian says, it knew favorite son Jackson could not win the caucus),[3] and this led to broad discussion of the matter. Virginia, where Ritchie's *Richmond Enquirer* supported Crawford, saw its General Assembly early in the process call on Virginia Republican congressmen to work to have a nominating caucus. Maine, New York, and Georgia's legislatures issued similar calls.[4]

The elephant in the room was Crawford's health. While visiting with Senator James Barbour of Virginia at his Barboursville plantation (conveniently located short rides from both Jefferson's Monticello and Madison's Montpellier) in September 1823, Crawford came down with "a severe case of erysipelas." A physician apparently administered an overdose of lobelia (though there is some indication it may have been an overdose of calomel), which left the secretary of the treasury "speechless, nearly blind and immobile." Crawford was also bled twenty-three times. (Recall that in 1799 George Washington, hale and hearty in the morning, died after a few hours of Virginia physicians' expert ministrations—including numerous bleedings.) The public was kept in the dark about the severity of Crawford's malady, which kept him from Cabinet meetings for two months, and when he returned, he was obviously impaired—his "speech was still thick and hesitant, and his memory uncertain." He later said that a May relapse had left him "deranged." He did not resign his office, however, because doing so would have killed his presidential campaign, and President Monroe did not replace him lest he seem to be taking sides in the contest (!).[5]

Crawford was the particular favorite of hardline Jeffersonians unhappy with Monroe for his significant efforts to end party disputation. (Senator Martin Van Buren, R-NY, called advocacy of a party-less polity "the Monroe heresy.")[6] Men such as Thomas Ritchie, Philip P. Barbour, and the like were unlikely to appreciate Monroe's effort to paper over the constitutional differences between the parties on internal improvements, for example, and they certainly disliked his tax, naval, and other policies. (Though he insisted it not be made public, Thomas Jefferson preferred Crawford too.)[7] Their views were reflected by the congressional caucus's nomination of Crawford for president, with sixty-two votes for him and four scattered among other candidates. It chose Gallatin for vice president.[8]

Ultimately Calhoun's candidacy was doomed by Pennsylvania's endorsement of Andrew Jackson, alongside whom he was nominated for vice president. Once Pennsylvania formally broached that idea, other states followed. Margaret Bayard Smith said Calhoun "feels very deeply the disappointment of his ambition," which, however, did not sleep yet.[9]

Clay in his "American System" speech looked beyond official Washington to the entire American electorate. He laid out a vision for active government involvement in the American economy—a kind of neo-Hamiltonianism without the Report on Manufactures—that would guide one party in America's two-party politics for several decades to come. Clay's program had three components: a national bank, a protective tariff, and internal improvements. The last of those he assumed to be constitutional without the constitutional amendment President Monroe, like President Madison before him, said must precede it. Clay envisioned a commanding role for the government in society, at one point vowing that he would make five hundred thousand farmers into manufacturing workers—a promise that would come back to haunt him. Clay's advocacy of this program did result in a substantial increase in tariff rates under the new Tariff of 1824, which heightened Southerners' concerns about the direction the government was taking. He said that he understood that the South would derive little benefit from his program, instead paying disproportionate tariffs to fund a platform that would benefit the other sections, but he thought Southerners were patriotic enough to overlook this fact.[10]

Despite, or perhaps in part because of, his American System program, Speaker of the House Clay placed fourth in the Electoral College behind Crawford, Jackson, and Adams. The Constitution says that if no candidate wins a majority, the names of the top three vote-getters will go before the House, which will elect a president with each state having one vote. Clay's name did not go before the House, but as speaker he could be expected to have influence on the outcome.

Though his brief stint in Congress had not yielded any particular legislative results (and in fact anyone paying close attention could tell by his performance in the Senate that he did not have a political temperament), General Jackson's military exploits made him quite popular with the general public, despite his not having a program other than election—a phenomenon not unique in American history.[11] John Quincy Adams, meanwhile, had strong support in New England and played a winning hand in New York. Besides his exemplary record as secretary of state, Adams's candidacy also stood out on account of his known antislavery principles and his former identification with the Federalists, which won him support in the Middle States.

It was Middle States' support that ultimately won Adams the race. Despite the myth of nearly two centuries, besides ultimately winning the contest in the House of Representatives by a vote of Adams 13, Jackson 7, Crawford 4,[12] Adams had more proven popular support than any other candidate. His supporters in that state's legislature had about 40 percent of popular votes cast in New York, while Andrew Jackson—said by his supporters at the time and by scholars until very recently to have had more popular votes and more Electoral College votes than any other candidate—had virtually no New York support. Party propaganda has a long half-life.[13]

When in the wake of his election Adams tapped Clay for secretary of state, Jackson supporters dubbed the supposed arrangement between the speaker and Adams the "Corrupt Bargain." They left aside the fact that if Clay had preferred Adams to Crawford and Jackson when the matter was before the House, his judgment concerning their personal fitness for the post and the close sympathy between Clay's and Adams's programs could easily account for the choice, besides which it would have been highly uncharacteristic for Adams to have made such an arrangement.

In addition to the election of Adams, the other significant result of the Election of 1824 was the birth of the Democratic Party—today's Democratic Party. Rufus King traced the "Corrupt Bargain" idea to Crawford supporters' unhappiness with the election's outcome. They were the ones who pushed this idea on Jackson men, who proved only too willing to take it up and use it for their own political purposes. For disgruntled Republicans like Martin Van Buren, using Jackson's popularity as the cement of a new Jeffersonian coalition made perfect sense. Jackson's personality made him easy to persuade that he had been cheated somehow in 1824 too.

As these events transpired, the Marquis de Lafayette, young general of the Continental Army and hero of revolutionary France, mentioned in a letter to Monroe, "I often dream of the day when I will be able, without remorse, to enjoy the happiness of finding myself once again on American ground." Monroe immediately wrote that if he came, he would be "the Nation's guest." Wisely seeing that accepting Monroe's proffer of a ride on an American warship could cause the United States diplomatic problems, Lafayette traveled to New York on an American merchantman. When he arrived at New York, the crowd of ships waiting in the harbor and the throngs of people wanting to catch a glimpse of him left him stuck. Monroe realized that a route straight to the capital could have diplomatic ramifications too, in light of the French king's displeasure with Lafayette (Louis XVIII called him "that animal"), and so Monroe sent him on a circuitous route around

America. Meantime the president concocted a plan to have Congress award the nation's French friend American lands, money, or both. Born into a chateau, Lafayette had paid dearly for his services to the cause of *liberté*, American and French. Monroe found Lafayette "in good health & spirits, and less altered in his form, than I expected, and not at all in his mind."[14]

Lafayette toured the country as George Washington, onetime French Minister to the United States Edmond Charles Genet, and James Monroe had done. Wherever Lafayette went, veterans of the Revolution came out to see him and, as if he were a president, military men accompanied him, which slowed his traveling considerably: an expected three-week trip from Philadelphia to Monticello took five weeks, and a two-day trek from Yorktown to Monticello took two weeks. There were widely publicized events such as Lafayette's reunion with Thomas Jefferson at Monticello after so long a time.[15] As a young officer Lafayette had known James Monroe during the war too, and so their reunion evoked memories of the glorious founding of the United States, both from them and from citizens who saw or read about aspects of Lafayette's tour. At the end of December 1824, Congress responded to Monroe's request for a gift to Lafayette by awarding him twenty-four thousand acres of land in northern Florida and $200,000 worth of 6 percent bonds redeemable in ten years.[16] (Predictably, Lafayette did not live long enough to redeem the bonds.)

70

·┼· ⊛ ·┼·

By this point Monroe had delivered his final annual message.[1] More than one authority classifies it as "valedictory." Far the longest of his annual messages, this one was a *tour d'horizon* of the Federal Government's responsibilities and activities, with attention to military policy, trade policy, Indian policy, the Judicial Branch, Lafayette's visit, and the Western Hemisphere's prospects. Like Monroe's other annual messages and unlike modern ones, this address really did provide, in the words of Article II, Section 3 of the Constitution, "Information of the State of the Union."

Monroe began by considering the remarkable growth of America's population and expansion of its settled area. "We have daily gained strength by a native population in every quarter," he said, "—a population devoted to our happy system of government and cherishing the bond of union with internal affection." Where other expansive countries had been weakened by the multiplicity of their economic interests, America's heterogeneity of interests "can not fail to produce with us under wise regulations the opposite effect. What one portion wants the other may supply. . . ." So too the federal organization of American government yielded a situation in which "causes which might otherwise lead to dismemberment operate powerfully to draw us closer together."

The Federal Government's system of taxation, relying on tariffs and tonnage taxes, weighed lightly on the people. The country's foreign relations were in a happy state with all other nations. The country's fortifications and naval building programs proceeded apace. "For these blessings," he said, "we owe to Almighty God . . . our most grateful and unceasing acknowledgements."

American trade relations generally stood on the United States' preferred footing of reciprocity between nations—a principle "essentially connected with those upon which their independence was declared." Though negotiations with the British had not yet resulted in an agreement for cooperation in suppressing the slave trade, Monroe hoped they soon would yield "its entire extirpation forever." Foreign relations more generally were happy with all other nations, including newly independent Brazil—from whom a chargé d'affaires had recently been received. Britain had scrupulously lived up to the Treaty of Ghent, and indemnity from France was expected. As to his administration's greatest triumph, the territorial acquisition resulting from the Transcontinental Treaty, Monroe said, "Of the great advantages resulting from [it] . . . too high an estimate can not be formed."

In the next section Monroe itemized the government's major expenditures, concluding with a forecast that "[t]he last portion of the public debt will be redeemable on [January 1, 1835]." Monroe's prediction proved perfectly accurate, and Andrew Jackson—who happened to be the incumbent president at the time Monroe's plan came to fruition—commonly receives the credit for the debt's extinguishment then.

As had been characteristic of him throughout his tenure, Monroe devoted substantial attention to Indian policy in this final address. The difficulties recently encountered in relations with the tribes on the Upper Mississippi and Upper Lakes he attributed to hostility among different Indian groups there. His policy response was to try to pacify their relations with one another—"to bring about a general peace among them"—for the good of all. As to other Indians, he said, "our relations with all the others are on the same friendly footing, and it affords me great satisfaction to add that they are making steady advances in civilization and the improvement of their condition. Many of the tribes have already made great progress in the arts of civilized life. This desirable result has been brought about by the humane and persevering policy of the Government, and particularly by means of the appropriation for the civilization of the Indians." Among means for this achievement had been the establishment of "32 schools, containing 916 scholars, who are well instructed in several branches of literature, and likewise in agriculture and the ordinary arts of life." Monroe's successor, John Quincy Adams, supported this policy vector strongly.

Monroe next described the various deployments of the U.S. Navy, whose chief functions were suppression of piracy and interdiction of the slave trade. No American vessel had been captured slaving that year, though Monroe added, "It is well known, however, that the trade still exists under other flags."

Lafayette had been invited to visit America "in conformity with a resolution of Congress," the president observed, and beginning with his debarkation at New York, "he was received with the warmth of affection and gratitude to which his very important and disinterested services and sacrifices in our Revolutionary struggle so eminently entitled him." He had received similar expressions of admiration and affection "throughout every portion of our Union." In short, people could not get enough of him. Of particular note had been the outpouring of the remaining veterans of the Revolution wherever the old general appeared. "A more interesting spectacle," Monroe continued, "it is believed, was never witnessed, because none could be founded on purer principles, none proceed from higher or more disinterested motives. That the feelings of those who had fought and bled with him in a common cause should have been much excited was natural."

Monroe did not mention that Lafayette's imploring insistence to Jefferson, Madison, and Monroe himself that they free their slaves had yielded no tangible benefit. What Lafayette likely did not know is that in leaving the White House with a net negative personal fortune, Monroe shared a problem with Jefferson. It likely was legally impossible for either of them to satisfy the Frenchman's request.[2]

Monroe leant his name, at least, to the American Colonization Society (A.C.S.). As Monroe understood its program, that organization intended to resolve the slavery issue in a way analogous to the Monroe administration's answer to the question of how to deal with the relationship between American Indians and the U.S.A.: by removing them from the area of white settlement, in the A.C.S.'s case by sending them to Liberia. That West African state, whose capital, Monrovia, was then and is now named for James Monroe, was founded in the Jeffersonian era in an attempt to resolve the problem raised for Monroe and Jefferson by Gabriel's Rebellion: how "slavery [can] ever be extirpated."

Monroe in retirement allowed the A.C.S. to use his name, accepting honorary titles as president of his county's and his state's chapters of that organization. He wrote of the matter to a son of George Mason, the great Virginian Framer of the Virginia and U.S. Constitutions, who, like Jefferson, Madison, and Monroe, had decried the brutality of slavery and the slave trade while owning, and never manumitting, an enormous slave workforce himself. If slavery could be ended, Monroe asked, what would happen to the freedmen? Could Virginia send them to Liberia? Would they go willingly or have to be forced? If they stayed in Virginia, would they have "equal privileges & rights with the white population, or be held in an inferior grade?" Mason replied that freedmen should be sent to Liberia at federal expense, and then states should compensate former masters. Liberia should be analogous to an Indian reservation: inhabited by one people, but administered by the United States Government.[3]

The time was not too distant when, pressed to consider colonization by Jefferson's favorite (and namesake) grandson, the Virginia General Assembly would reject this scheme as impracticable. It chose instead to enforce slavery more energetically.[4]

"The struggle," Monroe continued, "was for independence and liberty, public and personal, and in this we succeeded." Bearing the common struggle in mind, he recommended, America ought to make some provision for Lafayette in his straitened fiscal circumstances.

Americans looked upon the Greeks' independence struggle with great sympathy. "The feeling of the whole civilized world," Monroe asserted, "is excited in a high degree in their favor." He hoped other countries could agree to accept Greece as an independent state. Yet "[s]eparated as we are from Europe by the great Atlantic Ocean, we can have no concern in the wars of the European Governments nor in the causes which produce them." America's interest was to be on a friendly footing with each European country.

He next asked that Congress consider reorganizing the federal judiciary. Supreme Court justices' circuit-riding obligation needed to be eliminated now that the country had expanded so considerably, he insisted. "The great interests of the nation seem to require that the judges of the Supreme Court should be exempted from every other duty than those which are incident to that high trust."

As to "the aboriginies within our limits, and especially those who are within the limits of any of the states," he said Americans had learned that they and the Indians could not live together unless "the tribes be civilized," besides that as American population grew, "their situation will become deplorable, if their extinction is not menaced." Thus "[t]heir civilization is indispensable to their safety," though "this can only be accomplished by degrees" and it must be commenced "with the infant state." Forcibly removing Indians from the lands they now occupied, "even with a view to their own security and happiness, would be revolting to humanity and utterly unjustifiable." He recommended that the tribes be induced to move to the great region between present American settlement and the Rocky Mountains, there to be educated "in literature and the arts of civilized life." Though likely quite expensive, this seemed the plan most likely to succeed.

In sum then "the situation of the United States is in the highest degree prosperous and happy." "The great object is to preserve these blessings, and to hand them down to the latest posterity." "Our institutions," Monroe insisted, "form an important epoch in the history of the civilized world," and in fact at the time Hispano-America was establishing its independence with similar institutions.

The last substantive passage of Monroe's message concerned the necessity in America's federal system of respecting the division of powers between the state and federal governments. He then closed with a personal observation about "this communication, the last of the kind which I shall have to make," noting that through all of the many trusts with which he had been honored in a long career, he had received abundant "instances of the public confidence and the generous support" of his "fellow citizens." Along the way "I have witnessed the great difficulties to which our Union has been" subjected. "From the present prosperous and happy state," he said, "I derive a gratification which I can not express." He then invoked "the Supreme Ruler of the Universe."

The end of Monroe's presidency closed the book on the Revolutionary generation, but (providentially?) the one of the first five presidents who had a son would see him inaugurated as the first post-Jeffersonian president. While the matter was pending before the House, thinking to share the moment with his new old friend at Monticello, the last Federalist president sent him a missive dated January 22, 1825.[5]

"The presidential election," John Adams began,

> has given me less anxiety than I, myself could have imagined. The next administration will be a troublesome one to whomsoever it falls. And our John has been too much worn to contend much longer with conflicting factions. I call him our John, because when you was at Cul de sac at Paris, he appeared to me to be almost as much your boy as mine. I have often speculated upon the consequences that would have ensued from my takeing your advice, to send him to William and Mary College in Virginia for an Education."

By the time Jefferson answered that generous note, the House had made its choice.[6] Jefferson said, "I sincerely congratulate you on the high gratific[atio]n which the issue of the late election must have afforded you. it must excite ineffable feelings in the breast of a father to have lived to see a son to whose educ[atio]n and happiness his life has been devoted so eminently distinguished by the voice of his country." He then pooh-poohed the likelihood of a rocky ride for the Adams administration.[7]

Soon enough, however, the younger Adams gave his Inaugural Address.[8] After beginning by saying he was about "to bind myself by the solemnities of religious obligation to the faithful performance of the duties allotted to me in the station to which I have been called," Adams referred to the Constitution as "this social compact" and said the Supreme Court had "settl[ed] in harmonious coincidence with the legislative will numerous weighty questions of construction which the imperfection of human language had rendered unavoidable."

The close of "that generation by which [the Constitution] was formed [has] been crowned with success equal to the most sanguine expectations of its founders," he continued. All of the aims named in the U.S. Constitution's Preamble "have been promoted by the Government under which we have lived." "From the experience of the past we derive instructive lessons for the future." One that Adams derived was that of the Federalists and Republicans, "the candid and the just w[ould] now admit that both have contributed splendid talents, spotless integrity, ardent patriotism, and disinterested sacrifices to the formation and administration of this Government, and that both have required a liberal indulgence for a portion of human infirmity and error."

After enumerating some of the principles he thought Americans held in common, Adams concluded that there still remained for past party partisans "one sacrifice of prejudice and passion, to be made. . . . It is that of discarding every remnant of rancor against each other, of embracing as countrymen and friends, and of yielding to talents and virtue alone that confidence which in times of contention for principle was bestowed only upon those who bore the badge of party communion."

In listing some of Monroe's notable achievements, Adams turned for an example of an area in which party concerns ought to be thrown aside to "the topic of internal improvement, emphatically urged by him at his inauguration." "The magnificence and splendor of their public works," Adams ruminated, "are among the imperishable glories of the ancient republics." Legislative discussion had brought people to general agreement that "the first national road" was constitutional, and he hoped that such discussion would lead to "all constitutional objections [to internal improvements] be[ing] removed."

When the new Congress came into session in December 1825, President Adams met it with an annual message pushing this line of thought further. The Federal Government ought to spend on further internal improvements, a national university, and a "lighthouse to the skies." In regard to this last idea, he pointed out that while Europe had over 130 such "lighthouses," the New World had none.[9]

Monticello is about a hundred miles away from Washington, D.C., as the crow flies, and its master finished reading Adams's message highly upset. Its proposals of seemingly constitutionally unjustified initiatives reflected the ideas behind Adams's claim in his Inaugural Address that party division was no longer desirable—that Republicans and Federalists alike should be considered as having contributed significantly to the United States and be treated as welcome participants in a political system in which, once the Supreme Court had "settl[ed constitutional questions] in harmonious coincidence with the legislative will," more or less any government initiative was permissible. In response Jefferson proposed the kind of answer he had prodded Virginians to counterpose to federal overreaching before: a formal legislative warning to the Federal Government that it was risking state government resistance by exercising power not granted to it through the Constitution as Jefferson read it, in this case power to construct internal improvements—power which Jefferson hoped the General Assembly would declare had never been granted to the Federal Government. What his "solemn Declaration and Protest of the Commonwealth of Virginia on the principles of the Constitution of the US. of America & on the violations of them" said was that Virginia had delegated specified powers to the Federal Government, that to "the distribution of it's powers, the Commonwealth of Virginia does religiously and affectionately adhere, opposing, with equal fidelity and firmness, the usurpation of either set of functionaries on the rightful powers of the other." The problem of the moment was that "the federal branch has, assumed in some cases, and claimed in others, a right of enlarging it's own powers by constructions, inferences, and indefinite deductions, from those directly given, which this assembly does declare to be usurpations of the powers retained to the independent branches, mere interpolations into the compact [that is, the U.S. Constitution], and direct infractions of it." Any reading of the Constitution that held Congress had power to engage in internal improvements was one of these "usurpations."[10]

Virginians did not want, Jefferson's resolutions said, to push matters to a breakup of the Union: "they would indeed consider such a rupture as among the greatest calamities which could befall them; but not the greatest. there is yet one greater, submission to a government of unlimited powers." Virginia, in Jefferson's estimation, did not hold that it should immediately push things to a separation, for "we are not at once to despair but that the will & the watchfulness of it's sounder parts will reform it's aberrations, recall it to original and legitimate principles, and restrain it within the rightful limits of self-government. and these are the objects of this Declaration and Protest."

Thomas Jefferson did not accept that the Federalists, if unreconstructed, should be folded into the political establishment the Republicans had come to dominate, let alone that any of their program's elements that he had argued for more than thirty years were unconstitutional should be treated as legitimate. While there is no evidence that he said so, Jefferson seems to have agreed with Martin Van Buren in rejecting the "Monroe Heresy" to the end of his days.

James Madison persuaded Jefferson to keep these resolutions to himself.[11] His day was past. Or so it seemed.

ACKNOWLEDGMENTS

Producing a book is a huge task requiring a team effort. Writing is only part of it. My team in creating *The Jeffersonians* started with my agent, Andrew Stuart, who did his customary first-class job. Andrew and I have now worked with executive editor Michael Flamini at St. Martin's Press on three books, and we are happy with all three. Associate editor Hannah Phillips and colleagues Lizz Blaise (managing editorial), Michelle Cashman (marketing), John Morrone (production), Gail Friedman (production), Gabrielle Gantz (publicity), Young Lim (jacket designer), and Nicola Ferguson (interior designer) did a fine job as well. You can see that the jacket design and interior design are beautiful, and I attest that the editorial staff helped me substantially in giving the text its ultimate polish. The SMP publicity and marketing effort has always been superb.

My employer, Western Connecticut State University, also gave me substantial support in this project during the five years I was working on it. That support took the forms of several course releases for research along the way and a sabbatical leave during the semester when I finally completed the drafting of the manuscript. In addition, part of this book's first chapter originally appeared as "Thomas Jefferson's Revolutionary First Inaugural Address," the 2018 Kartch/Jefferson Lecture at William Paterson University. My invited address, "The Jeffersonian Republicans vs. The Federalist Courts," presented at the University of St. Thomas Law Journal Symposium in Minneapolis in 2016, formed the nub of my discussion of related matters in this book. Most important, my paper "The Monroe Administration: The Case for Continuities," presented at the Lebanon Valley College Center for Political History Annual Conference for 2017, laid out my argument for the reperiodization of American history—considering the Jeffersonian era as an integral whole instead of seeing a breaking point in 1815—underlying this book. Thank you to the participants in that conference for their encouragement and perceptive comments.

Other colleagues in the field of the history of the early American Republic helped me in various ways as well. Professor Peter Kastor of the Department of History at Washington University in St. Louis, a friend from grad school days at the University of Virginia, let me pick his brain about the Voyage of Discovery, aka the Lewis & Clark Expedition, at an early point in my work. Professor Richard Samuelson of the History Department at California State University–San Bernadino, another friend from the University of Virginia, was ever ready to answer my questions about all things Adams, among other matters. Panelists in the "Contrary to the Law of Nature: The Missouri Crisis & the Politics of Slavery" symposium at the CUNY Graduate Center in 2019 threw off abundant insights into the history of that pivotal event in the history of the Jeffersonian era, many of which I found useful.

Finally, my thanks to the teachers who first interested me in this and related topics. I think Michael Holt, emeritus Langbourne M. Williams Professor of American History at the University of Virginia, will see here that my version of William Branch Giles has at last come to resemble his understanding of Thomas Hart Benton—which does not flatter either Giles or Benton. Professor J. C. A. Stagg, editor of *The Papers of James Madison*, will find that I have relied heavily upon his versions of events in the War of 1812 both major and minor. From Professor Ed Ayers, I learned not only a certain skepticism of John C. Calhoun but to consider the prose in which an argument is made an essential buttress of that argument. My fixation on this particular subfield of American history I blame on Thomas Jefferson Memorial Foundation Professor Emeritus Peter S. Onuf, whose "conflicted" appreciation of the Virginian cohort of "the Founding Guys" I seem to have come at last to share. This book is dedicated to my son, Cyril—at last.

NOTES

Chapter 1

1. Thomas Jefferson (hereafter TJ) to the House of Representatives, February 20, 1801, *The Papers of Thomas Jefferson,* ed. Julian P. Boyd (Princeton, NJ: Princeton University Press, 1950) (hereafter *PTJ*), 33:25.

2. Fisher Ames to John Rutledge Jr., January 26, 1801, *Works of Fisher Ames,* ed. Seth Ames (Indianapolis, IN: Liberty Fund, 1983), 2:1404–06, at 1405. Interestingly, Ames proposed that congressional Federalists make a condition of Federalist acquiescence in Jefferson's election that Jefferson pledge "he wd. not countenance democratic amendmts.," which perhaps explains the otherwise mysterious stillbirth of Edmund Pendleton, "The Danger Not Over" (1801), in which the prominent Virginia patriot proposed eight amendments to foreclose adoption of measures such as those to which Republicans objected in the 1790s.

3. Nancy Isenberg, *Fallen Founder: The Life of Aaron Burr* (New York: Penguin, 2007), 220.

4. Rep. James A. Bayard is quoted to this effect in *PTJ, 33*, n. at 3–4. As we will see, the question of the political fate of Bayard's correspondent, Collector of the Port of Wilmington Allen McLane, would be a major thorn in President Jefferson's political side.

5. James Madison (hereafter JM) to TJ, January 10, 1801, *PTJ,* 32:436–39, at 437.

6. Michael A. Bellesiles, "'The Soil Will Be Soaked With Blood': Taking the Revolution of 1800 Seriously," in James Horn, et al., eds., *The Revolution of 1800: Democracy, Race, and the New Republic* (Charlottesville: University of Virginia Press, 2002), 75.

7. Joseph E. Ellis, *American Sphinx: The Character of Thomas Jefferson* (New York: Alfred A. Knopf, 1996).

8. TJ to JM, February 18, 1801, *PTJ, 33*:16.

9. In a letter to his son-in-law the next day, Jefferson said that House Federalists' behavior had "done in one week what very probably could hardly have been effected by years of mild and impartial administration": making most Federalists into Republicans. TJ to Thomas Mann Randolph, February 19, 1801, *PTJ,* 33:20–21, at 21. He repeated this idea in TJ to Thomas Lomax, February 25, 1801, *PTJ,* 33:66–67.

10. JM to TJ, February 28, 1801, *PTJ,* 33:99–100, at 100. Also see JM to TJ, January 10, 1801, *PTJ,* 33:436–39, at 436–37.

11. TJ to Henry Dearborn, February 18, 1801, *PTJ,* 33:13.

12. TJ to Meriwether Lewis, February 23, 1801, *PTJ,* 33:51.

13. TJ to Robert Livingston, February 24, 1801, *PTJ,* 33:61 and note; George Dangerfield,

Chancellor Robert R. Livingston of New York, 1746–1813 (New York: Harcourt, Brace, 1960), 309–94.

14. TJ to John Wayles Eppes, February 22, 1801, *PTJ*, 33:37–38, at 38.

15. TJ to the Senate, February 28, 1801, *PTJ*, 33:101.

16. TJ to Spencer Roane, September 6, 1819, Founders Online (National Archives), https://founders.archives.gov/documents/Jefferson/98-01-02-0734.

17. The most colorful account is Richard Brookhiser, *Founding Father: Rediscovering George Washington* (New York: Free Press, 1996). See also Ron Chernow, *Washington: A Life* (New York: Penguin, 2010), 561–65.

18. George Washington (hereafter, GW), First Inaugural Address, in James D. Richardson, ed., *Messages and Papers of the Presidents, 1789–1897* (Washington, 1896), 1:51–54. The "Virginian" elements included avowals of Washington's want of preparation and lack of proper qualification. Compare, besides Jefferson's First Inaugural Address, Edmund Pendleton's speeches on assuming the presidencies of the Virginia Convention of 1776 and Virginia Ratification Convention of 1788 and GW's speech upon being selected by the Continental Congress to command its army.

19. GW, Second Inaugural Address, in Richardson, *Messages and Papers*, 1:138.

20. John Ferling, *John Adams: A Life* (New York: Henry Holt, 1992), 334–35.

21. John Adams (hereafter JA), Inaugural Address, in Richardson, *Messages and Papers*, 1:228–32.

22. JA to TJ, December 6, 1787, Founders Online (National Archives), https://founders.archives.gov/documents/Adams/99-02-02-0281.

23. A full-length account by a rhetoric scholar is Stephen Howard Browne, *Jefferson's Call for Nationhood: The First Inaugural Address* (College Station: Texas A&M University Press, 2003).

24. Ellis, *American Sphinx*, 170.

25. Ian W. Toll, *Six Frigates: The Epic History of the Founding of the U.S. Navy* (New York: W. W. Norton, 2006), 264.

26. Margaret Bayard Smith to Her Sister, October 5, 1800, http://bobarnebeck.com/mbs.html (accessed October 22, 2018).

27. Margaret B. Smith to Susan B. Smith, in Margaret Bayard Smith, *The First Forty Years of Washington Society*, ed. Gaillard Hunt, 2nd edition (New York: Frederick Ungar, 1965), 25–7, at 25–6.

28. Isenberg, *Fallen Founder*, 208.

29. Alexander Hamilton (hereafter, AH) to Gouverneur Morris, December 26, 1800, Founders Online (National Archives), https://founders.archives.gov/documents/Hamilton/01-25-02-0145.

30. AH to Gouverneur Morris, December 24, 1800, Founders Online (National Archives), https://founders.archives.gov/documents/Hamilton/01-25-02-0141.

31. TJ, First Inaugural Address, March 4, 1801, *PTJ*, 33:148–52. For the term "social intercourse," see Caspar Wistar to TJ, February 18, 1801, *PTJ*, 33:19–20, at 19. For more along the same lines, see William Jackson to TJ, February 24, 1801, *PTJ*, 33:58–59, at 58.

32. Andrew Burstein, *The Inner Jefferson: Portrait of a Grieving Optimist* (Charlottesville: University Press of Virginia, 1995); Douglas L. Wilson, "Jefferson and the Republic of Letters," in Peter S. Onuf, ed., *Jeffersonian Legacies* (Charlottesville: University Press of Virginia, 1993), 50–76.

33. For Morris's unsentimental estimation of commoners generally, see Richard Brookhiser, *Gentleman Revolutionary: Gouverneur Morris, the Rake Who Wrote the Constitution* (New York: Free Press, 2004), 20.

34. For Republicans' "Gallomania," see David Waldstreicher, *In the Midst of Perpetual Fetes: The Making of American Nationalism, 1776–1820* (Chapel Hill: University of North Carolina Press, 1997); for burning Bibles, Edward J. Larson, *A Magnificent Catastrophe: The Tumultuous Election of 1800, America's First Presidential Campaign* (New York: Free Press, 2007), 169.

35. Peter S. Onuf, *Jefferson's Empire: The Language of American Nationhood* (Charlottesville: University Press of Virginia, 2000), 46.

36. For Jefferson and freedom of conscience, see Kevin R. C. Gutzman, *Thomas Jefferson—Revolutionary: A Radical's Struggle to Remake America* (New York: St. Martin's Press, 2017), chapter 2.

37. The best account is Peter Onuf and Nicholas Onuf, *Federal Union, Modern World: The Law of Nations in an Age of Revolutions* (Madison, WI: Madison House, 1993).

38. Browne, *Jefferson's Call for Nationhood*.

39. Forced to choose, Jefferson would opt for Virginia's rights over the Union. Peter S. Onuf, *Jefferson and the Virginians: Democracy, Constitutions, and Empire* (Baton Rouge: Louisiana State University Press, 2018). Also see Gutzman, *Thomas Jefferson—Revolutionary*, chapter 1.

40. Kevin R. C. Gutzman, *Virginia's American Revolution: From Dominion to Republic, 1776–1840* (Lanham, MD: Lexington Books, 2007), chapter 4.

41. Compare TJ, Revised Draft, *PTJ*, 33:146, and 148, n. 20. Madison had counseled Jefferson against "the steps toward [Adams] which you seem to be meditating," and perhaps his advice played a role here as well. JM to TJ, January 10, 1801, *PTJ*, 32:436–39, at 436. For what Jefferson had been "meditating" regarding Adams, TJ to JM, December 19, 1800, *PTJ*, 32:321–23, 323.

42. John Strode to TJ, February 26, 1801, *PTJ*, 33:83.

43. At the news of it bells rang from around 11:00 AM until sundown in Lancaster, Pennsylvania. Thomas McKean to TJ, February 20, 1801, *PTJ*, 33:28–29, at 28. Bells and cannon heralded the news in Philadelphia. Stephen Sayre to TJ, February 20, 1801, *PTJ*, 30–31, at 30. The young men of William & Mary paraded gleefully down the old Virginia capital Williamsburg's main street. Gutzman, *Virginia's American Revolution*, 137.

44. The contemporary publication of Jefferson's First Inaugural Address is a subject of Noble E. Cunningham Jr., *The Inaugural Addresses of President Thomas Jefferson, 1801 and 1805* (Columbia and London: University of Missouri Press, 2001), 17–38.

Chapter 2

1. Russell Kirk, *John Randolph of Roanoke: A Study in American Politics, with Selected Speeches and Letters*, 4th edition (Indianapolis, IN: Liberty Fund, 1997), 31.

2. Gordon S. Wood, *The American Revolution: A History* (New York: Modern Library, 2003), 127–28.

3. "Jay and Slavery," *The Papers of John Jay*, Columbia University Libraries, http://www.columbia.edu/cu/libraries/inside/dev/jay/JaySlavery.html.

4. For Jefferson and slavery's future, see Kevin R. C. Gutzman, *Thomas Jefferson—Revolutionary: A Radical's Struggle to Remake America* (New York: St. Martin's Press, 2017),

chapter 3; and Cara J. Rogers, "Jefferson's Sons: "Notes on the State of Virginia and Virginian Antislavery, 1760–1832" (PhD diss., Rice University, 2018).

5. TJ to JM, December 19, 1800, *The Papers of Thomas Jefferson,* ed. Julian P. Boyd (Princeton, NJ: Princeton University Press, 1950), 32:321–23, at 322.

6. JM to TJ, January 10, 1801, *PTJ,* 32:436–39, at 438–39.

7. JM to TJ, February 28, 1801, *PTJ,* 33:99–100, at 99.

Chapter 3

1. Robert M. S. McDonald, *Confounding Father: Thomas Jefferson's Image in His Own Time* (Charlottesville: University of Virginia Press, 2017), 13–14.

2. For the party's story, Lance Banning, *The Jeffersonian Persuasion: Evolution of a Party Ideology* (Ithaca, New York: Cornell University Press, 1980).

3. Merrill Peterson, *Thomas Jefferson & the New Nation: A Biography* (New York: Oxford University Press, 1970), 444–46 (quotation at 446).

4. Though there really is no substitute for reading Taylor's own writings, including for this period his pamphlets and letters, besides the record of debates on the Virginia Resolutions in the Virginia House of Delegates in 1798, the best introduction to Taylor in this period remains Robert E. Shalhope, *John Taylor of Caroline: Pastoral Republican* (Columbia: University of South Carolina Press, 1980), 70–107.

5. TJ to JM, September 21, 1795, Founders Online (National Archives), https://founders.archives.gov/documents/Jefferson/01-28-02-0375.

6. For the Pacificus-Helvidius debate, see Kevin R. C. Gutzman, *James Madison and the Making of America* (New York: St. Martin's Press, 2012), 266.

7. For the coalescence of a proto-party around Madison in the House of Representatives by 1792, see Mary P. Ryan, "Party Formation in the United States Congress, 1790–1796: A Quantitative Analysis," *William and Mary Quarterly* 28 (1971): 523–42.

8. For Madison, see Gutzman, *James Madison and the Making of America,* chapters 1–6.

9. JM to TJ, January 22, 1786, Founders Online (National Archives), https://founders.archives.gov/documents/Madison/01-08-02-0249.

10. William Lee Miller, *The Business of May Next: James Madison and the Founding* (Charlottesville: University Press of Virginia, 1992).

11. JM, "Notes on Ancient and Modern Confederacies," (April–June) 1786, Founders Online (National Archives), https://founders.archives.gov/documents/Madison/01-09-02-0001; JM, "Vices of the Political System of the United States," 1787, Founders Online (National Archives), https://founders.archives.gov/documents/Madison/01-09-02-0187.

12. For Madison, Washington, and the creation of the Constitution, see Stuart Leibiger, *Founding Friendship: George Washington, James Madison, and the Creation of the American Republic* (Charlottesville: University Press of Virginia, 1999), chapter 3.

13. The following account of Madison's role in the Philadelphia Convention relies on Gutzman, *James Madison and the Making of America,* 49–131.

14. Charles F. Hobson, "The Negative on State Laws: James Madison, the Constitution, and the Crisis of Republican Government," *The William and Mary Quarterly* 36 (1979): 215–35.

15. For Madison and the ratification campaign up to the Richmond Convention, Gutzman, *James Madison and the Making of America*, 133–86. For Madison in the Richmond Convention, Gutzman, *James Madison and the Making of America*, 187–237.

16. Fisher Ames to George Richards Minot, May 3, 1789, *Works of Fisher Ames, as Published by Seth Ames*, ed. W. B. Allen (Indianapolis, IN: Liberty Fund, 1983), 1:567–69, at 569. For Madison during the Washington and Adams administrations, Gutzman, *James Madison and the Making of America*, 239–77.

17. Charles Rappleye, *Robert Morris: Financier of the American Revolution* (New York: Simon & Schuster, 2010).

18. See especially Lance Banning, *The Jeffersonian Persuasion;* Joyce Appleby, *Capitalism and a New Social Order* (New York: NYU Press, 1984); Stanley Elkins and Eric McKitrick, *The Age of Federalism: The Early American Republic, 1788–1800* (New York: Oxford University Press, 1993); Richard Buel, *Securing the Revolution: Ideology in American Politics, 1789–1815* (Ithaca, NY: Cornell University Press, 1972); and James Roger Sharp, *American Politics in the Early Republic: The New Nation in Crisis* (New Haven, CT: Yale University Press, 1993).

19. Ryan, "Party Formation in the United States Congress," 523–42, says that by 1792, a couple of dozen House members voted consistently with Rep. Madison across the gamut of issues. This, she says, was the proto-Republican Party.

20. In a crowded field the best account of Hamilton's tenure at Treasury is Forrest McDonald, *Alexander Hamilton: A Biography* (New York: W. W. Norton, 1982), 117–306. It makes the financial program clear.

21. Thomas K. McCraw, *The Founders and Finance: How Hamilton, Gallatin, and Other Immigrants Forged a New Economy* (Cambridge, Massachusetts: Harvard University Press, 2012), 109.

22. Ibid., chapter 3 and passim; Herbert Sloan, *Principle and Interest: Thomas Jefferson and the Problem of Debt* (New York: Oxford University Press, 1995).

23. TJ to JM, September 6, 1789, *The Papers of Thomas Jefferson*, ed. Julian P. Boyd (Princeton, NJ: Princeton University Press, 1950), 15:392–97, at 392–93.

24. For analysis of the entire exchange, see Lance Banning, *Jefferson & Madison: Three Conversations from the Founding* (Madison, WI: Madison House Publishers, 1995), 27–55.

25. Gutzman, *Virginia's American Revolution*, 116–17.

26. Sloan, *Principle and Interest: Thomas Jefferson and the Problem of Debt*, 142–44.

27. Peterson, *Thomas Jefferson & the New Nation*, 442.

28. Ibid., 485.

29. TJ to JM, June 23, 1793, Founders Online (National Archives), https://founders.archives.gov/documents/Jefferson/01-26-02-0318.

30. Gutzman, *James Madison and the Making of America*, 266.

31. TJ to Francis Hopkinson, March 13, 1789, Founders Online (National Archives), https://founders.archives.gov/documents/Jefferson/01-14-02-0402.

32. For popular politics in the 1790s, see David Waldstreicher, *In the Midst of Perpetual Fetes: The Making of American Nationalism, 1776–1820* (Chapel Hill: University of North Carolina Press, 1997); and Simon P. Newman, *Parades and the Politics of the Street:*

Festive Culture in the Early American Republic (Philadelphia: University of Pennsylvania Press, 1997).

33. McDonald, *Confounding Father,* 13–14.

Chapter 4

1. For Madison in the General Assembly, Kevin R. C. Gutzman, *James Madison and the Making of America* (New York: St. Martin's Press, 2013), 276–80; for the Sedition Act Crisis generally, Kevin R. C. Gutzman, *Virginia's American Revolution* (Lanham, MD: Lexington Books, 2007), chapter 4; and Wendell Bird, *Criminal Dissent: Prosecutions Under the Alien and Sedition Acts of 1798* (Cambridge, Massachusetts: Harvard University Press, 2020).

2. The best account of the Madisonian experiment in foreign policy is Peter Onuf and Nicholas Onuf, *Federal Union, Modern World: The Law of Nations in an Age of Revolutions* (Madison, Wisconsin: Madison House Publishers, 1993). Also see Robert W. Tucker and David C. Hendrickson, *Empire of Liberty: The Statecraft of Thomas Jefferson* (New York: Oxford University Press, 1990).

3. Ian W. Toll, *Six Frigates: The Epic History of the Founding of the U.S. Navy* (New York: W. W. Norton, 2006), 186.

4. For Northern "democrats," Henry Adams, *History of the United States of America During the Administrations of Thomas Jefferson* (New York: Library of America, 1986), 440, 443, and passim.

5. Gregory May, *Jefferson's Treasure: How Albert Gallatin Saved the New Nation from Debt* (Washington, DC: Regnery, 2018), 7.

6. Raymond Walters Jr., *Albert Gallatin: Jeffersonian Financier & Diplomat* (New York: Macmillan, 1957), 1.

7. May, *Jefferson's Treasure,* 7.

8. Adams, *History of the United States of America During the Administrations of Thomas Jefferson,* 80.

9. For the slight speciousness of the assertion concerning Pennsylvanians' reasons for distilling, Thomas K. McCraw, *The Founders and Finance: How Hamilton, Gallatin, and Other Immigrants Forged a New Economy* (Cambridge, MA: Harvard University Press, 2012), 197. For the claim that this accounted for their distilling, Albert Gallatin, "Petition Against Excise," 1792, *The Writings of Albert Gallatin,* ed. Henry Adams (Philadelphia: J.B. Lippincott, 1879), 1:2–4.

10. May, *Jefferson's Treasure,* 43; AH to GW, August 5, 1794, Founders Online (National Archives), https://founders.archives.gov/documents/Washington/05-16-02-0357.

11. McCraw, *The Founders and Finance,* 196–97.

12. May, *Jefferson's Treasure,* 44–45.

13. Ibid., 46–7.

14. Albert Gallatin, "The Speech of Albert Gallatin, a Representative from the County of Fayette, in the House of Representatives of the General Assembly of Pennsylvania [January 3, 1795,] . . . ," *The Writings of Albert Gallatin,* 3:1–53, at 7, Online Library of Liberty (Liberty Fund), https://oll.libertyfund.org/titles/gallatin-the-writings-of-albert-gallatin-vol-3.

15. May, *Jefferson's Treasure,* 49.

16. McCraw, *The Founders and Finance,* 199.

17. Albert Gallatin, "Declaration of the Committees of Fayette County," September 1794, *The Writings of Albert Gallatin,* 1:4–9; May, *Jefferson's Treasure,* 54.

18. May, *Jefferson's Treasure,* 55.

19. Ibid., 69, 72.

20. Ibid., 35–7.

21. Ibid., 66.

22. AH to Robert Morris, April 30, 1781, Founders Online (National Archives), https://founders.archives.gov/documents/Hamilton/01-02-02-1167.

23. May, *Jefferson's Treasure,* 67.

24. Ibid., 68.

Chapter 5

1. The following discussion of Gallatin's pamphlet relies heavily on Thomas K. Mc-Craw, *The Founders and Finance: How Hamilton, Gallatin, and Other Immigrants Forged a New Economy* (Cambridge, MA: Harvard University Press, 2012), 205–17, and on Gregory May, *Jefferson's Treasure: How Albert Gallatin Saved the New Nation from Debt* (Washington, DC: Regnery, 2018), 74–76.

2. JM to TJ, January 31, 1796, Founders Online (National Archives), https://founders.archives.gov/documents/Madison/01-16-02-0125.

3. For Livingston's rejection and the reasons for it, Robert R. Livingston to TJ, January 7, 1801, *The Papers of Thomas Jefferson,* ed. Julian P. Boyd (Princeton, NJ: Princeton University Press, 1950), 32:406–09, at 408–09; for the offer to Smith, TJ to Samuel Smith, March 9, 1801, *PTJ,* 33:234; Samuel Smith to TJ, *PTJ,* 33:339–40, at 339. Also see TJ to JM, March 12, 1801, *The Papers of James Madison: Secretary of State Series* (hereafter, *PJMSS*), ed. Robert A. Rutland, et al. (Charlottesville: University Press of Virginia, 1986–), 1:12–13.

4. Merrill D. Peterson, *Thomas Jefferson & the New Nation* (New York: Oxford University Press, 1970), 662.

5. TJ to Wilson Cary Nicholas, June 11, 1801, *PTJ,* 34:308–10, at 309.

6. TJ to James Monroe, June 20, 1801, *PTJ,* 34:398–99.

7. James Sterling Young, *The Washington Community, 1800–1828* (New York: Columbia University Press, 1966), 23–24.

8. Ibid., 25.

9. Ibid., 26.

10. Ibid., 68 and Figure 3, 69.

11. Entry for October 31, 1803, *John Quincy Adams: Diaries, 1779–1821,* ed. David Waldstreicher (New York: Library of America, 2017), 101.

12. Entry for December 20, 1803, *John Quincy Adams: Diaries,* 102.

13. Young, *The Washington Community, 1800–1828,* 73.

14. TJ to the Senate, March 5, 1801, *PTJ,* 33:188–89.

15. May, *Jefferson's Treasure,* 97; Nancy Isenberg, *Fallen Founder: The Life of Aaron Burr* (New York: Penguin, 2007), 226. Isenberg quotes Gallatin telling his wife that of the pending appointments, the "most obnoxious to the other party, and the only one which I think will be rejected, is . . . a certain friend of yours."

16. Among studies arguing that mishandling the patronage led to enormous problems are Joel Silbey, *Storm Over Texas: The Annexation Controversy and the Road to Civil War* (New York: Oxford University Press, 2005) (Polk's mistakes led to the Civil War); and T. Harry Williams, *Lincoln and His Generals* (New York: Vintage, 1952) (chiefly political selections of Union generals early on by Lincoln and governors go far toward explaining early Union battlefield setbacks). Washington, as Stuart Leibiger, *Founding Friendship: George Washington, James Madison, and the Creation of the American Republic* (Charlottesville: University Press of Virginia, 1999), shows, relied extensively on advice from Madison.

17. William Jay, *The Life of John Jay* (New York: J. & J. Harper, 1833), 274.

18. For Bolingbroke's concept and the early presidency, Ralph Ketchum, *Presidents Above Party: The First American Presidency, 1789–1829* (Chapel Hill: University of North Carolina Press, 1987).

19. William Branch Giles to TJ, March 16, 1801, *PTJ*, 33:310–12, at 311.

20. Walter Jones to TJ, March 14, 1801, *PTJ*, 33:283–88, at 285–88.

21. Ibid., n. at 33:288.

22. TJ to Walter Jones, March 31, 1801, *PTJ*, 33:506.

Chapter 6

1. Cf. TJ, Notes on New York Patronage, [after February 17, 1801], *The Papers of Thomas Jefferson,* ed. Julian P. Boyd (Princeton, NJ: Princeton University Press, 1950), 33:11; TJ, Notes on New Jersey Patronage, *PTJ*, [ca. March 5, before June 1801], 183; TJ, List of John Adams's Judicial Appointments, [February 18, 1801], *PTJ*, 33:15; TJ, List of John Adams's Appointments, February 23, 1801, *PTJ*, 33:52; Jacob Wagner's Memorandum on State Department Clerks, [March 1801], *PTJ*, 33:512; TJ, Notes on South Carolina Patronage, [March–November 1801], *PTJ*, 33:513–14; TJ, Notes on Patronage in New Hampshire, November 10, 1801, *PTJ*, 35:601.

2. TJ to William Duane, July 24, 1803, *PTJ*, 41:107–10, at 108.

3. Forrest McDonald, *The Presidency of Thomas Jefferson* (Lawrence: University Press of Kansas, 1976), 34.

4. TJ, "Circular Letter to Midnight Appointees," after March 4, 1801, *PTJ*, 33:172–73.

5. For this sentence and the next paragraph, TJ to Archibald Stuart, April 8, 1801, *PTJ*, 33:555.

6. TJ to Wilson Cary Nicholas, June 11, 1801, *PTJ*, 34:308–10, at 309.

7. Nancy Isenberg, *Fallen Founder: The Life of Aaron Burr* (New York: Penguin, 2007), 243–51.

8. Far the most dramatic account of the friendship-gone-wrong culminating in the "interview in Weehawken" is Thomas Fleming, *Duel: Alexander Hamilton, Aaron Burr, and the Future of America* (New York: Basic Books, 1999). Also see *Interview in Weehawken: The Burr-Hamilton Duel as Told in the Original Documents,* Harold C. Syrett and Jean G. Cooke, eds. (Middletown, Connecticut: Wesleyan University Press, 1960).

9. John Page to TJ, May 25, 1804, *PTJ*, 43:488.

10. TJ to John Page, June 25, 1804, *PTJ*, 43:652–53.

11. Abigail Adams to TJ, May 20, 1804, *PTJ*, 43:458–59. Jefferson's son-in-law forwarded this letter along with his own characterizing Mrs. Adams as remarkable, "The successful rival of her husband in public estimation could not under any circumstances excite sympathy in

the breast of an ordinary female. . . ." John Wayles Eppes to TJ, June 14, 1804, *PTJ*, 43:582–84, at 584.

12. TJ to Abigail Adams, June 13, 1804, *PTJ*, 43:578–80.

13. The book that persuaded most scholars of the general truth of the Hemings tale is Annette Gordon-Reed, *Thomas Jefferson & Sally Hemings: An American Controversy* (Charlottesville: University of Virginia Press, 1997). For the state of the controversy before Gordon-Reed's book, see Edward L. Ayers and Scott French, "The Strange Career of Thomas Jefferson: Race and Slavery in American Memory, 1943–1993," in *Jeffersonian Legacies*, ed. Peter S. Onuf (Charlottesville: University Press of Virginia, 1993), 418–56. Several scholars' dissents are collected in *The Jefferson-Hemings Controversy: Report of the Scholars Commission*, ed. Robert F. Turner (Durham, NC: Carolina Academic Press, 2001, 2011).

14. Gordon-Reed, *Thomas Jefferson & Sally Hemings*, 2.

15. Ibid., 59, 63.

16. Ibid., 61.

17. Ibid., 61–62.

18. For the whole sad story see Dumas Malone, *Jefferson the President: First Term, 1801–1805* (Boston: Little, Brown, 1970), 216–23.

19. TJ to Robert Smith, July 1, 1805, Founders Online (National Archives), https://founders.archives.gov/documents/Jefferson/99-01-02-2005.

20. TJ to Abigail Adams, July 22, 1804, *The Adams-Jefferson Letters: The Complete Correspondence Between Thomas Jefferson and Abigail and John Adams*, ed. Lester Cappon (Chapel Hill: University of North Carolina Press, 1987), 274–76.

21. So, for example, under the "Constitution" query of *Notes on the State of Virginia*, he had referred to provisions of Virginia's constitution "which when they transgress their acts shall become nullities." TJ, *Notes on the State of Virginia* (Philadelphia, 1788), 137, Documenting the American South (https://docsouth.unc.edu/southlit/jefferson/jefferson.html#p137).

22. Abigail Adams to TJ, August 18, 1804, *The Adams-Jefferson Letters*, 276–78, at 277–78.

23. TJ to Abigail Adams, September 11, 1804, *The Adams-Jefferson Letters*, 278–80, at 278–79.

24. Ibid., 278–80, 279.

25. Ibid., 278–80, at 280.

26. Abigail Adams to TJ, October 25, 1804, *The Adam-Jefferson Letters*, 280–82, at 281–82.

Chapter 7

1. William Duane to TJ, May 10, 1801, *The Papers of Thomas Jefferson*, ed. Julian P. Boyd (Princeton, NJ: Princeton University Press, 1950), 34:71–73.

2. Henry Adams, *History of the United States of America During the Administrations of Thomas Jefferson* (New York: Library of America, 1986), 432.

3. Ibid., 433–34.

4. Raymond Walters Jr., *Albert Gallatin: Jeffersonian Financier & Diplomat* (New York: Macmillan, 1957), 240.

5. For Jefferson and the Alien and Sedition Acts Crisis, Kevin R. C. Gutzman, *Virginia's American Revolution: From Dominion to Republic, 1776–1840* (Lanham, MD: Lexington Books, 2007), chapter 4; for Jefferson and the Cabell presentment, Kevin R. C. Gutzman, *Thomas*

Jefferson—Revolutionary: A Radical's Struggle to Remake America (New York: St. Martin's Press, 2017), 44–46.

6. TJ to Justice William Johnson, June 12, 1823, *Thomas Jefferson: Writings* (New York: Library of America, 1984), 1469–77, at 1474.

7. R. Kent Nemyer, *John Marshall and the Heroic Age of the Supreme Court* (Baton Rouge: Louisiana State University Press, 2001), 134.

8. Theodore J. Crackel, "The Military Academy in the Context of Jeffersonian Reform," in *Thomas Jefferson's Military Academy: Founding West Point* (Charlottesville: University of Virginia Press, 2004), 99–117, at 105.

9. For discontinuation of the Duane prosecution, TJ to Edward Livingston, November 1, 1801, *PTJ*, 35:543–44.

10. Cf. TJ, Pardon for David Brown, March 12, 1801, *PTJ*, 251–52.

11. Jefferson at first thought himself lacking in authority to return the money. TJ, "A Bill for the Relief of Sufferers under Certain Illegal Prosecutions," *PTJ*, 36:258–59.

12. TJ, Pardon for James Thomson Callender, March 16, 1801, *PTJ*, 309–10.

13. *Papers of James Madison: Secretary of State Series,* ed. Robert A. Rutland, et al. (Charlottesville: University Press of Virginia, 1986-), 1:120, n. 1.

14. James Thomson Callender to TJ, February 23, 1801, *PTJ*, 33:46–47, at 46; Callender to JM, April 27, 1801, *PJMSS,* 1:117–20.

15. *PJMSS,* 1:117–20, n. 6.

16. JM to James Monroe, May 6, 1801, *PJMSS,* 1:143.

17. James Monroe to JM, May 17, 1801, *PJMSS,* 1:190–91, at 191.

18. This and the following paragraph rely on James Monroe to JM, June 4, 1800, *PJMSS,* 8:537–38. The fine was not so draconian as Callender imagined, if the case of David Brown is any indication. TJ, Pardon for David Brown, March 12, 1801, *PTJ*, 33:251–52. (Although he had served his eighteen-month sentence, Brown remained in prison because he was unable to pay his fine of $400.)

19. James Monroe to JM, May 23, 1801, *PJMSS,* 1:222–24, at 222, 223.

20. Ibid., 1:236, n. 1.

21. Albert Gallatin to JM, [May 29, 1801], *PJMSS,* 1:236.

22. JM to James Monroe, June 1, 1801, *PJMSS,* 1:244–46, at 244–45.

23. Ibid., 1:266, n. 1.

24. James Monroe to JM, June 6, 1801, *PJMSS,* 1:265–66.

25. Leonard D. White, *The Jeffersonians: A Study in Administrative History, 1801–1829* (New York: Macmillan, 1951), 356.

Chapter 8

1. TJ to George Jefferson, March 27, 1801, *The Papers of Thomas Jefferson,* ed. Julian P. Boyd (Princeton, NJ: Princeton University Press, 1950), 33:465.

2. TJ to Benjamin Rush, March 24, 1801, *PTJ*, 33:436–38.

3. TJ to Wilson Cary Nicholas, June 11, 1801, *PTJ*, 34:308–10, at 309.

4. TJ to William Duane, July 24, 1802, *PTJ*, 41:107–10, at 108.

5. "Remonstrance of the New Haven Merchants," June 18, 1801, *PTJ*, 34:381–83, and n. at 383.

6. C. Peter Magrath, *Yazoo: Law and Politics in the New Republic—The Case of Fletcher v. Peck* (New York: W. W. Norton, 1966), 23–24. See also "Abraham Bishop's *Georgia Speculation Unveiled*," in Magrath, *Yazoo*, 151–71.

7. TJ to the New Haven Merchants, July 12, 1801, *PTJ*, 34:554–56.

8. TJ to Pierpont Edwards, July 12, 1801, *PTJ*, 34:606–07. For Edwards's communication of information to Jefferson, Pierpont Edwards to TJ, May 12, 1801, *PTJ*, 34:90–94, and Pierpont Edwards to TJ, June 10, 1801, *PTJ*, 34:301–02.

9. TJ to William Duane, July 24, 1802, *PTJ*, 41:107–10, at 108–09.

Chapter 9

1. The following account relies on Daniel L. Dreisbach, *Thomas Jefferson and the Wall of Separation Between Church and State* (New York: NYU Press, 2002), 9–17.

2. Ibid., 161, n. 16.

3. Philip Hamburger, *Separation of Church and State* (Cambridge, MA: Harvard University Press, 2002), 157, n. 25.

4. The details that follow are at "Presentation of the 'Mammoth Cheese,'" Editorial Note, *The Papers of Thomas Jefferson*, ed. Julian P. Boyd (Princeton, NJ: Princeton University Press, 1950), 36:246–49, at 248, unless otherwise noted; Jefferson's address is TJ To the Committee of Cheshire, Massachusetts, January 1, 1802, *PTJ*, 36:252.

5. For Jefferson in this paragraph, TJ to John Wayles Eppes, January 1, 1802, *PTJ*, 36:261.

6. Dreisbach, *Thomas Jefferson and the Wall of Separation*, 14.

7. Maurizio Valsania, *Jefferson's Body: A Corporeal Biography* (Charlottesville: University of Virginia Press, 2017).

8. The following discussion is based on The Danbury Baptist Association to TJ, October 17, 1801, *PTJ*, 35:407–08 and n. at 409.

9. TJ, "A Bill for Establishing Religious Freedom," *PTJ*, 2:545–47.

10. TJ, Draft Reply to the Danbury Baptist Association, on or before December 31, 1801, *PTJ*, 36:254–55.

11. TJ to Levi Lincoln, January 1, 1802, *PTJ*, 36:256–57. Though there is no extant letter to Gideon Granger, the contents of Granger's response make clear that it closely resembled Jefferson's letter to Lincoln.

12. Jeremy D. Bailey describes the uses to which Jefferson put responses to addresses such as the one from the Danbury Baptists in *Thomas Jefferson and Executive Power* (New York: Cambridge University Press, 2007), 225–58, considering this one at 239.

13. Soon enough the experiment was repeated among the populations of Washington, Richmond, Philadelphia, various other American towns, and Indian tribes. Merrill Peterson, *Thomas Jefferson & the New Nation: A Biography* (New York: Oxford University Press, 1970), 683–84.

14. Gideon Granger to TJ, December 31, 1801, *PTJ*, 36:256.

15. Levi Lincoln to TJ, January 1, 1802, *PTJ*, 36:257.

16. The Danbury Baptists were not the first such group to write to Jefferson at the White House. Connecticut's religious establishment made receipt of the Danbury letter a ripe opportunity to lay out Jefferson's views regarding government and religion. From the Delaware Baptist Association, June 26, 1801, *PTJ*, 34:458–59.

17. Editorial Note, "Reply to the Danbury Baptist Association," *PTJ*, 36:253–54, at 254.

18. TJ To the Danbury Baptist Association, January 1, 1802, *PTJ*, 36:258.

19. *Everson v. Board of Education of the Township of Ewing*, 330 U.S. 1 (1947).

20. The quotations are from TJ to the Members of the Baltimore Baptist Association, October 17, 1808, *The Complete Jefferson—Containing His Major Writings, Published and Unpublished, Except His Letters* (hereafter, *The Complete Jefferson*), ed. Saul K. Padover (New York: Duell, Sloan & Pearce, 1943), 537; and TJ to the General Meeting of Correspondence of the Six Baptist Associations Represented at Chesterfield, Virginia, November 21, 1808, *The Complete Jefferson*, 538–39. Also see TJ to the Members of the Ketocton Baptist Association, October 18, 1808, *The Complete Jefferson*, 537–38.

21. "S" to TJ, April 20, 1802, *PTJ*, 37:294.

22. One might note that ignoring the president's statements about state religion policies was perfectly in line with Jefferson's thinking about such matters. See Thomas E. Woods Jr. and Kevin R. C. Gutzman, *Who Killed the Constitution?: The Fate of American Liberty from World War I to George W. Bush* (New York: Crown Forum, 2008), 103–117; and Kevin R. C. Gutzman, *Thomas Jefferson—Revolutionary: A Radical's Struggle to Remake America* (New York: St. Martin's Press, 2017), 62.

Chapter 10

1. TJ to the Speaker of the House of Representatives and the President of the Senate, December 8, 1801, *The Papers of Thomas Jefferson*, ed. Julian P. Boyd (Princeton, NJ: Princeton University Press, 1950), 36:57.

2. TJ, "Notes on the Bank of the United States and Internal Revenues," November 10, 1801, *PTJ*, 35:602–03.

3. Editor's Note, "Drafting the Annual Message to Congress," *PTJ*, 35:612–17, at 614; TJ to JM, November 12, 1801, *PTJ*, 35:621–22; TJ to Albert Gallatin, November 14, 1801, *PTJ*, 35:622; TJ to Levi Lincoln, November 27, 1801, *PTJ*, 35:650.

4. TJ, Preliminary Draft: Naturalization, before November 12, 1801, *PTJ*, 35:618.

5. TJ, Partial Draft: Appointments and Post Office, before November 12, 1801, *PTJ*, 35:618–19.

6. TJ, Partial Draft: Judiciary, Juries, and Naturalization, before November 12, 1801, *PTJ*, 35:620.

7. TJ, Calculation of Annual Debt Payment, ca. November 15, 1801, *PTJ*, 35:624–26.

8. Notes on Circuit Cases, *PTJ*, 35:658.

9. Levi Lincoln's Remarks on the Message, ca. November 27–December 8, 1801, *PTJ*, 35:651–52, at 652.

10. The following discussion is based on TJ, Fair Copy, First Annual Message to Congress, December 8, 1801, *PTJ*, 35:641–49; and TJ, First Annual Message to Congress, December 8, 1801, *PTJ*, 36:58–65.

11. For Jefferson's assimilationism, Kevin R. C. Gutzman, *Thomas Jefferson—Revolutionary: A Radical's Struggle to Remake America* (New York: St. Martin's Press, 2017), chapter 4.

12. Note, *PTJ*, 35:589. For the jubilation of the navy secretary's senator brother at the news, Samuel Smith to TJ, November 14, 1801, *PTJ*, 35:663–64. For Jefferson's joyous commendation of the naval officer, TJ to Andrew Sterrett, December 1, 1801, *PTJ*, 36:3. For young

Sterrett in action, Ian W. Toll, *Six Frigates: The Epic History of the Founding of the U.S. Navy* (New York: W. W. Norton, 2006), 118.

13. GW, To the United States Senate and House of Representatives, January 8, 1790, Founders Online (National Archives), https://founders.archives.gov/documents/Washington /05-04-02-0361.

14. Dearborn had told TJ in November that while legally authorized to have as many as 5,036 enlisted personnel, the army counted only 4,195. The number the two of them had agreed they wanted was 3,210. *PTJ*, 35:600, n.

15. Bernard Bailyn, *The Ideological Origins of the American Revolution: Fiftieth Anniversary Edition* (Cambridge, MA: Harvard University Press, 2017); Lance Banning, *The Jeffersonian Persuasion: Evolution of a Party Ideology* (Ithaca, NY: Cornell University Press, 1978).

16. In 1798–1800 the legislatures of Virginia and Kentucky had led the way in laying out the Republicans' objections to the Alien and Sedition Acts as unconstitutional, and they had been followed by those of Tennessee and Georgia, besides one house of the North Carolina Legislature. South Carolina did not officially weigh in only because its sympathetic legislature received the Virginia Resolutions on the last day of the 1798 session. Wendell Bird, *Press and Speech Under Assault: The Early Supreme Court Justices, the Sedition Act of 1798, and the Campaign Against Dissent* (New York: Oxford University Press, 2016), 323–325.

17. TJ, Notes on District Court Cases, November 12, 1801, *PTJ*, 35:658; TJ to JM, with Madison's Reply, February 26, 1802, *PTJ*, 36:654–55.

18. For the Cabell matter, Gutzman, *Thomas Jefferson—Revolutionary,* 45–46.

19. "Asia and Africa, have long expelled her—Europe regards her like a stranger, and England hath given her warning to depart. O! receive the fugitive, and prepare in time an asylum for mankind." Thomas Paine, *Common Sense,* Liberty Fund (Online Library of Liberty), https://oll.libertyfund.org/pages/1776-paine-common-sense-pamphlet.

Chapter 11

1. TJ to John Wayles Eppes, January 1, 1802, *The Papers of Thomas Jefferson,* ed. Julian P. Boyd (Princeton, NJ: Princeton University Press, 1950), 36:261.

2. TJ to the Senate, December January 6, 1802, *PTJ*, 331–36.

3. TJ to Albert Gallatin, October 11, 1809, *The Papers of Thomas Jefferson: Retirement Series,* ed. J. Jefferson Looney (Princeton, NJ: Princeton University Press, 2004) (hereafter, *PTJRS*), 1:597–99, at 598.

4. Albert Gallatin to TJ, November 11, 1809, *PTJRS*, 1:664–65, at 664.

5. Enclosure, "Estimate of Receipts and Expenditures for 1801," *PTJ*, 33:277–81.

6. Albert Gallatin to TJ, March 14, 1801, *PTJ*, 33:275–76.

7. Theodore J. Crackel, "The Military Academy in the Context of Jeffersonian Reform," in *Thomas Jefferson's Military Academy: Founding West Point* (Charlottesville: University of Virginia Press, 2004), 111–12.

8. TJ to Nathaniel Macon, May 14, 1801, *PTJ*, 34:109–10, at 110.

9. Crackel, "The Military Academy in the Context of Jeffersonian Reform," 112.

10. Robert M. S. McDonald, Preface, *Thomas Jefferson's Military Academy: Founding West Point,* ix-xix, at xi.

11. Peter S. Onuf, "Thomas Jefferson's Military Academy: A Summary View," in *The Mind of Thomas Jefferson* (Charlottesville: University of Virginia Press, 2007), 178–201, at 189.

12. David P. Currie, *The Constitution in Congress: The Jeffersonians, 1801–1829* (Chicago: University of Chicago Press, 2001), 39–65, clearly explains all of the issues Congress considered in drafting the Twelfth Amendment.

13. Editorial Note, *The Papers of John Marshall*, ed. Herbert A. Johnson, et al. (Chapel Hill: University of North Carolina Press , 1974–2006), 6:69–73, at 69.

14. F. Thornton Miller, *Juries and Judges vs. The Law: Virginia's Provincial Legal Perspective, 1783–1828* (Charlottesville: University Press of Virginia, 1994), 66–67.

15. John Marshall to William Paterson, April 6, 1802, *The Papers of John Marshall*, 6:105–06, at 106.

16. John Marshall to William Paterson, April 19, 1802, *The Papers of John Marshall*, 6:108–09.

17. Samuel Chase to John Marshall, April 24, 1802, *The Papers of John Marshall*, 6:109–16.

18. For the precedent to which Chase referred, *The Papers of John Marshall*, 6:116, n. 2.

19. From Hannah Cushing to Abigail Adams, June 25, 1802, *The Papers of John Marshall*, 6:116, n. 5.

20. John Marshall to William Paterson, May 3, 1802, *The Papers of John Marshall*, 6:117–18.

21. Ibid., 118, n.

22. Ibid., 121, n. 1.

23. 5 U.S. 299 (1803), 309.

Chapter 12

1. TJ to Joel Barlow, May 3, 1802, *The Papers of Thomas Jefferson*, ed. Julian P. Boyd (Princeton, NJ: Princeton University Press, 1950), 37:399–401, at 400–01.

2. Gordon S. Wood, *Empire of Liberty: A History of the Early Republic, 1789–1815* (New York: Oxford University Press, 2009), 554.

3. Hannah Spahn, *Thomas Jefferson, Time, and History* (Charlottesville: University of Virginia Press, 2011).

4. *PTJ*, 37:297, notes.

5. The best accounts are James Sidbury, *Plowshares into Swords: Race, Rebellion, and Identity in Gabriel's Virginia, 1730–1810* (New York: Cambridge University Press, 1997), and Douglas R. Egerton, *Gabriel's Rebellion: The Virginia Slave Conspiracies of 1800 & 1802* (Chapel Hill: The University of North Carolina Press, 1993), 68–115.

6. Egerton, *Gabriel's Rebellion*, 69.

7. Ibid., 114.

8. James Monroe, "General Orders," September 15, 1800, *The Papers of James Monroe: Selected Correspondence and Papers*, ed. Daniel Preston, et al. (Santa Barbara, CA: ABC-Clio, 2012-), 4:409–10.

9. For this and the following paragraph, Thomas Jefferson to James Monroe, September 20, 1800, *The Papers of James Monroe*, 4:413.

10. Kevin R. C. Gutzman, *Thomas Jefferson—Revolutionary: A Radical's Struggle to Remake America* (New York: St. Martin's Press, 2017), chapter 3.

11. For the 1801 law, *PTJ*, 34:347, n. The discussion that follows is based on James Monroe to TJ, June 15, 1801, *PTJ*, 34:345–47.

12. Characterization of slavery as a curse entailed upon the South by its former British rulers remained a commonplace in Southern political circles for a generation after this. It appeared most famously in South Carolina U.S. Senator Robert Y. Hayne's arguments in the Webster-Hayne Debate of 1830. Daniel Webster, Robert Y. Hayne, et al., *The Webster-Hayne Debate on the Nature of the Union*, ed. Herman Belz (Indianapolis, IN: Liberty Fund, 2000).

13. Gutzman, *Thomas Jefferson—Revolutionary*, 141.

14. James Monroe to TJ, June 15, 1801, *The Papers of James Monroe*, 522–23, and n.

15. John Chester Miller, *The Wolf by the Ears: Thomas Jefferson and Slavery* (New York: Free Press, 1977), 127. Not everyone among the Virginia political elite reacted with such empathy for the slaves. See particularly Joseph Jones [James Monroe's uncle] to James Monroe, September 9, 1800, *The Papers of James Monroe*, 4:404–05.

16. TJ to Rufus King, July 13, 1802, *PTJ*, 38:54–56, at 55–56, is the source of this paragraph and the next one.

17. Christopher Gore to TJ, October 10, 1802, *PTJ*, 38:473–75.

18. Rufus King to Alexander Hamilton, April 8, 1802, *The Papers of Alexander Hamilton*, ed. Harold C. Syrett, et al. (New York: Columbia University Press, 1961–1979), 25:598; Rufus King to JM, August 5, 1802, *PJMSS*, 3:457.

19. Miller, *Wolf by the Ears*, 138.

Chapter 13

1. In a letter to the French foreign minister, a French diplomat in Washington lamented "*ce deffaut de dignité qui fait aller M. Jefferson à pied, à cheval, sans domestiques, et qui le fait a recevoir chez lui à toute heure dans un négligé inconvenant, le plus souvent en pantoufles, et l'impolitesse affectée de ses manieres.*" Louis Pichon to Charles Maurice de Talleyrand-Périgord, February 24, 1802, *The Papers of Alexander Hamilton*, ed. Harold C. Syrett, et al. (New York: Columbia University Press, 1961–1979), 25: 561, n. Unbeknownst to them, Jefferson, for his part, highly disliked "the profusion of gold lace on [their] clothes." Entry for November 23, 1804, *John Quincy Adams: Diaries, 1779–1821*, ed. David Waldstreicher, (New York: Library of America, 2017), 1:24–25.

2. TJ to Destutt de Tracy, January 26, 1811, *The Papers of Thomas Jefferson: Retirement Series* (hereafter, *PTJRS*), ed. J. Jefferson Looney, et al. (Princeton, NJ: Princeton University Press, 2004), 3:334–39, at 336–37.

3. Forrest McDonald, *The Presidency of Thomas Jefferson* (Lawrence: University Press of Kansas, 1976), 36–37.

4. Extract from John F. Kennedy's Remarks at a Dinner Honoring Nobel Prize Winners of the Western Hemisphere, April 29, 1962, Jefferson Quotes & Family Letters (Monticello .org), https://tjrs.monticello.org/letter/1856.

5. Robert M. Johnstone Jr., *Jefferson and the Presidency: Leadership in the Young Republic* (Ithaca, NY: Cornell University Press, 1978), 144.

6. Ibid., 145–46.

7. Adams's diary entries span the period 1779–1848. In fifty-one volumes, they come to more than fourteen thousand manuscript pages. The Diaries of John Quincy Adams: A

Digital Collection, Massachusetts Historical Society, https://www.masshist.org/jqadiaries
/php/. The following accounts rely on Entry for November 23, 1804, *John Quincy Adams:
Diaries,* 1:113–14.

8. John Quincy Adams, "Reply to the Appeal of the Massachusetts Federalists," in *Documents Relating to New-England Federalism, 1800–1815,* ed. Henry Adams (Burt Franklin
Research and Source Works Series #89, American Classics in History and Social Science
#8), 107–329, at 154.

9. The following account is from JM to James Monroe, January 19, 1804, *PJMSS,* 6:361–66.

10. Catherine Allgor, *Parlor Politics: In Which the Ladies of Washington Help Build a City
and a Government* (Charlottesville: University Press of Virginia, 2000), 36.

11. As Jefferson described the event in a section of his Draft Autobiography, March 16,
[1821], "it was impossible for anything to be more ungracious than their notice of Mr. Adams
and myself. I saw at once that the ulcerations in the narrow mind of that mulish king left nothing to be expected on the subject of my attendance; and on the first conference with the Marquis of Caermarthen, his Minister of foreign affairs, the distance and disinclination which he
betrayed in his conversation, the vagueness & evasions of his answers to us, confirmed me in
the belief of their aversion to have anything to do with us." "Autobiography," *Thomas Jefferson: Writings,* (New York: Library of America, 1984), 3–122, at 57–58.

12. JM to James Monroe, February 16, 1804, *PJMSS,* 6:484–86.

13. Margaret Bayard Smith, *The First Forty Years of Washington Society,* ed. Gaillard
Hunt, 2nd edition (New York: Frederick Ungar, 1965), 46.

14. Dumas Malone, *Jefferson the President: First Term, 1801–1805* (Boston: Little, Brown,
1970), 382–83.

15. Both Allgor, *Parlor Politics,* and Andrew Burstein and Nancy Isenberg, *Madison
and Jefferson* (New York: Random House, 2010), 401, blame Jefferson for resisting what the
latter calls "a diplomat's forceful wife attempting to insinuate herself into *what he regarded as*
[emphasis added] a strictly masculine political setting." Allgor's version of the Smith passage
quoted above omits the part about Mrs. Merry making a "masculine" impression and enough
of the physical description that the overwhelming effect of her ostentatious dress is absent.

16. James Monroe to JM, July 1, 1804, *The Papers of James Monroe,* 5:238–40, at 239.

17. Henry Adams, *History of the United States of America During the Administrations of
Thomas Jefferson* (New York: Library of America, 1986); Henry Adams, *John Randolph: A
Biography* (Armonk, NY: M. E. Sharpe, 1996). See also Malone, *Jefferson the President: First
Term,* 143, et seq.

18. Margaret L. Coit, *John C. Calhoun: American Portrait* (Boston: Houghton Mifflin, 1950), 162.

19. K[evin]. R. Constantine Gutzman, "The Randolph-Clay Duel," *Southern Partisan*
18 (4th Quarter 1998): 16–20.

20. David Johnson, *John Randolph of Roanoke* (Baton Rouge: Louisiana State University Press, 2012), 112.

21. William Plumer, *William Plumer's Memorandum of Proceedings in the United States
Senate, 1803–1807* (New York: Macmillan, 1923), 23–25.

22. McDonald, *The Presidency of Thomas Jefferson,* 40.

23. The best brief account remains Arthur M. Schlesinger Jr., *The Age of Jackson* (Boston:
Little, Brown, 1945), chapter III, "Keepers of the Jeffersonian Conscience," 18–29.

Chapter 14

1. The following account relies on Editorial Note, *Marbury v. Madison, The Papers of John Marshall,* ed. Herbert A. Johnson, et al. (Chapel Hill: University of North Carolina Press, 1974–2006), 6:160–65 unless otherwise specified; and Opinion, *Marbury v. Madison,* February 24, 1803, *The Papers of John Marshall,* 6:165–85.

2. The court alludes to U.S. Constitution, Article III, Section 2.

3. Kevin R. C. Gutzman, *James Madison and the Making of America* (New York: St. Martin's Press, 2012), 286.

4. Editorial Note, *Marbury v. Madison, The Papers of John Marshall,* 6: 160–65, at 164.

Chapter 15

1. TJ, Second Annual Address, December 15, 1802, *The Papers of Thomas Jefferson,* ed. Julian P. Boyd (Princeton, NJ: Princeton University Press, 1950), 39:162–68, at 166.

2. Gallatin's Remarks on the Draft, November 19–21, 1802, *PTJ,* 39:18–22, quotations at 19.

3. TJ, Notes on a Cabinet Meeting, May 15, 1801, *PTJ,* 34:114–15.

4. Robert W. Tucker and David C. Hendrickson, *Empire of Liberty: The Statecraft of Thomas Jefferson* (New York: Oxford University Press, 1990), 98.

5. JM to Robert R. Livingston, September 28, 1801, *The Papers of James Madison: Secretary of State Series,* ed. Robert A. Rutland, et al. (Charlottesville: University Press of Virginia, 1986–), 2:142–47, passages cited at 144–46.

6. TJ to Robert R. Livingston, April 18, 1802, *PTJ,* 37:263–66.

7. For "mere" declaration and George's responsibility, see Pauline Maier, *American Scripture: Making the Declaration of Independence* (New York: Alfred A. Knopf, 1997).

8. Pierre S. du Pont de Nemours to TJ, April 30, 1802, *PTJ,* 37:367–72.

9. TJ to Pierre S. Du Pont de Nemours, May 5, 1802, *PTJ,* 37:418–19.

10. TJ to Livingston, May 5, 1802, *PTJ,* 37:421–22.

11. Dumas Malone, *Jefferson the President: First Term, 1801–1805* (Boston: Little, Brown, 1970), 239–40.

12. TJ to James Monroe, January 10, 1803, *PTJ,* 39:306.

13. Harry Ammon, *James Monroe: The Quest for National Identity* (Charlottesville: University Press of Virginia, 1971), 203.

14. Forrest McDonald, *The Presidency of Thomas Jefferson* (Lawrence: University Press of Kansas, 1976), 66.

Chapter 16

1. TJ to James Monroe, January 13, 1803, *The Papers of Thomas Jefferson,* ed. Julian P. Boyd (Princeton, NJ: Princeton University Press, 1950), 39:328–30.

2. TJ, Commission for James Monroe and Robert R. Livingston, January 12, 1803, *PTJ,* 39:320–21.

3. Harry Ammon, *James Monroe: The Quest for National Identity* (Charlottesville: University Press of Virginia, 1971), 206.

4. Rufus King to JM, April 2, 1803, *The Papers of James Madison: Secretary of State*

Series, ed. Robert A. Rutland, et al. (Charlottesville: University Press of Virginia, 1986–), 4:474–75, at 475.

5. Robert W. Tucker and David C. Hendrickson, *Empire of Liberty: The Statecraft of Thomas Jefferson* (New York: Oxford University Press, 1990), 113.

6. TJ to Livingston, April 18, 1802, *PTJ,* 37:263–66.

7. Tucker and Hendrickson, *Empire of Liberty,* 114–16.

8. Robert R. Livingston to JM, May 28, 1802, *PJMSS,* 3:264–65.

9. Robert R. Livingston to JM, May 12, 1803, *PJMSS,* 4:590–94, at 591.

10. Henry Adams, *History of the United States of America During the Administrations of Thomas Jefferson* (New York: Library of America, 1986), 255, 256.

11. Ibid., 279, 280.

12. Tucker and Hendrickson, *Empire of Liberty,* 131.

13. Forrest McDonald, *The Presidency of Thomas Jefferson* (Lawrence: University Press of Kansas, 1976), 67.

14. Memorial of the Kentucky Legislature, December 1, 1802, *PTJ,* 39:104–05. For the intendant's lack of authorization from the Spanish government to take this step, Dumas Malone, *Jefferson the President: First Term, 1801–1805* (Boston: Little, Brown, 1970), 240.

15. JM to Monroe and Livingston, March 2, 1803, *PJMSS,* 4:364–78.

16. James Monroe to JM, April 15, 1803, *PJMSS,* 4:520–22, at 521.

17. This paragraph and the next three are based on Robert R. Livingston to JM, April 11, 1803, *PJMSS,* 4:500–02.

18. Robert R. Livingston to James Monroe, April 10, 1803, *The Papers of James Monroe: Selected Correspondence and Papers,* ed. Daniel Preston, et al. (Santa Barbara, CA: ABC-Clio, 2012–), 5:26–27.

19. *PJMSS,* 4:xxviii. Though it rejected that motion, the Senate did agree to resolutions authored by Senator John Breckinridge, R-KY, authorizing Jefferson to raise eighty thousand militiamen for no stated purpose. Likely Livingston's use of this information fulfilled the Senate's expectations. See Robert R. Livingston to JM, April 11, 1803, *PJMSS,* 4:500–02, at 501.

20. *PJMSS,* 4:522–23, n. 3.

21. Robert R. Livingston to JM, April 17, 1803, *PJMSS,* 4:524–27.

22. John Beckley to JM, May 5, 1803, *PJMSS,* 4:574; for the currency of this impression in France, see Robert R. Livingston to JM, May 12, 1803, *PJMSS,* 4:590–94, at 591.

23. The Louisiana Treaty, May 2, 1803, *The Papers of James Monroe,* 5:50–53.

24. Robert R. Livingston and James Monroe to JM, May 13, 1803, *PJMSS,* 4:601–06.

25. James Monroe to Stevens Thomson Mason, Wilson Cary Nicholas, and John Breckinridge, May 25, 1803, *The Papers of James Monroe,* 5:76–77, at 76.

26. Robert R. Livingston to JM, May 20, 1803, *PJMSS,* 5:18–20, at 19.

27. James Monroe to Charles Pinckney, May 16, 1803, *The Papers of James Monroe,* 5:70.

28. James Monroe to JM, May 18, 1803, *The Papers of James Monroe,* 5:71–72, at 72.

Chapter 17

1. TJ to Heads of Departments, December 31, 1802, *The Papers of Thomas Jefferson,* ed. Julian P. Boyd (Princeton, NJ: Princeton University Press, 1950), 39:241.

2. Levi Lincoln to TJ, January 10, 1803, *PTJ,* 39:302–05.

3. Albert Gallatin to TJ, January 13, 1803, *PTJ*, 39:324–26.

4. TJ to Albert Gallatin, January 13, 1803, *PTJ*, 39:327–28, at 328.

5. Editorial Note, Constitutional Amendment on Louisiana, *PTJ*, 40:681–85, at 682.

6. Alexander Hamilton, "Purchase of Louisiana," July 5, 1803, *The Papers of Alexander Hamilton*, ed. Harold C. Syrett, et al. (New York: Columbia University Press, 1961–1979), 26:129–36.

7. TJ, Draft Amendment, on or before July 9, 1803, *PTJ*, 40:685.

8. JM, Proposed Constitutional Amendment, ca. July 9, 1803, *The Papers of James Madison: Secretary of State Series,* ed. Robert A. Rutland, et al. (Charlottesville: University Press of Virginia, 1986–), 5:156.

9. TJ to Albert Gallatin, July 9, 1803, *PTJ*, 688–89.

10. TJ and JM, Revised Amendment, ca. July 9, 1803, *PTJ*, 40:686–88.

11. Robert Smith to TJ, July 9, 1803, *PTJ*, 40:704–05.

12. JM, Proposed Constitutional Amendment, ca. July 9, 1803, *PJMSS*, 5:156.

13. For the date of receipt, Dumas Malone, *Jefferson the President: First Term, 1801–1805* (Boston: Little, Brown, 1970), 315, n. 11.

14. *PTJ*, n. at 40:473.

15. TJ to John Breckinridge, August 18, 1803, *PTJ*, 41:209; TJ to JM, August 18, 1803, *PTJ*, 41:219. TJ to Thomas Paine, August 18, 1803, *PTJ*, 41:221 repeats the first point in Jefferson's letter of that date to Breckinridge.

16. JM to TJ, August 20, 1803, *PTJ*, 41:233–34, at 233.

17. Albert Gallatin to TJ, August 31, 1803, *PTJ*, 41:296–301, at 297. The president had informed the secretary of the treasury of Livingston's in TJ to Albert Gallatin, August 23, 1803, *PTJ*, 41:243–44.

18. TJ to John Breckinridge, August 12, 1803, Ibid., 41:184–86.

19. Ibid., at 185–86.

20. TJ to William Ludlow, September 6, 1824, Founders Online (National Archives), https://founders.archives.gov/documents/Jefferson/98-01-02-4523.

21. John Breckinridge to TJ, September 10, 1803, *PTJ*, 41:357–58.

22. Wilson Cary Nicholas to TJ, September 3, 1803, *PTJ*, 41:312–14.

23. TJ to Wilson Cary Nicholas, September 7, 1803, *PTJ*, 41:346–48. By this point, Jefferson had drafted for Congress a plain annexation amendment, which eventually found its way into the Breckinridge Family Papers. Resolution for Introduction of Constitutional Amendment [August 1803 ?], *PTJ*, 41:305.

Chapter 18

1. William Plumer, *William Plumer's Memorandum of Proceedings in the United States Senate, 1803–1807* (New York: Macmillan, 1923), 1.

2. Editorial Note, Drafting the Annual Message to Congress, *The Papers of Thomas Jefferson,* ed. Julian P. Boyd (Princeton, NJ: Princeton University Press, 1950), 41:438–40.

3. James Madison's Remarks on the Draft, October 1, 1803, *PTJ*, 41:442–44, at 442–43.

4. Annual Message to Congress, October 17, 1803, *PTJ*, 41:534–39.

5. Plumer, *William Plumer's Memorandum*, 1–2.

6. So, for example, Speaker of the House Nathaniel Macon told Jefferson, "The acquisition

of Louisiana has given general satisfaction. . . ." Nathaniel Macon to TJ, September 3, 1803, *PTJ*, 41:311–12, at 312.

7. Entry for October 21, 1803, *John Quincy Adams: Diaries, 1779–1821,* ed. David Waldstreicher (New York: Library of America, 2017), 1:100.

8. Dumas Malone, *Jefferson the President: First Term, 1801–1805,* (Boston: Little, Brown, 1970), 328.

9. Ibid., 330.

10. Levi Lincoln to TJ, September 10, 1803, *PTJ*, 41:359–61, at 360.

11. The following discussion of Senate proceedings on the Louisiana Purchase Treaty is based on Plumer, *William Plumer's Memorandum,* 3–14. Plumer's riff on Montesquieu is one more data point against the widespread assumption that Madison's *Federalist* #10 lay at the root of Americans' decision to ratify the U.S. Constitution. In fact, "[b]efore 1815, no Massachusetts Federalist was known to accept Madison's bold thesis, best expressed in the *Tenth Federalist,* that large territorial boundaries might be the very guarantor of republican government." James M. Banner Jr., *To the Hartford Convention: The Federalists and the Origins of Party Politics in Massachusetts, 1789–1815* (New York: Alfred A. Knopf, 1970), 28.

12. In referring to this treaty as "one of the best," Morris must have had in mind the triumph of his and Livingston's fellow New Yorker John Jay in winning the Mississippi River as the United States' western border.

13. Gouverneur Morris, *The Diary and Letters of Gouverneur Morris,* ed. Anne Cary Morris (New York: Charles Scribner's Sons, 1888), 2:444.

14. Malone, *Jefferson the President: First Term,* 323–24.

15. Ibid., 330–32. The foremost scholar of Jefferson's thinking about Executive power, Jeremy Bailey, arrives at the markedly different conclusion that although devoted to serious constitutionalism—what nowadays is called "strict construction"—Jefferson left space for the fugitive emergency in which a chief executive must act while he could, then—as Senator Taylor put it during the Louisiana Affair—throw himself on the mercy of his countrymen. Adams may be forgiven his unfamiliarity with Jefferson's record as war governor of Virginia, when he had acted on this understanding. Jeremy Bailey, *Thomas Jefferson and Executive Power* (New York: Cambridge University Press, 2007), 28–64 (for his war governorship), 171–94 (regarding the Louisiana Purchase).

Chapter 19

1. The following account relies upon Reply of John Quincy Adams to the Letter of Massachusetts Federalists, December 30, 1828, in *Documents Relating to New-England Federalism, 1800–1815,* ed. Henry Adams (Burt Franklin Research and Source Works Series #89, American Classics in History and Social Science #8), 46–62, at 52, et seq.

2. Henry H. Simms, *Life of John Taylor, The Story of a Brilliant Leader in the Early Virginia State Rights School* (Richmond, VA: William Byrd Press, 1932), 61–62; Robert E. Shalhope, *John Taylor of Caroline: Pastoral Republican* (Columbia: University of South Carolina Press, 1980), 84.

3. This account is from William Plumer to John Quincy Adams, December 20, 1828, *Documents Relating to New-England Federalism, 1800–1815,* ed. Henry Adams 143–15.

4. TJ, entry for January 2, 1804, *The Anas of Thomas Jefferson,* ed. Franklin B. Sawvel (New York: Da Capo Press, 1970), 223.

5. TJ, entry for January 26, 1804, *The Anas of Thomas Jefferson,* 224–28.

6. TJ, Fourth Annual Message, November 8, 1804, *The Complete Jefferson,* ed. Saul K. Padover (New York: Duell, Sloan & Pearce, 1943), 406–10.

7. Forrest McDonald, *The Presidency of Thomas Jefferson* (Lawrence: University Press of Kansas, 1976), 87.

8. John Taylor to TJ, December 26, 1804, Founders Online (National Archives), https://founders.archives.gov/documents/Jefferson/99-01-02-0899; TJ to John Taylor, January 6, 1805, *The Works of Thomas Jefferson,* ed. Paul Leicester Ford (New York: G. P. Putnam's Sons, 1904–05), 10:124–26. For Taylor to have criticized Jefferson for selfishness on this ground would have come with ill grace, for the younger man habitually served short stints in office and then returned to his famous plantation for further agricultural experimentation. For example, each of his first two stints as a U.S. senator was of two years' duration. For Taylor's preference for farming over politics, Robert E. Shalhope, *John Taylor of Caroline: Pastoral Republican* (Columbia: University of South Carolina Press, 1980), 34. One of their contemporaries, James Monroe, complained to Taylor during one of the latter's hiatuses from public life that his wealth both enabled him to serve in high office and "increase[d] the obligation on [him] so to do." James Monroe to John Taylor, March 6, 1803, *The Papers of James Monroe: Selected Correspondence and Papers,* ed. Daniel Preston, et al. (Santa Barbara, CA: ABC-Clio, 2012), 5:22–23.

9. TJ, Second Inaugural Address, March 4, 1805, in *The Complete Jefferson* 410–15, quotations at 411.

10. "Jefferson's notes for his draft of this inaugural address," *The Complete Jefferson,* 410, n. 1.

11. For Jefferson's attitudes toward and policy for Indians generally, Kevin R. C. Gutzman, *Thomas Jefferson—Revolutionary: A Radical's Study to Remake America* (New York: St. Martin's Press, 2017), chapter 4, "Assimilation," 175–94.

Chapter 20

1. C. Peter Magrath, *Yazoo: Law and Politics in the New Republic—The Case of Fletcher v. Peck* (New York: W. W. Norton, 1966) remains the best study of the controversy and the case.

2. Ibid., 7.

3. Ibid., 7–13, quotation at 13.

4. Ibid., 15.

5. Ibid., 15–17.

6. Ibid., 32.

7. For Framers' and Ratifiers' concern to ban enactment of such statutes, see Kevin R. C. Gutzman, *James Madison and the Making of America* (New York: St. Martin's Press, 2012), 146.

8. Magrath, *Yazoo: Law and Politics,* headnote at 149. Hamilton's opinion is at 149–50.

9. For the contemporary attitude on these two issues, consider that the Northwest Ordinance, in Section 14, Article 2, said, "[N]o law ought ever to be made, or have force in the [Northwest] territory, that shall, in any manner whatever, interfere with or affect private contracts or engagements, *bona fide,* and without fraud, previously formed." Northwest Ordinance, July 13, 1787, Avalon Project (Yale Law School), https://avalon.law.yale.edu/18th_century/nworder.asp.

10. Magrath, *Yazoo: Law and Politics*, 33–34.

11. Ibid., 34–35.

12. Forrest McDonald, *The Presidency of Thomas Jefferson* (Lawrence: University Press of Kansas, 1976), 47.

13. Raymond Walters Jr., *Albert Gallatin: Jeffersonian Financier & Diplomat* (New York: Macmillan, 1957), 177–78.

14. The entire speech is found at Russell Kirk, *John Randolph of Roanoke: A Study in American Politics, with Selected Speeches and Letters,* 4th edition (Indianapolis, IN: Liberty Fund, 1997), 294–311.

15. Randolph here uses "job" in the sense of "a public or official act or decision carried through for the sake of improper private gain," "job, n." definition 10, Dictionary.com (accessed September 23, 2021).

Chapter 21

1. TJ to the House of Representatives, February 3, 1803, *The Papers of Thomas Jefferson,* ed. Julian P. Boyd (Princeton, NJ: Princeton University Press, 1950), 39:443 and n.; Lynn W. Turner, *William Plumer of New Hampshire, 1759–1850* (Chapel Hill: University of North Carolina Press, 1962), 125–26.

2. William Plumer, *William Plumer's Memorandum of Proceedings in the United States Senate, 1803–1807* (New York: Macmillan, 1923), 97.

3. Ibid., 150.

4. Dumas Malone, *Jefferson the President: First Term, 1801–1805* (Boston: Little, Brown, 1970), 461.

5. Ibid., 163.

6. Ibid., 176.

7. Forrest McDonald, *The Presidency of Thomas Jefferson* (Lawrence: University Press of Kansas, 1976), 80. Some scholars read the relevant materials as showing that Judge Pickering's incapacity resulted from alcohol abuse. R. Kent Newmyer, *The Supreme Court Under Marshall and Taney* (New York: Thomas Y. Crowell, 1968), 32.

8. Plumer, *William Plumer's Memorandum,* 179.

9. Ibid.

10. Henry Adams, *John Randolph* (Armonk, New York: M. E. Sharpe, 1996), 65.

11. *Calder v. Bull,* 3 U.S. 386 (1798).

12. Scott Douglas Gerber, *Seriatim: The Supreme Court Before John Marshall* (New York: NYU Press, 1998).

13. *PTJ,* 40:372–73, n.

14. TJ to Joseph H. Nicholson, May 13, 1803, *PTJ,* 40:371–72, at 372.

15. Malone, *Jefferson the President: First Term,* 402–408, 460.

16. This entire conversation is found at Entry for December 21, 1804 , *John Quincy Adams: Diaries, 1779–1821,* ed. David Waldstreicher (New York: Library of America, 2017), 1:116–17.

17. Plumer, *William Plumer's Memorandum,* 100–01.

18. This and the following two paragraphs are based on Plumer, *William Plumer's Memorandum,* 101–03.

19. John Gay, "Fables, Part II, Number VII, The Countryman and Jupiter, Fable VII: To Myself," line 52. (Thanks to Greg Heineken for identifying the verse.)

20. Plumer, *William Plumer's Memorandum,* 213.

21. David Johnson, *John Randolph of Roanoke* (Baton Rouge: Louisiana State University Press, 2012), 88. For *Fletcher v. Peck* as a set-up case in which Martin appeared before the court "so drunk . . . that Marshall had the Court adjourn until the counsel regained his sobriety—the only recorded incident of its kind in Supreme Court history" (this was written in 1966), C. Peter Magrath, *Yazoo: Law and Politics in the New Republic—The Case of Fletcher v. Peck* (New York: W. W. Norton, 1966), 67, 69. It was to Martin that Marshall referred as "counsel for Maryland" in his opinion for the court in *McCulloch.* Either Martin or Marshall mischaracterized the "Principles of '98" as claiming that the state *governments* had created the U.S. Constitution. (Of course, Republicans said that via the Article VII ratification process, the sovereign states through constituent ratification conventions created the U.S. Constitution.) Having described Martin's (?) position inaccurately, Marshall mocked it. Opinion, *McCulloch v. Maryland,* March 6, 1819, *The Papers of John Marshall,* ed. Herbert A. Johnson, et al. (Chapel Hill: University of North Carolina Press, 1974–2006), 8:259–79, at 261.

22. Plumer, *William Plumer's Memorandum,* 216–18. For a full account of House consideration and passage of the articles and appointment of managers, see *Annals of Congress,* 8th Congress, 2nd Session, 728–761 (https://memory.loc.gov/cgi-bin/ampage?collId=llac&fileName =014/llac014.db&recNum=361, et seq.).

Chapter 22

1. *Annals of Congress,* 8th Congress, 2nd Session, Senate, 101–150 (https://memory.loc .gov/cgi-bin/ampage?collId=llac&fileName=014/llac014.db&recNum=48, et seq.).

2. William Plumer, *William Plumer's Memorandum of Proceedings in the United States Senate, 1803–1807* (New York: Macmillan, 1923), 275.

3. *Annals of Congress,* 8th Congress, 2nd Session, Senate, 151 (https://memory.loc.gov /cgi-bin/ampage?collId=llac&fileName=014/llac014.db&recNum=73). (Plumer's notes of the House response describe it as "conceived in very bitter, indecent, & abusive language," which if correct indicates that Randolph's oral presentation of it differed from the actual script. Senators were only given printed copies the following day. Plumer, *William Plumer's Memorandum,* 277, 278.)

4. Plumer, *William Plumer's Memorandum,* 280–81.

5. Ibid., 284.

6. Ibid., 291.

7. John Marshall, Testimony in the Trial of Samuel Chase, February 16, 1805, *The Papers of John Marshall,* ed. Herbert A. Johnson, et al. (Chapel Hill: University of North Carolina Press, 1974–2006), 6:350–57, at 353.

8. Ibid., 6:350–57, at 354.

9. Ibid., 6:350–57, at 356.

10. Raoul Berger, *Impeachment: The Constitutional Problems* (Cambridge, MA: Harvard University Press, 1973), 228, n. 18.

11. Ibid., 225.

12. Ibid., 229–30. For the Cooper trial see Peter Charles Hoffer, *The Free Press Crisis of 1800: Thomas Cooper's Trial for Seditious Libel* (Lawrence: University Press of Kansas, 2011).

13. Berger, *Impeachment,* 231.

14. Joseph Jones to JM, January 7, 1804, *The Papers of James Madison: Secretary of State Series,* ed. Robert A. Rutland, et al. (Charlottesville: University Press of Virginia, 1986), 8:460.

15. Irving Brant, *James Madison: Secretary of State, 1800–1809* (New York: Bobbs-Merrill, 1953), 249.

16. Dumas Malone, *Jefferson the President: First Term, 1801–1805,* (Boston: Little, Brown, 1970), 483.

17. Ibid., 479.

18. Richard E. Ellis, *The Jeffersonian Crisis: Courts and Politics in the Young Republic* (New York: W. W. Norton, 1971).

19. Malone, *Jefferson the President: First Term,* 483.

20. Entry for March 1, 1805, *The Diary of John Quincy Adams, 1794–1845,* ed. Allan Nevins (New York: Charles Scribner's Sons, 1951), 32–34.

21. Plumer, *William Plumer's Memorandum,* 311.

22. Brant, *James Madison: Secretary of State,* 250.

23. JM to an Unidentified Correspondent, May 29, 1805, *PJMSS,* 9:416.

24. Entry for March 3, 1805, *The Diary of John Quincy Adams, 1794–1845,* 34–36, at 35.

25. TJ to William Branch Giles, April 20, 1807, *The Works of Thomas Jefferson,* ed. Paul Leicester Ford (New York: G. P. Putnam's Sons, 1904–05), 10:383–88, at 387.

26. TJ to Spencer Roane, September 6, 1819, *The Papers of Thomas Jefferson: Retirement Series,* ed. J. Jefferson Looney (Princeton, NJ: Princeton University Press, 2004-), S, 15:16–18, at 17. Supreme Court justices typically rate the Chase impeachment as one of the most important precedents in American constitutional law, as it essentially gave them free rein in their behavior on the bench. William H. Rehnquist, *Grand Inquests: The Historic Impeachments of Justice Samuel Chase and President Andrew Johnson* (New York: William Morrow, 1992), 275–78; Sandra Day O'Connor, *The Majesty of the Law* (New York: Random House, 2003), 83.

27. Henry Adams, *John Randolph: A Biography* (Armonk, NY: M. E. Sharpe, 1996), 94.

28. Entry for March 2, 1805, *The Diary of John Quincy Adams, 1794–1845,* 1:34.

29. Plumer: *William Plumer's Memorandum,* 312–13.

Chapter 23

1. Lawrence S. Kaplan, *Thomas Jefferson: Westward the Course of Empire* (Wilmington, DE: SR Books, 1999), 40; Dumas Malone, *Jefferson and the Rights of Man* (Charlottesville: University of Virginia Press, 2005), 27–32.

2. American Commissioners to John Jay, March 28, 1786, Founders Online (National Archives), https://founders.archives.gov/documents/Jefferson/01-09-02-0315.

3. Ian W. Toll, *Six Frigates: The Epic History of the Founding of the U.S. Navy* (New York: W. W. Norton, 2006), 165.

4. Kaplan, *Thomas Jefferson: Westward the Course of Empire,* 43–44.

5. Norman K. Risjord, *Jefferson's America, 1760–1815* (Lanham, MD: Rowman & Littlefield, 2002), 345.

6. TJ to JM, August 28, 1801, *The Papers of Thomas Jefferson,* ed. Julian P. Boyd (Princeton, NJ: Princeton University Press, 1950), 35:162–63.

7. Toll, *Six Frigates,* 168–69.

8. Albert Gallatin to TJ, August 16, 1802, *PTJ,* 38:229–32, at 231; Cabinet Meeting Notes, May 8, 1803, *PTJ,* 40:330–31; TJ to JM, March 22, 1803, *PTJ,* 40:101.

9. Toll, *Six Frigates,* 186–87.

10. Ibid., 190–92.

11. Ibid., 200.

12. Ibid., 204–05.

13. Ibid., 206.

14. Ibid., 207.

15. This entire account of Decatur's mission is based on Toll, *Six Frigates,* 208–11. The quotation is at 211.

16. Forrest McDonald, *The Presidency of Thomas Jefferson* (Lawrence: University Press of Kansas, 1976), 78.

17. Toll, *Six Frigates,* 251–52.

18. Ibid., 223.

19. McDonald, *The Presidency of Thomas Jefferson,* 78.

20. Toll, *Six Frigates,* 258.

21. Ibid., 224.

22. Ibid., 228.

23. Ibid., 259–63.

24. Ibid., 10.

25. The following discussion draws on McDonald, *The Presidency of Thomas Jefferson,* 101; Dumas Malone, *Jefferson the President: Second Term, 1805–1809* (Boston: Little, Brown, 1974), 59–60; and, especially, Merrill D. Peterson, *Thomas Jefferson & the New Nation* (New York: Oxford University Press, 1970), 806–08.

26. Peterson, *Thomas Jefferson & the New Nation,* 805.

27. JM to James Monroe, March 6, 1805, *The Papers of James Madison: Secretary of State Series,* ed. Robert A. Rutland, et al. (Charlottesville: University Press of Virginia, 1986–), 9:109–114, at 109.

Chapter 24

1. C. Edward Skeen, *John Armstrong, Jr.: A Biography* (Syracuse, NY: Syracuse University Press, 1981), 73.

2. Ibid., 74.

3. Richard Brookhiser, *Founding Father: Rediscovering George Washington* (New York: Free Press, 1996) 30.

4. Entry for March 17, 1806, *John Quincy Adams: Diaries, 1779–1821,* ed. David Waldstreicher, (New York: Library of America, 2017), 1:132.

5. *The Papers of James Monroe: Selected Correspondence and Papers,* ed. Daniel Preston, et al. (Santa Barbara, CA: ABC-Clio, 2012-), 5:243, n. 3.

6. Skeen, *John Armstrong, Jr.,* 51.

7. Ibid., 59–60.

8. JM to James Monroe, October 10, 1803, *The Papers of James Madison: Secretary of State Series,* ed. Robert A. Rutland, et al. (Charlottesville: University Press of Virginia, 1986), 5:504–05, at 505.

9. JM to James Monroe, December 26, 1803, *PJMSS,* 6:212–13, at 213.

10. JM to James Monroe, October 10, 1803, *PJMSS,* 5:504–05, at 505.

11. The rest of this and all of the following paragraph are based on JM to James Monroe, January 5, 1804, *PJMSS,* 6:282–306.

12. This and the following paragraph are based on James Monroe, Diplomatic Diary, April 2, 1804, *The Papers of James Monroe,* 5:209–12.

13. JM to James Monroe, March 6, 1805, *The Papers of James Monroe,* 5:344–47, at 345.

14. TJ to James Monroe, January 8, 1804, *The Papers of James Monroe,* 5:183–86, at 186.

15. TJ to Alexander I, April 19, 1806, *Thomas Jefferson: Writings* (New York: Library of America, 1984), 1161–62.

16. TJ, Fifth Annual Message, December 3, 1805, *The Complete Jefferson—Containing His Major Writings, Published and Unpublished, Except His Letters,* ed. Saul K. Padover (New York: Duell, Sloan & Pearce, 1943), 415–20.

17. TJ, entry for November 12, 1805, *The Anas of Thomas Jefferson,* ed. Franklin B. Sawvel (New York: Da Capo Press, 1970), 232–33.

18. Henry Adams, *History of the United States of America During the Administrations of Thomas Jefferson* (New York: Library of America, 1986), 694.

19. Timothy Pickering to Fisher Ames, March 24, 1806, *Works of Fisher Ames,* ed. Seth Ames (Indianapolis, IN: Liberty Fund, 1983), 2:1521–24, at 1524.

20. Merrill Peterson, *Thomas Jefferson & the New Nation: A Biography* (New York: Oxford University Press, 1970), 813.

21. Norman K. Risjord, *The Old Republicans: Southern Conservatism in the Age of Jefferson* (New York: Columbia University Press, 1965), 46–47.

22. Adams, *History of the United States of America During the Administrations of Thomas Jefferson,* 695–97.

23. Ibid., 697–98; JM to John Armstrong and James Bowdoin, March 13, 1806, *PJMSS,* 11:378–80.

Chapter 25

1. JM, 1806, "An Examination of the British Doctrine, Which Subjects to Capture a Neutral Trade, Not Open in Time of Peace," *The Writings of James Madison, Comprising His Public Papers and His Private Correspondence,* ed. Gaillard Hunt (New York: G. P. Putnam's Sons, 1908), 7:204–375.

2. Peter Onuf and Nicholas Onuf, *Federal Union, Modern World: The Law of Nations in an Age of Revolutions, 1776–1814* (Madison, WI: Madison House, 1993), 201 and n. 63. The following discussion relies both on this book's treatment of the pamphlet, 201–211, and on the pamphlet itself.

3. Ibid., 202, 204.

4. JM, 1806, "An Examination of the British Doctrine, Which Subjects to Capture a Neutral Trade, Not Open in Time of Peace," *The Writings of James Madison,* 7:346.

5. Harry Ammon, *James Monroe: The Quest for National Identity,* (Charlottesville: Uni-

versity Press of Virginia, 1971), 248. Ammon's account of the negotiations culminating in the Monroe-Pinkney Treaty, the treaty's contents, and the president's decision about it is at 248–69.

6. This account is taken from James Monroe to JM, August 7, 1804, *The Papers of James Monroe: Selected Correspondence and Papers,* ed. Daniel Preston, et al. (Santa Barbara, CA: ABC-Clio, 2012), 5:244–46.

7. Ibid., 5:247, n. 4.

8. Ibid., 5:214, n. The Project of a Convention Relative to Seamen &c. [April 7, 1804] is at *The Papers of James Monroe,* 5:213–14.

9. JM to James Monroe, January 13, 1806, *The Papers of James Monroe,* 5:444. Monroe sent it along to the new British foreign minister soon thereafter. James Monroe to Charles J. Fox, *The Papers of James Monroe,* 5:464.

10. James Monroe to JM, January 28, 1806, *The Papers of James Monroe,* 5:446–47, at 447.

11. James Monroe to JM, February 2, 1806, *The Papers of James Monroe,* 5:448–52.

12. Ibid., 5:145, n. 6.

13. Ibid., 5:456, n. 4.

14. TJ to James Monroe, JM to James Monroe, January 13, 1806, *The Papers of James Monroe,* 5:462.

15. Ibid., 5:462, n. 2.

16. Ibid., 5:462, n. 3.

17. Ibid., 5:436, n. 2.

18. Journal of Negotiation, November 5, 1806, *The Papers of James Monroe,* 5:540.

19. Ibid., 5:540, n. 1.

20. Lord Holland and Lord Auckland to James Monroe and William Pinkney, November 8, 1806, *The Papers of James Monroe,* 5:541.

21. James Monroe and William Pinkney to JM, November 11, 1806, *The Papers of James Monroe,* 5:542–46.

22. Treaty of Amity Commerce and Navigation between His Britannic Majesty and the United States of America, December 31, 1806, *The Papers of James Monroe,* 5:554–61; James Monroe and William Pinkney to James Madison, January 3, 1807, *The Papers of James Monroe,* 5:562–72 (section regarding impressment and compensation to shipowners at 569, 570).

23. Lord Howick to James Monroe, January 10, 1807, *The Papers of James Monroe,* 5:572.

Chapter 26

1. *The Papers of James Monroe: Selected Correspondence and Papers,* ed. Daniel Preston, et al. (Santa Barbara, CA: ABC-Clio, 2012), 5:587, n. 2.

2. Lawrence S. Kaplan, *Thomas Jefferson: Westward the Course of Empire* (Wilmington, DE: SR Books, 1999), 160.

3. TJ to James Monroe, March 21, 1807, *The Papers of James Monroe,* 5:588.

4. Irving Brant, *James Madison: Secretary of State, 1800–1809* (New York: Bobbs-Merrill, 1953), 370.

5. Ibid., 372.

6. Ibid., 376–77.

7. Ibid., 378–79; Raymond Walters Jr., *Albert Gallatin: Jeffersonian Financier & Diplomat* (New York: Macmillan, 1957), 195.

8. Joseph Nicholson to James Monroe, April 12, 1807, *The Papers of James Monroe,* 5:591–92.

9. Kevin R. C. Gutzman, *Thomas Jefferson—Revolutionary: A Radical's Struggle to Re-make America* (New York: St. Martin's Press, 2017), chapter 4.

10. Meriwether Lewis: Estimated Costs of Missouri River Expedition, January 18, 1803, *The Papers of Thomas Jefferson,* ed. Julian P. Boyd (Princeton, NJ: Princeton University Press, 1950), 39:342.

11. Stephen E. Ambrose, *Undaunted Courage: Meriwether Lewis, Thomas Jefferson, and the Opening of the American West* (New York: Simon & Schuster, 1996), 79.

12. TJ to the Senate and House of Representatives, January 18, 1803, *PTJ,* 350–53, at 352–53.

13. Peter J. Kastor, "The Many Wests of Thomas Jefferson," *Seeing Jefferson Anew—In His Time and Ours,* John B. Boles and Randal L. Hall, eds. (Charlottesville: University of Virginia Press, 2010), 66–94, at 88.

14. Ibid., 66–94, at 82, 84.

15. Ambrose, *Undaunted Courage,* 397, 399.

16. Ibid., 399–400.

17. TJ, "Sixth Annual Message," December 2, 1806, *The Complete Jefferson—Containing His Major Writings, Published and Unpublished, Except His Letters,* ed. Saul K. Padover (New York: Duell, Sloan & Pearce, 1943), 421–26, at 423–24 (Lewis and Clark), 424 (slavery), 425–26 (education, improvements, and amendment), 426 (military preparation).

18. Ibid., 421–26, at 422.

19. The most exhaustive effort to plumb the depths of Burr's conspiracy took the author to "roughly fifty state and local historical societies, college and university special collections departments, history museums, and research centers" over nearly twenty years. James E. Lewis Jr., *The Burr Conspiracy: Uncovering the Story of an Early American Crisis* (Princeton, NJ: Princeton University Press, 2017), 463. Ultimately this book became an account of what people had thought Burr was doing, rather than a history of the conspiracy, because it became clear that Burr, superb lawyer that he was, knew how to cover his tracks.

20. Merrill Peterson, *Thomas Jefferson & the New Nation: A Biography* (New York: Oxford University Press, 1970), 847.

21. TJ, "Sixth Annual Message," *The Complete Jefferson,* December 2, 1806, 421–26, at 422.

22. R. Kent Newmyer, *The Treason Trial of Aaron Burr: Law, Politics, and the Character Wars of the New Nation* (New York: Cambridge University Press, 2012), 1. Newmyer's is the best account.

23. TJ, Entry for October 22, 1806, *The Anas of Thomas Jefferson,* ed. Franklin B. Sawvel (New York: Da Capo Press, 1970), 245–47, at 246–47.

24. Newmyer, *The Treason Trial of Aaron Burr,* 7; Forrest McDonald, *The Presidency of Thomas Jefferson,* (Lawrence: University Press of Kansas, 1976), 121.

25. TJ, Entries for October 24 and 25, 1806, *The Anas of Thomas Jefferson,* 247–48.

Chapter 27

1. Merrill Peterson, *Thomas Jefferson & the New Nation,* (New York: Oxford University Press, 1970), 842, says Burr's goal was "creating an independent confederacy south of the Ohio." Burr's friendliest biographer, however, says his goal was to drive the Spanish out

of Mexico and the Floridas. Nancy Isenberg, *Fallen Founder: The Life of Aaron Burr* (New York: Penguin, 2007), 290–92.

2. Forrest McDonald, *The Presidency of Thomas Jefferson* (Lawrence: University Press of Kansas, 1976), 121.

3. Peterson, *Thomas Jefferson & the New Nation*, 848.

4. McDonald, *The Presidency of Thomas Jefferson*, 124; Peterson, *Thomas Jefferson & the New Nation*, 849.

5. R. Kent Newmyer, *The Treason Trial of Aaron Burr: Law, Politics, and the Character Wars of the New Nation* (New York: Cambridge University Press, 2012), 8. McDonald, *The Presidency of Thomas Jefferson*, 125.

6. R. Kent Newmyer, *The Treason Trial of Aaron Burr: Law, Politics, and the Character Wars of the New Nation*, 8.

7. McDonald, *The Presidency of Thomas Jefferson*, 127.

8. Ibid., 128; TJ, Special Message, January 22, 1807, *The Complete Jefferson—Containing His Major Writings, Published and Unpublished, Except His Letters*, ed. Saul K. Padover (New York: Duell, Sloan & Pearce, 1943), 427–31.

9. Newmyer, *The Treason Trial of Aaron Burr*, 56, et seq.

10. Ibid., 154.

11. Ibid., 146–48.

12. Ibid., 165.

13. Ibid., 178.

14. Ibid., 167.

15. TJ to Albert Gallatin, January 13, 1807, *The Works of Thomas Jefferson*, ed. Paul Leicester Ford (New York: G. P. Putnam's Sons, 1904–05), 10:339–40.

16. Lawrence S. Kaplan, *Thomas Jefferson: Westward the Course of Empire*, (Wilmington, Delaware: SR Books, 1999), 160.

17. Ibid., 161–62.

18. JM, Draft "Chesapeake" Proclamation, June 29, 1807, *The Works of Thomas Jefferson*, 10:447–48, fn.

19. Ian W. Toll, *Six Frigates: The Epic History of the Founding of the U.S. Navy* (New York: W. W. Norton, 2006), 294–98 (block quotation at 296).

20. TJ, "Chesapeake" Proclamation, July 2, 1807, *The Works of Thomas Jefferson*, 10:434–47.

21. Resolutions on the Chesapeake-Leopard Affair, August 3, 1807, *The Papers of John C. Calhoun*, ed. Robert L. Meriwether, et al. (Columbia: University of South Carolina Press, 1959–2003), 1:34–7, and n. at 37.

22. Irving H. Bartlett, *John C. Calhoun: A Biography* (New York: W. W. Norton, 1993), 57.

23. Norman K. Risjord, *Thomas Jefferson* (Lanham, MD: Rowman & Littlefield, 1994), 166.

24. Burton Spivak, *Jefferson's English Crisis: Commerce, Embargo, and the Republican Revolution* (Charlottesville: University Press of Virginia, 1979), 102.

25. TJ, Special Message on Commercial Depredations, December 18, 1807, *The Works of Thomas Jefferson*, 10:530–31.

26. Spivak, *Jefferson's English Crisis*, 105–06.

27. Ibid., 107.

28. Albert Gallatin to Joseph H. Nicholson, July 17, 1807, *The Writings of Albert Gallatin*, ed. Henry Adams (Philadelphia: J. B. Lippincott, 1879), 1:338–40, at 338–39.

29. Spivak, *Jefferson's English Crisis,* 107–08; Irving Brant, *James Madison: Secretary of State, 1800–1809* (New York: Bobbs-Merrill, 1953), 401–03 (this and the next paragraph). As is nearly always the case, Brant approves of Madison's argument.

30. R. B. Bernstein, *Thomas Jefferson* (New York: Oxford University Press, 2003), 167.

31. Gregory May, *Jefferson's Treasure: How Albert Gallatin Saved the New Nation from Debt* (Washington, DC: Regnery, 2018), 167, 168.

32. TJ, Eighth Annual Message, November 8, 1808, *The Works of Thomas Jefferson,* 11:56–72, at 56–64.

33. May, *Jefferson's Treasure,* 172.

34. Ibid., 174–75.

Chapter 28

1. Entry for March [4], 1809, Margaret Bayard Smith, *The First Forty Years of Washington Society,* ed. Gaillard Hunt, 2nd edition (New York: Frederick Ungar, 1965), 58–64, at 59. Madison as orator often proved inaudible. Kevin R. C. Gutzman, *James Madison and the Making of America* (New York: St. Martin's Press, 2012), 201.

2. "President's House Forty Years Ago," 1841, Margaret Bayard Smith, *The First Forty Years of Washington Society,* 383–412, at 410.

3. JM, First Inaugural Address, [March 4, 1809], *The Papers of James Madison: Presidential Series,* ed. Robert A. Rutland, et al. (Charlottesville: University Press of Virginia, 1984–) (hereafter, *PJMPS*), 1:15–18.

4. In Madison's day, commas commonly were used to mark pauses in spoken prose. As the chief author of George Washington's First Inaugural Address (Gutzman, *James Madison and the Making of America,* 242) and a close collaborator of Thomas Jefferson, Madison knew whereof he spoke.

5. Wilson Cary Nicholas to JM, ca. March 3, 1809, *PJMPS,* 1:10–11.

6. Irving Brant, *James Madison: The President, 1809–1812* (New York: Bobbs-Merrill, 1956), 23. For Giles, see Dice Robins Anderson, *William Branch Giles: A Study in the Politics of Virginia and the Nation from 1790 to 1830* (Menasha, WI: George Banta, 1914).

7. Brant, *James Madison: The President,* 22.

8. William Branch Giles to JM, February 27, 1809, Founders Online (National Archives), https://founders.archives.gov/documents/Madison/99-01-02-4071.

9. Donald R. Hickey, *The War of 1812: A Forgotten Conflict—Bicentennial Edition* (Urbana: University of Illinois Press, 2012), 70.

10. Ralph Ketcham, *James Madison: A Biography* (Charlottesville: University Press of Virginia, 1990), 482.

11. Hickey, *The War of 1812,* 70.

12. Andrew Burstein and Nancy Isenberg, *Madison and Jefferson* (New York: Random House, 2010), 521.

13. Henry Lee to JM, February 2, 1827, Founders Online (National Archives), https://founders.archives.gov/documents/Madison/99-02-02-0898.

14. Madison's reply, which his editor oddly consigned to a pages-long footnote, is JM to Henry Lee, February 1827, *The Writings of James Madison, Comprising His Public Papers*

and His Private Correspondence, ed. Gaillard Hunt (New York: G.P. Putnam's Sons, 1910), 9:277–80, n.1.

Chapter 29

1. The leading study is Catherine Allgor, *Parlor Politics: In Which the Ladies of Washington Help Build a City and a Government* (Charlottesville: University Press of Virginia, 2000), though we need not be quite so impressed with Mrs. Madison's political significance as Allgor. For example, "[w]e may wonder if it occurred to Dolley and James Madison, as they wandered through echoing rooms, that the condition of the President's House might be a fitting metaphor for the political situation Jefferson had bequeathed to them." Allgor, *Parlor Politics,* 48–9. Also consider "both Madisons . . . entered the executive mansion in 1809 and then guided the nation through war." Allgor, *Parlor Politics,* 52. Allgor also heads a section of her Dolley Madison chapter "Last of the Founders," thus both alluding to the title of the foremost Madison book and putting Dolley Madison in the company of George Washington, John Adams, Thomas Jefferson, and her husband. Allgor, *Parlor Politics,* 94; Drew McCoy, *The Last of the Fathers: James Madison & the Republican Legacy* (New York: Cambridge University Press, 1989).

2. Allgor, *Parlor Politics,* 63.

3. Ibid., 71, 255, n. 57, 62.

4. William W. Freehling, *The Road to Disunion, Volume 1: Secessionists at Bay, 1776–1854* (New York: Oxford University Press, 1990), 167–68.

5. Allgor, *Parlor Politics,* 95.

6. Ibid., 72.

7. Ibid., 76.

8. Annette Gordon-Reed, *Thomas Jefferson & Sally Hemings: An American Controversy* (Charlottesville: University of Virginia Press, 1997), 197; Appendix B, 245–48, at 247.

9. Catherine Allgor, *Dolley Madison: The Problem of National Unity* (Boulder, CO: Westview Press, 2013), 99.

10. Ibid.

11. Elizabeth Dowling Taylor, *A Slave in the White House: Paul Jennings and the Madisons* (New York: Palgrave Macmillan, 2012), 226.

12. Paul Jennings, "A Colored Man's Reminiscences of James Madison," in Taylor, *A Slave in the White House,* Appendix A, 229–36, at 235, 236.

13. Ralph Ketcham, *James Madison: A Biography* (Charlottesville: University Press of Virginia, 1990), 477.

14. Irving Brant, *James Madison: The President, 1809–1812,* (New York: Bobbs-Merrill, 1956), 38–39.

15. JM to William Pinkney, March 17, 1809, *The Papers of James Madison: Presidential Series,* ed. Robert A. Rutland, et al. (Charlottesville: University Press of Virginia, 1984-), 1:55–57.

16. An excellent account of New England's role in American foreign policy at this time is Richard Buel Jr., *America on the Brink: How the Political Struggle Over the War of 1812 Almost Destroyed the Young Republic* (New York: Palgrave Macmillan, 2005).

17. The following description relies upon Editorial Note, "Presidential Proclamation Restoring Commerce with Great Britain, 15–19 April 1809," *PJMPS,* 1:117–18.

18. Albert Gallatin to JM, April 14, 1809, *PJMPS*, 1:118.

19. JM, Presidential Proclamation, April 19, 1809, *PJMPS*, 1:125–26.

20. Ibid., 1:137, n. 1.

21. JM to the Mother Superior of the Ursuline Convent, April 24, 1809, *PJMPS*, 1:136; JM to TJ, April 24, 1809, *PJMPS*, 1:135–36.

22. TJ to JM, April 27, 1809, *PJMPS*, 1:139–40.

23. Ibid., 1:202, n. 1.

24. JM to Congress, May 23, 1809, *PJMPS*, 1:199–202.

25. JM to TJ, May 30, 1809, *PJMPS*, 1:213–14, at 214.

Chapter 30

1. Madison had received indication that something was odd a few days before. JM to TJ, June 12, 1809, *The Papers of James Madison: Presidential Series*, ed. Robert A. Rutland, et al. (Charlottesville: University Press of Virginia, 1984–), 1:239–40. For the bombshell's arrival on June 19, JM to TJ, June 20, 1809, *PJMPS*, 1:261–62, and n. 1.

2. Ibid., 1:308, n. 1.

3. William Eustis to JM, July 27, 1809, *PJMPS*, 1:308.

4. JM to Albert Gallatin, July 28, 1809, *PJMPS*, 1:309–10.

5. Irving Brant, *James Madison: The President, 1809–1812* (New York: Bobbs-Merrill, 1956), 44.

6. Erskine indicated to Gallatin that Madison's statement about George's honor had in fact been the basis of British refusal of Erskine's agreement. Albert Gallatin to JM, July 31, 1809, *PJMPS*, 1:313–14, at 314.

7. JM to Albert Gallatin, July 28, 1809, *PJMPS*, 1:309–10, at 310.

8. JM, Presidential Proclamation, August 9, 1809, *PJMPS*, 1:320–21.

9. Ibid., 1:374, n. 2.

10. JM to Robert Smith, September 15, 1809, *PJMPS*, 1:378.

11. Ralph Ketcham, *James Madison: A Biography* (Charlottesville: University Press of Virginia, 1990), 496.

12. JM to Albert Gallatin, October 5, 1809, *PJMPS*, 2:3 and n. 1; JM to TJ, October 6, 1809, *PJMPS*, 2:5.

13. Caesar A. Rodney to JM, October 17, 1809, *PJMPS*, 2:17–18, at 18.

14. Smith to Francis James Jackson, summary note, *PJMPS*, 2:11.

15. Ketcham, *James Madison*, 496–97. Ketcham, sometimes relying on Henry Adams, credits Madison with the letters to Jackson. The editors of the authoritative edition of Madison's papers, however, are uncertain how completely letters in Smith's handwriting should be credited to Madison. Editorial Note, "Madison, Francis James Jackson, and Robert Smith, 9 October–11 November 1809," *PJMPS*, 2:8–11.

16. Draft of Robert Smith to William Pinkney, ca. November 9, 1809, *PJMPS*, 2:65–7, and n. 1.

17. Garry Wills, *James Madison* (New York: Times Books, 2002), 86–87.

18. JM to Congress, January 3, 1810, *PJMPS*, 2:158 and n. 2.

19. Wills, *James Madison*, 87.

20. JM to TJ, May 25, 1810, *PJMPS*, 2:353–54, at 353.

21. Armstrong to Robert Smith, August 5, 1810, *PJMPS*, 2:463, n. 1.

22. Paul Hamilton to JM, September 25, 1810, *PJMPS*, 2:554, and n. 1. A letter from a friend in Paris confirming the French news soon followed. Lafayette to JM, September 26, 1810, *PJMPS*, 2:559–60, at 560.

23. JM, Presidential Proclamation, November 2, 1810, *PJMPS*, 2:612–13.

24. JM to William Pinkney, October 30, 1810, *PJMPS*, 2:603–05.

25. Robert Allen Rutland, *The Presidency of James Madison* (Lawrence: University Press of Kansas, 1990), 64–67.

26. For Francophilia, Henry Adams, *History of the United States of America During the Administrations of James Madison* (New York: Library of America, 1986), 42.

27. Good general accounts are Ketcham, *James Madison,* 500–02; and Brant, *James Madison,* 173–89. Also see Editorial Note, Madison and the Collapse of the Spanish-American Empire: The West Florida Crisis of 1810, April 20, 1810, *PJMPS*, 2:305–20.

28. JM, Presidential Proclamation, October 27, 1810, *PJMPS*, 2:595–96.

29. This instruction took the form of an interlineation in Smith's instructions to Claiborne in Madison's hand. *PJMPS,* 2:596, n. 4.

30. Brant, *James Madison: The President,*189.

31. Dumas Malone, *Jefferson and His Time, vol. 6: The Sage of Monticello* (Boston: Little, Brown, 1981), 87–88; *PJMPS,* 3:95, n. 4.

Chapter 31

1. For Madison's opposition to the Bank Bill during the Washington administration, Kevin R. C. Gutzman, *James Madison and the Making of America* (New York: St. Martin's Press, 2012), 256–60. For his omission to advocate re-charter in 1811, Irving Brant, *James Madison: The President, 1809–1812* (New York: Bobbs-Merrill, 1956), 269–70.

2. Robert Allen Rutland, *The Presidency of James Madison* (Lawrence: University Press of Kansas, 1990), 68–69.

3. Brant, *James Madison: The President,* 269.

4. Gregory May, *Jefferson's Treasure: How Albert Gallatin Saved the New Nation from Debt* (Washington, DC: Regnery, 2018), 191–92.

5. The chief evidence is JM, Memorandum on Robert Smith, ca. April 11, 1811, *The Papers of James Madison: Presidential Series,* ed. Robert A. Rutland, et al. (Charlottesville: University Press of Virginia, 1984–), 3:255–63.

6. Ibid., 3:143, n. 2.

7. See Littleton W. Tazewell to James Monroe, October 8, 1808, *The Papers of James Monroe: Selected Correspondence and Papers,* ed. Daniel Preston, et al. (Santa Barbara, CA: ABC-Clio, 2012–), 5:720–23; and James Monroe to Littleton W. Tazewell, October 30, 1808, *The Papers of James Monroe,* 5:725–29.

8. James Monroe to John Taylor, January 9, 1809, *The Papers of James Monroe,* 5:733–34.

9. "I see with infinite grief a contest arising between yourself and another who have been very dear to each other, and equally so to me." TJ to James Monroe, February 18, 1808, *The Papers of James Monroe,* 5:670–71.

10. TJ to James Monroe, April 11, 1808, *The Papers of James Monroe,* 702–04, at 704.

11. Tim McGrath, *James Monroe: A Life* (New York: Penguin, 2020), 290.

12. Chapman Johnson to James Monroe, January 12, 1811, *The Papers of James Monroe,* 5:784–85.

13. James Monroe to Chapman Johnson, January 14, 1811, *The Papers of James Monroe,* 5:785–86. (This letter appeared in the *Richmond Enquirer,* the Commonwealth's leading newspaper, on January 17, 1811.)

14. James Monroe to Littleton Waller Tazewell, January 15, 1811, *The Papers of James Monroe,* 5:786, n.

15. The following account depends on McGrath, *James Monroe,* 290–91; James Monroe to John Taylor, September 10, 1810, *The Papers of James Monroe,* 5:766–775, at 774–75; James Monroe to John Taylor, November 19, 1810, *The Papers of James Monroe,* 5:778–80, at 779–80; John Randolph to James Monroe, January 14, 1811, *The Papers of James Monroe,* 5:786; *The Papers of James Monroe,* 5:787, n. 3; John Randolph to James Monroe, January 15, 1811, *The Papers of James Monroe,* 5:787.

16. Harry Ammon, *James Monroe: The Quest for National Identity* (Charlottesville: University Press of Virginia, 1990),

17. TJ to James Monroe, January 25, 1811, *The Papers of James Monroe,* 5:791.

18. Richard Brent to James Monroe, ca. March 8–12, 1811, *The Papers of James Monroe,* 5:797; James Monroe to Littleton Waller Tazewell, March 17, 1811, *The Papers of James Monroe,* 5:797–98.

19. Littleton Waller Tazewell to James Monroe, March 17, 1811, *The Papers of James Monroe,* 5:798–800.

20. Ibid., 5:800, n.

21. Enclosure, March 18, 1811, *The Papers of James Monroe,* 5:800–01, and n.; James Monroe to Richard Brent, March 18, 1811, *The Papers of James Monroe,* 5:800–01.

22. JM to James Monroe, March 20, 1811, *The Papers of James Monroe,* 5:801–02.

23. James Monroe to JM, March 23, 1811, *The Papers of James Monroe,* 5:802.

24. JM to James Monroe, March 26, 1811, *The Papers of James Monroe,* 5:803.

25. Ibid., 5:805, n; James Monroe to Joseph J. Monroe, December 6, 1811, *The Papers of James Monroe,* 6:93–94, at 93. Monroe confided that he hoped his service would "promot[e] harmony at least in the republican party." James Monroe to TJ, April 3, 1811, *The Papers of James Monroe,* 5:806.

26. Meredith Henne Baker, *The Richmond Theater Fire: Early America's First Great Disaster* (Baton Rouge: Louisiana State University Press, 2012), 19.

Chapter 32

1. JM to the House of Representatives, February 21, 1811, *The Papers of James Madison: Presidential Series,* ed. Robert A. Rutland, et al. (Charlottesville: University Press of Virginia, 1984–), 3:176, and 3:177, n. 1; JM to the House of Representatives, February 28, 1811, *PJMPS,* 3:193 and n. 1.

2. Henry Adams, *History of the United States of America During the Administrations of James Madison,* (New York: Library of America, 1986), 247.

3. James Haw, Francis F. Beirne, Rosamond R. Beirne, and R. Samuel Jett, *Stormy Patriot: The Life of Samuel Chase* (Baltimore: Maryland Historical Society, 1980), 243.

4. Ibid., 248.

5. G. Edward White, *The Marshall Court and Cultural Change, 1815-1835* (New York: Oxford University Press, 1991, abridged edition), 322.

6. Ibid., 325-27.

7. Thomas Jefferson to James Madison, October 15, 1810, *PJMPS*, 2:580-81, at 581.

8. R. Kent Newmyer, *Supreme Court Justice Joseph Story: Statesman of the Old Republic* (Chapel Hill: University of North Carolina Press, 1985), 62-63.

9. Ibid., 63.

10. Ibid., 71, for the nominees; for Adams's turning down the appointment, Robert Allen Rutland, *The Presidency of James Madison* (Lawrence: University Press of Kansas, 1990), 57. (Both Newmyer and Rutland explain Adams's decision by reference to his presidential ambitions.)

11. Albert Gallatin to JM, ca. November 1, 1811, *PJMPS*, 3:535-38; navy passage at 537.

12. Ralph Ketcham, *James Madison: A Biography* (Charlottesville: University Press of Virginia, 1990), 529-30.

13. JM, Annual Message to Congress, November 5, 1811, *PJMPS*, 4:1-5.

14. Ibid. 4:6, n. 2.

Chapter 33

1. *The Papers of James Monroe: Selected Correspondence and Papers*, ed. Daniel Preston, et al. (Santa Barbara, CA: ABC-Clio, 2012-), 6:91, n. 1.

2. James Monroe to Jonathan Russell, Joel Barlow, George Erving, and John Quincy Adams, November 27, 1811, *The Papers of James Monroe,* 6:90.

3. Ibid., 6:91, n. 2.

4. An interesting account of the charismatic brothers' overall situation is Gregory Evans Dowd, *A Spirited Resistance: The North American Indian Struggle for Unity, 1745-1815* (Baltimore, MD: Johns Hopkins University Press, 1993).

5. Margaret L. Coit, *John C. Calhoun: American Portrait* (Boston: Houghton Mifflin, 1950), 73.

6. James Monroe to Jonathan Russell, November 27, 1811, *The Papers of James Monroe,* 6:91. For the likely effect of arming merchant ships, Ralph Ketcham, *James Madison: A Biography* (Charlottesville: University Press of Virginia, 1990), 513.

7. Report on Relations with Great Britain, November 29, 1811, *The Papers of John C. Calhoun* ed. Robert L. Meriwether, et al. (Columbia: University of South Carolina Press, 1959-2003), 1:63-69, resolutions at 68-69.

8. The following account is based on the transcript at Henry Adams, *John Randolph: A Biography* (Armonk, New York: M. E. Sharpe, 1996), 205-09.

9. Henry Clay, Amendment to, and Speech on, the Bill to Raise an Additional Military Force, December 31, 1811, *The Papers of Henry Clay,* James F. Hopkins, et al., eds. (Lexington: University of Kentucky Press, 1959-1991), 1:602-09. Many of the arguments the speaker made here were in answer to those made by Rep. John Randolph on December 9-10. *The Papers of John C. Calhoun,* 1:85, n. 48.

10. John C. Calhoun to Dr. James Macbride, February 16 [17?], 1812, *The Papers of John C. Calhoun,* 1:90-91.

11. James Monroe to Lord Holland, November 29, 1811, *The Papers of James Monroe,* 6:92-93.

12. JM to TJ, February 7, 1812, *The Papers of James Madison: Presidential Series*, ed. Robert A. Rutland, et al. (Charlottesville: University Press of Virginia, 1984–), 4:168–69 and notes 1 and 2.

13. *PJMPS*, 4:169–70, n. 3.

14. Ketcham, *James Madison*, 514–15.

15. Ibid., 521.

16. This and the following paragraph depend on Albert Gallatin to TJ, March 10, 1812, *PTJRS*, 4:547.

17. The best account of domestic opposition to the War of 1812 is Richard Buel Jr., *America on the Brink* (New York: Palgrave Macmillan, 2005).

Chapter 34

1. The following account relies on Richard Buel Jr., *America on the Brink* (New York: Palgrave Macmillan, 2005), 139–41; also see Irving Brant, *James Madison: The President, 1809–1812* (New York: Bobbs-Merrill, 1956), 413–21. Madison's letter is JM to Congress, March 9, 1812, *The Papers of James Madison: Presidential Series*, ed. Robert A. Rutland, et al. (Charlottesville: University Press of Virginia, 1984–), 4:235.

2. John Henry to James Monroe, February 20, 1812, *The Papers of James Monroe: Selected Correspondence and Papers*, ed. Daniel Preston, et al. (Santa Barbara, CA: ABC-Clio, 2012), 6:119.

3. Buel Jr., *America on the Brink*, 141.

4. Henry Adams, *History of the United States of America During the Administrations of James Madison* (New York: Library of America, 1986), 420–21.

5. This paragraph relies on Ralph Ketcham, *James Madison: A Biography* (Charlottesville: University Press of Virginia, 1990), 524, except for Madison's message, which is JM to Congress, April 1, 1812, *PJMPS*, 4:279.

6. Ketcham, *James Madison*, 536.

7. Adams, *History of the United States of American During the Administrations of James Madison*, 440–41.

8. Robert Allen Rutland, *The Presidency of James Madison* (Lawrence: University Press of Kansas, 1990), 93.

9. Preface, *PJMPS*, 4:xxv–xxxi, at xxx.

10. Albert Gallatin to Joseph H. Nicholson, May 21, 1812, *The Writings of Albert Gallatin*, ed. Henry Adams (Philadelphia: J. B. Lippincott, 1879), 1:518.

11. Rutland, *The Presidency of James Madison*, 93.

12. JM to Congress, June 1, 1812, *PJMPS*, 4:432–38.

13. Kevin R. C. Gutzman, *James Madison and the Making of America* (New York: St. Martin's Press, 2012), 118. For Madison and restrained executive power, see Ralph Ketcham, *Presidents Above Party: The First American Presidency, 1789–1829* (Chapel Hill: University of North Carolina Press, 1984), 113–23.

14. *PJMPS*, 4:438, n. 1.

15. Augustus John Foster to James Monroe, April 15, 1812, *The Papers of James Monroe*, 6:150.

16. Ibid., 6:150, n. 4.

17. Ibid., 6:185, n.

18. JM to Congress, June 1, 1812, *PJMPS*, 4:432–38.

Chapter 35

1. Alexander Hamilton and James Madison, *The Pacificus-Helvidius Debates of 1793–1794* (Indianapolis, IN: Liberty Fund, 2007).

2. J. C. A. Stagg, *The War of 1812: Conflict for a Continent* (New York: Cambridge University Press, 2012). Stagg credits the chief State Department clerk, John Graham, with writing most of the report; the editors of Calhoun's papers assert that Calhoun drafted most of it and note good reasons for rejecting both the claim for Graham and the idea that Monroe drafted the report. *The Papers of John C. Calhoun,* ed. Robert L. Meriwether, et al. (Columbia: University of South Carolina Press, 1959–2003), 1:122–25, n. 66.

3. *The Papers of John C. Calhoun.*

4. Irving Brant, *James Madison: The President, 1809–1812* (New York: Bobbs-Merrill, 1956), 476.

5. Ibid., 477.

6. Ralph Ketcham, *James Madison: A Biography* (Charlottesville: University Press of Virginia, 1990), 529.

7. Bill to Declare War on Great Britain, *The Papers of John C. Calhoun,* 1:125, n. at 125–26.

8. Presidential Proclamation, June 19, 1812, *The Papers of James Madison: Presidential Series,* ed. Robert A. Rutland, et al. (Charlottesville: University Press of Virginia, 1984–) *PJMPS,* 4:489–90.

9. Stagg, *The War of 1812,* 47.

10. The following account is based on Richard Buel Jr., *America on the Brink* (New York: Palgrave Macmillan, 2005), 156–60.

11. Jonathan Russell to James Monroe, June 25, 1812, *The Papers of James Monroe: Selected Correspondence and Papers,* ed. Daniel Preston, et al. (Santa Barbara, CA: ABC-Clio, 2012), 6:206, and n.

12. Jonathan Russell to James Monroe, June 26, 1812, *The Papers of James Monroe,* 6:209–10.

13. James Monroe to John Quincy Adams, July 1, 1812, *The Papers of James Monroe,* 6:214–15.

14. J. C. A. Stagg, perhaps in the minority in this regard, judges Britain's continued insistence that it had a right to re-impose the orders justification enough for the American war declaration. Madison's purpose, he insists, was to make Britain disavow its trade restrictions on neutral nations such as America. Thus, after the revocation, "the case for war remained almost as strong as it had ever been." J. C. A. Stagg, *Mr. Madison's War: Politics, Diplomacy, and Warfare, 1783–1830* (Princeton, NJ: Princeton University Press, 1983), 118–19, quotation at 119.

15. Stagg, *The War of 1812,* 48.

Chapter 36

1. James Monroe to Jonathan Russell, June 26, 1812, *The Papers of James Monroe: Selected Correspondence and Papers,* ed. Daniel Preston, et al. (Santa Barbara, CA: ABC-Clio, 2012-), 6:208–09.

2. J. C. A. Stagg, *The War of 1812: Conflict for a Continent* (New York: Cambridge University Press, 2012), 49.

3. The following discussion is based on Josiah Quincy and James A. Bayard, from "An Address of the Minority to Their Constituents, on the Subject of War with Great-Britain," Late June, 1812, *The War of 1812: Writings from America's Second War of Independence,* ed. Donald R. Hickey (New York: Library of America, 2013), 46–53.

4. This paragraph and the next are based on Timothy Pickering to Edward Pennington, July 12, 1812, *Documents Relating to New-England Federalism, 1800–1815,* ed. Henry Adams (Burt Franklin Research and Source Works Series #89, American Classics in History and Social Science #8, 1877), 388–90.

5. Caleb Strong to William Eustis, August 5, 1812, *The War of 1812: Writings from America's Second War of Independence,* ed. Donald R. Hickey (New York: Library of America, 2013), 105–09 (information about Eustis to Strong in headnote).

6. *The Papers of James Madison: Presidential Series,* ed. Robert A. Rutland, et al. (Charlottesville: University Press of Virginia, 1984–), 4:544, n. 1.

7. Richard Rush's Proposal that Thomas Jefferson become Secretary of State, May 24, 1812, *The Papers of Thomas Jefferson: Retirement Series,* ed. J. Jefferson Looney, et al. (Princeton, NJ: Princeton University Press, 2004–), 5:78.

8. James Barbour to James Monroe, July 13, 1812, *The Papers of James Monroe,* 6:224–25.

9. George Hay to James Monroe, July 13, 1812, *The Papers of James Monroe,* 6:225–27.

10. J. C. A. Stagg, *Mr. Madison's War: Politics, Diplomacy, and Warfare, 1783–1830* (Princeton, NJ: Princeton University Press, 1983), 164.

11. Robert Allen Rutland, *The Presidency of James Madison* (Lawrence: University Press of Kansas, 1990), 108.

12. Hickey, *The War of 1812,* 67–68.

13. TJ to William Duane, August 4, 1812, *PTJRS,* 5:293–94, at 293.

14. John C. Calhoun, Speech on the Albany Petition for Repeal of the Embargo, May 6, 1812, *The Papers of John C. Calhoun,* ed. Robert L. Meriwether, et al. (Columbia: University of South Carolina Press, 1959–2003), 1:102–07, at 104–05.

15. Ralph Ketcham, *James Madison: A Biography* (Charlottesville: University Press of Virginia, 1990), 535.

16. Hickey, *The War of 1812,* 80; and Stagg, *Mr. Madison's War,* 190–91.

Chapter 37

1. Henry Adams, *History of the United States of America During the Administrations of James Madison* (New York: Library of America, 1986), 503–04.

2. J. C. A. Stagg, *Mr. Madison's War: Politics, Diplomacy, and Warfare, 1783–1830* (Princeton, NJ: Princeton University Press, 1983), 165.

3. Adams, *History of the United States of America During the Administrations of James Madison,* 505.

4. Robert Allen Rutland, *The Presidency of James Madison* (Lawrence: University Press Kansas, 1990), 111.

5. Stagg, *Mr. Madison's War,* 198.

6. Ibid., 198–99.

7. William Hull, Proclamation, July 13, 1812, *The War of 1812: Writings From America's Second War of Independence,* ed. Donald R. Hickey (New York: Library of America, 2013), 85–87.

8. Ibid., 85, n.; 80–81.

9. Stagg, *Mr. Madison's War,* 201.

10. Ibid., 203.

11. Hickey, *The War of 1812,* 81–82.

12. Stagg, *Mr. Madison's War,* 205; Hickey, *The War of 1812,* 83.

13. JM to Henry Dearborn, August 9, 1812, *The Papers of James Madison: Presidential Series,* ed. Robert A. Rutland, et al. (Charlottesville: University Press of Virginia, 1984–), 5:133–34.

14. JM to Albert Gallatin, ca. August 26, 1812, *PJMPS,* 5:208.

15. Stagg, *Mr. Madison's War,* 244–45.

16. Moses Smith, from *Naval Scenes in the Last War, The War of 1812: Writings from America's Second War of Independence,* ed. Donald R. Hickey (New York: Library of America, 2013), 121–29 (introduction at 121).

17. Henry Adams seems to have proven the American account correct. Adams, *History of the United States of America During the Administrations of James Madison,* 313–21.

18. Rutland, *The Presidency of James Madison,* 108–09.

19. Adams, *History of the United States of America During the Administrations of James Madison,* 528, 534.

20. Hickey, *The War of 1812,* 83.

Chapter 38

1. JM to TJ, August 17, 1812, *The Papers of James Madison: Presidential Series,* ed. Robert A. Rutland, et al. (Charlottesville: University Press of Virginia, 1984–), 5:165–66.

2. James Monroe to Henry Clay, August 28, 1812, *The Papers of James Monroe: Selected Correspondence and Papers,* ed. Daniel Preston, et al. (Santa Barbara, CA: ABC-Clio, 2012–), 6:246.

3. Ibid., 6:246–47, n. 3.

4. J. C. A. Stagg, *The War of 1812: Conflict for a Continent* (New York: Cambridge University Press, 2012), 70.

5. Jared Willson to Alvan Stewart, November 9, 1812, *The War of 1812: Writings from America's Second War of Independence,* ed. Donald R. Hickey (New York: Library of America, 2013), 160–62 (biographical information in headnote).

6. Robert Allen Rutland, *The Presidency of James Madison* (Lawrence: University Press of Kansas, 1990), 113; Hickey, *The War of 1812,* 86 (Van Rensselaer quotation).

7. Hickey, *The War of 1812,* 86–87.

8. Ralph Ketcham, *James Madison: A Biography* (Charlottesville: University Press of Virginia, 1990), 543–44.

9. Henry Adams, *History of the United States of America During the Administrations of James Madison* (New York: Library of America, 1986), 548–49.

10. Henry Dearborn to JM, December 13, 1812, *PJMPS*, 5:503–04.

11. Adams, *History of the United States of America During the Administrations of James Madison*, 582.

12. Albert Gallatin to TJ, December 18, 1812, *The Writings of Albert Gallatin*, ed. Henry Adams (Philadelphia: J. B. Lippincott, 1879), 1:530–31.

13. For Madison's assistance to historians in his retirement years, Ralph Ketcham, *The Madisons at Montpelier: Reflections on the Founding Couple* (Charlottesville: University of Virginia Press, 2009), 101–05.

14. Henry Lee to JM, February 2, 1827, Founders Online (National Archives), https://founders.archives.gov/documents/Madison/99-02-02-0898.

15. JM to Henry Lee, February 1827, *The Writings of James Madison, Comprising His Public Papers and His Private Correspondence*, ed. Gaillard Hunt (New York: G. P. Putnam's Sons, 1908), 9:277–80, n. 1.

Chapter 39

1. James Monroe to JM, September 2, 1812, *The Papers of James Monroe: Selected Correspondence and Papers*, ed. Daniel Preston, et al. (Santa Barbara, CA: ABC-Clio, 2012-), 6:252–53.

2. JM to James Monroe, September 5, 1812, *The Papers of James Monroe*, 6:257–58.

3. James Monroe to JM, September 7, 1812, *The Papers of James Monroe*, 6:260–61.

4. James Monroe to JM, September 8, 1812, *The Papers of James Monroe*, 6:262–63.

5. William Eustis to JM, September 7, 1812, *The Papers of James Madison: Presidential Series*, ed. Robert A. Rutland, et al. (Charlottesville: University Press of Virginia, 1984-), 5:282–83, at 283.

6. JM to James Monroe, September 8, 1812, *PJMPS*, 5:287–88.

7. Announcement, James Monroe, September 9, 1812, *The Papers of James Monroe*, 6:264, and n.

8. James Monroe to JM, September 10, 1812, *The Papers of James Monroe*, 6:266, and n. 2.

9. James Monroe to Henry Clay, September 17, 1812, *The Papers of James Monroe*, 6:268–69.

10. George Hay to James Monroe, October 9, 1812, *The Papers of James Monroe*, 6:281–83.

11. Charles Royster, *Light-Horse Harry Lee and the Legacy of the American Revolution* (New York: Alfred A. Knopf, 1981), chapter 4.

12. In addition to the chapter of Royster's book, this account draws on the headnote to SILENCING THE ANTI-WAR PRESS: BALTIMORE, SUMMER 1812, *Maryland House of Delegates, Committee of Grievances and Courts of Justice Report on the Baltimore Riots*, in *The War of 1812: Writings from America's Second War of Independence*, ed. Donald R. Hickey (New York: Library of America, 2013), and on the document itself, 54–68.

13. Hickey, *The War of 1812*, 62.

14. Ibid., 57, 59, 62.

15. Ibid., 63.

16. Ibid., 64.

17. John Montgomery to JM, August 9, 1812, *PJMPS*, 5:135; JM to John Montgomery, August 13, 1812, *PJMPS*, 5:150.

Chapter 40

1. J. C. A. Stagg, *Mr. Madison's War: Politics, Diplomacy, and Warfare, 1783–1830* (Princeton, NJ: Princeton University Press, 1983), 276–77.

2. Irving Brant, *James Madison: Commander in Chief, 1812–1836* (Indianapolis, IN: Bobbs-Merrill, 1961), 126–27.

3. Albert Gallatin to JM, January 4, 1813, *The Papers of James Madison: Presidential Series,* ed. Robert A. Rutland, et al. (Charlottesville: University Press of Virginia, 1984–), 5:552.

4. Albert Gallatin to JM, January 7, 1813, *PJMPS,* 5:557–58.

5. JM to John Armstrong, January 14, 1813, *PJMPS,* 5:576; John Armstrong to JM, January 17, 1813, *PJMPS,* 5:593.

6. C. Edward Skeen, *John Armstrong, Jr., 1758–1845: A Biography* (Syracuse, NY: Syracuse University Press, 1981), 124.

7. Brant, *James Madison: Commander in Chief, 1812–1836,* 126.

8. Ralph Ketcham, *James Madison: A Biography* (Charlottesville: University Press of Virginia, 1990), 546.

9. David G. Chandler, *The Campaigns of Napoleon* (New York: Macmillan, 1966), 754–55.

10. Ibid., 739.

11. Ibid., 808.

12. Ibid., 852, 853.

13. Henry Adams, *History of the United States of America During the Administrations of James Madison* (New York: Library of America, 1986), 286–91 (Caulaincourt quotation at 290).

14. Entry for September 21, 1812, *John Quincy Adams: Diaries, 1779–1821,* ed. David Waldstreicher (New York: Library of America, 2017), 1:247–49.

15. Entry for December 7, 1812, *John Quincy Adams: Diaries,* 1:257–58.

16. Entry for November 20, 1813, *John Quincy Adams: Diaries,* 1:279–80.

17. William Harris Crawford to JM, March 3, 1813, *PJMPS,* 6:79–80.

18. Ibid., 6:80, n. 1.

19. JM, Second Inaugural Address, March 4, 1813, *PJMPS,* 6:85–87.

20. Ibid., 6:87, n.

21. An account that finds Madison's grounds for war to be inconsistent with Just War Theory is Jonathan Den Hartog, "The War of 1812," in *America and the Just War Tradition,* Mark David Hall and J. Daryl Charles, eds. (Notre Dame, IN: University of Notre Dame Press, 2019), 74–96.

22. For this theme in American war propaganda during the Madison administration, Paul A. Gilje, *Free Trade and Sailors' Rights in the War of 1812* (New York: Cambridge University Press, 2013).

Chapter 41

1. Richard Buel Jr., *America on the Brink: How the Political Struggle Over the War of 1812 Almost Destroyed the Young Republic* (New York: Palgrave Macmillan, 2005), 186.

2. Ibid., 186.

3. Ibid., 187.

4. This and the next paragraph are based on Albert Gallatin to James Monroe, January 4, 1813, *The Papers of James Monroe: Selected Correspondence and Papers,* ed. Daniel Preston, et al. (Santa Barbara, CA: ABC-Clio, 2012), 6:337–38.

5. J. C. A. Stagg, *The War of 1812: Conflict for a Continent* (New York: Cambridge University Press, 2012), 86.

6. Norman K. Risjord, *The Old Republicans: Southern Conservatism in the Age of Jefferson* (New York: Columbia University Press, 1965), 146.

7. JM to Congress, May 25, 1813, *The Papers of James Madison: Presidential Series,* ed. Robert A. Rutland, et al. (Charlottesville: University Press of Virginia, 1984), 6:339–43.

8. Ibid., 5:573, n. 2.

9. Donald R. Hickey, *The War of 1812: A Forgotten Conflict—Bicentennial Edition* (Urbana: University of Illinois Press, 2012), 95–96.

10. Henry Adams, *History of the United States of America During the Administrations of James Madison* (New York: Library of America, 1986), 821.

11. Kevin R. C. Gutzman, *James Madison and the Making of America* (New York: St. Martin's Press, 2012), 2.

12. Hickey, *The War of 1812,* 115–16; Stagg, *The War of 1812,* 95 (quotation).

13. Ralph Ketcham, *James Madison: A Biography* (Charlottesville: University Press of Virginia, 1990), 557–58.

14. Alan Taylor, *The Internal Enemy: Slavery and War in Virginia, 1772–1832* (New York: W. W. Norton, 2013), 4.

15. Ibid., 178.

16. Ketcham, *James Madison,* 558, citing Dolley Madison to Edward Coles, May 12, 1813.

17. *Annals of Congress,* 13th Congress, First Session, 86–90; Raymond Walters Jr., *Albert Gallatin: Jeffersonian Financier & Diplomat* (New York: Macmillan, 1957), 269.

18. *PJMPS,* 6:388, n. 2.

19. JM to the Senate, July 6, 1813, *PJMPS,* 6:406–07.

20. Ian W. Toll, *Six Frigates: The Epic History of the Founding of the U.S. Navy* (New York: W. W. Norton, 2006), 418–19.

21. Hickey, *The War of 1812,* 131.

22. Tecumseh: Speech to Henry Procter, September 1813, Hickey, *The War of 1812,* 323–24.

23. Headnote, "John Robinson: from *War of 1812,*" in Hickey, *The War of 1812,* 325.

24. The following account relies on Hickey, *The War of 1812,* 131–32, except where noted.

25. Stagg, *The War of 1812,* 92–93.

26. Michael F. Holt, *The Rise and Fall of the American Whig Party: Jacksonian Politics and the Onset of the Civil War* (New York: Oxford University Press, 1999), 43.

27. Stagg, *The War of 1812,* 93.

28. David G. Chandler, *The Campaigns of Napoleon* (New York: Macmillan, 1966), 865–941.

Chapter 42

1. James Madison, Annual Message, December 7, 1813, *The Papers of James Madison: Presidential Series,* ed. Robert A. Rutland, et al. (Charlottesville: University Press of Virginia, 1984–), 7:82–89.

2. J. C. A. Stagg, *The War of 1812: Conflict for a Continent* (New York: Cambridge University Press, 2012), 107; *PJMPS,* 7:89.

3. Irving Brant, *James Madison: Commander in Chief, 1812–1836* (New York: Bobbs-Merrill, 1961), 238; JM to Congress, January 6, 1814, *PJMPS,* 7:178.

4. Brant, *James Madison: Commander in Chief,* 240.

5. Ralph Ketcham, *James Madison: A Biography* (Charlottesville: University Press of Virginia, 1990), 568.

6. Ibid., 570.

7. John C. Calhoun, Speech on the Dangers of "Factious Opposition," January 15, 1814, *The Papers of John C. Calhoun,* ed. Robert L. Meriwether, et al. (Columbia: University of South Carolina Press, 1959–2003), 1:189–200.

8. David G. Chandler, *The Campaigns of Napoleon* (New York: Macmillan, 1966), 1001–02; Kevin R. Gutzman, "An Emperor Betrayed: Marmont's Perfidy Became Part of the Language," *Military History* (June 1992), 18–24, 32, 89–90.

9. Albert Gallatin to Henry Clay, April 22, 1814, *The Papers of Henry Clay,* James F. Hopkins, et al., eds. (Lexington: University of Kentucky Press, 1959–1991), 1:883–84.

10. Merrill D. Peterson, *The Great Triumvirate: Webster, Clay, and Calhoun* (New York: Oxford University Press, 1987), 39.

11. Ibid.

12. Garry Wills, *James Madison* (New York: Times Books, 2002), 126–27.

13. JM to John Armstrong, June 3, 1814, *PJMPS,* 7:534–35; JM to William Jones, June 3, 1814, *PJMPS,* 535–36; JM to James Monroe, June 3, 1814, *PJMPS,* 536.

14. John Armstrong to JM, June 4, 1814, *PJMPS,* 7:537; William Jones to JM, June 6, 1814, *PJMPS,* 7:543.

15. *PJMPS,* 7:537, n. 1.

16. Ibid., 7:543, n. 1.

17. JM, Memorandum on Cabinet Meeting, June 7, 1814, *PJMPS,* 7:545.

18. William Jones to JM, June 8, 1814, *PJMPS,* 7:549, and n. 1, 7:549–50.

19. J. C. A. Stagg, *Mr. Madison's War: Politics, Diplomacy, and Warfare, 1783–1830* (Princeton, NJ: Princeton University Press, 1983), 388.

20. Ibid., 392.

21. Ibid., 393.

22. Ibid.

23. Ibid., 396.

24. JM to John Armstrong, August 13, 1814, *PJMPS,* 8:98–101.

25. Stagg, *The War of 1812,* 121.

26. Though he had not raised the issue in the Cabinet, Navy Secretary Jones had ordered Chauncey to focus on gaining command of Lake Ontario from the Royal Navy. Stagg, *Mr. Madison's War,* 403–4.

27. Ibid., 401.

28. Donald R. Hickey, *The War of 1812: A Forgotten Conflict—Bicentennial Edition* (Urbana: University of Illinois Press, 2012), 188–89.

Chapter 43

1. Donald R. Hickey, *The War of 1812: A Forgotten Conflict—Bicentennial Edition* (Urbana: University of Illinois Press, 2012), 189–91.

2. Ibid., 191–94, quotation at 194.

3. Ralph Ketcham, *James Madison: A Biography* (Charlottesville: University Press of Virginia, 1990), 572–74.

4. *The Papers of James Madison: Presidential Series,* ed. Robert A. Rutland, et al. (Charlottesville: University Press of Virginia, 1984), 7:494, n. 3.

5. JM to John Armstrong, May 20, 1814, *PJMPS,* 7:502–04, at 503.

6. JM, Memorandum on Defense of the City of Washington, *PJMPS,* 8:2. The Monroe letter discussed hereafter is at n. 1.

7. J. C. A. Stagg, *Mr. Madison's War: Politics, Diplomacy, and Warfare, 1783–1830* (Princeton, NJ: Princeton University Press, 1983), 408.

8. This paragraph relies on Stagg, *Mr. Madison's War,* 408–09.

9. JM to John Armstrong, July 2, 1814, *PJMPS,* 8:5.

10. Stagg, *Mr. Madison's War,* 409.

11. C. Edward Skeen, *John Armstrong, Jr.: A Biography* (Syracuse, NY: Syracuse University Press, 1981), 189.

12. Robert Wright to John Armstrong, July 14, 1814, *PJMPS,* 8:34–5 and note.

13. Resolution of the Aldermen and Common Council of the City of Washington, July 18, 1814, *PJMPS,* 8:45–46.

14. Stagg, *Mr. Madison's War,* 413; JM to James Monroe, August 21, 1814, *PJMPS,* 8:128.

15. Headnote to James Scott, from *Recollections of a Naval Life,* in Hickey, *The War of 1812,* 490.

16. JM to James Monroe, 8:00 AM, August 21, 1814, *PJMPS,* 8:128; James Monroe to JM, August 21, 1814, *PJMPS,* 8:129; James Monroe to JM, 11:00 PM, August 21, 1814, *PJMPS,* 8:130–31; JM to James Monroe, 5:00 AM, August 22, 1814, *PJMPS,* 8:131; JM to James Monroe, 10:00 AM, August 22, 1814, *PJMPS,* 8:132; James Monroe to JM, August 22, 1814, *PJMPS,* 8:133. For Arnold and Jefferson, Dumas Malone, *Jefferson the Virginian* (Boston: Little, Brown, 1948), 336–40 (the Commonwealth's public records at 340).

17. Stagg, *Mr. Madison's War,* 416–17.

18. Hickey, *The War of 1812,* 205. Actually the rider, William Simmons, had recently been fired by Madison from his position as an accountant in the War Department. *PJMPS,* 8:137, n. 5.

19. The following relies on James Scott, from *Recollections of a Naval Life,* in Hickey, *The War of 1812,* 490–501. Barney's account is excerpted in the first note at 501, and the account of Madison's battlefield behavior is in the last note on that page.

20. Donald R. Hickey says the rockets' practical effect was scant, while their effect on morale was significant. Hickey, *The War of 1812,* 206.

21. *PJMPS,* 8:137, n. 6.

22. The following account draws on Henry Adams, *History of the United States of America During the Administrations of James Madison* (New York: Library of America, 1986), 1011–13.

23. For these numbers, Tim McGrath, *James Monroe: A Life* (New York: Penguin, 2020), 338.

Chapter 44

1. Tim McGrath, *James Monroe: A Life* (New York: Penguin, 2020), 338.

2. Elizabeth Dowling Taylor, *A Slave in the White House: Paul Jennings and the Madisons* (New York: Palgrave Macmillan, 2012), 50–51.

3. Ralph Ketcham, *James Madison: A Biography* (Charlottesville: University Press of Virginia, 1990), 579.

4. Ibid., 578.

5. Henry Adams, *History of the United States of American During the Administrations of James Madison* (New York: Library of America, 1986), 1014–15.

6. JM, Memorandum of Conversations with John Armstrong, August 24, 1814, *The Papers of James Madison: Presidential Series,* ed. Robert A. Rutland, et al. (Charlottesville: University Press of Virginia, 1984), 8:134–36; JM, Memorandum of a Conversation with John Armstrong, August 29, 1814, *PJMPS,* 8:153–55; James Monroe's Draft Memoranda on the Events of 24–28 August at Washington, post-28 August, *PJMPS,* 8:149–52. The editors of Madison's papers say that despite their dates, Madison's memoranda are likely to have been written later; he probably did not have time to write them in the middle of the events described above—as the memoranda themselves make clear. *PJMPS,* 8:136:1.

7. The following account is based on Memorandum of Conversations with John Armstrong, August 24, 1814, *PJMPS,* 8:134–36 and notes at 136–37.

8. Ibid., 8:136, n. 2.

9. JM to John Armstrong, August 13, 1814, *PJMPS,* 8:98–101.

10. This last point and the following discussion are based on Editorial Note, "The Madisons' Travels in Virginia during the British Occupation of Washington, 24–26 August 1814," *PJMPS,* 8:137–41, at 140–41.

11. JM, Memorandum of a Conversation with John Armstrong, August 29, 1814, *PJMPS,* 8:153–55.

12. Ibid., 8:156, n. 1.

13. John Armstrong to JM, September 4, 1814, *PJMPS,* 8:178.

14. Ibid., 8:178, n. 1.

15. Andrew Burstein and Nancy Isenberg, *Madison and Jefferson* (New York: Random House, 2010), 541.

16. From the *Georgetown Federal Republican,* October 4, 1814, *PJMPS,* 8:279.

17. C. Edward Skeen, *John Armstrong, Jr.: A Biography* (Syracuse, New York: Syracuse University Press, 1981), 201.

18. Presidential Proclamation, September 1, 1814, *PJMPS,* 8:166–68. Attorney General Richard Rush aided in the composition. Burstein and Isenberg, *Madison and Jefferson,* 542.

19. Burstein and Isenberg, *Madison and Jefferson,* 531.

20. Ketcham, *James Madison,* 589.

21. J. C. A. Stagg, *Mr. Madison's War: Politics, Diplomacy, and Warfare, 1783–1830* (Princeton, NJ: Princeton University Press, 1983), 428. Stagg notes that in their understandable though

regrettable fixation on Chesapeake events in these weeks, Madison, Monroe, and Jones completely lost track of the Niagara front, where General George Izard's strategic mistake opened Upstate New York and Vermont to invasion. For once, local militia proved adequate to the emergency. Stagg, *Mr. Madison's War,* 427.

22. I here rely on Marc Leepson, *What So Proudly We Hailed: Francis Scott Key, A Life* (New York: St. Martin's Press, 2014), 61–65; Garry Wills, *James Madison* (New York: Times Books, 2002), 140; and Donald R. Hickey, *The War of 1812: A Forgotten Conflict—Bicentennial Edition* (Urbana: University of Illinois Press, 2012), 210–11.

23. Hickey, *The War of 1812,* 212.

24. Francis Scott Key, Original Manuscript of "Star Spangled Banner," digital file from original negative (Library of Congress) www.loc.gov/resource/hec.04307.

25. Leepson, *What So Proudly We Hailed,* 66–67.

Chapter 45

1. Ralph Ketcham, *James Madison: A Biography* (Charlottesville: University Press of Virginia, 1990), 588–89.

2. Ibid., 590.

3. Richard Buel Jr., *America on the Brink: How the Political Struggle Over the War of 1812 Almost Destroyed the Young Republic* (New York: Palgrave Macmillan, 2005), 210–11.

4. Ibid., 215–18.

5. Ketcham, *James Madison,* 592.

6. Wilson Cary Nicholas to JM, November 11, 1814, *The Papers of James Madison: Presidential Series,* ed. Robert A. Rutland, et al. (Charlottesville: University Press of Virginia, 1984–), 8:372–74.

7. Madison acted upon Nicholas's advice regarding the Springfield Armory. Minutes of a Conversation Between James Monroe and Robert Swartwout, January 10, 1815, *Papers of James Monroe: Selected Correspondence and Papers,* ed. Daniel Preston, et al. (Santa Barbara, CA: ABC-Clio, 2012), 7:271.

8. JM to Wilson Cary Nicholas, November 26, 1814, *PJMPS,* 8:401–02.

9. The following account relies primarily on J. C. A. Stagg, *The War of 1812: Conflict for a Continent* (New York: Cambridge University Press, 2012), 150–54 (Cochrane's intentions for New Orleans at 150).

10. Ibid., 151 and 151, n. 10.

11. Henry Adams, *The History of the United States During the Administrations of James Madison* (New York: Library of America, 1986), 1171–72.

12. Andrew Jackson to James Monroe, January 9, 1815, *The Papers of James Monroe,* 7:268–70, at 269.

13. For Pakenham, Donald R. Hickey, *The War of 1812: A Forgotten Conflict—Bicentennial Edition* (Urbana: University of Illinois Press, 2012), 221–22.

14. Irving Brant, *James Madison: Commander-in-Chief, 1812–1836* (New York: Bobbs-Merrill, 1961), 358–59; James Monroe to JM, January 10, 1815, *PJMPS,* 8:501 and n. 1.

15. Buel, *America on the Brink,* 299.

16. Donald R. Hickey, *The War of 1812: A Forgotten Conflict—Bicentennial Edition* (Urbana: University of Illinois Press, 2012), 280–81.

17. Garry Wills, *James Madison* (New York: Times Books, 2002), 146.

18. Hickey, *The War of 1812,* 281; see Robert Y. Hayne's speeches in *The Webster-Hayne Debate on the Nature of the Union: Selected Documents,* ed. Herman Belz (Indianapolis, IN: Liberty Fund, 2000).

Chapter 46

1. JM to Congress, February 18, 1815, *The Papers of James Madison: Presidential Series,* ed. Robert A. Rutland, et al. (Charlottesville: University Press of Virginia, 1984-), 8:599-601.

2. JM, Presidential Proclamation, January 16, 1815, *PJMPS,* 8:594-99. John Quincy Adams told his British opposite numbers at Ghent that he hoped they had just concluded "the last treaty of peace between Great Britain and the United States." Whether he expected that two centuries and more later the two countries would long have been the best of friends is doubtful. Ralph Ketcham, *James Madison: A Biography* (Charlottesville: University Press of Virginia, 1990), 598. Madison's partnership with Washington is the subject of Stuart Leibiger, *Founding Friendship: George Washington, James Madison, and the Creation of the American Republic* (Charlottesville: University Press of Virginia, 1999).

3. Ian W. Toll, *Six Frigates: The Epic History of the Founding of the U.S. Navy* (New York: W.W. Norton, 2006), 456-57; Henry Adams, *History of the United States of America During the Administrations of James Madison* (New York: Library of America, 1986), 1253.

4. Unfortunately, the dey of Algiers repudiated the treaty in April 1816. *PJMPS,* 10:xix.

5. JM, Annual Message to Congress, December 5, 1815, *PJMPS,* 10:66-72.

6. Ibid., 10:73, n. 14.

7. Ibid., 10:74, n. 15 mentions proposed protection of American hat manufacturers, cabinet- and wooden-ware makers, carriage makers, makers of leather goods, and paper manufacturers.

8. Kevin R. C. Gutzman, *James Madison and the Making of America* (New York: St. Martin's Press, 2012), 49-131, 247-55.

9. Robert Allen Rutland, *The Presidency of James Madison* (Lawrence: University Press of Kansas, 1990), 197.

10. Dice Robins Anderson, *William Branch Giles: A Study in the Politics of Virginia and the Nation from 1790 to 1830* (Menasha, WI: George Banta, 1914), 204-05.

11. Ketcham, *James Madison,* 605.

12. John C. Calhoun, Speech Introducing the Bank Bill, February 26, 1816, *Papers of John C. Calhoun,* ed. Robert L. Meriwether, et al. (Columbia: University of South Carolina Press, 1959-2003), 1:331-39.

13. See Charles M. Wiltse, *John C. Calhoun: Nationalist, 1782-1828* (Indianapolis, IN: Bobbs-Merrill, 1944); Charles M. Wiltse, *John C. Calhoun: Nullifier, 1829-1839* (Indianapolis, IN: Bobbs-Merrill, 1949); Charles M. Wiltse, *John C. Calhoun: Sectionalist, 1840-1850* (Indianapolis, IN: Bobbs-Merrill, 1951).

14. Andrew Burstein and Nancy Isenberg, *Madison and Jefferson* (New York: Random House, 2010), 558; JM to the Senate, January 30, 1815, *PJMPS,* 8:541-43.

15. *Papers of John C. Calhoun,* 1:346-47, n.; Preface, *PJMPS,* 10:xix-xxiv, at xxi.

16. Henry Clay, Remarks on Bill Increasing Compensation to Members of Congress, March

7, 1816, *The Papers of Henry Clay,* James F. Hopkins, et al., eds. (Lexington: University of Kentucky Press, 1959–1991), 2:171.

17. John C. Calhoun, Speech on Compensation of Members, March 8, 1816, *Papers of John C. Calhoun,* 1:343–45 and n. Clay and Calhoun were not alone in making the family argument, nor did that argument pass uncontested. *The Papers of Henry Clay,* 2:172, n.

18. Irving H. Bartlett, *John C. Calhoun: A Biography* (New York: W. W. Norton, 1993), 84–85.

19. Ketcham, *James Madison,* 606.

Chapter 47

1. Except where otherwise noted, the following account relies on F. Thornton Miller, *Juries and Judges versus the Law: Virginia's Provincial Legal Perspective, 1783–1828* (Charlottesville: University Press of Virginia, 1994), 74–86. (For a refutation of the claim in that book's title, see Kevin R. C. Gutzman, *Thomas Jefferson—Revolutionary: A Radical's Struggle to Remake America* (New York: St. Martin's Press, 2017), chapter 1.)

2. Kevin R. C. Gutzman, *Virginia's American Revolution: From Dominion to Republic, 1776–1840* (Lanham, MD: Lexington Books, 2007), 129–30.

3. R. Kent Newmyer, *Supreme Court Justice Joseph Story: Statesman of the Old Republic* (Chapel Hill: University of North Carolina Press, 1985), 106–07. The rest of this discussion will draw on 108–10.

4. *Martin v. Hunter's Lessee* (1816), Legal Information Institute (Cornell Law School) https://www.law.cornell.edu/supremecourt/text/14/304.

5. The following account relies on Andrew H. Browning, *The Panic of 1819* (Columbia: University of Missouri Press, 2019), chapter three, "Volcano Weather," 75–102.

Chapter 48

1. Tim McGrath, *James Monroe: A Life* (New York: Penguin, 2020), 375–76.

2. JM, Annual Message to Congress, December 3, 1816, *The Papers of James Madison: Presidential Series,* ed. Robert A. Rutland, et al. (Charlottesville: University Press of Virginia, 1984–), 11:532–39.

3. For the biography's authorship, see Robert Elder, *Calhoun: American Heretic* (New York: Basic Books, 2021), 401–03; the account of Calhoun and the Bonus Bill is at [John C. Calhoun & R. M. T. Hunter,] *Life of John C. Calhoun . . .* (New York: Harper & Brothers, 1843), 21.

4. JM to the House of Representatives, March 3, 1817, *PJMPS,* 11:701–03; Henry Clay to JM, March 3, 1817, *PJMPS,* 11:703–04.

5. Alexander Hamilton, James Madison, and John Jay, *The Federalist,* ed. Jacob E. Cooke (Middletown, Connecticut: Wesleyan University Press, 1961), 308–14.

6. *PJMPS,* 11:703, n. 1.

7. Norman K. Risjord, *The Old Republicans: Southern Conservatism in the Age of Jefferson* (New York: Columbia University Press, 1965), 173.

8. Ibid., 169–70; Ralph Ketcham, *James Madison: A Biography* (Charlottesville: University Press of Virginia, 1990), 670.

Chapter 49

1. Tim McGrath, *James Monroe* (New York: Penguin, 2020), 377.

2. Noble E. Cunningham Jr., *The Presidency of James Monroe* (Lawrence: University Press of Kansas, 1996), 19.

3. The following discussion is based on James Monroe to Andrew Jackson, December 14, 1816, *The Papers of James Monroe: Selected Correspondence and Papers,* ed. Daniel Preston, et al. (Santa Barbara, CA: ABC-Clio, 2012), 7:635–38.

4. Merrill D. Peterson, *The Great Triumvirate: Webster, Clay, and Calhoun* (New York: Oxford University Press, 1987), 85.

5. Peterson, *The Great Triumvirate,* 86–87.

6. *Salem* (Massachusetts) *Gazette,* July 4, 1817, *The Papers of James Monroe,* 1:365; Peterson, *The Great Triumvirate,* 86.

7. *The Papers of Henry Clay,* James F. Hopkins, et al., eds. (Lexington: University of Kentucky Press, 1959–1991), 2:320, n. Monroe's leading biographer ascribed responsibility for the House's decision to Clay, irked at not being made secretary of state. Harry Ammon, *James Monroe: The Quest for National Identity* (Charlottesville: University Press of Virginia, 1990), 367–68.

8. Ammon, *James Monroe,* 369.

9. Here Monroe had in mind Thomas Jefferson and James Madison. George Washington, for one, had done no such thing.

10. Later in the speech Monroe made clear his meaning that the "Government . . . protects every citizen in the full enjoyment of his rights," though of course some of them were the province of the states, not the Federal Government. Thus Connecticut's Standing Order would be abolished the following year, but Massachusetts's religious establishment would endure until 1833—the fifth year of Andrew Jackson's administration.

11. James Monroe to JM, December 22, 1817, *The Papers of James Madison: Retirement Series,* David B. Mattern, et al., eds. (Charlottesville: University of Virginia Press, 2009) (hereafter *PJMRS*), 1:178–79.

12. David L. Holmes, *The Religion of the Founding Fathers* (Ash Lawn-Highland: The Home of James Monroe and The Clements Library, The University of Michigan, 2003), 126–27.

Chapter 50

1. *The Writings of James Monroe,* ed. Stanislaus Murray Hamilton (New York: G. P. Putnam's Sons, 1898–1903), 6:15, n.

2. Harry Ammon, *James Monroe: The Quest for National Identity* (Charlottesville: University Press of Virginia, 1971), 396–97.

3. Entries for November 20 and November 21, 1817, *John Quincy Adams:Diaries, 1779–1821,* ed. David Waldstreicher (New York: Library of America, 2017), 1:425–26.

4. Ammon, *James Monroe,* 647, n. 3.

5. Ibid., 398–99.

6. TJ to James Monroe, April 13, 1817, *The Papers of Thomas Jefferson: Retirement Series,* ed. J. Jefferson Looney (Princeton, NJ: Princeton University Press, 2004), 11:257–58; TJ to James Monroe, April 15, 1817, *PTJRS,* 11:262.

7. Not only had the place belonged to Monroe, whose house still stands on the Grounds, but it had belonged to George Nicholas, who as a state legislator filed the motion to investigate the Jefferson administration's performance during Benedict Arnold's invasion and later was an eminent Virginia Ratification Convention Federalist. Though Nicholas's motion struck Jefferson very hard, his brother Wilson Cary Nicholas had by 1817 contributed a son to the Jefferson kin network, and it was Governor Wilson Cary Nicholas who appointed Jefferson's choices to the Board of Visitors. As a U.S. senator, Wilson Cary Nicholas would be an important ally of President James Monroe.

8. Editorial Note, The Founding of the University of Virginia: Central College, 1816–1819, *The Papers of James Madison: Presidential Series*, ed. Robert A. Rutland, et al. (Charlottesville: University Press of Virginia, 1984), 11:314–15. The best account of the general subject is in Jennings L. Wagoner Jr., *Jefferson and Education* (Charlottesville, VA: Thomas Jefferson Foundation, Inc., 2004).

9. Ammon, *James Monroe*, 371.

10. James Monroe to Thomas Jefferson, April 23, 1817, *The Papers of James Monroe: Selected Correspondence and Papers*, ed. Daniel Preston, et al. (Santa Barbara, CA: ABC-Clio, 2012), 1:13–14, at 14.

11. Joseph G. Swift Memoirs, March 25, 1817, April 4, 1817, and April 9, 1817, *The Papers of James Monroe*, 1:9.

12. Nicholas Biddle to James Monroe, April 10, 1817, *The Papers of James Monroe*, 1:10–11.

13. *Baltimore Patriot*, April 18, 1817, *The Papers of James Monroe*, 1:12; *Richmond Enquirer*, April 18, 1817, *The Papers of James Monroe*, 1:12.

14. Harrison Gray Otis to James Monroe, April 22, 1817, *The Papers of James Monroe*, 1:12–13.

15. *Georgetown* (DC) *Messenger*, May 31, 1817, *The Papers of James Monroe*, 1:33; (Washington) *National Intelligencer*, June 2, 1817, *The Papers of James Monroe*, 1:33–34.

16. Charles Bagot to Viscount Castlereagh, June 3, 1817, *The Papers of James Monroe*, 1:35.

17. James Monroe to William Jones, April 22, 1817, *The Papers of James Monroe*, 1:13.

18. (Washington) *National Intelligencer*, April 23, 1817, *The Papers of James Monroe*, 1:14–15.

19. *Baltimore Federal Republican*, April 24, 1817, *The Papers of James Monroe*, 1:16.

20. David Humphreys to James Monroe, April 25, 1817, *The Papers of James Monroe*, 1:16–17. Europeans did indeed watch Monroe's progress with that issue in mind. Charles Bagot to Viscount Castlereagh, May 5, 1817, *The Papers of James Monroe*, 1:26.

21. *Salem Gazette*, April 25, 1817, *The Papers of James Monroe*, 1:17.

22. *Boston Patriot*, April 26, 1817, *The Papers of James Monroe*, 1:18–19, and n. at 19–20.

23. *Boston Patriot*, May 7, 1817, *The Papers of James Monroe*, 1:26–27.

24. James Monroe to Andrew Jackson, May 21, 1817, *The Papers of James Monroe*, 1:30–31.

25. George Graham to Jacob Brown, May 30, 1817, *The Papers of James Monroe*, 1:32; William H. Crawford, May 31, 1817, *The Papers of James Monroe*, 1:32–33.

Chapter 51

1. *Washington Register*, May 31, 1817, *The Papers of James Monroe: Selected Correspondence and Papers*, ed. Daniel Preston, et al. (Santa Barbara, CA: ABC-Clio, 2012), 1:33; *George-*

town (DC) *Messenger,* June 2, 1817, *The Papers of James Monroe,* 1:33; (Washington) *National Intelligencer,* June 2, 1817, *The Papers of James Monroe,* 1:33–34.

2. *Richmond Enquirer,* June 3, 1817, *The Papers of James Monroe,* 1:35.

3. (Springfield, MA) *Hampden Federalist,* June 12, 1817, *The Papers of James Monroe,* 1:107.

4. *Baltimore American,* June 1, 1817, *The Papers of James Monroe,* 1:36; *Baltimore Patriot,* June 2, 1817, *The Papers of James Monroe,* 1:37; Joseph G. Swift, *Memoirs, The Papers of James Monroe,* 1:37.

5. *Baltimore American,* June 3, 1817, *The Papers of James Monroe,* 1:39.

6. *Baltimore Patriot,* June 6, 1817, *The Papers of James Monroe,* 1:41–42; *Baltimore Patriot,* June 3, 1817, *The Papers of James Monroe,* 1:43.

7. Caesar A. Rodney to James Monroe, June 4, 1817, *The Papers of James Monroe,* 1:98–99.

8. Ibid., 1:24, n.

9. *National Intelligencer,* June 17, 1817, *The Papers of James Monroe,* 1:52.

10. *New Jersey Journal,* June 10, 1817, *The Papers of James Monroe,* 1:57.

11. This account draws on the (New York) *Columbian*'s correction of that day's *New-York Gazette*—the latter calling for splendor, the former gainsaying it. *The Papers of James Monroe,* 1:58–59.

12. Rufus King to Christopher Gore, June 12, 1817, *The Papers of James Monroe,* 1:72–73.

13. James Monroe to George Graham, June 15, 1817, *The Papers of James Monroe,* 1:87–88.

14. Rufus King to Christopher Gore, June 21, 1817, *The Papers of James Monroe,* 1:95.

15. John Adams to Benjamin Waterhouse, June 18, 1817, *The Papers of James Monroe,* 1:101.

16. John Adams to James Monroe, June 23, 1817, *The Papers of James Monroe,* 1:162.

17. *Baltimore American,* June 14, 1817, *The Papers of James Monroe,* 1:110.

18. *Hartford Times,* July 1, 1817, *The Papers of James Monroe,* 1:132–34.

19. (Hartford) *Connecticut Courant,* July 8, 1817, *The Papers of James Monroe,* 1:134–35, at 135. Newport, Rhode Island Federalists' consistency in not saying anything particularly positive in their town's address to Monroe irked local Republicans too. (New York) *National Advocate,* July 25, 1817, *The Papers of James Monroe,* 1:152.

20. James Monroe, Reply to the Mayor, Aldermen, and Common Council, of the City of New-London, June 25, 1817, (New London) *Connecticut Gazette,* July 2, 1817, *The Papers of James Monroe,* 1:143.

21. *Salem Gazette,* July 8, 1817, *The Papers of James Monroe,* 1:159; (Newport) *Rhode Island Republican,* August 6, 1817, *The Papers of James Monroe,* 1:159.

22. A similar event occurred in Hagerstown, Maryland, as Monroe progressed back to Washington, D.C. Two men were "very much burnt and lacerated," as they were "engaged in the act of charging one of the cannon." (Hagerstown) *Maryland Herald,* September 17, 1817, *The Papers of James Monroe,* 1:475.

Chapter 52

1. *Albany Argus,* August 22, 1817, *The Papers of James Monroe: Selected Correspondence and Papers,* ed. Daniel Preston, et al. (Santa Barbara, CA: ABC-Clio, 2012), 1:160.

2. Jeremiah Mason to Jesse Appleton, July 3, 1817, *The Papers of James Monroe,* 1:165. Newspapers commonly referred to then-president Monroe as "Col. Monroe." (Lexington) *Kentucky Gazette,* July 26, 1817, *The Papers of James Monroe,* 1:390.

3. (Lexington) *Kentucky Gazette*, June 28, 1817, *The Papers of James Monroe*, 1:170–71.

4. *Baltimore American*, June 25, 1817, *The Papers of James Monroe*, 1:181–82.

5. *The Papers of James Monroe*, 1:180, n.

6. Ibid., 1:195–96.

7. Ibid., 1:196.

8. Ibid., 1:205.

9. Ibid., 1:206.

10. James Monroe to John Adams, July 4, 1817, *The Papers of James Monroe*, 1:207.

11. Christopher Gore to Jeremiah Mason, July 4, 1817, *The Papers of James Monroe*, 1:208.

12. Abigail Adams to Francis Vanderkamp, January 24, 1818, *The Papers of James Monroe*, 1:231.

13. John Kenrick to James Monroe, July 5, 1817, *The Papers of James Monroe*, 1:220 and 1:221, n.

14. Eliza Susan Quincy Diary, July 6, 1817, *The Papers of James Monroe*, 1:221.

15. Joseph G. Swift, *Memoirs*, July 7, 1817, *The Papers of James Monroe*, 1:221.

16. (Boston) *Columbian Centinel*, July 9, 1817, *The Papers of James Monroe*, 1:224.

17. (Boston) *Columbian Centinel*, July 12, 1817, *The Papers of James Monroe*, 1:226.

18. Christopher Gore to Rufus King, July 8, 1817, *The Papers of James Monroe*, 1:233.

19. (Boston) *Columbian Centinel*, July 16, 1817, *The Papers of James Monroe*, 1:233–34.

20. Jeremiah Mason to Rufus King, July 24, 1817, *The Papers of James Monroe*, 1:416–17, at 417.

21. James Monroe to Thomas Jefferson, July 27, 1817, *The Papers of James Monroe*, 1:417–18, at 418.

22. *Boston Patriot*, July 11, 1817, *The Papers of James Monroe*, 1:371–72. An equally persuasive Federalist argument to the same effect is *Dedham* (MA) *Gazette*, July 11, 1817, *The Papers of James Monroe*, 1:373–74.

23. (Portsmouth) *Oracle*, July 31, 1817, *The Papers of James Monroe*, 1:271.

24. *Richmond Enquirer*, July 18, 1817, *The Papers of James Monroe*, 1:381.

25. (Boston) *Columbian Centinel*, July 23, 1817, *The Papers of James Monroe*, 1:281.

26. Moses Merrill Diary, July 15, 1817, and George Thacher, et al., address to James Monroe, July 15, 1817, *The Papers of James Monroe*, 1:284.

27. (Portland) *Eastern Argus*, July 22, 1817, Address of Selectmen of Saco to James Monroe, July 15, 1817, and Response of James Monroe to Selectmen, July 15, 1817, at *The Papers of James Monroe*, 1:287–88.

28. (Portland) *Eastern Argus*, June 24, 1817, *The Papers of James Monroe*, 1:292.

29. Diary of Sarah Connell Ayer, *The Papers of James Monroe*, 1:299.

30. William Plumer to James Monroe, July 18, 1817, *The Papers of James Monroe*, 1:314–15.

31. *Salem Gazette*, July 22, 1817, *The Papers of James Monroe*, 1:321. So too did the *Salem* (Massachusetts) *Gazette* of August 1, 1817, *The Papers of James Monroe*, 1:393.

32. *New Hampshire Patriot*, July 22, 1817, *The Papers of James Monroe*, 1:320–21.

33. (Charleston, South Carolina) *Southern Patriot*, August 9, 1817, *The Papers of James Monroe*, 1:405.

Chapter 53

1. *Boston Intelligencer*, July 26, 1817, *The Papers of James Monroe: Selected Correspondence and Papers*, ed. Daniel Preston, et al. (Santa Barbara, CA: ABC-Clio, 2012), 1:325.

2. Francis Brown to James Monroe, August 30, 1817, *The Papers of James Monroe*, 1:330.

3. *Concord* (New Hampshire) *Gazette*, July 21, 1817, *The Papers of James Monroe*, 1:326.

4. *The Papers of James Monroe*, 1:348–60.

5. *A Narrative of a Tour of Observation, Made During the Summer of 1817, by James Monroe, President of the United States* (Philadelphia, 1818), 187–91, at *The Papers of James Monroe*, 1:354–55.

6. Lewis Grant to James Monroe, August 5, 1817, *The Papers of James Monroe*, 1:360.

7. Lewis Grant to Charles Bagot, August 15, 1817, *The Papers of James Monroe*, 1:362. Surely none of these British officials was unaware that the president's purpose was, as a Cincinnati newspaper put it, to "make such improvements in our fortifications as will prove invulnerable to either British or savage attacks." *Liberty Hall and Cincinnati Gazette*, July 21, 1817, *The Papers of James Monroe*, 1:384. Yet their policy was that Monroe should be received "with the Military Honours [*sic*] usually paid to a sovereign." John C. Sherbrooke to Charles Bagot, August 17, 1817, *The Papers of James Monroe*, 1:502.

8. Richard Rush to James Monroe, July 13, 1817, *The Papers of James Monroe*, 1:410–11, and n.

9. James Monroe to Richard Rush, July 20, 1817, *The Papers of James Monroe*, 1:413–14, at 413.

10. Charles Bagot to Viscount Castlereagh, August 8, 1817, *The Papers of James Monroe*, 1:426–27.

11. *Detroit Gazette*, August 22, 1817, *The Papers of James Monroe*, 1:431. For the basis of Monroe's/Republicans' argument, Kevin R. C. Gutzman, *Thomas Jefferson—Revolutionary: A Radical's Struggle to Remake America* (New York: St. Martin's Press, 2017), chapter 1.

12. James Monroe to Richard Rush, August 16, 1817, *The Papers of James Monroe*, 1:435.

13. Letter to the editor, *Western Intelligencer and Columbus Gazette*, August 21, 1817, *The Papers of James Monroe*, 1:437.

14. *Liberty Hall and Cincinnati Gazette*, September 22, 1817, *The Papers of James Monroe*, 1:458.

15. *Georgetown* (D.C.) *Messenger*, September 19, 1817, *The Papers of James Monroe*, 1:477–78, and n.

16. *National Intelligencer*, September 19, 1817, *The Papers of James Monroe*, 1:480.

17. (Washington) *National Intelligencer*, September 19, 1817, *The Papers of James Monroe*, 1:481.

18. (Lexington) *Kentucky Gazette*, September 20, 1817, *The Papers of James Monroe*, 1:495–96.

19. George Hay to Richard Rush, August 19, 1817, *The Papers of James Monroe*, 1:503.

20. (Washington) *National Intelligencer*, October 3, 1817, *The Papers of James Monroe*, 1:499–500.

21. James Monroe to Andrew Jackson, September 27, 1817, *The Papers of James Monroe*, 1:508.

22. James Monroe to the Members of the Cabinet, *The Writings of James Monroe*, 6:31–32.

23. Noble E. Cunningham Jr., *The Presidency of James Monroe* (Lawrence: University Press of Kansas, 1996), 43–44.

24. Entry for November 28, 1817, *The Diaries of John Quincy Adams* (Massachusetts Historical Society online).

Chapter 54

1. James Monroe to Jacob Brown, December 2, 1817, *The Papers of James Monroe: Selected Correspondence and Papers*, ed. Daniel Preston, et al. (Santa Barbara, CA: ABC-Clio, 2012), 1:514.

2. James Monroe, First Annual Message, December 2, 1817, Miller Center (University of Virginia online).

3. For Jefferson, see Kevin R. C. Gutzman, *Thomas Jefferson—Revolutionary: A Radical's Struggle to Remake America* (New York: St. Martin's Press, 2017), chapter 4.

4. Noble E. Cunningham Jr., *The Presidency of James Monroe* (Lawrence: University Press of Kansas, 1996), 47.

5. JM to James Monroe, December 9, 1817, *The Papers of James Madison: Retirement Series,* David B. Mattern, et al., eds. (Charlottesville: University of Virginia Press, 2009-), 1:171.

6. Gutzman, *Thomas Jefferson—Revolutionary,* 187.

7. James Monroe to Andrew Jackson, October 5, 1817, *The Papers of Andrew Jackson,* ed. Harold D. Moser, et al. (Knoxville: University of Tennessee Press), 4:144–48, at 147–48.

8. James Monroe to JM, December 22, 1817, *PJMRS,* 1:178–79.

9. Thomas Todd to JM, July 17, 1817, *PJMRS,* 1:96–97 and n. 2 at 98.

10. James Monroe to JM, December 22, 1817, *PJMRS,* 1:178–79.

11. Henry St. George Tucker to JM, December 18, 1817, *PJMRS,* 1:175–76. The pamphlet was his report "on so much of the President's message as relates to roads, canals, and seminaries of learning." *PJMRS,* n. 1. Tucker would in time be Virginia's leading legal/constitutional expert—author of numerous legal treatises and longtime professor of law at Mr. Jefferson's University. *PJMRS,* n. 2.

12. JM to Henry St. George Tucker, December 23, 1817, *PJMRS,* 1:181.

13. JM to James Monroe, December 27, 1817, *PJMRS,* 1:190–91.

14. David P. Currie, *The Constitution in Congress: The Jeffersonians, 1801–1829* (Chicago: University of Chicago Press, 2001), 271–74.

Chapter 55

1. Entry for December 31, 1817, *John Quincy Adams: Diaries, 1779–1821,* ed. David Waldstreicher (New York: Library of America, 2017), 1:430–31.

2. Entry for January 5, 1818, *John Quincy Adams: Diaries,* 1:431–32.

3. David S. Heidler and Jeanne T. Heidler, *Old Hickory's War: Andrew Jackson and the Quest for Empire* (Baton Rouge: Louisiana State University Press, 2003), 94–95, 101.

4. Samuel Flagg Bemis, *John Quincy Adams and the Foundations of American Foreign Policy* (New York: Alfred A. Knopf, 1949), 307.

5. Entry for January 6, 1818, *John Quincy Adams: Diaries,* 1:432–33.

6. James Monroe, Special Message to Congress, January 13, 1818, The American Presidency Project online (UC Santa Barbara), https://www.presidency.ucsb.edu/node/206561.

7. Bemis, *John Quincy Adams and the Foundations of American Foreign Policy,* 301.

8. My account of the First Seminole War and its aftermath relies, unless otherwise noted, on Merrill Peterson, *The Great Triumvirate: Webster, Clay, and Calhoun* (New York: Oxford University Press, 1987), 55–56; and Heidler and Heidler, *Old Hickory's War,* passim.

9. Heidler and Heidler, *Old Hickory's War,* 90.

10. Noble E. Cunningham Jr., *The Presidency of James Monroe* (Lawrence: University Press of Kansas, 1996), 56–57.

11. Entry for December 26, 1817, *John Quincy Adams: Diaries,* 428–29.

12. Cunningham Jr., *The Presidency of James Monroe,* 58–59.

13. James Monroe to Fulwar Skipwith, April 21, 1818, *The Papers of James Monroe: Selected Correspondence and Papers,* ed. Daniel Preston, et al. (Santa Barbara, CA: ABC-Clio, 2012), 1:521; James Monroe to Charles Everett, March 30, 1818, *The Papers of James Monroe,* 1:520, n.; Benjamin Crowninshield to James Beatty, May 12, 1818, *The Papers of James Monroe,* 1:522.

14. (Washington) *National Intelligencer,* May 29, 1818, *The Papers of James Monroe,* 1:514.

15. (Annapolis) *Maryland Gazette,* June 4, 1818, and *Baltimore American,* June 2, 1818, *The Papers of James Monroe,* 1:525; (Annapolis) *Maryland Gazette,* June 4, 1818, *The Papers of James Monroe,* 1:525–27.

16. *Baltimore American,* June 2, 1818, *The Papers of James Monroe,* 1:528; James Monroe to John Quincy Adams, May 30, 1818, *The Papers of James Monroe,* 1:529.

17. Joseph G. Swift, *Memoirs,* June 5–6, 1818, 174–75, *The Papers of James Monroe,* 1:530.

18. Joseph G. Swift, *Memoirs,* June 7–8, 1818, 175, *The Papers of James Monroe,* 1:532.

19. (Norfolk) *American Beacon,* June 9, 1818, *The Papers of James Monroe,* 1:532–33.

20. *Auto-biography of Lemuel Sawyer,* 21–22, cited at *The Papers of James Monroe,* 1:538–39.

21. (Norfolk) *Herald,* June 15, 1818, *The Papers of James Monroe,* 1:540–44.

22. Ibid., 1:547.

23. Ibid., 1:549.

Chapter 56

1. Entry for July 15, 1818, *John Quincy Adams: Diaries, 1779–1821,* ed. David Waldstreicher (New York: Library of America, 2017), 1:445–46.

2. John C. Calhoun to Andrew Jackson, December 26, 1817, *The Papers of John C. Calhoun,* ed. Robert L. Meriwether, et al. (Columbia: University of South Carolina Press, 1959–2003), 2:39–40.

3. Entry for July 16, 1818, *John Quincy Adams: Diaries,* 1:446–48.

4. David Johnson, *Irreconcilable Founders: Spencer Roane, John Marshall, and the Nature of America's Constitutional Republic* (Baton Rouge: Louisiana State University Press, 2021), 50–51.

5. Noble E. Cunningham Jr., *The Presidency of James Monroe,* (Lawrence: University Press of Kansas, 1996), 60–62.

6. James Monroe to Andrew Jackson, July 19, 1818, *The Writings of James Monroe,* 6:54–61.

7. Andrew Jackson to James Monroe, August 19, 1818, *The Papers of Andrew Jackson,* 4:236–39.

8. Cunningham Jr., *The Presidency of James Monroe,* 64.

Chapter 57

1. Merrill D. Peterson, *The Great Triumvirate: Webster, Clay, and Calhoun* (New York: Oxford University Press, 1987), 55–56.

2. The following account relies on Samuel Flagg Bemis, *John Quincy Adams and the Foundations of American Foreign Policy* (New York: Alfred A. Knopf, 1949), 317–40 and Map 7.

3. James Monroe, Second Annual Message, November 16, 1818, The American Presidency Project online (UC Santa Barbara), https://www.presidency.ucsb.edu/documents/second-annual-message-1.

4. TJ to James Monroe, January 18, 1819, *The Papers of Thomas Jefferson: Retirement Series,* ed. J. Jefferson Looney (Princeton, NJ: Princeton University Press, 2004), 13:586–87, at 587; James H. Hutson, "John Adams's Title Campaign," *The New England Quarterly* 41 (1968): 30–39.

5. Bemis, *John Quincy Adams and the Foundations of American Foreign Policy,* quotation at 329.

6. The following account is based on Entry for February 22, 1819, *John Quincy Adams: Diaries, 1779–1821,* ed. David Waldstreicher (New York: Library of America, 2017), 1:474–77.

7. Richard B. Bernstein, *The Education of John Adams* (New York: Oxford University Press, 2020), 66.

8. Entry for November 1, 1818, *John Quincy Adams: Diaries,* 1:456.

9. Entry for November 2, 1818, *John Quincy Adams: Diaries,* 1:456–57.

Chapter 58

1. Entry for February 22, 1819, *John Quincy Adams: Diaries, 1779–1821,* ed. David Waldstreicher (New York: Library of America, 2017), 1:475.

2. G. Edward White, *The Marshall Court and Cultural Change, 1815–1835,* abridged edition (New York: Oxford University Press, 1991), 182.

3. Andrew Browning, *The Panic of 1819: The First Great Depression* (Columbia: University of Missouri Press, 2019), 115–16.

4. Browning, *The Panic of 1819,* 158.

5. Richard E. Ellis, *Aggressive Nationalism: McCulloch v. Maryland and the Foundation of Federal Authority in the Young Republic* (New York: Oxford University Press, 2007), 63.

6. Ellis, *Aggressive Nationalism,* 65, 69.

7. White, *The Marshall Court and Cultural Change,* 246.

8. Ibid., 247, n. 215; 248–49.

9. Ellis, *Aggressive Nationalism,* 76. Ellis concludes that only Marshall "had the stature, the influence, or the power to operate behind the scenes to channel a case as important as this one in a particular direction."

10. Merrill D. Peterson, *Thomas Jefferson & the New Nation* (New York: Oxford University Press, 1970), 432–36.

11. Ellis, *Aggressive Nationalism,* 88.

12. Ibid., 89.

13. Ibid., 90.

14. R. Kent Newmyer, *John Marshall and the Heroic Age of the Supreme Court* (Baton Rouge: Louisiana State University Press, 2001), 296–97.

15. Entry for January 8, 1820, *John Quincy Adams: Diaries,* 1:518–23, at 520.

16. David Johnson, *Irreconcilable Founders: Spencer Roane, John Marshall, and the Nature of America's Constitutional Republic* (Baton Rouge: Louisiana State University Press, 2021), 80–81.

Chapter 59

1. John Taylor, *Construction Construed, and Constitutions Vindicated* (Richmond, VA: Shepherd and Pollard, 1820).

2. *John Marshall's Defense of* McCulloch v. Maryland, ed. Gerald Gunther (Stanford, CA: Stanford University Press, 1969), 11–12.

3. Ibid., 12–13.

4. Ibid., 64–77, quotations at 73, 74, final point at 75.

5. This discussion is based on David Johnson, *Irreconcilable Founders: Spencer Roane, John Marshall, and the Nature of America's Constitutional Republic* (Baton Rouge: Louisiana State University Press, 2021), 81–86.

6. Kevin R. C. Gutzman, "Edmund Randolph and Virginia Constitutionalism," *Review of Politics* 66 (2004): 469–97.

7. Spencer Roane to TJ, August 22, 1819, *The Papers of Thomas Jefferson: Retirement Series,* ed. J. Jefferson Looney (Princeton, NJ: Princeton University Press, 2004), 14:626–27.

8. TJ to Spencer Roane, September 6, 1819, *PTJRS,* 15:16–18.

9. Kevin R. C. Gutzman, *Thomas Jefferson—Revolutionary: A Radical's Struggle to Remake America* (New York: St. Martin's Press, 2017), chapter 5. One wonders whether Jefferson had a twinge of self-doubt in saying these things to Patrick Henry's son-in-law and ideological heir, for which see Peter S. Onuf, *Jefferson and the Virginians: Democracy, Constitutions, and Empire* (Baton Rouge: Louisiana State University Press, 2018), chapter 2.

10. Spencer Roane to JM, August 22, 1819, *The Papers of James Madison: Retirement Series,* David B. Mattern, et al., eds. (Charlottesville: University of Virginia Press, 2009-), 1:499.

11. JM to Spencer Roane, September 2, 1819, *PJMRS,* 1:500–03.

Chapter 60

1. John R. Van Atta, *Wolf by the Ears: The Missouri Crisis, 1819–1821* (Baltimore: Johns Hopkins University Press, 2015), 16, 4.

2. Merrill D. Peterson, *The Great Triumvirate: Webster, Clay, and Calhoun* (New York: Oxford University Press, 1987), 59.

3. Robert Ernst, *Rufus King: American Federalist* (Chapel Hill: University of North Carolina Press, 1968), 369; Rufus King to Colonel Pickering, November 4, 1803, *The Records of the Federal Convention of 1787,* ed. Max Farrand (New Haven, CT: Yale University Press, 1966), 3:399–400, at 399. King had been dispassionate in opposing slave imports in the Philadelphia Convention as well. Richard Beeman, *Plain, Honest Men: The Making of the American Constitution* (New York: Random House, 2009), 323–24.

4. Peterson, *The Great Triumvirate,* 59.

5. Van Atta, *Wolf by the Ears,* 75–76.

6. From Ephraim Bateman, March 4, 1819, *Circular Letters of Congressmen to Their Constituents, 1789–1829,* ed. Noble E. Cunningham Jr. (Chapel Hill: University of North Carolina Press, 1978), 3:1067–77.

7. Harry Ammon, *James Monroe: The Quest for National Identity* (Charlottesville: University Press of Virginia, 1971), 450.

8. James Monroe to Fulwar Skipwith, November 28, 1818, *The Papers of James Monroe: Selected Correspondence and Papers,* ed. Daniel Preston, et al. (Santa Barbara, CA: ABC-Clio, 2012-), 1:555.

9. Worden Pope to James Monroe, March 1, 1819, *The Papers of James Monroe,* 1:555–56.

10. John C. Calhoun to James Gadsden, March 25, 1819, *The Papers of James Monroe,*

1:557; *City of Washington Gazette,* March 26, 1819, *The Papers of James Monroe,* 1:557; James Monroe to John Mason, March 27, 1819, *The Papers of James Monroe,* 1:558.

11. John Quincy Adams Diary, March 30, 1819, *The Papers of James Monroe,* 1:559.

12. *City of Washington Gazette,* March 31, 1819, *The Papers of James Monroe,* 1:559.

13. (Norfolk) *American Beacon,* March 31, 1819 and April 1, 1819, *The Papers of James Monroe,* 1:561–62; (Norfolk) *American Beacon,* April 3, 1819, *The Papers of James Monroe,* 1:562–66.

14. *Edenton Gazette,* April 13, 1819, *The Papers of James Monroe,* 1:568.

15. Ibid., 1:569–70.

16. (New Bern) *Carolina Centinel,* May 8, 1819, *The Papers of James Monroe,* 1:585–88.

17. *Charleston Courier,* April 29, 1819, *The Papers of James Monroe,* 1:613; Samuel F. B. Morse to James Monroe, December 11, 1819, *The Papers of James Monroe,* 1:773; Noble E. Cunningham Jr., *The Presidency of James Monroe* (Lawrence: University Press of Kansas, 1996), 124; https://www.whitehousehistory.org/photos/james-monroe.

18. James Monroe to George Hay, May 2, 1819, *The Papers of James Monroe,* 1:618–20 is the source for this paragraph and the next.

19. *Charleston Courier,* March 4, 1819, *The Papers of James Monroe,* 1:621.

20. Guerdon Gates Journal, September 4, 1817, *The Papers of James Monroe,* 1:461.

21. (Salem, Massachusetts) *Essex Register,* May 15, 1819, *The Papers of James Monroe,* 1:621–22, at 621.

Chapter 61

1. (Lexington) *Kentucky Gazette,* July 2, 1819, *The Papers of James Monroe: Selected Correspondence and Papers,* ed. Daniel Preston, et al. (Santa Barbara, CA: ABC-Clio, 2012), 1:707.

2. *Savannah Republican,* March 11, 1819, *The Papers of James Monroe,* 1:633.

3. *Savannah Republican,* March 17, 1819, *The Papers of James Monroe,* 1:634–35, at 635.

4. "An Observer," *Savannah Republican,* March 23, 1819, *The Papers of James Monroe,* 1:636.

5. "Americanus," *Savannah Republican,* April 30, 1819, *The Papers of James Monroe,* 1:637.

6. *Charleston Courier,* May 13, 1819, *The Papers of James Monroe,* 1:637–38, at 638.

7. Ibid., 1:640.

8. *Savannah Republican,* June 1, 1819, *The Papers of James Monroe,* 1:660.

9. Spring Place Mission, May 25, 1819, *The Papers of James Monroe,* 1:661.

10. Ibid., 1:662.

11. James Monroe to Return J. Meigs, May 27, 1819, *The Papers of James Monroe,* 1:663 and n.

12. James Monroe to John Quincy Adams, June 14, 1819, *The Papers of James Monroe,* 1:679.

13. James Monroe to John Quincy Adams, July 5, 1819, *The Papers of James Monroe,* 1:720.

14. (Lexington) *Western Monitor,* July 12, 1819, *The Papers of James Monroe,* 1:725.

15. Cf., (Lexington) *Western Monitor,* July 4, 1819, *The Papers of James Monroe,* 1:712.

16. For example, James M. Denny and Charles B. King to James Monroe, June 23, 1819, *The Papers of James Monroe,* 1:687.

17. *City of Washington Gazette,* August 9, 1819, *The Papers of James Monroe,* 1:728.

18. John Quincy Adams Diary, August 8, 1819, *The Papers of James Monroe,* 1:728.

19. (Washington) *National Intelligencer,* August 11, 1819, *The Papers of James Monroe,* 1:728–30.

20. James Monroe, Third Annual Message, December 7, 1819, Miller Center (University of Virginia Online).

21. Tim McGrath, *James Monroe: A Life* (New York: Penguin, 2020), 439.

22. Northwest Ordinance, Article V, Avalon Project (Yale Law School), https://avalon.yale.edu/18th_century/nworder.asp.

23. Harry Ammon, *James Monroe: The Quest for National Identity* (Charlottesville: University Press of Virginia, 1971), 451–52.

24. Noble E. Cunningham Jr., *The Presidency of James Monroe* (Lawrence: University Press of Kansas, 1996), 94.

25. Ibid., 94–95.

26. Entry for January 8, 1820, *John Quincy Adams: Diaries, 1779–1821,* ed. David Waldstreicher (New York: Library of America, 2017), 1:518–23.

Chapter 62

1. Noble E. Cunningham Jr., *The Presidency of James Monroe* (Lawrence: University Press of Kansas, 1996), 96.

2. Entry for January 16, 1820, *John Quincy Adams: Diaries, 1779–1821,* ed. David Waldstreicher (New York: Library of America, 2017), 1:525–26.

3. Cunningham Jr., *The Presidency of James Monroe,* 98–99.

4. Ibid.

5. John R. Van Atta, *Wolf by the Ears: The Missouri Crisis, 1819–1821* (Baltimore, MD: Johns Hopkins University Press, 2015), 97.

6. James Barbour to JM, February 10, 1820, *The Papers of James Madison: Retirement Series,* David B. Mattern, et al., eds. (Charlottesville: University of Virginia Press, 2009), 2:8–9; JM to James Barbour, February 14, 1820, *PJMRS,* 2:10–11.

7. Van Atta, *Wolf by the Ears,* 98.

8. Ibid., 101; also see Kevin R. Gutzman, "Preserving the Patrimony: William Branch Giles and Virginia versus the Federal Tariff," *The Virginia Magazine of History and Biography* 104 (1996), 341–72. A cogent attack on Clay's program along proto-public-choice grounds is John Taylor, *Tyranny Unmasked* (Washington: Davis and Force, 1822).

9. Entry for February 24, 1820, *John Quincy Adams: Diaries,* 1:534–35.

10. James Monroe to TJ, February 19, 1820, *The Writings of James Monroe,* 6:115–16.

11. George Dangerfield, *The Era of Good Feelings* (Chicago: Elephant Paperbacks, 1952), 229; K[evin] R. Constantine Gutzman, "The Randolph-Clay Duel," *Southern Partisan* 18 (Fourth Quarter 1998), 16–20 (cover story).

12. Robert Pierce Forbes, *The Missouri Compromise and Its Aftermath* (Chapel Hill: University of North Carolina Press, 2007), 98–9.

13. Merrill D. Peterson, *The Great Triumvirate: Webster, Clay, and Calhoun* (New York: Oxford University Press, 1987), 62.

14. This account relies on Entry for March 3, 1820, *John Quincy Adams: Diaries,* 1:537–45.

15. This understanding was reflected not only in popular culture, but in Southern states' highest law. For this principle in Section 1 of Virginia's 1776 Declaration of Rights—the first

American declaration of rights, see Kevin R. C. Gutzman, *Virginia's American Revolution: From Dominion to Republic, 1776–1840* (Lanham, Maryland: Lexington Books, 2007), 27–28. Perhaps Calhoun knew this story.

Chapter 63

1. Harry Ammon, *James Monroe: The Quest for National Identity* (Charlottesville: University Press of Virginia, 1971), 460.

2. Robert Pierce Forbes, *The Missouri Compromise and Its Aftermath* (Chapel Hill: University of North Carolina Press, 2007), 112–15.

3. Noble E. Cunningham Jr., *The Presidency of James Monroe* (Lawrence: University Press of Kansas, 1996), 107.

4. United States Elections Project (University of Florida), http://www.electproject.org/national-1789-present.

5. Forbes, *The Missouri Compromise and Its Aftermath,* 115–17.

6. Ibid., 118.

7. John C. Calhoun to Charles Tait, October 26, 1820, *The Papers of John C. Calhoun,* ed. Robert L. Meriwether, et al. (Columbia: University of South Carolina Press, 1959–2003), 5:412–14, at 413.

8. Robert Elder, *Calhoun: American Heretic* (New York: Basic Books, 2021), 189–90.

9. Alongside the following account, consider Michael J. Klarman, "How Great Were the 'Great' Marshall Court Decisions?" *Virginia Law Review,* vol. 87, no. 6 (Oct. 2001): 1111–1184.

10. 4 Wheaton 518.

11. The following account relies primarily on R. Kent Newmyer, *John Marshall and the Heroic Age of the Supreme Court* (Baton Rouge: Louisiana State University Press, 2001), 244–53.

12. Editorial Note, Dartmouth College v. Woodward, *The Papers of John Marshall,* ed. Herbert A. Johnson, et al. (Chapel Hill: University of North Carolina Press , 1974–2006), 8:217–23, at 221.

13. 6 Wheat 264 (1821).

14. The following case description is based on David Johnson, *Irreconcilable Founders: Spencer Roane, John Marshall, and the Nature of America's Constitutional Republic* (Baton Rouge: Louisiana State University Press, 2021), 99–100.

15. Article III, Section 2, Clause 1 of the U.S. Constitution says, "The Judicial Power shall extend to all Cases, in Law and Equity, *arising under* this Constitution, the Laws of the United States, and Treaties made, or which shall be made, under their Authority. . . ." (Emphasis added.)

16. The following discussion is based on Charles F. Hobson, *The Great Chief Justice: John Marshall and the Rule of Law* (Lawrence: University Press of Kansas, 1996), 127–32 except where otherwise noted. The House of Delegates resolution denying the Supreme Court's jurisdiction in the matter is at *The Papers of Thomas Jefferson: Retirement Series,* ed. J. Jefferson Looney (Princeton, NJ: Princeton University Press, 2004), 16:593, n.

17. James Madison, for his part, held that if "the legitimate meaning of the Instrument" could not be "derived from the text itself," "it must be not in the opinions or intentions of the Body which planned & proposed the Constitution, but in the sense attached to it by the people in their respective State Conventions where it recd. all the authority which it pos-

sesses" that "a key is to be sought." JM to Thomas Ritchie, September 15, 1821, *PJMRS*, 2:381–82, at 381.

18. Johnson, *Irreconcilable Founders*, 101–102, citing Dumas Malone, *Jefferson and His Time*, vol. 6, *The Sage of Monticello* (Boston: Little, Brown, 1981), 357.

Chapter 64

1. TJ to Archibald Thweatt, January 19, 1821, *The Papers of Thomas Jefferson: Retirement Series*, ed. J. Jefferson Looney (Princeton, NJ: Princeton University Press, 2004), 16:556.

2. John Taylor, *Construction Construed, and Constitutions Vindicated* (Richmond: Shepherd & Pollard, 1820).

3. TJ to Spencer Roane, March 9, 1821, *PTJRS*, 17:31.

4. Spencer Roane to JM, April 17, 1821, *The Papers of James Madison: Retirement Series*, David B. Mattern, et al., eds. (Charlottesville: University of Virginia Press, 2009), 2:302.

5. JM to Spencer Roane, May 6, 1821, *PJMRS*, 2:317–21.

6. The following discussion relies on David Johnson, *Irreconcilable Founders: Spencer Roane, John Marshall, and the Nature of America's Constitutional Republic* (Baton Rouge: Louisiana State University Press, 2021), 103–05.

7. Apparently, Roane did not espy the difficulty posed by this theory that Justice James Iredell highlighted in *Calder v. Bull*, 3 U.S. 386 (1798).

8. JM to Spencer Roane, June 29, 1821, *PJMRS*, 2:347–48.

9. TJ to William Johnson, October 27, 1822, Founders Online (National Archives), https://founders.archives.gov/documents/Jefferson/98-01-02-3118.

10. William Johnson to TJ, December 10, 1822, Founders Online (National Archives), https://founders.archives.gov/documents/Jefferson/98-01-02-3203.

11. TJ to William Johnson, March 4, 1823, Founders Online (National Archives), https://founders.archives.gov/documents/Jefferson/98-01-02-3373.

12. Thomas Jefferson to Joel Barlow, May 3, 1802, Founders Online (National Archives), https://founders.archives.gov/documents/Jefferson/01-37-02-0318.

13. William Johnson to TJ, April 11, 1823, Founders Online (National Archives), https://founders.archives.gov/documents/Jefferson/98-01-02-3448.

14. TJ to William Johnson, June 12, 1823, Founders Online (National Archives), https://founders.archives.gov/documents/Jefferson/98-01-02-3562.

15. Donald G. Morgan, *Justice William Johnson: The First Dissenter* (Columbia: University of South Carolina Press, 1954), 306–07.

Chapter 65

1. This and the next paragraph rely primarily on Jean Edward Smith, *John Marshall: Definer of a Nation* (New York: Henry Holt, 1996), 473–75.

2. G. Edward White, *The Marshall Court and Cultural Change, 1815–1835*, abridged edition (New York: Oxford University Press, 1991), 571. The following discussion relies on White's account, 571–80.

3. Michael J. Klarman, "How Great Were the 'Great' Marshall Court Decisions?" *Virginia Law Review*, vol. 87, no. 6 (Oct. 2001): 1111–1184, at 1144.

4. Entry for March 3, 1821, *John Quincy Adams: Diaries, 1779–1821,* ed. David Waldstreicher (New York: Library of America, 2017), 1:596–99.

5. Noble E. Cunningham Jr., *The Presidency of James Monroe* (Lawrence: University Press of Kansas, 1996), 111–12.

6. Merrill D. Peterson, *The Great Triumvirate: Webster, Clay, and Calhoun* (New York: Oxford University Press, 1987), 93.

7. Entry for March 4, 1821, *John Quincy Adams: Diaries,* 2:1.

8. Entries for February 23, 1821 and March 1, 1821, *The Diaries of John Quincy Adams* (Massachusetts Historical Society online).

9. Entry for March 5, 1821, *John Quincy Adams: Diaries,* 2:1–3.

10. Harry Ammon, *James Monroe: The Quest for National Identity* (Charlottesville: University Press of Virginia, 1971), 473–74.

11. James Monroe, Second Inaugural Address, *The Writings of James Monroe,* 6:163–74.

12. John C. Calhoun to Henry Clay, December 5, 1818, *The Papers of John C. Calhoun,* ed. Robert L. Meriwether, et al. (Columbia: University of South Carolina Press, 1959–2003), 3:341–55, at 350.

Chapter 66

1. Irving Bartlett, *John C. Calhoun: A Biography* (New York: W. W. Norton, 1993), 97. Calhoun's posture is particularly interesting in light of the fact that his paternal grandmother and a paternal uncle had been killed and "most inhumanely butchered" by upcountry South Carolina Indians. Robert Elder, *Calhoun: American Heretic* (New York: Basic Books, 2021), 12.

2. John Quincy Adams to Henry Middleton, July 5, 1820, *The Writings of James Monroe,* 6:347–50.

3. James Monroe to TJ, April 14, 1823, *The Writings of James Monroe,* 6:304–07.

4. John Quincy Adams to Richard Rush, July 28, 1823, *The Writings of James Monroe,* 6:357–61.

5. Richard Rush to John Quincy Adams, August 19, 1823, *The Writings of James Monroe,* 6:361–65.

6. George Canning to Richard Rush, August 20, 1823, *The Writings of James Monroe,* 6:365–66.

7. James Monroe to TJ, October 17, 1823, *The Writings of James Monroe,* 6:323–25.

8. TJ to James Monroe, October 24, 1823, *The Works of Thomas Jefferson,* ed. Paul Leicester Ford (New York: G. P. Putnam's Sons, 1905), 12:318–21.

9. JM to James Monroe, October 30, 1823, *The Writings of James Monroe,* 6:394–95. See also Irving Brant, *James Madison: Commander in Chief* (Indianapolis, IN: Bobbs-Merrill, 1961), 438–39.

10. Richard Rush to George Canning, August 23, 1823, *The Writings of James Monroe,* 6:366–67.

11. Richard Rush to John Quincy Adams, August 23, 1823, *The Writings of James Monroe,* 6:368–69.

12. George Canning to Richard Rush, August 23, 1823, *The Writings of James Monroe,* 6:369.

13. Richard Rush to George Canning, August 27, 1823, *The Writings of James Monroe*, 6:369-70.

14. Richard Rush to John Quincy Adams, August 28, 1823, *The Writings of James Monroe*, 6:370-72.

15. George Canning to Richard Rush, August 31, 1823, *The Writings of James Monroe*, 6:372-74.

16. Richard Rush to John Quincy Adams, September 8, 1823, *The Writings of James Monroe*, 6:374.

17. Richard Rush to James Monroe, September 15, 1823, *The Writings of James Monroe*, 6:374-77.

18. Brant, *James Madison: Commander in Chief*, 572, n. 4; Entry for November 7, 1823, *The Diaries of John Quincy Adams*, Massachusetts Historical Society, https://www.masshist.org /jqadiaries/php/, 2:47-49.

Chapter 67

1. Entry for November 21, 1823, *The Diaries of John Quincy Adams*, Massachusetts Historical Society, https://www.masshist.org/jqadiaries/php/, 2:49-52.

2. Albert Gallatin to James Monroe, October 26, 1823, *The Writings of James Monroe*, 6:323, n. 1.

3. Noble E. Cunningham Jr., *The Presidency of James Monroe* (Lawrence: University Press of Kansas, 1996), 153.

4. Ibid., 156.

5. James Monroe, Seventh Annual Message, December 3, 1823, *The Writings of James Monroe*, 6:325-42.

6. Francis Walker Gilmer to Dabney Carr, January 15, 1811, *The Papers of James Madison: Retirement Series*, David B. Mattern, et al., eds. (Charlottesville: University of Virginia Press, 2009), 2:180-81, n. 1.

7. Harry Ammon, *James Monroe: The Quest for National Identity* (Charlottesville: University Press of Virginia, 1971), 369.

Chapter 68

1. Noble E. Cunningham Jr., *The Presidency of James Monroe* (Lawrence: University Press of Kansas, 1996), 160-62.

2. James Monroe, "To Congress—Massachusetts' Claim for Military Compensation," February 24, 1824, *The Writings of James Monroe*, 7:8-11, at 8, 11.

3. Donald R. Hickey, *The War of 1812: A Forgotten Conflict—Bicentennial Edition* (Champaign: University of Illinois Press, 2012), 272.

4. James Monroe, Veto Message, May 4, 1822, The American Presidency Project online (UC Santa Barbara), https://www.presidency.ucsb.edu/documents/veto-message.

5. Cunningham Jr., *The Presidency of James Monroe*, 166.

6. Donald G. Morgan, *Justice William Johnson: The First Dissenter* (Columbia: University of South Carolina Press, 1954), 122-24. "Today" was 1954. The pamphlet is at "Views on the Subject of Internal Improvements," *The Writings of James Monroe*, 6:216-84.

7. James Monroe to Congress, March 30, 1824, *The Writings of James Monroe*, 7:14-17.

Chapter 69

1. Donald Ratcliffe, *The One-Party Presidential Contest: Adams, Jackson, and 1824's Five-Horse Race* (Lawrence: University Press of Kansas, 2015) 154.

2. Ibid., 261–62.

3. Ibid., 151.

4. Chase C. Mooney, *William H. Crawford, 1772–1834* (Lexington: University Press of Kentucky, 1974), 249–53.

5. Harry Ammon, *James Monroe: The Quest for National Identity* (Charlottesville: University Press of Virginia, 1971), 530 and n. 4.

6. Ibid., 497.

7. Dumas Malone, *Jefferson and His Time: The Sage of Monticello* (Boston: Little, Brown, 1981), 432.

8. Ratcliffe, *The One-Party Presidential Contest,* 154.

9. Robert Elder, *Calhoun: American Heretic* (New York: Basic Books, 2021), 209–10.

10. Kevin R. C. Gutzman, "Preserving the Patrimony: William Branch Giles and Virginia vs. the Federal Tariff," *The Virginia Magazine of History and Biography* 104 (1996): 341–372 (figure at 353).

11. Kevin R. C. Gutzman, "General Ignorance," *The American Conservative* online, August 10, 2012, https://www.theamericanconservative.com/articles/general-ignorance/.

12. Tim McGrath, *James Monroe: A Life* (New York: Penguin, 2020), 549.

13. Ratcliffe, *The One-Party Presidential Contest,* 5.

14. McGrath, *James Monroe,* 542–44.

15. Malone, *Jefferson and His Time,* 403.

16. McGrath, *James Monroe,* 553.

Chapter 70

1. James Monroe, Eighth Annual Message, December 7, 1824, The American Presidency Project online (UC Santa Barbara), https://www.presidency.ucsb.edu/documents/eighth-annual-message-1.

2. Regarding Monroe, see Tim McGrath, *James Monroe: A Life* (New York: Penguin, 2020), 553, 566. The exchange with Madison is at 566–67.

3. Ibid., 566–67.

4. Alison Goodyear Freehling, *Drift Toward Dissolution: The Virginia Slavery Debate of 1831–1832* (Baton Rouge: Louisiana State University Press, 1982).

5. John Adams to TJ, January 22, 1825, *The Adams-Jefferson Letters, The Complete Correspondence between Thomas Jefferson and Abigail and John Adams* (Chapel Hill: University of North Carolina Press, 1959), 606–07.

6. Donald Ratcliffe, *The One-Party Presidential Contest: Adams, Jackson, and 1824's Five-Horse Race* (Lawrence: University Press of Kansas, 2015), 252.

7. TJ to John Adams, February 15, 1825, *The Adams-Jefferson Letters,* 608–09, at 609.

8. John Quincy Adams, Inaugural Address, March 4, 1825, Avalon Project (Yale Law School), https://avalon.law.yale.edu/19th_century/qadams.asp.

9. John Quincy Adams, First Annual Address, December 6, 1825, Miller Center (The Uni-

versity of Virginia), https://millercenter.org/the-presidency/presidential-speeches/december
-6-1825-first-annual-message.

10. TJ, December 24, 1825, "Solemn Declaration and Protest of the Commonwealth of
Virginia," Founders Online (National Archives), https://founders.archives.gov/documents
/Jefferson/98-01-02-5764.

11. Kevin R. C. Gutzman, *Thomas Jefferson—Revolutionary: A Radical's Struggle to Remake America* (New York: St. Martin's Press, 2017), 95–6.

INDEX